Lecture Notes in Computer Science 13320

More information about this series at https://link.springer.com/bookseries/558

Vincent G. Duffy (Ed.)

Digital Human Modeling and Applications in Health, Safety, Ergonomics and Risk Management

Health, Operations Management, and Design

13th International Conference, DHM 2022
Held as Part of the 24th HCI International Conference, HCII 2022
Virtual Event, June 26 – July 1, 2022
Proceedings, Part II

Springer

Editor
Vincent G. Duffy
Purdue University
West Lafayette, IN, USA

ISSN 0302-9743   ISSN 1611-3349 (electronic)
Lecture Notes in Computer Science
ISBN 978-3-031-06017-5   ISBN 978-3-031-06018-2 (eBook)
https://doi.org/10.1007/978-3-031-06018-2

This Springer imprint is published by the registered company Springer Nature Switzerland AG
The registered company address is: Gewerbestrasse 11, 6330 Cham, Switzerland

Foreword

Human-computer interaction (HCI) is acquiring an ever-increasing scientific and industrial importance, as well as having more impact on people's everyday life, as an ever-growing number of human activities are progressively moving from the physical to the digital world. This process, which has been ongoing for some time now, has been dramatically accelerated by the COVID-19 pandemic. The HCI International (HCII) conference series, held yearly, aims to respond to the compelling need to advance the exchange of knowledge and research and development efforts on the human aspects of design and use of computing systems.

The 24th International Conference on Human-Computer Interaction, HCI International 2022 (HCII 2022), was planned to be held at the Gothia Towers Hotel and Swedish Exhibition & Congress Centre, Göteborg, Sweden, during June 26 to July 1, 2022. Due to the COVID-19 pandemic and with everyone's health and safety in mind, HCII 2022 was organized and run as a virtual conference. It incorporated the 21 thematic areas and affiliated conferences listed on the following page.

A total of 5583 individuals from academia, research institutes, industry, and governmental agencies from 88 countries submitted contributions, and 1276 papers and 275 posters were included in the proceedings to appear just before the start of the conference. The contributions thoroughly cover the entire field of human-computer interaction, addressing major advances in knowledge and effective use of computers in a variety of application areas. These papers provide academics, researchers, engineers, scientists, practitioners, and students with state-of-the-art information on the most recent advances in HCI. The volumes constituting the set of proceedings to appear before the start of the conference are listed in the following pages.

The HCI International (HCII) conference also offers the option of 'Late Breaking Work' which applies both for papers and posters, and the corresponding volume(s) of the proceedings will appear after the conference. Full papers will be included in the 'HCII 2022 - Late Breaking Papers' volumes of the proceedings to be published in the Springer LNCS series, while 'Poster Extended Abstracts' will be included as short research papers in the 'HCII 2022 - Late Breaking Posters' volumes to be published in the Springer CCIS series.

I would like to thank the Program Board Chairs and the members of the Program Boards of all thematic areas and affiliated conferences for their contribution and support towards the highest scientific quality and overall success of the HCI International 2022 conference; they have helped in so many ways, including session organization, paper reviewing (single-blind review process, with a minimum of two reviews per submission) and, more generally, acting as goodwill ambassadors for the HCII conference.

This conference would not have been possible without the continuous and unwavering support and advice of Gavriel Salvendy, founder, General Chair Emeritus, and Scientific Advisor. For his outstanding efforts, I would like to express my appreciation to Abbas Moallem, Communications Chair and Editor of HCI International News.

June 2022   Constantine Stephanidis

HCI International 2022 Thematic Areas and Affiliated Conferences

Thematic Areas

- HCI: Human-Computer Interaction
- HIMI: Human Interface and the Management of Information

Affiliated Conferences

- EPCE: 19th International Conference on Engineering Psychology and Cognitive Ergonomics
- AC: 16th International Conference on Augmented Cognition
- UAHCI: 16th International Conference on Universal Access in Human-Computer Interaction
- CCD: 14th International Conference on Cross-Cultural Design
- SCSM: 14th International Conference on Social Computing and Social Media
- VAMR: 14th International Conference on Virtual, Augmented and Mixed Reality
- DHM: 13th International Conference on Digital Human Modeling and Applications in Health, Safety, Ergonomics and Risk Management
- DUXU: 11th International Conference on Design, User Experience and Usability
- C&C: 10th International Conference on Culture and Computing
- DAPI: 10th International Conference on Distributed, Ambient and Pervasive Interactions
- HCIBGO: 9th International Conference on HCI in Business, Government and Organizations
- LCT: 9th International Conference on Learning and Collaboration Technologies
- ITAP: 8th International Conference on Human Aspects of IT for the Aged Population
- AIS: 4th International Conference on Adaptive Instructional Systems
- HCI-CPT: 4th International Conference on HCI for Cybersecurity, Privacy and Trust
- HCI-Games: 4th International Conference on HCI in Games
- MobiTAS: 4th International Conference on HCI in Mobility, Transport and Automotive Systems
- AI-HCI: 3rd International Conference on Artificial Intelligence in HCI
- MOBILE: 3rd International Conference on Design, Operation and Evaluation of Mobile Communications

List of Conference Proceedings Volumes Appearing Before the Conference

1. LNCS 13302, Human-Computer Interaction: Theoretical Approaches and Design Methods (Part I), edited by Masaaki Kurosu
2. LNCS 13303, Human-Computer Interaction: Technological Innovation (Part II), edited by Masaaki Kurosu
3. LNCS 13304, Human-Computer Interaction: User Experience and Behavior (Part III), edited by Masaaki Kurosu
4. LNCS 13305, Human Interface and the Management of Information: Visual and Information Design (Part I), edited by Sakae Yamamoto and Hirohiko Mori
5. LNCS 13306, Human Interface and the Management of Information: Applications in Complex Technological Environments (Part II), edited by Sakae Yamamoto and Hirohiko Mori
6. LNAI 13307, Engineering Psychology and Cognitive Ergonomics, edited by Don Harris and Wen-Chin Li
7. LNCS 13308, Universal Access in Human-Computer Interaction: Novel Design Approaches and Technologies (Part I), edited by Margherita Antona and Constantine Stephanidis
8. LNCS 13309, Universal Access in Human-Computer Interaction: User and Context Diversity (Part II), edited by Margherita Antona and Constantine Stephanidis
9. LNAI 13310, Augmented Cognition, edited by Dylan D. Schmorrow and Cali M. Fidopiastis
10. LNCS 13311, Cross-Cultural Design: Interaction Design Across Cultures (Part I), edited by Pei-Luen Patrick Rau
11. LNCS 13312, Cross-Cultural Design: Applications in Learning, Arts, Cultural Heritage, Creative Industries, and Virtual Reality (Part II), edited by Pei-Luen Patrick Rau
12. LNCS 13313, Cross-Cultural Design: Applications in Business, Communication, Health, Well-being, and Inclusiveness (Part III), edited by Pei-Luen Patrick Rau
13. LNCS 13314, Cross-Cultural Design: Product and Service Design, Mobility and Automotive Design, Cities, Urban Areas, and Intelligent Environments Design (Part IV), edited by Pei-Luen Patrick Rau
14. LNCS 13315, Social Computing and Social Media: Design, User Experience and Impact (Part I), edited by Gabriele Meiselwitz
15. LNCS 13316, Social Computing and Social Media: Applications in Education and Commerce (Part II), edited by Gabriele Meiselwitz
16. LNCS 13317, Virtual, Augmented and Mixed Reality: Design and Development (Part I), edited by Jessie Y. C. Chen and Gino Fragomeni
17. LNCS 13318, Virtual, Augmented and Mixed Reality: Applications in Education, Aviation and Industry (Part II), edited by Jessie Y. C. Chen and Gino Fragomeni

39. CCIS 1582, HCI International 2022 Posters - Part III, edited by Constantine Stephanidis, Margherita Antona and Stavroula Ntoa
40. CCIS 1583, HCI International 2022 Posters - Part IV, edited by Constantine Stephanidis, Margherita Antona and Stavroula Ntoa

http://2022.hci.international/proceedings

Preface

Software representations of humans, including aspects of anthropometry, biometrics, motion capture and prediction, as well as cognition modelling, are known as Digital Human Models (DHM), and are widely used in a variety of complex application domains where it is important to foresee and simulate human behavior, performance, safety, health and comfort. Automation depicting human emotion, social interaction and functional capabilities can also be modeled to support and assist in predicting human response in real world settings. Such domains include medical and nursing applications, education and learning, ergonomics and design, as well as safety and risk management.

The 13th Digital Human Modeling & Applications in Health, Safety, Ergonomics & Risk Management (DHM) Conference, an affiliated conference of the HCI International Conference 2022, encouraged papers from academics, researchers, industry and professionals, on a broad range of theoretical and applied issues related to Digital Human Modelling and its applications.

The research papers contributed to this year's volume spans across different fields that fall within the scope of the DHM Conference. In the context of anthropometry, human behavior, and communication, the physical aspects emphasized build on human modeling lessons of the past, whereas attentional aspects are providing evidence for new theories and applications. The study of DHM issues in various application domains has yielded works emphasizing task analysis, quality and safety in healthcare, as well occupational health and operations management. Digital human modeling in interactive product and service design is also discussed in this year's contributions. There are applications of interest shown across many industries, while multi-disciplinary and systems-related challenges remain for validation and generalizability in future work. Sensors-based modeling, information visualization, collaborative robots, and intelligent interactions are among the human-technology modeling and results reporting efforts this year.

Two volumes of the HCII 2022 proceedings are dedicated to this year's edition of the DHM Conference, entitled Digital Human Modeling and Applications in Health, Safety, Ergonomics and Risk Management: Anthropometry, Human Behavior, and Communication (Part I), and Digital Human Modeling and Applications in Health, Safety, Ergonomics and Risk Management: Health, Operations Management, and Design (Part II). The first volume focuses on topics related to ergonomic design, anthropometry, and human modeling, as well as collaboration, communication, and human behavior. The second volume focuses on topics related to task analysis, quality and safety in health-care, as well as occupational health and operations management, and Digital Human Modeling in interactive product and service design.

Papers of these volumes are included for publication after a minimum of two single–blind reviews from the members of the DHM Program Board or, in some cases, from members of the Program Boards of other affiliated conferences. I would like to thank all of them for their invaluable contribution, support and efforts.

June 2022   Vincent G. Duffy

13th International Conference on Digital Human Modeling and Applications in Health, Safety, Ergonomics and Risk Management (DHM 2022)

Program Board Chair: **Vincent G. Duffy,** Purdue University, USA

- Mária Babicsné Horváth, Budapest University of Technology and Economics, Hungary
- Joan Cahill, Trinity College Dublin, Ireland
- André Calero Valdez, RWTH Aachen University, Germany
- Yaqin Cao, Anhui Polytechnic University, China
- Damien Chablat, CNRS and LS2N, France
- Genett Isabel Delgado, Institución Universitaria ITSA, Colombia
- H. Onan Demirel, Oregon State University, USA
- Martin Fleischer, Technical University of Munich, Germany
- Martin Fränzle, Oldenburg University, Germany
- Afzal Godil, NIST, USA
- Fu Guo, Northeastern University, China
- Michael Harry, Loughborough University, UK
- Sogand Hasanzadeh, Purdue University, USA
- Mingcai Hu, Jiangsu University, China
- Sandy Ingram, University of Applied Sciences of Western Switzerland, Switzerland
- Alexander Mehler, Goethe University Frankfurt, Germany
- Sonja Miesner, KAN - Commission for Occupational Health and Safety and Standardization, Germany
- Fabian Narvaez, Universidad Politecnica Salesiana, Ecuador
- Peter Nickel, Institute for Occupational Safety and Health of the German Social Accident Insurance (IFA), Germany
- T. Patel, North Eastern Regional Institute of Science and Technology, India
- Manikam Pillay, RESMEERTS, Australia
- Qing-Xing Qu, Northeastern University, China
- Caterina Rizzi, Università of Bergamo, Italy
- Joni Salminen, Qatar Computing Research Institute, Qatar
- Beatriz Santos, University of Aveiro, Portugal
- Deep Seth, Mahindra University, India
- Leonor Teixeira, University of Aveiro, Portugal
- Renran Tian, IUPUI, USA
- Alexander Trende, OFFIS - Institute for Information Technology, Germany
- Dustin Van der Haar, University of Johannesburg, South Africa
- Kuan Yew Wong, Universiti Teknologi Malaysia, Malaysia
- Shuping Xiong, Korea Advanced Institute of Science and Technology, South Korea
- James Yang, Texas Tech University, USA

The full list with the Program Board Chairs and the members of the Program Boards of all thematic areas and affiliated conferences is available online at

http://www.hci.international/board-members-2022.php

HCI International 2023

The 25th International Conference on Human-Computer Interaction, HCI International 2023, will be held jointly with the affiliated conferences at the AC Bella Sky Hotel and Bella Center, Copenhagen, Denmark, 23–28 July 2023. It will cover a broad spectrum of themes related to human-computer interaction, including theoretical issues, methods, tools, processes, and case studies in HCI design, as well as novel interaction techniques, interfaces, and applications. The proceedings will be published by Springer. More information will be available on the conference website: http://2023.hci.international/.

General Chair
Constantine Stephanidis
University of Crete and ICS-FORTH
Heraklion, Crete, Greece
Email: general_chair@hcii2023.org

http://2023.hci.international/

Contents – Part II

Occupational Health and Operations Management

Contents – Part I

Collaboration, Communication, and Human Behavior

Task Analysis, Quality and Safety
in Healthcare

Human-Centered Participatory Co-design of a Dosimetry-Quality Assurance Checklist in an Academic Cancer Center

Karthik Adapa[1,2]([✉]) [iD], Gregg Tracton[2], Prithima Mosaly[3], Fei Yu[4] [iD],
Ross McGurk[2], Carlton Moore[5], John Dooley[2], Shiva Das[2], and Lukasz Mazur[1,2,3]

[1] Carolina Health Informatics Program, University of North Carolina, Chapel Hill, NC, USA
karthikk@live.unc.edu
[2] Department of Radiation Oncology, University of North Carolina, Chapel Hill, NC, USA
[3] Ben Allegretti Consulting, Inc., Stafford, VA, USA
[4] School of Information and Library Science, University of North Carolina, Chapel Hill, NC, USA
[5] Department of Medicine, School of Medicine, University of North Carolina, Chapel Hill, NC, USA

Abstract. Most radiation oncology centers use in-house quality assurance (QA) checklists to ensure patient safety. Unfortunately, most of these QA checklists are often implemented in clinical settings without formal usability evaluation. We applied a human-centered participatory co-design framework to identify design changes to a dosimetry QA checklist (DQC) currently deployed in an academic radiation oncology center and develop a user-focused functional prototype of an enhanced DQC. We found that the human-centered participatory co-design framework used in this study holds promise in improving the usability of QA checklists currently deployed in clinical settings.

Keywords: Human-centered participatory co-design · Checklist · Radiation oncology

1 Introduction

Radiation therapy (RT) plays an important role in the curative and palliative management of many types of cancer [1]. In the US ≈600,000 people receive RT annually [1]. Errors in RT occur in ≈1–5% of patients with harm occurring in ≈1 of 1,000–10,000 patients annually [2]. A review of single [3] and multi-institutional [4] incident learning systems reveals that the majority of errors in radiation oncology originate in the treatment planning stage of the care path. The predominant approach to minimize errors is to perform well-established quality assurance (QA) processes such as pretreatment dosimetry and physics QA processes between treatment planning and treatment delivery [5]. However, there are inter and intra-institutional variations in how these QA processes are performed, and checklists have been promoted by radiation oncology professional

V. G. Duffy (Ed.): HCII 2022, LNCS 13320, pp. 3–20, 2022.
https://doi.org/10.1007/978-3-031-06018-2_1

organizations such as the American Society of Radiation Oncology and the American Association of Physics in Medicine to facilitate standardization [6].

Multiple academic institutions have designed, developed, and implemented QA checklists, as the processes, software, and hardware used for treatment planning and delivery vary based on institutional practice [7]. Most institutions typically use in-house QA checklists to optimize cognitive workload and reduce human errors [8]. However, these QA checklists are often implemented in clinical settings without formal human-computer interaction (HCI) and human factors (HF) engineering evaluations. We recently reported that our institutional dosimetry-QA checklist (DQC) has suboptimal usability and meets only 3 out of 9 recommended HCI standards [9]. The HCI field offers alternative approaches to improve QA checklists' usability and optimize users' cognitive workload, improve performance, and care coordination [10].

In aviation and medicine, checklists have been studied extensively. Despite initial success stories involving checklists in medical settings [11, 12], multiple studies [13, 14] have highlighted the role of socio-cultural and technical barriers such as organizational processes, workflow alignment, user motivation, unintended impact on clinician roles, and culture impact the usability and efficacy of checklists. For example, Borchard et al. found that aligning checklists to roles and creating opportunities for user empowerment during checklist design and implementation were critical factors in the success of surgical checklists [13]. Drawing on participatory methods widely used in HCI, researchers have been co-designing checklists to address some of the key challenges impacting the usability and efficacy of medical checklists. Among recent studies, Kuo et al. co-designed a diagnostic checklist for intradialytic hypertension through a series of interviews and focus groups with nurses, clinicians, patients, and other stakeholders [10]. Madaio et al. co-designed an artificial intelligence fairness checklist using a series of semi-structured interviews and co-design workshops [15]. In this study, we applied a human-centered participatory co-design framework to identify design changes to a DQC deployed in a radiation oncology clinic and developed a user-focused functional prototype of an enhanced DQC.

2   Theoretical Framework

2.1   Human-Centered Design Process

In user-centered design (UCD) philosophy, an end-user is at the center of the design process. The term was coined in the 1980s by Donald Norman who proposed guidelines for achieving good usability outcomes [16]. Subsequently, various methodologies and techniques have been proposed to involve the end-user in the design process, with the end-user being defined as the "person who will ultimately be using the product." International Organization for Standardization (ISO) in the ISO 9241-210 standards, extended the definition of UCD to "address impacts on many stakeholders, not just those typically considered as users," referring to the design approach as human-centered design (HCD) [17]. Per the ISO 9241-210 standards HCD has four defined activity phases (Fig. 1): (1) Analyze users and their context; (2) Identify the user requirements; (3) Produce design solutions to meet user requirements, and (4) Evaluate the usability of the interface. The main goal of HCD is to increase the usability of the product to create maximum user satisfaction and increase the safety performance of the product.

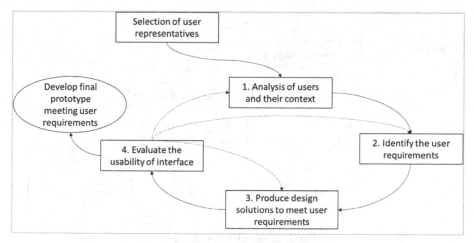

Fig. 1. Human-centered design process

HCD approaches to the design of healthcare technology have been widely described in the literature. For example, Schaeffer et al. employed an HCD methodology where they used surveys and focus groups to gather user requirements and create interface prototypes for an insulin pump [18]. Castilla et al. described an HCD process for a telepsychology app, where they presented end-users with icon and interface concepts in the first step of their design process before moving on to a cognitive walkthrough methodology to evaluate the navigation of the interface. These and many other examples like them [19, 20] indicate a wide variance in the application of HCD to health care technology. However, in checklist design literature and more specifically in re-designing existing checklists to improve their usability, there is a lack of descriptive detail of the methods to be carried out within the design process.

2.2 Participatory Design

Participatory design is based on the Scandinavian approach to democratic system design [21]. It seeks to involve not only end-users but a wide range of stakeholders and actors to shape the changes from several perspectives. The participatory design facilitates collaborative designing and provides guidance to deal with conflicting constraints and values and makes visible diverse stakeholders' interests and knowledge [22]. This approach often requires a designer to spend time with diverse stakeholders and contextual details in place of doing laboratory experiments. Also, this approach provides research-based design as a methodological approach involving four iterative phases – contextual inquiry, participatory design, product design, and prototype as hypothesis (Fig. 2) [21].

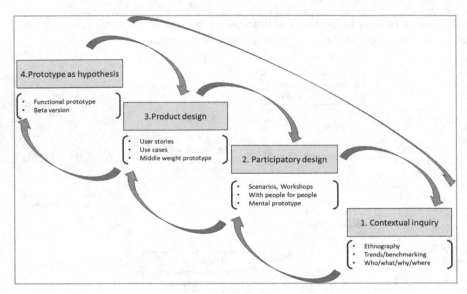

Fig. 2. Research-based design

2.3 Human-Centered Participatory Co-design

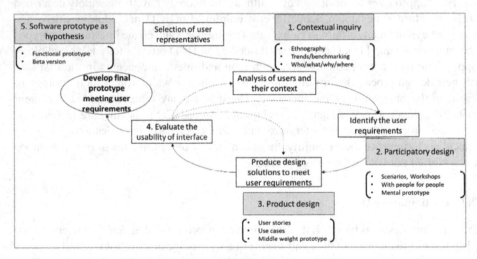

Fig. 3. Human-centered participatory co-design

In the recent years, HCD and participatory design have been used together to become what is often termed human-centered participatory co-design, which is defined as "the creativity of designers and people not trained in design working together in design development process" [23]. Research-based design methods originally developed as participatory design methodology have been modified as participatory co-design framework. We propose to utilize methods from the participatory co-design framework and overlay it on the HCD process to identify design changes to the current DQC and develop a user-focused functional prototype of an enhanced DQC (Fig. 3).

The objectives of this study are: 1) to apply a human-centered participatory co-design framework to design DQC, 2) to explain the design process in which multi-phased key stakeholders' participation informed design decisions, and 3) to identify design changes to currently deployed DQC in an academic radiation oncology clinic and develop a user-focused functional prototype of an enhanced DQC.

3   Methods

3.1   Study Settings

We conducted the study in a radiation oncology clinic to learn and account for interruptions and collaborations between members of the interdisciplinary care team. We obtained approval from the Institutional Review Board at the University of North Carolina for this study.

3.2   Pre-treatment Dosimetry QA Process

Dosimetrists perform the following QA tasks in the pre-treatment dosimetry QA process, which includes a varying number of checks:

Pre-planning. During this QA check, dosimetrists investigate the electronic medical record (e.g., MOSAIQ©) to assess the physician's intent (ideal treatment goals), planning note (the radiation plan that can be safely delivered), and the prescription (delivery directive to the therapists).

Planning. Dosimetry planning is the process of determining the amount, rate, and distribution of radiation emitted from a source of ionizing radiation based on the physician's prescription for a specific patient. In this QA task, dosimetrists verify parameters in plan design, check isocenters, beams, digitally reconstructed radiographs (DRRs), and set up beams, guard leaf, optimization, etc. Dosimetrists have a vital role in ensuring that an appropriate radiation dose is administered to the target area.

Pre-MD Approval. Before submitting the plan to a physician (MD) for approval, dosimetrists perform additional checks in the treatment planning software (e.g., RayStation©) such as comparing the treatment plan in RayStation with the planning note in MOSAIQ.

Post-MD Approval. After the physician (MD) approval, most checklist items are cross-checked based on data from the treatment planning system (RayStation©), electronic medical record (MOSAIQ©), and departmental policy.

3.3   Current Dosimetry QA Checklist (DQC)

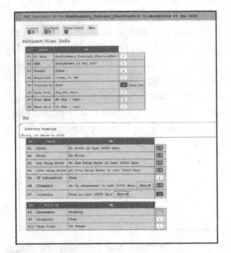

Fig. 4. dosCheckV2 (Color figure online)   **Fig. 5.** Electronic checklist

Currently, two distinct checklists are deployed in the radiation oncology clinic to perform the pre-treatment dosimetry QA process described in Sect. 3.4. To perform pre-planning and planning QA tasks, Tracton et al. developed a dosimetry checklist (dosCheck V2) with inputs from physicists and dosimetrists as well as unstructured interviews with the chair of the physics division (Fig. 4) [8]. In the pre-planning tab of this checklist, the patient's context is presented along with physician intent, planning note, and prescription. The dosimetrists are also provided information regarding previous radiation, pregnancy, and pacemakers (3-Ps) to prepare them for the planning process. In the planning tab, this checklist has automated some of the key checks and provides colored flags to indicate whether a check is safe to the patient (green), absolutely unsafe (red), of unknown status due to missing input (yellow), in need of an additional safety check (orange), or just for general information (white). The clinic also utilizes a second electronic checklist with ~35 items to perform pre-MD and post-MD QA tasks for different external beam radiation therapies (Intensity Modulated Radiation Therapy (IMRT), Volumetric Modulated Arc Therapy (VMAT), Stereotactic Body Radiation Therapy, 3-D Conformal Radiation Therapy (CRT) and Tomotherapy) on a Microsoft Word document (Fig. 5). Thus, this checklist includes both specific and non-specific items for each radiation therapy and like most checklists poses items as binary: "yes" or "not applicable".

3.4 Data Collection

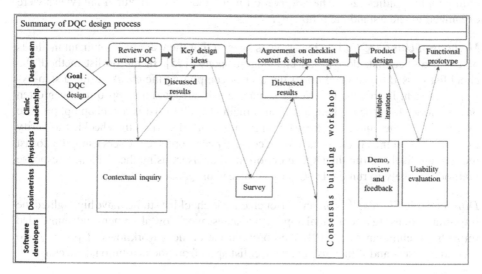

Fig. 6. DQC co-design process

The key stakeholders involved in the DQC design process were: (1) the design team (including two human factors experts and an experienced software developer) (2) clinic leadership which oversaw the project management (including the chair of the physics division) (3) physicists (n = 9) review the plan designed by dosimetrists to improve the safety and quality of the plan and are the secondary users of DQC (4) dosimetrists (n = 5) are involved in designing a treatment plan for each patient and are the primary users of the DQC (5) experienced software developers (n = 2) who were involved in building dosCheckV2 (Fig. 6). Based on previous studies highlighting the impact of socio-cultural and technical barriers on the usability and effectiveness of checklists, the design process began with the goal of identifying design changes to the currently deployed DQC in an academic radiation oncology clinic. We reviewed the checklist content and key design ideas in the current DQC and the HCI approaches to further improve the usability and effectiveness of DQC.

Contextual Inquiry. The primary purpose of the contextual inquiry was to better understand the context in which DQC is being used and help recognize possible challenges and design opportunities. Accordingly, the focus in this phase was to assess how primary and secondary users utilized the current DQC and to examine the gaps in the current DQC as well as the individual differences in the clinical workflow. In this phase, we conducted contextual inquiries first with dosimetrists (n = 5) and then with physicists (n = 4). We observed them for four to five hours each during their clinical duty and performed semi-structured interviews to gain a deeper understanding of the end-users' challenges with the current DQC. A total of ~40 h of observations were completed, and information was collected using a field note-taking procedure established in previous ethnographic studies [24]. The observation notes and semi-structured interviews were organized to understand the following.

Methods of Using DQC. Previous studies suggest that there are two dominant methods of using a checklist: do-list and challenge-response [25]. In the do-list method, the checklist is used to lead and direct the user in completing the checks using a step-by-step approach. In this method, if the sequence is interrupted a skipped item can often pass unnoticed. In the challenge-response method, a checklist is a backup option. The user performs the entire check based on memory and then uses the checklist to verify that all items on the checklist have been correctly accomplished. Users using the do-list method are likely to run the DQC more often while users using the challenge-response method are likely to run the DQC only at the end of QA tasks.

Differences in Clinical Workflows. Prior electronic checklist studies have highlighted the importance of using a contextual approach to assess workflow alignment and unintended impacts on clinician roles [10]. We observed the clinical workflows of primary and secondary users and if they used any checklist apart from the institutional checklist.

Differences in When (Pre-plan, Planning, Pre-MD, and Post-MD) and How the Current DQC Was Used. Since the current DQC has two distinct checklists, we wanted to understand the individual variation in the use of both checklists and their use during the different QA tasks.

Gaps in the Current DQC. At the end of the naturalistic observation, participants were asked open-ended questions on what they liked and disliked about the current DQC and the changes they would suggest for the current DQC. At the end of the contextual inquiry process, the main results and findings were discussed with the clinic leadership, and the first set of key design ideas was developed.

Participatory Design. In this phase, results from the contextual inquiry process were discussed and developed further by involving end-users. The primary purpose of this phase was to seek maximum input from key end-users, focusing on actual and practical design. In this study, we presented the results from the contextual inquiry to dosimetrists to discuss the design changes suggested by the end-users. This phase included surveys and consensus-building workshops. Surveys were administered to assess the level of agreement on the key changes suggested, and consensus-building workshops were aimed at resolving disagreements between users, prioritizing key design changes, and producing design solutions to key end-user challenges.

Survey. The design changes suggested by dosimetrists and physicists for the current DQC and the extent of agreement to each of the proposed changes were assessed using a survey. As primary users of the DQC, all dosimetrists were invited to participate in the survey. To quantify the strength of agreement between dosimetrists on the suggested design changes and checklist content (checklist items requiring changes and new checklist items), we conducted a content validity index (CVI) exercise [26]. CVI is a widely reported approach for content validity in instrument development. Generally, item-CVI is calculated as the number of experts giving a rating of "very relevant" for each item divided by the total number of experts [27]. In our study, dosimetrists (n = 5) were asked to rate their agreement on each item (checklist content and design changes) using a validated 5-point ordinal scale (1 = strongly disagree, 2 = disagree, 3 = neither agree nor disagree, 4 = agree, 5 = strongly agree). A minimum of 80% (4 out of 5 participants) was required to endorse design changes and checklist content by a rating of at least 4 out of 5 to establish content validity beyond the 0.05 level of significance. This approach was previously utilized by Bowie et al. in designing a preliminary safety checklist for general practice [26].

Consensus-Building Workshops. The results from the survey were analyzed, and a consensus-building workshop was conducted to discuss the major disagreements between dosimetrists. The goal of this workshop was to understand the major disagreements, gauge user needs, and assess the technical and organizational feasibility of the suggested design changes. The consensus-building workshop involved multi-disciplinary experts including dosimetrists (n = 5), physicists (n = 3), software engineers (n = 2), and human factors engineers (n = 2) along with clinic leadership. Study participants were involved in in-depth critical discussion on major disagreements, and consensus on major design changes was discussed during a 2-h workshop. To resolve some of the key issues, we used forced ranking, a structured and objective approach to helping achieve consensus while satisfying the varied needs of the users [16]. Additional features to improve the usability of the DQC were proposed and discussed. Participants were asked to anonymously provide individual rankings to issues that could not be resolved even after discussion, and the number of votes received for/against each issue was reviewed as a group. The workshop moderator (KA) also took notes, selected members of the research team, reviewed the notes, and finalized the design ideas and checklist content.

Product Design. We used data from contextual inquiries, surveys, and workshops to develop use cases. This phase aimed to give a more concrete form to the ideas presented in the earlier stages of the design process. We used agile software development methods to develop use cases and basic interactions using prototypes. In this phase, all the design ideas presented during the contextual inquiry and further agreed upon in the survey and consensus-building workshop were further developed and presented to dosimetrists and physicists for review and feedback. After multiple iterations, the middle-level fidelity or semi-functioning prototypes were built for further testing and refinement efforts.

Usability Evaluation. In this phase, the improved semi-functioning prototypes were presented to end-users. User testing was conducted over Zoom with both dosimetrists and physicists. Three short testing cycles (i.e., 3 cohorts) were conducted with 3 participants in each cycle. End users were asked to think aloud as they evaluated the prototypes. Each user was asked to randomly choose any of the external beam radiation therapy plans (IMRT/VMAT/SBRT/3D-CRT/Tomotherapy). The user's screen and audio recordings were employed to record the user's interaction with the prototype. The interview guide was developed in consultation with a qualitative research expert. The video and audio recordings of user verbalizations were reviewed with annotations and time stamps to demarcate key user actions, system responses, and other interesting aspects of user-system interaction. We used Kushniruk et al.'s video coding scheme to analyze the usability, usefulness, safety & technology-induced errors [28]. We present some important comments from the think-aloud sessions as a comprehensive analysis of this data is out of scope for this paper.

End users evaluated the perceived usability using the System Usability Scale (SUS), which is the most effective and widely used tool to measure usability. It is a validated post-test questionnaire that measures user satisfaction. SUS provides a score (range: 0–100) based on a participant's rating of 10 statements regarding usability with higher scores indicating greater satisfaction with usability [29]. A SUS score of 68 is considered the average benchmark, and a SUS of 80 is considered the above-average benchmark. SUS is relatively easy and quick for study participants to complete in clinical settings or over Zoom and is also easy to score [29]. Therefore, SUS was used to quantify the overall perceived usability of the semi-functioning prototype. Problems identified during the testing were prioritized and addressed in turn by the development team.

Functional Prototype. In this phase, the development team used agile software development methods to release small functional pieces of software. Subsequently, a user-focused functional prototype was built as a script using Python and JavaScript, which included all the key design changes that were suggested by the participants during the contextual inquiry, survey, workshop, product design, and usability evaluation.

4   Results

4.1   Contextual Inquiries

Methods of Using DQC. We observed that five (3 dosimetrists, 2 physicists) out of nine participants adopted a challenge-verify method, while the remaining four (2 dosimetrists, 2 physicists) adopted a do-list method.

Differences in Clinical Workflows. Two out of five dosimetrists utilized their checklists in addition to the institutional DQC. All physicists only used the institutional checklist. There were no significant variations in the clinical workflow between the dosimetrists. In some checks, dosimetrists used different functionalities in MOSAIQ but ultimately completed QA tasks with identical efficiency as measured by the time taken to complete the tasks.

Differences in When (Pre-plan, Planning, Pre-MD, and Post-MD) and How the Current DQC is Used. There was variation in how dosimetrists were using the current DQC. We noted that dosimetrists used the current DQC at different stages of the radiation therapy plan process. Between dosCheckV2 and the electronic checklist, dosCheckV2 was being used mostly in the planning task, while the electronic checklist was used only at the post-MD task. More specifically, only one dosimetrist used dosCheckV2 in the pre-planning task (1/5), while all five dosimetrists used dosCheckV2 in the planning task. The electronic checklist was used at the end of the pre-MD task by two dosimetrists while all dosimetrists this electronic checklist at the end of the post-MD task.

Gaps in Current DQC. Participants identified multiple gaps in the current DQC. The key gaps within the current DQC and the suggested key design ideas for improvement are presented in Table 1.

Table 1. Key suggested design features

Design features	Gaps in current DQC	Key design ideas
1. Checklist components	Includes two distinct checklists	Merge both the checklists and design per the clinic's workflow (Pre-plan, In-plan, Pre-MD, Post-MD)
2. Initial selection	Users select the site of the clinic (academic vs non-academic site settings)	Allow users to select the MOSAIQ plans and RayStation beam sets and the treatment options (IMRT, VMAT, SBRT, 3CRT, Tomotherapy)
3. User options	The current checklist offers users only two options: Yes and N/A	Provide enhanced options supported by distinct colors to represent user decisions: All Okay (AOK), Attention (Attn), and Not applicable (N/A)
4. Improved communication and care coordination	Lack of standardized mode of communication. For instance, dosimetrists and physicists use the phone/email/in-person to communicate over the checklist	Support communication between dosimetrists and physicists. For instance, users should be able to write a brief note to reviewers to draw their attention and these notes can be discussed during bi-weekly departmental quality improvement meetings
5. User feedback	DQC does not provide any feedback if the users forget to select a checklist and the number of checklist items that have been completed	Users suggested feedback may be provided if any item is unfilled on the checklist
6. Memory aids to facilitate the checklist process	Users perform tasks on two different information systems (MOSAIQ and RayStation) and often must compare results from both information systems. The tool lacks adequate memory aids	Users suggested making data from MOSAIQ and RayStation readily available to cross-check and decide
7. Declutter the checklist	Users felt that the electronic checklist was cluttered and was not specific for RT. They cannot filter the status and are forced to scan the entire tab	Users shared their preference to disable options that are not required to be checked for specific RT plans. They wanted a filter by status to trim the report and focus only on warning flags
8. Personalization of checklist	Users cannot customize the checklist items to match their workflow	Users shared a preference to personalize the order and the number of checklist items (over and beyond the institutional checklist items)

4.2 Participatory Design

Survey.
Design Changes: All the design changes suggested in Table 1 were evaluated by dosimetrists. All five dosimetrists rated 7 key design changes with a >4 score on the

5-point scale and the overall CVI ratio for these 7 design changes was 0.96. However, on personalization or customization of DQC to individual dosimetrists, only 3 dosimetrists rated >3 on the 5-point scale.

Checklist Content: The checklist content was assessed to determine whether additional checklist items were needed or if existing checklist items required changes. For instance, during contextual inquiry, dosimetrists suggested changes to 12 checklist items. On 5/12 checklists items, all dosimetrists rated >4 on the 5-point scale. However, on remaining checklist items, there was no agreement among the dosimetrists. Further, during the contextual inquiry, participants suggested two additional checklist items. All five dosimetrists rated >4 on the 5-point scale for including these two checklist items. The overall CVI ratio for checklist content was 0.75.

Consensus-Building Workshop. During the consensus-building workshop, there was a major discussion on the personalization or customization of the checklist. End users were divided on whether the checklist should be customized to each user and match their clinical workflow. However, the software developers clarified that this feature may not be technically feasible then as the plan was to develop the checklist as a RayStation script, and it would require individual login for each user. Dosimetrists also highlighted the need to remove checklist items such as goal sheet and IMRT QA form which is not part of their work. Clinic leadership clarified the purpose of these checks and after further deliberation, all those checklist items on which there was no consensus were put to voting. Software developers suggested that do-list users tend to run the script many times. To reduce the time to fire up the script, they suggested including a new *bail on error* feature that would focus on the earliest sections of planning workflow with significant errors or warnings or missing status and would not run the tests on the later sections. This would reduce the processing time and allow users to correct errors in the order in which planning tasks occur. They also suggested additional features such as a comprehensive MOSAIQ calendar with all related activities such as weekly chart checks, clinical closings, chart check QCLs, and planned fraction sessions by site as an interactive calendar. The rest of the team provided other suggestions (check tracked and planned doses, the patient is charged by clinical location, etc.) which were discussed, and a consensus was reached during the workshop.

4.3   Product Design

The design ideas presented during the contextual inquiry were further agreed upon in the survey and consensus-building workshop. After multiple reviews, feedback, and iterations from dosimetrists and physicists, the product design was developed. The key design idea and the artifacts from the product design are shown in Table 2.

Table 2. Design ideas and artifacts from product design

Key design idea	Artifacts from product design
Merge both the checklists and design per the clinic's workflow (Pre-plan, In-plan, Pre-MD, Post-MD)	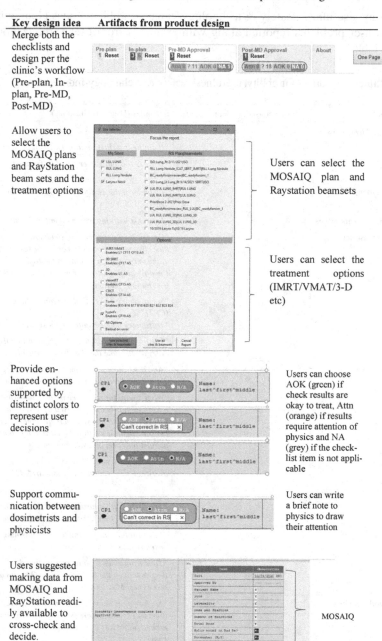
Allow users to select the MOSAIQ plans and RayStation beam sets and the treatment options	Users can select the MOSAIQ plan and Raystation beamsets
	Users can select the treatment options (IMRT/VMAT/3-D etc)
Provide enhanced options supported by distinct colors to represent user decisions	Users can choose AOK (green) if check results are okay to treat, Attn (orange) if results require attention of physics and NA (grey) if the checklist item is not applicable
Support communication between dosimetrists and physicists	Users can write a brief note to physics to draw their attention
Users suggested making data from MOSAIQ and RayStation readily available to cross-check and decide.	MOSAIQ — RayStation

4.4 Usability Evaluation

The usability, usefulness, safety & technology-induced problem codes along with the number of user problems reported along with examples from user verbalizations are shown in Table 3.

Table 3. Coding of usability, usefulness, safety & technology-induced errors

Problem codes	Number of user problems reported	Examples (User verbalizations)
A. Usability problem codes		
Navigation	4	"If a note is written in attn, how is it preserved?"
Meaning of icons	2	"What is this thing over here? (referring to stale QCLs)"
Visibility of system status	3	"I wonder if this is different from this, would it show up?"
Understanding error messages	6	"I got this warning which I don't understand"
Understanding instructions	3	"I'm thinking to myself like you know, there are times like where you have certain boxes like CA2 to at the very top. I'm looking at the treatment site and I'm only getting site information from mosaic, but not from ray station"
Workflow issues	2	"Set up beams (A5) should be after Check Iso (CP7)" "Dosimetry note be shifted to post-MD"
Layout	3	"The box is so small that they wouldn't really know every all the note that has been written right."
Speed/response time	1	"And it's been a while since I ran something new, I don't know how long it takes to open the tool"
Color	2	"What's hard for me to see is you know what information is being displayed by mosaic, and which is race Asian so like yes, there are color-coded here, but sometimes it's a little bit hard to not think it's all merged into one, and so I have to."
Overall ease of use	2	"The one page would be too long and overwhelming. Can this be summarized?"
B. Usefulness of content code		
Accuracy	5	"The MDs don't approve the site they check the diagnosis and they approve the prescription."
Relevance	7	"I don't think that's going to mean anything to anybody outside of you know."
Timeliness	2	"Time from when a patient is simulated to when they're treated the first fraction or QA days about two weeks. May be a 30-day window"
Impact on work activities	3	"So, having it in one places there's a good, but I think the, I think, where people are going to get most excited about it is if it's doing their job for them, you know."
C. Safety and technology-induced error codes		
Slip	4	"I am really good at breaking things"

(continued)

Table 3. (*continued*)

Problem codes	Number of user problems reported	Examples (User verbalizations)
Mistake	12	*"I clicked on the yellow button and the box came."*
Workaround	5	*"Yeah I just I developed a workaround and I just keep rolling"*

Descriptive statistics for subjective assessments of usability were calculated using Microsoft Excel. We compared the perceived usability in three cohorts (3 participants each) with HCI standards for SUS (Table 4) and found that the usability scores for cohorts 2 and 3 matches the SUS benchmark scores.

Table 4. Usability scores

Number of participants	Cohort 1	Cohort 2	Cohort 3
Participant 1	77.5	80	90
Participant 2	75	82.5	85
Participant 3	75	80	85
Mean (SD)	75.83 (1.44)	80.83 (1.44)	86.67 (2.89)
SUS benchmark score	80	80	80

4.5 Functional Prototype

After four additional iterations with dosimetrists and physicists, and correcting all the usability, usefulness, safety, and technology-induced errors, product designs were finalized and a user-focused functional prototype of enhanced DQC was developed with all the suggested major key designs features.

5 Discussion

Through an iterative human-centered participatory co-design process, involving contextual inquiries, surveys, consensus-building workshops, product design, usability evaluation, we developed a functional prototype of DQC. Participants suggested key design changes, shared disagreements, negotiated removing checklist items, and identified key usability, usefulness, and safety and technology-induced errors. The result of this comprehensive evidence-based theoretical approach is an enhanced DQC that meets above-average SUS benchmark standards. This study demonstrates that current DQC's usability can be improved using a human-centered participatory co-design process.

Our study results are similar to previous checklist studies [10, 11] that highlight the importance of socio-technical barriers in design process. We incorporated existing workflows, tools, and organizational policies in the enhanced DQC. Thus, the enhanced DQC is likely to better integrate into our institution's socio-technical system. In our study, the primary objective was to identify design changes to the current DQC and thus, we emphasized context more than is typical in design research where researchers often develop new tools. Leinonen et al. argue that stakeholders and designers propose key design changes during participatory design phase as they deepen their understanding of the context during this phase [21, 22]. But in our study, stakeholders were using current DQC in a clinical setting and had clear insights on improvements needed to the current DQC. Thus, they proposed key design ideas during the contextual inquiry phase and resolved disagreements during the participatory design phase.

Our study findings are significant as it supports a specific type of thinking during the checklist process rather than a consistent task completion which is the key focus in most checklist studies. For instance, the design idea of cross-matching data from two different health information systems (MOSAIQ© and RayStation©) encourages the user to maintain "relaxed focused attention" [30] during the checklist process. This study also represents a major shift in checklist design as it focuses on improving communication between dosimetrists and physicists, emphasizes a collaborative checklist process between clinicians (dosimetrists and physicists in our case) rather than focusing on a specific clinician group to complete the checklist.

This study has several limitations. First, this study is based on participants from a single academic medical center. Second, there are inter-institutional differences in how QA processes and checks are performed. Third, this checklist has only undergone rapid usability testing and its integration into the clinical environment would require additional testing. Third, we have not evaluated the checklist in the clinical environment though we gathered feedback from multiple stakeholders throughout the design process.

6   Conclusion

Improving the usability of a checklist currently deployed in the clinic environment requires an understanding of the socio-cultural and technical barriers impacting its usability and effectiveness. We used a human-centered participatory co-design framework to improve the usability of a DQC through innovative design ideas generated by key stakeholders. This methodology proved to have tremendous potential to improve the usability and effectiveness of medical checklists in general. Future research will include assessing the impact of enhanced DQC on patient safety, users' cognitive workload, and performance in simulation and near-live settings before its clinical implementation.

References

1. Marks, L.B., et al.: The challenge of maximizing safety in radiation oncology. Pract. Radiat. Oncol. 1(1), 2–14 (2011)
2. Yeung, T.K., Bortolotto, K., Cosby, S., Hoar, M., Lederer, E.: Quality assurance in radiotherapy: evaluation of errors and incidents recorded over a 10 year period. Radiother. Oncol. 74(3), 283–291 (2005)
3. Das, P., et al.: Rate of radiation therapy events in a large academic institution. J. Am. Coll. Radiol. 10(6), 452–455 (2013)

4. Cunningham, J., Coffey, M., Knöös, T., Holmberg, O.: Radiation Oncology Safety Information System (ROSIS)–profiles of participants and the first 1074 incident reports. Radiother. Oncol. **97**(3), 601–607 (2010)
5. Ford, E.C., Terezakis, S., Souranis, A., Harris, K., Gay, H., Mutic, S.: Quality control quantification (QCQ): a tool to measure the value of quality control checks in radiation oncology. Int. J. Radiat. Oncol. Biol. Phys. **84**(3), e263–e269 (2012)
6. Ford, E., et al.: Strategies for effective physics plan and chart review in radiation therapy: report of AAPM Task Group 275. Med. Phys. **47**(6), e236–e272 (2020)
7. Liu, S., et al.: Optimizing efficiency and safety in external beam radiotherapy using automated plan check (APC) tool and six sigma methodology. J. Appl. Clin. Med. Phys. **20**(8), 56–64 (2019)
8. Tracton, G.S., Mazur, L.M., Mosaly, P., Marks, L.B., Das, S.: Developing and assessing electronic checklists for safety mindfulness, workload, and performance. Pract. Radiat. Oncol. **8**(6), 458–467 (2018)
9. Adapa, K., et al.: Evaluating the usability of a dosimetry quality assurance checklist and associated workload, performance and patient safety in clinical settings. Int. J. Radiat. Oncol. -Biol.-Phys. (Red J.) (2021), https://doi.org/10.1016/j.ijrobp.2021.07.1391
10. Kuo, P.-Y., et al.: Development of a checklist for the prevention of intradialytic hypotension in hemodialysis care: design considerations based on activity theory. In: Proceedings of the 2019 CHI Conference on Human Factors in Computing Systems - CHI 2019, pp. 1–14. ACM Press, New York (2019)
11. Hales, B.M., Pronovost, P.J.: The checklist–a tool for error management and performance improvement. J Crit Care. **21**(3), 231–235 (2006)
12. Haynes, A.B., et al.: A surgical safety checklist to reduce morbidity and mortality in a global population. N. Engl. J. Med. **360**(5), 491–499 (2009)
13. Borchard, A., Schwappach, D.L.B., Barbir, A., Bezzola, P.: A systematic review of the effectiveness, compliance, and critical factors for implementation of safety checklists in surgery. Ann. Surg. **256**(6), 925–933 (2012)
14. Burian, B.K., Clebone, A., Dismukes, K., Ruskin, K.J.: More than a tick box: medical checklist development, design, and use. Anesth. Analg. **126**(1), 223–232 (2018)
15. Madaio, M.A., Stark, L., Wortman Vaughan, J., Wallach, H.: Co-designing checklists to understand organizational challenges and opportunities around fairness in AI. In: Proceedings of the 2020 CHI Conference on Human Factors in Computing Systems, pp. 1–14. ACM, New York (2020)
16. Norman, D.: Cognitive engineering. In: Norman, D., Drapers, S.W., (eds.) User Centered System Design, pp. 31–61 (1986)
17. ISO - ISO 9241-210:2010 - Ergonomics of human-system interaction—Part 210: Human-centred design for interactive systems. https://www.iso.org/standard/52075.html. Accessed 10 Feb 2022
18. Schaeffer, N.E.: The role of human factors in the design and development of an insulin pump. J. Diabetes Sci. Technol. **6**(2), 260–264 (2012)
19. Zickler, C., Halder, S., Kleih, S.C., Herbert, C., Kübler, A.: Brain painting: usability testing according to the user-centered design in end users with severe motor paralysis. Artif. Intell. Med. **59**(2), 99–110 (2013)
20. Katsulis, Z., et al.: Iterative user centered design for development of a patient-centered fall prevention toolkit. Appl. Ergon. **56**, 117–126 (2016)
21. Leinonen T. Designing Learning tools. Methodological insights (2010)
22. Leinonen, T., Durall-Gazulla, E.: Design thinking and collaborative learning. Comunicar: Revista Científica de Comunicación y Educación. **21**(42), 107–116 (2014)
23. Durall, E., Perry, S., Hurley, M., Kapros, E., Leinonen, T.: Co-designing for equity in informal science learning: a proof-of-concept study of design principles. Front. Educ. **6**, 204 (2021)

24. Franklin, A., et al.: Opportunistic decision making and complexity in emergency care. J. Biomed. Inform. **44**(3), 469–476 (2011)
25. Degani, A., Wiener, E.L.: Cockpit checklists: concepts, design, and use. Hum. Factors **35**(2), 345–359 (1993)
26. Bowie, P., et al.: Participatory design of a preliminary safety checklist for general practice. Br. J. Gen. Pract. **65**(634), e330–e343 (2015)
27. Zamanzadeh, V., Ghahramanian, A., Rassouli, M., Abbaszadeh, A., Alavi-Majd, H., Nikanfar, A.-R.: Design and implementation content validity study: development of an instrument for measuring patient-centered communication. J. Caring Sci. **4**(2), 165–178 (2015)
28. Kushniruk, A.W., Borycki, E.M.: Development of a video coding scheme for analyzing the usability and usefulness of health information systems. Stud. Health Technol. Inform. **218**, 68–73 (2015)
29. Brooke, J.: SUS: a "quick and dirty" usability scale. In: Usability Evaluation in Industry, 189–194 (1996)
30. Lippelt, D.P., Hommel, B., Colzato, L.S.: Focused attention, open monitoring and loving kindness meditation: effects on attention, conflict monitoring, and creativity - a review. Front. Psychol. **5**, 1083 (2014)

Increase Therapy Understanding and Medication Adherence for Patients with Inflammatory Skin Diseases Through Augmented Reality

Yannick Roger Deiss[1]($\boxtimes$), Safak Korkut[2] (ID), and Terry Inglese[2]

[1] Salted GmbH, 4600 Olten, Switzerland
deiss@salted.ch

[2] University of Applied Sciences and Arts Northwestern Switzerland, 4052 Basel, Switzerland
{safak.korkut,terry.inglese}@fhnw.ch

Abstract. Augmented Reality (AR) offers an incomparable user experience by projecting digital content in a user's real environment. Like AR, dermatology is a visual field, and the integration of AR technology into the daily lives of patients and dermatologists promises synergy opportunities. Patients with inflammatory skin diseases as atopic dermatitis and psoriasis face complex challenges to adhere to their therapy. The lack of understanding about the specific disease and the unknowledge of the potential worsening process leads to uncertainty in therapy and place an additional burden on therapy management.

The benefits of AR as an enabler of learning experiences have been discussed in various fields as professional education in healthcare. Studies have been conducted regarding the potential impact of and opportunities provided by AR for patients with inflammatory skin diseases. According to the design science research framework, dermatologists and patients have been interviewed to investigate and evaluate an AR prototype in the context of therapy understanding and medication adherence for patients. A visual framework of a mobile application and the AR prototype were demonstrated to dermatologists and patients based on semi-structured interviews. The added value of AR in the analysis was reported to be beneficial to increase not just patients' understanding about their disease but also the motivation to be more adherent to the prescribed therapy. The AR visualizations of different manifestations of the affected skin were acknowledged as helpful, especially in the context of prevention of further worsening.

Keywords: Augmented Reality · Dermatology · Healthcare communication · Interactive learning experiences · Education and training

1 Introduction

1.1 Background Information

Inflammatory skin diseases are widespread dermatological issues and can limit the quality of life of patients (Schielein et al. 2019). Not only the optical change in the skin,

V. G. Duffy (Ed.): HCII 2022, LNCS 13320, pp. 21–40, 2022.
https://doi.org/10.1007/978-3-031-06018-2_2

but also the change in patients' psychological condition are important components in the treatment of skin diseases (p. 875). Therapy compliance in healthcare means taking medication as doctors prescribe it and further includes patients' ability to make recommended changes and complete planned investigations and can be a challenge for both patients and physicians (Goldsmith 1979, p. 297). According to Hilken et al. (2018, pp. 509–512), Augmented Reality (AR) can enable solving specific problems, such as the visualization of a situation, by enlarging the user's perceived environment. Similar to AR, dermatological treatments rely predominantly on visual feedback and thereby the combination of AR technology and dermatology offer a unique opportunity to leverage the users' experience in treatment (Obagi et al. 2020, p. 2).

1.2 Problem Statement

Atopic dermatitis (Capozza and Schwartz 2019, p. 58) and psoriasis (Zaghloul and Goodfield 2004, p. 411) patients' understanding of the medication used to treat their problems is often inadequate. Nearly one third of patients with atopic dermatitis do not adhere to the therapy for their lesions (Kolli et al. 2019, p. 75). According to Capozza and Schwartz (2019, p. 59), the reasons for low adherence are controversial and not well understood. Delivering the right amount of information is relevant for patients, as are education and explanations about the illness, the related treatments, and possible results (Deledda et al. 2013, p. 298). Even though AR applications have led to growing attention in the area of marketing, developers, managers, and academics have trouble with the argumentation of how AR delivers experiences that are valuable to customers in different ways from usual marketing approaches (Chylinski et al. 2020, p. 3).

1.3 Research Objective

This paper addresses dermatologists and proposes a new way for sharing valuable and necessary information with their patients and improve patient communication outside the clinical environment with the use of AR technology. A proof-of-concept highlights in what situation and context a mobile AR application provides opportunities to help patients with inflammatory skin diseases to better understand their lesions and possible treatments. Thus, the research objective brings together the opportunities provided by mobile AR to address the challenges in therapy understanding and medication adherence for patients with inflammatory skin diseases by creating new learning and information experiences.

To combine opportunities, experiences, knowledge and research, this paper focuses on dermatology as a specific indication area in the pharmaceutical industry and does not attempt to provide a clinical study. To create added value for an explicit target group, the literature research and the development of the prototype are concentrated on inflammatory skin diseases, especially atopic dermatitis and psoriasis. AR technology is implemented with the objective of enabling new learning experiences throughout a digital interaction and visualization of individual skin diseases to increase awareness and understanding of patients' lesions and treatments and thus motivate them to be more adherent to their therapy. Medication adherence is one of many aspects within therapy compliance and embodies the focus of this paper.

2 State of the Art

2.1 Inflammatory Skin Diseases

This section explores the work of Möbus et al. (2020) and states that some of the most widespread inflammatory skin diseases can be clustered and analysed together in terms of different perspectives, regarding development and genetic circumstances. Atopic dermatitis and psoriasis show similar effects in the human body. In a systematic literature review, Möbus et al. (2020) describe that atopic dermatitis and psoriasis not only develop for similar reasons, but also occur under similar genetic circumstances. Additionally, the authors outline a distinct profile regarding the epigenetic risk factors of atopic dermatitis and psoriasis but that they have a different genetic profile. Atopic dermatitis and psoriasis are the focus of the research due to their similarity and are categorised as inflammatory skin diseases (pp. 1049–1060). The individual characteristics and similarities of these lesions are explained in the following two sections.

Atopic Dermatitis. Ten to twenty percent of children and 5 to 10% of adults in Central Europe are affected by atopic dermatitis, which makes it one of the most widespread skin diseases (Möbus et al. 2020, p. 1049; Weidinger and Novak 2016, p. 1109). It usually begins in childhood, mainly affects children and in most cases declines with age. Patients have dry skin and are plagued by persistent itching; therefore, their quality of life is significantly limited. Skincare products are the main products used for medical treatment depending on the individual characteristics of the lesion (Krakowski et al. 2008, p. 812). Therapeutic possibilities are changing quickly due to new research and development, especially in the area of biologic therapies and novel small molecules, but most therapies do not have a standard protocol in terms of duration and treatment, which makes it difficult to compare different therapies (Lansang et al. 2019, pp. 20–23). Atopic dermatitis still cannot be cured, and the aim of therapies is to manage symptoms and achieve long-term disease control (Weidinger and Novak 2016, p. 1116).

Psoriasis. Like atopic dermatitis, psoriasis is an inflammatory skin disease that often places great burdens on patients and their relatives (Zaghloul and Goodfield 2004, p. 408). Of the world population, 1 to 3% percent are affected by this chronic inflammatory skin disorder (Möbus et al. 2020, pp. 1049–1050), which is characterised by scaly, itchy and often painful changes in the structure of the skin. The extent and location can change over time (Zaghloul and Goodfield, p. 408). Because of its systemic inflammation, psoriasis is often associated with an increased risk of cardiovascular diseases, obesity and diabetes. Therefore, the goal of the treatment is not only to heal the affected sites on the skin but to reduce patients' systemic inflammation. According to Korman (2020, p. 823), there are still no treatments or therapies that completely cure psoriasis, so ongoing treatment is important to control the extent of the disease.

Medication Adherence. Compliance in healthcare has been defined as the extent to which a person's behaviour coincides with health-related advice and includes the patient's ability to attend clinic appointments as scheduled, take medication as prescribed, make recommended lifestyle changes and complete recommended investigations (Goldsmith 1979, p. 297). Nonadherence to treatment represents a common issue for 30% of patients with atopic dermatitis, which are not taking their medication as prescribed (Kolli et al. 2019, p. 75). The reasons for low adherence among patients are controversial and not yet well understood (Capozza and Schwartz 2019, p. 58).

Moreover, in an open prospective study on 294 psoriasis patients starting a new treatment for the first time showed a significantly higher medication adherence compared to patients with a continuing treatment (Zaghloul and Goodfield 2004). Furthermore, the extent and location of the lesions were significantly important for the medication adherence since patients with more than three sites of lesions are more adherent to the planned medication (pp. 411–412). Weidinger and Novak (2016) have presented similar results. Their study of reports from January 2010 to March 2015 regarding atopic dermatitis and atopic eczema concluded that failure of therapy is common and is often related to irrational fears, such as possible adverse effects and insufficient information (p. 1116). A more recent randomised controlled study (Hiremath et al. 2021) with 68 psoriasis patients highlights the effect of education intervention, especially the information delivered by community pharmacists increased patients' knowledge about the disease and improved their quality of life, which resulted in better medication adherence.

To conclude, atopic dermatitis and psoriasis patients' understanding of their disease and the associated therapy, as well as information about the course of the disease and its possible manifestations, are key factors for higher medication adherence. In addition, patients' relationship of trust with the treating specialists is also highly relevant.

Patients are generally not well informed about their medication interactions and potential complications; therefore, they tend to trust doctors' decisions (Mira et al. 2012, p. 826). Not only does relevant information about diagnostic tests and causes of illness might lead to a trusting relationship between the treating doctor and patients, but also information about the origin and causes of illness and potential treatment complications is also crucial (Mira et al. 2012, pp. 831–835). These circumstances and expectations regarding the effectiveness of therapy and medication adherence are often not clear to patients.

2.2 Augmented Reality

Since the innovative technologies AR and virtual reality (VR) can visualize complex information, there are many opportunities for applications in dermatology (Obagi et al. 2020, p. 1). Furthermore, mobile AR applications enhance users' environment with digitally provided information without any restrictions of mobility or location (Abbas et al. 2020). The pharmaceutical and medical industry has already implemented some applications focusing on head-mounted devices and on education of professionals (Jorge et al. 2019, p. 2).

Augmented Reality in Dermatology. According to Sharma et al. (2019, p. 1216), AR is used in clinical medicine to enhance existing digital information represented with different devices, such as headsets or smartphones. Dermatology and AR are visual fields; therefore, applications that combine these two technologies might enhance familiarity and appropriate use in practice for dermatologists. Sharma et al. (2019) categorised already-deployed AR applications in dermatology in five different sectors: lesion measurement, lesion tracking, real-time procedure assistance, clinical education and patient education (Table 1).

Table 1. Categories of AR applications in the medical and pharmaceutical context (Sharma et al. 2019, p. 1219)

AR category	Category description
Lesion measurement	Programs digitally measure the size and other qualities of lesions and may include clinical decision support
Lesion tracking	Programs track the size, color and other qualities of lesions and may include clinical decision support
Real-time procedure assistance	Programs enhance surgical planning by creating rich 3D representations of patient anatomy
Clinical education	Programs create rich, interactive clinical education experiences through 3D visualizations of disease, often superimposed on healthy individuals in unexpected ways, simulating real-life disease identification and management
Patient education	Programs that can enhance patient education across a range of topics, including disease screening, self-care, disease management, explanation of imaging or other procedures, possible treatment outcomes and any other existing patient education efforts

Sharma et al. state that AR has different perspectives to create a positive effect on dermatologists in diagnostics and for the planning of procedures (2019, p. 1217–1220). In their study, Jorge et al. (2019) measured the performance of 54 nursing students in wound diagnostic parameters. The training-procedure was improved thanks to an integrated simulation with AR function, which was compared with a no simulation setting; the AR version showed promising results. The simulation of the growth of lesions and its digitally visualised responses to treatments on healthy skin provided for nonphysician trainees, such as the novice nurses, an enriched training experience. This experiment showed that AR applications were more efficient in teaching nonphysician trainees in dermatology, which also promoted a better and long-term knowledge retention. For these students, observing chronic wounds on one's own healthy skin might have a significantly positive impact also on how to handle a new device and its system, which could lead to an increased motivation to learn (pp. 1–3).

mARble. For disease patterns and health care topics that are visually oriented, Von Jan et al. (2012, p. 67) state that AR applications offer an interesting solution because then possibility to visualise almost lifelike digital cases have the potential to significantly improve the learning experience. Additionally, Von Jan et al. (2012) by using a mobile AR application observed that medical students were encouraged to become active learners using real case studies, due to the visualization of digitally provided content on their own healthy skin. The AR application provided features which students could use on their own bodies and explore their learning progress, by posting questions and browsing the internet for further pictures and information about the specific lesion or injury. The scholars concluded that mobile AR applications not only improve the learning process for visually oriented subjects in medical education, but also increase students' motivation to interact with the different topics (2012, pp. 68–69). Their research results were further supported by Jorge et al. (2019), which have shown that among professionals and students, visualising clinical pictures on their healthy skin not only produced positive learning effects, but also increased motivation and flexibility. The pursuit of a similar approach with patients in dermatology instead of professionals might anticipate similar results in terms of learning experiences and increased motivation to interact with the educational content.

mARble focused on providing dynamic learning experiences through AR applications for the professional training of students, nurses and doctors. AR captures, analyses and superimposes digital information onto the real case studies; thus, healthcare providers can create useful and unique perspectives with the aim of enhancing patients' awareness through visual diagnosis and procedural planning (Sharma et al. 2019, p. 1217).

FirstDerm. Several applications use image recognition to search in image databases to list differential diagnoses of the specific lesion and then utilise users' feedback to refine the quality of the provided image recognition. To create a deeper understanding of how these applications work and what users experience, the application FirstDerm was created, considering the work of Kassianos et al. (2015) and Ngoo et al. (2018). In fact, Kassianos et al. (2015) analysed another approach to treating patients across the world at any time and every day. These researchers published a review about smartphone health tools and found 40 available mobile applications. The study was based on previous articles, which concluded that earlier detection of melanoma improves the therapy outcome; therefore, the aim was to detect the elements of an application which could lead to better patient understanding and better detection of melanoma. Ngoo et al. (2018, p. 100) enhanced the results of Kassianos et al. (2015) assessing the available mobile applications for melanoma patients, clinician users in the field of skin cancer. Additionally, Ngoo et al. (2018, pp. 101–104) tested the available descriptions of the mobile applications, its functionality and user ratings. The main functionalities were the teaching of different states of the patients' lesion and then option to take photos of their skin and to log them with a date, as a control of the individual development.

In FirstDerm (2020), patients can upload pictures and descriptions within a mobile application and a board-certified professional on the FirstDerm team analyses any skin concern within hours. These professionals promise 'peace of mind on the move' or from the comfort of the user's home without seeing a specialist. A standardised form helps patients to describe their problems and afterwards to create an initial diagnosis based on the data entered by the patients (Comstock 2018). The focus of FirstDerm is not to create learning experiences or education, but to provide further information and ideas about the patients' lesions and based on this professional expertise about treatments of the skin. By combining the visualizations of the different stages of the diseases with additional information about the treatment the added value for patients can be increased. The founder of FirstDerm, Alexander Börve, highlights another added value for patients:

> Nobody likes to go to see a doctor. The ones that go to see a doctor, it's because of pain. Pain is the thing. Pain drives people to pay. Just having a rash isn't painful so people say: It will go away. I won't worry about it. (Alexander Börve on Comstock 2018)

Summarizing, multiple studies have documented that the extension of the reality offers unmistakable opportunities that might have a positive impact on learning experiences of patients and novice practitioners in the health care sector (Jorge et al. 2019, p. 3; Sharma et al. 2019, p. 1218; Santos et al. 2014, p. 15; von Jan et al. 2012, p. 68). These researchers enabled such learning experiences with mobile AR technology and evaluated them through observational evaluation. Due to the large number of different possibilities to make content and objects experienceable, AR learning experiences are subject to a great variability (Santos et al. 2014, p. 42). AR learning experiences can help people to memorise information on specific objects, and furthermore, the integration of multiple human senses can contribute to a more intensive learning experience (Santos et al. 2014, p. 51). Additionally, the interaction with AR functions can lead to an enhanced content understanding and long-term memory retention (Soltani and Morice 2020, p. 3).

2.3 Research Gap

According to Sharma et al. (2019, p. 1219), patient education means for the patients owing awareness and agency across various topics, such as disease management, explaining procedures and possible treatment outcomes, transfer of relevant information and knowledge to patients. When focusing on patient education added value for patients with inflammatory skin diseases, as well as for dermatologists, can be created. If the accessibility of the mobile AR application in the area of dermatology is free and no prior professional clarification is required, there is an opportunity for patients to consult the application for lower-threshold problems, such as small eczema or rashes instead of consulting a dermatologist or deciding for an inactive behaviour. By providing a mobile AR application that not only visualises treatments and possible developments of their diseases, but also offers patients advice and further information, healthcare companies can collect data about patients, their lesions and their reactions to possible treatments.

3   Research Design

This research is designed based on the design science research (Vaishnavi et al. 2004). This framework provides a clear structure from creating awareness of a problem and over-formulating preliminary suggestions for the mentioned research questions to developing a specific prototype and evaluating the outcome according to functional specifications.

To identify specific perspectives, as well as the challenges of the daily life of dermatologists, semi-structured and problem-centered interviews were held with two well-experienced dermatologists. Additionally, interviews with four patients were conducted. The results were used for developing a prototype. Six participants (four participants took part also in the previous phases) tested it and were interviewed, as part of the evaluation process.

3.1   Awareness Phase

According to Hevner and Chatterjee's (2010), the goal of the design science research framework is to promote awareness and gain deeper insights; therefore, interviews were also conducted with two dermatologists. The questions were open-ended and thus allowed the dermatologists to express themselves openly. First, the aim of the interviews was to understand the dermatologists' experiences and their opinions on therapy compliance and medication adherence. Second, the questions were intended to explore how then use of technologies influences the communication and the collaboration between dermatologists and patients. At the end of the interviews, the dermatologists were specifically asked whether they would like to share further ideas, considerations or experiences that were not previously addressed. In fact, several suggestions emerged. For example, when making the diagnosis and during the first consultation with the patient, it would be useful to provide appropriate visualizations and explanations of the current status of the disease and to show the possible development. The visualization of different development stages of the lesion would provide an opportunity to raise the patients' understanding and anchor the new knowledge more firmly, especially if patients can consult this function anytime and not just see it once during the diagnostic interview.

The specialists can also imagine using a mobile application to exchange images with patients. The patients could take and store pictures at regular intervals, which the treating doctors would have access to. In this way, the relationship between doctors and patients could be maintained outside of the agreed consultation hours, and doctors could intervene in case of abnormalities. The mobile phone is well suited as a medium for the exchange of visual information and advice. All interviewed patients were familiar with mobile devices and the use of high-quality cameras, especially if the first diagnosis has already been made.

From the interviews conducted during the awareness phase, different codes were identified (see Table 2). These codes were categorized in three "main themes": a) therapy compliance; b) use of technology and c) disease area. The assessment of the qualitative data set was used to develop the mobile AR prototype.

Table 2. Codes for qualitative data analysis in the awareness phase

Theme	Codes
Therapy compliance	Individual characteristics
	Restriction of quality of life
	Emotions of patients
	Affected body parts
	Personal behaviour
	Basic understanding
	Reasonableness
	Feasibility
	Period of therapy
	Trust
	Knowledge
	Imagination
	Control and surveillance
Technology	Specialists
	Connection of realities
	Visualizations
	Mobile devices
	Photo diary
	Management of the disease
	Platforms and tele dermatology
Disease area	Wide range of lesions
	Photodynamic therapy (oncology)
	Seborrheic eczema
	Wart therapies
	Increasing specialisation

3.2 Suggestion Phase

The suggestion phase included a discussion with two patients: one suffering from psoriasis and the other one with an inflammatory hand disease. The interviewed patients stated that from their dermatologists they usually receive insufficient information about their diseases, the problems and treatment options associated with them. Their trust in their dermatologists is high, and they would like to receive more information about the treatment or tips for daily life. Additionally, they also would appreciate receiving a visual comparison of the different stages of the healing development to classify oneself and obtain focused information. Furthermore, according to the patients, it would be also helpful to see how the skin looks like when the disease worsens, since this visualization could be a source of motivation for regular care, depending on where the disease appears on the surface of the skin (Santos et al. 2014, p. 52).

Table 3 provides an overview of the codes out extracted from the qualitative data analysis, conducted during the suggestion phase.

Table 3. Codes for qualitative data analysis in the suggestion phase

Theme	Codes
Information	Origin and causes Therapies and curability Descriptions Development Impact and effects Side effects Medication planning Lifestyle
Functions	Explanation Development and changes Mobile application Digital medication plan Push messages Sharing with doctor Newsletter Motivation
Trust	Data security Context of data

3.3 Requirements

Functions and Information. The aforementioned study of Kassianos et al. (2015, p. 1516) showed that for patients, applications can create added value in the utilization of patients' data regarding diagnosis and potential therapy. Furthermore, providing education and further information about the disease is relevant for patients (Kassianos et al. 2015, p. 1516). Further studies by Ngoo et al. (2018) included testing of functionalities and user ratings of existing applications. The teaching about different stages of the patients' lesions and taking photos of their skin and log them with a date would help to give them more control over their disease and its development (p. 101). Moreover, during the interviews, requirements were collected, and these are reported in Table 4.

Since these research results correspond with the suggestions of the interviewed dermatologists and patients, documenting patients' pictures of their diseases and providing relevant information are part of the artefact. The application prototype includes disease screening and supplies patients with hints about self-care and possible treatment outcomes. The application is providing functions and information for patients to create a better understanding of their disease and therefore to become more adherent to the medication plan. First, the artefact must contain basic AR functions allowing a comparison of different stages of the atopic dermatitis or the psoriasis. Furthermore, it must be designed in an understandable way to ensure a high-quality evaluation as a mobile application capable of running on a smartphone. Additionally, the artefact must document in detail what functions must be covered to create relevance for patients with inflammatory

Table 4. Patient-suggested functions and information

Type	Name	Description
Function	Visualization	A visualization of the different phases of the corresponding disease
Function	Digital medication plan	Digitally provided medication plan prescribed by the dermatologist
Function	Push messages	Information and reminders about medication planning or new reports on diseases or therapies
Function	Photo diary	Diary with photos as log data of all affected posts shared with the treating dermatologist
Function	Communication	Possibility of contacting the treating dermatologist with questions or uncertainties
Information	Nutrition	Hints and tips on adequate nutrition that leads to better disease control or a reduction of symptoms
Information	Origin	Facts and experiences concerning where the disease comes from and what leads to its spread
Information	Therapy and care	Testimonials and advice on the treatment and care of the affected areas on the skin

skin diseases. The prototype itself can be limited to only AR but must contain further relevant content and functions to ensure the integration into patients' daily life. The description of the artefact and its functions must also show opportunities for changing the communication between patients and their treating dermatologists.

According to Sharma et al.'s method of categorisation (2019, p. 1219), the prototype should consider two categories: lesion tracking and patient education. The photo diary function allows the stages of the disease to be recorded and compared over different time periods and body parts. Additionally, the analysis of these images for clinical decisions is conceivable. Enhancing patients' education, using the AR function, as well as the digital medication planning with push messages, justifies the categorisation in patient education.

Lastly, the requirement for the prototype is to provide mobile AR functions with the visualization of different stages of the lesion. BlippAR is considered as the platform for the development of the AR prototype. It provides a graphical user interface and common functions, such as drag and drop, and embodies a possible platform for developing a rudimentary mobile AR application (Blippar 2021).

3.4 Development Phase

The goal of the development phase is to create a rudimentary mobile AR application, as a prototype for a demonstration to patients with inflammatory skin diseases, as well as to dermatologists to evaluate the AR experience. Moreover, further functionalities are briefly described, so they could be designed as simple as possible. The development of the artefact not only includes an AR prototype, but also a documentation and a description of all other relevant functions suggested in Sects. 3.2 and 3.3, which aim to evaluate an integration of such a mobile application into patients' daily life.

In Fig. 1, we represent the core elements of the developed prototype. The central function and thus the main element of this work is the visualization of the different stages of diseases via mobile AR. The photo diary should be used to periodically record and document the stages and various locations of the diseases to understand the course of the disease and, if necessary, share the information with the treating doctor for further consultations. The medication plan is intended to enable patients to view their planned therapy at any time, and to allow push messages to support the most precise medication adherence. In addition, this mobile application provides further tips, ideas and findings from research for patients to ensure long-term sustainable therapy and thus ensure the relevance of the application in the medium or long term.

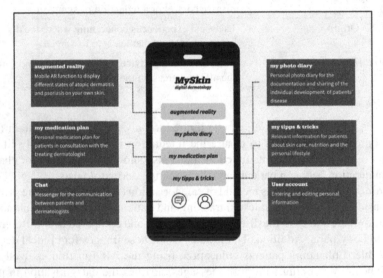

Fig. 1. Overview of all functions of the MySkin prototype

Mobile AR Function. Users can scan the artificial marker as the target for the visualization on a specific body part. After scanning the target, the first visualization appears, directly covering the marker to enable a fusion of the user's environment and the digitally provided visualization. The prototype then allows the user to switch between the four different steps of development of atopic dermatitis: non-lesional skin, acute lesion, subacute lesion and chronic lesional skin. According to Weidinger and Novak (2016, p. 1110), different body parts can be affected by atopic dermatitis, but mostly the hands, arms and face are affected. Therefore, the marker makes it possible to project the images of the disease on every part of the body but was tested with hands and arms during the development phase.

Figure 2 shows the interface design with the four main functions in the menu. When entering the AR function, users click the scan button and focus the camera of the mobile device on the artificial marker. After the mobile application recognises the marker, the AR visualization appears directly above the marker.

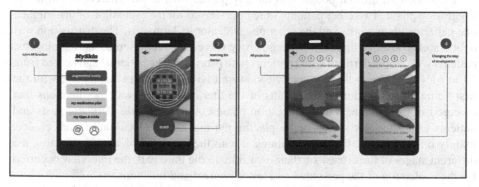

Fig. 2. AR function of the MySkin prototype

Other Content of the Prototype. During the interviews, patients and dermatologists mentioned the possibility of documenting the development of the respective disease with pictures. The dermatologists suggested giving patients the opportunity to describe the pictures and the circumstances, especially if there is a noticeable change, like a new symptom or a change in the skin surface. To facilitate communication between patients and dermatologists, the application allows pictures to be shared between them.

Dermatologists should be able to integrate the medication plan they provide individually for patients into the mobile application. This digital medication plan will allow patients to access and view their prescribed treatments at any time and improve their medication adherence. Notifications about important treatment components or medications can be activated in the form of push messages.

Patients are motivated to make lifestyle changes for better control and development of their disease. Therefore, the mobile application contains ideas and solutions suggested by dermatologists. These include nutritional experiences, such as lowering the end inflammation levels in the body or consuming the most important nutrients through diet. These ideas also comprise general experience values concerning exercise in sports, leisure time and practical advice about what can and should be done, for example, to reduce redness and itching or to prevent further spread of the disease.

3.5 Evaluation Phase

The goal of the evaluation phase was planned for patients and dermatologists to discuss and judge the idea of integrating AR technology, providing relevant information in a mobile application. The evaluation was conducted with a group of six people. In the evaluation group four people had already participated in the awareness and in the suggestion phase. Two other patients were interviewed for the evaluation of the artefact: one patient with psoriasis and the other one with atopic dermatitis. The distribution was deliberately chosen so that each response group was equally represented: dermatologists, patients with atopic dermatitis and patients with psoriasis. The patients' age ranged from 29 to 61 years. The evaluation interviews were divided into three sequences, with the first being a presentation of the results of the literature review and the functions that emerged in the awareness and suggestion phases. Afterwards, the dermatologists and patients tested the AR prototype by placing the marker at a location of their choice, mainly on the hand or forearm, scanning it with the mobile device and projecting the different stages of the disease on their own skin. In the third part, the interview occurred for the evaluation of the presented and tested content and functions.

The interviewees did not offer short and concise answers but shared detailed personal experiences and references to their problems and potential solutions. As a result, the evaluation of the functions, contents and problems led to diversified feedback. The many similarities regarding the user experience and the integration into patients and dermatologists' everyday life, as well as the uniformly positive evaluation of the artefact as a whole, may identify the need for new solutions in the field of dermatology.

> From my point of view, the most important things are really in the presented solution approach: that is, being reminded with push messages that I have to take the medication and applying the cremes. If I notice that it's progress, that I can share that with my doctor without having a physical meeting. I can do that during the break or when I am on holiday, and that's a huge help. Otherwise, you always have to call the doctor beforehand, and I also think the idea behind it, that you get information about nutrition, is strong, because it creates a holistic approach …
> (Patient 3, [translated from German])

Functions and Information. The AR visualization was the central function evaluated. According to the patients, the experimental character of experiencing the different stages on their own skin has a direct influence on their adherence to medication, because they want to counteract the worst development steps. For dermatologists, AR visualizations are helpful, because there are few suitable pictures and explanations of the stages of the disease that can be distributed to patients. It is not uncommon that a change in the appearance of the skin might lead to the discontinuation of a therapy, because although such changes are not necessarily negative, to the patient, they may appear to be an aggravation. With the AR function, patients could therefore be prepared in advance for potential changes that might appear on their skin, but continue their therapy as planned. According to the dermatologists, the choice of images can be a critical success factor for prevention: pictures of lesions that are too severe can trigger anxiety, which is an unhelpful starting point for therapy. Patients and dermatologists understood the

AR function and had no questions about the handling with the mobile AR application prototype. Regarding the quality of the experience, the interviewees agreed that the images must be adapted to the patient's skin appearance, in terms of color and shape, in a high quality. The interviewees indicated that a higher degree of immersion would enable a better AR learning experience. Another consistent evaluation experience was the use of the artificial marker. The AR prototype is based on a marker-based approach since the usability of marker-based AR is deemed better than the marker-less alternative (Brito and Stoyanova 2018, p. 819). However, the marker-based approach was not affirmed in the usability tests with dermatologists and patients. The placement of the marker does not seem practical but is rather inconvenient for the use of the AR function on different parts of the body. In terms of practicability, the mobile application is the right choice. All the participants interviewed use their mobile phones in everyday life both professionally and privately.

> Having these functions in a mobile application would be very practical because today nothing works without the mobile phone anyway … (Patient 2, [translated from German])

The choice of the device leads to less discussion than the presented functions. Both patients and dermatologists positively rated taking pictures of the affected areas on patients' bodies and documenting them in the application. While the patients did not identify any dangers or difficulties, the dermatologists highlighted potential risk factors. First, the quality of the images is crucial for an accurate evaluation of the problem since the surface texture of the skin is relevant for assessing the stage of the disease. On the other hand, several images should be taken per body part and from different distances to see the texture of the skin and the overall context.

> With photographic representation, a lesion can look totally different from what is, because dermatologists do not have the overall context of the patient. (Dermatologist 1, [translated from German])

With the semi-structured interview and open questions, the interviewees were finally invited to further share insights about the use of the application. Table 5 outlines the extracted codes from the interviews.

Table 5. Codes for qualitative data analysis in the evaluation phase

Theme	Codes
Patients' understanding	Pedagogical perspective Learning effects Visual learning Medication adherence
User experience	Emotions Extension Prevention Marker Mobile device Daily routine Testing with real application Privacy Data privacy Integration in daily life Holistic approach Specific solution Timesaving Cost reduction
Functions	Communication with dermatologists Reminder function AR visualization Photo diary AR quality Different development steps Medication planning Nutrition Scalability Connection to health insurance Image recognition Continuous development
Challenges for patients	Insufficient information Forgetfulness Discipline Anonymous reviews Insecurity and shame Communication with dermatologists (hurdle) Photo quality Costs Alternative medicine

(*continued*)

Table 5. (*continued*)

Theme	Codes
Challenges for dermatologists	Effort Integration in daily business Chargeability Tele-dermatology Exchange of data (interface management) Responsibility (alternative medicine) Isolated perspective
Community	Sharing experiences and knowledge Belonging Private contact

4 Conclusion

Brito and Stoyanova (2018, p. 823) state that AR applications could create new, efficient learning environments by allowing users to add, remove and modify digital content in the real environment. This added value might promote a more interactive learning experience and extend the previous capacities created by static images or printed information. Furthermore, Hilken et al. (2018, p. 512) describe that the fusion of realities helps to identify and explain problems that may not yet exist. Therefore, AR offers the possibility for patients to project the different stages of development of inflammatory skin diseases onto their own skin and thus prepare themselves for the onset of different stages. Patients learn with the AR function what possible skin lesions they might encounter and what these lesions can look like, and patients can compare the severity of their lesions with the AR visualizations.

Von Jan et al. (2012) observed different medical students using a mobile AR application that allowed them to visualise dermatological lesions on their own skin. Their study concluded that the AR experience improved the learning process in medical education and increased the participants' motivation to interact with dermatological topics. The interviewed dermatologists explained that few communication tools are available to highlight the diseases, their origin and their potential development for patients. Thus, by educating patients, the AR function can increase their medication adherence. In summary, patients with inflammatory skin diseases can better understand their disease with AR knowledge and anchor the knowledge for a longer period of time. Our research outlines that the visualization of the disease patterns on the patient's own skin through the usage of AR may potentially lead to a preventive effect and a stronger memorisation of knowledge. Therefore, it is presumable that patients' motivation will increase to adhere to their therapy to prevent their skin condition from worsening and to strive for an improvement of their skin condition initially and for a longer time.

4.1 Outlook

The literature review and the research have shown that AR increases patients' understanding of their disease and the associated therapy. In addition, AR learning experiences can have a positive impact on motivation to use therapy, resulting in increased and long-term medication adherence. The studies and experiments mentioned in the literature review focused on the education and training of professionals. The contribution of this paper to research and development is the design of solution approaches focusing on patients with inflammatory skin diseases to increase their therapy understanding and medication adherence with AR.

In the interviews, the patients mentioned the need for specific functions to expand the communication between dermatologists and patients. The evaluated ideas could thus be a first step towards the development of a mobile information and communication platform in the field of dermatology.

Acknowledgements. The work was first submitted as a Master Thesis in the Master of Science in Business Information Systems program at the UAS Northwestern Switzerland (FHNW) in 2020 by Yannick Roger Deiss (first author). Safak Korkut and Terry Inglese (co-authors) have been the supervisors of the thesis.

References

Schielein, M.C., Tizek, L., Seifert, F., Biedermann, T., Zink, A.: Versorgung von chronisch entzündlichen Hauterkrankungen. Hautarzt **70**(11), 875–882 (2019). https://doi.org/10.1007/s00105-019-04481-6

Goldsmith, C.H.: The effect of compliance distributions on therapeutic trials. In: Compliance in Health Care, pp. 297–308. John Hopkins University Press, Baltimore, MD (1979)

Hilken, T., Heller, J., Chylinski, M., Keeling, D.I., Mahr, D., de Ruyter, K.: Making omnichannel an Augmented Reality: the current and future state of the art, pp. 509–523. Maastricht University School of Business and Economics, Netherlands and School of Marketing, UNSW Business School, Sydney, Australia (2018)

Obagi, Z.A., Rundle, C.W., Dellavalle, R.P.: Widening the scope of virtual reality and augmented reality in dermatology. Dermatol. Online J. **26** (2020). Accessed https://escholarship.org/uc/item/6mz1s20x

Capozza, K., Schwartz, A.: Does it work and is it safe? Parents' perspectives on adherence to medication for atopic dermatitis. Pediatric Dermatol. **37**, 58–61 (2019). https://doi.org/10.1111/pde.13991

Zaghloul, S.S., Goodfield, M.J.: Objective assessment of compliance with psoriasis treatment. Arch Dermatol. **140**(4), 408–414 (2004). https://doi.org/10.1001/archderm.140.4.408

Kolli, S.S., Pona, A., Cline, A., Strowd, L.C., Feldman, S.R.: Adherence in atopic dermatitis. In: Feldman, S.R., Cline, A., Pona, A., Kolli, S.S. (eds.) Treatment Adherence in Dermatology. UCD, pp. 75–84. Springer, Cham (2019). https://doi.org/10.1007/978-3-030-27809-0_8

Deledda, G., Moretti, F., Rimondini, M., Zimmermann, C.: How patients want their doctor to communicate. A Literature review on primary care patients' perspective. Patient Educ. Couns. **90**, 297–306 (2013). https://doi.org/10.1016/j.pec.2012.05.005

Chylinski, M., Hilken, T., Heller, J., Keeling, D., de Ruyter, K., Mahr, D.: Augmented reality marketing: a technology-enabled approach to situated customer experience. Australas. Mark. J. **28**, 374–384 (2020). https://doi.org/10.1016/j.ausmj.2020.04.004

Möbus, L., Weidinger, S., Emmert, H.: Epigenetic factors involved in the pathophysiology of inflammatory skin diseases. J. Allergy Clin. Immunol. **145**(4), 1049–1060 (2020). https://doi.org/10.1016/j.jaci.2019.10.015

Krakowski, A.C., Eichenfield, L.F., Dohil, M.A.: Management of atopic dermatitis in the pediatric population. Pedriatics Official J. Am. Acad. Pediatrics **122**, 812–824 (2008). https://doi.org/10.1542/peds.2007-2232

Lansang, P., Lam, J.M., Marcoux, D., Prajapati, V.H., Spring, S., Lara-Corrales, I.: Approach to the assessment and management of pediatric patients with atopic dermatitis: a consensus document. J. Cutan. Med. Surg. **23**, 19–31 (2019). https://doi.org/10.1177/1203475419882647

Weidinger, S., Novak, N.: Atopic dermatitis, pp. 1109–1122. Department of Dermatology and Allergy, University Hospital Schleswig-Holstein, Kiel, Germany (2016). https://doi.org/10.1016/s0140-6736(15)00149-x

Korman, N.J.: Management of psoriasis as a systemic disease: what is the evidence? Br. J. Dermatol. **182**, 840–848 (2020). https://doi.org/10.1111/bjd.18245

Hiremath, A.C., Bhandari, R., Wali, S., Ganachari, M., Doshi, B.: Impact of clinical pharmacist on medication adherence among psoriasis patients: a randomized controlled study. Clin. Epidemiol. Global Health **10**, 100687 (2021). https://doi.org/10.1016/j.cegh.2020.100687

Mira, J.J., Guilabert, M., Pérez-Jover, V., Lorenzo, S.: Barriers for an effective communication around clinical decision making: an analysis of the gaps between doctors' and patients' point of view. Health Expect. **6**, 826–839 (2012). https://doi.org/10.1111/j.1369-7625.2012.00809.x

Abbas, A., Seo, J., Kim, M.: Impact of mobile augmented reality system on cognitive behaviour and performance during rebar inspection tasks. J. Comput. Civ. Eng. **34**, 04020050 (2020). https://doi.org/10.1061/%28asce%29cp.1943-5487.0000931

Jorge, N.R., Morgado, L., Gaspar, P.J.S.: E-learning and augmented reality (AR) for chronic wound assessment: promoting learning and quality of care. In: Virtual and Augmented Reality in Mental Health Treatment (2019). https://doi.org/10.4018/978-1-5225-7168-1.ch014

Sharma, P., Vleugels, R.A., Nambudiri, V.E.: Augmented Reality in dermatology: are we ready for AR? J. Am. Acad. Dermatol. **81**, 1216–1222 (2019). https://doi.org/10.1016/j.jaad.2019.07.008

Von Jan, U., Noll, C., Behrends, M., Albrecht, U.-V.: mARble – augmented reality in medical education. Biomedizinische Technik/Biomed. Eng. **57** (2012). https://doi.org/10.1515/bmt-2012-4252

Kassianos, A.P., Emery, J.D., Murchie, P., Walter, F.M.: Smartphone applications for melanoma detection by community, patient and generalist clinician users: a review. Br. J. Dermatol. **172**, 1507–1518 (2015). https://doi.org/10.1111/bjd.13665

Ngoo, A., Finnane, A., McMeniman, E., Soyer, P.H., Janda, M.: Fighting melanoma with smartphones: a snapshot of where we are a decade after app stores opened their doors. Int. J. Med. Inform. **118**, 99–122 (2018). https://doi.org/10.1016/j.ijmedinf.2018.08.004

FirstDerm. Online Dermatologist. How it works (2020). https://www.firstderm.com/how-it-works/. Accessed 14 Dec 2020

Comstock, J.: In-Depth: Advances and challenges in digital dermatology. mobihealthnews (2018). https://www.mobihealthnews.com/content/depth-advances-and-challenges-digital-dermatology. Accessed 14 Dec 2020

Brito, P.Q., Stoyanova, J.: Marker versus markerless Augmented Reality. Which has more impact on users? Int. J. Hum.-Comput. Interact. **34**, 819–833 (2018). https://doi.org/10.1080/10447318.2017.1393974

Soltani, P., Morice, A.H.P.: Augmented reality tools for sports education and training. Comput. Educ. **155**, 103923 (2020). https://doi.org/10.1016/j.compedu.2020.103923

Vaishnavi, V., Kuechler, B., Petter, S.: Design science research in information systems. In: Integrated Series in Information Systems, vol. 22, pp. 9–22 (2004). https://doi.org/10.1007/978-1-4419-5653-8_2

Hevner, A., Chatterjee, S.: Design science research in information systems. In: Hevner, A., Chatterjee, S. (eds.) Design Research in Information Systems, pp. 9–22. Springer, Boston (2010). https://doi.org/10.1007/978-1-4419-5653-8_2

Santos, M.E., Chen, A., Taketomi, T., Yamamoto, G., Miyazaki, J., Kato, H.: Augmented reality learning experiences: survey of prototype design and evaluation. IEEE Trans. Learn. Technol. **7**, 38–56 (2014). https://doi.org/10.1109/TLT.2013.37

Blippar. We augment reality (2021). https://www.blippar.com/. Accessed 25 Apr

Design of an Intelligent Intravenous Infusion Hemostat for Elderly Patients with Chronic Diseases Based on Image Recognition Technology

Minting Fu and Jing Luo[✉]

School of Arts and Design, Shenzhen University, Shenzhen, Guangdong, China
luojng@szu.edu.cn

Abstract. In the wave of global technological development, artificial intelligence technology is developing very rapidly [1]. Image recognition technology, a core aspect of AI technology, is also becoming more and more popular in people's daily lives [2]. If the healthcare industry takes advantage of the new technology, it will greatly contribute to the development of healthcare services. The global trend towards ageing is evident, and in China, the elderly are often treated with intravenous injections. Currently, venipuncture needle extraction compressions are still performed manually to stop bleeding. However, the compression component is often not valued by healthcare professionals and elderly patients [3]. Chronic geriatric patients also suffer from subcutaneous bruising as a result of their own illnesses and the ageing of their bodies, such as problems with skin laxity and poor vascular elasticity, as well as incorrect methods of compression to stop bleeding [4]. To reduce patient discomfort and improve patient satisfaction with hospital services, it is necessary to design a smart hemostat in conjunction with new technology.

Keywords: Image recognition · Intravenous infusion · Hemostat · Geriatric patients

1 Introduction

As an important tool in clinical disease care and an essential part of basic nursing practice for nurses, intravenous infusion is a rapid and efficient way of rehydrating and administering medication [5]. In current clinical practice, intravenous infusion needle extraction compressions are still performed manually. Hemostatic compressions are usually applied by healthcare professionals to patients with infusion patches, and then the patient applies the compressions themselves. As a result of the patient's failure to apply appropriate and effective compressions, manual compressions lead to bleeding, petechiae, and even subcutaneous hemostasis at the puncture site [6]. The busy and understaffed healthcare staff is unable to perform compressions. In addition, blood bruises on the hands can occur when family members cannot accompany the patient or when the force, position, or timing of the purchase is incorrect.

© The Author(s), under exclusive license to Springer Nature Switzerland AG 2022
V. G. Duffy (Ed.): HCII 2022, LNCS 13320, pp. 41–53, 2022.
https://doi.org/10.1007/978-3-031-06018-2_3

As venipuncture needle extraction pressure stasis has gained attention, various methods of improving pressure stasis have been proposed. Early on, researchers used existing compression strips and medical items to modify them and designed a new venipuncture needle extraction compression strip. The band was made up of a wide rubber band, a medical gauze block, and Velcro stitching, which could be used to apply pressure to the puncture site instead of manually. However, the band requires occasional rounds by healthcare professionals, and additional equipment is needed to set the compression time [7]. Uniform and moderate compressions are particularly important as the traditional "one-point" compression and displacement of compressions lead to local bruising, hematoma, and pain. Subsequently, some researchers have proposed an alternative solution. Based on this pain point, researchers have designed an alternative tourniquet using materials such as medical elastic bandages, adhesive snap fasteners, and cloth buckles. The innovation of this tourniquet is that the nylon snap is repeatedly pressed over the eye of the needle and moved parallel to the puncture point to achieve even pressure. Yet it still requires the healthcare provider to wrap his finger around the hand quickly, which may lead to missing the best moment to apply pressure [8].

In addition to tourniquet compression at the puncture site, researchers have designed compression devices with a mechanical structure to assist patients. The researchers first proposed a pen-operated venipuncture needle puller, which has been in clinical practice for a long time. The compression device is a recycled sterile medical sponge brush with a handle fixed to medical gauze with universal glue. After the needle is removed by the nurse, the patient or family member holds the handle of the presser placed on the infusion patch to apply pressure to the puncture site [9]. Although it reduces the time for the tourniquet to wrap around the fixation step to be able to apply pressure promptly, the external handle compression method is still not fully automated. Furthermore, other researchers have developed a shrapnel-type venous compression tourniquet that applies compression to puncture sites by applying downward pressure to the shrapnel [10]. Not only does this design simplify compression procedures and free the patient's hands, but it also allows freedom of movement for compression site fixation. Nevertheless, the design is effective in reducing the probability of blood stasis on compression but still requires manual retraction of the spring and autonomous monitoring of time. Additionally, researchers have designed a multifunctional infusion stopper that holds the needle during infusion and applies pressure to the post-injection site to stop bleeding. The design significantly reduces the need for staff to adhere to the infusion patch, while the firm fixation allows for freedom of movement of the limb.

With the continuous advancement of science and technology, the application of artificial intelligence in healthcare is vast and has an important role to play in improving human health [11]. The intervention of artificial intelligence assistive technology, especially image recognition technology incorporating the experience of clinical health care professionals, is an important guide to healthcare [12]. Image recognition technology reduces the time it takes to recognize images. Furthermore, increasing recognition accuracy opens the door to medical applications [13]. Among them, model recognition is used more often in the medical clinical field [14]. Using this technology simplifies the image recognition process and analyses and processes the information in the image, which is impossible with traditional image processing. Moreover, dorsal hand vein recognition is still a relatively new method of biometric identification for clinical medical purposes [15]. This technology is of great relevance to the medical field as it accomplishes the identification of veins mainly by extracting their skeletal and geometric features [16, 17]. It provides the basis for a fully automated intravenous technique that facilitates venipuncture localization, venous extraction, and pressure localization. Accordingly, an intelligent IV hemostat can replace manual pressure to stop bleeding in elderly patients. The design reduces the workload of healthcare workers in assisting compressions, dictating, and making rounds and helps to simplify the compression steps for elderly patients and reduce the probability of inappropriate compressions leading to blood stasis.

There is a consensus that designers should adopt human-centered design guidelines in the design of medical device products. To avoid secondary injuries due to the use of the device, a reasonable fit between the device and the patient's body should be ensured [18]. In addition, it is important to ensure the ease of use and maintenance of the product by healthcare professionals and the comfort of the patient in using it. In the design of the intelligent intravenous infusion hemostasis device, ergonomics should be fully considered to ensure the function of basic pressure to stop bleeding while also ensuring the safety and stability of the product. For elderly patients, scientific intravenous infusion needle extraction pressure is still difficult. Patients may feel intimidated and uncomfortable if intelligent products are used instead of manual compression due to the unfamiliarity and coldness of the machine. Some might fear harm if they make a mistake when using the machine for the first time since it is different from previous operations. Therefore, the design of medical device products must take into account the psychological characteristics of elderly patients and ease the user's tension through humanized design.

Based on previous research, this paper intends to design an intelligent IV needle extraction device to stop bleeding in elderly patients suffering from chronic diseases. This process takes into account cutting-edge image recognition technology, human dimensions, as well as a thorough understanding of elderly user psychology, ensuring the feasibility, safety, and comfort of the product. First, the user research was conducted by observing the users in the field and conducting interviews with them. Afterward, the user research results are combined with ergonomic guidelines to find the best design solution.

2 User Research

The user study consisted of two parts: (a) Observation: By observing current patient behavior during intravenous needle extraction, the designer was able to identify and sum up the problems in the existing behavioral process. Design insights based on these observations were sought. (b) Interviews: Through interviews with healthcare staff and elderly patients, the design insights from part (a) were validated and multiple design ideas were explored.

2.1 Observation

The designer observed and recorded two complete intravenous procedures and watched carefully as the patient removed the needle and applied pressure. Participant A completed a series of actions such as paying fees, receiving the infusion medication, and waiting for the infusion to be dispensed according to the prescription for the intravenous infusion treatment. The infusion patient first goes to the infusion window to be punctured by the health care provider and then selects a comfortable infusion seat for the infusion. Second, the healthcare provider tells the infusion patient to be extracted when the infusion is complete so that pressure can be applied to stop bleeding. During this process, the designer found that the infusion patch would fall off due to hand movement. What's more, patients with a poor grasp of the position, timing, and strength of the compressions, resulting in poor compressions, would have problems with blood stasis.

2.2 Interviews

The design staff interviewed infusion patients and healthcare staff separately. The interviews were used to understand the patients' views on the manual IV stop product and their expectations of the automatic IV stop product, which will help in the next step of design and exploration. During the interviews with healthcare staff, the designer learned that due to the large number of patients waiting for an infusion, healthcare staff are often too busy preparing for the infusion to keep an eye on each patient's pressure to stop bleeding after the needle is removed from the IV. Additionally, medical staff often suggest that bleeding be stopped by applying scientific pressure. But there is nothing they can do in the face of some patients who do not comply. Therefore, they wanted to design a product that could be fully automated to stop bleeding after an IV infusion, which would reduce the workload of the healthcare staff. Interviews with elderly infusion patients revealed that they are often unable to apply scientific pressure to stop bleeding due to cognitive deterioration, poor disease status, and physical fatigue, resulting in subcutaneous blood

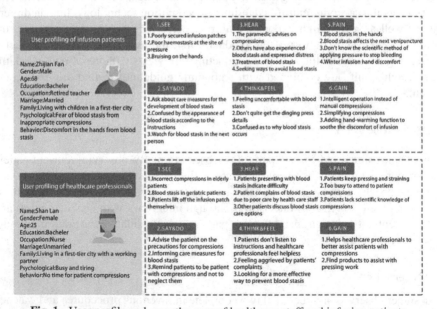

Fig. 1. User profile and empathy map of healthcare staff and infusion patients

stasis. The infusion of cold fluids causes stiffness in the patient's hands, making it more uncomfortable to apply pressure to stop bleeding, especially in winter.

Through field observations and user interviews, the designer created user-profiles and empathy maps (Fig. 1) of healthcare staff and infusion patients, analyzing the users' behavior and psychology.

The following are the specific design issues that emerged from the studies of users. First, they wanted a device that is easy to operate and includes clear instructions, without adding to the burden on staff or increasing learning costs. Second, the product was adjustable for patients of all ages and physical conditions. Lastly, the product is also capable of replacing manual work to perform fully intelligent hemostasis, which is closely sterilized after each use.

3   Design Process

Through literature review and user research, we have summarized the workflow of intravenous infusion (Fig. 2).

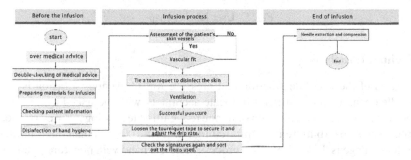

Fig. 2. Workflow diagram for intravenous infusion

3.1   User Journey Mapping Interviews

The analysis of the user journey for IV infusion informed the conceptual design. As shown in the diagram below (Fig. 3), this study identified different pain points at different stages of the IV infusion during the analysis. Intravenous infusion mainly includes the pre-infusion preparation, the infusion process, and the stopping of bleeding after the needle is removed from the infusion. In gaining insight into the whole process, it was found that the existing infusion patches mainly serve to stop bleeding and fixation and are closely related to the three processes of IV infusion. Therefore, it is important to provide users with intelligent pressure to stop bleeding and to address the auxiliary functions of fixing and soothing hand discomfort during the infusion process.

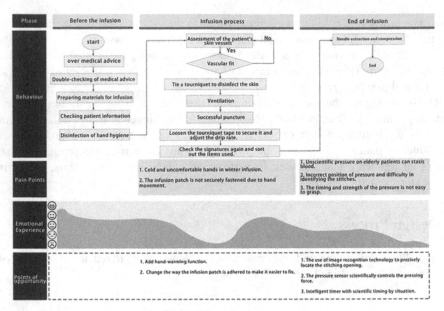

Fig. 3. User journey map

3.2 Technical Analysis

The location of the needle extraction and pressure for intravenous infusion is not the skin needle opening and is difficult to locate accurately with the naked eye, so precise positioning is achieved with the help of image recognition technology. Based on medical principles, veins absorb more near-infrared light at 700–1000 nm than other tissues, so the captured image is darker [19]. The process of dorsal hand vein puncture point recognition involves image acquisition, preprocessing, feature extraction, and completion of recognition based on template matching. The process will first extract and profile the veins in segments and then annotate the appropriate sections based on the characteristics of the venous puncture points [20, 21]. The system block diagram of the IV puncture point recognition system is shown below (Fig. 4).

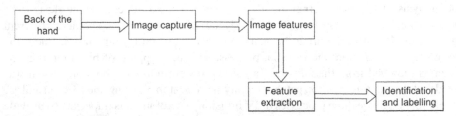

Fig. 4. Block diagram of the intravenous infusion puncture point identification system

Because of the special sensitivity of the veins on the back of the hand to near-infrared light, the image acquisition system consists of a near-infrared LED light source, a lens, and an image sensor. A diagram of the image acquisition system at the puncture point of an IV infusion is shown below (Fig. 5).

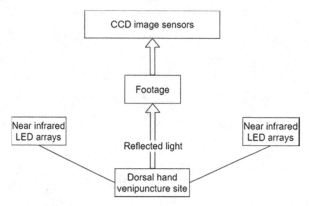

Fig. 5. Diagram of the intravenous infusion puncture point image acquisition system

A hardware and software platform consisting of a MATLAB-controlled Raspberry Pi and its supporting camera and image sensor was used to complete the acquisition, processing, and recognition of the vein images. From the recognition results on the back of the hand vein recognition system, it can be seen that the recognition rate of the system is as high as 96.67%. Secondly, the total time of the recognition process for image processing and recognition annotation is less than 2 s.

In response to the results of the user research and technical analysis, we have defined a process and functional principle as follows: After the healthcare worker has completed the IV puncture, the puncture point is identified using the venous puncture point identification module of the hemostat. The hemostat is then placed on the area of compression as indicated by the light of the identifier and adjusted for the size of the patient's hand to complete the fixation. During the infusion process, the hand-warming function can be activated in winter or in the case of hand discomfort, which will improve the comfort of the patient during the infusion. The hand warming function is based on heated patches at the ends of the wristband. At the end of the infusion, the hemostat automatically toggles the pressure plate to apply simultaneous pressure to the puncture point after the needle has been removed by the healthcare professional. Finally, the hemostat will automatically disconnect the pressure when the time is up, as the patient's condition dictates. After the hemostat has been used, it can be disinfected and reused.

Using the design principles discussed above, as well as the user flow and functional principles, we have come up with the following conceptual design sketch scheme (Fig. 6).

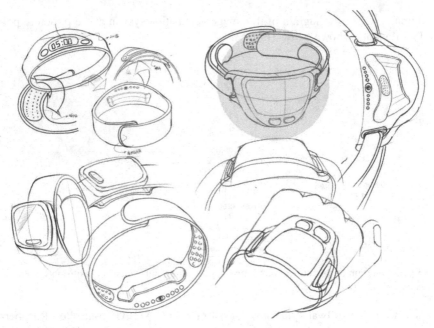

Fig. 6. Sketch of the conceptual design of the intravenous infusion hemostat

3.3 CMF Analysis

Designing a system that properly addresses intravenous infusion pressure needs for elderly patients requires taking into account both their physiological and psychological characteristics, as well as the hospital's environmental characteristics. The hemostat is a medical product in terms of color, and the color not only makes people feel clean, approachable, and durable, but it also makes them feel clean and approachable. At the same time, to meet the psychological needs of the elderly, low-saturation solid colors are chosen as the main colors, with bright colors used as accent colors at key buttons and to highlight information [22]. The choice of materials will take into account the processing, the skin-friendly affinity, and the wear-resistant material of the medical casing. Good materials will prolong the life of the product and, at the same time, enhance the comfort of the patient's use. The design of a medical product for the elderly is based on simplicity, safety, and aging appropriateness. A rendering of the final concept design prototype is shown in Fig. 7. Figure 8 shows the structure of the various parts of the product. The flow of use of the product is shown in Fig. 9.

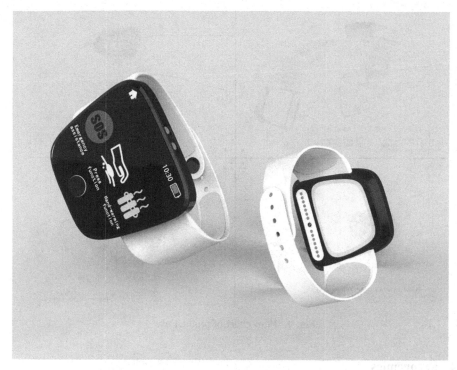

Fig. 7. Rendering of the conceptual design prototype

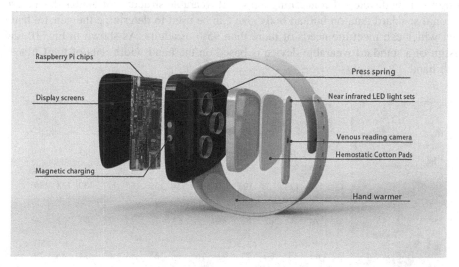

Fig. 8. Exploded view of the product

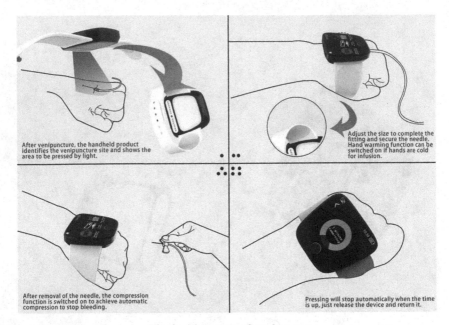

Fig. 9. Flow chart of product use

3.4 Ergonomics

Considering that the Smart IV Needle Pulling and Pressing Hemostat needs to meet all the functions of fixing the infusion needle, stopping bleeding and relieving discomfort in the hand, as well as conforming to the atmosphere of being placed in a hospital, the design will be developed concerning the smart wearable structure of the hand. Chinese national standard data on human body size can be used to determine the general hand size, which can meet the needs of more than 95% of adults. As shown in Fig. 10, the design of a standard wearable device is based on the hand width data of the Chinese adult hand.

GROUPING / PERCENTILE / MEASURING PROJECT	Male(18~60years old)							Female(18~55years old)						
	1	5	10	50	90	95	99	1	5	10	50	90	95	99
Hand Length	164	170	173	183	193	196	202	154	159	161	171	180	183	189
Hand Width	73	76	77	82	87	89	91	67	70	71	76	80	82	84
Index Finger Length	57	60	61	66	71	72	76	60	63	64	69	74	76	79

Fig. 10. Hand size chart for adults in China (part)

Secondly, the details of the human-computer interaction of the medical device are analyzed from a human-centered design concept [23]. In this design, the users of the product are elderly patients and healthcare professionals, and the special characteristics of elderly patients, in particular, should be considered comprehensively. One thing you should consider is the screen resolution of the device and the font and button sizes. Also, raising the hand and avoiding sharp right angles will increase screen safety. The human-machine interface of the design consists of three main functions: the press to stop bleeding, the hand-warming function, and the emergency assistance function. The main function of the product is to stop bleeding by pressing, selecting different pressing times according to the elderly person's condition, and showing the remaining time. The main interface is shown in Fig. 11.

Fig. 11. Diagram showing the main interaction interfaces of the product

4 Design Evaluation

This design focuses on the use of image recognition technology to accurately locate venipuncture points and provides a more scientific needle extraction and compression service for elderly patients to reduce the probability of blood stasis. At the same time, it solves the problems of needle fixation and cold hand discomfort during intravenous infusion and optimizes the infusion experience. However, the design has the following deficiencies:

Firstly, the design solution has not been prototyped, and the problems that arise in practical application are unpredictable.

Secondly, to achieve precise positioning of the press position, the design incorporates hardware and software for image recognition technology, which will inevitably increase the cost.

5 Conclusion

This research focuses on the design of an intelligent IV hemostasis product, which aims to incorporate image recognition technology to achieve fully intelligent compression hemostasis instead of manual compression hemostasis. Not only does this free up the patient's hands, but it also reduces the burden on healthcare professionals. According to user research, the design does meet the real needs of users, and transfusion patients are willing to try it out. The design also provides a reference for the design of similar products by determining the required dimensions through ergonomic and other relevant knowledge.

References

1. Yang, C., Huang, C.: Quantitative mapping of the evolution of AI policy distribution, targets and focuses over three decades in China. Technol. Forecast. Soc. Change **174**, 121188 (2022)
2. Zhang, Z., Zhao, L., Yang, T.: Research on the application of artificial intelligence in image recognition technology. J. Phys.: Conf. Ser. **1992**(3), 032118 (2021)
3. Chen, J., Ye, F., Wu, Y., et al.: Effect of thumb pressing on hemostasis after needle pulling out of intravenous infusion. J. Nurs. **13**(9), 93 (2006)
4. Wang, H.: Analysis of causes and countermeasures of subcutaneous congestion after intravenous infusion in elderly patients with chronic diseases. Health Nutr. **27**(12), 288–289 (2017). (in Chinese). https://doi.org/10.3969/j.issn.1004-7484.2017.12.476
5. Li, X., Huang, X.: Study on the method of removing needle pressure from intravenous infusion. Chin. J. Pract. Nurs. **21**(7), 1–3 (2005)
6. Wu, S.: Design and application of automatic post-intravenous infusion tourniquet set_Wu Su. Contemp. Nurse **28**(10), 181–182 (2021)
7. Qiu, Z.: The production and use of venipuncture needle extraction compression strips. J. Nurs. **21**(4), 77–78 (2014)
8. Production and use of a pressure tourniquet_Liu Yuanyuan
9. Li, S.: Application of homemade pen-operated venipuncture needle puller to stop bleeding after intravenous infusion needle pulling. J. Bengbu Med. Coll. **44**(1), 113–115 (2019)
10. Hu, S.: Effectiveness of a bullet-type intravenous compression tourniquet in clinical use_12. Contemp. Nurse **27**(9), 188–189 (2020)
11. Jia, S., Wang, Y., Wang, W., Zhang, Q., Zhang, X.: Value of medical imaging artificial intelligence in the diagnosis and treatment of new coronavirus pneumonia. Expert Syst. **39**, e12740 (2021). https://doi.org/10.1111/exsy.12740
12. Artificial Intelligence Versus Clinicians in Disease Diagnosis: Systematic Review-Web of Science Core Collection. https://www-webofscience-com.ezproxy.lib.szu.edu.cn/wos/woscc/full-record/WOS:000488621000012. Accessed 14 Jan 2022
13. Wu, Y.: Application of voice and image recognition and artificial intelligence in medical industry. Technol. Innov. (9), 157–158 (2018). https://doi.org/10.15913/j.cnki.kjycx.2018.09.157
14. Qiu, Y.: Application analysis of image recognition technology under artificial intelligence. Comput. Program. Skills Maintenance **37**(3), 123–124, 159 (2021)
15. Zhang, X., Guo, Y.H., Li, G., et al.: Automatic image recognition and annotation for dorsal hand intravenous injection. Infrared Technol. **37**(9), 751–755 (2015)
16. Li, L.: Simulation study of improved finger vein image recognition algorithm. J. Comput. Simul. **28**(3), 310–312 (2011)
17. Jia, X., Xue, D.Y., Cui, J.J., et al.: Algorithm for dorsal hand vein recognition based on chunked ridge wave transform. Pattern Recogn. Artif. Intell. **24**(3), 346–352 (2011)
18. Qian, W.C.: Exploring the application of ergonomics in medical device design. Sci. Tech. Innov. She. **17**(15), 62–63 (2020)
19. Yao, L.B.: Low-illumination CMOS image sensor technology [1]. Infrared Technol. **35**(3), 125–132 (2013)
20. Wang, H., Tao, L., Zhou, J.: Retinex and wavelet decomposition based dorsal hand vein recognition method. Syst. Eng. Theory Pract. **34**(2), 428–436 (2014)

21. Zhou, Y., Liu, Y., Yang, F., et al.: Palm vein recognition based on directional features [3]. Chin. J. Graph. Graph. **19**(2), 243–252 (2014)
22. Gao, G., Dong, X.: Research on the design of wearable health care products for the elderly based on the concept of humanization. Ind. Des. **16**, 71–72 (2020)
23. Tang, X.: Application of ergonomics in the design of medical devices. Jushe **28**(36), 171 (2017)

How Does Robot-Assisted Laparoscopic Surgery Impact Pain and Burnout Among Minimally Invasive Surgeons? A Survey Study

Jaime Hislop[1](✉) (iD), Chris Hensman[2,3,4], Mats Isaksson[1], Oren Tirosh[5,6], and John McCormick[7]

[1] Department of Mechanical Engineering and Product Design Engineering, Swinburne University of Technology, Melbourne, Australia
jhislop@swin.edu.au
[2] Department of Surgery, Monash University, Melbourne, Australia
[3] Department of Surgery, University of Adelaide, Adelaide, Australia
[4] LapSurgery Australia, Melbourne, Australia
[5] School of Health Sciences, Swinburne University of Technology, Melbourne, Australia
[6] Institute for Health and Sport, Victoria University, Melbourne, Australia
[7] Centre for Transformative Media Technologies, Swinburne University of Technology, Melbourne, Australia

Abstract. Pain is experienced by 77.8% and 53.8% of surgeons performing Traditional Laparoscopic Surgery (TLS) and Robot-Assisted Laparoscopic Surgery (RALS), respectively. Contributing factors include equipment design issues and lacking ergonomic knowledge among surgeons. This study investigated the burnout and discomfort experienced by laparoscopic surgeons. A survey composed of the Nordic Musculoskeletal Questionnaire (NMQ) and the Copenhagen Burnout Inventory (CBI) was distributed via social media groups of laparoscopic surgeons between October 2020 and January 2021. Results were analyzed in Microsoft Excel and RStudio. In total, 164 responses were provided by surgeons practicing TLS, 48 of whom also practiced RALS. Intraoperative pain was experienced by 91.5% and 75% of TLS and RALS surgeons, respectively. The main sites of complaint were the neck for RALS (35.4%) and the shoulders for TLS (64.6%). Average burnout scores from the CBI were between 25.8 and 36.5 out of 100 for the three dimensions of burnout. Surgeons practicing both RALS and TLS experienced discomfort at more anatomic sites in total and greater work-related burnout than those who only practiced TLS. In this study, RALS was associated with a lower prevalence of pain than TLS for all anatomic sites, although physical complaints were alarmingly common for both modalities. On average, respondents were experiencing low levels of burnout. The neck symptoms, increased multi-site discomfort, and higher work-related burnout among RALS surgeons suggest the need to investigate console design and cumulative workload experienced by RALS surgeons across modalities.

Keywords: Robot-Assisted Laparoscopic Surgery (RALS) · Traditional Laparoscopic Surgery (TLS) · Ergonomics · Pain · Burnout

V. G. Duffy (Ed.): HCII 2022, LNCS 13320, pp. 54–66, 2022.
https://doi.org/10.1007/978-3-031-06018-2_4

1 Introduction

The da Vinci console (Intuitive Surgical, Inc., Sunnyvale, CA, USA) is currently the most widely used system in Robot-Assisted Laparoscopic Surgery (RALS), with Intuitive Surgical holding 80.6% of the market share in robotic surgical systems and accessories [1]. The device allows the surgeon to operate while seated at a console that has dexterous controls and 3D visualization. The lightweight hand controls require minimal force to operate and may be repositioned during the procedure to allow the surgeon to work with their upper extremities at a more comfortable angle. The surgeon's motions are relayed to several wristed instruments housed in a patient-side cart [2]. This overcomes the drawbacks associated with Traditional Laparoscopic Surgery (TLS) including a limited range of motion, uncomfortable handle design and poor force transferal in the tools, awkward postures caused by table and monitor position, and a lack of depth perception [3]. Despite the benefits of RALS, there are recognized deficits in its human-computer interface. The downward viewing angle of the robotic console and 3D visual display, although intended to improve immersion and intuitiveness, can cause neck and eye strain. The limited adjustability of the console is inadequate for surgeons who are not between 175 and 200 cm tall [4]. Even though there are concerns regarding console design, RALS is associated with a lower physical demand than TLS [5–7].

The prevalence of pain and injury has been thoroughly investigated among TLS and RALS surgeons; a meta-analysis showed that 77.8% of TLS surgeons and 53.8% of RALS surgeons experienced physical symptoms while operating [8]. This is caused by the awkward and static postures maintained by surgeons throughout procedures due to poor equipment design and a lack of ergonomic knowledge among surgeons [9–11].

Burnout, which is defined as "a state of physical and emotional exhaustion caused by long-term involvement in situations that are emotionally demanding" [12], has been associated with a twofold increase in the risk of developing musculoskeletal pain. This was demonstrated during longitudinal studies where individuals experiencing burnout at the beginning of the studies were twice as likely to report physical pain and injury during the follow-up period as those who were not experiencing burnout [13, 14]. Burnout is not purely a measure of stress; it has numerous possible contributing factors for surgeons that may include dynamics and stressors within the operating room [15], the impact of adverse events [16], work-life balance [17], and existential doubt [18]. The largest known study of burnout among surgeons was conducted by Shanafelt et al. [19] where 7,905 individuals were surveyed, 40% of whom were showing signs of burnout.

The purpose of this study was to investigate the possible association between burnout and the physical symptoms experienced by RALS and TLS surgeons. Burnout is not considered to be solely caused by physical pain or vice versa. However, the relationship between burnout and physical symptoms may contribute to a better understanding of surgeon health and wellbeing. Additionally, a subgroup analysis was performed to determine whether increased use of the robotic console impacted the overall physical and cognitive symptoms the surgeons experienced in their practices.

2 Method

This study was approved by the institutional review board at Swinburne University of Technology, the Swinburne University Human Research Ethics Committee (SUHREC). Previously validated questionnaires were used to investigate pain and burnout among laparoscopic surgeons. The survey was composed of the Nordic Musculoskeletal Questionnaire (NMQ) [20], adapted to specifically ask about the pain experienced at each anatomical site during TLS and RALS procedures individually, and the Copenhagen Burnout Inventory (CBI) [21]. An existing single-item measure of burnout was also included to determine how it compared with the results of the CBI [22]. A summary of the questionnaire is included in Table 1. A sample size calculation was conducted before distributing the survey using data from a previous meta-analysis [8], with α equal to 0.05 for a confidence level of 95% and β equal to 0.2 for a power of 80%. Additionally, an adjustment was made based on the assumption that only one-third of respondents would have experience in RALS, producing the desired response rate of 116 TLS surgeons, 39 with RALS experience.

Table 1. Survey summary

Question summary	Answer format
1. Consent statement	Multiple Choice (MC)
2. In which country do you currently reside?	MC
3. Biological sex	MC
4. Age	Text-entry
5. Height	Text-entry
6. What is your surgical specialty?	MC
7. Years of experience in Traditional Laparoscopic Surgery (TLS)	MC
8. On average how many hours per week do you perform TLS?	MC
9. Have you at any time in the last 12 months had trouble (such as ache, pain, discomfort, numbness) while performing TLS in your:	Matrix table for neck, shoulders, upper back, lower back, elbows, wrists/hands, hips/thighs, knees, ankles/feet
10. Years of experience in Robot-Assisted Laparoscopic Surgery (RALS)	MC
11. On average how many hours per week do you perform RALS?	MC
12. Have you at any time in the last 12 months had trouble (such as ache, pain, discomfort, numbness) while performing RALS in your:	Matrix table for neck, shoulders, upper back, lower back, elbows, wrists/hands, hips/thighs, knees, ankles/feet

(continued)

Table 1. (*continued*)

Question summary	Answer format
13. Based on your previous answers: a. During the last 12 months have you been prevented from carrying out normal activities (e.g. job, housework, hobbies) because of this trouble in your: b. During the last 12 months have you seen a physician for this condition c. During the last 7 days have you had trouble in:	Matrix table for neck, shoulders, upper back, lower back, elbows, wrists/hands, hips/thighs, knees, ankles/feet
14. Personal burnout: a. How often do you feel tired? b. How often are you physically exhausted? c. How often are you emotionally exhausted? d. How often do you think "I can't take it anymore"? e. How often do you feel worn out? f. How often do you feel weak and susceptible to illness?	Matrix table – frequency
15. Work-related burnout (part 1): a. Is your work emotionally exhausting? b. Do you feel burnt out because of your work? c. Does your work frustrate you?	Matrix table – severity
16. Work-related burnout (part 2): a. Do you feel worn out at the end of the working day? b. Are you exhausted in the morning at the thought of another day at work? c. Do you feel that every working hour is tiring? d. Do you have enough energy for family and friends during leisure time?	Matrix table – frequency
17. Patient-related burnout (part 1): a. Do you find it hard to work with patients? b. Do you find it frustrating to work with patients? c. Does it drain your energy to work with patients? d. Do you feel that you give more than you get back when you work with patients?	Matrix table – severity

(*continued*)

Table 1. (*continued*)

Question summary	Answer format
18. Patient-related burnout (part 2): a. Are you tired of working with patients? b. Do you sometimes wonder how long you will be able to continue working with patients?	Matrix table – frequency
19. Signs of burnout included increased frustration or cynicism about work, emotional distance, physical symptoms such as headaches or intestinal issues, emotional or physical exhaustion, or reduced performance at work. Please consider these factors and select the most suitable response	MC

From October to November 2020, a link to the survey composed in Qualtrics was distributed online via professional laparoscopic social media groups. The requirement for inclusion was that the respondent had experience in and regularly practice either TLS or RALS, although not necessarily both. The response of any participant indicating that they had no experience in either TLS or RALS was excluded from the analysis. Incomplete responses were automatically submitted after one month of inactivity, these responses were manually reviewed to determine whether they would be included in the analysis. A response was considered valid if the participant successfully answered the demographic questions as well as the questions regarding pain experienced during either TLS or RALS, as a minimum requirement.

For analysis, all responses were exported into Excel (Microsoft Corporation, Redmond, WA, USA) where the statistics regarding the discomfort among surgeons while operating were obtained. The CBI was scored as recommended. The Likert responses for each question were assigned a corresponding value (0, 25, 50, 75, or 100), with one question on the 19-item questionnaire being reverse-scored. For each of the three sub-scales (personal burnout, work-related burnout, and patient-related burnout), scores were averaged to produce a single value for each measure [21]. To determine any relationships that were present in the survey responses, Fisher's exact test and Pearson's correlation coefficient were calculated in the RStudio statistical computing program (RStudio, Inc., Boston, MA, USA) [23] depending on whether the data being compared were continuous or categorical. Subgroup analysis was completed between those that only practiced TLS and those that practiced TLS and RALS using Welch's t-test to determine whether there were any differences in the multisite pain, ongoing impact of symptoms, or severity of burnout between groups.

3 Results

3.1 Summary of Survey Responses

Between October 2020 and January 2021, 196 survey responses were collected. Upon review, 32 responses were excluded as invalid. This yielded 164 valid responses, with 48 participants also having experience with RALS. Further dropout was observed, with only 146 respondents completing the entire survey. However, since the number of responses remained constant for a given section of the survey it was decided to retain the 18 incomplete responses. The analysis for each section was done using the number of respondents

Table 2. Respondent demographics

Biological sex (% male)		80.5	
Age (mean ± standard deviation)		45.7 ± 10.0	
Height (cm) (mean ± standard deviation)		173.7 ± 11.3	
Continent	Africa	1	
	Asia	98	
	Australia/Oceania	8	
	Europe	13	
	North America	42	
	South America	2	
Specialty	Bariatric	19	
	Colorectal	3	
	Gastrointestinal	29	
	General	94	
	Gynecology	1	
	Urology	1	
	Other	17	
		TLS (n = 164)	RALS (n = 48)
Years' experience	1 to 3	9	21
	3 to 5	21	12
	5 to 10	31	10
	10 to 15	28	5
	15+	75	0
Hours operating per week	1 to 5	28	26
	5 to 10	43	5
	10 to 15	50	10
	15 to 20	23	5
	20+	20	2

who had valid responses to the relevant questions of the survey. Most commonly the bio-logical sex of respondents was male, their location of practice was in Asia, specifically India (53%), and their specialty was general surgery. There was a significant difference (p < 0.01) for both the years' experience and hours operating per week between TLS and RALS surgeons. Only 31.3% of surgeons with RALS experience had more than 5 years of experience in this modality, compared with 81.7% for TLS. The majority of RALS surgeons (64.6%) operated with RALS less than 10 h each week, whereas most TLS surgeons (56.7%) operated over 10 h per week. The demographics and work characteristics of these 164 respondents are included in Table 2.

It was found that physical symptoms (defined in the survey to possibly include ache, pain, discomfort, or numbness) were experienced by 91.5% and 75% of surgeons while performing TLS and RALS procedures, respectively. A consistently higher prevalence of

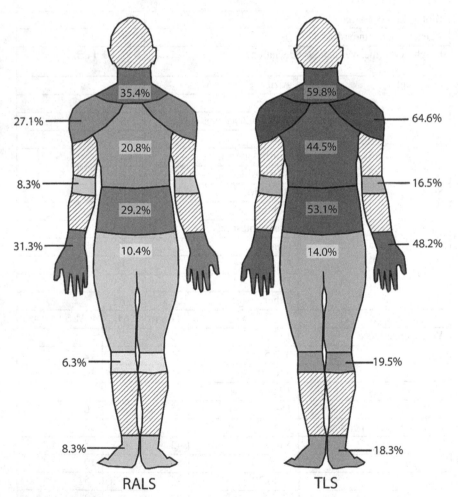

Fig. 1. Prevalence of pain experienced by surgeons during RALS (n = 48) and TLS (n = 164) procedures for each anatomic region

discomfort was found with TLS than with RALS for each anatomic region; these results are reported in full in Fig. 1. Complaints during TLS were most commonly associated with the shoulders; the prevalence of discomfort was also above 50% for the neck and lower back for TLS. The greatest area of concern for RALS surgeons was the neck. Of those who had experienced symptoms, between 10% and 30% reported that it had an impact on daily living and had affected them in the last seven days; less than 15% had consulted a doctor about that complaint, depending on the anatomic region. Data relating to the impact of operating using TLS and RALS is included in Table 3.

Table 3. Ongoing impact of pain by anatomic region

	During the last 12 months have you been prevented from carrying out normal activities because of this trouble in your…?		During the last 12 months have you seen a physician for this condition?		Based on your previous answers: - During the last 7 days have you had trouble in your…?		Total respondents
	n	(%)	n	(%)	n	(%)	
Neck	27	29.35	13	14.13	23	25.00	92
Shoulders	23	23.71	14	14.43	22	22.68	97
Upper back	14	19.72	4	5.63	11	15.49	71
Lower back	22	26.83	9	10.98	23	28.05	82
Elbows	4	15.38	1	3.85	7	26.92	26
Wrists/hands	8	10.00	5	6.25	14	17.50	80
Hips/thighs	4	14.81	0	0.00	7	25.93	27
Knees	8	27.59	4	13.79	6	20.69	29
Ankles/feet	6	20.69	3	10.34	5	17.24	29

Average scores of 36.5, 31.9, and 25.8 were obtained for the measures of personal, work-related, and patient-related burnout, respectively. It should be noted that patient-related burnout was scored as the equal or sole lowest measure of burnout by 61.5% of respondents. A score of above 50 out of 100 was reached by 34.7% of surgeons for at least one individual measure of the CBI, suggesting possible burnout. Scores above 75 were observed for 6.8% of respondents. For the single-item measure, 23.3% indicated that they were experiencing symptoms of burnout to some degree. There was a strong positive correlation ($|r| > 0.5$, $p < 0.01$) between the CBI and the single item burnout measure, suggesting surgeons could accurately assess their level of burnout.

There was a significant relationship found between discomfort and practice length for RALS ($p < 0.01$); those with less RALS experience, particularly those who had been operating with RALS for less than 3 years, tended to be less likely to report pain while operating. The number of sites where a surgeon indicated they had experienced pain in the last 12 months, regardless of the modality to which they attributed it, was used to compare the number of multisite injuries with the dimensions of burnout. There was a small, statistically significant positive correlation between the number of sites of discomfort and all three measures of burnout ($0.3 < |r| < 0.5$, $p < 0.05$). Additionally, there was a small statistically significant negative correlation found between age and personal burnout ($0.3 < |r| < 0.5$, $p < 0.01$).

3.2 Subgroup Analysis

When comparing those that only practiced TLS and those that practiced TLS and RALS, there was no statistically significant difference between the two groups in terms of biological sex, average age, or height. It was also found that the two groups had similar expertise in TLS in terms of years' experience and weekly caseload. For those operating with both modalities, an estimate of hours per week was obtained by adding together the mean of the range of hours indicated for TLS and RALS (i.e. if the surgeon worked 10 to 15 h using TLS and 5 to 10 h with RALS this would be taken as $12.5 + 7.5 = 20$ and their workload would be approximated as 15 to 20 h). Those that practiced TLS and RALS had a significantly higher workload than those that only practiced TLS using this method of extrapolation ($p = 0.02$). The total number of multisite injuries, regardless of whether they were attributed to TLS or RALS, was compared between groups. On average, those that practiced RALS experienced discomfort in more areas of the body than those that only operated using TLS; this result almost reached statistical significance (4.0 vs 3.3, $p = 0.054$). The pain was considered to have a notable impact if the surgeon had been prevented from carrying out everyday activities in the last 12 months, had sought medical intervention, or had been affected by symptoms in the last seven days. There was no significant difference in the number of surgeons impacted by their discomfort between the two groups.

Those operating with both TLS and RALS experienced significantly more work-related burnout than those only experienced in TLS based on the scores from the CBI (38.0 vs 29.4, $p = 0.01$). There was no significant difference found between the groups for the other two dimensions of burnout assessed with the CBI.

When determining the correlation between the total number of multisite injuries and the dimensions of burnout for each of the two groups, a small, statistically significant positive correlation between discomfort and all three measures of burnout ($0.3 < |r| < 0.5$, $p < 0.01$) was observed for those who only practiced TLS. This relationship did not exist for those operating with both modalities.

For those that practiced both TLS and RALS, there was a significant overlap between injuries reported for RALS and those reported for TLS. Most notably, 100% of surgeons reporting shoulder symptoms during RALS also reported shoulder discomfort during TLS. The rest of these results are shown in Table 4. There was no correlation found between the number of multisite injuries experienced by a surgeon and the ratio of hours operating with RALS in comparison to TLS in their surgical practice.

Table 4. Overlap in injuries between RALS and TLS among surgeons who practice both modalities (n = 48)

	TLS only	RALS only	Both
Neck	18	3	14
Shoulders	18	0	13
Upper back	15	4	6
Lower back	17	3	11
Elbows	5	2	2
Wrists/hands	15	7	8
Hips/thighs	4	4	1
Knees	12	1	2
Ankles/feet	5	2	2

4 Discussion

The prevalence of physical strain during TLS (91.5%) and RALS (75.0%) reported in this study was higher than the averages reported in a previous meta-analysis of 77.8% and 53.8% [8]. The main sites of complaint were the shoulders (64.6%) for TLS, possibly due to the abduction and rotation of the shoulders while operating [24, 25]. The neck was associated with the highest prevalence of discomfort for RALS (35.4%), likely due to the downward viewing angle of the visual display [4]. This current study found a positive correlation between physical complaints during RALS and experience. This contradicts the findings of Takayasu et al. [26] who showed that medical students with no RALS knowledge were significantly more likely to extend their wrists beyond 50° while completing RALS tasks than surgeons with over 15 years of experience, and significantly less likely to reposition the camera view or hand controls which could lead to discomfort. The average levels of burnout observed in this study are lower than those observed by Shanafelt et al. [19]. The scores above 75 on the dimensions of the CBI reported by a small number of respondents indicate significant burnout. This raises concerns about the health and wellbeing of these surgeons. Additionally, pain and burnout have previously been shown to have an impact on patient care [27, 28]. The majority of surgeons obtained the lowest, or equal lowest, score for the patient-related burnout measure. This may be because treating patients provides a feeling of significance for medical staff, as was found in a study of Israeli nurses [18]. The negative relationship between personal burnout and age has also been demonstrated in previous studies [17]. Burnout was positively correlated with multisite injury; this relationship requires further investigation.

It may have been expected that RALS surgeons regularly experiencing the technical benefits of the console (the articulated tools and controls, the 3D visualization, and the supported position) would experience less physical and mental strain while operating. Even though these surgeons still perform TLS, their cumulative workload and ergonomic exposure from performing both TLS and RALS would be lower than those only performing TLS for the equivalent amount of time. It was hypothesized that they would therefore develop less severe mental symptoms and fewer sources of pain and injury over time. However, increased multisite pain and work-related burnout were observed among those that practiced RALS and TLS in comparison to those who only practiced TLS. This may be because the projected hours among those that practiced both approaches were significantly higher than those that only practiced one; although it should be noted that there may be other procedures or work-related exposures that were not accounted for in this study. It is also possible that more surgeons are practicing RALS because of chronic pain they have experienced during open or TLS procedures. Musculoskeletal pain has previously been shown to have an impact on the choice of operating modality for some surgeons. Plerhoples et al. [29] found that pain contributed to the process of selecting a surgical modality for 30% of participants. Bagrodia and Raman [30] stated that 25% of respondents allowed physical symptoms to influence how they performed a procedure. When comparing open surgery, TLS, and RALS, only 3% considered RALS to cause the most discomfort.

Survey design is a strength of this study. It was estimated that the survey should only take 10 min to complete. Conditional logic was used, meaning that surgeons were not required to answer questions that did not apply to them based on their previous responses. This streamlined the process of completing the survey. Response validation meant that respondents were not able to skip questions. Submitting surveys after a month of inactivity and manually reviewing progress also enabled the inclusion of additional responses for some sections of the survey. As with any survey, this study is limited by recall bias. Regarding the NMQ, the questions were asked concerning the previous 12 months. For the CBI, the questions required a response indicating the frequency or severity of an experience with no specific period indicated. Selection bias was also a limitation of this study, as those experiencing physical pain or burnout are more likely to respond to a survey investigating these issues. While there was variation in age, location, and characteristics of surgical practice among respondents, the majority of respondents were male, from India, and specializing in general or gastrointestinal laparoscopic surgery. This, coupled with the small sample size, prohibits the generalization of the results to a larger population of laparoscopic surgeons. Despite this, the thresholds provided in the sample size analysis were reached. Additionally, these results are considered important as they demonstrate an exacerbation of pain and injury among surgeons while performing TLS and RALS, which is consistent with previous studies.

In conclusion, this study showed that TLS was consistently associated with a higher prevalence of pain than RALS for all anatomic regions examined. Additionally, over one-third of surgeons were experiencing burnout. The relationship between burnout and pain found in these survey results requires additional investigation. Subgroup analysis did not suggest that increased use of the RALS console would reduce the physical and cognitive symptoms of surgeons. The current human-computer interface of the RALS console includes a variety of features that improve the technical ability of the surgeon; however, the physical design of the console requires attention to preserve the health and wellbeing of laparoscopic surgeons. Additionally, it is important to consider the cumulative workload surgeons experience in their practice. It would be valuable to conduct further high-powered, high-quality research of a similar nature among surgeons who primarily, or only, operate using RALS. This is because surgeons did experience fewer injuries while operating with RALS, although overall still experienced similar, if not higher, levels of injury and burnout as their colleagues who only operated with TLS even though RALS has consistently been associated with a lower workload and prevalence of pain in the literature.

Acknowledgments. Ms. Jaime Hislop would like to acknowledge Ph.D. funding received from Mulgrave Private Hospital and Healthe Care during this study.

References

1. Medtech Insight, Informa Pharma Intelligence: Market Intel: Medtech Giants Ready To Battle Frontrunner Intuitive Surgical In 'Soft Surgery Robotics.' Informa UK Ltd. (2020)
2. Freschi, C., Ferrari, V., Melfi, F., Ferrari, M., Mosca, F., Cuschieri, A.: Technical review of the da Vinci surgical telemanipulator. Int. J. Med. Robot. **9**, 396–406 (2013). https://doi.org/10.1002/rcs.1468
3. Quinn, D., Moohan, J.: Optimal laparoscopic ergonomics in gynaecology. Obstetrician Gynaecologist **17**, 77–82 (2015). https://doi.org/10.1111/tog.12176
4. Van't Hullenaar, C.D.P., Hermans, B., Broeders, I.A.M.J.: Ergonomic assessment of the da Vinci console in robot-assisted surgery. Innov. Surg. Sci. **2**, 97–104 (2017). https://doi.org/10.1515/iss-2017-0007
5. Hubert, N., Gilles, M., Desbrosses, K., Meyer, J.P., Felblinger, J., Hubert, J.: Ergonomic assessment of the surgeon's physical workload during standard and robotic assisted laparoscopic procedures. Int. J. Med. Robot. **9**, 142–147 (2013). https://doi.org/10.1002/rcs.1489
6. Lee, G.I., Lee, M.R., Clanton, T., Sutton, E., Park, A.E., Marohn, M.R.: Comparative assessment of physical and cognitive ergonomics associated with robotic and traditional laparoscopic surgeries. Surg. Endosc. **28**, 456–465 (2014). https://doi.org/10.1007/s00464-013-3213-z
7. Zárate Rodriguez, J.G., et al.: Ergonomic analysis of laparoscopic and robotic surgical task performance at various experience levels. Surg. Endosc. **33**(6), 1938–1943 (2019). https://doi.org/10.1007/s00464-018-6478-4
8. Hislop, J., Hensman, C., Isaksson, M., Tirosh, O., McCormick, J.: Self-reported prevalence of injury and discomfort experienced by surgeons performing traditional and robot-assisted laparoscopic surgery: a meta-analysis demonstrating the value of RALS for surgeons. Surg. Endosc. **34**(11), 4741–4753 (2020). https://doi.org/10.1007/s00464-020-07810-2
9. Liang, B., et al.: Ergonomic status of laparoscopic urologic surgery: survey results from 241 urologic surgeons in China. PLoS ONE **8**, e70423 (2013). https://doi.org/10.1371/journal.pone.0070423
10. Wauben, L.S.G.L., van Veelen, M.A., Gossot, D., Goossens, R.H.M.: Application of ergonomic guidelines during minimally invasive surgery: a questionnaire survey of 284 surgeons. Surg. Endosc. **20**, 1268–1274 (2006). https://doi.org/10.1007/s00464-005-0647-y
11. Park, A., Lee, G., Seagull, F.J., Meenaghan, N., Dexter, D.: Patients benefit while surgeons suffer: an impending epidemic. J. Am. Coll. Surg. **210**, 306–313 (2010). https://doi.org/10.1016/j.jamcollsurg.2009.10.017
12. Pines, A., Aronson, E.: Career Burnout: Causes and Cures. Free Press, New York (1988)

13. Melamed, S.: Burnout and risk of regional musculoskeletal pain—a prospective study of apparently healthy employed adults. Stress Health **25**, 313–321 (2009). https://doi.org/10.1002/smi.1265
14. Armon, G., Melamed, S., Shirom, A., Shapira, I.: Elevated burnout predicts the onset of musculoskeletal pain among apparently healthy employees. J. Occup. Health Psychol. **15**, 399–408 (2010). https://doi.org/10.1037/a0020726
15. Kurmann, A., Tschan, F., Semmer, N.K., Seelandt, J., Candinas, D., Beldi, G.: Human factors in the operating room – the surgeon's view. Trends Anaesth. Crit. Care. **2**, 224–227 (2012). https://doi.org/10.1016/j.tacc.2012.07.007
16. Luu, S., et al.: Waking up the next morning: surgeons' emotional reactions to adverse events. Med. Educ. **46**, 1179–1188 (2012). https://doi.org/10.1111/medu.12058
17. Campbell, D.A., Sonnad, S.S., Eckhauser, F.E., Campbell, K.K., Greenfield, L.J.: Burnout among American surgeons. Surgery **130**, 696–705 (2001). https://doi.org/10.1067/msy.2001.116676
18. Malach-Pines, A.: Nurses' burnout: an existential psychodynamic perspective. J. Psychosoc. Nurs. Ment. Health Serv. **38**, 23–31 (2000)
19. Shanafelt, T.D., et al.: Burnout and career satisfaction among American surgeons. Ann. Surg. **250**, 463–471 (2009)
20. Kuorinka, I., et al.: Standardised Nordic questionnaires for the analysis of musculoskeletal symptoms. Appl Ergon. **18**, 233–237 (1987). https://doi.org/10.1016/0003-6870(87)90010-X
21. Kristensen, T., Borritz, M., Villadsen, E., Christensen, K.: The Copenhagen Burnout Inventory: a new tool for the assessment of burnout. Work Stress **19**, 192–207 (2005). https://doi.org/10.1080/02678370500297720
22. Dolan, E.D., et al.: Using a single item to measure burnout in primary care staff: a psychometric evaluation. J. Gen. Intern. Med. **30**(5), 582–587 (2015). https://doi.org/10.1007/s11606-014-3112-6
23. RStudio Team: RStudio: Integrated Development Environment for R. RStudio, Inc., Boston, MA (2019)
24. Nguyen, N.T., et al.: An ergonomic evaluation of surgeons' axial skeletal and upper extremity movements during laparoscopic and open surgery. Am. J. Surg. **182**, 720–724 (2001). https://doi.org/10.1016/s0002-9610(01)00801-7
25. Szeto, G.P.Y., Cheng, S.W.K., Poon, J.T.C., Ting, A.C.W., Tsang, R.C.C., Ho, P.: Surgeons' static posture and movement repetitions in open and laparoscopic surgery. J. Surg. Res. **172**, e19–e31 (2012). https://doi.org/10.1016/j.jss.2011.08.004
26. Takayasu, K., Yoshida, K., Mishima, T., Watanabe, M., Matsuda, T., Kinoshita, H.: Analysis of the posture pattern during robotic simulator tasks using an optical motion capture system. Surg. Endosc. **32**(1), 183–190 (2018). https://doi.org/10.1007/s00464-017-5655-1
27. Davis, W.T., Fletcher, S.A., Guillamondegui, O.D.: Musculoskeletal occupational injury among surgeons: effects for patients, providers, and institutions. J. Surg. Res. **189**, 207–212e6 (2014). https://doi.org/10.1016/j.jss.2014.03.013
28. West, C.P., Dyrbye, L.N., Erwin, P.J., Shanafelt, T.D.: Interventions to prevent and reduce physician burnout: a systematic review and meta-analysis. Lancet **388**, 2272–2281 (2016). https://doi.org/10.1016/S0140-6736(16)31279-X
29. Plerhoples, T.A., Hernandez-Boussard, T., Wren, S.M.: The aching surgeon: a survey of physical discomfort and symptoms following open, laparoscopic, and robotic surgery. J. Robot. Surg. **6**, 65–72 (2012). https://doi.org/10.1007/s11701-011-0330-3
30. Bagrodia, A., Raman, J.D.: Ergonomics considerations of radical prostatectomy: physician perspective of open, laparoscopic, and robot-assisted techniques. J. Endourol. **23**, 627–633 (2009). https://doi.org/10.1089/end.2008.0556

The Bigger Picture of Digital Interventions for Pain, Anxiety and Stress: A Systematic Review of 1200+ Controlled Trials

Najmeh Khalili-Mahani[1,2,3](✉) 🆔 and Sylvain Tran[3]

[1] Technoculture, Arts and Games, The Milieux Institute for Arts, Culture and Technology, Concordia University, Montreal, QC, Canada
najmeh.khalili-mahani@concordia.ca
[2] Department of Electrical and Computer Engineering, Concordia University, Montreal, QC, Canada
[3] Department of Computer Science and Software Engineering (CSSE), Concordia University, Montreal, QC, Canada

Abstract. The aim of this systematic scoping review was to gain a better understanding of research trends in digital mental health care. We focused on comorbid conditions: depression, anxiety, and pain–which continue to affect an estimated 20% of world population and require complex and continuous social and medical care provisions. We searched all randomized controlled trials on PubMed until May 2021 for any articles that used a form of information and communication technology (ICT) in relation to primary outcomes anxiety, pain, depression, or stress. From 1285 articles that satisfied the inclusion criteria, 890 were randomized trials with nearly 70% satisfactory outcomes. For depression and anxiety, the most frequently reported, were web-based, or mobile apps used for self-monitoring, and guided interventions. For pain, VR-based interventions or games were more prevalent, especially as tools for distraction, or as stimuli for mechanistic studies of pain or anxiety. We discuss gaps in knowledge and challenges that relate to the human factors in digital health applications, and underline the need for a practical and conceptual framework for capturing and reporting such variations.

Keywords: mHealth · Depression · Pain · Anxiety · Stress · Mental health · Digital health · Self-help · Therapy · Randomized controlled trials · Game · VR · ICT

1 Introduction

Conditions such as chronic pain, depression and anxiety disorders continue to resist treatment, and scientists are yet to find purely biological models for these prevalent conditions [1, 2]. As such, search for technology-driven strategies to facilitate citizen science, and patient-centered and personalized care has begun [3–5].

The ubiquity of information and communication technologies (ICT) has triggered an exponential surge of digital health applications, especially for mental healthcare.

© The Author(s) 2022
V. G. Duffy (Ed.): HCII 2022, LNCS 13320, pp. 67–78, 2022.
https://doi.org/10.1007/978-3-031-06018-2_5

In a 2018 opinion paper by the former director of the National Institute of Mental Health who left NIMH to join Google's Life Science, Tom Insel asked: *"What does this technology revolution have in store for psychiatry? Will brick-and-mortar clinics be replaced by teleclinicians? Will smartphones become the new clinical interface for diagnosis and treatment? Will psychiatrists be replaced by artificial intelligence (AI)-engineered conversational bots trained on millions of clinical interviews and treatment sessions?"* [6].

Among the possibilities for digital interventions in mental health are: digital phenotyping [7] and citizen science [3, 8, 9], remote care to rural communities by offering more timely response, guided treatment and adherence monitoring [10], as well as providing information and social support, which are important factors in coping with illness [11].

Today, the use of self-monitoring and behavioral training applications has become commonplace. At the time of writing this article (Feb 2022), Google Play and Apple Store offer more than 106,000 mobile apps listed under health and wellness (Source, Statistia reports in Dec 21, 2021). Several of these applications are heavily commercialized and advertised, with some data to support their efficacy, for cognitive behavioral training for weight loss [12], mindfulness [13], and game-based cognitive training [14].

Several systematic reviews in the clinical literature have tried to examine the clinical effectiveness of ICT interventions and have found promising possibilities for providing digital care for mental healthcare [15], especially for anxiety and depression [16] or chronic pain [17, 18]. However, the majority of the existing systematic reviews are designed to address specific research questions about a particular outcome, or particular population under study, and as such the search strategies do not provide a long-shot perspectives on the trends, commonalities and differences among applications that target comorbid conditions, nor the existing knowledge gaps.

In this current review, we have aimed to conduct a systematic, but broad scoping review of any studies that are listed under the category of Randomized Controlled Trials (RCTs) involving any ICT intervention. Without any specific priors other than those categories that guided the search, we have used an inductive coding methodology to identify themes that emerge from the existing literature, and might guide the development of a pragmatic framework for collaborative and inclusive digital mental healthcare solutions.

2 Methods

2.1 Systematic Review Procedure

Our systematic review search and data extraction were guided by [19] (Box 1) and search results are reported according to PRISMA guidelines [20] (Fig. 1).

> **Box 1**
>
> **Research question**
> What themes and patterns will emerge from existing data about different modes of ICT interventions in mental healthcare?
>
> **What articles can answer this question?**
> Any articles that are listed under a randomized controlled trial category.
>
> **What key concepts address the research question?**
> Identifying the ICT modalities used per clinical outcomes (depression, stress, pain and anxiety); and the types of research objectives that seek to explore or establish their efficacy in mental healthcare.
>
> **Which elements can provide an overview of research trends and gaps?**
> Sampling Characteristics; Aim of the study; Type of ICT Intervention; Target Outcome; Effectiveness of the Intervention.
>
> **Appropriate database**
> We have limited the search to PubMed-indexed peer reviewed articles.
>
> **Search terms**
> (App OR mobile OR "Mobile App" OR game OR Videogame OR web or Website OR smartphone OR VR OR "virtual reality") AND (Depression, Anxiety, Pain)
>
> **Filters**
> Randomized Controlled Trials; English; Abstract Available.

2.2 Article Selection and Data Retrieval

Because we were interested in health-related trials, we limited our search to the PubMed database (up to and including published articles on May 18, 2021) using the search query: "(anxiety OR depression OR pain) AND (app OR mobile OR game OR web OR smartphone OR VR OR "virtual reality"). Search was limited to Randomized Controlled Trials, and it resulted in a total of 1,932 peer-reviewed articles. No [tiab] annotations were used to ensure that our search was not limited by the words in the title or abstract only.

We used a quasi-automated information extraction method and used the PubMed export query tool to automatically generate a base list of results and sorted abstracts. We then programmed a Java file extraction routine to remove headers abd extract the results, and methods sections of each entry using Google Sheets API. Those articles that did not have structured abstracts were coded manually. If sufficient data was not available in the abstracts, and the articles were open-access, we searched methods and results for finding more information about sample size and demographics.

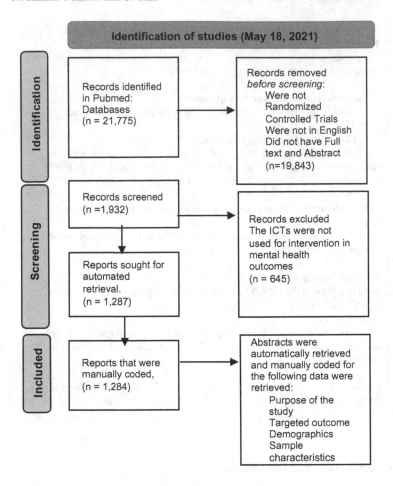

Fig. 1. Systematic review flow chart

2.3 Inductive Coding of Themes in Abstracts

Each abstract was reviewed by two coders. In the first pass ST coded the abstracts for outcome variable studied (Pain, Depression, Anxiety or Stress), sample size, sample characteristics (age range, patient or healthy control) and the type of ICT that was used (app, web, virtual reality, game, artificial intelligence, augmented reality, Computer, video, handheld devices, phone mobile text, console, Fitbit, etc.); as well as the reason for which the ICT intervention was designed (general distraction, immersion, visualization, manipulation, hypnosis, talking to a chatbot, socialization, etc.), the benefits that were provisioned (education, training, therapy, tracking, physical training, cognitive behavioral therapy, self-management, clinical follow-up and adherence monitoring, or data collection and diagnostics).

The second coder NKM, reviewed inductive codes and scanned the abstracts for reports of significant effectiveness. A study was classified as *Effective* if it reported a "significant improvement" as a result of ICT-based intervention; *Non-effective* if "no significant effects" were reported; and *Mixed*, if the primary outcomes (e.g., pain reduction, anxiety and depression scores, engagement) were modified based on specific experimental contexts, such as characteristics of population under study, baseline variations in clinical status, or experimental design. In addition, abstracts were inductively coded if the objective of the study was something other than a clinical evaluation of the pre-post intervention.

Because the age groups were not consistently reported, we categorized the population into child (<10 or identified as child in the study), adolescent (between 10–18, or if identified as adolescent in the study), adult (between 18–60) and senior (+60 or if identified as such). Because sex or gender were not consistently reported in the abstracts, we did not examine these variables.

2.4 Statistical Analysis and Synthesis of Results

We used NVIVO (for Mac); and Gephi 0.9 to examine the interrelations between themes that emerged from the review. Results were explored in terms of counts and occasionally as percentages (ratio of part to whole).

Within this review, several ICTs were designed or tested for more than one outcome. This provided an opportunity to examine and cross-functionalities between different implementations (e.g., game, web, app, etc.) for different applications (e.g., pain, anxiety, depression), and different age groups. We created an adjacency matrix with each cell representing the number of times that any two themes appeared in the same Abstract. We used Gephi to compute the network modularity (the structure emerging from the likelihood of node correlations, dividing a network into clusters forming from more correlated nodes) and eigenvector centrality (the importance of each node in terms of its within-cluster connections, as well as connection to the hubs of other clusters.) These variables were used to depict the prevalence of themes that emerged in the review, and the relations between them.

3 Results

3.1 Summary of Sample Characteristics

Within the abstracts reviewed, only 1,221 studies had specified the age group. The majority of individuals tested were adults (18–64 years old), 88.53% ($n = 1081$); followed by children (1–11 years old), 7.29% ($n = 89$), adolescents (12–17 years old), 3.77% ($n = 46$), and seniors (65 years and older), 0.41% (n = 5).

Figure 1 shows the distribution of sample size in each study, which indicates a moderate growth over time (exponential fit). The average sample size among the 1142 studies that reported the sample size was (279 ± 1178), with the median = 93. The large standard deviation is explained by the large variations from case studies ($n = 1$) to large-scale open access smoking secession studies ($n = 23,213$, albeit with high dropout rate) [21], or more structured large-scale longitudinal trials ($n = 6451$) reporting effectiveness of intervention [22].

Number of Subjects Per Study

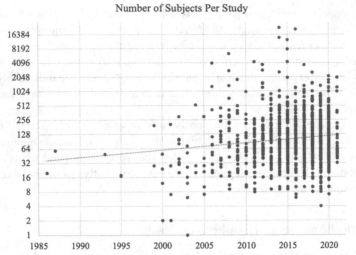

Fig. 2. Progression of sample size over time. Number of participants in the study (Y-axis) is scaled logarithmically.

Overall, 212 studies compared patients with specific clinical conditions to healthy controls, 198 studies studied only healthy controls, 823 studies included patients only.

The prevalence of studies targeting Depression was the highest (645 studies) followed by Anxiety (493 studies), Pain (337 studies) and Stress (131 studies); with significant overlap between them, the largest being Anxiety and Depression (269 studies).

3.2   Types of ICTs Studied

Within this review, 44% of studies deployed Web-based interventions (n = 561), followed by Apps (27%; $n = 346$), VR (21%; $n = 271$), Gamified interventions (10%; $n = 131$); text messaging ($n = 32$) and other types of interventions (such as Augmented Reality, $n = 5$; telephones, $n = 4$ or multimedia, $n = 10$); with a few using multimodal interventions.

The prevalence of each modality being used for a specific type of study is reported in Table 1. As it can be seen, the total number of counted outcomes and interventions is greater than the number of articles and this indicates co-occurrence of conditions or modes of intervention.

3.3   Application of ICT in Clinical Mental Health Care

While coding the studies, we noted a significant degree of overlap between different conditions, or multimodal interventions that used hybrid forms of interaction with patients while offering digital interventions. As Fig. 3 illustrates, our network-based illustrations showed that Depression was the most central condition (n = 645) within the themes of this review. Web- and App-based interventions, Therapy and Self-Management clustered together with themes related to Depression, Anxiety and Stress; as well as Expert-guided interventions and Cognitive Behavioral Therapy (CBT) (magenta). On the other hand,

Table 1. Type of ICT used for RCT interventions (not mutually exclusive).

	Web	App	VR	Game	SMS	Other	Total
Distraction	12	15	126	31	1	7	**192**
Diagnostic tool	31	25	2	5	1	0	**64**
Physical training	40	37	51	45	2	1	**176**
Tracking	40	96	7	6	4	0	**153**
Data generation	41	27	41	26	1	2	**138**
Clinical follow-up	51	49	7	13	10	1	**131**
CBT	109	59	23	11	1	0	**203**
Expert-guided	144	59	12	5	7	2	**229**
Training	189	75	32	26	9	3	**334**
Self-management	248	128	9	7	5	3	**400**
Therapy	257	135	119	49	10	2	**572**

VR and Games clustered together with condition of Pain, with the of Distraction, Physical training and Data Generation (black). To use ICTs for Tracking and Clinical follow-up and diagnosis formed a separate cluster (green). This modular representation indicates

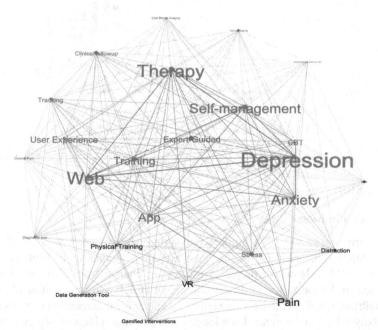

Fig. 3. Clustering Themes. The size of the letter indicated centrality (i.e., importance and frequency of connections), lines depict the frequency of connections. Colors indicate the likelihood of belonging to the same theme cluster. (Color figure online)

that there is a certain degree of bias in what type of ICT was preferred for which type of clinical condition. As well, the fact that the network seems to have low modularity suggests that possibilities for multi-modal interventions for these correlated conditions were being explored.

3.4 Evolution of Study Targets and Outcomes Over Time

As Fig. 4 shows, there has been a steady growth of both the number of controlled trials (70% of articles reviewed here, $n = 890$), as well as positive reports of the interventions having been effective on reducing the symptoms or improving patient's quality of life or care ($n = 638$). Proportionately, the number of studies that have not satisfied the efficacy criterion is small ($n = 97$). A relatively small portion of studies have also revealed complexities in administration or uptake of the interventions related to participant characteristics ($n = 155$). Notably, starting in 2007, a new category of publication, Protocol ($n = 177$), has started to emerge with the highest peak in 2015–2016.

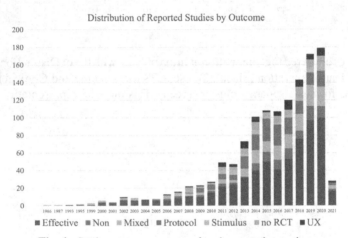

Fig. 4. Study outcomes measured and reported over time

4 Discussion

4.1 The Key Findings

Our results are consistent with a similar systematic review of literature in 2015, which identified Depression and CBT as the most prevalent themes in ICT-related mental health research [23]. However they also illustrate a change from 2016 when another review failed to demonstrate consistent efficacy of ICT based interventions [24]. Our review confirms that ICTs have been extensively tested for therapeutic purposes in pain and mood disorders; and extends knowledge by illustrating a larger research landscape where inter-relations between comorbid conditions and multimodal interventions are explored.

A few key concepts are as follows:

- Depression and Anxiety are the most studied conditions, with web- and app-based interaction being implemented for providing CBT, or guided therapies.
- Applications such as games and VR have been most extensively studied in pain to create analgesia or in surgical planning to reduce acute anxiety. These interventions have also been used to serve in physical training, as well as in creating simulated fear or anxiety responses in studying vulnerability to anxiety or mood disorders.
- The experience of users is more likely to have been considered in therapeutic studies of depression and anxiety, but specifics of user experiences are seldome a part of the experimental designs.
- All ICTs listed here have the potential to be data-collection tools. However, this modality of application does not have a significant weight in the body of literature reviewed here (RCTs on PubMed).

4.2 The Bigger Picture

The bigger picture emerging from this review is the remaining gaps that need to be addressed:

ICTs Are Not Integrated in Clinical Care for Pain, Anxiety, and Depression. This review shows that despite evidence growing in favor of increasing healthcare capacity by adding ICTs, by the time of this review, they are not integrated in the healthcare system.

The World Health Organization's first agenda on eHealth (involving 58 nations) was announced in May 2005 (WHA58.28), urging member states to draw long-term strategies and multisectoral collaborations for developing legal, logistical and technological plans for developing and implementing various range of eHealth services [25]. As Fig. 4 illustrates, the number of PubMed-indexed RCT publications has begun rising coincidentally.

However, the relatively small sample sizes (Fig. 2), study protocols without a unifying data-collection/harmonization strategy, ambiguities in data interpretation due to variations in experimental design, expert-guiding and adherence to ecological data gathering, suggest that clinical eHealth implementations at least in mood, anxiety and pain conditions are still lagging.

'Controlled' Trials in Digital Mental Healthcare Remain Challenging. The point of controlled trials is to minimize the sources of variation among the study participants, to record changes that are observed by modifying one single element in the study. To control for variations in mental health research often translates to careful stratification of sample in terms of age, gender, and clinical diagnosis, and controlling for moderating factors such as personality, cognitive and affective states, etc. However, unlike pharmacological therapies, ICT-based therapies involve a complex range of active decision making and executive agency which play a role in the phenomenology of a given experience with technology. To date, these factors remain difficult to characterize and quantify. However, this review reveals an emerging trend of studies which use adaptive algorithms towards diagnostics or experimental manipulation of user experience (e.g., by changing the intensity of VR imagery, or using it as a stimulus to induce anxiety.) Within this review, examples of these applications (Chatbots, VR-induced hypnosis, or data-driven decision support systems) in RCTs are still too few.

Human Factors Pose a Challenge But Are Not Always Considered in Trial Design and Interpretation. Given that more than 80% of the studies here were in adults (18–60), and that gender, culture or geopolitical or socioeconomic variations were not consistently measured or reported as control variables of interest, the bulk of existing evidence is not generalizable. More specifically, within this review, 61 studies were solely about evaluation of user experience in a clinical context. A smaller portion of these were related to specific outcomes measures (38/890; i.e., less than 4%), and considered user experience, acceptance, and adherence in their analyses; and 27 of those produced mixed results. It should be noted that nearly 28% of the clinical trials reported negative or mixed results, perhaps due to individual or contextual differences mediating the results.

A discussion of possible human factors that can impact clinical efficacy (e.g., baseline severity; dyadic procedures; personality factors; presence of co-morbidities or medications; or even blinding and placebo effect) are beyond the scope of this article, however these are critical factors that must be considered in provisioning adaptive and person-centered design of such applications. On the other hand, clinicians must also account for variations that arise from interindividual variations in human-computer interactions (HCI) [26].

Confounding Effects of ICT-Alone or Expert-Guided Longitudinal Care Are not Always Explored. By nature, information and communication technologies involve social interactions with professionals. Most studies reviewed here have a longitudinal design, or an Intervention versus a wait-list design. In either case, patients benefit from extended access to healthcare providers. Most interventions reviewed here include either an expert or peer involved in real-time or asynchronous communications (e.g., via video conferencing, SMS, or through social and peer support). We noted (not reported here) that in many of the effective interventions (e.g., those in which the effects were sustained after 12 months), the effects improved if the ICTs were added to the regular therapeutic procedures. It is plausible to postulate that when used as a complementary tool in patient care, ICT increases the capacity of patients to learn from interactive communication with experts, and then personalize their own care (by self-monitoring, and improved decision making about treatment options, or compliance with rehabilitation or pharmacological interventions.) Whether stand-alone technologies may produce clinically significant outcomes is an important factor that can be studied only if the human factors are carefully considered in both experimental design, and phenomenological assessment of the ICT usage in different individuals.

4.3   Limitations and Future Work

This review is limited by its own scale, which served to offer a long-shot perspective on the progression of the eHealth in clinical care for comorbid conditions: pain, anxiety, depression, and stress. As such, it remains to more closely examine the experimental factors that may inform the development of a unifying framework for collaborative and international research and development into digital therapeutics.

It should also be noted that this review is based on an inductive qualitative methodology where the themes for interventions and study objectives are coded based on keywords in the abstract and two coders. In this paper, we have reported only the first set of our code hierarchy. In the future work, we will be delving more closely into clinical elements of these studies.

5 Conclusion

This review illustrates a rapidly growing interest in applying ICTs in care for hard-to-treat conditions such as pain, anxiety, and depression; and suggests that the evidence is mostly promising. However, there is a lack of an experimental or conceptual framework to account for variations in human factors. These variations may arise from the quality and quantity of the interactions among patients and their caregivers, as well as from personal or clinical factors that may influence the experience of individuals while adopting these technologies into their care. Methods to account for such variations are needed.

References

1. Thompson, P.M., et al.: ENIGMA and global neuroscience: a decade of large-scale studies of the brain in health and disease across more than 40 countries. Transl. Psychiatry 10(1), 1–28 (2020). https://doi.org/10.1038/s41398-020-0705-1
2. Craig, K.D., et al.: Pain in persons who are marginalized by social conditions. Pain 161(2), 261–265 (2020). https://doi.org/10.1097/j.pain.0000000000001719
3. Khalili-Mahani, N., et al.: Play the pain: a digital strategy for play-oriented research and action. Front. Psychiatry 12, 746477 (2021). https://doi.org/10.3389/fpsyt.2021.746477
4. Katapally, T.R.: The SMART framework: integration of citizen science, community-based participatory research, and systems science for population health science in the digital age. JMIR mHealth uHealth 7(8), e14056 (2019). https://doi.org/10.2196/14056
5. Ilioudi, S., Lazakidou, A., Tsironi, M.: Information and communication technologies for better patient self-management and self-efficacy. Int. J. Electron. Healthc. 5(4), 327–339 (2010). https://doi.org/10.1504/IJEH.2010.036205
6. Hirschtritt, M.E., Insel, T.R.: Digital technologies in psychiatry: present and future. Focus 16(3), 251–258 (2018). https://doi.org/10.1176/appi.focus.20180001
7. Insel, T.R.: Digital phenotyping. JAMA 318(13), 1215–1216 (2017). https://doi.org/10.1001/jama.2017.11295
8. Brañas-Garza, P., et al.: Citizen Social Lab: a digital platform for human behavior experimentation within a citizen science framework. PLoS ONE 13(12), e0207219 (2018). https://doi.org/10.1371/journal.pone.0207219
9. Tran, V.-T., et al.: Patients' perspective on how to improve the care of people with chronic conditions in France: a citizen science study within the ComPaRe e-cohort. BMJ Qual. Saf. 28(11), 875–886 (2019). https://doi.org/10.1136/bmjqs-2018-008593
10. Rauseo-Ricupero, N., et al.: Case studies from the digital clinic: integrating digital phenotyping and clinical practice into today's world. Int. Rev. Psychiatry 33(4), 394–403 (2021). https://doi.org/10.1080/09540261.2020.1859465
11. Rains, S.A.: Coping with Illness Digitally. MIT Press, Cambridge (2018)
12. Chin, S.O., et al.: Successful weight reduction and maintenance by using a smartphone application in those with overweight and obesity. Sci. Rep. 6(1), 1–8 (2016). https://doi.org/10.1038/srep34563
13. Mani, M., et al.: Review and evaluation of mindfulness-based iPhone apps. JMIR mHealth uHealth 3(3), e4328 (2015). https://doi.org/10.2196/mhealth.4328

14. Anguera, J.A., et al.: Video game training enhances cognitive control in older adults. Nature **501**(7465), 97–101 (2013). https://doi.org/10.1038/nature12486
15. Miralles, I., et al.: Smartphone apps for the treatment of mental disorders: systematic review. JMIR mHealth uHealth **8**(4), e14897 (2020). https://doi.org/10.2196/14897
16. Lattie, E.G., et al.: Digital mental health interventions for depression, anxiety, and enhancement of psychological well-being among college students: systematic review. J. Med. Internet Res. **21**(7), e12869 (2019). https://doi.org/10.2196/12869
17. Devan, H., et al.: Evaluation of self-management support functions in apps for people with persistent pain: systematic review. JMIR Mhealth Uhealth **7**(2), e13080 (2019). https://doi.org/10.2196/13080
18. Pfeifer, A.-C., et al.: Mobile application-based interventions for chronic pain patients: a systematic review and meta-analysis of effectiveness. J. Clin. Med. **9**(11), 3557 (2020). https://doi.org/10.3390/jcm9113557
19. Bramer, W.M., et al.: A systematic approach to searching: an efficient and complete method to develop literature searches. J. Med. Libr. Assoc. **106**(4), 531 (2018). https://doi.org/10.5195/jmla.2018.283
20. Beller, E.M., et al.: PRISMA for abstracts: reporting systematic reviews in journal and conference abstracts. PLoS Med. **10**(4), e1001419 (2013). https://doi.org/10.1371/journal.pmed.1001419
21. Mañanes, G., Vallejo, M.A.: Usage and effectiveness of a fully automated, open-access, Spanish web-based smoking cessation program: randomized controlled trial. J. Med. Internet Res. **16**(4), e3091 (2014). https://doi.org/10.2196/jmir.3091
22. Rabius, V., et al.: Comparing internet assistance for smoking cessation: 13-month follow-up of a six-arm randomized controlled trial. J. Med. Internet Res. **10**(5), e1008 (2008). https://doi.org/10.2196/jmir.1008
23. Hallberg, S.C., et al.: Systematic review of research investigating psychotherapy and information and communication technologies. Trends Psychiatry Psychother. **37**(3), 118–125 (2015). https://doi.org/10.1590/2237-6089-2014-0055
24. Breslau, J., Engel, C.C.: Information and communication technologies in behavioral health: a literature review with recommendations for the Air Force. RAND Health Q. **5**(4), 17 (2016)
25. WHO. Fifty-Eight World Health Assembley, 5461 (2005)
26. Jalil, S., et al.: Complementing a clinical trial with human-computer interaction: patients' user experience with telehealth. JMIR Hum. Factors **6**(2), e9481 (2019). https://doi.org/10.2196/humanfactors.9481

Multimodal Data Fusion for Automatic Detection of Alzheimer's Disease

Ivan Krstev, Milan Pavikjevikj, Martina Toshevska[✉], and Sonja Gievska

Faculty of Computer Science and Engineering, Ss. Cyril and Methodius University,
Skopje, North Macedonia
{ivan.krstev.1,milan.pavikjevikj}@students.finki.ukim.mk,
{martina.toshevska,sonja.gievska}@finki.ukim.mk

Abstract. The viability of multimodal fusion of linguistic and acoustic biomarkers in speech to help in identifying a person with probable Alzheimer's dementia symptoms have been explored in this research. For capturing the effect of dementia on person's language and verbal abilities, a novel way of disease detection was explored based on visual analysis of images of spectrogram extracted from patient's interview recordings. We put forward three fusion methods, which allow the major advancements in representation learning to be utilized. The objective of the empirical study and ensuing discussion presented in this paper was threefold: 1) to examine the potential of state-of-the-art transformer-based architectures and transfer learning to assist the disease diagnosis, 2) to map the problem of acoustic analysis into the realm of image processing, by transforming spectrograms into images and employing pretrained deep neural networks, such as ResNet to extract visual patterns, and 3) to investigate the sound interplay of multi-modal biomarkers of Alzheimer's dementia when fusing the learned representations in different modalities. We present the results of independent evaluations of the unimodal methods against which the fusion methods have been compared to.

Keywords: Alzheimer's dementia · Audio · Text · Multimodal fusion · Machine learning · Deep learning · Transformers

1 Introduction

Alzheimer's disease (AD) [13] is the most common neurodegenerative disorder causing dementia, affecting millions of people worldwide. Clinical symptoms include progressive dementia, irritability, confusion, and memory loss [20]. Age has been reported as a major factor correlated with high probability of being diagnosed with AD dementia. According to the latest 2021 Alzheimer's Association report, 13.8% of people age 75–84 and 34.6% of people age 85 are diagnosed with Alzheimer's dementia in the US [41]. Early detection of dementia has a crucial importance in bringing timely medical care and support to the patient and allowing their family and friends to adjust to the changes. Clinical diagnostic tests and neuropsychological examinations (currently achieving accuracy of

V. G. Duffy (Ed.): HCII 2022, LNCS 13320, pp. 79–94, 2022.
https://doi.org/10.1007/978-3-031-06018-2_6

95%) [27] are timely and costly and face challenges when it comes to detecting early stages of the disease (mild cognitive impairment). Computational predictive methods are viewed as a faster and less obtrusive diagnostic alternative.

The list of proposed linguistic and acoustic biomarkers that might be associated with amnestic and non-amnestic cognitive impairment in patients with probable Alzheimer's still lack comprehensiveness. The performance of the methods experimented in the past is typically strongly affected by the predictive power of the selected handcrafted features indicative of the disease [38]. Various linguistic features have been experimented with, from simple word frequencies to part-of-speech tags and grammatical dependencies [22,24]. What early research work in the field lacks is standardization and reproducibility [38]. While feature engineering and traditional ML are still in use as baseline methods, distributed and contextual word vector representation [28,43] are hailed as much more scalable and generalizable approach recurrently yielding superior performance advantage.

We have examined the ways in which both traditional and deep learning techniques might complement, or be helpful in diagnosing this incurable neurodegenerative disease that has a progressive devastating effect on patient's verbal and cognitive abilities. This paper explores a multimodal early detection of Alzheimer's disease on the clinical dataset from Dementia Bank, which consists of demographic data, namely, the age and gender of the participants in the study, as well as the 551 recorded interviews and transcripts elicited from 292 participants. There are 309 recordings labeled as samples belonging to patients with probable Alzheimer's disease, while 242 samples were gathered from 99 healthy patients from the control group. The notable difference between the two groups is that AD patients exhibit difficulties in communicating their thoughts, finding words or coherently describing a visual scene.

While the performance achievements of the proposed unimodal methods for AD detection in user's speech were positive and inline with previous research, fusing acoustic and language cues has also been considered to be a more viable approach to assess patients' probable cognitive deficits from their recorded interviews. We have also explored the possibility of using state-of-the-art computer vision architectures for detecting AD based on images of patient's MEL spectrogram. The early fusion approach i.e. feature-based fusion was performed by concatenating multimodal features. Late fusion acts as a "soft voter", i.e. the probability yielded by the three unimodal models was aggregated at a decision level. The Sentence-based model and our joint fusion model, incorporating Sentence-BERT embeddings [34] and the final hidden states of the ResNet34 network [15] for learning the audio representation of the spectrogram images yielded the best results. After a brief review of research studies most related to our own presented in Sect. 2, we give a description of the DementiaBank dataset used for training and evaluating the models in Sect. 3. The details of the unimodal and fusion methods explored in this work are laid out in Sect. 4. The discussion of the findings are presented in Sect. 5, while the last section concludes the paper.

2 Related Work

Many researchers follow the idea of using features of multiple modalities for Alzheimer's Disease (AD) detection [22, 23].

A multimodal approach for AD detection was proposed by [24]. Several ML models were explored with various feature categories: acoustic features, TF-IDF features, readability features, and Doc2Vec embeddings. The reported results suggest that TF-IDF features were the best performing among all feature categories. However, specific types of acoustic features and readability scores have shown to boost the overall performances, and early fusion of the features led to better performances than unimodal approaches. Doc2Vec embeddings have shown poor performances possibly due to a very small train dataset.

Apart from frequently used features, such as features obtained at utterance level and voice activity, audio embeddings have also been utilized [33]. The authors have used x-vectors obtained by a Time Delay Neural Network (TDNN), and emotional embeddings obtained by a PAD (Pleasure, Arousal, and Dominance)-based model [26]. For linguistic features, two transformer-based language models were used: BERT [9] and ELECTRA [7]. BERT is trained to predict the correct input token that has been masked, while ELECTRA is trained to discriminate between real and fake input words. The acoustic-only and linguistic-only model obtained similar performance results. However, there was a performance gain with early fusion of both acoustic and linguistic features. An additional analysis was performed to explore the influence of the interviewer in the conversations. The models were evaluated on datasets containing patients' utterances only, interviewers' utterances only and the entire interview. The findings suggest that the interviewer is important for smoother interactions.

Attention-based networks composed of three standalone deep neural networks represented as a self-attention layer followed by a convolutional layer were proposed in [40]. Each of the networks is responsible for a specific feature set: acoustic features, linguistic features, and embeddings (sentence embeddings of the automatically transcribed speech recordings, and audio embeddings). The experimental results show that using both audio embeddings and linguistic features is the best approach for this setting. Although handcrafted linguistic features perform better than sentence embedding representations, using only the latent text-based features does not perform as well as using only audio embeddings.

Wav2Vec [4] achieves comparable performance to traditional automatic speech recognition systems by self-supervised learning the representation of speech data without the need for massive datasets. Wav2BERT, a combination of Wav2Vec to extract semantic information from speech and BERT to detect dementia, was proposed in [43]. To preserve non-semantic information, the model is extended with pause preservation and embedding conversion. This extension led to better performances. However, the impact of the in-sentence pauses was negative possibly due to the limited training data. A study [11] exploring models based on acoustic features including Wav2Vec has concluded that Wav2Vec is superior compared to all unimodal and multimodal methods.

3   Dataset

For training and evaluating our models, we have used the DementiaBank collection [5] of 551 recorded interviews and transcripts from 292 patients evaluated for probable Alzheimer's disease. The dataset contains a balanced number of samples; 309 audio samples belong to 193 patients with probable Alzheimer's disease, while the healthy control group consists of the 242 recorded interviews with 99 patients.

DementiaBank[1] is a valuable database of multimodal interactions related to clinical trials on early diagnosing AD or dementia patients. The particular dataset targeted in our study was collected as part of several longitudinal studies on interaction patterns exhibited by patient with Alzheimer's disease and dementia, conducted by the School of Medicine, University of Pittsburg. A number of data from patient's medical records, including neuropsychological examinations results associated with participants in the studies is also available, although for this particular research we have used two demographics data only, age and gender, as specified in the INTERSPEECH 2021 task [23].

The content of the recorded interviews relates to patient describing a Cookie Theft image, part of the Boston Diagnostic Test for Aphasia (BDAE) [14], which is clinically relevant for diagnosing and assessing linguistic deficiency in patients with Alzheimer's and Aphasia. Participants were asked to describe the content of the image in English, while the verbal statements of the patients were recorded and later transcribed by CHAT, a computational tool for automatic transcription of audio data.

Given the fact that the risk of Alzheimer's disease in elderly population is more prominent, the screening was conducted on a group of patients with ages varying between 46–90 years, with a mean age of 68.43. Gender differences in incidence numbers are preserved, namely, the dataset includes 342 number of samples from female and 209 recordings from male patients. Our models were trained on 257 samples from patients classified as probable AD, while the remaining 52 samples, labeled with other types of dementia were excluded. The entire set of 241 recordings from the control group was included. The quartile distribution of the patients with AD follows the overall distribution of the dataset.

The dataset was initially split into training and test sets in a 80:20 ratio. The test set was used exclusively for evaluation of the already trained models, whilst grid search and cross validation for parameter tuning was done only with the train set.

4   Methodologies

In this study, the information carried out by different channels of communications has been explored to unify the multimodal aspects previously considered by others [24,40] and suggests new fusion approaches based on state-of-the-art deep learning architectures.

---

[1] https://dementia.talkbank.org/, last visited: 10.02.2022.

At the onset of our study, we set two baseline models based on linguistic and acoustic features frequently used in previous research with the addition of two demographic features, age and gender. These models served as our baselines that other methods will be compared to. While age correlation with dementia occurrence has been well documented, understanding gender-specific trends in dementia and Alzheimer's disease might be particularly useful in identifying preclinical risk factors aimed at preventing disease as well as gender-related differences in disease progression.

The description presented henceforth report on the models we propose for multimodal detection of Alzheimer's disease.

4.1   Linguistic Model

Psycholinguistic features, such as the amount of nouns, pronouns, verbs, as well as lexical richness are prominent features in a linguistic style profile of each individual [6]. Exploiting the difference in syntax, morphology, and word choices used by individuals assists in discriminating between healthy and AD patients. Psycholinguistic features have been successfully applied in many tasks focused on classification of diseases that affect the behaviour of patients: identifying depressed users in online forums [36], and classification of patients with aphasia [3].

Following this line of research, 10 psycholinguistic characteristics were extracted from the transcripts of each participant. First, the *total number of words* were computed, as well as *total number of nouns, verbs*, and *adjectives*. The *number of unique word stems was* included as it indicates the lexicon richness used by a participant. Apart from these, the feature set is extended with the *number of questions asked*, the *number of times that noisy and unclear things were said*, and *phrases like "uh", "um", or similar*. Since the transcripts include a person describing an image related to cookies, the *number of times the word "cookie" has been said* was also calculated. Considering that age is the main risk factor, and women are more prone to AD than man [39], *age* and *gender* are also included.

The linguistic model with 10 psycholinguistic and 2 demographic features was evaluated by five machine learning (ML) algorithms: Support Vector Machines (SVM), Naive Bayes Classifier, Random Forests, K Nearest Neighbors (KNN) and XGBoost. Grid Search combined with 3-fold cross-validation was used for optimization and training of the models.

4.2   Acoustic Model

The linguistic features for dementia prediction captures language deficits including discourse coherence at a lexical and syntactic level (e.g., word repeat, syntactic complexity, and vocabulary richness). However, behavioral symptoms of language impairment in individuals with probable onset of AD are reflected both at linguistic and acoustic level [24,33,40]. Our acoustic model was based on a number of features that were extracted to account for tangible AD indicators in patient's voice recordings. The selection of acoustic cues draws upon previous theoretical and empirical research that point to their relevance for AD recognition in speech.

A set of 210 acoustic features belonging to two categories, namely prosodic and spectral, has been included in the second acoustic baseline model. Variations in pitch, loudness, tempo, and rhythm in speech reveal meanings that complement the information conveyed by speaker's word choices. Supra-segmental acoustic (prosodic) features of speech are considered indicative of the emotional state of the speaker. Our list of this category included: *zero crossing rate (ZCR)*, *spectral roll off (bellow 85%)*, *chroma frequencies* and *spectral bandwidth*. Similarly, variations in resonant frequencies that result in slow or not distinctive formants are evidence of health-related difficulties. Consequently, short-term spectrum features, such as *Mel Frequency Cepstral Coefficient (MFCC)* were exploited as paralinguistic cues that can further enrich the AD detection analysis. The choice to include a statistical functional (e.g., mean, median, min, max, standard deviation) was guided the results of our exploratory study.

The acoustic model based on the spectral and prosodic feature set has been evaluated using five machine learning algorithms. A matrix of 210-feature vectors, one vector per frame, was input to our implementations of the Naïve Bayes, Random Forest, Support Vector Machine (SVM), K-Nearest Neighbors (KNN) and XGBoost classifier. Grid Search combined with 3-fold cross validation was used to optimize the classification models that were previously subjected to PCA dimensionality reduction. We extracted the acoustic features from the audio files using the Python Librosa library [25].

4.3   Language Representation-Based Model

Word and sentence embeddings have shown to improve the performances in almost every NLP area. There is a variety of pretrained language models that provide word as well as sentence embeddings. The embeddings used for our experiments are GloVe [29] and FastText [19] as distributed word embeddings, and Sentence-BERT [34] and FLAIR [2] as contextualized embeddings.

Three approaches to create representation for the transcripts were utilized. In the first approach, the representation from the final hidden state of an LSTM model was used. The embeddings of the words in a document are stacked on top of each other and are then fed into an LSTM model that generates the representation with its final hidden state. The second approach is focused on document pooled embeddings [1]. A matrix is formed using the embeddings of each word in a document. Pooling operation is further performed on each column thus creating the final embedding representation. The last approach includes mapping each transcript into a dense vector using sentence transformer models [34], namely BERT that was pretrained on the Stanford Natural Language Inference (SNLI) corpus.

The embeddings created with the previously-described approaches were fed into a separate Gated Recurrent Unit (GRU) network. The hyperparameters of GRU-based models were trained with an initial learning rate of 0.5 and 50%

annealing factor. The maximum number of epochs was set to 100, however, each of the models converged in less than 100 epochs. For document embeddings, we have used the FLAIR framework [2].

4.4   Visual Spectrogram Analysis Model

We introduce a novel approach based on visual processing of speech spectrograms that contrasts traditional speech analysis for dementia detection. By doing so, the problem of distinction between healthy participants and patients with probable AD-related dementia is mapped in the realm of computer vision. While spectrograms were previously reported to carry relevant psychophysiological manifestations pertaining to speaker's emotional state [32], no prior work has attempted to analyze speech for the task of AD or dementia prediction.

A spectrogram is a two-dimensional graphical representation of an audio signal; time-varying spectral information such as energy, pitch, and formants are woven into its compact visual display. In an attempt to understands what type of evidence is preserved in a spectrogram that might be used to complement language representation learning in our fusion models, a Mel frequency spectrogram of all audio samples were transformed into images. Figure 1 shows a sample of MEL spectrogram of a healthy patient and one of a patient with a probable diagnosis of Alzheimer's disease.

Machine vision is one of the stellar use cases of deep learning. Recent advances in very deep pretrained convolutional neural networks (CNNs) [15,18,37] have already become industry standards in the fields of computer vision. For the purpose of extracting features and patterns found in the spectrogram images representing audio samples we have adopted the same approach. Finetuning pretrained models, such as ResNet34 [15], SqueezeNet [18] and VGG16 [37] have been used for training the model to distinguish between spectrogram images that belong to both classes of patients, healthy and probable AD patients.

FastAI [16] implementations of ResNet30, SqueezeNet and VGG16 were used as pretrained models on the ImageNet dataset [8]. By doing so, low-level image features were learned in the first pass by training the first layer of the network on the ImageNet. In the second phase, the weights of the first layer were preloaded and other layers were unfrezeed, so that the entire network could be trained to learn the representation of the input images i.e., spectrograms.

4.5   Fusion Models

The problem addressed by our research is challenging as it involves modeling behavioral symptoms of different modality exhibited by a patient with probable Alzheimer's disease. Extensive prior works on integrating multimodal data in various application domains, such as affective analysis [12,30,31], fake news detection [2,10], graph proteins [42], disease diagnosis [17] warranted an exploration into the potential of fusion approaches for the problem under investigation.

Broadly, methods for fusing multimodal data fall into three categories and this research conducts an exploration into all three categories of fusion tailored

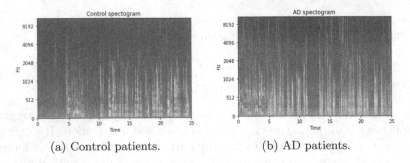

(a) Control patients.   (b) AD patients.

Fig. 1. Spectrograms generated from the audio files from one control patient and 3 AD patients.

to the specifics of our problem. Feature-based (early) fusion refers to simple concatenation of multimodal features, while decision-based (late) fusion combines the unimodal decisions based on a certain aggregation criteria (e.g., average, weighted, maximum). With the advances in deep learning architectures and transfer learning, joint fusion has received heightened attention in the last decade. In joint fusion, unimodal data are encoded by a suitable choice of modality-specific network into an embedded representations; modality-specific models are trained jointly through a loss function.

Our feature-based fusion model builds a multimodal representation by concatenating the acoustic features extracted from a given audio sample along with the psycholinguistic features and FastText word embedding of the transcript. Two demographic data were added i.e., the age and gender of the patient an audio sample belongs to. The process of early fusion is shown in Fig. 2 (on the left). The same set of five traditional machine algorithms used in our baseline models were used as classifiers. While this united feature set carries richer information, the correlation between heterogeneous features is elusive to capture by this simple form of fusion.

Decision-based (late) fusion model combines the predictions of the two unimodal baseline models as shown in Fig. 2 (on the right). The final prediction is obtained in a soft voting manner by averaging the estimates of the two models. The criteria for combining the outputs is not restricted to any strategy per se as other strategies (e.g., weighted, best) can be plugged in and further investigated for the task under consideration. Even though the entire psycholinguistic and acoustic feature set were included, the correlation information that might offer valuable insights under different scenarios are likely to be lost with late fusion.

Motivated by the successes in computer vision that rely on transfer learning and powerful deep neural networks pretrained on massive datasets, the joint fusion model leverages the state-of-the-art transformer architecture for language modeling in conjunction with the pretrained architectures used in computer vision. For our joint fusion model, a patient's transcript was encoded by the Sentence-BERT transformer architecture, while the audio recordings were represented by the final hidden state of the ResNet34 that was fed with the Mel spectrogram images. In this way, the two unimodal representations generated by the pretrained architectures were projected into a joint latent space. The final prediction of whether the patient is likely to have Alzheimer's disease is performed by a simple Feed Forward Neural Network (FFNN) as shown in Fig. 3. The most important changes brought about by the joint fusion lies in the training procedure. By jointly learning through a loss function, the model is expected to capture the complex relationships between different modalities pertaining to AD recognition.

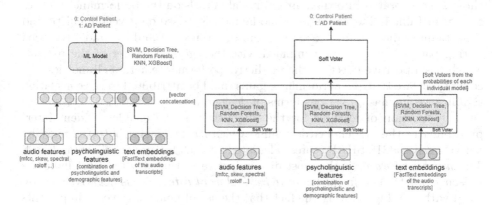

Fig. 2. General architecture of **Early Fusion Model** (shown on the left) and **Late Fusion Model** (shown on the right).

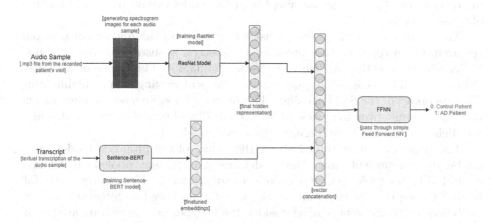

Fig. 3. General architecture of the **Joint Fusion Model**.

5   Results and Discussion

An exploratory study was conducted to assess the performance standing of our deep learning based models for automatic prediction of Alzheimer's disease. We also compare our models to two unimodal baselines evaluated on the same DementiaBank dataset consisting of 551 audio samples and transcripts from 292 patients with probable AD and 192 individuals in the healthy, control group. Traditional metrics precision, accuracy, recall and F1-measure have been selected for comparative performance analyses. The results concerning the effects of various choices incorporated into the four unimodal models on the performance metrics appear in Table 1. Two baseline unimodal models, based on psycholinguistic and acoustic prosodic features extracted from the transcript and the audio recorded during patient's visit, were combined with the age and gender of the patient, which has a positive effect on the predictive performance across all metrics. We could speculate that the performance gains could be attributed to the correlation significance age has on various forms of dementia.

The selection of features for the linguistic baseline enables evident interpretability of the models i.e. determine which features contribute the most by SHAP analysis [21]. SHAP scores calculated for each feature are shown in Fig. 4. The *number of words* is the most discriminative feature; higher value indicates presence of AD. The *frequency of individual word categories* is negatively correlated with AD, highlighting the fact that the use of nouns and verbs in patients with probable AD is sparse. *Lexical diversity* is not as descriptive as expected i.e. control patients are still more "lexically diverse" than AD patients, but the difference is insignificant. The models' performance drops when demographic characteristics (age and gender) are removed from the feature set. Overall, the psycholingustic features have consistent performance among all machine learning algorithms. The best performing Linguistic model variant uses SVM and has obtained accuracy of 73%.

The results obtained by the acoustic baseline echo the findings of previous research, which reported that prosodic and spectral acoustic features a resound indicarsto frf detecting Alzheimer's disease [24,33,40]. The choice of ML algorithm resulted in inconsistent performance effects of varying degree, highlighting the superiority of the SVM classifier. The Acoustic baseline model achieves accuracy in the range from 57% yielded by KNN to 73% obtained by the SVM, which parallels the results of the linguistic baseline model.

The third section of Table 1 shows the results of the proposed model based on language representation. The models using document pooled embeddings exhibited better performance compared to traditional LSTM, although still fall behind the superior performance of the transformer-based architecture, such as Sentence-BERT. Sentence-BERT yielded the best performances compared to all other models evaluated in this work. Its performances are close to the best performing model on the task [35].

The results concerning the effects of the proposed model based on visual spectrograms are shown in the last category box of Table 1. The current findings demonstrate lower performance achieved by the model compared to the best

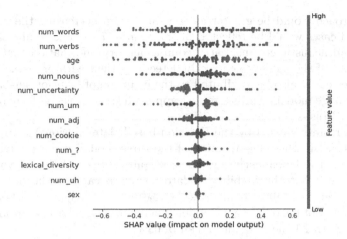

Fig. 4. SHAP analysis of the feature importance of the Psycholinguistic and demographic features. Blue color implies lower values of the given feature, red color denotes the higher values for the same feature. (Color figure online)

results achieved by the unimodal baselines and the superior models using word embeddings. Across five pretrained convolutional networks used, the numbers of incorrect classifications were consistently higher for more complex ResNet-50 architecture, as well as 18-layer SqueezeNet. While the results show weaker evidence for the relationship between the visual cues extracted from spectrogram images and the disease, improvement of performance through fusion was hypothesized.

The findings of the four unimodal models presented in Table 1 were compared with the evaluation results of the fusion models. The values obtained in a set of experiments focusing on evaluating the three fusion models are presented in Table 2, along with the results of the best performing unimodal methods.

The effectiveness of a variety of psycholinguistic and acoustic features for predicting the phenotype of probable Alzheimer's have been well documented. Although promising results have been reported, we hypothesize that the fusion models could bring further improvements of the performance of the unimodal models. One of the major limitations of unimodal methods is their inability to capture a comprehensive set of biomarkers indicative of early stages of the disease that so often elude even the standard neuropsychological diagnostic tools.

The simplest bimodal feature-based fusion model of linguistic and acoustic cues has produced significant improvements across all performance metrics compared to the performance of unimodal baselines, which is consistent with the evidence presented in the related research [33,40]. The system has shown F1 value of 76%. It was intuitively assumed that the performance metrics of the hybrid approach would be greater as the gains from decreasing the number of misclassified cases would be reflected in the recall (77%). The results show that linguistic and acoustic channel carry complementary information that improve the capability of the model to correctly detect a patient with probable AD. The higher values could also be attributed to the inclusion of transformer-based pre-trained language models that is a robust approach that brings performance gains to many NLP tasks.

Yet, the results yielded by the Decision-based (late) Fusion Model does not quite seems satisfactory. The training of the three modality-specific models has been performed independently and their outputs subjected to soft voting. We could speculate that the inability of late fusion to capture the dependencies between different modality channels is the reason behind the results being lower than the ones obtained by each model independently. The late fusion model underscores with F1 measure and recall of 68%.

Overall, the multimodal Joint Fusion Model that combines Sentence-BERT representation of textual information and ResNet representation of visual information extracted from spectrogram images performed optimally, although without the gains we have expected. Across all evaluation metrics the joint fusion model matches the performance of the best performing unimodal Sentence-BERT model. The advantage of joint fusion was evident only on improving the recall value by 0.1%. We consider the result encouraging as dealing with uncertain situation and distinguishing between situations when dichotomy between the modalities exist is crucial for advancing the current standing of the model. Our current efforts are directed towards more extensive experimentation with various combination of pretrained representation models through fusion.

Overall, this research has provided insights into the roles different modality-specific data play in discriminating between healthy patients and patients with probable Alzheimer's disease. Findings show general performance gains with early fusion compared with unimodal approaches based on traditional machine learning. Finetuning Sentence-BERT transformer architecture for the task at hand has outperformed all other unimodal methods, including the feature-based and decision-based fusion models. The comparable results obtained by the joint fusion model that was based on state-of-the-art pretrained neural architectures for transfer learning reinforce the notion that further advances in telediagnostic tools for AD screening are within reach.

Table 1. Evaluation results for the models trained with linguistic and demographics features, audio and demographics features, language representation features, and visual spectrogram features.

Features	Model	Accuracy	Precision	Recall	F1
Linguistic + demographics	**SVM**	0.73	0.73	0.72	0.72
	Naive Bayes	0.70	0.70	0.70	0.70
	Random Forest	0.72	0.72	0.71	0.71
	KNN	0.67	0.66	0.66	0.66
	XGBoost	0.71	0.71	0.71	0.71
Acoustic + demographic	**SVM**	0.73	0.73	0.73	0.73
	Naive Bayes	0.68	0.68	0.67	0.67
	Random Forest	0.65	0.67	0.64	0.63
	KNN	0.57	0.57	0.57	0.57
	XGBoost	0.66	0.66	0.66	0.66
Language representation	**Pooled (GloVe)**	0.71	0.72	0.72	0.70
	LSTM (GloVe)	0.67	0.67	0.67	0.67
	Pooled (GloVe + FLAIR)	0.68	0.71	0.66	0.66
	LSTM (GloVe + FLAIR)	0.67	0.66	0.66	0.66
	Pooled (FastText)	0.77	0.78	0.78	0.77
	LSTM (FastText)	0.53	0.53	0.53	0.53
	Sentence-BERT	0.82	0.81	0.80	0.81
Visual spectrogram	**ResNet-18**	0.60	0.60	0.61	0.59
	ResNet-34	0.61	0.62	0.63	0.61
	ResNet-50	0.55	0.56	0.57	0.55
	SqueezeNet	0.54	0.58	0.56	0.53
	VGG16	0.62	0.66	0.64	0.62

Table 2. Evaluation results for fusion models compared with the best performing models from each feature set.

Model	Accuracy	Precision	Recall	F1
SVM (psycholingustic + demographics features)	0.73	0.73	0.72	0.72
SVM (audio + demographics features)	0.73	0.73	0.73	0.73
GRU (Sentence-BERT)	0.82	0.81	0.80	0.81
VGG16 (spectrogram images)	0.62	0.66	0.64	0.62
Early fusion	0.76	0.76	0.77	0.76
Late fusion	0.69	0.68	0.68	0.68
Joint fusion	0.81	0.81	0.82	0.80

6 Conclusion

The potential of having an automated telediagnostic method for detecting probable AD carries the benefits of ubiquitous screening of elder population on a larger scale without the cost of manual neuropsychological examination. Moreover the clinical significance of diagnosing a patient in early stages of the disease and before clinically visible symptoms develop has an enormous potential for early treatment and adjustments of the patient and her family.

This work conducts an exploration into methods suitable for analyzing audio recordings and transcripts of patients describing a Cookie Theft image (part of the Boston Diagnostic Test for Aphasia) for the purpose of distinguishing between probable AD patients and healthy patients. This research study reflects on some of the lessons and findings achieved while we have conducted an extensive experimentation with various unimodal models as well as three fusion models. We have also explored a novel way of analysing spectrograms images that contrasts traditional approach in which low-level acoustic features are extracted from speech. As expected, using pretrained transformer architectures results in substantially higher performance scores.

There are no easy guidelines to follow when it comes to selecting the right architecture and fusion model that effectively learns the predictive features for Alzheimer's disease detection. Difficulties in understanding and interpreting deep learning models preclude easy replication and qualitative comparison between research studies. However, the analysis has suggested several directions that can be pursued to extend the current research. One research question that could be particularly useful investigating is a strategy for selecting the best multimodal fusion method suitable for patient's stage of AD progression.

References

1. Akbik, A., Bergmann, T., Vollgraf, R.: Pooled contextualized embeddings for named entity recognition. In: NAACL 2019, 2019 Annual Conference of the North American Chapter of the Association for Computational Linguistics, pp. 724–728 (2019)
2. Akbik, A., Blythe, D., Vollgraf, R.: Contextual string embeddings for sequence labeling. In: COLING 2018, 27th International Conference on Computational Linguistics, pp. 1638–1649 (2018)
3. Alyahya, R.S., Halai, A.D., Conroy, P., Ralph, M.A.L.: Mapping psycholinguistic features to the neuropsychological and lesion profiles in aphasia. Cortex **124**, 260–273 (2020)
4. Baevski, A., Zhou, Y., Mohamed, A., Auli, M.: wav2vec 2.0: a framework for self-supervised learning of speech representations. Adv. Neural Inf. Process. Syst. **33**, 12449–12460 (2020)
5. Becker, J.T., Boiler, F., Lopez, O.L., Saxton, J., McGonigle, K.L.: The natural history of Alzheimer's disease: description of study cohort and accuracy of diagnosis. Arch. Neurol. **51**(6), 585–594 (1994)
6. Bucks, R.S., Singh, S., Cuerden, J.M., Wilcock, G.K.: Analysis of spontaneous, conversational speech in dementia of Alzheimer type: evaluation of an objective technique for analysing lexical performance. Aphasiology **14**(1), 71–91 (2000)
7. Clark, K., Luong, M., Le, Q.V., Manning, C.D.: ELECTRA: pre-training text encoders as discriminators rather than generators. CoRR abs/2003.10555 (2020). https://arxiv.org/abs/2003.10555
8. Deng, J., Dong, W., Socher, R., Li, L.J., Li, K., Fei-Fei, L.: ImageNet: a large-scale hierarchical image database. In: 2009 IEEE Conference on Computer Vision and Pattern Recognition, pp. 248–255. IEEE (2009)

9. Devlin, J., Chang, M., Lee, K., Toutanova, K.: BERT: pre-training of deep bidirectional transformers for language understanding. CoRR abs/1810.04805 (2018). http://arxiv.org/abs/1810.04805

10. Eyben, F., Wöllmer, M., Schuller, B.: OpenSmile: the Munich versatile and fast open-source audio feature extractor. In: Proceedings of the 18th ACM International Conference on Multimedia, pp. 1459–1462 (2010)

11. Gauder, L., Pepino, L., Ferrer, L., Riera, P.: Alzheimer disease recognition using speech-based embeddings from pre-trained models. In: Proceedings of Interspeech 2021, pp. 3795–3799 (2021). https://doi.org/10.21437/Interspeech.2021-753

12. Gievska, S., Koroveshovski, K.: The impact of affective verbal content on predicting personality impressions in YouTube videos. In: Proceedings of the 2014 ACM Multi Media on Workshop on Computational Personality Recognition, pp. 19–22 (2014)

13. Goedert, M., Spillantini, M.G.: A century of Alzheimer's disease. Science **314**(5800), 777–781 (2006)

14. Goodglass, H., Kaplan, E., Weintraub, S.: BDAE: The Boston Diagnostic Aphasia Examination. Lippincott Williams & Wilkins, Philadelphia (2001)

15. He, K., Zhang, X., Ren, S., Sun, J.: Deep residual learning for image recognition. In: Proceedings of the IEEE Conference on Computer Vision and Pattern Recognition, pp. 770–778 (2016)

16. Howard, J., Gugger, S.: FastAI: a layered API for deep learning. Information **11**(2), 108 (2020)

17. Huang, S.C., Pareek, A., Zamanian, R., Banerjee, I., Lungren, M.P.: Multimodal fusion with deep neural networks for leveraging CT imaging and electronic health record: a case-study in pulmonary embolism detection. Sci. Rep. **10**(1), 1–9 (2020)

18. Iandola, F.N., Moskewicz, M.W., Ashraf, K., Han, S., Dally, W.J., Keutzer, K.: SqueezeNet: AlexNet-level accuracy with 50x fewer parameters and <1mb model size. CoRR abs/1602.07360 (2016). http://arxiv.org/abs/1602.07360

19. Joulin, A., Grave, E., Mikolov, P.B.T.: Bag of tricks for efficient text classification (2016)

20. Khachaturian, Z.S.: Diagnosis of Alzheimer's disease. Arch. Neurol. **42**(11), 1097–1105 (1985)

21. Lundberg, S.M., Lee, S.I.: A unified approach to interpreting model predictions. In: Proceedings of the 31st International Conference on Neural Information Processing Systems, pp. 4768–4777 (2017)

22. Luz, S., Haider, F., de la Fuente, S., Fromm, D., MacWhinney, B.: Alzheimer's dementia recognition through spontaneous speech: the adress challenge. arXiv preprint arXiv:2004.06833 (2020)

23. Luz, S., Haider, F., de la Fuente, S., Fromm, D., MacWhinney, B.: Detecting cognitive decline using speech only: the ADReSSo challenge. In: Proceedings of Interspeech 2021, pp. 3780–3784 (2021). https://doi.org/10.21437/Interspeech.2021-1220

24. Martinc, M., Pollak, S.: Tackling the ADReSS challenge: a multimodal approach to the automated recognition of Alzheimer's dementia. In: INTERSPEECH, pp. 2157–2161 (2020)

25. McFee, B., et al.: Thassilo: librosa/librosa: 0.8.1rc2, May 2021. https://doi.org/10.5281/zenodo.4792298

26. Mehrabian, A.: Pleasure-arousal-dominance: a general framework for describing and measuring individual differences in temperament. Curr. Psychol. **14**(4), 261–292 (1996)

27. Mucke, L.: Alzheimer's disease. Nature **461**(7266), 895–897 (2009)

28. Pan, Y., et al.: Using the outputs of different automatic speech recognition paradigms for acoustic-and BERT-based Alzheimer's dementia detection through spontaneous speech. In: Proceedings of Interspeech, pp. 3810–3814 (2021)
29. Pennington, J., Socher, R., Manning, C.D.: GloVe: global vectors for word representation. In: Proceedings of the 2014 Conference on Empirical Methods in Natural Language Processing (EMNLP), pp. 1532–1543 (2014)
30. Poria, S., Cambria, E., Bajpai, R., Hussain, A.: A review of affective computing: from unimodal analysis to multimodal fusion. Inf. Fusion **37**, 98–125 (2017)
31. Poria, S., Cambria, E., Howard, N., Huang, G.B., Hussain, A.: Fusing audio, visual and textual clues for sentiment analysis from multimodal content. Neurocomputing **174**, 50–59 (2016)
32. Poria, S., Chaturvedi, I., Cambria, E., Hussain, A.: Convolutional MKL based multimodal emotion recognition and sentiment analysis. In: 2016 IEEE 16th International Conference on Data Mining (ICDM), pp. 439–448. IEEE (2016)
33. Pérez-Toro, P., et al.: Influence of the interviewer on the automatic assessment of Alzheimer's disease in the context of the ADReSSo challenge. In: Proceedings of Interspeech 2021, pp. 3785–3789 (2021). https://doi.org/10.21437/Interspeech.2021-1589
34. Reimers, N., Gurevych, I.: Sentence-BERT: sentence embeddings using Siamese BERT-networks. In: Proceedings of the 2019 Conference on Empirical Methods in Natural Language Processing. Association for Computational Linguistics, November 2019. https://arxiv.org/abs/1908.10084
35. Sarawgi, U., Zulfikar, W., Soliman, N., Maes, P.: Multimodal inductive transfer learning for detection of Alzheimer's dementia and its severity. arXiv preprint arXiv:2009.00700 (2020)
36. Shrestha, A., Serra, E., Spezzano, F.: Multi-modal social and psycho-linguistic embedding via recurrent neural networks to identify depressed users in online forums. Netw. Model. Anal. Health Inform. Bioinform. **9**(1), 1–11 (2020). https://doi.org/10.1007/s13721-020-0226-0
37. Simonyan, K., Zisserman, A.: Very deep convolutional networks for large-scale image recognition. In: Bengio, Y., LeCun, Y. (eds.) 3rd International Conference on Learning Representations, ICLR 2015, San Diego, CA, USA, 7–9 May 2015, Conference Track Proceedings (2015). http://arxiv.org/abs/1409.1556
38. Stark, B.C., et al.: Standardizing assessment of spoken discourse in aphasia: a working group with deliverables. Am. J. Speech Lang. Pathol. **30**(1S), 491–502 (2021)
39. Vina, J., Lloret, A.: Why women have more Alzheimer's disease than men: gender and mitochondrial toxicity of amyloid-β peptide. J. Alzheimers Dis. **20**(s2), S527–S533 (2010)
40. Wang, N., Cao, Y., Hao, S., Shao, Z., Subbalakshmi, K.: Modular multi-modal attention network for Alzheimer's disease detection using patient audio and language data. In: Proceedings of Interspeech 2021, pp. 3835–3839 (2021). https://doi.org/10.21437/Interspeech.2021-2024
41. Wiley, J.: Alzheimer's disease facts and figures. Alzheimers Dement. **17**, 327–406 (2021)
42. Zhou, G., Wang, J., Zhang, X., Yu, G.: DeepGOA: predicting gene ontology annotations of proteins via graph convolutional network. In: 2019 IEEE International Conference on Bioinformatics and Biomedicine (BIBM), pp. 1836–1841. IEEE (2019)
43. Zhu, Y., Obyat, A., Liang, X., Batsis, J.A., Roth, R.M.: WavBERT: exploiting semantic and non-semantic speech using wav2vec and BERT for dementia detection. In: Proceedings of Interspeech 2021, pp. 3790–3794 (2021)

Research on Service Design for COVID-19 Nucleic Acid Test Needs of the Public

Ruohui Li[✉], Ting Shen, and Hanjing Li

College of Furnishings and Industrial Design, Nanjing Forestry University, Nanjing, China
dongdzhouz@sina.com

Abstract. Taking the whole city nucleic acid test process in Nanjing as the starting point, this paper explores the main characteristics of the existing nucleic acid test process. Then it analyzes the main process of nucleic acid test and the user needs of community residents, volunteers and medical staff in nucleic acid detection. Based on this, a new design idea is proposed to optimize the nucleic acid test process for the public. Using the design methods of service blueprint and stakeholder analysis, this paper finally puts forward a set of service design process based on the combination of online mobile application terminal and offline self-service nucleic acid detection equipment. By optimizing the nucleic acid test service process, we can alleviate the shortage of medical manpower resources and cross infection between doctors and patients under the outbreak of COVID-19. At the same time, we also help users achieve a safe, fast and efficient nucleic acid detection process experience.

Keywords: COVID-19 · Nucleic acid test · Service design · User experience

1 Introduction

Since the outbreak of COVID-19 in 2019, it has spread to more than 200 countries and regions worldwide. The explosion of the epidemic has made significant changes in social life, and the attendant problems have also affected the development of all walks of life, especially in human life and health [1]. Because of the characteristics of COVID-19, it has been infected with infected people only in a matter of ten seconds, and its high infection effect is scarce. To screen out all cases the first time after the outbreak, the nucleic acid test has become one of the most essential contents of COVID-19's prevention and control. And it is of great significance for the prevention and treatment of epidemic diseases.

In China, because the epidemic situation is often repeated everywhere, especially in cities, once there are concentrated cases, large-scale nucleic acid testing of the whole city must be started immediately. In the process of nucleic acid test, there are many problems such as maintaining the order of residents waiting in line, great demand for medical staff, and high risk of cross-infection. Therefore, it is important to explore its existing issues, optimize the problems and find new improvement schemes because of the current urban nucleic acid test service process.

V. G. Duffy (Ed.): HCII 2022, LNCS 13320, pp. 95–111, 2022.
https://doi.org/10.1007/978-3-031-06018-2_7

Based on this, this paper takes the nucleic acid test in Chinese cities as theme. It takes the ordinary residents, volunteers and medical personnel in the test process as the object, trying to make an in-depth analysis of the user needs and experience problems in the existing nucleic acid test process. From the perspective of service design, this paper puts forward a systematic service design scheme to optimize the current nucleic acid test process, in order to improve the public experience, cut down the risk of cross-infection and reduce the demand for medical personnel.

2 Main Characteristics of Nucleic Acid Test

The substance of nucleic acid detection is a viral nucleic acid. A nucleic acid test is to find out whether there are invading virus nucleic acids in the respiratory tract, blood, or feces of patients, to determine whether they are infected by COVID-19. Therefore, once detected as nucleic acid "positive", it can prove a virus in the patient's body. After COVID-19 infects the human body, it will first propagate in the respiratory tract, so it can detect whether the human body is infected with the virus by detecting the nucleic acid in the sputum and nasopharyngeal swabs. Consequently, the positive detection of nucleic acid can be used as a new diagnostic standard for New Coronavirus infection.

According to the existing nucleic acid detection processes in various countries, it mainly has the following characteristics:

1. The detection process involves a wide range of personnel and many people. Because the novel coronavirus pneumonia is very infectious, it may spread rapidly and cause a wide range of infections once a case is in the crowd. Therefore, the relevant close contacts and residents in the surrounding area need to be tested, whether they are students, or office workers or retirees. All age groups and occupational groups need nucleic acid screening immediately to ensure that infected persons are isolated and treated in time.
2. There are many testing times, and it is required to feedback the results quickly. Once COVID-19 breaks out, it is necessary to carry out nationwide testing. Its coverage must cover all kinds of people, so as to complete accurate screening and achieve effective control. At present, the transmission of the new virus is enhanced. To curb the spread of the epidemic in time, the detection time needs to be as short as possible, and the results should be obtained as soon as possible to realize rapid screening. The government needs to isolate the infected people and announce their whereabouts as soon as possible.
3. The risk of cross-infection is high. Due to a large number of people for nucleic acid testing in the city, the demand for medical staff also increases. Crowd congestion is easy to occur in the crowd gathering place, and the possibility of cross-infection is greatly improved. Although volunteers in protective clothing guide the crowd to queue up in order at each nucleic acid testing point for sample collection, problems such as doctor-patient cross infection and population secondary transmission still exist.

3 Current Main Process of Nucleic Acid Test—Taking Nanjing as an Example

3.1 Introduction to COVID-19 in Nanjing

In 2019, COVID-19 broke out in Wuhan, Hubei, and spread to other cities. In controlling the spread of COVID-19, nucleic acid testing and screening have become essential means adopted by local governments. After several months of closure, isolation, research and rescue, the epidemic situation in China has been well controlled, but there are still small-scale outbreaks from time to time. On July 20, 2021, nine positive samples were detected in the regular nucleic acid test of the staff of Nanjing Lukou International Airport. Then, Nanjing quickly carried out the nucleic acid test of the whole city and isolated the infected people for medical treatment for the first time. From the daily new cases, the maximum number of cases can reach dozens. By early August, the cumulative number of confirmed instances in Nanjing reached more than 160, and some areas such as Jiangning District were listed as medium and high-risk areas. In addition, with the spread of the epidemic, Yangzhou and other cities in Jiangsu have also been affected. After the efforts of all parties, the number of new cases has been decreasing, and by the middle of August 2021, there has been no breakthrough in single-day cases. Nanjing COVID-19 has been well controlled.

3.2 Methods of Nucleic Acid Test During the Outbreak of COVID-19 in Nanjing

Novel coronavirus pneumonia was detected in five rounds in Nanjing to block the spread of the new crown pneumonia epidemic effectively. The first round of testing was after the confirmed cases appeared in Lukou Airport. That night, Nanjing organized and coordinated the establishment of nucleic acid testing sampling points in districts. 9.3 million residents in the city need to queue up for testing at the designated open-air nucleic acid testing points according to the community where they live. Each nucleic acid testing point has arranged five medical staff to take samples, and about seven community volunteers to maintain order and guide residents to queue up and receive test tubes. Due to the large number of people who need to be tested, much tested personnel, medical personnel and volunteers stayed up all night, which helped the epidemic prevention work. In the second round of nucleic acid detection in cities, to reduce the possibility of cross-infection and improve the queuing situation, community residents need to be organized by the community and go to the indoor sampling points in batches. In addition, the nucleic acid test can be arranged flexibly according to the 24-h arrival time of each resident. In the third round of nucleic acid testing of the whole city, Jiangning District and Lishui District, two areas with the serious epidemic situation, which were taken as the key areas of nucleic acid testing, was started in advance. And other low-risk areas such as Xuanwu District, Qinhuai District and Jianye District were arranged at another time. The tested personnel shall be tested according to the principle of "1:1 single test for people in high-risk areas, 1:5 mixed test for people in medium-risk areas and 1:10 mixed test for people in low-risk areas". The sampling sites have also been optimized. According to the principle of "convenience for the majority and care for the very few", each district scientifically and reasonably adjusted the sampling sites according to the first two rounds of nucleic acid sampling, detection volume, personnel distribution and composition, average waiting time, etc. each sampling point was set as a dry sampling unit. The sampling points were kept open or well ventilated, and they timely adjusted or added temporary sampling sites according to climate change. Based on fixed sampling points, the government adopted grid management mode, refined and improved the layout through entering schools, enterprises and units, to facilitate citizens' sampling and improve sampling efficiency. The first three rounds of nucleic acid testing in Nanjing were all nucleic acid testing. With the gradual improvement of the epidemic situation, the fourth and fifth rounds of nucleic acid testing were only carried out in some high-risk areas.

3.3 Main Process of Nucleic Acid Test in Nanjing

After issuing the instruction of nucleic acid test in the whole city, the community sent this information to the residents' mobile phones through SMS for the first time, and issued announcements on Weibo, Wechat and other online public platforms. Considering that some residents did not pay attention to the information and some elderly residents were without mobile phones, community staff used loudspeakers to broadcast the notice of nucleic acid detection in the whole city. To save residents' time and avoid a large number of people gathering at the test point, the nucleic acid test adopted the time arrangement of the staggered peak test. Residents could freely choose their free time to arrive at the nucleic acid test point for the test within one day of the specified date. After arriving at the nucleic acid test point, residents needed to queue up according to the guidance of volunteers and get the test tube for nucleic acid test. On queuing, they could register their identity information on the applet. After entering the nucleic acid detection area, volunteers would verify the identity information of residents and stick the bar code with resident identity information on the test tube. Residents needed to take the test tube into the sampling room, let the medical staff take samples, and recover the sample test tube. The recovered sample test tubes would be sent to the testing center for inspection by special medical personnel. After the test results come out, if they were positive, the residents would be notified in the form of SMS and quarantined immediately; If there were no infection with COVID-19, the residents would not be informed, and residents who need it would have to log in by themselves.

According to the existing nucleic acid test process, this paper draws the flow chart shown in Fig. 1. The whole nucleic acid test process can be visualized through the flow chart [2]. It reveals the process steps of the entire nucleic acid test and presents the relationship between each cycle. The whole nucleic acid test process is divided into ten degrees, and each degree needs to be carried out in sequence. Residents need to obey the command of volunteers on-site and accept nucleic acid tests in an orderly manner according to the requirements of the nucleic acid tests. The whole process considers the various needs of residents, but there are still some places that can be improved in terms of queuing, sample collection and result acquisition.

Fig. 1. Flow chart of existing nucleic acid test

4 Analysis of User Experience in Nucleic Acid Test in Nanjing

4.1 Persona Analysis

Persona was proposed by Alan Cooper, and its core work is data tagging. By cleaning and sorting all kinds of raw data collected, we can extract user attributes. Finally, we can mine user tags from user attributes and use these tags to build a persona [3]. Alan Cooper believes that persona has four core functions: generating a common language; making the user image no longer changeable and inconclusive; letting the design have a clear goal orientation, not for everyone; stopping team members from arguing about the priority and execution order of design content. For a set of service designs, the persona should be built from the initial process planning stage. The persona's role can radiate to all phrases of service design, including initial planning of service system, process setting and optimization, specific service design, later promotion, etc.

In the whole process of nucleic acid test, there are three main groups involved: ordinary community residents, volunteers and medical staff. To understand the needs of all kinds of personnel and improve the experience of service design of the new nucleic acid test process, this paper selects these three types of subjects to draw personas. Through the analysis and interview of ten community residents, ten volunteers and ten medical staff and the investigation of network information, the research results are summarized, and the persona is drawn. As shown in Fig. 2, user A is an ordinary community resident and a software engineer. He is usually busy and often needs to work overtime. After receiving the notice of nucleic acid detection, he queued up late at night, resulting in his poor spirit at work the next day. Here are his main pain points: 1. The work task is heavy, and there is no time to queue up at the detection point for a long time; 2. We need to get the nucleic acid report in time and devote ourselves to our work. User B is a volunteer at the nucleic acid detection point and a community worker. When she was resting at home, she received a temporary notice from her superior leaders and needed to volunteer at the nucleic acid detection point. She is responsible for maintaining on-site order, guiding residents to queue up, scanning code registration information, issuing nucleic acid test tubes, etc. Here are her main pain points: 1. Some repeated similar questions of residents need to be answered; 2. Working for a long time is mentally tired. User C is a medical worker and a doctor urgently dispatched from other areas for support. After receiving the dispatch notice, he rushed to the responsible nucleic acid detection point for nucleic acid detection at the first time. Here are his main pain points: 1. The sampling action is not rigorous enough due to long-time work, and the error of invalid sampling may occur; 2. Worry about the situation of relatives at home.

Fig. 2. Persona

4.2 User Journey Map Analysis

User experience journey refers to a method that describes the user's experience of using products or receiving services in the form of narrative stories from the perspective of users, displays them in the form of visual graphics, finds the pain points and satisfaction points of users in the whole use process, and finally extracts the optimization points and design opportunities in products or services. It allows designers to understand the users' seeing, thinking, listening and doing in the use process, so that they can consider the whole service design process from the perspective of users. As one of the commonly used tools in service design, a user journey map can help us find out the pain points of users by analyzing the behavior and emotional changes in the process of user service experience [4]. By analyzing the psychological changes of community residents, volunteers and medical staff through user journey map, on the one hand, it can visually process the abstract data such as psychology and emotion of the target population to enhance the cognition of abstract information; On the other hand, we can summarize and sort out the psychological experience and pain points of the people who carry out nucleic acid testing, to find out the common characteristics and experiences of the three types of people investigated, and find solutions to these pain points [5].

According to the habits and behavior characteristics of community residents, the user journey map of community residents is further established. As shown in Fig. 3, community residents mainly go through six stages: receiving notice, arriving at the detection point, waiting for detection, testing, testing completion and obtaining the report. After an in-depth analysis of the behavior and emotion of community residents, the following key points are summarized: 1. The current situation of the epidemic is not very clear and anxious; After working overtime, people are physically and mentally exhausted, and the large number of people queuing is prohibitive. 2. The number of people gathered is significant. They are worried about the possibility of cross-infection; The mask is muggy, the air environment is poor, and the weather is hot; There is something unclear about the process. 3. The medical staff may feel throat discomfort due to their rough and straightforward sampling methods. 4. I was anxious when waiting for the nucleic acid results, hoping to obtain information for the first.

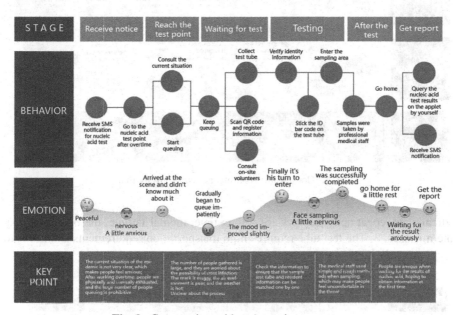

Fig. 3. Community residents' user journey map

As shown in Fig. 4, community volunteers mainly go through four stages: receiving notice, going to the testing point, volunteering and ending their work. After in-depth analysis of the behavior and emotion of community volunteers, the following key points are summarized: 1. Protective clothing, masks, eye masks and other protective measures make people feel stuffy; 2. Due to the flow of people, disinfection treatment needs to be done frequently; 3. Residents queue up disorderly and need timely guidance; Residents have many puzzles about nucleic acid detection and need to answer some similar questions repeatedly; Verification of identity information not only increases the workload, but also takes more time for residents. 4. The storage requirements of test tubes are high and they need to be appropriately kept.

As shown in Fig. 5, the medical staff mainly went through four stages: receiving the notice, arriving at the detection point, sampling, and the end of the work. After in-depth analysis of the behavior and emotion of medical staff, the following key points are summarized: 1 Protective clothing, masks, eye masks and other protective measures make medical staff feel stuffy and uncomfortable; 2. When sampling, the medical team may accidentally hurt the throat of the residents and make the residents feel uncomfortable;

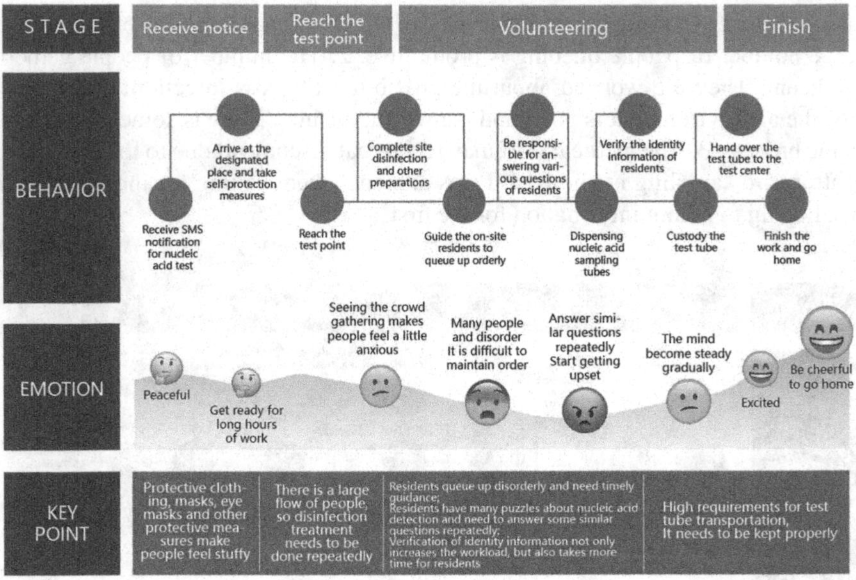

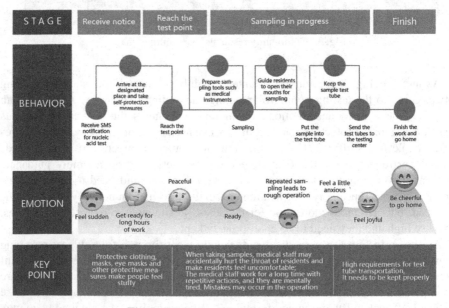

Fig. 4. Community volunteers' user journey map

Medical staff repeat actions, work for a long time, mental fatigue, the operation may make mistakes. 3. The test tube requires high transportation requirements and needs to be kept properly.

Fig. 5. Medical staff's user journey map

4.3 Summary of User Experience

Through the investigation and analysis of several types of users, we can sum up the following user experience problems:

- It is prone to cross-infection. When people queue up for sampling at the detection point, they often have the characteristics of a dense population and long gathering time. At this stage, cross-infection is easy to occur, allowing the epidemic to spread further. Therefore, disinfection measures must be put in place, and the volunteers need to maintain order in the queue.
- Time liberalization. Because nucleic acid detection involves a wide range of people, it is likely to bring a lot of inconvenience to residents' work, study and life to concentrate on nucleic acid detection in a certain period.
- Residents have any doubts about the process of nucleic acid detection and the current development of the epidemic. Volunteers need to answer similar questions repeatedly.
- Improve efficiency and accuracy. In the process of nucleic acid detection, many medical staff are needed to assist, which consumes a lot of human and material resources. In addition, due to the long-term and continuous hard work of medical staff, it is effortless to lead to fatigue and manual operation errors, and even discomfort residents.
- Pick up information more directly. In the existing nucleic acid detection process, residents need to register their identity information on the applet, and volunteers will map the information to the sample test tube. There are two main situations for obtaining nucleic acid reports. First, do not directly inform the results. If there is any situation, isolate it the first time. Second, go to the applet to view the report results. In either case, people cannot obtain the information of nucleic acid test report at the first time, and the process is cumbersome.
- Volunteers and medical staff need to wear protective clothing, masks, eye masks and other protective measures, making it muggy in hot weather.
- The storage and transportation of sample tubes need the proper care of volunteers and medical staff.

In general, although the user experience of the current nucleic acid test process has some advantages, there are still inconveniences and inefficiencies in some details. Therefore, it is necessary to optimize the existing nucleic acid detection process.

5 Design Concept

5.1 Optimized Direction

Given the existing nucleic acid testing process analysis and pain points in user experience, this paper proposes the following optimization objectives:

1. Realize multi-location test and residents can be tested at any time within 24 h. To avoid excessive concentration of people, nucleic acid testing sites can be set up in multiple locations throughout the city. Residents can freely choose testing sites for testing according to their actual situation and queuing conditions at various

monitoring sites, so as to facilitate the personal needs of users and reduce the risk of cross-infection.

2. Reduce the participation of medical personnel and volunteers as much as possible. Non-medical personnel testing should be carried out to reduce the cost of human medical resources. Residents should conduct self-operation by themselves to reduce the possibility of doctor-patient cross-infection.
3. Optimize the acquisition of nucleic acid test results. Samples should be sent to the testing center for inspection in time to ensure timeliness; The detection results can be synchronized to the mobile terminal of the mobile phone, so that people can obtain the nucleic acid test results for the first time, and it is also convenient to retrieve and search at any time.

5.2 Basic Design Idea

Based on the above optimization direction, the following design ideas are proposed. First, it is necessary to plan the location of nucleic acid testing sites reasonably, implement 24-h testing, and explore the use of online mobile applications for test notification, test point query, queue number prompt, test appointment, etc. The second is to explore the feasibility of unmanned self-service test by the public; Third, the sample submission process should be optimized so that the sample results can be associated with the platform, nucleic acid test information can be received synchronously, and notification can be sent to residents' mobile phones for easy viewing.

5.3 Design Expansion

Optimization of Testing Process. The service design of the new nucleic acid testing process should be based on the needs of user experience, starting from the user behavior of user experience, and aiming at satisfying the real vision and emotional experience of users [6]. Based on this, the new nucleic acid testing process attempts to use the combination of offline self-service testing equipment and online nucleic acid testing-related applications.

As shown in Fig. 6, after the user applies for the detection code on the mobile app, the user can independently check the distribution of nearby detection devices and the number of queuing people at each detection point on the mobile phone, and select the relatively idle detection point to make an appointment. When the detection time is up, the user can go to the detection device to check the identity information by scanning the detection code, perform operations according to the intelligent voice reminder and video demonstration on the detection device, and take the sample collection tool for self-service sample collection as prompted. People should carry out the whole process under the equipment detection, and the final detection process is given by the machine is standard qualified information, to ensure that the sample is valid and effective. After passing the test, the sample container will be placed in the designated position, sealed by the machine, waiting for volunteers to take it out at a fixed time, and sent it to the testing center. After the testing center finishes the test, the nucleic acid test report will be input into the mobile app first, and users can access and view it at any time.

Fig. 6. Flow chart of new nucleic acid test

Service Blueprint. The service blueprint is a detailed analysis and display of service operation. Through the service blueprint, we can clearly know every action of users, service providers and other stakeholders during service operation, so as to analyze the service process [7]. The service blueprint is roughly divided into four parts:

- Physical touchpoint: the physical part that the user touches.
- User behavior: the journey of users in the service process.
- Front desk: the service interface that users are exposed to.
- Background: actions performed by service providers that cannot be seen by users.
- Support system: other support and actions of collaborators.

In the whole service design process, as shown in Fig. 7, users bind their personal identifiable information through the mobile app, upload the information to the platform system, and identify it in the form of two-dimensional code. After users scan the QR code on the self-service nucleic acid testing machine, the machine can determine the identity information associated with the QR code and record it. After nucleic acid sampling by the self-service sampling machine, the sampling tool is handed over to the device for recycling. In the recycling process, the number of recovered samples will correspond to the previously identified identification information by the device and be recorded in the platform system. After passing the above process, the nucleic acid sample has been successfully bound with the identity information of people in the platform system. After the testing center completes the final sample testing, the results are uploaded to the corresponding personage information in the platform system. After the APP gets the updated data of the platform system, the user will get the nucleic acid test report from their mobile phones.

Stakeholder Analysis. Given the unique background of COVID-19, relevant subjects in the nucleic acid testing process are analyzed. As shown in Fig. 8, the related components of the overall service process are summarized and visually displayed about each other. Among them, user-centered, self-service nucleic acid testing machines and mobile apps constitute the main body of the service design. In contrast, community volunteers, medical staff, testing centers and platform systems are secondary subjects.

Due to the shortage of medical staff brought by large-scale nucleic acid testing, most of the work at the testing site was replaced by self-service nucleic acid testing machines, with only a small number of community volunteers to guide and maintain the order on site. Medical staff focused on rescuing patients and testing samples. Secondly, users need to register information on the APP before arriving at the detection point, which can not only improve the efficiency of self-service nucleic acid testing, but also facilitate

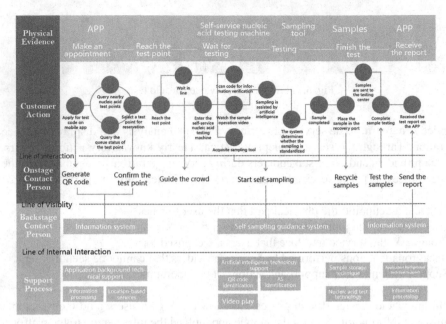

Fig. 7. Service blueprint

the reception of subsequent nucleic acid reports. The data of the testing center and the data on the APP are interconnected and correlated through the platform system. All the medical information of users is included in the platform system.

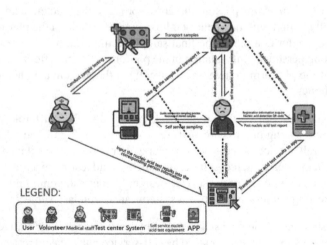

Fig. 8. Stakeholders

5.4 Online Application Design and Analysis

According to the data of "2020–2026 China Mobile APP Industry Market Prospect Planning and Market Prospect Trend Analysis Report" released by Zhiyan Consulting, it can be seen the APP usage of Chinese netizens of all ages. Among mobile Internet users aged 15–19, there are 84 mobile apps per capita. Among mobile Internet users aged 20–29, the average number of mobile apps is 65. Among mobile Internet users aged 60 and above, the average number of mobile apps is 37. It can be seen from these data that mobile applications have been integrated into the daily life of most people, so it is feasible to integrate online nucleic acid testing applications into the new nucleic acid testing process service system [8]. As an essential part of the new nucleic acid testing process service design, the interactive interface is the primary embodiment of user experience design. In the interface design, we need to consider the simplicity of the screen, the convenience of operation, the easy recognition of functions and other principles. The interface conforms to the habit of human-computer interaction [9].

The functional architecture of the app is shown in Fig. 9, which is mainly divided into four parts: Home page, QR code, map and mine. The home page mainly displays the navigation bar, some shortcut entrances, real-time updates of the epidemic and notification information. The map shows the distribution of the disease across the country, as well as the distribution of nucleic acid testing sites around residents. QR code can quickly retrieve nucleic acid test code, health code, travel card and other daily needs. My page is filled with user information, shortcut buttons and Settings that are common to all apps.

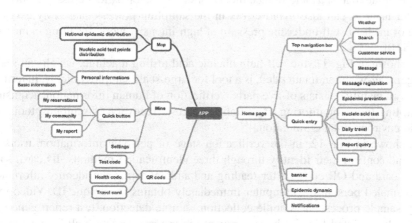

Fig. 9. Functional graph

The APP is mainly used to assist the nucleic acid testing process. Its core functions include test code application, nucleic acid test site reservation, nucleic acid test report query, and quick access to QR code. (As shown in Fig. 10) In the test code application interface, users can obtain a QR code after inputting necessary identity information, such as name, ID number, contact phone number, community and home address, for subsequent code scanning and information input on the self-service nucleic acid testing machine. If there is any error, you can also click the change button at the bottom to modify it in time. On the interface of reserving nucleic acid test sites, you can view all nucleic acid test sites around the current location. Each nucleic acid test site is marked with the number of people waiting in line for reservation, and color is used as a reminder. Large numbers are red, medium numbers are yellow, and small numbers are green. After the user clicks the small circular icon of any test point, the interface will display the specific information of the test point, the estimated queuing time and the number of people waiting. The user can select a specific time at the nucleic acid test point to reserve the nucleic acid test service at the bottom of the page. In the interface for querying nucleic acid test reports, users can first see their nucleic acid test status, with green indicating safety, and the bottom part showing some personal information of users. If you need to view detailed data reports or electronic export documents of the words, you can click the bottom part of the page to query more information. In the QR code interface, users can quickly retrieve the QR code they need, and simply and efficiently open the health code or travel card for inspection by epidemic prevention personnel when entering and leaving public places.

5.5 Design and Analysis of Offline Self-service Testing Equipment

With the active exploration of artificial intelligence in the medical field, self-service nucleic acid testing equipment, as a new nucleic acid testing mode to take samples instead of medical staff, has gradually been known to people. In the case of an epidemic outbreak, the use of a self-service nucleic acid testing machine can reduce the workforce shortage of medical staff and reduce the situation of doctor-patient cross-infection; On the other hand, it can also avoid errors in the sampling process caused by excessive fatigue of medical staff under the pressure of high-intensity work, resulting in incorrect results [10].

As shown in Fig. 11, the self-help nucleic acid testing machine, which can realize intelligent, all-weather, unattended, is a tool for large-scale samples quickly. In terms of function, it mainly consists of five parts: verification of human information, acquisition of sampling tools, monitoring of sampling process, recovery of sampling tools, and internal environmental elimination.

As shown in Fig. 12, in the verification stage of personal information, users can verify and confirm their identity through three identification methods: ID card, social security card and QR code. After reading and authenticating the identity information of the sampled person, the computer immediately obtains the unique ID. Video monitoring, sample processing, sample collection, sample detection, test report generation and sampling-related files in the subsequent sampling process are all associated with this ID to ensure the correspondence between sample data and personal information. At the stage of obtaining sampling tools, all the sampling tools are disposable products. To ensure the safety of users, hand disinfection is required before using the sampling tools. In the monitoring and sampling process stage, the user will need to get the sampling tools placed in the mouth, the sampling tools after arriving on swab sampling area user sampling should be carried out according to the prompt operation, to ensure that the epithelial cells collected, to ensure that the sample qualified, effective user needs in artificial intelligence under the guide of video-assisted sampling, and effective by

Fig. 10. APP interface

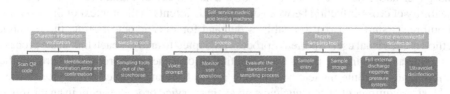

Fig. 11. Function diagram of self-service nucleic acid testing machine

artificial intelligence determine whether the sample code. In the recovery stage of sampling tools, after collecting qualified samples, the user will place the sampling tools at the specified location. After each placement, the devices will undergo high-temperature disinfection treatment, and the pieces will be automatically collected, encapsulated and saved by robots. The machine's internal sample tube storage box, sample tool storage box, sample processing bin, sample tube recycling box, sampling tool recycling box are also independent, to ensure timely disinfection. In terms of internal environment disinfection, to avoid cross-infection, the sample processing warehouse adopts the leading full external discharge negative pressure system and ultraviolet disinfection system, and the intake and exhaust are equipped with independent filtration membrane. In the operation process, the air is filtered into the kit first, while the polluted air in the equipment is filtered out to the outside, which can avoid aerosol pollution.

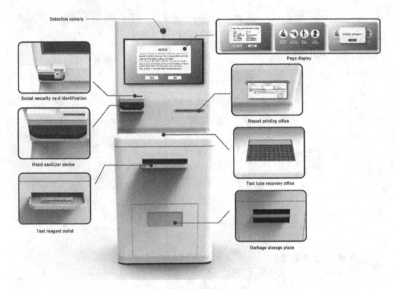

Fig. 12. Self-service nucleic acid testing machine

6 Conclusion

This paper addresses the problems of insufficient medical human resources and the possibility of cross-infection between doctors and patients in the context of the COVID-19 outbreak. Starting from the public's demand for nucleic acid testing, the research method of the visual user experience process is adopted to analyze each link in the process of nucleic acid testing by users, and an optimization scheme is proposed. Through the combination of online nucleic acid testing application and offline self-service nucleic acid testing equipment, a new nucleic acid testing service process is built in an all-round way, connecting users with online and offline service contacts in the testing process, to help users achieve a safe, fast and efficient nucleic acid testing process experience.

Acknowledgements. This paper is supported by: The youth science and technology innovation fund project of Nanjing Forestry University (CX2019014), The special research project for young liberal arts teachers of Nanjing Forestry University (D2021YB05)

References

1. Jiang, J., Li, Y., Wang, X.: Design thinking for elderly home care service system based on internet+ in the context of pandemic. Design **33**(11), 78–81 (2020)
2. Liu, Y., Deng, R.: Study on service design strategy of home care for elderly. Design **32**(20), 116–118 (2019)
3. Li, R.: Review of user portrait research. Sci. Technol. Innov. (23), 4–9+12 (2021)
4. Hu, H., Jin, Y., Duan, H., Zhou, Z.: Design of emotional computing psychological rescue robot based on user journey. Design **34**(19), 150–153 (2021)
5. User experience journey map: concept, practice & template. http://www.woshipm.com/user-research/1640253.html. Accessed: 19 Nov 2018
6. Gao, Y., Xu, X.: Service design: a new concept of contemporary design. Lit. Art Stud. **6**, 140–147 (2014)
7. Guo, M.: Research on medical monitoring product design of children's asthma based on service design concept. Hubei University of Technology (2020)
8. Gong, B., Deng, S.: Interactive interface design of 'new user ceremony' in mobile application terminal. J. Zhejiang Normal Univ. (Nat. Sci.) **45**(01), 35–41 (2022)
9. Zhang, J., Wang, J.: Research on intelligent medical terminal service design based on user experience. Ind. Des. **08**, 104–107 (2021)
10. Li, Y., Jiang, K.: Design and research of intelligent diagnosis guidance robot service system based on epidemic background. Design **34**(14), 121–123 (2021)

Health Technology Use in Germany Among Older Adults (Part I): Short Time Changes in Information and Communication Technology

Alexander Mertens[1(✉)] ⓘ, Peter Rasche[1,4] ⓘ, Sabine Theis[1] ⓘ, Tobias Seinsch[1],
Maximilian Boddin[1], Rebecca Küpper[1], Christina Bröhl[1] ⓘ, Matthias Wille[1] ⓘ,
Axel Zweck[2], Christopher Brandl[1,3] ⓘ, Verena Nitsch[1,3] ⓘ, and Katharina Schäfer[1] ⓘ

[1] Institute of Industrial Engineering and Ergonomics, RWTH Aachen University,
Eilfschornsteinstraße 18, 52062 Aachen, Germany
a.mertens@iaw.rwth-aachen.de
[2] Future and Innovation, Institute of Sociology, Eilfschornsteinstr. 7, 52062 Aachen, Germany
[3] Fraunhofer Institute for Communication, Information Processing and Ergonomics FKIE,
Campus-Boulevard 55, 52074 Aachen, Germany
[4] Institute of General Practice and Family Medicine (Abteilung für Allgemeinmedizin),
Ruhr-University Bochum, Universitätsstraße 150, 44801 Bochum, Germany

Abstract. The technology use of older people is marked by stigmas. Whether in literature, films or even in science, the narrative of older people who cannot manage the simplest clicks and handles is omnipresent. Independent information search? Unrealistic - children and grandchildren are rather called for help. What if they no longer have a landline but only a cell phone? How should they be served? - But what does it look like in reality? Is this view, which has existed for decades, outdated? Should it not give way to a new narrative? It is the focus of a longitudinal study, concentrating on the usage of information and communication technology (ICT) by the elderly (older people) (60+) in Germany. This study, conducted by the interdisciplinary research team Tech4Age, consists of two surveys from 2016/2017 (survey I) and 2018/2019 (survey II). The article presents the results of the second survey by comparing both surveys as well as potential changes. The sample consisted of $N = 649$ participants (54.6% male and 45.4% female) with an average age of 66.11 years ($SD = 5.45$ years). A fundamental aspect of both surveys was to examine use of health-related information and levels of trust, general and mHealth applications used by older adults as well as information and communication technology used by older adults. Due to larger scopes of the surveys and their results, the latter will be presented in two separate articles. This paper focuses on the third aspect: the information and communication technology used by older adults.

An essential aspect of survey II was to examine the integration of information and communication technologies (ICT) of older and very old citizens. While survey I of 2016/2017 [1] was still based on preliminary studies (for example [2, 3]), survey II of 2018/2019 was based on a more in-depth analysis [4–6]. Overall, it showed that these main questions were of importance: (1) How is ICT used among older adults and what are reasons for technology acquisition? (2) If ICT is used, who administrates ICT products? (3) Do older adults use the Internet and if so,

V. G. Duffy (Ed.): HCII 2022, LNCS 13320, pp. 112–128, 2022.
https://doi.org/10.1007/978-3-031-06018-2_8

when? (4) Which everyday activities do older adults perform with the help of ICT? The purpose of this paper is to present and discuss the results, focusing especially on the use of Information and communication technology. Results suggest that respondents of survey II integrate ICT into their daily lives, using devices as computers, smartphones and also navigation systems or e-book readers. Reasons for usage are to communicate and out of practical reasons or curiosity. Additionally, participants use the Internet at home as well as mobile Internet ranging from 15 min up to more than two hours daily.

Keywords: Older adults · Germany · ICT · Information-seeking behavior · Health · Ergonomics

1   Introduction[1]

Hardly any other phenomenon is and has been discussed as much as demographic change. Predictions say that the proportion of older people in Germany will increase significantly by 2060 [7, 8]. Considering demographic change in the context of digitisation, it is safe to say that:

"Demographic change and increasing digitalization are two of the current mega-trends directly impacting the every-day life of people. While the shift in age distribution among the German population towards an ever-increasing average age, and therefore also the significantly increasing prevalence and incidence of chronic diseases, represent an ongoing complication for the standard of high-quality healthcare processes, the diffusion of mobile information and communication technologies, e.g. in the form of smartphones and tablets, offers great potential for implementing low-threshold, location-independent and patient-specific healthcare in terms of electronic health ('e-health')" Mertens et al. [4].

For this, it is necessary to identify the needs of users and the context of application. This is relevant for the area of digital health applications, since the risk of being stigmatised as, for example, needy, can be high and can have an influence on the acceptance of independent technology use in a negative way. Impacts can be seen in adhesion and social environments of users.

Therefore, in 2016/2017, Mertens et al. [4] conducted a longitudinal study (referred to as "survey I"), trying to address this challenge by examining the usage of information and communication technology of older and very old people (60+) in Germany.[2] This study was repeated in 2018/2019 (referred to as "survey II"). Both surveys aimed to collect comprehensive data on the status quo of the interaction-specific use of mobile

---

[1] In this contribution and in the contribution "Health technology use in Germany among older adults (Part I): short time changes in health-related information and mHealth applications" in this congress proceedings do exist congruent text passages. It is due to the fact that they are based on the same study and different aspects have been analyzed in the contributions. Nevertheless, each contribution should be complete and understandable on its own.

[2] The survey was developed and conducted by an interdisciplinary team consisting of engineers, computer scientists, psychologists, sociologists and medics, focusing on the ergonomic design of human-computer interfaces of digital health systems and services (see also Wille et al. 2016).

health applications and technologies together with individual user characteristics, needs, and context-specific influencing factors of older adults in Germany. The assumption was that new, innovative, and user-centred systems are needed to integrate new digital technologies into the healthcare system.

The article presents the results of the second survey with regard on the comparison of both surveys as well as on potential changes. The sample consisted of N = 649 participants (54.64% male and 45.36% female) with an average age of 66.11 years (SD = 5.45 years). A fundamental aspect of both surveys was to examine the use of health-related information and levels of trust, the general and mHealth applications used by older adults as well as the information and communication technology used by older adults. Due to the large scope of the surveys and their results, the latter will be presented in two separate articles. This paper focuses on the third aspect: the information and communication technology used by older adults.

An essential aspect of survey II was to examine the integration of information and communication technologies (ICT) of older and very old citizens. While 2016/2017 survey I [1] was still based on preliminary studies (for example [2, 3]), 2018/2019 survey II was based on a more in-depth analysis [4–6]. Overall, it showed that the main questions were of great importance: (1) How is ICT used among older adults and what are the reasons for technology acquisition? (2) If ICT is used, who administrates ICT products? (3) Do older adults use the Internet and if so, in what kind of situations? (4) Which everyday activities do older adults perform with the help of ICT? The purpose of this paper is to present and discuss the results, focusing particularly on the use of Information and communication technology. Results suggests that respondents of survey II integrate ICT into their daily lives by using devices as computers or smartphones but also navigation systems or e-book readers. Reasons for usage are primarily due to communicational purposes, practical reasons or because of curiosity. Additionally, participants use the Internet at home as well as mobile Internet ranging from 15 min up to more than two hours daily.

In this conference proceedings, a second article entitled "Health technology use in Germany among older adults (Part I): short time changes in health-related information and mHealth applications" presents the results around health related information's and mHealth applications.

2   Method

The following section gives a brief introduction to the method. A more detailed description can be found in the contribution "Health technology use in Germany among older adults (Part I): short time changes in health-related information and mHealth applications" in these conference proceedings.

2.1   Questionnaire Construction

In order to assess user- and context-dependent parameters of technology-usage, the Tech4Age questionnaire was developed and tested in 2015 by five independent examiners with regard to wording [4, 9]. Existing tools of validation were combined with standard demographic and health-related items as well as with newly included items. Most questions had closed-ended responses that required participants to check one or more predetermined answers or rate statements on a Likert scale. Open-ended questions were used to gain insight into motivational background and behavioural reasons. Some questions for the second survey of 2018/2019 were changed to improve reading comprehension, and one question on net household income was added.

2.2 Procedure

In a first step, the existing questionnaire was checked for topicality. Segments that were not up to date were revised and modified. Together with an one-page cover letter, describing the reason for contacting and request for participation in survey II, a paper-based questionnaire was sent in a second step by postal mail to adults aged 60 years or older. On this introductory page, the participants were informed that the study's aim was to explore modern digital technologies in the German healthcare sector. Thus, the questionnaire did not differ in structure from the first one in 2016/2017 [4]. Participants' addresses were randomly selected, restricted by age criteria (equal age or above 60 years) and with the help of a balanced gender distribution within Germany by a service provider. No remuneration was offered to the participants for their participation; only the return of the questionnaire by post was paid for. All participants were informed about duration of the survey, data storage, and the lead examiner. Returned surveys were digitalised by a Remark Office software OMR (Gravic, Malvern, USA). In cases of uncertainty of the Remark output, a questionnaire was inspected visually and its values transcribed by hand. The data matrix output of Remark was subsequently analysed with SPSS Statistic 25 (IBM, Armonk, USA). An ethics vote was obtained for this study at RWTH Aachen University.

2.3 Restriction

A total of 649 out of 5000 participants responded to the questionnaire of 2018/2019. The participation rate was 13%; in the previous survey I it was 11%. Accordingly, one restriction of survey II was that the query was available as a paper version only. Another restriction of survey II was the exclusive availability in Germany, making it difficult for non-native speakers living in Germany to participate. A further restriction was that survey II did not include the same interviewed people as in the first survey.

2.4 Participants

The mean age of the sample from 2018/2019 (N = 649) was 66.11 years (SD = 4.54). The gender ratio was approximately balanced with 54.6% male and 45.4% female participants in 2018/2019, which corresponds approximately to the results from 2016/2017. Most participants lived in their own home or flat (N = 475; 73.2%), followed by participants living in a rented apartment (N = 169; 26%). The same applies to the place of living: 59.3% (N = 385) participants lived in an urban area while 40.2% (N = 261) lived in a rural setting. 440 (67.8%) participants stated being retired, 86 (13.3%) persons said working part-time or earning up to 450 euros monthly, while 193 (29.7%) participants were still working and 16 (2.5%) participants abstained from answering.

Participants' global technology affinity showed a mean of 3.22 ($SD = .69$) on a five-point Likert scale (1 = strongly agree, 5 = strongly disagree) in 2018/2019 compared to 3.23 ($SD = .70$) in 2016/2017. Whereas average rate on subscale acceptance was $M = 2.71$ ($SD = .90$), participants' competence scored on average $M = 3.38$ ($SD = 1.01$) and their locus of control dimension had a mean value of $M = 3.53$ ($SD = .85$). Compared to survey I from 2016/2017, the participants' subscale acceptance was $M = 2.71$ ($SD = .97$), participants' competence scored on average $M = 3.36$ ($SD = 1.03$) and the locus of control dimension had a mean value of $M = 3.59$ ($SD = .87$). Social desirability of the answers was on average 5.08 ($SD = .65$) on a seven-point Likert scale in 2018/2019. In 2016/2017, it was 5.18 ($SD = .672$). The participants' subscales self-delusion ($M = 5.04$, $SD = .72$) and external delusion ($M = 5.13$, $SD = .97$) had similar average values in 2018/2019 with a self-delusion of ($M = 5.08$, $SD = .753$) and external delusion of ($M = 5.28$, $SD = .97$). Technological affinity [11] and social desirability [12] will be discussed in Sect. 3.2.

3 Results

3.1 Information and Communication Technology Used by Older Adults

A fundamental aspect of survey II was to examine the integration of information and communication technologies (ICT) of older and very old citizens. While 2016/2017 survey I was still based on preliminary studies [1–3, 13, 14], 2018/2019 survey II was based on a more in-depth analysis [4–6] of the first 2016/2017 analysis, revealing weaknesses in the questionnaire and therefore resulting in small modifications of the second survey. Overall, however, it showed that the main questions were still relevant: (1) How is ICT used among older adults and what are the reasons for technology acquisition? (2) If ICT is used, who administrates ICT products? (3) Do older adults use the Internet and if so, in which situations? (4) Which everyday activities do older adults perform with the help of ICT?

ICT Used Among Older Adults and Their Reasons for Acquisition. The use of mobile devices indicated a slight trend towards new media when comparing both studies. In survey ii of 2018/2019, ownerships of desktop computers, tablets and especially smartphones increased (see Table 1). In addition, the use of common mobile devices (e.g., smartphones or tablets), the use of (health) technologies like navigation systems, activity trackers or home automation systems was analysed. Results of both surveys are presented in Table 2. An interesting aspect of the second survey is that a total of 158 participants (24.4%) stated not using any of the devices listed below.

Table 1. Ownership of mobile devices (multiple answers allowed)

Year	2016/2017 ($N = 551$)		2018/2019 (N = 649)	
Mobile devices	Percent of sample	N in sample	Percent of sample	N in sample
Desktop computer	77.7	428	88.3	573
Smartphone	49.2	271	77.7	504
Mobile Phone (without touch display)	55.4	305	47.6	309
Tablet-PC	28.3	156	39.3	255
Smartwatch	1.1	6	4.3	28

Table 2. Technological devices used by older adults (multiple answers allowed)

Year	2016/2017 ($N = 551$)		2018/2019 ($N = 649$)	
Technological devices	Percent of sample	N in sample	Percent of sample	N in sample
Navigation system	52.3	288	55.5	360
E-book reader	18.3	101	22.3	145
Blood glucose meter	18.3	101	24.0	156
Activity tracker	7.3	40	13.6	88
House emergency call	1.6	9	0.6	4
Home automation system	0.7	4	2.6	17

Participants were asked about their reasons for acquiring technological devices. Open-ended answers were coded in the same way as in 2016/2017. The three most frequently mentioned reasons for a renewal of survey II can be found in Table 3. "Communication and accessibility" represent private usages by participants, including communication with friends, family and also contacts in cases of emergency. Curiosity, entertainment, and new technical possibilities acquire new technical methods (emails, searches on the Internet, storage of photos, etc.). External circumstances, for example, are receiving new devices as gifts, desires to keep up with technology, or an old, defective device. Practical reasons are related to operability of devices. The last reason for the acquisition of technological devices is because of entertaining purposes. Motivations for using e-book readers and smartwatches are similar to the ones mentioned above, complemented by reasons as profession and communication.

Table 3. Reasons for acquiring an ICT device in 2018/2019 (coded open-ended answers)

ICT device	Reason	Percent of sample	N in sample
Smartphone (N = 462)	Communication and availability	66.0	305
	Practical reasons	12.1	56
	Curiosity, fun, and new technical possibilities	8.9	52
Tablet (N = 224)	Curiosity, fun, and new technical possibilities	30.8	69
	Practical reasons	27.2	61
	Research	15.2	34
Desktop computer/Laptop (N = 494)	Practical reasons	25.5	126
	Profession	21.9	108
	Communication and availability	17.6	87
Smartwatch (N = 25)	Fitness	72.0	18
	Indicate Time	12.0	3
	External circumstances (gift, …)	8.0	2
E-book reader (N = 133)	For hobbies only	49.6	66
	Practical reasons	45.9	61
	External circumstances (gift, …)	2.3	3

Administration of ICT Devices. Besides reasons for acquisition and reasons for using ICT devices, their administration was also questioned, as can be seen in Table 4. In most cases, older adults themselves or their relatives are in charge of administrating ICT products, making relatives and friends a relevant source to rely on when administrating ICT devices.

Use of Internet. By repeating survey II, 99.1% of the participants stated having access to Internet at home (N = 643). This shows an increase compared to 2016/2017 survey I, in which 84% (N = 458) had internet access. Reasons against domestic use of Internet, asked as an open-ended question, have decreased equally compared to the results of survey II. Merely the reasons 'lack of interest' (N = 1), 'missing technical requirements' (N = 1) and 'not using personally but my wife or husband' were answered with the same frequency (N = 1). What was new, though, was "too expensive" (N = 1) as a reason for not using internet. In Table 5, daily at home internet usages of the sample are described.

Table 4. Administration of technical products in percent of sample (multiple answers allowed)

ICT device	Year	N in sample	I myself	Family member	Friend	Service provider	Other
Smartphone	2016/2017	309	63.1	45.6	8.1	6.8	1.6
	2018/2019	516	63.8	47.3	9.9	4.5	0.6
Tablet	2016/2017	180	63.3	46.1	7.2	7.2	0.6
	2018/2019	275	58.5	42.5	7.3	6.2	0.7
Desktop computer/Laptop	2016/2017	440	50.2	50.5	16.1	15.9	1.8
	2018/2019	569	54.0	46.4	11.6	13.2	0.4
Smartwatch	2016/2017	13	61.5	30.8	7.7	7.7	
	2018/2019	35	80.0	20.0	2.9		
E-book reader	2016/2017	100	78.0	27.0	6.0	4.0	
	2018/2019	141	83.0	24.8	3.5	0.7	

Table 5. Durations of fixed internet use per day

Year	2016/2017 ($N = 534$)		2018/2019 ($N = 630$)	
Duration of fixed Internet use per day	Percent of sample	N in sample	Percent of sample	N in sample
No use	18.7	100	8.3	52
Up to 15 min	17.8	95	11.7	74
15 min up to 30 min	20.4	109	20.2	127
30 min up to 60 min	20.6	110	28.4	179
1 h up to 2 h	14.4	77	20.2	127
More than 2 h	8.1	43	11.3	71

In addition, 98.5% ($N = 639$) of the participants also stated that they have mobile internet access. This may be explained by the establishment of the smartphone and its increase in use, now being at 77.7% ($N = 504$). Asked about reasons for not using mobile Internet, coded open-ended questions reported reasons like 'missing technical requirements' ($N = 24$), 'lack of interest' ($N = 12$), and 'not using personally but my wife or husband' ($N = 2$) does. Further, a decrease in open response categories of the years 2016/2017 can be observed [4]. Table 6 illustrates daily durations of mobile internet use within the sample.

Table 6. Durations of mobile Internet use per day

Year	2016/2017 ($N = 519$)		2018/2019 (N = 631)	
Durations of mobile Internet use per day	Percent of sample	N in sample	Percent of sample	N in sample
No use	53.5	295	37.7	238
Up to 15 min	23.5	122	31.7	200
15 min up to 30 min	8.1	42	13.9	88
30 min up to 60 min	6.9	36	9.8	62
1 h up to 2 h	1.7	9	3.3	21
More than 2 h	2.9	15	3.5	22

In 2016/2017, participants preferred having access to internet at home since the t-test revealed ($t(515) = 20.783, p < .001$). For survey II, the result was $t(634) = 12.995, p < .001$), indicating that participants still prefer using internet at home, although this seems to be a decreasing trend.

Activities Performed via ICT. In 2016/2017, participants were asked on their preferred methods for performing a variety of different activities. The idea behind this question was to determine which aspects of everyday life are digitally assisted and which ones are likely to be performed in manually. The same questions were also asked in 2018/2019. Results of 2018/2019 are shown in Table 7.

Table 7. Devices for performing everyday activities. The higher percentage in the sample is because of multiple responses (2018/2019)

Activity (number in request)	Smartphone	Tablet	Desktop computer/Laptop	Other (e.g., face-to-face)	I don't perform such an activity	Cumulative percentage
Banking ($N = 750$)	8.0	7.2	53.5	25.6	21.3	115.6
Timetable information (bus, train, etc.) ($N = 854$)	37.6	17.4	47.3	10.0	19.3	131.6
Ticket booking (bus, train, etc.) ($N = 709$)	9.7	6.0	38.4	17.3	37.9	109.2

(continued)

Table 7. (*continued*)

Activity (number in request)	Smartphone	Tablet	Desktop computer/Laptop	Other (e.g., face-to-face)	I don't perform such an activity	Cumulative percentage
Navigation ($N = 745$)	46.7	6.3	21.3	20.6	19.9	114.8
Playing games ($N = 709$)	16.5	12.9	23.1	5.5	51.2	109.2
Writing letters ($N = 703$)	5.2	8.2	69.0	9.2	16.6	108.3
Purchasing goods ($N = 757$)	10.8	11.7	44.8	22.5	26.8	116.6
Watching videos (YouTube, etc.) ($N = 752$)	20.5	17.7	34.5	5.9	37.3	115.9
Sharing of confidential information ($N = 682$)	7.9	2.8	19.3	19.0	56.2	105.1
Watching TV ($N = 648$)	2.6	7.4	14.6	32.2	43.0	99.8
Listening to music ($N = 734$)	18.8	10.5	17.3	31.0	35.6	113.1
Reading messages ($N = 978$)	42.2	24.3	48.1	26.7	9.4	150.7
Searching for information ($N = 906$)	35.1	21.7	44.8	22.5	15.4	139.6
Calendar ($N = 768$)	44.2	7.4	17.7	22.5	26.5	118.3

(*continued*)

Table 7. (*continued*)

Activity (number in request)	Smartphone	Tablet	Desktop computer/Laptop	Other (e.g., face-to-face)	I don't perform such an activity	Cumulative percentage
Taking notes* (*N* = 720)	30.8	6.2	17.6	24.7	31.7	110.9

Note: * = Not queried in survey I of 2016/2017, but given as a response to choose from open-ended questions, leading to an inclusion in survey II of 2018/2019.

Comparing the data from 2016/2017 and 2018/2019, a slight increase of ICT-usage can be observed, especially for the use of smartphones and desktop PCs. Overall, however, the sample from 2018/2019 is digitised in the same way as the sample from 2016/2017. The activities included in both studies have not changed: performing bank-related tasks, using ICT for mobility reasons, and receiving information are considered to be the main activities.

3.2   Correlation of Factors

This section reveals important correlation results based on the methodical approach of Boyer et al. [15], Cohen [16, 17] and Schäfer and Schöttker-Königer [18]. Results from "Health technology use in Germany among older adults (Part I)" are included here, while paying careful attention to facets of computer literacy, affinity for technology, and social desirability in the sample of 2018/2019, with respect to handling of technology and applications. Furthermore, significant correlations will be compared with the help of a Fisher's z-transformation in order to obtain differences from the first survey. Scrutinised variables are scaled differently. Therefore, correlation coefficients were calculated for at least one variable with nominal scaling Eta coefficient, for ordinal scaling Spearman's-Rho and for interval scaling Bravias-Pearson.

The main scales of affinity for technology and computer literacy display high positive correlations ($r = .427, p < .001$), showing no differences ($F = -0.663, p = .508$) between the two samples compared to survey I of 2017/2017. As a result, it can be concluded that the affinity rate for technology is likely to be higher when people 60+ have better computer skills. In comparison to both data sets, results were confirmed, and a similar linear correlation was found. Further significant correlations can be seen in the analysis of sociodemographic data. With regard to the test person's genders, a correlation was found between affinity for technology ($\eta = .111, p = .003$) and computer knowledge ($\eta = .306, p < .001$), indicating that women show less technical affinity and less technical knowledge in the 60+ sample. The results of this age class of 2016/2017 were compared to the results of 2018/2019 of this age class ($F = -0.478, p = .633$), proving that with increasing age, examinees showed less affinity for technology ($r = -.109, p = .007$) and computer knowledge ($r = -.259, p < .001$). In addition, in 2018/2019, the educational attainment was newly surveyed as a variable correlating positively with affinity for technology ($r_s = .279, p < .001$) and computer skills ($r_s = .191, p < .001$).

Looking at affinities for technology, positive correlations can be seen regarding availabilities of Internet use at home ($r_s = .311, p < .001$), mobile Internet use ($r = .270, p < .001$) as well as frequencies of computer and laptop usages ($r_s = .214, p < .001$), e-book readers ($r_s = .171, p = .030$) and smart watches ($r = .371, p = .003$). According to usages of smartphones ($r_s = .069, p = .125$) and tablets ($r_s = .051, p = .403$), no significant results were observed in terms of usage behaviours. This is also evident in the results from survey I of 2016/2017, as there are significantly different correlations compared to the second survey of 2018/2019 (smartphone: $F = 3,566, p < .001$; tablet: $F = 3,329, p < .001$). The data indicate that older people 60+ own and use smartphones and tablets more often, possibly leading to a better and more adaptive manageability. Empirical evidence also showed that numbers of apps on smartphones ($r_s = .290, p < .001$) and tablets ($r_s = .307, p < .001$) as well as frequencies of app usages (smartphone: $r_s = .290, p < .001$; tablet: $r_s = .254, p < .001$) correlate positively with technological affinity. Here, the correlations of the first survey exemplify similar gradient coefficients as those of the second survey.

Additionally, the data on computer knowledge may hold empirically interesting correlations. Here, too, a positive correlation can be seen in the use of internet at home ($r_s = .236, p < .001$). When comparing this to the sample of 2016/2017, the frequency of use of smartphones, tablets, smartwatches, and e-book readers did not show any significant correlations, except for computers and laptops with frequencies of usages of $r_s = .145, p = .001$. This could be attributable to the trend considering computers and laptops as main devices for work. Furthermore, in the data of 2016/2017, the number of applications (smartphone: $r_s = .261, p < .001$; tablet: $r_s = .249, p < .001$) and the frequency of application usages on smartphones ($r_s = .295, p < .001$) and tablets ($r_s = .213, p < .001$) were to be replicated.

With regard to mHealth apps usages for reasons of technological affinity (smartphone: $r_s = .146, p = .002$; tablet: $r_s = .213, p < .001$) and computer skills (smartphone: $r_s = .106, p = .023$; tablet: $r_s = .172, p = .003$), low correlations were observed. There are slight correlations in the number of mHealth apps considering affinity for technology (smartphone: $r_s = .149, p = .001$; tablet: $r_s = .186, p = .001$). Subjects using mHealth apps use them platform-independently on both smartphones and tablets. Other conclusions can be drawn with regard to the intensity of the use of smartwatches, since here medium to high correlations can be found with pre-installed mHealth Apps on smartphones ($r_s = .413, p = .001$) and frequencies of their usages (smartphone: $r_s = .579, p < .001$; tablet: $r_s = .304, p = .042$). Based on this, the results suggest that smartwatches may be the main information source for health-conscious users, because of being easily portable. Furthermore, no correlations regarding numbers of chronic diseases of the test persons could be shown empirically.

Social desirability was surveyed as a control indicator to check whether test persons responded intuitively and freely of external influences. Apart from factors as gender ($\eta = .147, p < .001$) and satisfaction with information on health-related topics ($r_s = -.134, p = .001$), there were no correlations with other variables of the questionnaire. As a result, older male examinees are slightly more interested in responding to social desirability. Respondents who were dissatisfied more with the availability of health information show a slight plus in social desirability. Adding on to that, results suggest that honest answers were given within the sample.

4   Discussion

Survey II of the Tech4Age project – as survey I of 2016/2017 – corresponds to design rec-ommendations within the framework of the human-centred development process accord-ing to DIN EN ISO 9241-210. Mertens et al. [4] discussed the relevance of similar studies in the context of development of new technical products as well as changes in attitudes towards technology and acceptance of usage. In the next section, results of this study are compared with results of other studies, followed by a presentation of limitations.

4.1   Comparison with Other Surveys

This section compares our findings with established results by other researchers, tar-geting older adults as well while also examining use of ICT and health-related issues. Differences and similarities between these studies will be identified to compare the results with regard to the use of digital technologies in Germany on the one hand and on the other, to compare the use of ICT technologies in Germany. The first study in these research fields is to be compared first, followed by more recent results.

The quantitative study by Rockmann, Gewald and Brune [19] on IT usage in tran-sition of age with specific focus on causes and effects of individual differences was conducted in 2015 in Germany as well as in the US with the aim to examine acceptance of technology along with the usage behaviour of the ageing population starting at age 50. Especially factors like computer anxiety, personal interest, and computer-related self-efficacy expectations represent key components when it comes to using IT. Rockman, Gewald and Brune [19] regard computer anxiety in terms of individual digital compe-tences, while at the same time acceptance and usage of IT lead to individuals with greater computer anxiety and more usability problems.

The data does not provide insight into the latter items being directly linked with searching for information online. Considering the types of mHealth apps used by our participants, a wider variety of apps comes into play, emphasising the recognition of the explorative plus extended behaviour of older adults as Rockman, Gewald and Brune [19] put it. For them [19], digital technologies play a comparably smaller role in the context of health information and mHealth while stating that people's health status is linked to their use of technology whereas our contributions suggest that increasing competencies in the area of digitization are linked to searching for information in the digital context.

In a report by Destatis, 'Ältere Menschen in Deutschland und der EU, 2016' [Older people in Germany and the EU, 2016] [20], which is a report of the German federal office for statistics, the focus is on presenting demographic change in Germany. In addition to the demographic data, labour force participation, financial situation, health status and lifestyle of older and very old people are also taken into consideration. Comparing the ages of participants in the Destatis report with our study, it is striking that in the Destatis report, 52–55% percent of female participants had an age of 60–79 years, whereas women in our survey II aged 60 to 90 years were represented by 48%. According to Destatis, 72% of people older than 65 years have a desktop computer. This finding does not align with ours, since here more than 88% are in possession of a desktop computer. When questioned on spending time online in 2015, 49% aged older than 65 years agreed to this question in the Destatis report, while participants in 2018/2019 agreed 91%. This result indicates a clear tendency towards being more online between the years of 2016 and 2018/2019. Nevertheless, there is not much discrepancy between the two studies when comparing aims and actions performed when being online and using ICT. Destatis declared that 90% of participants write emails, while 85% search for information online, 67% use the Internet for media online, 44% carry out online banking and 39–49% shop online. The difference between Destatis and our survey II is the fact that their data is relatable to online users only, while ours take the complete sample into consideration. Overall, a comparison of these two studies shows that their results are broadly similar. The positive digitization trend from the Destatis study seems to continue in our study, as shown, for example, by the ownership of a desktop PC.

In a qualitative long-term field study by Ogonowski et al. [21], researchers looked at an ICT-based fall prevention system for older adults. Twelve participants between 65–80 years old were supposed to exercise daily for mobility reasons and to prevent falls. As in survey II, participants made use of ICT products, but in contrast to our questionnaire they included an ICT based training program on a daily routine as a substitution for exercise. Outcomes of Ogonowski et al. [21] reveal that the training system has potential to decrease fall risks of those who are likely to fall more easily when using the system regularly. In addition, the successful integration of the ICT training program exemplifies the increasing tendency of using ICT daily, as can be seen in our survey II, since here, older adults are continually incorporating ICT into their daily lives. Furthermore, products as smartwatches, activity trackers or blood glucose meters, which record a rising tendency in usages between 2016/2017 and 2018/2019, also emphasise the older adults' desire to make use of ICT and their intention to get acquainted with technology (not just generally, but effectively) – even if the majority of participants stated they have not installed any mHealth apps on their tablets or smartphones. All in all, the findings by Ogonowskis et al. [21] are in line with the first Tech4Age survey from 2016/2017. However, a decreasing trend of ICT technologies becomes not visible here, which may be due to the limited time span of the survey.

A study much referred to is the 'ARD-ZDF-online Study'[3], an online survey by German public service broadcast companies, with the aim of researching internet use of all age groups in the two years of 2016/2017, questioning 1508 attendees. The main findings were that the group of 50 to 69 year old respondents spent an average amount of 85 min online, whereas participants aged 70 years and older were online for an average of 28 min. Since our inquiry did not examine the minutes spent online but categorises the duration of being online ('0 = no use', '1 = up to 15 min', '2 = 15–30 min', '3 = 30–60 min', '4 = 1–2 h', '5 = more than 2 h'), the results are not directly comparable. In our survey II of 2018/2019, respondents between 60–69 ($N = 840$) years have a mean value of 2.66 ($SD = 1.43$), indicating that their time spent online corresponds to 15 to 30 and 30 to 60 min. Compared to the results of the ARD-ZDF online study, it must be considered that the examinees of survey II were older, 60–69 years compared to 50–69 years of the ARD-ZDF online study.

For the age group from 70 years upwards, the mean value of categorical data is 2.04 ($SD = 1.61$), representing a duration between 1 min and 30 min of being online. When comparing the results of both studies, participants of survey II spent less time online.

---

[3] http://www.ard-zdf-onlinestudie.de/.

Questioned on activities done online by the age group of 70+ in the ARD-ZDF-online study, 30% play games online, 22% stated seeking for information,17% communicated while 15% used the Internet for media purposes or for online shopping. The categories implemented in our study display identical results while considering more in-depth categories. The only activity carried out online, which is not mentioned in the ARD-ZDF online study but is ranked second in survey II, is using the Internet for mobility reasons. In summary, we can conclude that the results of the ARD study indicate the participants' Internet usage being higher than in surveys I and II. This may be due to a sampling effect or to the size of the sample. With regard to reasons for using digital media, both studies are almost identical.

The comparison of the studies (survey I and survey II) makes it clear that the results of the papers in this congress proceedings seem to apply to the German population and not only to German subgroups. Adding on to that, the digitization trend continues to increase in the temporal context. Both, the Tech4Age longitudinal surveys I and II emphasise and exemplify the older adults' increasing tendency of familiarising themselves with smart-phones and other digital tools and applying information and communication technology in the context of health care into their daily lives. Additionally, when considering the general rise of digital technology in this group of age, it becomes evident that within the two years the surveys took place, it has become more important and attractive for older adults to use ICT, indicating developers and designers to provide products specifically for the needs and demands of the elderly.

4.2 Limitations

Limitations of survey I in 2016/2017 also apply to the reproduced survey II in 2018/2019, including the limitation regarding self-selected participation, missing remainders for participation (such as reminder e-mails), and missing questions on depth of engagement with healthcare apps. Furthermore, a transferability towards the total population of Germany is only possible to a limited extent, as the 5000 questionnaires were sent out randomly. This means that certain demographic characteristics may potentially correlate with the decision of answering the questionnaire. It is therefore possible that certain profile factors are not or even overrepresented in survey II and do not accurately reflect the reality of the status quo in this population group in Germany.

However, this limitation can never be ruled out for corresponding study designs in which participation is voluntary and requires a certain degree of personal initiative. The samples from both studies remain independent of each other, due to the fact that because of an external service provider, 5000 people over 60 years were contacted in both studies. As a result, there may be overlaps within the sample, but this is not mandatory.

Accordingly, it is difficult to derive clear developments and trends from the data and therefore difficult to draw conclusions about the development of the data over time. A further limitation is the timing of survey II, as the survey took place two-and-a-half years after survey I. The reason for this is the assumption that society is changing more rapidly within the digitisation process.

5 Conclusion

The aim of this article was to present the descriptive results of survey II, conducted in 2018/2019, with specific consideration of information and communication technology used by older adults as well as correlation of factors. Concluding our results in regard of the findings of two years prior, it is safe to say that usage of ICT along with usage of digital technology has significantly increased. By having an increased rate of respondents to the questionnaire of 2018/2019 compared to 2016/2017, the results of 2016/2017 are subjected to a check whereas the results of 2018/2019 receive verification, proving the overall acceptance of survey II among the participants.

The digitization trend is continually progressing among older and very old people in Germany, since an increase in use of digital devices can be observed even in the short period from 2016/2017 to 2018/2019. This is particularly the case in the context of healthcare. It is reasonable to assume that both studies apply to the German population - at least in this age cohort.

Acknowledgement. The interdisciplinary research group Human Factors Engineering and Ergonomics in Healthcare (HFE^{2}H) is part of the Institute of Industrial Engineering and Ergonomics of RWTH Aachen University. The project Tech4Age is funded by the German Federal Ministry of Education and Research (BMBF) under Grant No. 16SV7111. For more details and information, please visit www.tech4age.de.

References

1. Wille, M., Theis, S., Rasche, P., Bröhl, C., Schlick, C., Mertens, A.: Best practices for designing electronic healthcare devices and services for the elderly. i-com. **15**(1), 67–78 (2016). https://doi.org/10.1515/icom-2016-0009
2. Rasche, P., et al.: Wandel von Technikakzeptanz und -nutzung im hohen Alter [Change in technology acceptance and usage in old age]. Zeitschrift für Gerontologie und Geriatrie (49), 130ff (2016)
3. Bröhl, C., Mertens, A., Ziefle, M.: How do users interact with mobile devices? An analysis of handheld positions for different technology generations. In: Zhou, J., Salvendy, G. (eds.) Human Aspects of IT for the Aged Population. Applications, Services and Contexts. LNCS, vol. 10298, pp. 3–16. Springer, Cham (2017). https://doi.org/10.1007/978-3-319-58536-9_1
4. Mertens, A., Rasche, P., Theis, S., Bröhl, C., Wille, M.: Use of information and communication technology in healthcare context by older adults in Germany: initial results of the Tech4Age long-term study. i-com. **16**(2), 165–180 (2017). https://doi.org/10.1515/icom-2017-0018
5. Schäfer, K., et al.: Datenbasierte Personas älterer Endbenutzer für die zielgruppenspezifische Entwicklung innovativer Informations- und Kommunikationssysteme im Gesundheitssektor [Data-based personas of older end users for the development of innovative information and communication systems in the health sector for specific target groups]. Zeitschrift für Arbeitswissenschaft **73**(2), 177–192 (2019). https://doi.org/10.1007/s41449-019-00150-5
6. Schäfer, K., et al.: Survey-based personas for a target-group-specific consideration of elderly end users of information and communication systems in the German health-care sector. Int. J. Med. Inform. **132**, 103924 (2019). https://doi.org/10.1016/j.ijme-dinf.2019.07.003

7. Schmidt, A., Wolf-Ostermann, K.: Ambulante Versorgung von Menschen mit Demenz–ein Überblick [Outpatient care for people with dementia – an overview]. In: Pfannstiel, M.A., Focke, A., Mehlich, H. (eds.) Bedarfsplanung und ganzheitliche regionale Versorgung und Zusammenarbeit. Management von Gesundheitsregionen/Mario A. Pfannstiel, Axel Focke, Harald Mehlich Herausgeber, vol. 4, pp. 59–76. Springer Gabler, Wiesbaden (2018)
8. Pötzsch, O., Rößger, F.: Germany's Population by 2060: Results of the 13th Coordinated Population Projection, Wiesbaden (2015)
9. Rasche, P., et al.: Prevalence of health app use among older adults in Germany: national survey. JMIR Mhealth Uhealth 6(1), e26 (2018). https://doi.org/10.2196/mhealth.8619
10. Sengpiel, M., Dittberner, D.: The computer literacy scale (CLS) for older adults—development and validation. In: Herczeg, M., Kindsmüller, M.C. (eds.) Mensch und Computer 2008. 8. fachübergreifende Konferenz für interaktive Medien - Viel Mehr Interaktion. Naturwissenschaft und Technik II 6-2010, pp. 7–16. Oldenbourg Wissenschaftsverlag, München (2010)
11. Neyer, F.J., Felber, J., Gebhardt, C.: Entwicklung und Validierung einer Kurzskala zur Erfassung von Technikbereitschaft [Development and validation of a short scale for the registering of technical readiness]. Diagnostica 58(2), 87–99 (2012). https://doi.org/10.1026/0012-1924/a000067
12. Winkler, N., Kroh, M., Spiess, M.: Entwicklung einer deutschen Kurzskala zur zweidimensionalen Messung von sozialer Erwünschtheit [Development of German Short Scale for Two-Dimensional Measurement of Social Desirability], 579. http://www.econstor.eu/bitstream/10419/18472/1/dp579.pdf
13. Schäfer, K., et al.: Age-related shift in adoption and use of information and communications technology (2016). https://www.researchgate.net/publication/305881017_Age-related_Shift_in_Adoption_and_Use_of_Information_and_Communications_Technology. Accessed 20 Dec 2021
14. Bröhl, C., Theis, S., Rasche, P., Wille, M., Mertens, A., Schlick, C.M.: Neuroergonomic analysis of perihand space: effects of hand proximity on eye-tracking measures and performance in a visual search task. Behav. Inf. Technol. 36(7), 737–744 (2017). https://doi.org/10.1080/0144929X.2016.1278561
15. Boyer, J.E., Palachek, A.D., Schucany, W.R.: An empirical study of related correlation coefficients. J. Educ. Stat. 8(1), 75–86 (1983). https://doi.org/10.3102/10769986008001075
16. Cohen, J.: Statistical Power Analysis for the Behavioral Sciences. Lawrence Erlbaum Associates, 2nd edn. L. Erlbaum Associates, Hillsdale, NY (1988)
17. Cohen, J., Cohen, P., West, S.G., Aiken, L.S.: Applied Multiple Regression/Correlation Analysis for the Behavioral Sciences, 3rd edn. L. Erlbaum Associates, Mahwah, NJ (2003)
18. Schäfer, A., Schöttker-Königer, T.: Statistik und quantitative Methoden für Gesundheitsfachberufe. Springer, Heidelberg (2015). https://doi.org/10.1007/978-3-662-45519-7
19. Rockmann, R., Gewald, H., Brune, P.: Gesundheitsbezogene IT-Nutzung im Altersübergang – Ursachen und Auswirkungen individueller Differenzen [Health-related IT use in the transition of age – causes and effects of individual discrepancies]. In: Schneider, W. (ed.) Der Altersübergang Als Neuarrangement Von Arbeit und Leben -Kooperative Dienstleistungen Für das Alter(n) in Vielfalt [Health-Related IT Use in the Transition of Age - Causes and Effects of Individual Discrepancies], pp. 177–198. Vieweg, Wiesbaden (2019)
20. Haustein, T., Mischke, J., Schönfeld, F., Willand, I.: Ältere Menschen in Deutschland und der EU. [Older people in Germany and the EU], Wiesbaden (2016). https://www.bmfsfj.de/resource/blob/93214/95d5fc19e3791f90f8d582d61b13a95e/aeltere-menschen-deutschland-eu-data.pdf
21. Ogonowski, C., et al.: ICT-based fall prevention system for older adults. ACM Trans. Comput.-Hum. Interact. 23(5), 1–33 (2016). https://doi.org/10.1145/2967102

Health Technology Use in Germany Among Older Adults (Part II): Short Time Changes in Health-Related Information and mHealth Applications

Katharina Schäfer[1]([✉]) [iD], Peter Rasche[1,4] [iD], Sabine Theis[1] [iD], Tobias Seinsch[1], Maximilian Boddin[1], Rebecca Küpper[1], Christina Bröhl[1] [iD], Matthias Wille[1] [iD], Axel Zweck[2], Christopher Brandl[1,3] [iD], Verena Nitsch[1,3] [iD], and Alexander Mertens[1] [iD]

[1] Institute of Industrial Engineering and Ergonomics, RWTH Aachen University, Eilfschornsteinstraße 18, 52062 Aachen, Germany
k.schaefer@iaw.rwth-aachen.de
[2] Future and Innovation, Institute of Sociology, Eilfschornsteinstr. 7, 52062 Aachen, Germany
[3] Fraunhofer Institute for Communication, Information Processing and Ergonomics FKIE, Campus-Boulevard 55, 52074 Aachen, Germany
[4] Institute of General Practice and Family Medicine (Abteilung für Allgemeinmedizin), Ruhr-University Bochum, Universitätsstraße 150, 44801 Bochum, Germany

Abstract. Demographic change in Germany has been discussed on a grand scale in the past years. Feared and denied at first; research was conducted; approaches were presented, and measures derived. The health care sector is an area of special interest because demographic change is affecting it twice: on the one hand, more elderly patients have to be treated while at the other hand, less medical staff is being trained. It is expected that digitization can provide a solution. But is this true? How can digitization help to relieve the burden on medical staff in particular? Are digital services and available information used by older people? Or do they reject them? Finding answers to these questions is the aim of this longitudinal study. The focus was on the usage of information and communication technology (ICT) by the elderly (older people) (60+) in Germany. This study by the interdisciplinary research team "Tech4Age" consists of two surveys from 2016/2017 (survey I) and 2018/2019 (survey II). The article presents the results of the second survey, focusing on the comparison of both surveys as well as on potential changes. The sample consisted of $N = 649$ participants (54.6% male and 45.4% female) with an average age of 66.11 years ($SD = 5.45$ years). A fundamental aspect of the surveys was to examine the use of health-related information and levels of trust, the general (smartphone and tablet) applications and mHealth applications used by older adults plus information and communication technology used by older adults. Due to the large scope of both the surveys and the results, the latter will be presented in two separate articles. This paper concentrates on the first two aspects: the use of health-related information and levels of trust as well as on general and mHealth applications used by older adults.

© The Author(s), under exclusive license to Springer Nature Switzerland AG 2022
V. G. Duffy (Ed.): HCII 2022, LNCS 13320, pp. 129–147, 2022.
https://doi.org/10.1007/978-3-031-06018-2_9

In order to examine the use of health-related information and levels of trust, health literacy (HL) was taken into account. The focus here is on coping strategies in the context of health. HL is the ability to obtain, understand, and use health information for decision-making [1]. In contrast, Health Information Seeking Behaviour (HISB) encompasses individual abilities [2–4]. The research questions from 2016/2017 were adopted and compared with each other: (1) What kind of health information needs do older adults have? (2) How do older adults seek information on healthcare topics? (3) Which levels of health competences do older adults in Germany have? Results indicate that older adults are still satisfied with the information they receive on healthcare. The data shows that doctors and pharmacists are number one sources older adults rely on regarding reliability of information on healthcare. Information sources as Internet, TV or newspapers and magazines show an increase in demand.

The second aim was to look at the potential of ICT-use by older and very old end users. Here, the use of apps and mHealth ("mobile Health") apps was put into focus. mHealth can be defined as "the system built around the mobile technology to manage healthcare information" [5]. To further deepen these results, the following research questions were examined: (1) Do older adults use (smartphone and tablet) applications? If so, do they use mHealth applications? (2) What are the reasons for not using mHealth applications? (3) If mHealth applications are used by older adults, what type of applications do they use? (4) How do older adults find out about (smartphone and tablet) applications? Results show that the age group of older adults uses applications on smartphones as well as on tablets, but there seems to be a decreasing trend by the usage of mHealth applications compared to 2016/2017. Nevertheless, mHealth applications are still regularly used. Especially applications installed on smartphones tend to be used daily. Considering mHealth applications, fitness apps are used the most although apps for measuring calories, first aid apps or applications on health insurance companies provide a considerable increase in usage.

Keywords: Older adults · Germany · ICT · Information-seeking behavior · Health · Ergonomics

1 Introduction[1]

Hardly any other phenomenon is and has been discussed as much as demographic change. Predictions say that the proportion of older people in Germany will increase significantly by 2060 [6, 7]. Considering demographic change in the context of digitisation, it is safe to say that:

"Demographic change and increasing digitalization are two of the current megatrends directly impacting the every-day life of people. While the shift in age distribution among the German population towards an ever-increasing average age, and therefore also

---

[1] In this contribution and in the contribution "Health technology use in Germany among older adults (Part II): short time changes in information and communication technology" in this congress proceedings do exist congruent text passages. It is due to the fact that they are based on the same study and different aspects have been analyzed in the contributions. Nevertheless, each contribution should be complete and understandable on its own.

the significantly increasing prevalence and incidence of chronic diseases, represent an ongoing complication for the standard of high-quality healthcare processes, the diffusion of mobile information and communication technologies, e.g. in the form of smartphones and tablets, offers great potential for implementing low-threshold, location-independent and patient-specific healthcare in terms of electronic health ('e-health')" Mertens et al. [8].

For this, it is necessary to identify the needs of users and the context of (smartphone and tablet) application. This is relevant for the area of digital health applications, since the risk of being stigmatised as, for example, needy, can be high and can have an influence on the acceptance of independent technology use in a negative way. Impacts can be seen in adhesion and social environments of users.

Therefore, in 2016/2017, Mertens et al. [8] conducted a longitudinal study (referred to as "survey I"), trying to address this challenge by examining the usage of information and communication technology of older and very old people (60+) in Germany.[2] This study was repeated in 2018/2019 (referred to as "survey II"). Both surveys aimed to collect comprehensive data on the status quo of the interaction-specific use of mobile health applications and technologies together with individual user characteristics, needs, and context-specific influencing factors of older adults in Germany. The assumption was that new, innovative, and user-centred systems are needed to integrate new digital technologies into the healthcare system.

The article presents the results of the second survey with regard on the comparison of both surveys as well as on potential changes. The sample consisted of N = 649 participants (54.64% male and 45.36% female) with an average age of 66.11 years (SD = 5.45 years). A fundamental aspect of the surveys was to examine the use of health-related information and levels of trust, the general and mHealth applications used by older adults as well as the information and communication technology used by older adults. Due to the large scope of the surveys and the results, latter will be presented in two separate articles. This paper focuses on the first two aspects: the use of health-related information and levels of trust as well as general and mHealth applications used by older adults.

In order to examine the use of health-related information and levels of trust, health literacy (HL) was taken into account. The focus here is on coping strategies in the context of health. HL is the ability to obtain, understand, and use health information for decision-making [1]. In contrast, the Health Information Seeking Behaviour (HISB) encompasses individual abilities [2–4]. The research questions from 2016/2017 were adopted and compared with each other: (1) What kind of health information needs do older adults have? (2) How do older adults seek information on healthcare topics? (3) Which levels of health competences do older adults in Germany have? Results indicate that older adults are still satisfied with the information they receive on healthcare. Data shows that doctors and pharmacists are number one sources older adults rely on regarding reliability of information on healthcare. Information sources as Internet, TV or newspapers and magazines show an increase in demand.

---

[2] The survey was developed and conducted by an interdisciplinary team consisting of engineers, computer scientists, psychologists, sociologists and medics, focusing on the ergonomic design of human-computer interfaces of digital health systems and services (see also Wille et al., 2016).

The second aim was to look at the potential of ICT-use by older and very old end users. Here, the use of apps and mHealth ("mobile Health") apps was put into focus. mHealth can be defined as "the system built around the mobile technology to manage healthcare information" [5]. To further deepen these results, the following research questions were examined: (1) Do older adults use (smartphone and tablet) applications and do they use mHealth applications? (2) What are the reasons for not using mHealth applications? (3) If mHealth applications are used by older adults, what type of (smartphone and tablet) applications do they use? (4) How do older adults find out about applications? Results show that the age group of older adults uses applications on smartphones as well as on tablets, but there seems to be a decreasing trend on the usage of mHealth applications compared to 2016/2017. Nevertheless, mHealth applications are still used regularly. Especially applications installed on smartphones tend to be used daily. Considering mHealth applications, fitness apps are to be used most although apps for measuring calories, first aid apps or applications on health insurance companies provide a considerable increase in usage.

In this conference proceedings, a second article entitled "Health technology use in Germany among older adults (Part II): short time changes in information and communication technology" presents the results on information and communication technology.

2   Method

2.1   Questionnaire Construction

In order to assess user- and context-dependent parameters of technology-usage, the Tech4Age questionnaire was developed and tested in 2015 by five independent examiners with regard to wording [8, 9]. Existing validating tools were combined with standard demographic and health-related items as well as with newly included items. Most questions had closed-ended responses that required participants to check one or more predetermined answers or rate statements on a Likert scale. Open-ended questions were used to gain insight into motivational background, reasons for people's behaviour or to collect responses beyond those already known. Demographic items, such as age, gender, education, net household income, and health status, measured by number and type of chronic diseases participants might have, were queried. Additionally, the health competency of participants was measured using the (short version) European Health Literacy Survey (EU-HLS-Q16). To characterise participants' attitude towards technology in more detail, technology readiness and computer literacy scales were included. Additionally, information sources participants use to access (personal) health information [2–4] were requested. Other relevant topics were the computer literacy scale (CLS, [10]), which indicates the familiarity of participants with computer symbols, a section on technological affinity [11] and a section on social desirability [12]. At the end of the questionnaire, participants had the option to give further remarks. A more detailed description of the original questionnaire can be found in Mertens et al. [8]. Some questions have been changed for survey II in 2018/2019 to improve reading comprehension, and one question on net household income was added. For example, based on the results of survey I, the following questions were added: "What is your nationality? What is your monthly income?". In addition, the response options for, questions as "What is your highest educational qualification?" were adjusted and supplemented by the question "What vocational training qualifications do you have?". The 2018/2019 paper-based questionnaire included 110 items distributed across 15 different pages.

2.2 Procedure

In a first step, the existing questionnaire was checked for topicality. Segments that were not up to date were revised and modified. Together with an one-page cover letter, describing the reason for contacting and request for participation in survey II, a paper-based questionnaire was sent in a second step by postal mail to adults aged 60 years or older. On this introductory page, the participants were informed that the study's aim was to explore modern digital technologies in the German healthcare sector. Thus, the questionnaire did not differ in structure from the first one in 2016/2017 [8]. Participants' addresses were randomly selected, restricted by age criteria (equal age or above 60 years) and with the help of a balanced gender distribution within Germany by a service provider. No remuneration was offered to the participants for their participation; only the return of the questionnaire by post was paid for. All participants were informed about duration of the survey, data storage, and the lead examiner. Returned surveys were digitalised by a Remark Office software OMR (Gravic, Malvern, USA). In cases of uncertainty of the Remark output, a questionnaire was inspected visually and its values transcribed by hand. The data matrix output of Remark was subsequently analysed with SPSS Statistic 25 (IBM, Armonk, USA). An ethics vote was obtained for this study at RWTH Aachen University.

2.3 Restriction

A total of 649 out of 5000 participants responded to the questionnaire of 2018/2019. The participation rate was 13%; in the previous survey I it was 11%. Accordingly, one restriction of survey II was that the query was available as a paper version only. Another restriction of survey II was the exclusive availability in Germany, making it difficult for non-native speakers living in Germany to participate. A further restriction was that survey II did not include the same interviewed people as in the first survey.

2.4 Participants

The mean age of the sample from 2018/2019 ($N = 649$) was 66.11 years ($SD = 4.54$). Thus, on average, the participants are three years younger than in the previous survey I ($M = 69.17$ years, $SD = 5.79$). The gender ratio was approximately balanced with 54.6% male and 45.4% female participants in 2018/2019, which corresponds approximately to the results from 2016/2017. Regard the housing situation, data from 2018/2019 show no major differences compared to data from 2016/2017: most participants lived in their own home or flat ($N = 475; 73.2\%$), followed by participants living in a rented apartment ($N = 169; 26\%$). The same applies to the place of living: 59.3% ($N = 385$) participants lived in an urban area while 40.2% ($N = 261$) lived in a rural setting.

Table 1 compares the highest educational achievement of the participants. However, there is a change within the two surveys considering the specification of the retirement age of the participants. Thus, in survey II of 2018/2019, 440 (67.8%) participants stated they were retired, 86 (13.3%) persons said they have a part-time job or earn up to 450 euros monthly, while 193 (29.7%) participants were working and 16 (2.5%) participants abstained from answering. In comparison, only 109 out of 551 (19.8%) were employed during survey I from 2016/2017. Table 2 shows the vocational qualification of the participants and Table 3 indicates the (previous) professional domains comparing the two surveys.

Table 1. Highest educational achievement

Year	2016/2017 (*N* = 549)		2018/2019 (*N* = 644)	
Educational achievement	Percent of sample	N in sample	Percent of sample	N in sample
No achievement	0.2	1	1.7	11
Secondary school (*Hauptschule*)	10.0	55	24.4	157
Secondary school (*Realschule*)	16.0	88	27.0	174
Apprenticeship	31.9	176	*	*
University-entrance diploma (*Abitur*)	5.8	32	31.2	201
Academic studies	33.2	183	13.7	88
Other	2.5	14	2.0	13

Note: * = This value was not collected because the construct was split into questions on the highest school-leaving qualification and the highest vocational qualification.

Table 2. Vocational qualification

Year	2018/2019 (*N* = 641)	
Graduation	Percent of sample	Number of responses
In vocational training	3.8	34
Visit vocationally-oriented secondary schools/technical schools	2.4	21
Apprenticeship completed	37.4	334
Public administration service	7.4	66

(continued)

Table 2. (*continued*)

Year	2018/2019 ($N = 641$)	
Graduation	Percent of sample	Number of responses
Degree in social work or health care (*Ausbildungsberuf*)	5.3	47
Completion of a technical college/master craftsman/technical school/administration and business academy or technical academy	12.9	115
Bachelor	0.9	8
Diploma	15.9	142
Master/magister/state examination	6.3	56
Promotion	2.5	22
No vocational qualification and not in vocational training	1.7	15
Another professional qualification	3.7	33
Total	**100**	**893**

Table 3. Field of work

Year	2016/2017 ($N = 526$)		2018/2019 ($N = 638$)	
Field of work	Percent of sample	N in sample	Percent of sample	N in sample
Homemaker/housewife	2.0	11	1.4	9
Handcraft	12.2	67	11.0	70
Trading/administration	37.9	209	27.3	174
Technical/natural science	14.9	82	14.4	92
Social/humanities	11.8	65	6.7	43
Medical (-care)	7.6	42	8.6	55
Others	9.1	50	18.2	116

3   Results

3.1   Use of Health-Related Information and Levels of Trust

As in the first survey in 2016/2017, the repeated survey II took health literacy (HL) into account. The focus here is on coping strategies in the context of health. Health literacy is the ability to obtain, understand, and use health information for decision-making [1]. In contrast, the Health Information Seeking Behaviour (HISB) encompasses individual abilities [2–4]. The research questions from 2016/2017 were adopted and compared with each other: (1) What health information needs do older adults have? (2) How do older adults seek information about healthcare topics? (3) What levels of health competences do older adults in Germany have?

Information Need: What Do Older Adults Want to Know About Health? Older adults in Germany are still content with information they receive on (personal) health. N = 636 valid answers were given to the question on how satisfied participants in general are with the information they have access to about healthcare topics. Sixty percent (60.2%) claim to be 'very satisfied' and 'satisfied', while 32.9% consider their satisfaction as 'neutral'. Forty-four participants are 'unsatisfied' and 'very unsatisfied'. The five-level Likert scale, with a rating of 1 = "very satisfied" to 5 = "very dissatisfied", was answered by the elderly on average with 2.37 ($SD = .71$). These results are not significantly different ($t(1156) = .160, p < .873$) in their response behaviour compared to the first sample survey I in 2016/2017 ($N = 522$).

Health-Information-Seeking Behavior: Which Behavior Do Older Adults Have, with Whom Do They Communicate, and to What Extent Are Information Sources Used and Trusted? Descriptive results suggest that older adults in Germany receive information about healthcare primarily from their doctors and pharmacists or from TV. A comparison of the two surveys indicates a slight increase in the assessment of trustworthiness of the Internet (see Table 4). There were also marginal changes in the satisfaction with information on specific healthcare topics and questions (see Table 5). In survey II, the persons/institutions with whom older and very old persons share their healthcare information differed only marginally. Doctors/pharmacists and family/friends are still the main reference persons. Significances can be found in Table 6. There are also marginal differences between the two surveys in the level of activity when searching for information (see Table 7).

Table 4. Reliability of sources of information on healthcare

Date of survey	2016/2017	2018/2019	Significance level of the difference
TV	$N = 509$, $M = 2.92, SD = .83$	$N = 612$, $M = 2.94, SD = .87$	$\chi^2(1) = 4.94, p = .26, \varphi = .26$
Newspapers & Magazines	$N = 492$, $M = 3.30, SD = .80$	$N = 565$, $M = 3.26, SD = .86$	$\chi^2(1) = 4.94, p = .26, \varphi = .26$
Internet	$N = 449$, $M = 2.86\ SD = .82$	$N = 571$, $M = 2.97, SD = .86$	$\chi^2(1) = 4.94, p = .26, \varphi = .26$
Doctors & Pharmacies	$N = 539$, $M = 1.96, SD = .67$	$N = 638$, $M = 1.82, SD = .66$	$t(1175) = 3.559, p < .001$

(*continued*)

Table 4. (*continued*)

Date of survey	2016/2017	2018/2019	Significance level of the difference
Friends & Family	$N = 493$, $M = 2.80, SD = .81$	$N = 586$, $M = 2.70, SD = .81$	$t(1045.039) = 2.001$, $p < .046$
Other: e.g., Radio, Health Insurance, Flyer,...	$N = 47$, $M = 2.66, SD = 1.26$	$N = 41$, $M = 2.93, SD = 1.42$	$t(80.556) = -.929$, $p < .356$

Note: The answer options of the items were "very high" (= 1), "high" (= 2), "neutral" (= 3), "low" (= 4) and "very low" (= 5).

Table 5. Satisfaction with information on the following topics

Date of survey	2016/2017	2018/2019	Significance level of the difference
Medical diagnoses	$N = 540$, $M = 2.27, SD = .75$	$N = 636$, $M = 2.22, SD = .77$	$t(1153.698) = .977$, $p < .329$
Accounting of medical treatments	$N = 516$, $M = 3.05, SD = .93$	$N = 617$, $M = 3.15, SD = .94$	$t(1099.375) = -1.780$, $p < .075$
Clinical pictures/progressions	$N = 519$, $M = 2.68 SD = .75$	$N = 623$, $M = 2.63, SD = .80$	$t(1124.847) = 1.062$, $p < .289$
Experiences others make on health	$N = 510$, $M = 2.90, SD = .59$	$N = 614$, $M = 2.88, SD = .60$	$t(1093.156) = .633$, $p = .527$
(Interaction of) medicines	$N = 528$, $M = 3.15, SD = .90$	$N = 623$, $M = 3.18, SD = .98$	$t(1149) = -.536$, $p < .592$
Therapy & treatment options	$N = 530$, $M = 2.66, SD = .83$	$N = 626$, $M = 2.64, SD = .88$	$t(1141.756) = .565$, $p < .572$
Meaning of my treatment results	$N = 535$, $M = 2.37, SD = .72$	$N = 631$, $M = 2.38, SD = .80$	$t(1164) = -.110$, $p < .913$

Note: The answer options of the items were "very satisfied" (= 1), "satisfied" (= 2), "neutral" (= 3), "dissatisfied" (= 4) and "very dissatisfied" (= 5).

Table 6. Sharing information about healthcare and diseases in number of requests (multiple answers allowed)

Date of survey	2016/2017 N in sample	2018/2019 N in sample
With nobody	20	11
Doctor/pharmacist	405	481

(*continued*)

Table 6. (*continued*)

Date of survey	2016/2017 N in sample	2018/2019 N in sample
Health insurance	65	102
Family/friends	494	608
Acquaintance	139	135
Strangers	2	5
Social network	3	10
Self-help groups/forums	13	11
With someone else, e.g., colleagues, spouses, relevant forums*	*	16

Note: * = Was not collected in 2016/2017.

Table 7. Relevant characteristics (degree of activity, causal link, and regularity) of the information search

Date of survey	2016/2017	2018/2019	Significance level of the difference
I am looking for information about health/illness…			
… actively	$N = 387$, $M = 2.70, SD = 1.37$	$N = 537$, $M = 2.67, SD = 1.36$	$t(827.797) = .312, p < .755$
… rather casually	$N = 424$, $M = 2.71, SD = 1.22$	$N = 525$, $M = 2.89, SD = 1.24$	$t(913.277) = -2.245$, $p < .025$
… regularly	$N = 361$, $M = 3.30, SD = 1.39$	$N = 483$, $M = 2.63, SD = 1.35$	$t(766.090) = -1.175, p < .240$

Note: The answer possibilities of the items were "true" (= 1), "rather true" (= 2), "partly true" (= 3), "rather not true" (= 4) and "not true" (= 5).

Health Literacy: What Do Older Adults Know About Healthcare? Descriptive results on participants' health literacy suggest that older adults in Germany have little problems understanding information regarding health topics. The questions of the health literacy scale queried how participants would rank easiness by which information on different topics can be interpreted. On a scale from 1 = 'very good' to 5 = 'very bad', they primarily ranked 'credibility of the media' ($M = 3.34$, $SD = 1.49$, $N = 639$) and 'advantages and disadvantages of treatment methods' ($M = 3.04$, $SD = 1.41, N = 637$) with an average score above three. Topics they were able to understand best included 'dealing with unhealthy behaviour' ($M = 1.35$, $SD = .64$, $N = 640$) and 'preventive medical check-ups' ($M = 1.47, SD = .75, N = 641$). Table 8 shows relevant information frames for older people in comparison of the two studies considering the t-tests.

Table 8. Relevance of health information topics for older adults in Germany (21 items)

	2016/2017	2018/2019	T-Test
Symptom/illnesses information	$N = 519$, $M = 2.15, SD = .91$	$N = 633$, $M = 1.77, SD = 1.06$	$t(1147.562) = 6.571, p < .001, d = .388$
Doctor understanding	$N = 526$, $M = 2.10, SD = .76$	$N = 635$, $M = 1.93, SD = .97$	$t(1156.161) = 3.215, p = .001, d = .189$
Medical leaflets understanding	$N = 530$, $M = 2.60, SD = 1.05$	$N = 633$, $M = 2.56, SD = 1.38$	$t(1161) = .551, p = .582, d = .032$
Medical emergency	$N = 528$, $M = 2.46, SD = .88$	$N = 635$, $M = 2.32, SD = 1.25$	$t(1161) = 2.149, p = .027, d = .126$
Treatment dis-/advantages	$N = 527$, $M = 3.06, SD = .92$	$N = 637$, $M = 3.04, SD = 1.41$	$t(1162) = .204, p = .838, d = .012$
Media credibility	$N = 527$, $M = 3.25, SD = .96$	$N = 639$, $M = 3.34, SD = 1.49$	$t(1164) = 1.259, p = .208, d = .074$
Following medication intake	$N = 527$, $M = 1.93, SD = .79$	$N = 639$, $M = 1.59, SD = .76$	$t(1106.804) = 7.495, p < .001, d = .451$
Handling harming behaviour	$N = 530$, $M = 1.84, SD = .71$	$N = 640$, $M = 1.35, SD = .64$	$t(1081.938) = 12.297, p < .001, d = .748$
Psychological problems	$N = 526$, $M = 2.43, SD = .93$	$N = 633$, $M = 2.14, SD = 1.47$	$t(1157) = 3.910, p < .001, d = .230$
Vaccinations	$N = 530$, $M = 2.27, SD = .94$	$N = 638$, $M = 1.97, SD = 1.15$	$t(1165.463) = 4.861, p < .001, d = .285$
Medical check-ups	$N = 528$, $M = 2.17, SD = .70$	$N = 641$, $M = 1.47, SD = .75$	$t(1167) = 14.430, p < .001, d = .845$
Advice from family/friends	$N = 528$, $M = 2.58, SD = .86$	$N = 638$, $M = 1.81, SD = 1.07$	$t(1162.465) = 13.760, p < .001, d = .807$
Health support at work	$N = 451$, $M = 2.52, SD = .82$	$N = 638$, $M = 1.97, SD = 1.17$	$t(1086.820) = 9.087, p < .001, d = .551$
Food package information	$N = 529$, $M = 2.96, SD = 1.10$	$N = 638$, $M = 2.93, SD = 1.50$	$t(1165) = .413, p = .679, d = .024$
Assessing own lifestyle	$N = 530$, $M = 2.27, SD = .84$	$N = 640$, $M = 2.04, SD = 1.12$	$t(1157.261) = 3.926, p < .001, d = .231$
Professional help	*	$N = 641$, $M = 2.15, SD = 1.18$	*
Obtaining a second opinion	*	$N = 640$, $M = 2.54, SD = 1.38$	*
Decision concerning illnesses	*	$N = 641$, $M = 2.32, SD = 1.25$	*

(*continued*)

Table 8. (*continued*)

	2016/2017	2018/2019	T-Test
Following instructions	*	$N = 640$, $M = 1.70, SD = .81$	*
Media information on disease prevention	*	$N = 640$, $M = 2.41, SD = 1.37$	*
Mental well-being	*	$N = 638$, $M = 2.34, SD = 1.50$	*

Note: * = Was not collected in 2016/2017.

3.2 General and mHealth Applications Used by Older Adults

The second aim was to look at the potential of ICT-use by older and very old end users. Here, the use of apps and mHealth ("mobile Health") apps was put into focus. mHealth can be defined as "the system built around the mobile technology to manage healthcare information" [5]. To further deepen these results, the following research questions were examined: (1) Do older adults use (smartphone and tablet) applications and do they use mHealth applications? (2) What are the reasons for not using mHealth applications? (3) If mHealth applications are used by older adults, what type of applications do they use? (4) How do older adults find out about applications?

Use of Applications and mHealth Applications. Among older adults, the use of applications is limited. The majority uses up to ten general (smartphone and tablet) applications on smartphones or tablets. In the case of mHealth applications, the majority does not use any applications (see Figs. 1 and 2).

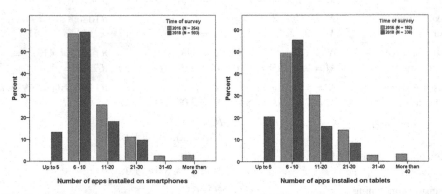

Fig. 1. Number of apps installed on smartphones and tablets according to apps in general

Although the majority uses only a small number of apps, the frequency of use remains quite high in survey II. Almost every third participant of the study uses an (smartphone and tablet) application daily. At the same time, there has been a slight increase in general

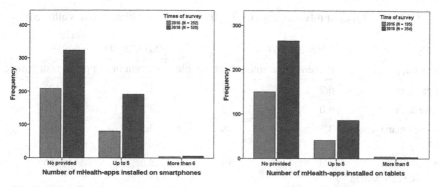

Fig. 2. Number of apps installed on smartphones and tablets according mHealth Apps

app use of smartphones. In the case of mHealth applications, the frequency of use is different. The majority of the small group of mHealth application users uses them on a weekly or monthly (see Table 9).

Table 9. Percentage of app usage requests in general and mHealth apps

Year	2016/2017 ($N = 551$)				2018/2019 ($N = 649$)			
	Apps in general		mHealth apps		Apps in general		mHealth apps	
Technological devices	Smart-phone	Tablet	Smart-phone	Tablet	Smartphone	Tablet	Smart-phone	Tablet
Daily	58.0 ($N = 166$)	42.9 ($N = 82$)	3.7 ($N = 10$)	3.8 ($N = 6$)	62.6 ($N = 326$)	32.0 ($N = 118$)	7.0 ($N = 34$)	1.6 ($N = 5$)
Every 2–3 days	19.2 ($N = 55$)	21.5 ($N = 41$)	5.6 ($N = 15$)	2.8 ($N = 5$)	10.7 ($N = 56$)	15.4 ($N = 57$)	9.8 ($N = 48$)	8.1 ($N = 26$)
Weekly	6.3 ($N = 18$)	17.8 ($N = 34$)	10.0 ($N = 27$)	8.4 ($N = 15$)	6.7 ($N = 35$)	14.6 ($N = 54$)	9.2 ($N = 45$)	6.9 ($N = 22$)
Monthly	6.3 ($N = 18$)	6.8 ($N = 13$)	7.8 ($N = 21$)	12.8 ($N = 23$)	2.7 ($N = 14$)	8.4 ($N = 31$)	12.9 ($N = 63$)	11.9 ($N = 38$)
Never	10.1 ($N = 29$)	11.0 ($N = 21$)	73.0 ($N = 197$)	72.6 ($N = 130$)	17.3 ($N = 90$)	29.5 ($N = 109$)	61.1 ($N = 299$)	71.6 ($N = 229$)
Total request N	286	191	270	179	521	369	489	320

Type of mHealth Applications Used by Older Adults. In survey II are differences in the mHealth applications of diverse apps. There is a slight increase in the use of fitness apps, first aid apps, and calorie trackers. However, this slight increase is not significant and thus reflects the results of 2016/2017 (see Table 10).

Table 10. Types of mHealth apps used by participants (multiple answers allowed)

Year	2016/2017 ($N = 551$)		2018/2019 ($N = 649$)	
Type of app	Percent of sample	N in sample	Percent of sample	N in sample
Fitness apps	6.7	37	15.7	102
Rating apps	6.0	33	7.2	47
Diabetes management apps	3.3	18	2.2	14
Apps of health insurance companies	3.3	18	8.6	56
Pulse measuring apps	3.1	17		
Calorie trackers	3.1	17	9.6	62
First aid apps	2.7	15	8.2	53
Diagnosis apps	2.5	14	3.1	20
Emergency health card	2.4	13		
Dairy apps	1.8	10	2.0	13
Medication reminder	1.6	9	1.7	11
Audiometry or visual test apps	0.9	5		
Communication apps to contact physician	0.7	4		
Apps for relaxations			4.8	31
Search for information			6.0	39
Disease management in general			4.6	30

One aim of this survey II was to examine which sources of information older adults use to retrieve information on (smartphone and tablet) applications. Results indicate that contacting family and friends is the preferred source of information (see Table 11). These results indicate no change in the second survey compared to the first. App-stores and Internet also continue to be important factors for older people when searching for healthcare information.

Reasons for not Using mHealth Applications. In this section, participants were asked why they do not use mHealth apps. The results show that a lack of trust in mHealth apps is the main reason for avoidance (see Table 12). An interesting aspect of the 2018/2019 survey II is the increase in number of people who stated not being interested in mHealth apps.

Table 11. Sources used by older adults to retrieve information about apps (multiple answers allowed)

Year	2016/2017 ($N = 551$)		2018/2019 ($N = 649$)	
Source	Percent of sample	N in sample	Percent of sample	N in sample
Family and friends	43.7	241	61.0	396
App store	21.6	119	31.0	201
Internet	20.2	111	30.8	200
Magazines or newspapers	13.4	74	12.3	80
Television	5.8	32	5.9	38
Experts	4.9	27	5.2	34

Table 12. Reasons for avoiding the use of mHealth apps

Year	2016/2017 ($N = 551$)		2018/2019 ($N = 649$)	
Reason	Percent of sample	N in sample	Percent of sample	N in sample
Lack of trust	44.1	243	53.0	344
Data privacy	18.0	99	32.7	212
Fear of misdiagnosis	10.5	58	15.6	101
Too complex to use	8.5	47	8.9	58
Lack of self-confidence	5.6	31	6.0	39
No interest[a]	1.8	10	25.1	163

Note: [a]Open-ended answers coded for analysis.

4   Discussion

Survey II of the Tech4Age project – as the 2016/2017 survey I – corresponds to the design recommendations within the framework of the human-centred development process according to DIN EN ISO 9241-210. Mertens et al. [8] discussed the relevance of similar studies in the context of development of new technical products as well as changes in attitudes towards technology and acceptance of usage. In this way, the cohort effect that inevitably occurs in longitudinal studies can be noted. Research questions can be raised in the context of the respective period in which the individual runs were carried out. This continuous "monitoring" ensures the validity and reliability of design patterns explored in longitudinal studies, especially when interactions between human and context-related factors and technology uses have been identified. In the following, a presentation of the importance of studies in the context of scientific work is given. An in-depth discussion and the limitations of the survey can be found in "Health technology use in Germany among older adults (Part II): short time changes in information and communication technology" in this congress proceedings.

Survey I (2016/2017) was integrated into various research activities. One such example is agent-based simulation of healthcare systems. Due to the demographic change, the demand for age-differentiated healthcare services increases. Promising solutions refer to modern, digital, and technology-supported forms of patient-physician interaction and promises to make treatment processes more efficient from initial contact up through therapy, prevention and rehabilitation. The success of introducing new digital solutions in healthcare services depends heavily on patients' general acceptance of ICT tools, health and computer literacy, and the resulting usage readiness, which can be challenging, especially for older target groups.

At the same time, testing processes based on pilot studies in the field of patient-centred development are extremely complex, expensive and – because of very high demands on data protection and ensuring informational self-determination – can only be carried out with systems already having a high level of technological readiness. Thus, in the incremental and iterative development of innovative digital concepts for healthcare, many decisions of the developers are rather based on gut feeling, since no relevant information is available in short term while at the same time information is difficult to empirically predict.

A promising approach to quantify the influence of new supply systems and the influence of system changes, which lies between the conflicting fields of theoretical considerations and empirical studies, is agent-based simulation. Simulations allow a detailed modelling of the interactions between patients and physicians, taking place in the healthcare system over a given period of time. Individual patient- or physician-specific characteristics and behaviours can be modelled by using defined probability distributions. Consequently, it is possible to analyse and evaluate specific questions and concrete cause-effect relationships. Especially age-differentiated disposition characteristics and behavioural patterns can be taken adequately into account.

The problem, however, often lies in the lack of representative and encompassing patient- and physician-specific data sets. Here, corresponding quantitative studies such as the Tech4Age project on potential user groups of innovative ICT tools offer an important starting point to identify empirically collected and evidence-based causal relationships to model these in corresponding simulations. Studies designed as longitudinal are particularly relevant for validity and reliability, reviewing and updating their results at regular intervals while raising awareness of new developments and changes within the target group.

Also, data from survey I were used to develop so-called personas [13, 14]. Survey I delivers quantified results on the current situation and needs of older people in the health sector while at the same time the survey refers to the level of digitalisation and general use of ICT. Personas are archetypal user groups with goals, needs, and fears [15, 16]. These archetypes have emerged in the context of development and evaluation of new software with the question of potential users [17]. The description is designed by developers on the basis of empirical data and fictional elements [18–20].

Eight data-supported personas were created in order to develop a best-practice app-roach. The personas are used in research and development to encounter problems outlined in the introduction. Short and long versions of the profiles are available to offer users as many variations as possible. The personas shall represent what older and very old German end users of digital products look like, what their needs and wishes are, and how they behave in certain situations. Personas should sensitise product developers, but also researchers. In addition, the personas' database, resulting from the longitudi-nal survey I in 2016/2017, was compared with the second survey from 2018/2019. The result indicated no significant changes towards the previous survey I since the time lag between first and second survey is too short for major social developments. Therefore, the personas are still valid.

Furthermore, results of these studies are used in interdisciplinary training of mHealth experts [21]. The increasing digitalisation of the healthcare system combined with grow-ing demands of a growing number of elderly people and steadily decreasing financial covers results in developers needing to be trained in an interdisciplinary manner. Results of the studies in 2016/2017 and in 2018/2019 represent an important cornerstone in the context of training, as they allow an up-to-date picture to be drawn of digital transfor-mation of older people by taking personas into account. Further applications could be in the fields of innovation and future research. Future research shows possible, probable, or desired future developments. The aim here is to minimise uncertainties of the informa-tion base for decision-making beyond the state of the art. Moreover, future research aims at increasing the information base for decision-makers by illustrating the consequences of decisions in politics, economies, and societies. For this purpose, methods to identify first hints on upcoming trends are necessary.

Apart from validating results by repeated surveys, the importance in future research is to identify first hints on upcoming trends from an early stage on. These hints have to be verified by additional surveys before they can be designated as serious trends. Trends limit the number of probable development paths – or in case of elaborated analyses – of scenarios in further research processes, which are a possibility to reduce the number of developments to more probable ones.

5 Conclusion

The aim of this contribution was to present the descriptive results of survey II, conducted in 2018/2019, by considering use of health-related information, levels of trust as well as general and mHealth applications used by older adults. Having an increased rate of respondents to the questionnaire of 2018/2019 compared to 2016/2017, the results of 2016/2017 are subjected to a check whereas the results of 2018/2019 receive verification, proving the overall acceptance of survey II.

In fact, looking at the extent to which accessibility of technical devices in the health-care sector has changed, it has become clear that accessibility regarding technical devices is likely to be of more importance than in 2016/2017, when considering increased own-erships of mobile devices and usages of technological devices. What cannot be said with certainty is whether the rise in both categories is attributable to the lower average age of the participants, being three years younger than in the first run – or if the expansion of digitalisation alone has led to the increase.

Speaking of mobile end-devices which show a tendency to become the focus of this much older group over time, smartphones and desktop PCs along with tablets are the most relevant usage but also for retrieving information online on healthcare topics, indicating that owning a device like these makes it easier for older adults to have access to healthcare information.

Acknowledgement. The interdisciplinary research group Human Factors Engineering and Ergonomics in Healthcare (HFE^{2}H) is part of the Institute of Industrial Engineering and Ergonomics of RWTH Aachen University. The project Tech4Age is funded by the German Federal Ministry of Education and Research (BMBF) under Grant No. 16SV7111. For more details and information, please go to www.tech4age.de.

References

1. Sørensen, K., et al.: Health literacy in Europe: comparative results of the European health literacy survey (HLS-EU). Eur. J. Pub. Health **25**(6), 1053–1058 (2015). https://doi.org/10.1093/eurpub/ckv043
2. Wilson, T.D.: On user studies and information needs. J. Doc. **37**(1), 3–15 (1981)
3. Wilson, T.D.: Models in information behaviour research. J. Doc. **55**(3), 249–270 (1999). https://doi.org/10.1108/EUM0000000007145
4. Wilson, T.D.: Activity theory and information seeking. Ann. Rev. Inf. Sci. Technol. **42**(1), 119–161 (2008). https://doi.org/10.1002/aris.2008.1440420111
5. Cameron, J.D., Ramaprasad, A., Syn, T.: An ontology of and roadmap for mHealth research. Int. J. Med. Inform. **100**, 16–25 (2017). https://doi.org/10.1016/j.ijmedinf.2017.01.007
6. Schmidt, A., Wolf-Ostermann, K.: Ambulante Versorgung von Menschen mit Demenz–ein Überblick [Outpatient Care for People With Dementia – An Overview]. In: Pfannstiel, M.A., Focke, A., Mehlich, H. (eds.) Bedarfsplanung und ganzheitliche regionale Versorgung und Zusammenarbeit. Management von Gesundheitsregionen, vol. 4, pp. 59–76. Springer Gabler, Wiesbaden (2018). https://doi.org/10.1007/978-3-658-16901-5_5
7. Pötzsch, O., Rößger, F.: Germany's Population by 2060: Results of the 13th Coordinated Population Projection, Wiesbaden (2015)
8. Mertens, A., Rasche, P., Theis, S., Bröhl, C., Wille, M.: Use of information and communication technology in healthcare context by older adults in Germany: initial results of the tech4age long-term study. i-com. **16**(2), 165–180 (2017). https://doi.org/10.1515/icom-2017-0018
9. Rasche, P., et al.: Prevalence of health app use among older adults in Germany: national survey. JMIR Mhealth Uhealth **6**(1), e26 (2018). https://doi.org/10.2196/mhealth.8619
10. Sengpiel, M., Dittberner, D.: The computer literacy scale (CLS) for older adults — development and validation. In: Herczeg, M., Kindsmüller, M.C. (eds.) Mensch und Computer 2008. 8. fachübergreifende Konferenz für interaktive Medien - Viel Mehr Interaktion. Naturwissenschaft und Technik II 6-2010, pp. 7–16. Oldenbourg Wissenschaftsverlag, München (2010)
11. Neyer, F.J., Felber, J., Gebhardt, C.: Entwicklung und Validierung einer Kurzskala zur Erfassung von Technikbereitschaft [Development and validation of a short scale for the registering of technical readiness]. Diagnostica **58**(2), 87–99 (2012). https://doi.org/10.1026/0012-1924/a000067
12. Winkler, N., Kroh, M., Spiess, M.: Entwicklung einer deutschen Kurzskala zur zweidimensionalen Messung von sozialer Erwünschtheit [Development of German Short Scale for Two-Dimensional Measurement of Social Desira-bility], 579 (2006). http://www.econstor.eu/bit stream/10419/18472/1/dp579.pdf

13. Schäfer, K., et al.: Datenbasierte Personas älterer Endbenutzer für die zielgruppenspezifische Entwicklung innovativer Informations- und Kommunikationssysteme im Gesundheitssektor [Data-Based Personas of Older End Users for the Development of Innovative Information and Communication Systems in the Health Sector for Specific Target Groups]. Zeitschrift für Arbeitswissenschaft. **73**(2), 177–192 (2019). https://doi.org/10.1007/s41449-019-00150-5

14. Schäfer, K., et al.: Survey-based personas for a target-group-specific consideration of elderly end users of information and communication systems in the German health-care sector. Int. J. Med. Inform. **132**, 103924 (2019). https://doi.org/10.1016/j.ijmedinf.2019.07.003

15. Blomquist, Å., Arvola, M.: Personas in action. In: Bertelsen, O.W. (ed.) Proceedings of the Second Nordic Conference on Human-Computer Interaction. The Second Nordic Conference, 19 October 2002–23 October 2002, Aarhus, Denmark, p. 197. ACM, New York (2002). https://doi.org/10.1145/572020.572044

16. Junior, P.T.A., Filgueiras, L.V.L.: User modeling with personas. In: Baranauskas, M.C.C. (ed.) Proceedings of the 2005 Latin American Conference on Human-Computer Interaction. The 2005 Latin American Conference, 23 October 2005–26 October 2005, Cuernavaca, Mexico, pp. 277–282. ACM, New York (2005). https://doi.org/10.1145/1111360.1111388

17. Nunes, F., Silva, P.A., Abrantes, F.: Human-computer interaction and the older adult. In: Makedon, F. (ed.) Proceedings of the 3rd International Conference on Pervasive Technologies Related to Assistive Environments. The 3rd International Conference, 23 June 2010–25 June 2010, Samos, Greece, p. 1. ACM, New York (2010). https://doi.org/10.1145/1839294.183 9353

18. Konstan, J.A., Chi, E.H., Höök, K.: Proceedings of the 2012 ACM Annual Conference on Human Factors in Computing Systems (2012)

19. Pruitt, J., Grudin, J.: Personas. In: Arnowitz, J. (ed.) Proceedings of the 2003 Conference on Designing for User Experiences. The 2003 Conference, 6 June 2003–7 June 2003, San Francisco, California, pp. 1–15. ACM, New York (2003). https://doi.org/10.1145/997078.997089

20. Coney, M.B., Steehouder, M.: Role playing on the web: guidelines for designing and evaluating personas online. Soc. Tech. Commun. **47**, 327–340 (2000)

21. Greven, A., Rasche, P., Droege, C., Mertens, A.: Digital health engineering and entrepreneurial innovation – education for the development of ICT for older adults. In: Stephanidis, C., Antona, M., Gao, Q., Zhou, J. (eds.) HCI International 2020 – Late Breaking Papers: Universal Access and Inclusive Design, vol. 12426, pp. 538–548. Springer, Cham (2020). https://doi.org/10.1007/978-3-030-60149-2_41

Occupational Health and Operations Management

Automatic Classification of Working Activities for Risk Assessment in Large-Scale Retail Distribution by Using Wearable Sensors: A Preliminary Analysis

Giuseppe Andreoni[1] , Giorgio Cassiolas[2] , Carlo Emilio Standoli[1] ,
Stefano Elio Lenzi[3] , Paolo Perego[1] , and Nicola Francesco Lopomo[2]([✉])

[1] Dipartimento di Design, Politecnico di Milano, Milan, Italy
[2] Dipartimento di Ingegneria dell'Informazione, Università degli Studi di Brescia, Brescia, Italy
nicola.lopomo@unibs.it
[3] Dipartimento di Neuroscienze, Biomedicina e Movimento, Università di Verona, Verona, Italy

Abstract. Providing reliable information on human activities and behaviors is an extremely important goal in various application areas such as healthcare, entertainment, and security. Within the working environment, a correct identification of the actual performed tasks can provide an effective support in the assessment of the risk associated to the execution of the task itself, and thus preventing the development of work-related musculoskeletal diseases. In this perspective, wearable-based Human Activity Recognition systems have been representing a prominent application. This study aimed to compare three different classification approaches appointed from supervised learning techniques, namely k-Nearest Neighbors, Support Vector Machine and Decision Tree. Motion data, related to several working activities realized in the large-scale retail distribution, were collected by using a full-body system based on 17 Inertial Measurement Units (MVN Analyze, XSens). Reliable features in both time- and frequency-domain were first extracted from raw 3D accelerations and angular rates data, and further processed by Principal Component Analysis, with 95% threshold. The classification models were validated via 10-fold cross-validation on a defined training dataset. k-Nearest Neighbors classifier, which provide the best results on the training session, was eventually tested for generalization on additional data acquired on few specific tasks. As a result, considering 5 main macro activities, k-Nearest Neighbors provided a classification accuracy of 80.1% and a computational time of 1865.5 s. To test the whole assessment process, the activities labelled by the classification model as handling of low loads at high frequency were automatically evaluated for risk exposure via OCRA Checklist method.

Keywords: Human activity classification · Wearable technology · Machine learning · Risk assessment · Work-related diseases · Large-scale retail distribution

V. G. Duffy (Ed.): HCII 2022, LNCS 13320, pp. 151–164, 2022.
https://doi.org/10.1007/978-3-031-06018-2_10

1 Introduction

During the last decade, the astounding development that microelectronics has been having in terms of computational power, performance, size, and costs, has been allowing
more and more people to easily and seamlessly interact with "smart" devices and systems
that can be even worn and used during their daily life activities [1, 2]. In parallel, the large
amount of data deriving from the use of these technologies has led to the new rebirth of
artificial intelligence through the implementation of machine learning and deep learning
algorithms, applied - for example - to the recognition of the activities carried out during
the day [3–5].

The Human Activity Recognition (HAR) mainly started with the analysis of video
sequences, and complex image analysis algorithms have been the focus of extensive
research for many years due to their great range of possible applications, even including
the identification of hand gestures for the development of "natural" user interfaces [6].
Indeed, the shift towards wearable-based HAR solutions is considered a key requirement
in many daily life applications, including health and wellness, and presents a fundamental
impact in many scientific fields such as biomechanics, ergonomics, remote monitoring,
safety, sports science, etc. [5, 7].Therefore, to ensure the expected outcomes for these
fields of interest, it is necessary to design and implement accurate and reliable solutions
able to correctly capture human motion, track the body movement and recognize each
specific task.

The most paradigmatic examples of wearable sensors used in HAR applications are
accelerometers, gyroscopes, and magnetometers, usually integrated in inertial measurement units (IMUs) or magneto-inertial measurement units (M-IMUs). Scientific literature reports different solutions which include the use of different kind of sensors usually
in an integrated fashion and textiles; therefore, not only the movements are acquired
but also physiological parameters (e.g., heart rate), global position and environmental
conditions (e.g., temperature and relative humidity) result to be detected and analyzed,
providing additional information that can be used even for ontological reasoning [8–
10].). IMUs have been representing the gold standard solution embedded in several
wearable technologies, including smartphones, and smartwatches or smartbands, and
widely exploited for the recognition of several daily activities, such as standing, walking, sitting, running, cycling, lying, etc. [11, 12] IMUs have been adopted also for proper
human motion analysis applications [13, 14], where several sensors are usually fixed on
different landmarks of the human body and – thanks to specific calibration phases – joint
angles are available for defined further assessments.

However, this approach (and the related tools) is apparently not generally applicable
to unstructured daily life to observe long-term and multi-task activities, due to the limiting setup, which could somehow annoy the subject, or because wearing such devices
can alter the comfort of the person and the naturalness of performing any gesture. On
the other hand, this approach can be used in the recognition of human activities in well-
defined contexts, such as the clinics, sports, and industry [10]. Focusing on industrial
context, the use of wearable technologies and dedicated analytical algorithms have been
demonstrated to be able to provide information for the risk assessment addressing the
activities performed by the employees, in a perspective of risk mitigation and prevention

of the development of work-related diseases [15, 16]. In this picture, wearable technologies can be used to quantitatively support the standard assessment of the risk, usually performed via technical standards [17–19]; a quantitative measurement of the performed task in terms of posture, duration, joint angles, velocities, and frequencies may provide even real-time indications on the exposure to a specific risk [16, 22] and preventing work-related diseases.

In addition to sensors, it is fundamental to focus on both the type and the quality of the data acquired and, above all, the algorithms and models that can be used for the recognition of the specific activities. From the data perspective, an activity recognition system can be broadly defined as a structured "organizer" that can be used to classify individual tasks with respect to similar characteristics. Also in wearable-based HAR, recognition can be performed by exploiting machine learning classification paradigms and many approaches are present in scientific literature covering several types of applications and input data [7, 10]; in general, two main methodologies based on machine learning techniques have been exploited for these applications: supervised and unsupervised approaches [23]. Supervised learning models included, for instance, k-Nearest Neighbors (kNN), Support Vector Machine (SVM) and Decision Tree; on the other hand, unsupervised learning models covered the use of Gaussian Mixture Models (GMM) and Hidden Markov Models (HMM). Focusing on these solutions, in general the features extracted from the raw data (i.e., transformations of accelerations and/or angular rates in time, frequency or time-frequency domains) are used as input for the classification algorithms; in case of HAR, the patterns of input data are associated with the activities under consideration (i.e., classes).

Due to the aforementioned reasons, we hypothesized that by exploiting the use of wearable IMUs is possible to recognize the activities realized by an employee during a specific working shift, and thus support the assessment of the risk exposure by means of quantitative information. The main aim of the current work was therefore to compare different classification models able to automatically identify the working activities specifically realized in the large-scale retail distribution, by exploiting motion data acquired by means of a full-body IMU-based system, and then provide useful information to automatically support the definition of the OCRA (Occupational Repetitive Action) Checklist method, used for specific risk assessment [20].

2 Materials and Methods

2.1 Subjects

Addressing the necessity to identify the working activities performed by the employees involved in large-scale retail distribution, we performed a preliminary ethnographic analysis keeping into account the anthropometric distribution (5°, 50° and 95° height percentile) and the sex (males and females) of the workers, and the active wards [21]. To cover all the possible working tasks, we specifically chose to have at least 6 people for each ward (3 height percentile for each sex) and to identify any possible shared activity among the different departments, to optimize the acquisition protocol. Several activities could not be inherently monitored due to the presence of stab-gloves or aprons reinforced in stainless steel, or water which could have led to critical issues for the sensors. Furthermore, for the aim of this preliminary analysis, we specifically selected the activities by considering the characteristics defined in the technical standard ISO 11228.

2.2 On-Field Acquisition Setup

The acquisition of the movements realized by the involved employees was performed by using a commercial full body motion capture system exploiting magneto-inertial measuring units (MVN Analyze, XSens). The system allowed to have both the raw data acquired by each single unit in terms of 3D accelerations, 3D angular rates and 3D inclinations, and – through proper modelling and calibration phase–all the 3D joint angles. Data were transmitted wirelessly between each motion tracker and the base station with a sampling frequency of 60 Hz.

The full-body protocol was based on the use of 17 wireless motion trackers fixed to the body by means of elastic Velcro band and customized clothes. Following the protocol defined by the manufacturer, the sensors were specifically placed on feet, lower legs (i.e., shanks), upper legs (i.e., thighs), pelvis (i.e., sacrum), shoulders (i.e., scapulae), sternum, head, upper arms, forearms, and hands.

Before acquiring the working task, an anatomical measurements of the users and a two-step calibration phase (static N-pose and dynamic level walking) were realized to determine sensor-to-body alignment and size of each body segment, according to the monitoring system's functioning. After the calibration, an accurate biomechanical model of the subject was available for motion tracking. An example of the on-field acquisition and provided real-time feedback is reported in Fig. 1.

Fig. 1. Example of on-field acquisition and the corresponding biomechanical model, within the user interface (MVN studio, Xsens).

The used tracking system was able to estimate position, velocity, acceleration, orientation, angular velocity and angular acceleration of each body segment implemented in the biomechanical model. By means of custom-made functions developed in a high-level development environment (Matlab 2020, Mathworks Inc.), we were then able to import all the acquired information for the following processing and analysis steps. For the defined classification approach, we specifically used only the information related to the 3D acceleration and 3D angular rate expressed in the sensor frames, whereas for the risk assessment we used joint angles estimated through the calibrated biomechanical model.

2.3 Classification

Pre-processing and Windowing. To proceed with the working task classification, the data obtained from the acquisition system were manually segmented and labelled with the identifier of the corresponding task. Segmentation was manually realized by using the same acquisition software to mark each start and stop times through visual analysis, and then to export raw data, which therefore included a specific label associated to each defined task.

As previously reported, for the classification phase, we specifically considered only 3D accelerations and 3D angular rates acquired by each sensor for a total of 102 time series (17 sensors × 3 dimensions × 2 types of data). No conditioning approach was used to filter the time-domain information.

In order to support the correct extraction of the features to use in the classification phase, we implemented a 2s fixed-length sliding Hamming window with 25% of overlapping, so as to keep into account the overall dynamics of the tasks we acquired and the eventual transitions among the different activities [23, 24].

Features. To optimize classification performance and minimize computational time and complexity, several features were defined starting from what was reported in literature [25]. A total of 17 features were considered, as reported in Table 1.

Since the extracted features could have different offsets and scale factors, we normalized them by subtracting the mean value and scaling with respect to the variance, both calculated on the whole dataset [25].

After the features selection, to reduce the dimensionality of the problem, without losing discriminative capability, we applied the principal component analysis (PCA) approach, considering a threshold level corresponding to the 95% of the variance.

Classification Models. Starting from the analysis of literature [23], and considering the available type of data and the dimensionality of our problem, we implemented three main supervised classification models, namely a weighted k-Nearest Neighbors (kNN) with an Euclidean distance metric and k = 18, a Support Vector Machine (SVM) with an automatically scaled quadratic kernel function with a box constrain level of 1 and a Decision Tree (DT) with a maximum number of split of 20 based on Gini's diversity index. These models were preliminary tested considering several types of implementations (e.g., different SVM kernels) and hyperparameters (e.g., number of k neighbors), by exploiting a dedicated toolbox (ClassificationLearner, Mathworks Inc.).

Accuracy Assessment. The accuracy of the classification models was assessed by using a training dataset via 10-fold cross-validation approach. The possibility to generalize the models was then tested by using a test dataset based on working tasks performed by the same subjects but not included in the training dataset.

Table 1. List of the extracted features in both time- and frequency domain.

ID	Feature	Domain	Definition
1	Mean Value	Time	$\mu = \dfrac{1}{N} \sum\limits_{i=1}^{N} x_i$
2	Maximum Value	Time	$max = max(x)$
3	Minimum Value	Time	$min = min(x)$
4	Range	Time	$\Delta(x) = max - min$
5	Number of zero crossing	Time	$nzc = \sum\limits_{i=1}^{N} [sgn(x_i \cdot x_{i+1})]$ $sgn(x) = \begin{cases} 1 & x \geq 0 \\ 0 & otherwise \end{cases}$
6	Standard Deviation	Time	$\sigma = \sqrt{\dfrac{\sum_{i=1}^{N}(x_i - \mu)^2}{N-1}}$
7	Variance	Time	$\sigma^2 = \dfrac{\sum_{i=1}^{N}(x_i - \mu)^2}{N-1}$
8	Mean Absolute Deviation	Time	$mad = median(|x_i - median(x)|)$
9	First Quartile	Time	Splitting off the lowest 25% of data from the highest 75%
10	Third Quartile	Time	Splitting off the highest 25% of data from the lowest 75%
11	Skewness	Time	$skew = E\left[\left(\dfrac{x-\mu}{\sigma}\right)^3\right]$
12	Kurtosis	Time	$kurt = E\left[\left(\dfrac{x-\mu}{\sigma}\right)^4\right]$
13	Spectral Energy	Frequency	$E = \sum\limits_{i=1}^{M} Y_i^2$
14	Median Frequency	Frequency	$\sum\limits_{i=1}^{mdf} Y_i = \dfrac{1}{2} \sum\limits_{i=1}^{M} Y_i$
15	Mean Frequency	Frequency	$f_c = \dfrac{\sum_{i=1}^{M} f_i Y_i}{\sum_{i=1}^{M} Y_i}$
16	Peak Magnitude	Frequency	$P_m = max(Y_i)$
17	Peak Frequency	Frequency	$P_f = freq_{|Pm}$

2.4 Automatic Risks Assessment

As highlighted in the Introduction, the analysis of postures and movement assumed by workers is critical to correctly define the level of risk to develop any kind of disorders, associated to their specific working activities. This study focused on the OCRA Checklist method, a simplify version of the more complex OCRA approach, as defined by the ISO 11228 technical standard [17–19]. To correctly understand this method, it is important to underline that the percentage of time is considered cumulatively for the movements realized by a specific joint; further, a time span is defined as "the time in which the worker maintain an incorrect posture (whenever the corresponding angle overcomes one of the thresholds, as reported in Table 2)". The percentage of time corresponding to the maintaining of an awkward posture is computed as $t_\% = t_{error}/t_{tot}$, where t_{error} is the effective time span and t_{tot} is the length of the assessment period [16].

As previously reported, thanks to the biomechanical model, we were able to extract the joint angles throughout all the temporal segments [22] here identified by using the optimal classification model.

Table 2. Angular displacement thresholds as defined by the OCRA checklist method.

Joint	Movement	Thresholds
Shoulder	Flexion/extension	$>80°$
	Pronation/supination (as dynamic movement)	$>60°$
Elbow	Flexion/extension (as dynamic movement)	$>60°$
Wrist	Palmar flexion/Dorsal extension	$>45°$
	Ulnar deviation	$>20°$
	Radial deviation	$>15°$

3 Results and Discussion

3.1 Population and Tasks

From the ethnographic analysis, six wards were identified for the realization of this study, specifically: fruits and vegetables, grocery, delicatessen, butchery, bakery, and dairy products' wards. The on-field acquisitions were performed by using the full-body protocol during 27 working days, involving almost 10 different stores [21] - characterized by different size and number of employees which affect work activities and performances. Fifty-two subjects participated voluntarily and were then enrolled in the general study. In this preliminary analysis, without losing generality, we focused our assessment on specific sessions realized by the only subjects employed in the grocery ward.

Concerning the common activities (and therefore the corresponding labelled classes) we initially identified 5 main tasks: 1) handling of high loads (label "HIGH"), 2) handling of low loads at high frequency (label "LOW"), 3) walking (label "WALK"), 4) using a cart (label "CART") and 5) standing (label "STAND"). To highlight the capability of the classification models the low loads activities were then split into more specific tasks. Further, during the analysis, we grouped tasks 3), 4) and 5) under a general macro activity label, as to balance the dataset, and to focus better on the manual handling problem.

3.2 Classification Models

The comparison between the three identified classification models (i.e., DT, SVM and kNN) highlighted that the best performance in terms of accuracy and computational time was provided by the kNN model. The results of this comparison are reported in Table 3.

Table 3. Comparison among Decision Tree (DT), Support Vector Machine (SVM) and kNN.

Classifier	Accuracy [%]	Computational time [s]
Decision Tree	76.1	254.1
Quadratic SVM	76.7	48612.0
Weighted kNN	80.1	1865.5

From the previous table is evident that SVM model required very long computational time for training (in some declination, even $> 50'000$ s); despite the overall classification performances – that were very similar to those achieved by the DT and however lower with respect to kNN -, we considered both these models not suitable for this specific application. kNN represents one of the most well-known and used nonparametric classification models in machine learning and data mining tasks. Despite its simplicity, kNN demonstrated to be one of the most effective algorithms in pattern recognition and it has been considered one of the top 10 methods in data mining [26]. As previously underlined, the type of kNN (i.e., weighted) and the value of k $(= 18)$ were defined according to literature and preliminary assessment [27].

3.3 Overall Classification Accuracy

We started the analysis of classification performances by considering each individual task and the corresponding classes; in particular - besides high loads handling, low loads handling at high frequency, walking, using a cart and standing - we introduced further detailed labels about: unboxing, loading, packaging, labelling, replenishment, arrangement of products, displacement of boxes, arrangement of boxes and other activities. The confusion matrix related to the classification of all these tasks is reported in Fig. 2.

Considering all the 14 tasks, the overall performance of the identified classifier interm of accuracy was quite low (44.3%) with a computational time of 1530.4 s. This low performance was mainly due to the great unbalance of the dataset used in this first analysis, i.e., several activities contained many samples (e.g., replenishment) whereas others presented a reduced number of samples (e.g., displacement of the boxes); indeed, the number of samples for training and assessing different activity was not evenly distributed. This problem was mainly related to the distribution of the tasks along the daily shift and a general approach on the manual labelling process; to enhance the detailed classification of all the task a proper and well-defined labelling phase is required.

As next step in the analysis, we used to group to obtain the overall 5 main labels, namely "HIGH", "LOW", "WALK", "CART", "STAND", corresponding to handling of high loads, handling of low loads at high frequency, walking, using a cart, and staying

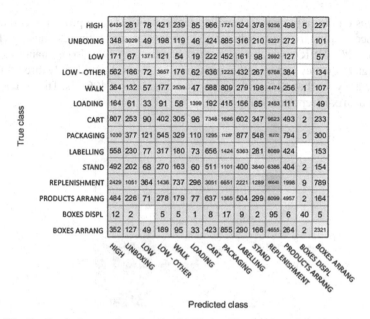

Fig. 2. Confusion matrix related to kNN classification by using 14 classes.

still, respectively. Clearly this choice allowed to correctly identify more activities, leading to an overall accuracy of 80.1% and a computational time of 1865.5s. The corresponding confusion matrix is reported in Fig. 3.

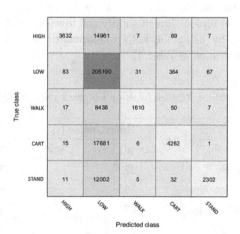

Fig. 3. Confusion matrix related to kNN classification by using three classes.

With this specific labelling, the mean Area under the Curve (AUC) value for the corresponding Receiver Operating Characteristic (ROC) was 0.73, that means that there was 73% chance that model will be able to distinguish between positive class and negative classes.

To focus on the only manual handling tasks, we tried to improve the classification performance groping the main tasks into 3 high level macro activities, namely "HIGH", "LOW" and "OTHER", which represented handling of high loads, handling of low loads at high frequency and any other activities, respectively. With only three classes the overall accuracy reached 81% with a computational time of 4068.7s. The corresponding confusion matrix is reported in Fig. 4.

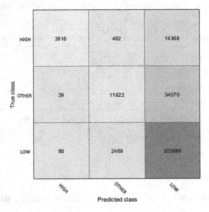

Fig. 4. Confusion matrix related to kNN classification by using three classes.

To generalize the performances obtained with the training dataset, the model was tested by using specific data extracted from four different sections recorded in different days. In particular, the identified working were: cash activity, hooks replenishment/supply, high shelves replenishment/supply and low shelves replenishment/supply. The accuracy obtained by using the kNN classification was 63.92% computed by averaging the results presented in Table 4.

Table 4. Performance obtained by using weighted kNN on the test dataset.

Task	Time duration [s]	Accuracy [%]
Cash activity	562 s	78.3
Hooks replenishment/supply	97	33.3
High shelves replenishment/supply	886	63
Low shelves replenishment/supply	671	57

Even in this real case, the performance of the classification model was limited by the presence of a reduced samples corresponding to the hooks' replenishment/supply, whereas the best performance was achieved when considering the activities performed by the cashiers.

3.4 Risk Assessment

Once classified the tasks in the correct way, it was possible to implement an automatic assessment of the risk associated to each specific activity and for the different percentile. Without losing generality, we reported here the possibility to implement the OCRA Checklist method, as previously described. The considered sequences were extracted from the testing dataset and in the table Table 5 are reported the % of time, when the joint angle is beyond the thresholds as defined in Table 2.

Table 5. Percentage of time in which the worker is in an awkward posture, as defined by OCRA checklist method.

Subject	Joint	Time [%]
S001	Left elbow	22.72
	Right elbow	22.72
	Left ehoulder	6.36
	Right ehoulder	0.00
	Left wrist	8.03
	Right wrist	53.42
S006	Left elbow	6.28
	Right elbow	12.12
	Left shoulder	1.14
	Right shoulder	0.00
	Left wrist	39.38
	Right wrist	33.28
S007	Left elbow	4.20
	Right elbow	4.96
	Left shoulder	0.00
	Right shoulder	0.61
	Left wrist	5.30
	Right wrist	12.84

4 Conclusions

In this preliminary study, the obtained performances, in terms of accuracy, seem to be lower with respect to the results reported in several related studies [9, 24, 28] However, comparing algorithms performance across different studies present in scientific literature is a quite difficult task for several reasons, including the differences in the experimental protocols, the application behind the HAR problem, the type of sensors used and their location on the body, the metrics used for the performance assessment and model validation, and the overall number of the activities to classify.

The here obtained reduced performance was basically due to the unbalance of available information within the dataset. As evident in the previous paragraphs, the activities labelled as "LOW" were the 90% of all the available dataset and among these activities there was high variability. By using the chosen classification model, the available dataset was not well dimensioned and balanced, since the disparity in terms of dimensions of classes did not allow the classifier to learn in a good way how to recognize the classes with the "smallest" size, and this was also affected by possible overtraining issues, that reflected on the lower performances obtained when the testing dataset was used.

A possible future implementation could be obtained by following an iterative application of the proposed method [28]. After the separation into main classes, the same approach could be applied to each single class to reduce the unbalance that could limit the accuracy. Therefore, the class "LOW" could be split into several subclasses, where the distribution is maintained more or less the same. To correctly perform this approach, it is necessary to acquire and segment/label precisely each single activity, in a way to create classes with well-balanced dimensionality. A further potential solution could be realized by using unsupervised learning methods, which could lead to the use of "deep learning" approaches, where there is no need of manual labelling of the dataset, and the algorithms are able to learn the inherent structure of the dataset from the input data. However, as main drawback of these approaches is the need of a huge amount of quality data.

Acknowledgement. Prof. Lopomo and all the authors would like to thank Simone Bertè for the efforts he realized in the preliminary analysis of the data, which defined the basis for this work.

References

1. John Dian, F., Vahidnia, R., Rahmati, A.: Wearables and the Internet of Things (IoT), applications, opportunities, and challenges: a survey. IEEE Access **2020**(8), 69200–69211 (2020). https://doi.org/10.1109/ACCESS.2020.2986329
2. Kumari, P., Mathew, L., Syal, P.: Increasing trend of wearables and multimodal interface for human activity monitoring: a review. Biosens. Bioelectron. **90**, 298–307 (2017). https://doi.org/10.1016/j.bios.2016.12.001
3. Rast, F.M., Labruyère, R.: Systematic review on the application of wearable inertial sensors to quantify everyday life motor activity in people with mobility impairments. J. NeuroEng. Rehabil. **17**(1), 1–19 (2020). https://doi.org/10.1186/s12984-020-00779-y
4. Baig, M.M., Afifi, S., Gholam Hosseini, H., Mirza, F.: A systematic review of wearable sensors and IoT-based monitoring applications for older adults–a focus on ageing population and independent living. J. Med. Syst. **43**(8), 1–11 (2019). https://doi.org/10.1007/s10916-019-1365-7
5. Wang, Y., Cang, S., Yu, H.: A survey on wearable sensor modality centred human activity recognition in health care. Expert Syst. Appl. **137**, 167–190 (2019). https://doi.org/10.1016/j.eswa.2019.04.057
6. Raval, R.M., Prajapati, H.B., Dabhi, V.K.: Survey and analysis of human activity recognition in surveillance videos. Intell. Decision Technol. **13**(2), 271–294 (2019). https://doi.org/10.3233/IDT-170035

7. Meng, Z., Zhang, M., Guo, C., Fan, Q., Zhang, H., Gao, N., et al.: Recent progress in sensing and computing techniques for human activity recognition and motion analysis. Electronics **9**, 1357 (2020). https://doi.org/10.3390/electronics9091357

8. Hassan, M.M., Uddin, M.Z., Mohamed, A., Almogren, A.: A robust human activity recognition system using smartphone sensors and deep learning. Futur. Gener. Comput. Syst. **81**, 307–313 (2017). https://doi.org/10.1016/j.future.2017.11.029

9. Yurtman, A., Barshan, B.: Activity recognition invariant to sensor orientation with wearable motion sensors. Sensors **17**, 1838 (2017). https://doi.org/10.3390/s17081838

10. Lara, O.D., Labrador, M.A.: A survey on human activity recognition using wearable sensors. IEEE Sens. J. **15**, 1192–1209 (2013). https://doi.org/10.1109/SURV.2012.110112.00192

11. Demrozi, F., Pravadelli, G., Bihorac, A., Rashidi, P.: Human activity recognition using inertial, physiological and environmental sensors: a comprehensive survey. IEEE Sens. J. **8**, 210816–210836 (2020). https://doi.org/10.1109/ACCESS.2020.3037715

12. Yuan, G., Wang, Z., Meng, F., Yan, Q., Xia, S.: An overview of human activity recognition based on smartphone. IEEE Sens. J. **39**, 288–306 (2019). https://doi.org/10.1108/SR-11-2017-0245

13. Lopez-Nava, I.H., Munoz-Melendez, A.: Wearable inertial sensors for human motion analysis: a review. IEEE Sens. J. **16**, 7821–7834 (2016). https://doi.org/10.1109/JSEN.2016.2609392

14. Sztyle, T., Stuckenschmidt, H., Petrich, W.: Position-aware activity recognition with wearable devices. Pervasive Mob. Comput. **38**, 281–295 (2017). https://doi.org/10.1016/j.pmcj.2017.01.008

15. Ranavolo, A., Draicchio, F., Varrecchia, T., Silvetti, A., Iavicoli, S.: Wearable monitoring devices for biomechanical risk assessment at work: current status and future challenges—a systematic review. Int. J. Environ. Res. Public Health **15**, 2001 (2018). https://doi.org/10.3390/ijerph15092001

16. Lenzi, S.E., Standoli, C.E., Andreoni, G., Perego, P., Lopomo, N.F.: Comparison among standard method, dedicated toolbox and kinematic-based approach in assessing risk of developing upper limb musculoskeletal disorders. In: Ahram, T.Z. (ed.) Advances in Human Factors in Wearable Technologies and Game Design. Advances in Intelligent Systems and Computing, vol. 795, pp. 135–145. Springer, Cham (2019). https://doi.org/10.1007/978-3-319-94619-1_13

17. ISO. 11228–1:2021. Ergonomics—Manual handling—Part 1: Lifting, lowering and carrying. International Organization for Standardization. Geneva, Switzerland (2021)

18. ISO. 11228–2:2007. Ergonomics—Manual handling—Part 2: Pushing and pulling. International Organization for Standardization. Geneva, Switzerland (2007)

19. ISO. 11228–3:2007. Ergonomics—Manual handling—Part 3: Handling of low loads at high frequency. International Organization for Standardization. Geneva, Switzerland (2007)

20. Colombini, D., Occhipinti, E.: The OCRA method (OCRA index and checklist). updates with special focus on multitask analysis. In: Karkwoski, W., Salvendy, G. (eds.) Conference Proceedings. AHFE 2008 Las Vegas, July 2008. ISBN 978–1- 60643–712–4 (2008)

21. Standoli, C.E., Lenzi, S.E., Lopomo, N.F., Perego, P., Andreoni, G.: The evaluation of existing large-scale retailers' furniture using DHM. In: Proceedings of the Congress of the International Ergonomics Association, Florence, Italy, August 2018. Springer, Cham (2018). eBook ISBN 978-3-319-96080-7, https://doi.org/10.1007/978-3-319-96080-7

22. Lenzi, S.E., Standoli, C.E., Andreoni, G., Perego, P., Lopomo, N.F.: A software toolbox to improve time-efficiency and reliability of an observational risk assessment method. In: Bagnara, S., Tartaglia, R., Albolino, S., Alexander, T., Fujita, Y. (eds.) Proceedings of the 20th Congress of the International Ergonomics Association (IEA 2018). Advances in Intelligent Systems and Computing, vol. 820, pp. 689–708. Springer, Cham (2019). https://doi.org/10.1007/978-3-319-96083-8_86

23. Attal, F., Mohammed, S., Dedabrishvili, M., Chamroukhi, F., Oukhellou, L., Amirat, Y.: Physical human activity recognition using wearable sensors. IEEE Sens. J. **15**, 31314–31338 (2015). https://doi.org/10.3390/s151229858https://doi.org/10.3390/s151229858

24. Zhang, M., Sawchuk, A.: A feature selection-based framework for human activity recognition using wearable multimodal sensors. In: Proceedings of the 6th International ICST Conference Body Area Networks (2011). https://doi.org/10.4108/icst.bodynets.2011.247018

25. Sarcevic, P., Pletl, S., Kincses, Z.: Comparison of time-and frequency-domain features for movement classification using data from wrist-worn sensors. In: 2 EEE 15th International Symposium on Intelligent Systems and Informatics (SISY) (2017). https://doi.org/10.1109/SISY.2017.8080564

26. Wu, X., Kumar, V., Ross Quinlan, J., Ghosh, J., Yang, Q., Motoda, H., et al.: Top 10 algorithms in data mining. Knowl. Inf. Syst. **14**, 1–37 (2008). https://doi.org/10.1007/s10115-007-0114-2

27. Garcia, S., Derrac, J., Cano, J.R., Herrera, F.: Prototype selection for nearest neighbor classification: taxonomy and empirical study. IEEE Trans. Pattern Anal. Mach. Intell. **34**(3), 417–435 (2012). https://doi.org/10.1109/TPAMI.2011.142

28. Garcia-Ceja, E., Brena, R.F.: An improved three-stage classifier for activity recognition. Int. J. Pattern Recognit. Artif. Intell. **32**(01), 1860003 (2018). https://doi.org/10.1142/S02180014 18600030

EMR Usage and Nurse Documentation Burden in a Medical Intensive Care Unit

Natalie Camilleri, Nate Henks, Kangwon Seo, and Jung Hyup Kim[✉]

Department of Industrial and Manufacturing Systems Engineering, University of Missouri,
Columbia, USA
{nrc6ng,nrhrhq}@mail.missouri.edu, {seoka,kijung}@missouri.edu

Abstract. Electronic medical records (EMRs) are a standard documentation system that contains vital patient health history. Although EMR system was implemented to improve nurse documentation, many healthcare workers feel the burden of EMR documentation. Due to the questions regarding the effectiveness of EMR from health care workers, it is necessary to investigate nurse EMR usage patterns and analyze timestamps in nurse documentation. In this study, a multi-factor observational study was conducted using EMR log data from five nurses working 12-h day shifts in an Intensive Care Unit (ICU). To study the deviances in timestamps of nurses, the Response Time Measurement System (RTMS) was used to examine nurse documentation time. The frequency of nurses' timestamps related to the patient medical record data was analyzed. The results showed that the frequency of the nurse EMR documentation was significantly higher at the beginning and end of the shifts than at mid-day. Also, we found that there is an association between the frequency of nurse documentation and time interval.

Keywords: Electronic medical records · Documentation burden · Nurses' workload · Real-time measurement system · Intensive care unit

1 Introduction

Electronic medical records (EMRs) are standard documentation systems containing vital patient history that allow healthcare workers to document and universally share data. The purpose of using EMR system is to store patient medical data such as diagnoses, medicines, tests, allergies, immunizations, and treatment plans. Previous studies have shown that the universal EMR implementation has increased documentation time and decreased patient care time, leading to the unintended consequences of documentation burden [1]. This electronic form of documentation significantly increases spending time on the computer rather than working directly with patients. Nurses' time pressure and burden to document medical records accurately and efficiently could decrease work performance through fatigue, self-doubt, and loss of motivation [2].

Among various concerns related to EMR documentation, the variability in nurse workload throughout 12-h shifts is an issue that has not been addressed well [3]. High workload variability throughout a day shift could result from fluctuations in the EMR documentation and lead to inaccurate medical documentation. In a medical ICU, nurses have a variety of patients with a range of severity of illnesses. Their main tasks are to monitor those patients constantly and be on their feet and ready to solve any possible problems.

Due to the overarching concern from health care workers about the effectiveness of the EMR, it is beneficial to study the efficiency of the EMR system by analyzing the frequency of timestamps of nurse documentation to determine the patterns in the Response Time Measurement System (RTMS) data. The RTMS data contains work patterns such as login and logout time, mouse and keyboard clicks, and pages accessed [4]. Our study uses an observational approach to analyze the frequency of nurse EMR documentation at the medical ICU throughout a shift. The frequencies of EMR documentation times were counted and grouped into four, three hour time intervals starting at 07:00 AM to understand their workload. Studying the patterns of documentation frequency is beneficial because it can detect the patterns in nursing workload throughout a shift to see points throughout the day when nurses have a heavy documentation burden.

Three hypotheses were tested in this study. Hypothesis #1 tested for any significant differences between the average frequencies of EMR documentation between the time intervals. Hypothesis #2 tested for significant differences of the proportion of EMR documentation time throughout a day shift between the time intervals. Hypothesis #3 tested for an association between the frequency of the nurse EMR documentation and the time intervals.

It is beneficial to study the efficiency of the EMR system by analyzing the frequencies of nurse EMR documentation throughout a shift. According to the study done by Yen, Pearl [3], they analyzed nurse stress levels and perceived workload with the EMR system by utilizing a stress monitoring device, administering workload questionnaires, and conducting a time-motion study. The study utilized a blood pulse wave tool to continuously monitor stress levels in the nurses during three, 4-h periods. One of the limitations of this study was that it did not consider other factors that might affect nurse stress levels from outside the workplace, including but not limited to family and health issues or financial problems. To reduce this gap, our study utilized the RTMS to analyze nurse documentation frequencies throughout a shift to study nurse workload. The RTMS data directly converts the information from nurse activity logs from the EMR data to timestamps of activities performed. These timestamps were counted and grouped into four to analyze nurse EMR documentation workload patterns throughout a shift.

In another similar study done by Momenipour and Pennathur [2], they investigated the balance between documentation and patient care tasks. The study used an observational approach to manually document work activity with corresponding clock times when activities were performed. A gap in this study was that the nurses could have experienced Hawthorne Effect, leading to abnormal task performance and biased data. The Hawthrone effect is the modification of a participant's behavior due to their awareness of being watched [5]. To overcome this gap, our study utilized the RTMS to automatically collect the EMR activity data and count the frequency of start times that the EMR documentation was performed. The RTMS method also omits the possibilities of human error in manually documenting work activity and clock times. In a similar matter, Guo and Kim [4] analyzed nurse experience levels and the influence of the documentation patterns in EMRs. They analyzed patterns in EMR documentation; however, instead of comparing mouse click frequency to nurse experience level, we compared the frequency of timestamps of EMR documentation to nurse workload. The nurse experience study [4] concluded that nurses' different experience levels had significant impacts on EMR documentation frequencies, and the findings suggested several EMR usability issues. On the other hand, our study analyzed EMR documentation frequencies to study nurse workload, and our results will analyze the work patterns throughout a shift that could lead to documentation burden and nurse burnout.

2 Methods

2.1 Participants

The participants for the study were ten ICU nurses working at the University of Missouri Hospital in Columbia, Missouri. Data from ten ICU nurses working at the University of Missouri was collected from 38 weekdays starting from Thursday, February 11th, 2021, to Friday, April 16th, 2021. The nurses who participated in the study worked a variety of day shifts (7:00:00 to 19:00:00) throughout the two months, ranging from one shift to eighteen shifts. From those ten nurses, we chose to analyze the data of nurses who worked five or more shifts; this approach was used to understand better the average proportion of the documentation frequencies throughout the shift for each nurse and during each three-hour time interval. Those nurses who worked less than five shifts were excluded from the analysis to lessen the likelihood of skewed average data. To keep the identification of each nurse confidential, the nurses were numbered as one to five.

2.2 Apparatus

The RTMS data was used to analyze the EMR documentation performed by each nurse. It is an efficient way to explore the input documentation time without interrupting the nurses. The use of the RTMS circumvents the risk of the Hawthorne Effect [1] that comes with in-person observational studies and prevents the risk of any human documentation error by using an automated data collection system rather than manually recording the time in which an EMR documentation occurs.

The RTMS apparatus collected many variables: start time, mouse clicks, double clicks, and task performed [6, 7]. We analyzed the "start-time" variable for this study, which collected the exact clock time in which a nurse went to the computer and documented something. Excel was used to organize the data extracted from R into a table containing five columns: nurse number, time interval, frequency, proportion, total per shift, displayed. Each CSV file determined the nurse number and the time interval corresponding to the total documentation frequency during each time interval for each CSV. The average shift for a day-shift nurse was from 7:00 AM to 7:00 PM. The 12-h shift was split into four, three-hour time intervals from [7:00 AM to 10:00 AM), [10:00 AM to 1:00 PM), [1:00 PM to 4:00 PM), and from [4:00 PM to 7:00 PM), and each time interval was numbered from one to four. After that, the statistical analysis was conducted by using the one-factor ANOVA test and Chi-Square for association tests to test the hypotheses.

2.3 Procedure

After collecting the RTMS data, the statistical software tool R was used to read each RTMS data file and extract the frequencies of each start time of documentation. The RTMS data collected from the study was organized into CSV (comma-separated values) files. Each CSV file corresponded to an individual nurse's documentation for a singular shift. Each CSV file was read into R and individually analyzed (Fig. 1).

```
1  ##This code loads a csv file for a nurse during one shift and analyzes the START_DATE variable.
2  ##It extracts the frequency of EMR documentation and organizes into 3 bins (3 hours each)
3  all_data<- read.csv(file.choose(),header = T, sep = ",")
4
5  ### Load Libraries
6  library(ggplot2)
7  library(chron)
8  ###################################################################
9  input_time <- data.frame(all_data$START_DATE)
10
11 ### reformat time to not have the date in it, just the time
12 new_time <- format(as.POSIXct(input_time$all_data.START_DATE),
13                    format= "%H:%M:%S")
14
15 #delete duplicated start time
16 unique <- new_time[!duplicated(new_time)]
17
18 # create function to convert raw time to clock time
19 timeToDecimal <- function(x){
20    sum(unlist(lapply(strsplit(x, split=":"),as.numeric)) * c(1, 1/60, 1/3600))}
21
22 #delete quotation marks around time we we can convert it
23 noquote <- noquote(unique)
24
25 #convert values into a list using timeToDecimal function
26 decimalNumber <- lapply(noquote,timeToDecimal)
27
28 #convert character string to numbers
29 not_list <- unlist(decimalNumber)
30
31 #create a chart with bins for each hour from 7:00 to 20:00
32 chart <- as.data.frame(table(cut(not_list, breaks=seq(7,20, by=1))))
33
34 #display frequencies on chart
35 ggplot(chart, aes(x= Var1, y=Freq))+ geom_col()
```

Fig. 1. R code used to extract EMR documentation frequencies

R was chosen as a statistical tool for the study to apply a systematic code to the RTMS data that analyzed total documentation frequency throughout the shift that was consistent for all CSV files. Due to the extensive size of the CSV files, it was necessary to use R to process the large CSV files that are too big for excel to analyze without crashing. The data extracted from R was recorded into an excel table that contained the nurse number, time interval number, and frequency EMR documentation. After all frequencies were recorded, each total frequency per shift and proportion (frequency of the i-th time interval/total frequency, $i = 1, 2, 3, 4$) of frequencies per shift were calculated in excel.

3 Results and Discussion

The Kolmogorov–Smirnov (KS) normality test was used to test the normality of the frequency and proportion data ($n = 264$). The p-value for the KS test was 0.064. Since the test result proved a normal distribution, the ANOVA and chi-square tests can be used to examine the data for statistical analysis.

According to the result of a one-way ANOVA, there was a statistical difference in the average EMR documentation frequencies between the time intervals during a nurse's shift (see Table 1).>).

Table 1. Frequency Comparisons between Time Intervals

	Time interval	Mean	F	p-value
Frequency	1 (7 AM – 10 AM)	91.24	7.08	<0.001
	2 (10 AM – 1 PM)	75.41		
	3 (1PM – 4 PM)	73.97		
	4 (4 PM – 7 PM)	101.82		

The p-value of this test was <0.001, which concluded that hypothesis #1 was accepted. It means that at least one of the average EMR documentation frequencies for a time interval was statistically different from the other time intervals. According to the Tukey Pairwise Comparison result, the four time intervals were split into two groups (A and B). Group A consisted of the higher mean documentation frequencies. Time intervals 7:00 AM–10:00 AM and 4:00 PM–7:00 PM were belonged to Group A, with a mean frequency of 91.24 and 101.82 documentations, respectively. Group B consisted of the lower mean frequencies, which consisted of 7:00 AM–10:00 AM, 10:00 AM–1:00 PM and 1:00 PM–4:00 PM, which had mean frequencies of 91.24, 75.41, and 73.97, respectively. Time interval one (7:00 AM–10:00 AM) was placed into both groups. This means that nurse documentation during the beginning of the shift was on average higher than documentation that occurred during the middle of the day, but not as high as the documentation at the end of the day. This average frequency pattern can be explained by nurses having to document more at the beginning and end of the shift. After the initial morning rounds of checking in on patients, the mid-day frequencies are expected to be lower because time of day usually includes lunch breaks, checking in on patients, and waiting for problems to attend to [8].

Hypothesis #2 was tested in the same way as hypothesis #1. However, the raw data extracted from R was converted into proportions of total frequency per shift for each nurse. Hypothesis #1 assumed that the studied nurses had experienced similar workdays over the two-month period that included the same number of patients, severity of illnesses, responsibility level, and level of training. For hypothesis #2, the proportions were calculated and tested to consider these potential routines and training. Hence, the nurses should spend similar proportions of documentation frequencies throughout a shift.

The frequency data for each of the nurse's shifts were converted into proportions, and the data was exported into Minitab to test hypothesis #2 using one-way ANOVA. The results from the test (see Table 2) resulted in a p-value of <0.001, which concluded that hypothesis #2 was accepted..

The results mean that at least one of the time intervals has a different proportion of documentation frequencies. Furthermore, the Tukey Pairwise Comparison grouped the mean proportions into three groups A, B, and C. Group A had the highest mean

Table 2. Proportion Comparisons between Time Intervals

	Time interval	Mean	F	p-value
Proportion	1 (7 AM – 10 AM)	0.265	17.21	<0.001
	2 (10 AM – 1 PM)	0.219		
	3 (1PM – 4 PM)	0.208		
	4 (4 PM – 7 PM)	0.307		

ratio of 0.3073, corresponding to time interval four (4:00 PM to 7:00 PM). Group B had the second highest mean proportion of 0.2651, corresponding to time interval one (7:00 AM to 10:00 AM). Group C had the lowest mean proportions of 0.21945 and 0.20814 for the time intervals two and three (10:00 AM to 1:00 PM and 1:00 to 4:00 PM), respectively. This outcome concludes that the frequencies for each time interval vary throughout the day, with the higher proportions being at the beginning and end of a shift. Even after taking the proportions into account, the average proportion of documentation frequencies was different for each time interval. Time interval four had the highest mean ratio of 30.73%, meaning that about 30% of total documentation was completed during the last three-hour stretch of nurses' day shifts. The findings of this test further support hypothesis #1 that the documentation frequencies differ throughout the day shift. It takes the analysis one step further into how each time interval varies. One possible explanation of this phenomenon is completing rounds that occur during these time periods. If the nurses get busy taking care of their patients, they must wait for the EMR documentation until the end of the shift. In a previous study done by Laitinen, Kaunonen [8], the peak time for EMR documentation was towards the end of a shift after all other work was finished. Similar to hypothesis #1, time interval one would have a higher proportion of EMR documentation frequency than the middle of the day. Another reason for the proportion of documentation frequency pattern could be the motivation change during the 12-h shift. Nurses could start the day with a high sense of motivation and be ready to tackle nursing tasks. As the day progresses and might be more chaotic, the morale decreases as stress increases, but as the end of the day shift approaches, nurses can see the light at the end of the tunnel effect and be more motivated to finish the documentation task.

The existence of an association between two variables, frequency and time interval, was tested using the chi-square test (Hypothesis #3). The chi-square test for association tested the independence between EMR documentation frequency of nurses and time interval performed. According to the result, the test concluded that the p-value for the test was 0.000, which means that hypothesis #3 was accepted, and the nurse documentation frequency and time intervals are dependent on each other. In other words, there is an association between the frequency of EMR documentation and the time intervals.

The frequency of EMR documentation was plotted to visualize this relationship (see Fig. 2). The graph plots the EMR documentation frequency for each time interval for five nurses. The legend to the right of the graph expresses the colors used for each nurse: blue for Nurse #1, red for Nurse #2, green for Nurse #3, purple for Nurse #4, and

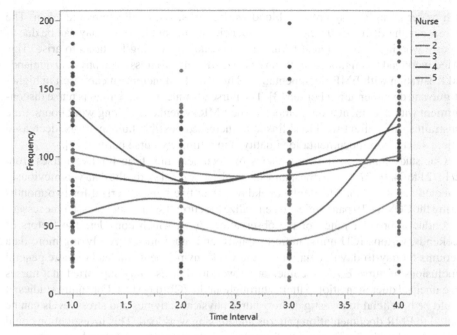

Fig. 2. Frequency vs. time interval with nurse comparison graphical analysis

orange for Nurse #5. Each nurse had a distinct total frequency pattern for their shifts, but overall, the lines followed similar patterns. For time interval one (7:00 AM–10:00 AM), the nurses' average EMR documentation frequencies varied. For example, Nurse #1's average was around 150, nurses #4 and #5 were around 100, and nurses #2 and #3 were around 50. This difference in the frequencies could be attributed to many factors, including the number of patients cared for, responsibility levels, and nurse experience. Despite these varying factors and frequency levels, the results showed a similar frequency documentation pattern throughout their day shifts. After time interval one, the nurses all showed a decline in average frequency documentation during either time intervals two or three. After the decline, the average frequency increased during time interval four. This means that the nurses experienced a higher workload at time intervals one and four compared to time intervals two and three. Even though each nurse had distinct average frequency documentation, the graph proved the results from the chi-square test that they follow similar patterns throughout a shift.

4   Conclusion

The results from hypotheses #1–#3 concluded that the nurse frequency of EMR documentation varies throughout a shift. It was particularly higher at the beginning and end of a shift. This variance in frequencies leads to the conclusion that nurse EMR documentation workload is higher during these times due to the completion of morning and evening rounds and documenting nursing activities completed during these rounds, such as recording any symptoms, blood work results, and medications are taken. The decrease in the EMR documentation frequencies in the middle of the day can be due to directly working with patients, taking lunch breaks, or waiting for tasks to arise. This varied workload throughout a shift can cause EMR-related stress from physical demands and frustration with EMR documentation. This workload increment can result in higher fatigue and documentation burden [3]. The nurse documentation burden is nurse discontentment with documentation methods in the EMR system due to long work hours, time constraints, and patient workload linked to increased possible human errors, decreased patient safety, poor documentation quality, and ultimately nurse burnout [9].

Our study analyzed the frequencies of documentation time for five nurses from 02/11/21 to 04/16/21. Due to the nature of the observational study, the data was previously collected and was limited to only weekdays when five nurses worked for two months during the COVID-19 pandemic. To generalize the current study outcomes, it is necessary to conduct a broader range of the observation study, which considers the factors of weekends, various ICU units, more hospitals, and more nurses. Analyzing more data accounts for day-to-day fluctuations of the work environment can lead to more general conclusions of nurse EMR documentation workload. This study supported that nurses have unequal documentation patterns throughout the ICU day shift. For future studies, it would be beneficial to investigate how nurse physical activities and stress levels can be related to EMR documentation patterns and nursing workload. This investigation could be combined with our findings to formulate whether nurses, in general, are less busy during certain times of their shifts, or if the decrease in EMR documentation could be from an increase in physical activities during that part of a shift.

Another limitation of the current study is that we only used the frequencies gathered from the RTMS system, which only records EMR documentation and not direct patient care. Patients are admitted and discharged, the number of patients fluctuates, and the number of healthcare workers varies along with the nurse experience. Due to the nature of the observational study, these factors were not considered in this study, and the only data analyzed was the frequency of timestamps for EMR documentation. Those factors can attribute to the variation in EMR documentation frequency. Further analysis should include collecting the data about these factors and analyzing their effects on documentation frequencies and nurse workload. Utilizing more factors such as the number of staff and patients can be combined with our findings to understand better whether the EMR documentation patterns are related to another factor such as the number of patients and staff available.

The current study analyzed the ICU nurse's EMR documentation patterns using RTMS data. Although there are several limitations in the data collection, the results concluded that the nurse workload related to EMR documentation varies throughout a shift because the frequency is particularly higher at the beginning and end of a day shift. The patterns of nurse workload found in this study can be used to analyze the nurse workload in a medical ICU.

References

1. Textbooks, C.o. and Publications: Association of schools and colleges of optometry*: june, 1954, annual reports of member institutions. Optom. Vis. Sci. **32**(3), 142–158 (1955)

2. Momenipour, A., Pennathur, P.R.: Balancing documentation and direct patient care activities: a study of a mature electronic health record system. Int. J. Ind. Ergon. **72**, 338–346 (2019)
3. Yen, P.-Y., et al.: Nurses' stress associated with nursing activities and electronic health records: data triangulation from continuous stress monitoring, perceived workload, and a time motion study. In: AMIA Annual Symposium Proceedings. American Medical Informatics Association (2019)
4. Guo, W., et al.: How nurse experience influences the patterns of electronic medical record documentation in an intensive care unit. In: Proceedings of the Human Factors and Ergonomics Society Annual Meeting. SAGE Publications Sage CA: Los Angeles, CA (2019)
5. Allen, R.L., Davis, A.S.: Hawthorne effect. In: Goldstein, S., Naglieri, J.A. (eds.) Encyclopedia of Child Behavior and Development, pp. 731–732. Springer, Boston, MA (2011). https://doi.org/10.1007/978-0-387-79061-9_1324
6. Kasaie, A., Kim, J.H., Guo, W., Nazareth, R., Shotton, T., Despins, L.: Different patterns of medication administration between inside and outside the patient room using electronic medical record log data. In: Duffy, V.G. (ed.) Digital Human Modeling and Applications in Health, Safety, Ergonomics and Risk Management. AI, Product and Service. Lecture Notes in Computer Science, vol. 12778, pp. 86–95. Springer, Cham (2021). https://doi.org/10.1007/978-3-030-77820-0_7
7. Kasaie, A., Kim, J.H., Guo, W., Nazareth, R., Shotton, T., Despins, L.: Comparing update assessment results in EMRs between inside and outside the patient room in an intensive care unit. In: Black, N.L., Patrick Neumann, W., Noy, I. (eds.) Proceedings of the 21st Congress of the International Ergonomics Association (IEA 2021). Lecture Notes in Networks and Systems, vol. 222, pp. 355–362. Springer, Cham (2021). https://doi.org/10.1007/978-3-030-74611-7_49
8. Laitinen, H., Kaunonen, M., Åstedt-Kurki, P.: The impact of using electronic patient records on practices of reading and writing. Health Inform. J. **20**(4), 235–249 (2014)
9. Androus, A.B.: What are some pros and cons of using electronic charting (EMR)?. https://www.registerednursing.org/articles/pros-cons-using-electronic-charting/ (2021). Accessed 28 Dec 2021

Simulation Model to Understand Nurses' Fatigue Level in an Intensive Care Unit

Vitor de Oliveira Vargas[1], Jung Hyup Kim[1(✉)], Laurel Despins[2], and Alireza Kasaie[1]

[1] Industrial and Manufacturing Systems Engineering Department, University of Missouri,
Columbia, MO, USA
{Vdvx55,skdx2}@umsystem.edu, kijung@missouri.edu
[2] Sinclair School of Nursing, University of Missouri, Columbia, MO, USA
despinsl@health.missouri.edu

Abstract. Although nursing is physically and mentally strenuous, only a few studies have been done to find the impacts of the fatigue level and nursing workflow corresponding to major healthcare activities in an intensive care unit (ICU). To address this need, the current study aims to understand the relationships among the key nursing activities that impact their fatigue levels in ICU. Nurses' time-study and real-time location data have been used to develop a simulation model in two different periods: February to March 2020 and July 2020. Two Hierarchical Task Analysis charts were developed from the collected data, one for each period, and used as the foundation for the fatigue-recovery simulation model. Different scenarios of all nursing activities' frequencies (number of conducted tasks during a shift) and task sequences (number of times tasks are conducted continuously prior to a break) were simulated in order to understand their impact on nurses' predicted average fatigue level reached in a shift. According to the results, the performing procedure, patient care, and peer support activities stand out as the most crucial drivers for fatigue during a nurse shift in an ICU.

Keywords: Fatigue-recovery simulation model · Intensive care unit · Hierarchical task analysis

1 Introduction

Within typical health organizations, nurses are the largest workforce and play a vital role in the quality of care and health promotion [1]. Generally, the nursing workload is determined by the time spent on patient care, nursing activities, and the skills needed to care for the patient. Nursing is physically and mentally strenuous, and high fatigue level is expected during the shift [2]. Fatigue and performance decrements are safety hazards for both patients and nurses in an intensive care unit (ICU). However, not many studies have been conducted on the connection between fatigue and nursing activities. Hence, this study is focused on the ICU nurses' workflow, which is analyzed based on three main characteristics: sequence of tasks under the same task group, frequency of the tasks, and tasks duration. The ICU is an environment that provides care for patients with severe clinical conditions [1]. ICU nurses are exposed to extremely high workloads, both physically and mentally.

This study is based on the ICU nurses' workflow using the Near Field Electro-magnetic Ranging (NFER) System and time study manual observation data collected during two different periods. The first period refers to February and March 2020, and the second one refers to July 2020. The tasks observed during the data collection were based on the task descriptions in a previous study [3]. NFER System is an indoor global positioning system. There are several applications to local positioning systems, partic-ularly in healthcare. They are used to find assets, caregivers, and patients, implying less time needed to look for people and medical equipment, reduce inventory and labor, and increase patient satisfaction [4].

The motivation for this work is to advance our understanding of the impact of the key task groups of nursing activities and sequence of tasks on nurses' average fatigue level during a shift. For that reason, this study aims to analyze that impact by simulated experi-ments varying the frequencies and sequences of nursing tasks in a screening experiment. Then, the main goal is to find the frequency and sequence task configurations that turn out high levels of fatigue risk. In this study, the instantaneous fatigue level is measured as a function of the task duration and its fatigue index, which in its turn, depends upon how mental, physical, and effort (focus) demanding the task is. In this study, the fatigue index determines how much time a worker is completely exhausted if s/he conducts the task without interruption. During the working shift, nurses switch between periods of fatigue accumulation and a few recovery periods, such as lunchtime. The fatigue level is negatively correlated to the task recovery index during a recovery period.

Two HTA (Hierarchical Task Analysis) charts were developed to develop simulation models using the Micro Saint Sharp software. With the models, the main simulation outcomes were compared with the collected data, and since there was statistical evidence that the simulations represented the observed data, simulate fatigue in both. After that, the simulation models were run 1,000 times for screening experiments. Finally, the contribution of each key factor over fatigue level was investigated.

2 Literature Review

Fatigue can take many forms such as mental fatigue, lack of alertness, specific muscular fatigue, or general body fatigue [5]. Moreover, human factors modeling is concerned with muscular fatigue accumulation and recovery [6]. Different aspects of fatigue can be included in human reliability analysis to identify potential risks, such as mental demand, physical demand, period performing a task, performance, and effort.

Studies showed the association among fatigue, work schedules, and perceived work performance among nurses, investigating the work-related fatigue by the Occupational Fatigue Exhaustion Recovery (OFER 15) scale [2]. Despite some similarities with the present study, as both investigate the same work/fatigue relationship, the outcomes of these other studies do not provide any forecast of fatigue during a work shift. That is why the assessment of the impacts on nurses' fatigue level and workflow makes this work so innovative.

Studies correlate human error and the interactions learning-forgetting and fatigue-recovery analytically, using the mathematical modeling called the learning–forgetting–fatigue–recovery model, but that work is focused only on the interactions fatigue-recovery [7, 8]. The current study does not aim to find or predict any worker error rate, but as mentioned before, to assess the impacts on nurses' fatigue level and work-flow, since fatigue is a safety hazard that has implications for both nurses and patients [2]. Other studies have applied the same mathematical model to simulate fatigue in a maintenance routine [9].

To calculate the accumulated fatigue, three levels of fatigue (or recovery) index are assumed, which determines how fast a worker gets exhausted (or recovers) under a work routine (or break): Slow, medium, and fast fatigue accumulation index levels [7]. The slow index assumes that the worker is completely exhausted after a 12-h working shift. Medium and fast indexes assume 8-h and 4-h working shifts, respectively. The recovery index has the same assumptions, that is, for the slow index, the worker will be completely recovered after a 12-h break, and so on. Since a normal ICU nurse shift lasts about 12 h, it is plausible to adopt the slow fatigue/recovery index.

2.1 National Aeronautics and Space Administration Task Load Index (NASA-TLX)

NASA-TLX is a subjective workload assessment tool that allows users to perform subjective workload assessments on a worker [10]. It derives an overall workload score based on a weighted average of ratings on six subscales, mental demand, physical demand, temporal demand, performance, effort, and frustration. In this study, a similar assessment tool was developed to define if an activity demands, is neutral to, or is invigorating in terms of mental demand, physical demand, and effort, qualitative analyzes instead of the quantitative NASA-TLX assessment.

3 Methodology

3.1 Data Collection

The data used in this study were collected using the same architecture applied in a previous study [3]. The NFER system was used to record the real-time location of nurses in an ICU, while the observers recorded the start time and end time of each task done by ICU. NFER technology is emerging as a preferred real-time locating system (RTLS) solution for operation in complicated indoor propagation environments, such as ICU [11]. NFER systems yield an accurate location within 1 m about 83% of the time, with the potential for 30 cm, which is completely acceptable for this study [12]. The NFER system architecture consists of tracking servers covering the whole ICU area, the tracking software installed in a laptop, and sensors that recognize nurses' location by tags they carry during their shifts. The servers receive and process the data to calculate a position of a tag.

During the data collection, the observers followed and monitored nurses' activities, recorded the start time and end time of each task done by them, and made notes for any special events during the observation. The observers organized the activities using the same codes used in a previous study [3].

3.2 Hierarchical Task Analysis

There are three principles governing the theory of Hierarchical Task Analysis (HTA) [13]. The first principle states that HTA is meant to describe a system in terms of its goals. The second principle is that HTA allows a system to be broken down in to sub-operations in a hierarchical manner. The last principle refers to an existing relationship among goals and sub-goals, and the rules to achieve sub-goals and the final objective. Based on that description, the development of the HTA chart allowed to build the simulation models as closely as possible to the reality.

The data set of the two periods was organized in two HTA charts, representing the data from February, March 2020, and July 2020 periods. The HTA charts aim to represent the nurses' workflow as a function of two main characteristics. The first one is the task frequencies, which are the number of times a task is repeated during a shift. The HTA charts order the tasks as a function of the greatest frequencies within each group of activities. The second feature refers to the task sequences, and the HTA charts reproduce those by the accomplishment plans for each group or subgroups of tasks.

The HTA charts organize both period workflows in the same seven main activity categories: Handoff, In-room activities, Out-of-room activities, Peer support, Patient clinical processes conversations, Teaching residents/students, and Non-nursing activities. However, the activities within the main tasks are placed in a different order for each period as a function of their frequencies, from the highest to the lowest one.

Handoff activity happens when the off-going nurses provide the oncoming nurse with a detailed review of the important issues about the patient's health condition. In-room activities contain all tasks performed inside the patient room and the tasks that support those kinds of activities. Out-of-room activities, as in-room activities, are related to patient care, but they are performed out of the patient rooms. Peer support activities, like the in-room activities, are conducted in the patient rooms, but this time the ICU nurse works as a peer supporter. Patient clinical processes conversations are related to patient care, but the patients are not part of those activities. As the data was collected at the University of Missouri Hospital, teaching residents/students are part of nurses' duties. Finally, non-nursing activities refer to all activities unrelated to patient care.

3.3 Simulation Model

The developed HTA charts are the foundation for developing two discrete event simulation models, one for each period, using the Micro Saint Sharp software. Discrete event simulation has been a standard technique in system analysis for more than 50 years [14]. Micro Saint Sharp program has been used in the health care industry, human factors, and ergonomics. While the simulation models were running, every time a task was accomplished, it calculated the nurse fatigue level and its contribution to the average fatigue level. Figure 1 shows an example of fatigue level outcome based on the Fatigue and Recovery effects. It also shows the nurse's average fatigue level for that shift.

3.4 Design of Experiment

The model-dependent variable is nurses' average fatigue level. This study aims to analyze its pattern by simulated experiments that randomly vary all nursing task frequencies

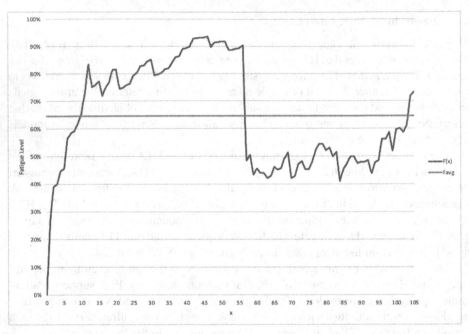

Fig. 1. Fatigue and Recovery effects during a shift.

and sequences, the independent variables, in a screening experiment. Besides the frequency variables, this study uses two independent sequence variables: the number of task sequences before lunch (*seq₀*) and after lunch (*seq₁*). A task sequence lasts while a nurse is conducting any activity related to the patient care, be it inside or outside the patient room, is supporting a peer, or is talking with someone else about a patient clinical condition. The task sequence finishes when the nurse initiates any non-value added activity. It is essential to clarify that if a nurse conducts 100 nursing activities during 5 task sequences in a shift, it averages 20 tasks/sequence. On the other hand, for the same 100 activities, but using 10 task sequences, it turns out 10 tasks/sequence. For a 12-h shift, the greater the number of task sequences, the greater the number of breaks between them.

For the experiment's accuracy, several adjustments were made. The three tasks (i.e., performing procedure, patient care, and closed curtain) were combined in one new variable, called *pc*. Also, the tasks within the category peer support were combined in the variable, called *ps*. Finally, tasks that might happen in- or out-of-room were counted together, such as EMR charting that turns out *emr*, using ASCOM phone that turns out *ascom*, talking with a physician that turns out *twp*, and talking with patient's family that turns out *twf*.

Each simulation model runs 1,000 times, and the simulated data were analyzed using JMP software, which turns out the response prediction expression (see Eq. 1). All independent variables were standardized using the transformation in Eq. 2. That transformation makes all independent variables have mean $= 0$ and standard deviation $= 1$, and the benefits of that are: $\hat{\beta}_0$ represents the average response and the estimated coefficients represent their variables' impact over the response, that is, the greater the coefficient, the larger the effect on the response.

$$\widehat{F}_{avg} = \widehat{\beta}_0 + \sum_{i=1}^{n} \widehat{\beta}_i z_i + \sum \sum_{i<j} \widehat{\beta}_{ij} z_i z_j, \begin{cases} i = 1, 2, \ldots, n. \\ j = 1, 2, \ldots, n. \end{cases} \quad (1)$$

where:

$\widehat{F}_{avg}$ = estimated average fatigue level during a shift.
$\widehat{\beta}_0$ = intercept (average response).
$\widehat{\beta}_i$ = estimated coefficients for the main effects.
$\widehat{\beta}_{ij}$ = estimated coefficient for the main effect interactions.
z_i = standardized independent variables.
n = number of independent variables.

$$z_{i,r} = \frac{x_{i,r} - \overline{x}_i}{S_i} \quad (2)$$

where:

$z_{i,r}$ = standardized variable z_i at run r.
$x_{i,r}$ = variable x_i at run r.
$\overline{x}_i$ = mean for variable x_i.
S_i = standard deviation for variable x_i.

4 Results

Average Fatigue Level. Two experiments, simulating the average fatigue level reached during a shift, were conducted with 1,000 runs for each period. This number of runs is significant enough to use the significance level of 0.01. It does not increase the probability of mistakenly concluding that both periods present the same average fatigue level pattern when they do not. Table 1 shows that the average fatigue level is different between the periods of interest ($\alpha = 0.01$), with the average fatigue level for the Feb, Mar-20 shifts being higher than the Jul-20 shifts.

Table 1. Comparison between simulated average fatigue level for Feb, Mar-20 and Jul-20 models.

Period	Average fatigue level	SD	Statistic	p
Feb, Mar-20	0.636	0.070	2.758	0.006
Jul-20	0.627	0.069		

Average Fatigue Level Screening. Although the models are different in their average fatigue level, they have some similarities. They have in common that seq_0, seq_1, pc, and ps variables are significant in both periods, outstanding as the most important drivers of fatigue for nurses.

Feb, Mar-20 Model

Equation 3 is the predicted average fatigue level as a function of the most significant independent variables ($p = 0.01$).

$$\widehat{F}_{avg} = 0.636 - 0.040z_{seq_1} - 0.039z_{seq_0} + 0.010z_{pc} + 0.009z_{emr} + 0.008z_{ps}$$
$$+ 0.005z_{twf} + 0.004z_{pc1} \tag{3}$$

Table 2 presents the most significant independent variables for the significance level of 0.01, in order of significance.

Table 2. Standardized parameter estimates (Feb, Mar-20 model).

Variable	Confidence interval	P
seq_1	$[-0.041, -0.038]$	<0.001
seq_0	$[-0.041, -0.038]$	<0.001
pc	$[0.009, 0.012]$	<0.001
emr	$[0.007, 0.010]$	<0.001
ps	$[0.007, 0.009]$	<0.001
twf	$[0.003, 0.006]$	0.0008
pc_1	$[0.003, 0.006]$	0.0024

Also, Eq. 3 tells that, for the variable seq_1, an increment of 1 standard deviation decreases the average fatigue level in 0.04, or it may be as great as 0.041 or as low as 0.038 (Table 2). For the variable seq_0, an increment of 1 standard deviation decreases the average fatigue level in 0.039, or it may be as great as 0.041 or as low as 0.038. For the variable pc, an increment of 1 standard deviation increases the average fatigue level in 0.01, or it may be as low as 0.009 or as great as 0.012. For the variable emr, an increment of 1 standard deviation increases the average fatigue level in 0.009, or it may be as low as 0.007 or as great as 0.010. For the variable ps, an increment of 1 standard deviation increases the average fatigue level in 0.008, or it may be as low as 0.007 or as great as 0.009. For the variable twf, an increment of 1 standard deviation increases the average fatigue level in 0.005, or it may be as low as 0.003 or as great as 0.006. For the variable pc_1, an increment of 1 standard deviation increases the average fatigue level in 0.004, or it may be as low as 0.003 or as great as 0.006.

Jul-20 Model

Equation 4 is the predicted average fatigue level as function of the most significant independent variables ($p = 0.01$).

$$\widehat{F}_{avg} = 0.627 - 0.036z_{seq_1} - 0.033z_{seq_0} + 0.018z_{pc} + 0.012z_{ps} + 0.006z_{pc12} \tag{4}$$

Table 3 presents the most significant independent variables for the significance level of 0.01, in order of significance.

Table 3. Standardized parameter estimates (Jul-20 model).

Variable	Confidence interval	P
seq_1	[−0.037, −0.034]	<0.001
seq_0	[−0.035, −0.031]	<0.001
pc	[0.016, 0.019]	<0.001
ps	[0.010, 0.013]	<0.001
pc_{12}	[0.005, 0.008]	<0.001

Also, Eq. 4 tells that, for the variable seq_1, an increment of 1 standard deviation decreases the average fatigue level in 0.036, or it may be as great as 0.037 or as low as 0.034. For the variable seq_0, an increment of 1 standard deviation decreases the average fatigue level in 0.033, or it may be as great as 0.035 or as low as 0.031. For the variable pc, an increment of 1 standard deviation increases the average fatigue level in 0.018, or it may be as low as 0.016 or as great as 0.019. For the variable ps, an increment of 1 standard deviation increases the average fatigue level in 0.012, or it may be as low as 0.01 or as great as 0.013. For the variable pc_{12}, an increment of 1 standard deviation increases the average fatigue level in 0.006, or it may be as low as 0.005 or as great as 0.008.

The variable pc is a significant fatigue driver in both periods and the differences presented in the dataset are not. The variable ps is other type of tasks that are important fatigue drivers in both periods and do not present significant differences between. The exception here is the number of patient transportation activities (pc_{12}) that do not present significant differences between periods, but it is only a significant fatigue driver for July 2020, which requires further investigation.

On the other hand, the variable emr is relevant only for the Feb, Mar-20 model, and when the periods' patterns are compared to each other, it is possible to identify that it decreased 16.5% in average during July 2020. Moreover, it is possible to identify the same pattern in the variable twf, that decreased 74.3% in average, and the variable pc_1, that decreased 72.2% in average, during July 2020.

Although the number of patient transportation activities does not present significant differences between periods, during the July 2020, that type of activity was, on average, more than 3 times longer than during February to March 2020.

5   Discussion

The main contribution of this study is that we identified three main factors influencing nurses' fatigue in an ICU shift: 1) the number of tasks conducted in a sequence without a break (number of task sequences), 2) the number of patient care or procedures, and 3) peer support activities performed during the shift. Besides knowing the key factors responsible for nurse's fatigue levels during an ICU shift in each period, it is also important to understand why some of them are present in both periods or in only one and how they differ in impact magnitude in both periods, recalling that July 2020 was in the middle of the COVID-19 pandemic and when new resident physicians began working in the hospital (an annual event in hospitals in the United States).

The total number of activities conducted during a shift was higher from February to March 2020. Since the shifts in both periods have the same average duration of 12 h, that suggests that nurses might spend longer time in non-valuable activities during July 2020, which explains why the average fatigue level of the data from February to March 2020 was slightly higher than July 2020 (see Table 1).

Recalling that the ICU in this study is a non-COVID-19 unit, and other studies have shown that non-COVID units became less busy during the pandemic in some health care units around the world, e.g., in a hospital in Demark, admissions for all non-COVID-19 disease groups decreased during compared with the pre-pandemic period [15]. Moreover, studies have found that non-COVID medical emergencies nearly halved during the British lockdown [16]. Also added, social distancing may have heralded the significant reductions in non-COVID and non-pneumonic infections in 2020 compared with 2017. Other studies also reinforce that non-COVID-19 ICUs have been less busy during the pandemic, insofar as changes in working patterns reduce risks associated with both long working hours and shift working [17]. It is worthwhile to mention that this concentrated effort on COVID-19 units could have entailed an increment of out-of-hospital mortality due to non-COVID diseases, particularly during the lockdown weeks [18].

The number of times tasks are conducted continuously without a break (number of task sequences), both before and after lunch, are the most significant factors to nurses' fatigue during a shift in an ICU for both periods. It is worthwhile mentioning that for a 12-h shift, the larger the number of task sequences, the shorter the sequences and the more often breaks occurred between them. For example, if during a shift, a nurse conducts 100 tasks using 5 task sequences, it turns out in average 20 tasks/sequence. On the other hand, for the same 100 tasks, but using 10 task sequences, it turns out 10 tasks/sequence. There was a negative correlation between the number of task sequences and the nurse's average fatigue level. This study also shows that the total number of activities during a period magnifies the effect of the number of task sequences. While during the first period (February to March 2020), when the nurses were busier, Eq. 3 shows that, for the variable seq_1, an increment of 1 standard deviation over the mean decreases the average fatigue level in 0.04, and for the variable seq_0, an increment of 1 standard deviation over the mean decreases the average fatigue level in 0.039, during the second period (July 2020), when nurses were less busy, Eq. 4 shows that, for the variable seq_1, an increment of 1 standard deviation over the mean decreases the average fatigue level in 0.036, and for the variable seq_0, an increment of 1 standard deviation over the mean decreases the average fatigue level in 0.033. The sequence length may explain this effect, given that during the first period (February to March 2020), in average nurse used to perform a total of 154.457 tasks in 19.327 task sequences (before and after lunch together). During the second period (July 2020), a total of 139.8 tasks in 21.106 task sequences (before and after lunch together), it turns out an average of 7.99 tasks/sequence during the first period (February to March 2020) and of 6.62 tasks/sequence during the second period.

The variables related to tasks' frequencies are positively correlated to nurses' fatigue levels, and in periods when nurses were less busy, as during the second period (July 2020), an increase in the number of tasks impacts more the nurses' fatigue than during periods when the nurses were busier, as in the first period (February to March 2020). For example, the variables pc and ps are significant for both periods and have coefficient estimates of 0.01 (Eq. 3) and 0.018 (Eq. 4) for Feb, Mar-20 and Jul-20 models, respectively. Moreover, it makes sense that those variables are significant in both models, since those activities do not present significant differences between periods.

However, some variables are significant in only one model. For instance, the variable emr is significant only for the Feb, Mar-20 model. So, in a further investigation, it is possible to note that during the Feb, Mar-20 period, nurses conducted more EMR charting activities than during the second period (July 2020). Similarly, the variable twf, the number of times the nurse talks to a patient's family, is also greater during the first period (February to March 2020) compared to the second one (July 2020). And lastly, the variable pc_1, the number of initial assessments, is also significant only for the first period (February to March 2020), when there was much more of this type of task than in the second one (July 2020). This pattern suggests that during the second period (July 2020), those variables' frequency ranges are not enough to impact the nurses' average fatigue level. Moreover, that observed difference should be strongly correlated to the need to avoid unnecessary contact with patients during the COVID-19 pandemic, that is, avoiding unnecessary contact with patients to prevent any contaminations, as described by precautionary measures that were disseminated during the pandemic [19]. Besides, during the pandemic, the nurses talked with the patient's family much less than before. This data suggests that during the pandemic, the access of patients' families to the hospital decreased considerably because of organizational visiting policy changes.

The only observed exception was that the variable pc_{12}, the number of times the nurse transported or prepared a patient to be transported, does not present significant differences in terms of frequency between periods, but it is only significant for the Jul-20 model. In a further investigation, it is possible to verify that during Jul-20, the time associated with the variable pc_{12} was much longer than during the first period (February to March 2020). This difference might not be related to whether the data is from the first period (February to March 2020) or second one (July 2020), but rather to the patients' clinical conditions in those specific periods, that is, the duration that a healthcare team takes to transport a patient might not be related to the period of the year the patient is in the ICU, but rather to the patient's clinical condition.

As previously mentioned, the number of sequences conducted in a shift is the most significant factor that leads to fatigue during a nurse ICU shift. Besides the number of sequences, both models have the variables pc and ps as fatigue drivers.

As the limitations of this study, the dataset does not present the ratio number of nurses/number of patients during the shifts, and these ratios might be strongly correlated to those variables. Therefore, it is recommended to include the ratios as an independent variable in the model. Another limitation in this study is regarding the fatigue and recovery indexes. In our current simulation models, we assumed three levels for the indexes (i.e., low, medium, and high) depending on the nature of the activity. Hence, it is recommended to capture a more precise fatigue and recovery index to improve our simulation results.

References

1. Moghadam, K.N., et al.: Nursing workload in intensive care units and the influence of patient and nurse characteristics. Wiley. British Association of Critical Care Nurses (2020)
2. Sagherian, K., Clinton, M.E., Huijer, H.A., Geiger-Brown, J.: Fatigue, work schedules, and perceived performance in bedside care nurses. Workplace Health Saf. **65**(7), 304–312 (2017)
3. Song, X., Kim, J.H.: A time-motion study in an intensive care unit using the near field electromagnetic ranging system. In: Industrial and Systems Engineering Conference (2017)
4. Kolodziej, K.W., Hjelm, J.: Local Positioning Systems: LBS Applications and Services, p. 95. CRC/Taylor & Francis, Boca Raton (2006)
5. Åhsberg, E.: Perceived fatigue related to work. Ph.D. diss, University of Stockholm, Sweden (1998)
6. Dode, P., Greig, M., Zolfaghari, S., Neumann, W.P.: Integrating human factors into discrete event simulation: a proactive approach to simultaneously design for system performance and employees' well being. Int. J. Prod. Res. **54**(10), 3105–3117 (2016). Department of Mechanical and Industrial Engineering, Ryerson University, Toronto, Canada
7. Givi, Z.S., Jaber, M.Y., Neumann, W.P.: Modelling worker reliability with learning and fatigue. Department of Mechanical and Industrial Engineering, Ryerson University, Toronto, Canada. Elsevier (2015)
8. Jaber, M.Y., Givi, Z.S., Neumann, W.P.: Incorporating human fatigue and recovery into the learning–forgetting process. Appl. Math. Model. **37**(12–13), 7287–7299 (2013)
9. Vargas, V., Kim, J.H.: Learning-forgetting-fatigue-recovery simulation model. In: Wright, J.L., Barber, D., Scataglini, S., Rajulu, S.L. (eds.) AHFE 2021. LNNS, vol. 264, pp. 135–142. Springer, Cham (2021). https://doi.org/10.1007/978-3-030-79763-8_16
10. https://humansystems.arc.nasa.gov/groups/tlx/
11. Schantz, H.G.: A real-time location system using near-field electromagnetic ranging. In: IEEE Antennas and Propagation Society International Symposium (2007)
12. Schantz, H.G., Weil, C., Unden, A.H.: Characterization of error in a near-field electromagnetic ranging (NFER) real-time location system (RTLS). In: IEEE Radio and Wireless Symposium (2011)
13. Staton, N.A.: Hierarchical task analysis: developments, applications and extensions. Applied Ergonomics **37**, 55–79 (2006). Human Factors Integration Defense Technology Centre, School of Engineering and Design, Brunel University, UK
14. Barnes, C.D., Laughery Jr., K.R.: Advanced uses for micro saint simulation software. In: 29th Conference on Winter Simulation (1997)
15. Bodilsen, J., et al.: Hospital admission and mortality rates for non-covid diseases in Denmark during covid-19 pandemic: nationwide population based cohort study. BMJ **373**, n1135 (2021)
16. Allison, M.C., et al.: Lockdown britain: evidence for reduced incidence and severity of some non-COVID acute medical illnesses. Clin. Med. (Lond.) **21**(2), e171 (2021)
17. Lemiere, C., Begin, D., Camus, M.: Occupational risk factors associated with work-exacerbated asthma in Quebec. Occ. Health Environ. Med. **69**, 901–907 (2012)
18. Santi, L., et al.: Non-COVID-19 patients in times of pandemic: emergency department visits, hospitalizations and cause-specific mortality in Northern Italy. PloS One **16**(3), e0248995 (2021)
19. Huang, L., Lin, G., Tang, L., Yu, L., Zhou, Z.: Special attention to nurses' protection during the COVID-19 epidemic. Crit. Care **24**, 120 (2020)

Digital Competencies for Therapists in Rehabilitation - A Case Study

Funda Ertas-Spantgar[1] , Jasmin Aust[1], Alexander Gabel[2] , Tom Lorenz[2] ,
Ina Schiering[2(✉)] , and Sandra Verena Müller[1]

[1] Faculty of Social Work, Ostfalia University of Applied Sciences,
Wolfenbüttel, Germany
[2] Faculty of Computer Science, Ostfalia University of Applied Sciences,
Wolfenbüttel, Germany
i.schiering@ostfalia.de

Abstract. Digitization provides a huge potential for rehabilitation and to foster inclusion. To this aim also digital competencies of therapists and caregivers are of utter importance. In the context of an mHealth app addressing deficits in structured executions of plans and goal-directed bevaviour, an iterative approach to develop training activities is presented. This is accompanied by an evaluation addressing usability, technology affinity and a semantic investigation of the individual workflows created by participants.

Keywords: Digitisation · Healthcare · Therapy · Digital competencies · Usability · Training

1 Introduction

Digital competencies of healthcare professionals and therapists are central elements in the context of digitization of healthcare. At the moment the adoption of eHealth and mHealth innovations is still relatively low [15]. Central barriers among others are knowledge concerning digital health services and usability of such services [17]. To this end digital health competencies for healthcare personal and therapists are investigated [13,18]. The focus there is merely on documentation as e.g. Electronic Health Records (EHR), basic computer and internet skills and general information literacy. When reflecting digital competencies as in the EU framework DigiComp 2.1 [6] beside these basic skills of information and data literacy also advanced competencies as content creation and problem solving are mentioned. In the ongoing discussions concerning DigiComp 2.2 also areas as Artificial Intelligence (AI), Safety and Digital Health are discussed.

Digital tools in the area of therapy provide the potential to integrate therapeutic interventions in daily life activities of patients and people with disabilities and therefore help them to gain self-efficacy and autonomy. For therapists this can be a cultural change from mainly explaining and monitoring therapeutic interventions to in addition planing and conceptualizing individual therapeutic

V. G. Duffy (Ed.): HCII 2022, LNCS 13320, pp. 185–196, 2022.
https://doi.org/10.1007/978-3-031-06018-2_13

activities in the context of digital tools. To this end therapists need specific competencies for realizing and adapting individualized training activities for patients or people with disabilities.

In the area of rehabilitation for people with disabilities and in the area of care and inclusion for people with intellectual disabilities the access and use of digital technologies depends on the attitude and competencies of their caregivers [12]. Especially caregivers with low affinity for technology and a traditional self-conception prefer accompanying people with disabilities instead of empowering them to foster their autonomy [3]. The importance of digital competencies and specific training in this area is stressed by Batz et al. [2]. They emphasize the need to incorporate digital skills in the curriculum.

Therefore the development of training activities for digital competencies and assistive technology are important. In the context of the RehaGoal app, an mHealth application addressing deficits in structured executions of plans and goal-directed behavior [9,11], training activities for therapists and the usability of the application from their point of view are developed. In this app individual daily activities of patients can be modeled via a visual programming interface [7]. Needed digital competencies beside usage of the interface are the modeling of activities and their representation in the RehaGoal app (see Fig. 1). The underlying therapeutic concept is the goal management training [14].

Training activities for therapists and caregivers are developed based on an iterative approach to foster their digital competencies in creating and adapting individual rehabilitation activities for patients and people with intellectual disabilities. This process incorporates a first phase with individual coaching and afterwards training activities improved in an iterative approach accompanied by evaluating usability and technology affinity. The aim is to derive insights how digital competencies in healthcare could be fostered.

2   Background

The RehaGoal app [11] is an mHealth application that addresses rehabilitation in the area of executive dysfunctions. Executive dysfunctions are deficits according to an acquired or congenital brain damage concerning "the selection and execution of cognitive plans, their updating and monitoring, the inhibition of irrelevant responses and problems with goal-directed behavior usually result in disorganized behavior, impulsivity and problems in goal management and self-regulation" [8, p. 17].

To address these deficits goal management training (GMT) [14] is a therapeutic measurement, where a goal is divided in subgoals until the granularity of the resulting tasks is appropriate for the patient. This is traditionally realized by paper-based checklists. The RehaGoal app provides a digitized version of GMT where the goal, single tasks and additional elements as repetitions, reminders and yes/no questions (if-then-else) (Table 1) can be used to describe an individual workflow for rehabilitation training, addressing goals of patients concerning activities of daily life (ADL) (Fig. 1). To this end the approach of block-based visual programming is employed based on *Google Blockly* [7,16].

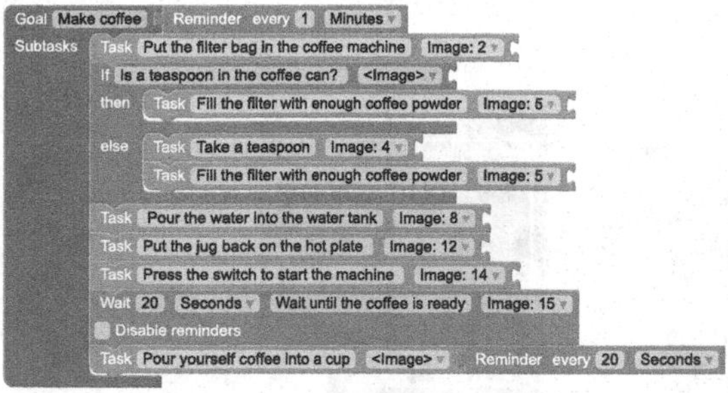

Fig. 1. Visual programming for modeling activities of daily life as workflows

Typical ADL which are modeled as workflows are cooking, taking public transport or cleaning. Each task contains a textual description and an optional additional image. These workflows can then be used on a smartphone to support patients in performing these activities fostering their autonomy (Fig. 2, Fig. 3). Textual descriptions can be read aloud via a text-to-speech engine. Workflows can be combined to sequences and the start can be triggered via a calendar module. Also user interfaces addressing perceptual disorders as e.g. neglect are available (Fig. 4).

Table 1. Overview of building blocks for workflows

block templates	description
	Initially the goal of the workflow is stated via a textual description
	Single tasks can be described by a textual description accompanied by an optional image
	It is possible to define a fixed number of repetitions of the blocks which are included
	Alternatively a repetition can be performed until a specific state is reached, e.g. water is cooking
	Activities that can be performed in an arbitrary order, e.g. in shopping or cooking activities
	Wait a defined time during a workflow or perform an action for a defined time
	Choose an alternative based on a yes/no question (also often called if-then-else) of the corresponding included blocks
	Blocks apart from waiting can be combined with a reminder

The RehaGoal app allows an individualized rehabilitation training which can be integrated in daily routines of patients. To realize the full potential of this concept for patients, healthcare professionals and therapists need specific digital

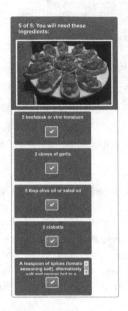

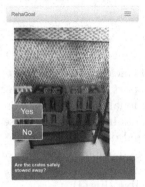

Fig. 2. Smartphone view of make coffee

Fig. 3. Example of arbitrary order block used for cooking

Fig. 4. User interface for neglect patients

competencies as structuring tasks and modeling workflows based on the given block templates (Table 1). To this end in the context of an agile development and participatory design approach a corresponding training concept was developed based on an iterative approach to address beside the needs of the patients also healthcare professionals and therapists.

3   Methodology

The aim of this case study is the development of a training concept and the investigation of the usability of the RehaGoal app for therapists. This training concept is developed and evaluated based on an iterative approach. Based on experience in coaching single therapists and several brief workshops a first version of a training activity (named as *workshop A*) was realized and a training of 13 participants with a background ranging from social science to healthcare was performed. This workshop lasted a whole day and the focus was to train features of the application in detail. For the evaluation of the application the system usability scale (SUS) [5] was used and the workflows which were developed during the training were analyzed afterwards. In addition it was asked very general whether participants feel confident with computers, smartphones, tablets or smart watches.

The training was optimized based on the feedback and specific difficulties identified in the analyzed workflows from workshop A. The focus was changed from merely explaining the usage of the application to training the concept of modeling daily activities. Also instead of a one-day workshop, a two hour initial workshop and two hour final workshop accompanied by coaching in smaller groups in between was performed. This second version of the training (named as *workshop B*) is used as a web-based training during the COVID-19 pandemic for 9 participants with a background in occupational therapy, physiotherapy and neurology. Since the user perception during the first training according to observations depended on affinity for technologies, instead of the very general questions of workshop A the affinity for technology interaction (ATI) scale [10] was used.

4   Results

These workshops were integrated in the participatory research process and ongoing evaluation (workshop A) and in the context of an evaluation study for the RehaGoal app. Workshop A was performed in the context of job coaches for people with intellectual disabilities whereas workshop B was in the context of clinical rehabilitation. Therefore there were differences about prior experience of the participants with the methodology of GMT respectively the RehaGoal app. Hence the following results are considered as a case study about usability of the RehaGoal app and digital competencies concerning individualizing rehabilitation training, structuring tasks and modeling workflows.

4.1   Participants, Usability and Affinity for Technology

Workshop A was held with 13 job coaches for inclusion of people with intellectual disabilities in the labor market in October 2020. Since they were integrated in the participatory design approach for the development of the RehaGoal app, several participants already had prior experience in creating workflows. There was a one-day workshop where technical details of the RehaGoal app were detailed and the participants worked on modeling workflow exercises. The SUS results are evaluated according to [4], the lines of the following table are colored according to the SUS as proposed in [1].

Usability of the RehaGoal app according to the SUS was in general considered as good. A summary about demographics, SUS and prior experience with the RehaGoal app is summarized in Table 2. Confidence with the use of computers, smartphones and smart watches was asked very general during workshop A (see Fig. 5).

Based on the reflection of workshop A it was considered that the huge difference in prior knowledge about the RehaGoal app was problematic and it is not useful to incorporate people with very different prior experience in one

Table 2. Participants of *workshop A* with additional information about gender, age, SUS Score (System Usability Scale) (excellent, good, ok) and number of workflows created before the workshop

Participant ID	Gender	Age	SUS	Created workflows
PA1	Female	40–50	87,5	4–9
PA2	Female	20–30	55	10–20
PA3	Female	20–30	67,5	10–20
PA4	Male	20–30	65	–
PA5	Female	–	55	4–9
PA6	Female	40–50	52,5	–
PA7	Female	50–60	65	–
PA8	Female	20–30	60	4–9
PA9	Female	20–30	72,5	0–3
PA10	Female	40–50	82,5	20+
PA11	Female	30–40	70	0–3
PA12	Male	20–30	70	20+
PA13	Female	20–30	80	4–9

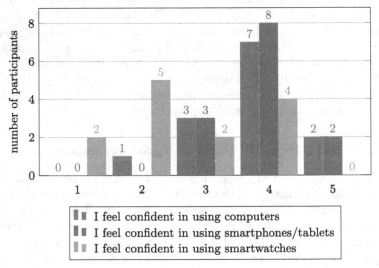

Fig. 5. Confidence concerning the usage of technological devices (5 strongly agree, ..., 1 strongly disagree)

workshop. Also for beginners it was difficult to memorize the basic blocks and directly afterwards already learn the methodology of structuring and modeling of workflows. To address the needs of beginners to get basic knowledge about the blocks, video tutorials presenting the blocks in the context of typical usage scenarios were created.

Workshop B was held in a clinical rehabilitation context with 9 participants in June and July 2021. The participants had no prior knowledge about the RehaGoal app, but the methodology of GMT was already used before in the traditional paper-based form. In a first workshop the methodology of GMT was summarized, the basic blocks were introduced based on typical use cases from the video tutorials and some example workshops were collaboratively created. Then the participants had three weeks time to gain experience with the RehaGoal app and were accompanied by a coaching approach in two smaller groups. In a final workshop at the end of the time, experiences, specific questions and example workflows were discussed between the participants.

Also in this group, the usability of the RehaGoal app according to the SUS was considered as good. The ATI score was in general only medium. A summary about demographics, SUS and ATI score is summarized in Table 3. To get an overview about the distribution of the ATI score see Fig. 6.

Table 3. Participants of the *workshop B* with additional information about gender, age, ATI Score (Affinity for Technology Interaction) and SUS Score (System Usability Scale) (good, ok)

Participant ID	Gender	Age	ATI	SUS
PB1	Female	20–30	3,88	70
PB2	Female	20–30	4,33	82,5
PB3	Female	50–60	3	82,5
PB4	Female	20–30	4	75
PB5	Female	40–50	2,66	80
PB6	Female	50–60	3,88	67,5
PB7	Female	30–40	3,33	80
PB8	Female	40–50	2	75
PB9	Female	20–30	3,88	72,5

4.2   Analysis of Workflows from Workshop A

As a basis for the video tutorials to introduce the basic blocks in typical usage scenarios, also hints concerning reasonable structuring and modeling of workflows are presented. As a basis for the creation of these workflows for usage scenarios also typical errors were analyzed. To this end workflows created in the context of *workshop A* were used. In the following some examples for such errors in modeling of workflows are presented

Alternative Block. Typical errors in using the yes/no question in the alternative block is that from reading the question and potential additional information

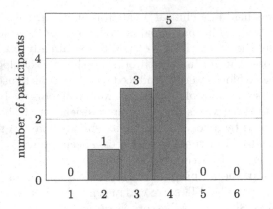

Fig. 6. Distribution of ATI Score in second workshop

from the optional image, it must be possible to answer the question with yes or no. Concerning the question *Do you have all the materials ready* (Fig. 7), it is not clear which material is needed. The question *Water hot enough* (Fig. 8) cannot be answered with yes or no since it is not clear which temperature is adequate. In this example also the question is repeated as a task in the else alternative. When using the workflow this means that the same text is repeated and an additional click for confirmation is needed. Sometimes this pattern was even used several times in a workflow resulting in a considerable amount of additional confirmations.

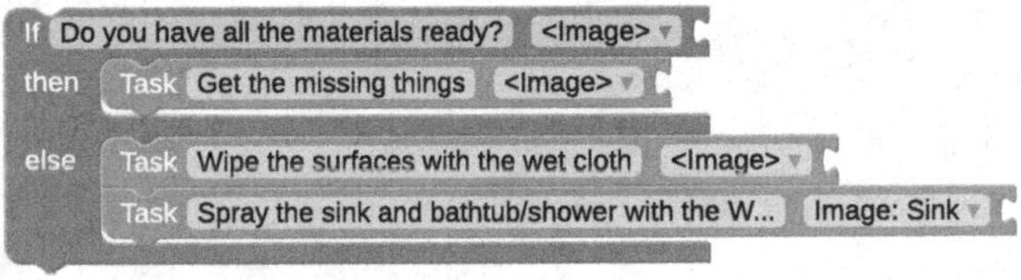

If Do you have all the materials ready?   <Image> ▾
then   Task Get the missing things   <Image> ▾

else   Task Wipe the surfaces with the wet cloth   <Image> ▾
        Task Spray the sink and bathtub/shower with the W...   Image: Sink ▾

Fig. 7. Question cannot be answered without additional information

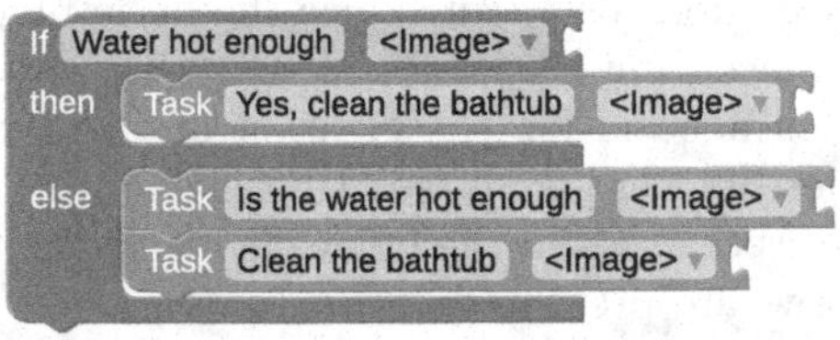

If Water hot enough   <Image> ▾
then   Task Yes, clean the bathtub   <Image> ▾

else   Task Is the water hot enough   <Image> ▾
        Task Clean the bathtub   <Image> ▾

Fig. 8. Unspecific question, repetition of question before the task

Arbitrary Order Block. A typical usage of this block which is not useful is when the list contains only one single item (Fig. 9). In combination with a repetition only few participants would profit from a workflow where a relatively long list of items need potentially several repeated checks (Fig. 10).

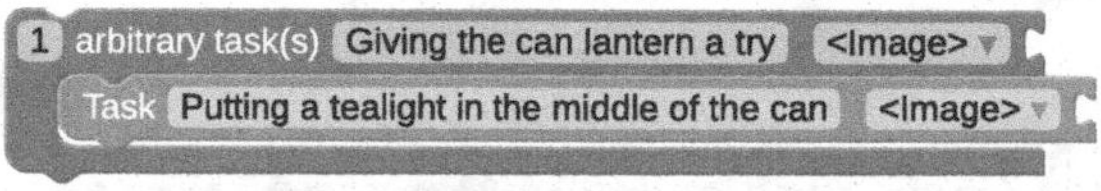

Fig. 9. Single task in block for a list of tasks to be performed in arbitrary order

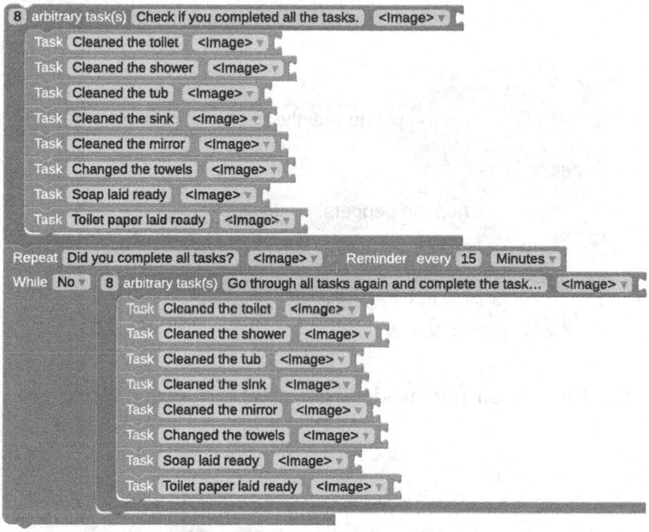

Fig. 10. Repeated checks needed

Repetition Block. A typical misconception concerning the usage of the repetition block is that a repetition block is conceptually wrong in the context. In the case of the question *Spray the can until it is completely covered with ...* (Fig. 11) this could be modeled as a single task. Also in the case of Fig. 12 the repetition block is not useful. In this scenario the task would be to get a certain number of potatoes, peppers and carrots in a first step, which could be modeled via a block for performing tasks in an arbitrary order. In a second arbitrary order block there could be tasks as *Peel all potatoes with the pealer.* As modeled here, a confirmation for every potato, pepper and carrot would be needed.

When the tasks in the repetition block are in addition stated before the repetition block this could lead to errors when workflows are adapted (Fig. 13, Fig. 8). It is important that workflows can be easily adapted according to changes of the tasks or to summarize several tasks because patients gained experience and need less granular support. When parts of the workflow are doubled, this could lead to errors when not all copies are changed.

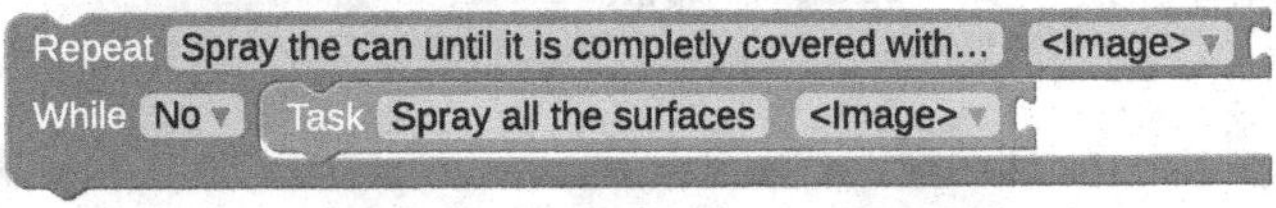

Fig. 11. Repetition not needed

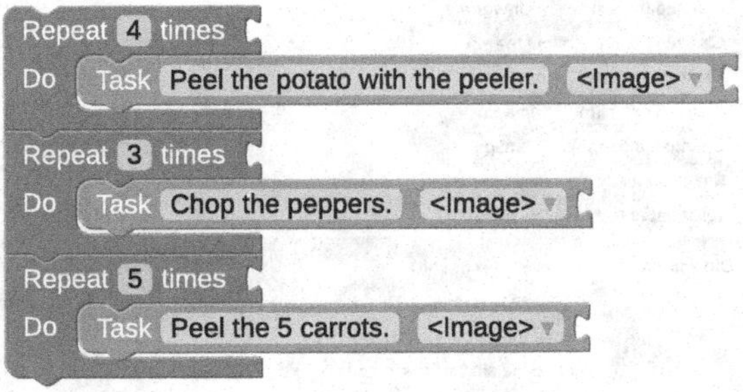

Fig. 12. Repetition not needed, use arbitrary order block instead

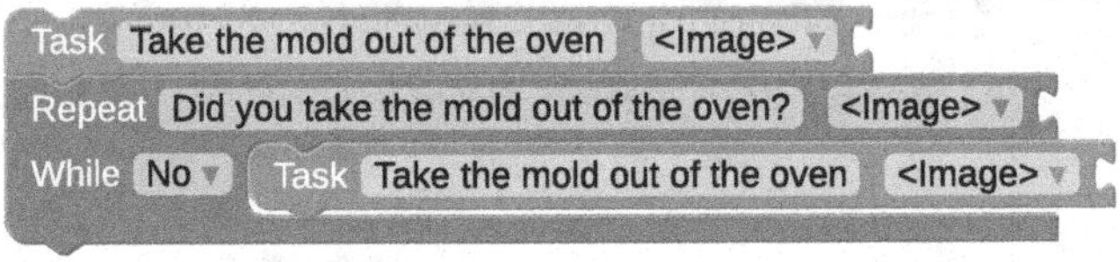

Fig. 13. Doubled task before the repetition

5   Discussion and Conclusion

As a general reflection from all training activities it can be summarized that the approach of *workshop B*, with a concise basic introduction, additional material as video tutorials and coaching to enhance personal experience and discuss workflows created by participants seems to be useful. The affinity for technology of healthcare professionals can be considered as in general only moderate. The usability of the RehaGoal app from their point of view is considered as good.

Additional means to foster digital competencies which could be helpful are to establish digital experts in the organization, which could provide guidance to others, and establish internal group coaching where participants can share experiences. Since especially longer and more complex workflows profit from review and potentially also restructuring, digital experts or such groups could be helpful for fostering the development of digital competencies in healthcare organization.

Acknowledgement. This work was funded by the German Ministry of Education and Research as part of the project *SmarteInklusion* under grant no. 01PE18011C and by the Ministry for Science and Culture of Lower Saxony as part of SecuRIn (VWZN3224).

References

1. Bangor, A., Kortum, P., Miller, J.: Determining what individual SUS scores mean: adding an adjective rating scale. J. Usability Stud. **4**(3), 114–123 (2009)
2. Batz, V., et al.: The digital competence of vocational education teachers and of learners with and without cognitive disabilities. In: Jia, W., et al. (eds.) SETE 2021. LNCS, vol. 13089, pp. 190–206. Springer, Cham (2021). https://doi.org/10. 1007/978-3-030-92836-0_17
3. Bosse, I., Haage, A.: Digitalisierung in der behindertenhilfe. Handbuch Soziale Arbeit und Digitalisierung **1**, 529–539 (2020)
4. Brooke, J.: SUS: a retrospective. J. Usability Stud. **8**(2), 29–40 (2013)
5. Brooke, J., et al.: SUS-a quick and dirty usability scale. Usability Eval. Ind. **189**(194), 4–7 (1996)
6. Carretero, S., Vuorikari, R., Punie, Y.: DigComp 2.1: the digital competence framework for citizens with eight proficiency levels and examples of use. European Commission, Joint Research Centre (2018). https://doi.org/10.2760/38842
7. Eckhardt, K., Schiering, I., Gabel, A., Ertas, F., Müller, S.V.: Visual programming for assistive technologies in rehabilitation and social inclusion of people with intellectual disabilities. In: Proceedings of Mensch und Computer 2019, MuC 2019, pp. 731–735. Association for Computing Machinery, New York, NY (2019). https:// doi.org/10.1145/3340764.3344899. ISBN 9781450371988
8. Emmanouel, A.: Look at the frontal side of life: anterior brain pathology and everyday executive function: assessment approaches and treatment. Ph.D. thesis, [Sl: sn] (2017)
9. Ertas, F., Aust, J., Lorenz, T., Schiering, I., Brunner, K., Müller, S.V.: Der Einsatz der RehaGoal App durch Menschen mit einer intellektuellen Beeinträchtigung bei der Arbeit zu Hause während der Corona-Pandemie. Z. Neuropsychol. **32**(1), 13–23 (2021). https://doi.org/10.1024/1016-264X/a000317
10. Franke, T., Attig, C., Wessel, D.: A personal resource for technology interaction: development and validation of the affinity for technology interaction (ATI) scale. Int. J. Hum.-Comput. Interact. **35**(6), 456–467 (2019). https://doi.org/10.1080/ 10447318.2018.1456150

11. Gabel, A., Pleger, M., Schiering, I.: RehaGoal App - Eine mHealth Anwendung zur Unterstützung bei Beeinträchtigungen in der Handlungsplanung. In: Luthe, E.W., Müller, S.V., Schiering, I. (eds.) Assistive Technologien im Sozial- und Gesundheitssektor, pp. 779–793. Gesundheit. Politik - Gesellschaft - Wirtschaft, Springer Fachmedien, Wiesbaden (2022). https://doi.org/10.1007/978-3-658-34027-8_31

12. Heitplatz, V.: Fostering digital participation for people with intellectual disabilities and their caregivers: towards a guideline for designing education programs. Soc. Inclusion 8(2) (2020). https://doi.org/10.17645/si.v8i2.2578

13. Jimenez, G., et al.: Digital health competencies for primary healthcare professionals: a scoping review. Int. J. Med. Inform. 143, 104260 (2020). https://doi.org/10.1016/j.ijmedinf.2020.104260

14. Levine, B., et al.: Rehabilitation of executive functioning: an experimental-clinical validation of goal management training. J. Int. Neuropsychol. Soc. 6(3), 299–312 (2000)

15. World Health Organization, et al.: Global strategy on digital health 2020–2025 (2020). https://www.who.int/docs/default-source/documents/gs4dhdaa2a9f352b0445bafbc79ca799dce4d.pdf

16. Pasternak, E., Fenichel, R., Marshall, A.N.: Tips for creating a block language with blockly. In: 2017 IEEE Blocks and Beyond Workshop (B&B), pp. 21–24. IEEE (2017). https://doi.org/10.1109/BLOCKS.2017.8120404

17. Schreiweis, B., Pobiruchin, M., Strotbaum, V., Suleder, J., Wiesner, M., Bergh, B.: Barriers and facilitators to the implementation of ehealth services: systematic literature analysis. J. Med. Internet Res. 21(11), e14197 (2019). https://doi.org/10.2196/14197. http://www.jmir.org/2019/11/e14197/

18. Sherbersky, H., Ziminski, J., Pote, H.: The journey towards digital systemic competence: thoughts on training, supervision and competence evaluation. J. Family Ther. 43(2), 351–371 (2021). https://doi.org/10.1111/1467-6427.12328

Scenario Design for Healthcare Collaboration Training Under Suboptimal Conditions

Jo E. Hannay[2](✉) [iD], Kristin S. Fuglerud[1] [iD], Wolfgang Leister[1] [iD], and Trenton Schulz[1] [iD]

[1] Norwegian Computing Center, Pb. 114 Blindern, 0314 Oslo, Norway
{kristin.skeide.fuglerud,wolfgang.leister,trenton.schulz}@nr.no
[2] Simula Metropolitan Center for Digital Engineering,
Center for Effective Digitalization of the Public Sector, OsloMet,
Pb. 4 St. Olavs plass, 0130 Oslo, Norway
johannay@simula.no

Abstract. Healthcare today usually consists of various services covering various parts of the total healthcare of a region or country. These services are required to coordinate and collaborate, often using procedures and IT collaboration tools that may not be designed for interoperating across the evolving wider landscape of healthcare services. We posit that it is necessary to train personnel in collaboration skills using whatever infrastructure is in place. To this end, we present design principles for simulation-based collaboration training scenarios that emphasizes the inclusion of suboptimal infrastructure elements. We applied the principles in a co-creational workshop with healthcare stakeholders from a hospital and surrounding municipalities in Norway where we discussed cases where collaboration training is perceived as critical. We elicited five training vignettes concerning the general case of detecting, and following up on, clinical deterioration in a patient at home or in a nursing home. We found that the design principles spurred highly relevant discussions among participants and that novel ideas for collaboration training were brought forth on the basis of these principles. We conclude that there is a potential in using these principles for eliciting training vignettes that address the actual situation more accurately.

Keywords: Scenario design · Healthcare collaboration · Procedures · IT services · Simulation-based training · Stakeholder journey analysis

1 Motivation

A patient's total healthcare is commonly provided by a number of different services across various parts of the public and private sectors. A seamless journey through these services is far from obvious. Collaboration and communication issues due to different fields of expertise, different work cultures, non-

V. G. Duffy (Ed.): HCII 2022, LNCS 13320, pp. 197–214, 2022.
https://doi.org/10.1007/978-3-031-06018-2_14

interoperable processes [4,13,14] and suboptimal, non-interoperable collaboration IT services [2,20,21] regularly lead to frustration for all involved, and may even cause health- and life-threatening situations.

It is common when collaboration problems arise in the public sector to launch large IT initiatives to develop common platforms for digitalized collaboration; several of which never get deployed, e.g., [32], or somehow get out of control in other ways, e.g., [33]. A uniform electronic patient record (EPR) system is often a central component of such systems. While we await the coming of future, successful collaborative IT platforms, healthcare must function in the present. We therefore argue that it is necessary to train personnel in the use of sub-optimal IT services.

A number of procedural tools, such as checklists and protocols, have been developed for guiding and standardizing the work of healthcare professionals. Successful collaboration often hinges on the joint use and understanding of these tools. There are also procedural tools for collaboration itself which can be used over various media, including the collaborative IT platforms mentioned above. In the particular case we are studying, the procedural tools are not uniformly in place and not jointly used and understood [34]. To address this situation, a model was introduced in the National healthcare sector for building procedural skills systematically and for training collaboration over those skills within and across healthcare services [3]. However, it is evident that even disseminating such procedural tools and building skills at the desired level across services will take time, and, again, healthcare collaboration must happen in the mean time.

We therefore present principles for designing simulation-based training for healthcare collaboration, in the face of (1) existing sub-optimal IT services and (2) sub-optimal levels and proliferation of procedural skills. We apply these design principles in scenario design in a co-creation workshop.

Beyond architectural guidelines for scenario design, e.g., [29], there is little information about how simulation-based training is actually developed in systematic reviews of the effects of simulation-based training [10,30]. However, it has been pointed out that it is important to develop training programs that are based on, and aligned with, the current needs of trainees, and the Delphi process has been suggested for selecting and prioritising what training to be included in a curriculum [22]. Others suggest that participatory approaches and co-creation is particularly well suited for design in healthcare, since the sharing of knowledge by all parties involved is regarded as a prerequisite for a good result [1,26].

The term co-creation is defined ambiguously in the existing literature on design and innovation [5,12,37]. We follow the definition that describes co-creation as an activity where actors jointly produce a mutually valued outcome, based on assessments of the risks and benefits of proposed courses of action and decisions based on dialogue, access to information and transparency [7].

Existing frameworks for co-creation stress that participation must happen at the same time and in the same context [1]. Thus, the most common activity for co-creation is a workshop. Workshops provide opportunities for using different methods to create and share ideas and foster joint solutions. Some possible methods that can be employed include role-playing, mixed-group teamwork, pro-

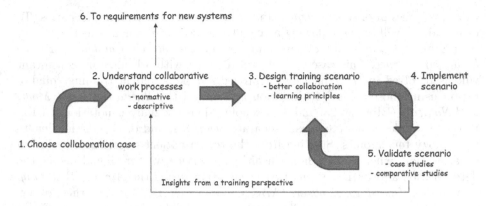

Fig. 1. Scenario design stages

totyping, creating personas, and creating stakeholder journeys. Co-creation can be a relevant way to create high-quality healthcare services since actors in healthcare must have a heightened understanding of each other's roles, motivations, knowledge and goals to collaborate and make decisions, but it is important that existing workshop methods be adapted to the specific settings under study [1].

2   Design Challenge

A scenario is a "description of the hypothetical or real area, environment, means, objectives, and events during a specified time frame related to events of interest" [29]. Scenario design for simulation-based training is non-trivial in the outset [28,29] and even more so for higher-level skills such as decision-making and collaboration; see pointers in [17]. To get to grasps with this in our setting, we follow the six high-level scenario design steps in Fig. 1. Together with healthcare stakeholders, we choose a collaboration case that is perceived to be of particular interest for improvement. For that case, we must then understand what should happen versus what actually happens. From this understanding, we design training scenarios aimed at training healthcare personnel to collaborate better within and across healthcare services, all according to learning principles such as deliberate practice and adaptive thinking [9,27]. Scenarios are then implemented in mixed reality and validated using stakeholder groups. Insights from the validations are also fed back to work process elicitation with the intent to provide input to requirements engineering for new collaborative systems.

Several collaboration cases will be studied, and therefore, Fig. 1 shows one increment or iteration of a concerted effort toward simulation-based training [16,25] for collaboration within and between healthcare services.

The rigorous way to design scenarios would be to (1) determine the normative work process, (2) determine the actual work process, and (3) work out the difference and design training with the aim to achieve the normative situation. The first two of those three steps are extensive fields of research conducted elsewhere by healthcare researchers. Our program of work is dedicated to describing work processes in only *sufficient* detail to design efficient training scenarios. To that end, we will in the following arrive at four scenario design principles.

Figure 2 shows a sketch of a work process for the case *clinical deterioration – home care service*. This case was elicited together with a healthcare consultant who is involved in the education of procedural skills and in training collaboration using those skills. The notation is a mix of the *Business Process Model and Notation* (BPMN) [23] and a stakeholder journey analysis notation [15, 18]. In our example, each actor has a separate *swimlane*, and orange circles denote technology touchpoints. Starting from the top, a patient experiences a clinical deterioration, whereupon a home healthcare service worker should detect the deterioration and initiate structured observations using the *Airway, Breathing, Circulation, Disability, Exposure* (ABCDE) approach [19]. Based on these observations, the worker should calculate the *National Early Warning Score* (NEWS) [24] and use that score and other observations to assess and decide further action. In Fig. 2, the further action involves communication with a general practitioner, emergency room or emergency response unit. During this communication, information is to be exchanged using the *Identify, Situation, Background, Assessment and Recommendation* (ISBAR) format [31] and entered into the electronic

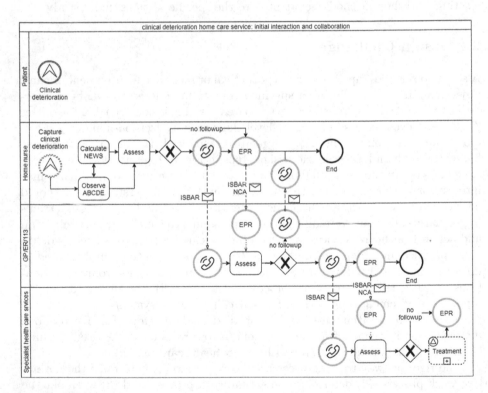

Fig. 2. Work process for a clinical deterioration collaboration case. Each actor has a separate *swimlane*, and orange circles denote technology touchpoints

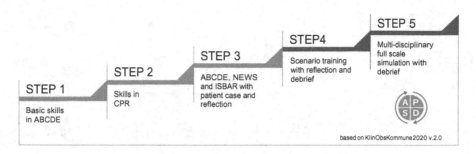

Fig. 3. Steps of the KlinObsKommune framework

patient record (EPR) system using *Nursing and Care* (NCA) messages [6]. Further collaboration with specialist healthcare services is illustrated in the bottom swimlane.

Recent research has uncovered that personnel in municipal healthcare services might not have the required skills regarding emergencies and general observation abilities [35]. Likewise, specialist staff at hospitals do not have sufficient knowledge about the skills of municipal healthcare personnel. The KlinObsKommune model [3] addresses the education of municipal and specialist healthcare personnel in a five-step model, shown in Fig. 3. In Steps 1 and 2, personnel train their skills in systematic patient observation (ABCDE) and cardiopulmonary resuscitation (CPR). In Step 3, the integration of ABCDE with NEWS for further clinical observation and decision-making is trained, together with the communication format ISBAR. Step 4 concerns training the ensuing collaboration within the municipal healthcare system to handle clinical patient deterioration, and Step 5 concerns training the ensuing collaboration between municipal and specialist healthcare systems. Steps 4 and 5 are the focus of our work.

A major challenge when designing training scenarios for higher-level skills such as collaboration, judgement and decision-making is that the number of conceivable situations that ostensibly need training is enormous. This contrasts with training procedural skills such as operating a medical instrument, assembling equipment, or performing ABCDE, NEWS and ISBAR correctly. While the work process in Fig. 2 appears structured and systematic, actual work processes are fraught with difficulties in practice. Various EPR systems may not always interoperate well, and even if the EPR systems work well together, other challenges based on other variables (e.g., unable to contact the person with whom to collaborate, not knowing the patient's previous status, inconsistent medicine lists, etc.) entail a combinatorial explosion of different sequences of events. Structured training often cannot be designed to cater for each specific contingency. This situation is exacerbated for simulation-based training that relies on synthetic (virtual reality) elements that require software development, because simulation systems development is time-consuming and traditionally does not cater well for the flexibility required in training [8,36].

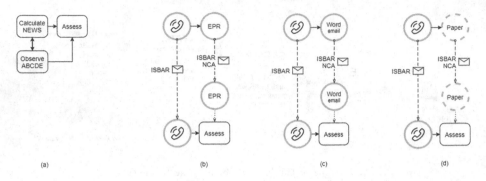

Fig. 4. Patterns of action and interaction that can be implemented as reusable modular vignettes.

To create simulation-based training that can be flexible and useful in the multitude of real-world situations that health-care workers will find themselves in, we start by positing the following design principles (DPs). Training scenarios should be

- composed of generic, reusable vignettes (DP1) and
- skills centered (DP2).

Vignettes can be described as small, reusable, temporally ordered set of events that are ideally self-contained, so that they can be reused in multiple scenarios [29]. When understanding the work processes in Stage 2 of our scenario design model (see Fig. 1), we have an explicit focus on identifying *action* and *interaction patterns* that form the basis for designing training vignettes. Further, these patterns should pertain to specific skills, so that vignettes can be designed with metrics to measure skill acquisition and improvement [17]. Figure 4 shows examples of an action pattern (a) and an interaction pattern (b) identified in Fig. 2. Working at identifying such patterns that target specific skills, rather than mapping out entire work processes, delineates our work against the more general task of defining normative and descriptive work processes as such.

Second, to ensure that training is performed on platforms that actually are in use, we state the principle that vignettes should

- include events that require the use of state-of-practice IT services (DP3).

This may seem trivial, but it is quite common that simulation-based training presents systems as they *are intended to be*, instead of *as they actually are*. Thus, vignettes must be designed so that practitioners can become better at using whatever suboptimal systems that are in place. For instance, practitioners might use *improvised* solutions such as using Microsoft Word or paper notes when cross-platform EPR systems are not functioning [11], as outlined in Fig. 4 (c) and (d).

Third, to ensure that training reflects actual levels and proliferation of procedural skills, we state the principle that vignettes should

– include events that require the use of state-of-practice procedures (DP4).

The KlinObsKommune model in Fig. 3 may lead one to think that everything has to be in place at the lower steps before one can start training on higher steps. Whether such a view is intended or, perhaps rather an artifact of the model graphics, we interpret the model as stating the structure of competence, rather than the order in which skills should be trained.

In sum, design principles DP3 and DP4 insist that trainees must collaborate in vignettes even under suboptimal circumstances caused by the present state of affairs of IT platforms, tools and procedural skills.

With the design principles spelled out, we can refine the high-level view of Fig. 1. To that effect, Fig. 5 shows the refined view, where Stage 2 is narrowed to understand collaborative work processes sufficiently for designing vignettes based on critical collaboration patterns. Further, the reusable vignettes are stored in a repository in various formats. The basic textual description of a vignette can be implemented in various materials, from simple scripts for discussion exercises and role playing to advanced software intended for mixed reality games. Implementing scenarios then involves using vignettes to compose larger scenarios.

3   Workshop for Eliciting Vignettes

In late autumn 2021, we conducted a co-creative workshop with the intent to elicit vignettes according to principles DP1–DP4 above. As we worked on the design principles and on planning the workshop, we were concerned that practitioners within each healthcare service did not necessarily have an overview of the overall collaborative process, and that there was large variation in which procedures and formats were familiar to everyone. Therefore, the workshop participants consisted of hand-picked practitioners with overall knowledge of the work processes and methods, rather than representatives for each actor in the

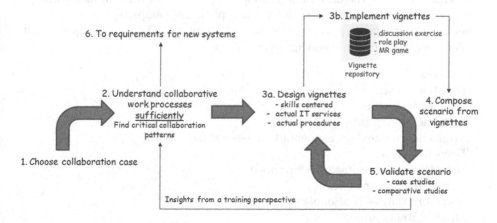

Fig. 5. Scenario design stages according to design principles

work process diagrams. Some participants also had experience from training practitioners in KlinObsKommune. The participants other than the researchers were general practitioners, nurses, and advisors in the municipalities' development centers for nursing homes and home healthcare. In total, nine participants and five researchers participated.

At the beginning of the workshop, the participants were familiarized with the notion of simulation-based training for healthcare collaboration and our ideas embedded in the four design principles. They received a walkthrough of an extended version of the stakeholder journey chart for the case discussed in Sect. 2 (see Fig. 2). We extended this to the general case of detecting, and following up on, clinical deterioration in a patient at home or in a nursing home. During this walkthrough, researchers pointed out repeating patterns of action and interaction. The researchers also emphasized that the chart was to be considered an example, since there are many variations of this case in practice.

The participants were then divided into three groups: one group of six (four participants and two researchers), one of five (three participants and two researchers), and one of three (two participants and one researcher). Each group was tasked with finding concrete instances of that case. For example, participants might visualize a patient with a specific condition and use this specific situation to discuss and identify the most crucial action and interaction patterns that need improvement.

The discussions were not recorded to avoid collecting personal data, but researchers took notes of issues that were raised underway. As discussions progressed, the groups were asked to suggest concrete training vignettes satisfying the design principles. This was facilitated by an online template prompting for relevant aspects of such vignettes. The template was prepared as an online spreadsheet that could be edited jointly. This was based on previous experience of performing co-creation workshops during Covid-19 lockdown based on video conferencing tools. The template was inspired by the customer journey method, with focus on how the various stakeholders collaborate around a particular patient case. In the current workshop, we planned for a physical workshop, with a virtual workshop as a possible backup-plan. The template was shared on a screen, and participants also brought their own laptops. The template prompted participants to enter the following information:

- Roles involved
- Situation
- Skills to be trained
- Relevant prerequisite skills
- Events and contextual elements trainees are faced with
- Tasks to perform
- Metrics to measure task performance
- How to measure metrics
- Hints for trainees (*optional*)
- Physical items present
- Other (*optional*)

The template was designed so that the participants could contribute by writing directly into the template, but in practice, the researchers wrote most of the entries in collaboration with the other participants. The introduction and walkthrough took 15 min. Several of the workshop participants had also participated in a full-day seminar the day before on the same topics. The groups were given one hour and 45 min to discuss and discover vignettes. After this, all the groups assembled again for a 30-min summary where each group presented their vignettes.

4   The Vignettes

A total of five vignettes were elicited using the above-mentioned case of detecting, and following up on, clinical deterioration in a patient at home or in a nursing home. The vignette descriptions below constitute the raw structured output from the workshop cosmetically edited for presentation. The purpose of presenting them in this discussion is to illustrate the first stages of the scenario design model (Fig. 5) and any effects of the design principles.

4.1   Vignette 1

Vignette 1 is about building trust and confidence between health services in a municipality on the one hand and the services run at the county or national level on the other hand. This was illustrated by a case where a municipality healthcare practitioner (e.g., a home care nurse or auxiliary nurse) visits the home of a patient with deteriorating health. After observing this, the healthcare practitioner is supposed to contact a doctor.

Roles involved: Two roles in the municipal healthcare system: 1) a municipal healthcare worker and 2) a municipal doctor (a general practitioner, an emergency room doctor, a doctor at the municipal emergency day care unit).
Situation: Clinical deterioration, not acute.
Skills to be trained: To structure communication in ISBAR and find common terminology during the initial phone call and to find empowerment to communicate lack of understanding to the other party. To structure information in ISBAR and use clear language when entering information in the EPR. In general, knowing when to place phone calls and when to send NCA messages.
Relevant prerequisite skills: Knowledge of ABCDE and ISBAR, but not necessarily NEWS.
Events and contextual elements trainees are faced with: Trainees experience that they do not share a common terminology with which to communicate with one another.
Tasks to perform: To find a common frame of reference for communication.
Metrics to measure task performance: The degree to which the severity of the situation is communicated successfully. The degree of mutual trust.
How to measure metrics: Self-assessment, mutual reflection, pre- and post-tests to measure changes in trust.
Physical items present: EPR system (either on PC, phone, or tablet)
Other: Use of VR for distributed training could support outcome.

4.2   Vignette 2

Vignette 2 builds upon the previous situation. The vignette's purpose is to ensure that the municipality healthcare practitioner has good decision-making skills and takes appropriate action when the municipal doctor does not respond.

Roles involved: Two roles in the municipal healthcare system: 1) A municipal healthcare worker and 2) a person other than a doctor.

Situation: Clinical deterioration, not acute.

Skills to be trained: Adaptive thinking.

Relevant prerequisite skills: Trainees are aware of the various channels for contact in the municipal healthcare system.

Events and contextual elements trainees are faced with: The doctor does not respond.

Tasks to perform: 1) Decide if further clinical assessment is called for. 2) Re-initiate contact with doctor. 3) Call other healthcare personnel that are available. 4) Use NEWS-determined response. 5) Retain responsibility or transfer that responsibility explicitly to someone else when necessary. 6) Systematically follow up the situation. 7) Report to EPR.

Metrics to measure task performance: 1) How well did the healthcare worker follow up on the patient (retaining responsibility)? Was the responsibility transferred to different personnel? 2) Completeness of EPR routine. 3) Across all trainees and training sessions: the number of patients who receive documented follow-ups or clarification.

How to measure metrics: (1) and (2) could possible be assessed automatically in a decision-tree-based game, (3) is still to be decided.

Physical items present: EPR system (either on PC, phone, or tablet)

Other: Use VR for distributed training.

4.3   Vignette 3

In Vignette 3, more context is given to the deterioration. The patient's medication list has not been updated after the patient has been dismissed from the hospital. The goal for the trainees is to understand each other's daily routines and systems, and how to spot an out-of-date medication list.

Roles involved: Two roles: 1) municipal healthcare personnel, including doctors on the one hand and 2) doctors in specialist roles on the other hand.

Situation: Clinical deterioration, not acute, with suspicion of the patients medication list not being up to date.

Skills to be trained: Structured communication with specialist doctor.

Relevant prerequisite skills: ABCDE

Events and contextual elements trainees are faced with: Clinical deterioration (breathing difficulty) triggered by inconsistent medication list after dismissal from the hospital.

Tasks to perform: 1) detect that the deterioration is caused by using the wrong medication. 2a) If available, locate the medication list; notice the list is not up-to-date and contact the hospital. 2b) If the list is not available, communicate suspicion via NCA message according to how acute the situation is. 3) Contact emergency room during vacations. 4) Report in EPR.

Metrics to measure task performance: 1) the degree of taking action. 2) Time until the medication list is updated. 3) Across trainees and training: the number of patient casualties caused by wrong medication.

How to measure metrics: (1) and (2) could possible be assessed automatically in a decision-tree-based game. (3) is still to be decided.

Physical items present: EPR system (either on PC, phone, or tablet)

Other: Use VR for distributed training.

4.4   Vignette 4

The purpose of Vignette 4 is to improve skills among municipality healthcare workers without a nursing certificate in potentially acute situations and to give them confidence to communicate directly to the emergency room on their own, especially in situations where the responsible nurse might be physically distant or busy with other urgent tasks. This vignette starts with a patient at home with a potentially life-threatening deterioration. Sepsis was chosen as a case because it is a common condition that might be difficult to detect. As for Vignette 1, this vignette will require the trainees to decide when to contact the emergency room and how to communicate essential information efficiently.

Roles involved: Two roles: 1) Municipality home healthcare workers and 2) nurses who take calls in the emergency room. Only the first role is under training.

Situation: Clinical deterioration, potentially acute. Specifically, the home healthcare worker visits a female patient in her eighties at home, who has symptoms of a urinary tract infection and seems disoriented. The documented patient status states that the patient is lucid, but suffers from heart disease. The municipality healthcare workers have not seen to the patient lately.

Skills to be trained: 1) Call the emergency room and communicate in ISBAR the results of ABCDE observations. 2) obtain the medication list and information about relevant diagnoses. 3) Raise awareness and reflect on what information home healthcare workers, versus the emergency room nurses, have access to. 4) Accept empowerment to request necessary information and to contribute to information quality in the user status.

Relevant prerequisite skills: Trainees know Level 1 of KlinObsKommune (i.e., ABCDE), but do not necessarily have much practice in it.

Events and contextual elements trainees are faced with: 1) It might not be possible to send messages between systems, because these systems do not communicate. 2) The trainee may not have all necessary medical equipment for ABCDE observations.

Tasks to perform: The home healthcare worker detects a strong odour, probably from the urinary tract and is then expected to do some observations before calling the emergency room. The possible observations are: check that airways are free, count respiration, observe heart rate (not possible), observe mental state (patient is disoriented), observe skin and lip colour (does not have blue lips). During the phone call, the home healthcare worker is guided by the emergency room nurse to communicate on ISBAR and to perform the ABCDE observations correctly.

Metrics to measure task performance: 1) The degree to which the gravity of the situation is communicated successfully. 2) The degree of mutual trust.

How to measure metrics: Self-assessment, mutual reflection, debriefing with facilitator. Check whether they perceive a tentative sepsis situation when guided. Trainee's assessment of the seriousness of the situation; in particular, whether they perceive that this is a serious situation with a potentially seriously ill patient, in which case they should call an ambulance without delay.

Hints for trainees: Pocket card with guidance on ISBAR, ABCDE and NEWS.

Physical items present: Access to a PC and a mobile phone with a clock that displays seconds. Access to user status in the mobile care solution, with the following information: Name and personal information, that she has a heart condition and is lucid. There are also some checklists in the mobile solution.

Other: Possible extension to this situation for calling an ambulance and communicating with the specialist healthcare.

4.5 Vignette 5

Vignette 5 addresses the emergency room aspect of the situation described in Vignette 4. The purpose of this vignette is for emergency room nurses to be trained on how to guide home healthcare workers in communication in ISBAR and on how to perform correct observations according to ABCDE.

Roles involved: Two roles: 1) Emergency room nurses and possibly emergency room doctors, 2) municipality home healthcare workers. Only the first role is under training.

Situation: Clinical deterioration, potentially acute. The emergency room nurse receives a call from a municipal home healthcare worker with a female patient in her eighties who has symptoms of a urinary tract infection and seems disoriented.

Skills to be trained: To guide a home healthcare worker during a phone call to communicate using ISBAR and to do correct ABCDE observations.

Relevant prerequisite skills: Trainees should know Level 1–3 of KlinObsKommune; i.e., they are familiar with ABCDE, NEWS and ISBAR.

Events and contextual elements trainees are faced with: 1) The ERP systems of the home healthcare worker and the emergency room ERP system do not communicate. 2) The home healthcare worker may not be have all necessary medical equipment for the ABCDE observations.

Tasks to perform: The emergency room nurse shall guide the home healthcare worker in communication in ISBAR, and on observation according to ABCDE observations.

Metrics to measure task performance: 1) How well the severity of the situation is communicated. 2) The degree of mutual trust.

How to measure metrics: The extent to which the emergency room nurse use the situation to explicitly guide the home healthcare worker in observation and communication according to ISBAR and NEWS, and the nurse's ability to detect possible sepsis without stressing the home healthcare worker.

Physical items present: Access to a PC, a phone

Vignettes 4 and 5 are the two opposing sides of a joint vignette. The fact that they are specified separately suggests that the role not under training can be simulated. Simulating one part of an interaction is sometimes desirable for added control over the learning situation.

5   Discussion

The design principles DP1 to DP4 were topics of discussion during the group work, often prompted by the researchers raising awareness of the principles. While DP1 to DP3 were generally accepted at face value, DP4 gave rise to two valuable discussion points that we emphasize here.

First, relating to the stepwise skills model in Fig. 3, DP4 states that it is important to train collaboration skills at Step 4 and 5, even when Steps 1–3 are not completed. This triggered conceptual discussions about the model itself, and in our opinion, these discussions heightened participants' awareness of DP4. The proposed vignettes rely on the presence of suboptimal procedural deployment and skills in several places.

Second, it was necessary to remind the participants of the fact that we were discussing vignettes for collaboration, *not* designing training for collaboration procedures. That is, although ISBAR is a protocol for communication and therefore collaboration (as are also ABCDE and NEWS in essence), we were not designing procedural training for ISBAR (nor for NEWS or ABCDE). Rather, we were designing training for interpersonal collaboration when these procedures are possibly lacking. Understanding this fact resulted in a relevant and innovative insight: Participants were concerned with how skilled personnel must guide less skilled personnel in using ISBAR and NEWS in a reassuring way to elicit the necessary information to evaluate the situation. This amounts to *in situ* training of procedural skills, within the training of interpersonal collaboration under suboptimal circumstances. This brings the idea of *just-in-time learning* to the knife's edge in that the procedural skill of Steps 1–3 in Fig. 3 are trained by necessity to ensure patient safety in a potentially critical situation. This idea is evident in Vignettes 4 and 5. If this is possible in practice, it may be a very good supplement to a more formalised learning of Steps 1–3 in the model in Fig. 3.

A third topic that arose more loosely from the discussions during the group work, was the participants' concern about the importance of training healthcare personnel so that they become aware of each other's different roles and access to information. This was perceived as an important step in developing mutual trust and building confidence to reveal personal short-comings and ask for information. A related topic that emerged was the need to train *systemic awareness*; that is, each individual's awareness of their significance and responsibility for the whole system to work better, both in a specific situation, but also by looking for ways to improve the quality of systemic artefacts (procedures, documentation, etc.).

We found that using an online and jointly shared spreadsheet to be an easy and effective way to structure the discussion and to gather information from the participants. Although devised for a virtual workshop in case of a Covid-19 lockdown, we ended up using this digital solution, after abandoning the white board, when we were, in fact, able to conduct the workshop physically. We found that it is important that the topics asked for in the spreadsheet (via the column names) are tailored to the goal and participants of the workshop. Although carefully designed by the researchers, some participants found that columns were overlapping in topic and asking for similar information. Better explanations before or joining or deleting some columns might have made the data collection even easier and faster. While we have not been able to compare this workshop method with, e.g., using storyboards as outlined by Schiza et al. [26], it seems that the threshold for engaging participants in the discussion using the spreadsheet was low. Quick and easy co-creation is an imperative when working with busy healthcare personnel.

The outcomes of our workshop were likely dependent on our selection of participants and that these participants understood the motivation for the workshop and the salience of the presented case. This resulted in effective participant dialogue and output, although we had limited time with the participants. The flipside of this has two issues: First, the results from this particular study may be replicable and generalizable only to groups consisting of individuals with similar backgrounds and experience. This is a threat to validity unless we are careful when applying our findings from this and ensuing similar studies. Second, although the case and its challenges resonated well with our particular participants, it is not given that healthcare personnel for which we are designing the vignettes will have the same degree of recognition of the importance of the case or its challenges. Indeed, they might perceive that the main issues are something else entirely. We picked the workshop participants precisely for the purpose of eliciting vignettes that address pressing needs and that are relevant for healthcare personnel, and we do have confidence that this is the case. Nevertheless, for the next steps of development, it is vital that representatives for the various roles under training are involved.

6   Final Remarks

The vignettes elicited in this study suggest training for specific healthcare roles. These vignettes will be presented to a stakeholder group that includes these roles. This second workshop will focus on validating the vignettes with these stakeholders and on distilling out a first validated vignette for further development in Stage 3 of our scenario design model, as outlined in Fig. 5. In Stage 3, the manner in which suboptimal procedures and IT services will be represented and implemented must be determined. Moreover, the details of embedding the just-in-time learning elements for *in situ* procedural training will have to be discussed, represented and implemented.

The vignette will be specified using a generic textual and graphical format. Then, this specification will initially be implemented as a role-playing exercise, which we will run with relevant stakeholders to adjust and refine the vignette. It is our aim to incorporate synthetic elements via virtual reality where this can enhance learning. There already exists virtual-reality solutions for procedural training of basic skills (ABCDE and ISBAR), and one interesting way forward would be to see whether these solutions can help us to embed the just-in-time learning of procedural skills mentioned above.

This first vignette will be the start of several iterations comprising of design, implementation and validation of vignettes that will span incrementally more of the desired training space.

We found that the design principles and vignette format helped us to address sub-optimal healthcare procedures and IT services and that the creation of the vignettes engaged the participants. We observed that the focus extended from sub-optimal IT services to the lack of training in procedures and communication in general. By listening carefully to the workshop participants, we were able to instantiate the design principles so that the vignettes would be suited to address the complexity of the healthcare work processes, as well as focusing on the municipal healthcare workers' skills.

The workshop method we used turned out to be a suitable technique for coming up with scenarios that are detailed enough to form a basis for further use. We plan on refining our workshop technique further in other projects where detailed and structured scenarios are needed.

Acknowledgements. The authors are grateful to the healthcare professionals, researchers and administrators for participating in the workshop. The authors are grateful to training coordinator and critical-care nurse Eva Linnerud for providing insights into the central aspects in our discussion and for organizing the workshop and its participants. This research is supported by the Norwegian Research Council under project number 321059 *Close the Gap – Simulation-based training for collaboration within and between healthcare services.*

References

1. Akoglu, C., Dankl, K.: Co-creation for empathy and mutual learning: a framework for design in health and social care. CoDesign **17**(3), 296–312 (2019). https://doi.org/10.1080/15710882.2019.1633358
2. Brattheim, B.J., Hellesø, R., Melby, L.: Planning for post-hospital care–local challenges to general benefits of e-messages: hospital staff's perspectives. In: Proceedings of the 3rd European Workshop on Practical Aspects of Health Informatics (PAHI) (2015)

3. Centre for Development of Institutional and Home Care Services: Klinisk observasjonskompetanse i kommunehelsetjenesten (2021). https://www. utviklingssenter.noklinisk-observasjonskompetanse
4. Davis, M.M., Devoe, M., Kansagara, D., Nicolaidis, C., Englander, H.: 'Did I do as best as the system would let me?' Healthcare professional views on hospital to home care transitions. J. Gen. Intern. Med. **27**, 1649–1656 (2012)
5. Dhaka, S.: Co-creation: literature review and research issues. Int. J. Res. - Granthaalayah **3**(2), 20–37 (2015). https://doi.org/10.29121/granthaalayah.v3.i2. 2015.3037
6. Direktoratet for e-helse: Bruk av pleie- og omsorgsmeldinger i pasientforløp. Technical report. HITS 80806:2012, Direktoratet for e-helse, Oslo, Norway, July 2012
7. Dugstad, J., Eide, T., Nilsen, E.R., Eide, H.: Towards successful digital transformation through co-creation: a longitudinal study of a four-year implementation of digital monitoring technology in residential care for persons with dementia. BMC Health Serv. Res. **19**(1), 366 (2019). https://doi.org/10.1186/s12913-019-4191-1
8. Edgren, M.G.: Cloud-enabled modular services: a framework for cost-effective collaboration. In: Proceedings of the NATO Modelling and Simulation Group Symposium on Transforming Defence through Modelling and Simulation-Opportunities and Challenges (STO-MP-MSG-094) (2012)
9. Ericsson, K.A., Charness, N., Feltovich, P.J., Hoffman, R.R. (eds.): The Cambridge Handbook of Expertise and Expert Performance. Cambridge University Press, Cambridge (2006)
10. Foronda, C.L., Fernandez-Burgos, M., Nadeau, C., Kelley, C.N., Henry, M.N.: Virtual simulation in nursing education: a systematic review spanning 1996 to 2018. Simul. Healthcare: J. Soc. Simul. Healthcare **15**(1), 46–54 (2020). https://doi.org/ 10.1097/SIH.0000000000000411
11. Fuglerud, K.S., Lauritzen, B.H., Eide, H.: Innovativ Rehabilitering i Indre Østfold, Nasjonalt forsøk med kommunal rehabilitering. Sluttrapport følgeevaluering; oppsummering av tjeneste og modell. Technical report, 71, Universitetet i Sørøst-Norge (2021)
12. Fuglerud, K.S., Schulz, T., Janson, A.L., Moen, A.: Co-creating persona scenarios with diverse users enriching inclusive design. In: Antona, M., Stephanidis, C. (eds.) HCII 2020. LNCS, vol. 12188, pp. 48–59. Springer, Cham (2020). https://doi.org/ 10.1007/978-3-030-49282-3_4
13. Gautun, H., Syse, A.: Earlier hospital discharge: a challenge for Norwegian municipalities. Nordic J. Soc. Res. **8**, 1–17 (2017)
14. Girdham, M.S.: District nurse views on improving the transfer of care from hospital to home. Primary Healthcare **26**, 23–27 (2016)
15. Halvorsrud, R., Kvale, K., Følstad, A.: Improving service quality through customer journey analysis. J. Serv. Theory Pract. **26**(6), 840–867 (2016)
16. Hannay, J.E., Brathen, K., Hyndøy, J.I.: On how simulations can support adaptive thinking in operations planning. In: Proceedings NATO Modelling and Simulation Group Symposium on M&S Support to Operational Tasks Including War Gaming, Logistics, Cyber Defence (STO-MP-MSG-133) (2015)
17. Hannay, J.E., Kikke, Y.: Structured crisis training with mixed reality simulations. In: Proceedings of the 16th International Conference on Information Systems for Crisis Response and Management (ISCRAM), pp. 1310–1319 (2019)
18. Hannay, J.E., Fuglerud, K.S., Østvold, B.M.: Stakeholder journey analysis for innovation. In: Antona, M., Stephanidis, C. (eds.) HCII 2020. LNCS, vol. 12189, pp. 370–389. Springer, Cham (2020). https://doi.org/10.1007/978-3-030-49108-6_27

19. Krarup, N.H.V., Grove, E.L., Rohde, C.V., Løfgren, B.: Initial assessment and treatment with the Airway, Breathing, Circulation, Disability, Exposure (ABCDE) approach. Int. J. Gener. Med. **5**, 117–121 (2012)
20. Lyngstad, M., Melby, L., Grimsmo, A., Hellesø, R.: Toward increased patient safety? Electronic communication of medication information between nurses in home healthcare and general practitioners. Home Healthcare Manag. Pract. **25**, 203–211 (2013)
21. Melby, L., Brattheim, B.J., Hellesø, R.: Patients in transition-improving hospital-home care collaboration through electronic messaging: providers' perspectives. J. Clin. Nurs. **24**(23–24), 3389–99 (2015)
22. Nayahangan, L.J., Stefanidis, D., Kern, D.E., Konge, L.: How to identify and prioritize procedures suitable for simulation-based training: experiences from general needs assessments using a modified Delphi method and a needs assessment formula. Med. Teach. **40**(7), 676–683 (2018). https://doi.org/10.1080/0142159X.2018.1472756
23. Object Management Group: Business Process Model and Notation 2.0.2. Technical report. formal/13-12-09, Object Management Group, Milford, Massachusetts, USA, December 2013
24. Royal College of Physicians: National Early Warning Score (NEWS) 2: Standardising the assessment of acute-illness severity in the NHS. Technical report, Royal College of Physicians, London, England (2017)
25. Salas, E., Wildman, J.L., Piccolo, R.F.: Using simulation-based training to enhance management education. Acad. Manag. Learn. Educ. **8**, 559–573 (2009)
26. Schiza, E.C., et al.: Co-creation of virtual reality re-usable learning objectives of 360° video scenarios for a clinical skills course. In: 2020 IEEE 20th Mediterranean Electrotechnical Conference (MELECON), pp. 364–367, June 2020. https://doi.org/10.1109/MELECON48756.2020.9140530
27. Shadrick, S.B., Lussier, J.W.: Training complex cognitive skills: a theme-based approach to the development of battlefield skills. In: Ericsson, K.A. (ed.) Development of Professional Expertise, chap. 13, pp. 286–311. Cambridge University Press (2009)
28. Siegfried, R., et al.: Scenarios in military (distributed) simulation environments. In: Spring Simulation Interoperability Workshop 2012 (2012 Spring SIW), Orlando, Florida, USA, pp. 119–130. Curran Associates Inc., March 2012
29. Simulation Interoperability Standards Organization: SISO-GUIDE-006-2018 - Guideline on Scenario Development for Simulation Environments (2018)
30. Stenseth, H.V., et al.: Simulation-based learning supported by technology to enhance critical thinking in nursing students: protocol for a scoping review (preprint). JMIR Preprints, January 2022. https://doi.org/10.2196/preprints.36725. http://preprints.jmir.org/preprint/36725
31. Stewart, K.: SBAR, communication, and patient safety: an integrated literature review. Honor's thesis, University of Tennessee Chattanooga, Chattanooga, Tennesee USA, December 2016
32. The National Audit Office: The National programme for IT in the NHS: an update on the delivery of detailed care records systems (2011), HC 888 Session 2010–2012
33. The Office of the Auditor General: Riksrevisjonens undersøkelser av: Sak 1: Helse- og omsorgsdepartementets styring av arbeidet med Én innbygger – én journal sak 2: Anskaffelser av konsulenttjenester i Direktoratet for e-helse (2021), 3, 14 (2020–2021)

34. Toppe, K., Navarsete, L.S.: Representantforslag om å be regjeringen evaluere samhandlingsreformen og fremme sak til Stortinget om nødvendige tiltak for at samhandlingsreformens intensjoner kan nås. Representantforslag Dokument 8, 19 S (2018–2019), Stortinget, Oslo, Norway, October 2018
35. Valdersnes, A.K., Venjum, M.L.: Konsept Kompetanse-sentralen: Trygg i egen kommune Designdrevet innovasjonsprosjekt DIP. Technical report, Kjeller Innovasjon, Kjeller, Norway (2016)
36. van den Berg, T.W., Huiskamp, W., Siegfried, R., Lloyd, J., Grom, A., Phillips, R.: Modelling and simulation as a service: rapid deployment of interoperable and credible simulation environments – an overview of NATO MSG-136. In: Winter Simulation Interoperability Workshop 2018 (2018 Winter SIW), Orlando, Florida, USA (2018)
37. Voorberg, W.H., Bekkers, V.J.J.M., Tummers, L.G.: A systematic review of co-creation and co-production: embarking on the social innovation journey. Public Manag. Rev. 17(9), 1333–1357 (2015). https://doi.org/10.1080/14719037.2014.930505

Hey Team: An E-Health Application for Promoting Quality of Life and Safety for Employees and Employers

Paulo Hermida[✉], Gabrielly Bessa, Mauro Teófilo, Ricardo Grunitzki,
and Andrea Medeiros

Mobile Innovation Lab, Sidia Institute of Science and Technology,
Manaus, AM, Brazil
{paulo.hermida,gabrielly.bessa,mauro.teofilo,ricardo.grunitzki,
andrea.medeiros}@sidia.com

Abstract. The COVID(19) pandemic created a sense of urgency for the early identification of its symptoms. Besides preventing the advancement of the disease, it allows for a more effective treatment for the patient. In this context, this work describes the Hey Team collaborative application: a strategy used by some companies in Brazil, and aims to provide support with information, contact with doctors, psychological support, among other features to its employees during the pandemic. Through the application, employees report their health situation daily so that they can be monitored individually. For this strategy to work, technological, legal, ethical, and cultural challenges were overcome. Comparing Hey Team with similar approaches through common indicators, we concluded that the use of a collaborative application, based on mutual trust, managed to achieve its goals, disseminating information and helping employees to get through this difficult time.

Keywords: Collaborative-health COVID-19 · Mobile-collaborative · Early diagnosis COVID-19

1 Introduction

E-health [3,12] is an area that brings together technology, health, and business to offer solutions that improve people's quality of life [8]. Despite being an area in constant evolution, it had a great boost due to the COVID-19 pandemic, where health has become a priority in people's lives. One of the main objectives of e-health applications in the context of the pandemic is to protect people against the worsening and consequent risk of life by observing their health status [10]. Under normal conditions, this monitoring takes place in hospitals, where equipment connected to patients assesses their clinical situation and the response they are having about the treatment they are undergoing. However, with the collapse of

Supported by Sidia Institute of Science and Technology http://www.sidia.com.

the healthcare system due to a large number of infected people, some of these tasks were partially transferred to the e-health applications [7, 13–16]. According to [4] the use of e-health has achieved good results in the early detection of infected people, in the dissemination of information on prevention protocols, in the rapid screening of individuals, in the exchange of information between health professionals and the public, for carrying out early diagnoses and mainly in reducing physical contact between people.

In the absence of known treatments, the approach most used by governments in the (COVID-19) pandemic was the use of alternative measures [9]. Social distancing, isolation of contaminated people, and, in some cases, the closing of public areas, prohibiting the movement of people, strongly affecting the economy [5], are examples of some of these measures.

Several applications were created by governments and research institutions to support public policies, scientific research, and above all help health services in a time of overload. According to [11] these applications can be classified into six categories, some of which may be present in more than one group. Table 1 describes these categories.

Table 1. Covid-19 app categories, according to [11]

App categories	Description
Symptoms	In this application category, you are guided by answering a number of questions about your health and exposure to coronavirus. Then he guides you according to your answers
Contact tracing	The focus of this application category is to track contact between people by measuring the distance between them using for this Bluetooth technology
Health monitoring	Using sensors, these applications monitor people's signals and then send them to analysis in medical centers
Prevalence	These applications provide information about the virus and also about health and safety resources. They bring relevant statistical data on the evolution of the pandemic
Research	Applications developed by colleges and universities to trace and study the dissemination of Covid-19 and its effects. Users send data about their health and symptoms to help researchers find ways to avoid future outbreaks
Telemedicine	This application category allows virtual access to your doctor and transmission of your vital information during this process

In its first versions, the Hey Team application fell into two of the categories in Table 1: Symptoms and Contact Tracing. However, using GPS technology and the focus being to register the presence of employees in risk areas. The use of contact tracing apps is an important tool for public health authorities and local communities in combating the spread of (Covid-19) [6]. Mobile applications, such as [1] and [2], were developed using Bluetooth technology to register when two phones approach, relating this fact to people. If one of the people subsequently shows symptoms of coronavirus, the other party is immediately notified, so they can self-isolate or seek health advice.

The present paper is organized as follows. Section 2 presents a summary of the work related to the development of applications to the Covid-19 pandemic. Section 3 highlights the motivation and problems that this research aims to solve. The Sect. 4 describes the Hey Team application, covering aspects of architecture, interface and design, security, functionality, and data privacy. Results and discussions are presented in Sect. 5. Section 6 summarizes what we have done so far to help people during this difficult time.

2   Related Works

Table 2 presents applications created to help in the fight against (Covid-19). These data show two trends that have reversed over the course of the pandemic. The first was the focus initially given to applications that monitored contact between people. This approach although valid as a tool to combat the pandemic has implications for individual data protection policies, which are already implemented in more than 120 countries. The Hey Team app itself in its current version has already disabled this functionality. The other trend was the empowerment of people to report their health situation. Initially, monitoring vital signs was a trend, as there was not enough information about the behavior of the disease. As the information accumulated and was massively passed on to the population, people were able to have enough knowledge to self-diagnose, reducing costs with remote sensing and increasing the accuracy of diagnoses. Data shows that apps focus on self-diagnosis, with people reporting their symptoms and sending massive amounts of information to users.

Table 2. Applications classified according to the criteria of [11]

Application name	Country	Symptoms	Contact tracing	Telemedicine	Prevalence
COVID-19 GOV PK	Pakistan	X	X		X
CORONAVIRUS-SUS	Brazil	X			X
Covid-19	Vietnam			X	X
Coronavirus Australia	Australia	X			X
COVIDSafe	Australia		X		
Tarassud	Oman	X			X
COVID-19 UAE	UAE	X	X		X
CDC	USA	X			X
JamCOVID19	Jamaica	X			X
Apple COVID-19	USA	X			X
Canada COVID-19	Canada	X			X
Hey Team	**Brazil**	**X**	**X**		**X**

3   Motivation

The Hey Team application is a self-assessment tool, through which employees must answer some pre-determined questions according to the directives of the World Health Organization and the Brazil Health Ministry, to identify and monitor any symptoms that could signify infection by the Coronavirus (COVID-19). Based on the answers to the questions, preventive actions can be taken, as well as the request for the employee to consult the company's medical department for further evaluation and definitive diagnosis. The purpose of the application is to increase the safety and protection of the work environment, through a more efficient screening based on the health self-assessment carried out periodically by the employee.

4   Hey Team: A Collaborative Application

The present paper proposes a mobile application called Hey Team, which provides support to employees who are experiencing the effects of the (COVID-19) pandemic and to the company's health department that can maintain daily contact with these employees through the application. This application serves two categories of users:

1. Company Employees (**CE**): Which are all company employees who previously accepted the support given by the application; and
2. Company medical support (**CMS**): Which are the employees who are part of the company's medical sector, whose objective is to give full support to the other employees.

4.1   Application Requirements

The requirements for this application have been based on the following questions:

1. During the period of the Covid-19 pandemic, with the closing of several essential services, the overload of the health system, with employees working from home, how to maintain the functional and emotional bond with these people so that they can feel welcomed by the company during this difficult period?
2. The company's medical department has kept in touch with employees through email, telephone, and in-person visits in some cases. However, this method is inefficient, as a lot of time is wasted depending on the number of employees and the speed with which the pandemic progresses. Can a digital solution help connect the company's medical sector with other employees to create a quick and mutually beneficial communication channel between them?

4.2 Actors

Hey-team application actors are identified as follows:

- CE Users: discussed in Sect. 4
- CMS Users: discussed in Sect. 4
- Unregisters users: the users who have not registered.
- Firebase: the server and database of the application.

An actor specifies a role played by a human user or any other systems that interact with the application, such as databases, devices, platforms, and servers.

4.3 Use Cases

The use cases for the Hey-team application are shown in Fig. 1.
    The use cases are described below:

1. **Register:** An unregistered user can register using their email address.
2. **Login:** A registered user (CE and CMS) can login using their email address.
3. **Answer Question:** A registered user (CE) can answer the set of questions about your health status.
4. **Register 1st Vaccine Dose:** A registered user (CE) can register your 1st Vaccine Dose, saving an image from his vaccine register status.
5. **Register 2nd Vaccine Dose:** A registered user (CE) can register your 2nd Vaccine Dose, saving an image from his vaccine register status.
6. **Green Passport:** A registered user (CE) receives the Green Passport to access the company's premises.
7. **Red Passport:** A registered user (CE) needs to contact the company's medical service in order to access the company's facilities.
8. **Dashboard:** A registered user (CMS) can access the dashboard information.

4.4 User Journey Map

In this section, we will detail the (CE) user journey, which follows two basic flows that start after the user login the app. The first flow is carried out daily and begins with the acceptance of the application's terms of use and legal. Then a sequence of ten questions is presented to the user to be answered, the content of the questions is related to their health status and each question has a relative weight. At the end of the process, the user declares the veracity of his answers, and a score is automatically generated. If the score value is above a threshold, the green passport is generated and is valid for 24 h, and the flow is terminated. If the result is below the threshold, the user receives the red passport and must contact the company's medical department to be evaluated again, and the flow is terminated.
    The second flow occurs when the user informs that he has already received the 1st or 2nd dose of the vaccine. In this case, it is requested that the image of the document with the vaccine information be captured. This information is

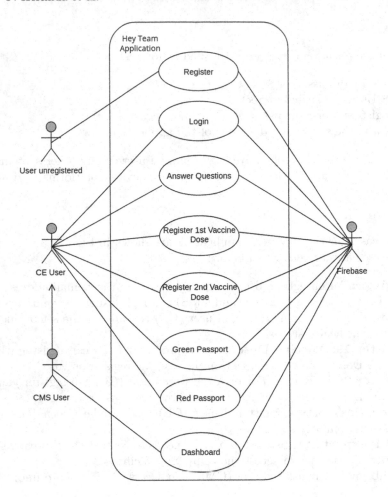

Fig. 1. Hey Team, high level use case.

saved and the flow ends. If the receipt of the 2nd dose is being informed, a permanent green passport is generated and the user no longer needs to answer daily questions about their health, unless they are experiencing a relevant symptom and wish to report this situation. The user journey (CE) is detailed in Fig. 2.

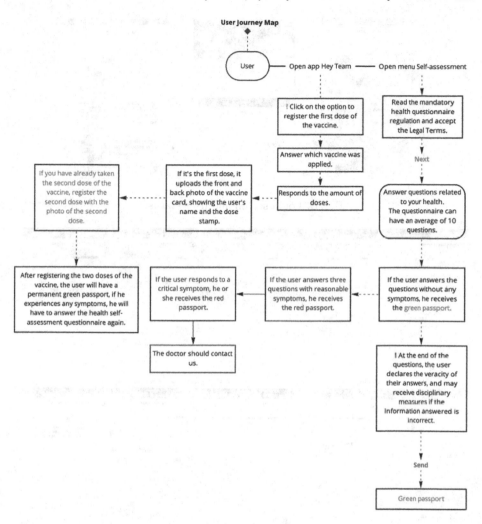

Fig. 2. Hey Team, (CE) user journey map.

4.5 Implementation

In this section, the application screens as well as the main operation flows will be detailed.

1. **Login Screen:** The user uses his email and password to log in to the application. Afterward, the status is verified, which is then returned to the main screen. If the user has already answered the questions on the current day and reached the minimum score, the green passport is presented. If he does not have yet answered the questions or has not reached the minimum score, the red passport will be presented. This sequence can be seen in Fig. 3.

Fig. 3. Login screen and user status.

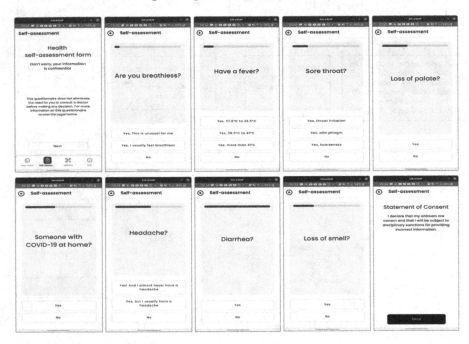

Fig. 4. Questions that the user must answer for the application to calculate his score.

2. **Questions Screens:** The user is initially informed that their data is confidential and that the information that will be collected below is not a substitute for a medical evaluation. From that point, a sequence of questions is presented to the user, each one with possible answer options. After answering the question, the application automatically moves on to the next one, and this flow repeats itself until the last question in the sequence. The last screen informs that the user is responsible for the information provided, and the process is completed. This sequence can be seen in Fig. 5. Then the score is calculated,

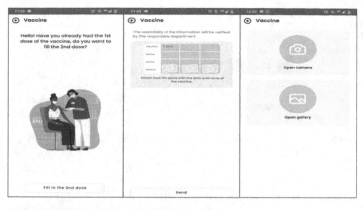

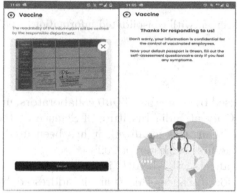

Fig. 5. Vaccine registration flow.

and the application returns to the home screen, presenting the green or red passport as explained in the previous item, Fig. 3.

3. **Vaccine registration:** The vaccine registration flow starts with the user choosing which type of vaccine they took. Then the dose is informed, and the application then asks the user to attach an image or use the camera to capture the vaccination record given at the health post. If it is the second dose, the green passport is permanently generated, and the user no longer needs to answer daily questions about their health, unless they have any symptoms. This sequence can be seen in Fig. 5.

4. **Dashboard:** This screen contains consolidated information that allows an overview of how the pandemic is affecting employees, as well as indicators that assess engagement with the application, the total number of vaccinated, among other important data that serve as a basis for decision-making. The dashboard can be seen in Fig. 6.

Fig. 6. Dashboard screen with consolidated information.

5   Results

The proposed tool is currently used by more than **5000** collaborators, in different companies in South America. Only at Sidia Institute of Science & Technology (Amazon - Brazil), where Hey Team was idealized, it has been used by more than 1300 collaborators since the first semester of 2020.

An important aspect that affects all e-health initiatives is the protection of individual data, in Brazil, for instance, this issue is addressed by federal law 13.709/2018, which was sanctioned in August 2018 and came into force in September 2020. With the implementation of LGPD[1], Brazil joins another 120 nations that have personal data protection policies. Before LGPD, Brazil only had some isolated topics on the subject within the civil engine of the Internet and the Consumer Defense Code. In this aspect, the personal data collected by the Hey Team application follows Brazilian legislation, so that all users authorized its collection and use for the specific purpose of fighting the pandemic. The legal persons responsible for this data are defined, as well as the period for which they were under the responsibility of the company. There are security measures that prevent unauthorized access to this information by unauthorized third parties.

Since its application, Hey Team has allowed Sidia to closely monitor the health of its employees, ensure their safety and also maintain the organization's operations in the face of the Covid-19 pandemic. Several benefits have been observed in the organization, of which it is worth noting:

1. A reduction in the company's medical costs, with activities related to supporting employees in the pandemic;
2. Massive implementation of the social distancing recommendation among employees;

---

[1] http://www.planalto.gov.br/ccivil_03/_ato2015-2018/2018/lei/l13709.htm.

3. Reduction in the time between detection of symptoms and application of tests to start medical support to the employee;
4. Daily monitoring of all employees, generating information for strategic decision-making;
5. Creating a collaborative link between the company and employees who recognize the importance of Hey Team application development and deployment;
6. Expansion of the user base to other countries besides Brazil.

6   Conclusion

The implementation of the Hey Team application took into account, from the beginning, the points that must be present in every e-health application, according to [8]. Efficiency was present when we reduced the cost of the company's medical sector, creating a digital tool that allows the management of hundreds of employees without costing more. This cost reduction, however, did not impact the quality of the service provided, on the contrary, the new tools allowed for an individualized service with a higher quality of care. The data generated by the application made decisions based on evidence, increasing its effectiveness. The direct contact between employees and the company's health sector generated a new relationship of mutual and collaborative trust, creating conditions for the implementation of preventive actions and reaching other scopes beyond the pandemic. And finally, the point that defines Hey-Team as a collaborative application is the equitable way in which all employees were treated, not considering factors other than those related to the health of each one.

References

1. Corona traker (2020)
2. Tracer together (2020)
3. Agyapong, V.I.O., et al.: Closing the psychological treatment gap during the Covid-19 pandemic with a supportive text messaging program: protocol for implementation and evaluation. JMIR Res. Protoc. **9**(6), e19292 (2020)
4. Asadzadeh, A., Kalankesh, L.R.: A scope of mobile health solutions in Covid-19 pandemics. Inform. Med. Unlocked **23**, 100558 (2021)
5. Bonaccorsi, G., et al.: Economic and social consequences of human mobility restrictions under Covid-19. Proc. Natl. Acad. Sci. **117**(27), 15530–15535 (2020)
6. Cho, H., Ippolito, D., Yu, Y.W.: Contact tracing mobile apps for Covid-19: privacy considerations and related trade-offs. arXiv preprint arXiv:2003.11511 (2020)
7. Drew, D.A., et al.: Rapid implementation of mobile technology for real-time epidemiology of Covid-19. Science **368**(6497), 1362–1367 (2020)
8. Eysenbach, G.: What is e-health? J. Med. Internet Res. **3**(2), e20 (2001)
9. Ferguson, N.M., et al.: Impact of non-pharmaceutical interventions (NPIS) to reduce Covid-19 mortality and healthcare demand. Imperial College COVID-19 Response Team, p. 20 (2020)
10. Gardner, R.M., Clemmer, T.P., Evans, R.S., Mark, R.G.: Patient monitoring systems. In: Shortliffe, E.H., Cimino, J.J. (eds.) Biomedical Informatics, pp. 561–591. Springer, London (2014). https://doi.org/10.1007/978-1-4471-4474-8_19

11. Nazario, B.: Coronavirus apps and dashboards (2022)
12. Rowland, S.P., Fitzgerald, J.E., Holme, T., Powell, J., McGregor, A.: What is the clinical value of mhealth for patients? NPJ Digit. Med. **3**(1), 1–6 (2020)
13. Schinköthe, T., et al.: A web-and app-based connected care solution for Covid-19 in-and outpatient care: qualitative study and application development. JMIR Public Health Surveill. **6**(2), e19033 (2020)
14. Timmers, T., Janssen, L., Stohr, J., Murk, J., Berrevoets, M., et al.: Using ehealth to support Covid-19 education, self-assessment, and symptom monitoring in the netherlands: observational study. JMIR Mhealth Uhealth **8**(6), e19822 (2020)
15. Yasaka, T.M., Lehrich, B.M., Sahyouni, R.: Peer-to-peer contact tracing: development of a privacy-preserving smartphone app. JMIR Mhealth Uhealth **8**(4), e18936 (2020)
16. Zamberg, I., Manzano, S., Posfay-Barbe, K., Windisch, O., Agoritsas, T., Schiffer, E.: A mobile health platform to disseminate validated institutional measurements during the covid-19 outbreak: utilization-focused evaluation study. JMIR Public Health Surveill. **6**(2), e18668 (2020)

Exploring Off-the-Shelf Data in Job Design: A Comparison of Metadata in Situation Awareness, Task Analysis and Data Visualization

Leena Naidu, Rachita Naidu, Sandeep Krishna Ramachandran,
and Vincent G. Duffy[✉]

Purdue University, West Lafayette, IN 47907, USA
{lnaidu,naidu4,ramach22,duffy}@purdue.edu

Abstract. This work presents a comparative analysis of three topics of interest in job design and three databases – Google Scholar, Scopus, and Crossref. The initial comparison is done using metadata indicating similarities and differences in the number of articles, relevance, popularity, trend, and other such factors sthat impact the research, a publication or its authors. These databases are commonly available to researchers. They are referred to here as 'off-the-shelf' and were not designed for this analysis. The study is conducted for the job design-related topics, Situation Awareness, Task Analysis and Data Visualization and were taken from the 'Handbook of Human Factors and Ergonomics, 5th edition. The topics selected are also of interest to researchers specializing in human-computer interaction. Bibliometric and statistical analysis were conducted for the articles using the dataset exported from Harzing's software. Using Microsoft Excel and Minitab inferences were drawn following analysis. The study checked for overlapping of authors from the chosen articles and the prescribed handbook selections and results were reported. The regression modeling included in analysis extends methodology beyond prior literature that showed metadata comparisons by observation using descriptive statistics. An illustration is shown that demonstrates differences in key articles of interest identified by search. Key articles identified in Scopus had the highest number of citations. In addition to differences that can be seen in numbers of articles and numbers of citations using the metadata from these databases, it should be noted that the articles of interest that may be identified or recognized by scholars with interest in the topic may also be different. From prior research, it was expected that many articles that were found in both Google Scholar and Scopus would have a higher number of citations in Google Scholar. However, articles of interest that were identified in Scopus had more citations in Google Scholar. This was the significant result found when comparing samples with known variance $(Z = -157, p < 0.0001)$. Articles of interest found in Scopus had more citations in Google Scholar than the articles of interest identified in Google Scholar. This suggests researchers should diversify their search among databases when conducting ergonomics and HCI-related literature reviews especially in the early stages of their research. The effort to diversify search can help early career researchers identify more impactful articles.

Keywords: Bibliometric analysis · Ergonomics · Job design · HCI · Human factors

V. G. Duffy (Ed.): HCII 2022, LNCS 13320, pp. 227–236, 2022.
https://doi.org/10.1007/978-3-031-06018-2_16

1 Introduction and Background

With the vast amount of data available for computation, data warehouses act as cloud storage that provides enhanced functionalities for processing data over physical servers. Data mining and research have become simpler by exploring off-the-shelf data that can be accessed easily through open-source search engines. These databases include metadata and metrics pertinent to the publications.

Over the years, there seems to be an increase in the big data about most study areas with the growing trend towards relevant search results and the quality of such results. The areas discussed in this work are contained within the scope of Human Factors and ergonomics. The three topics selected for the purpose of this study are **Situation Awareness, Task Analysis, and Data Visualization.** Definitions for the three topics are shown in more detail in the Handbook of Human Factors and Ergonomics, 5th ed. in related chapters (Pattanaik and Wiegand 2021; Endsley 2021; Hollnagel 2021). A Google Ngram for the three topics indicates the number of times the particular keyword has been referenced in books over the specified period viz. 1980–2019. The graph shows the percentage interaction between the three topics. It can be inferred that the popularity of 'Data-Visualization' has increased over the years while a steadily decreasing trend can be observed for 'Task Analysis' (Fig. 1).

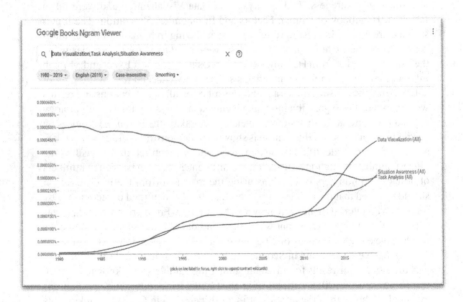

Fig. 1. Google Ngram result for the three topics

This study compares the yield from the three databases (**Google Scholar, Scopus, and Crossref**) on the selected topics including the count of search appearances, the number of citations, data concerning the authors, and the publications. Methods used for comparisons of databases are adapted from (Harzing and Alakangas 2016). Methods used for comparisons of topics using descriptive statistics are adapted from (Duffy 2021).

This study also documents detailed data mining procedures for getting these results. Two articles identified from each database search that are relevant to each topic (six from each database) were chosen and the yield for these is compared against the respective platforms. The study makes use of the Harzing software for providing extracting the dataset (metadata) that made possible numerous comparisons throughout the report.

2 Data Mining Procedure

The procedure involved using the topic as the keywords for the search. Different ways of writing the keywords impacted the results. For instance, in Scopus, inserting the word "AND" between two or more keywords ensures that all of those words are included in the results. The word "OR" implies that the result may include one or more of the suggested keywords.

These were used to find the most significant articles related to the topic. The results were filtered based on many factors. These include -

- Type of the article such as journals, dissertations, books, thesis, reviews, and conference papers.
- Date of publication which can be set from or for a specified period. The yield is reported for all dates as well as articles from 2015 and later.
- Other filters include language, authors, region, affiliation, publication stage, etc.

The table below shows the yield (number of articles) on the aforementioned topics across the three databases(Table 1).

Table 1. Number of articles compared on each database in different periods

Topic	Google scholar	Scopus	Crossref
Situation awareness			
All years	360000	27855	103987
2015 and above	39700	13220	71623
Task analysis			
All years	1070000	470	3069729
2015 and above	160000	205	1752653
Data visualization			
All years	363000	134083	900499
2015 and above	65100	62186	421540

It can be seen from the table above that the yield or the number of articles in each topic has increased over time, with an upward inclination in the yield from the year 2015 and above. This is an indication of the growing research in particular fields over the years.

The use of quotation marks alters the search results in all databases. Writing a word or phrase in quotation marks indicates that the user requires the given string of words in the exact order in the article's title or body. This is an important tool to filter the most relevant results. The following table shows a comparison of the yield of articles on Google Scholar with or without the quotations (Table 2).

Table 2. Number of articles on google scholar compared with and without quotations

Google scholar	With quotations	Without quotations
Situation awareness	4320	360000
Task analysis	6550	1070000
Data visualization	9000	363000

From the search results, the number of citations for each article can be inferred along with the source of the citations. It is possible to filter the search based on the number of citations to find the most cited articles. For instance, the table below shows the articles on the selected topics from Google Scholar, listed according to most cited to least cited. The list indicates articles sorted for all years- (Table 3)

Table 3. Articles from Google Scholar sorted from most-to-least cited

Title of articles identified from search in Google Scholar(GS)	Number of citations (in GS)
Applied cognitive task analysis (ACTA): a practitioner's toolkit for understanding cognitive task demands	740
A comparative analysis of SAGAT and SART for evaluations of situation awareness	343
Situation awareness in anesthesia: concept and research	219
Data analysis strategies for targeted and untargeted LC-MS metabolomics studies: Overview and workflow	206
The cognitive task analysis methods for job and task design: review and reappraisal	145
Multidimensional illumination functions for visualization of complex 3D environments	9

Two articles from each of three topics related to human factors and ergonomics were selected from all three databases. These were run through the Harzing dataset in "Publish or Perish" (Harzing's data mining software).

3   Bibliometric and Statistical Analysis

These analyses show results that extend beyond prior reports. Included in the analyses in this section is a comparison of results of the identified articles and authors. Results

// Harzing's Publish or Perish 6.42.6345.6928

File   Edit   Query   View   Help

Query	Source	Papers	Cites	Cites/ye...
My queries				
✓ A comparative analysis of SAGA...	G Google Sch...	1	343	14.29
Saved queries				
✓ Applied cognitive task analysis (...	G Google Sch...	1	740	30.83
Trash				
✓ Data analysis strategies for targ...	G Google Sch...	1	206	34.33
✓ Multidimensional illumination fu...	G Google Sch...	1	9	0.28
✓ Situation awareness in anesthesi...	G Google Sch...	1	219	24.33
✓ The cognitive task analysis meth...	G Google Sch...	1	145	8.06

Fig. 2. Comparison of Google Scholar articles on harzing data set

Author	Google Scholar	Scopus
Mica Endsley	73	35
Adrian W Gelb	62	52
Robert JB Hutton	12	3
Daniel J Levendousley	33	18
Carl Gutwin	73	47
Gerald Mathews	99	60
Joaquim Jaumat	33	28
Sumanta N. Pattnaik	34	22
Laura E Mauzen	15	13
Zhiyuan Wang	6	23

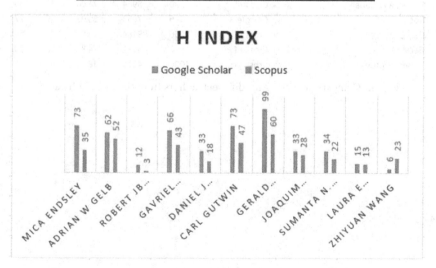

Fig. 3. Comparison of H Index of authors across two databases

show that the number of citations for articles identified in the three databases is highest for those identified in Scopus. These initial results suggest that Scopus may be more effective at emphasizing the most impactful articles during search (Fig. 2).

Harzing's Publish or Perish: Harzing's software is a unique and significant research software that helps in collecting data on several citations across numerous databases making it easier to compare and analyze the yield for various publications over the years. It includes metrics from a vast array of data like the number of citations, average citations, h, g-index, etc. This helps to get an idea of multiple aspects of a publication such as its popularity in a particular search engine, the quality level of the article, etc.

h-index is a performance metric that indicates the overall impact of an author's academic contribution and performance by measuring the quantity and quality of their scholarly work. Similarly, the g-index is another such metric that is focuses on the most-cited articles. It aids in signifying the relative impact of different authors based on their highly cited publications (Fig. 3).

The following figure was extracted using the Harzing dataset and it consists of data pertaining to seven authors compared against google scholar and Crossref. When entering the name of an author in the search bar, the software pulls out information from all sources making it easier to visualize and run relevant statistical analysis (Fig. 4).

Search terms	Source	Papers	Cites	Cites/ye...	h	g
✓ Mica Endsley	G Google Sch...	308	43357	1171.81	70	208
✓ Adrian Gelb	G Google Sch...	311	11542	288.55	54	104
✓ Sumanta Pattanaik	G Google Sch...	157	7710	226.76	32	87
✓ Mica Endsley	⮝ Crossref	1000	19018	213.69	54	125
✓ Carl Gutwin	G Google Sch...	423	21419	158.66	72	139
✓ Adrian Gelb	⮝ Crossref	1000	11117	106.89	56	83
✓ Sumanta Pattanaik	⮝ Crossref	1000	5964	71.00	35	55
✓ Robert Hutton	G Google Sch...	346	7053	50.02	39	77
✓ Carl Gutwin	⮝ Crossref	1000	9184	32.57	48	76
✓ Gerald Mathews	⮝ Crossref	1000	3781	24.88	28	50
✓ Robert Hutton	⮝ Crossref	1000	4375	18.70	34	57

Fig. 4. Comparison metrics for different authors from Harzing's software

A regression analysis was performed to measure the effect of cites per year in Google Scholar and CrossRef on the g-index of any particular author on Google Scholar. The following image shows the results of the analysis (Fig. 5 and Table 4).

Regression Equation

Google Scholar = 80.3 + 0.275 Cites/year(GS) - 0.843 Cites/year(CR)

Coefficients

Term	Coef	SE Coef	T-Value	P-Value	VIF
Constant	80.3	29.4	2.73	0.053	
Cites/year(GS)	0.275	0.101	2.72	0.053	6.55
Cites/year(CR)	-0.843	0.614	-1.37	0.242	6.55

Model Summary

S	R-sq	R-sq(adj)	R-sq(pred)
39.9179	79.86%	69.80%	0.00%

Analysis of Variance

Source	DF	Adj SS	Adj MS	F-Value	P-Value
Regression	2	25281	12641	7.93	0.041
Cites/year(GS)	1	11830	11830	7.42	0.053
Cites/year(CR)	1	3005	3005	1.89	0.242
Error	4	6374	1593		
Total	6	31655			

Fig. 5. Regression analysis on g-index and analysis of variance

A comparison of the means of number of citations shows Scopus helped emphasize articles for selection that were more impactful than the other two databases, Google Scholar or Crossref. Key articles identified in Scopus had the highest number of citations. In addition to differences that can be seen in numbers of articles and numbers of citations using the metadata from these databases, it should be noted that the articles of interest that may be identified or recognized by scholars with interest in the topic may also be different. From prior research, it was expected that many articles that were found in both Google Scholar and Scopus would have a higher number of citations in Google Scholar. However, articles of interest that were identified in Scopus had more citations in Google Scholar. This was a significant result statistically and a noticeable and practical difference ($Z = -157$, $p < 0.0001$; means for GS = 279.8 citations per identified article; SC = 6131.5 citations per identified article) found when comparing samples for a hypothesis test with known variance (Montgomery and Runger, 2018). Articles of interest found in Scopus had more citations in Google Scholar than the articles of interest identified in Google Scholar.

Table 4. Comparison of number of the number of articles across three databases and two time periods for each of the three topics. In total, 18 articles are compared Eighteen articles (3 × 2 × 3 = 18 articles) are shown in the table.

Database	Title	Number of Citations (in original database)	Year	Number of Citations in Google Scholar
SC5	Visualizing data using t-SNE.	14471 (SC)	2008	20685
SC3	Toward a theory of situation awareness in	4853 (SC)	1995	10173
SC6	Data-intensive applications, challenges, techniques and technologies: A survey on Big Data.	1781 (SC)	2014	3317
SC4	A descriptive framework of workspace	676 (SC)	2002	1444
SC1	EEG Correlates of Task Engagement and Mental Workload in Vigilance, Learning,	566 (SC)	2007	951
GS1	Applied cognitive task analysis (ACTA): a practitioner's toolkit for understanding	739 (GS)	1998	739
CR4	Situation Awareness: Review of Mica Endsley's 1995 Articles on Situation	94 (CR)	2008	417
GS2	A comparative analysis of SAGAT and SART for evaluations of situation	341 (GS)	1998	341
GS3	Situation awareness in anesthesia:	228 (GS)	2013	228
SC2	The Psychometrics of Mental Workload: Multiple Measures are Sensitive but	131 (SC)	2015	219
GS4	Data analysis strategies for targeted and untargeted LC-MS metabolomics studies:	214 (GS)	2016	214
GS5	The cognitive task analysis methods for job and task design: review and	148 (GS)	2004	148
CR6	Data visualization saliency model: A tool	3 (CR)	2017	36
CR3	Quantitative Analysis of Situation Awareness (QASA): Modelling and	4 (CR)	2018	16
GS6	Multidimensional illumination functions for visualization of complex 3D environments	9 (GS)	1990	9
CR2	Component-Total Task Relationships - Simple and Sequential Practice Effects	0 (CR)	1968	2
CR5	What Kinds of Questions do Students Ask	0 (CR)	2020	2
CR1	The Collection and Analysis of Human	0 (CR)	1970	0

4   Discussion and Conclusion

The regression analysis below, and the analysis of variance show that the g-index of the author in Google Scholar decreases as the number of cites/year increases in Crossref, and it has a linear relationship with the number of cites/year in Google Scholar.

The articles selected for the course of the study consisted of multiple authors that overlapped with those from the 'Handbook of Human Factors and ergonomics', Fifth Edition. Mica Endsley from Situation Awareness, Gavriel Salvendy from Task Analysis-related article in Behavior and Information Technology and co-editor of the handbook, and Sumantha Pattnaik from the Data Visualization chapter in the handbook appeared in both the search as well as the book. These authors along with others are included in the references in the aforementioned handbook.

Articles of interest found in Scopus had more citations in Google Scholar than the articles of interest identified in Google Scholar. This suggests researchers should diversify their search among databases when conducting ergonomics and HCI-related literature reviews especially in the early stages of their research. The effort to diversify search can help early career researchers identify more impactful articles.

References

Berka, C., et al.: EEG correlates of task engagement and mental workload in vigilance, learning, and memory tasks. Aviat. Space Environ. Med. **78**(5II), B231–B244 (2007)

Philip Chen, C.L., Zhang, Chun-Yang.: Data-intensive applications, challenges, techniques and technologies: a survey on big data. Inf. Sci. **275**, 314–347 (2014). https://doi.org/10.1016/j.ins.2014.01.015

(2022).https://search.crossref.org/

Duffy, V.G.: Digital human modeling in design. In: Salvendy, G., Karwowski, W. (eds.) Handbook of Human Factors and Ergonomics, 5th edn., pp. 761–781. Wiley, Hoboken (2021)

Edgar, G.K., et al.: Quantitative Analysis of Situation Awareness (QASA) modelling and measuring situation awareness using signal detection theory. Ergonomics **61**(6), 762–777 (2018)

Endsley, M.R.: Toward a theory of situation awareness in dynamic systems. Hum. Factors **37**(1), 32–64 (1995)

Endsley, M R., Selcon, S.J., Hardiman, T.D., Croft, D.G.: A comparative analysis of SAGAT and SART for evaluations of situation awareness In: Proceedings of the human factors and ergonomics society annual meeting, vol. 42(1), pp. 82–86. SAGE Publications, Los Angeles (1998)

Endsley, M.: Situation awareness. In: Salvendy, G., Karwowski, W. (eds.) Handbook of Human Factors and Ergonomics, 5th edn., pp. 434–455. Wiley, Hoboken (2021)

Geist, A.M., Zavala, A.: Component-total task relationships - simple and sequential practice effects (component total task relationships, analyzing simple and sequential practice effects with aid of melton complex coordinator). Hum. Factors **10**, 333–343 (1968)

Google nGram (2022). https://books.google.com/ngrams

Google Scholar (2022). https://scholar.google.com/

Gorrochategui, E., Jaumot, J., Lacorte, S., Tauler, R.: Data analysis strategies for targeted and untargeted LC-MS metabolomics studies: overview and workflow. TrAC Trends Anal. Chem. **82**, 425–442 (2016)

Gutwin, C., Greenberg, S.: A descriptive framework of workspace awareness for real-time groupware. Comput. Support. Coop. Work (CSCW) **11**(3), 411–446 (2002). https://doi.org/10.1023/A:1021271517844

Harzing, A.-W., Alakangas, S.: Google Scholar, Scopus and the Web of Science: a longitudinal and cross-disciplinary comparison. Scientometrics **106**(2), 787–804 (2016). https://doi.org/10.1007/s11192-015-1798-9

Hollnagel, E.: The changing nature of task analysis. In: Salvendy, G., Karwowski, W. (eds.) Handbook of Human Factors and Ergonomics, 5th edn., pp. 358–367. Wiley, Hoboken (2021)

Kastens, K.A., Zrada, M., Turrin, M.: What kinds of questions do students ask while exploring data visualizations? J. Geosci. Educ. **68**(3), 199–219 (2020)

Kempf, R.P.: The collection and analysis of human factors data in task analysis (06, 1970)

Matthews, G., Reinerman-Jones, L.E., Barber, D.J., Abich, J.: The psychometrics of mental work-load: multiple measures are sensitive but divergent. Hum. Factors **57**(1), 125–143 (2015). https://doi.org/10.1177/0018720814539505

Matzen, L.E., Haass, M.J., Divis, K.M., Wang, Z., Wilson, A.T.: Data visualization saliency model: a tool for evaluating abstract data visualizations. IEEE Trans. Visual Comput. Graphics **24**(1), 563–573 (2017)

Militello, L.G., Hutton, R.J.B.: Applied cognitive task analysis (ACTA): a practitioner's toolkit for understanding cognitive task demands. Ergonomics **41**(11), 1618–1641 (1998)

Montgomery, D., George, C.R.: Hypothesis Testing on the Difference in Means in Applied Statistics and Probability for Engineers, 7th edn., p. 247. Wiley, Hoboken (2018)

Mudur, S.P., Pattanaik, S.N.: Multidimensional illumination functions for visualization of complex 3D environments. J. Vis. Comput. Animat. **1**(2), 49–58 (1990)

Pattanaik, S.N., Paul Wiegand, R.: Data visualization. In: Salvendy, G., Karwowski, W. (eds.) Handbook of Human Factors and Ergonomics, pp. 893–946. Wiley (2021)

Scopus (2022). https://www.elsevier.com/solutions/scopus

Schulz, C.M., Endsley, M.R., Kochs, E.F., Gelb, A.W., Wagner, K.J.: Situation awareness in anesthesia: concept and research. J. Am. Soc. Anesthesiologists **118**(3), 729–742 (2013)

Van der Maaten, L., Hinton, G.: Visualizing data using t-SNE. J Mach Learn Res **9**(11), 2579–2605 (2008)

Wei, J., Salvendy, G.: The cognitive task analysis methods for job and task design: review and reappraisal. Behav. Inf. Technol. **23**(4), 273–299 (2004)

Wickens, C.D.: Situation awareness: review of Mica Endsley's 1995 articles on situation awareness theory and measurement. Hum. Factors **50**(3), 397 (2008)

Ways of Economical Production in Medical Institution Risk Management

Vasily Orel, Viktoriia Smirnova, Natalia Guryeva, Dmitriy Chentsov,
Liubov Sharafutdinova, Vladimir Zatulkin, and Sergey Lytaev

Department of Healthcare Organization, Saint Petersburg State Pediatric Medical University,
Saint Petersburg, Russia
physiology@gpmu.org, salytaev@gmail.com

Abstract. Priority tasks for the development of health care are the rational use of resources, increasing the availability and quality of medical care. The reform process should be based on the use of an innovative approach to the optimal use of available resources. This approach is lean manufacturing, which allows to address the causes of existing losses, minimize risks and costs. Wastage in healthcare is something that has no value both for the patient and the medical organization. The main losses in health care are considered to be overproduction, unnecessary actions, undue transportation, excess stocks, excessive processing, waiting, remaking/waste material. The practical implementation of losses elimination is possible with the use of lean manufacturing tools: mapping, just in time, visualization, standardization, 5C method. Application of the principles and tools of lean manufacturing in medical organizations providing primary health care to the population of St. Petersburg made it possible to address such problems as: difficulty of making an appointment with a doctor, lack of comfortable waiting areas, crossflows of patients, long-term preventive examinations. Thus, the introduction of lean manufacturing technologies made it possible to reduce time losses and create conditions that are followed by valuable interaction of a patient and a medical organization.

Keywords: Lean manufacturing · Losses · Value · Medical organization · Lean manufacturing tools · Value stream · Mapping · Innovative approach

1 Introduction

The priority tasks of healthcare development are to increase the efficiency of the use of state owned resources, create conditions for improving the availability and quality of medical care, and reduce the risks of negative events associated with the provision of medical care. In order to insure public satisfaction with the availability and quality of medical care, medical organizations transfer to patient-oriented medicine, which is characterized by an increase in the time of doctor's direct work with a patient and a reduction of time for performing actions that do not create value for the patient. In modern economic conditions, the reform process should be based on the use of an innovative approach to the management of a medical organization based on the principles of lean

© The Author(s), under exclusive license to Springer Nature Switzerland AG 2022
V. G. Duffy (Ed.): HCII 2022, LNCS 13320, pp. 237–248, 2022.
https://doi.org/10.1007/978-3-031-06018-2_17

manufacturing, which allows to achieve certain efficiency in addressing existing losses and minimizing costs [5, 11, 12, 22].

The idea of Lean Manufacturing was formulated and implemented by Henry Ford (1863–1947), an American industrialist who in 1914 created the world's first in-line production model using a FORD car production line. At the same period, A.K. Gastev (1882–1939) developed and launched a system of scientific organization of labor in the Soviet Union. Unlike Henry Ford, who dealt with improving production processes, A.K. Gastev focused on the human factor. He believed that the effectiveness of the organization as a whole starts with the personal effectiveness of each person in the workplace. The principles and ideas of lean manufacturing were then far ahead of their time and were not accepted by the business community. Later, in 1950, the Japanese manager Tai-ichi Ohno became the founder of the concept of lean manufacturing in its modern sense, who developed the production system for Toyota (Toyota Production System, TPS), which in Western interpretation became known as Lean Production, Lean Manufacturing, or simply Lean. Toyota company successfully implemented the first lean production experience and achieved tremendous economic success, which provoked interest in the technology and led to significant development, refinement, revision and modification of the original concept, as well as its combination with other various production optimization methodologies [14, 20]. First, the concept of lean manufacturing was applied in industries with discrete manufacturing, primarily in the automotive industry. The pioneers of Russian lean manufacturing are the Gorky Automobile Plant GAZ, then the Kama Automobile Plant KamAZ. Later the concept was adapted to the conditions of process production, and now this concept is actively used in the public administration sector, banking, education, trade and healthcare.

Lean production in healthcare is a system focused on increasing the satisfaction of consumers with medical services, reducing the labor losses of medical personnel, improving the quality and productivity of labor, and minimizing risks [5, 11].

The introduction of the basic principles of lean manufacturing in the work of medical organizations has a positive impact on both organizational and therapeutic - diagnostic processes (Table) [15].

The key principle of lean production in healthcare is the continuing production activity, without delays and queues, due to the uniform workload of personnel, rational logistics, optimal layout of the areas of a medical organization and elimination of all types of losses [5, 9, 22].

2   Methods

In order to eliminate all types of losses peculiar for each problem, indicators were selected that reflected the figures of current and target state of the process. Monitoring and audit of processes within the framework of the implementation and realization of improvement projects was carried out throughout the entire period of activity focused on elimination of losses.

Losses in healthcare is something that has no value for the patient and the medical organization. The main losses in healthcare are considered to be overproduction (16%), unnecessary actions (20%), undue transportation (10%), excess stocks (19%), excessive processing (6%), waiting (22%), remaking / defects (7%) (Fig. 1) (Table 1).

Table 1. Basic principles of lean manufacturing in healthcare

Basic principles of lean manufacturing	Application in healthcare system
Strategic focus	Analysis of the system of medical care
Focusing on creating value for the consumer	Any activity is considered from the position of increasing value for the patient (rule: Think like a customer")
Organization of the value stream for the customer	All processes and operations built in a continuous production flow must create value for the patient
Actions that create value	Professional actions of medical workers: collecting complaints, examining the patient, recommendations for treatment, performing diagnostic studies, sampling biomaterial
Actions that do not create value, but are inevitable for a number of reasons	Actions that must be performed during the professional activities of medical workers: applying a tourniquet, preparing medical papers, preparing for research
Activities that do not create value	Actions that do not create value for the patient (losses): queue at the registration office, long waiting time to be admitted in the doctor's office, registration to have diagnostic tests made, long stay in a medical organization, long time to have medical examination made
Pulling	Organization of processes for the provision of medical care, taking into account continuity, accessibility and rational use of medical organization resources
Continuous Improvement	Improving the activities of a medical organization in order to increase value for the patient, improve the value stream, reduce losses and involve staff in improvement projects
Building a corporate culture based on respect for people	Corporate culture helps to maintain the desire for continuous improvement in the employees of the medical organization

Target. To present the main types of losses in healthcare and tools for their elimination.

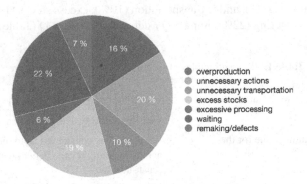

Fig. 1. The main types of losses in healthcare

Overproduction is the most unprofitable type of losses, which causes other losses. In the healthcare sector, this type of losses is manifested in uncallable and duplicated results of some laboratory and diagnostic tests; duplication of medical records; uneven workload on medical staff. Extra actions are all movements that are not part of a useful activity. This type of loss manifests itself in an unoptimized organization of work environment, improper organization of the ergonomics of workplaces and the labor process. The reasons for the presence of unnecessary actions are: irrational location of offices and departments; inconvenient location of equipment, office equipment, furniture in offices; lack of brief instructions, memos for medical personnel; lack of a precise and understandable software interface; lack of a clear algorithm for interaction between a doctor and a patient. Unnecessary transportation is a type of loss that is caused by the irrational location of the units of a medical organization; excessive transportation of paper documents; unnecessary transportation of laboratory tests; movement of the patient beyond the minimum necessary, including cases due to improperly organized process. Much attention must be paid to inventory management, as excesive stocks of drugs, consumable items, reagents, disinfectants, stationery, forms to be filled in, increase the costs associated with storage, movement, damage and disposal. Overprocessing is a type of losses that occurs when more work than is regulated by the requirements of the current procedures and standards for the provision of medical care is performed. Actual Losses Expectations in healthcare are associated with delayed completion of research; incorrect work of the information system; queues at doctors' offices; uneven distribution of workload among medical personnel. Losses from defects and alteration arise due to poor-quality documentation, re-testing due to violations of the rules of preparing for the study, the rules for taking biomaterials, storing and transporting biomaterials to the place of study. In addition, defects occur when there is a violation of the procedure for providing medical care, deviations from standards, non-compliance with clinical recommendations, mistakes in reports, incorrect codification, etc. To analyze and determine the share of each type of loss in the overall result of the improvement process, a Pareto chart is used, which allows to determine how much time from the overall process is taken by losses (Fig. 2).

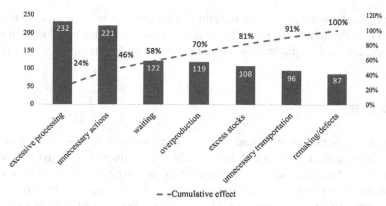

- -Cumulative effect

Fig. 2. Analysis of types of losses

Losses are also formed in case of adverse consequences associated with lack of organizational measures, technologies and risk management methods in a medical organization (Fig. 3).

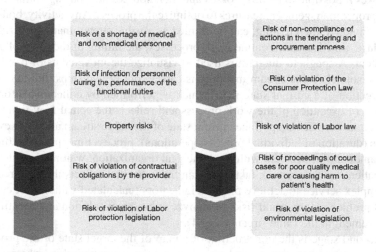

Fig. 3. Risks that form adverse consequences for a medical organization

In international standards, for example, ISO 9001:2015, the concept (risk based thinking) is used. By implementing a risk management policy, a medical organization identifies and minimizes factors that can affect routine work and cause adverse consequences [1, 4, 6, 7, 13]. Identified violations by regulatory organizations in the framework of strengthening supervisory functions, increasing the number of inspections, increasing penalties, can also be potential sources of risks.

The practical implementation of the elimination of losses is carried out by the introduction of lean manufacturing tools. To achieve the goal of diminishing losses, the main tools are used: mapping, just in time, visualization, standardization, the 5C method [15, 16].

3 Outcomes

The targeted implementation of lean manufacturing tools made it possible to organize patients' flows management, which led to reduction of queues at the reception desk, reduction in the time a patient spent in a medical organization, to create comfortable waiting areas, to organize convenient navigation and visualization, organize patients' advanced appointments to a doctor, introduce a remote appointment with doctors, reduce the time for laboratory and diagnostic studies, reduce the time for medical examinations and preventive examinations, implement clinical guidelines and standardize work processes [3].

The priority tool of lean manufacturing is mapping. Mapping is a tool for visualization and analysis of both material and information flows in the value creation process, which makes it possible to identify losses and their sources and, basing on the analysis, work out proper management measures to optimize the process. Any activity, both value-creating and non-value-creating, can be framed as a value stream map [10, 21, 22]. To detect delays, time losses in routine work processes, the timing of the route of patients is carried out. A spaghetti diagram is used to visualize the movements of patients and medical personnel. Value stream mapping is carried out in two steps: the first stage is the construction of a current state map, which is performed by collecting information at the place of execution of the work process and reflects the actual flow indicators at the date in question. The map of the current state of the value stream allows to evaluate: cycle time (duration of individual process operations); process time; process efficiency; patient's amount of movement within the medical organization; waiting time/downtime (for the patient/for the doctor); takt time - an indicator that reflects the required speed of the complex service to achieve planned indicators (calculated value); root causes of identified problems, losses and risks to analyze subsequent solution and identify areas for improvement in the value stream (Fig. 4).

The second stage is the construction of a map of the target state of the process. A target value stream map is produced for a specific date, in which the problems solved by the open improvement project are eliminated (Fig. 5).

Using innovative approaches, including in planning, the tool is used just in time, in this case, medical care is guaranteed to be performed in the exact sequence, at the required time and in the proper volume.

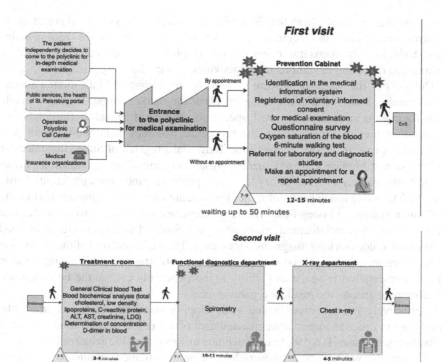

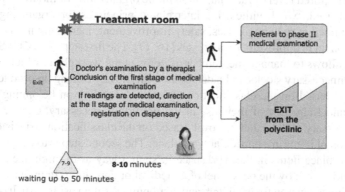

Process time = 162 minutes
Efficiency coefficient = 38%

Fig. 4. An example of a map of the current process and losses at different stages realization of the improvement project

The visualization tool allows to effectively solve the problems of visual presentation of information, ensuring the required level of security, Corporate culture helps to maintain the desire for continuous improvement in the employees of the medical organization searching and detecting deviations in the activities of a medical organization [1, 2, 16, 18]. The tools of the visual healthcare system are navigation and information stands. The information boards contain information about the medical organization, available options for making an appointment with specialists, routing of patients in the conditions of a particular medical organization, the procedure, volumes and conditions for providing medical care in accordance with the Territorial Program of State Guarantees of Free Provision of Medical Care to Citizens, higher and controlling organizations, insurance medical organizations, regulatory legal acts, preventive measures, preferential drug provision. The navigation system of a medical organization is an important part of the visualization system and one of the criteria for characterizing the quality of space. The system consists of an architectural and planning solution and navigation elements (road signs method, color marking, diagrams, signs, etc.). The main function of the navigation system is to create comfortable conditions for the patients' stay in a medical organization with quick orientation in space and ability to independently choose the best route for their movement around the medical organization.

To effectively use resources aimed at developing standards, rules, requirements, technologies in order to improve the management of a medical organization, the **standardization** tool is used [16, 19]. Standardization makes it possible to increase labor productivity, improve working conditions, reduce the number of medical mistakes, improve the quality of diagnostics and preventive measures, and rationally use the resources of a medical organization. Standardization of processes is presented in the form of regulatory documents: algorithms, instructions, block diagrams, standard operating procedures.

To achieve the required level of rationalization in the organization of the workspace, the **5C method** is used, which unites five interrelated principles for organizing the workplace/space, aimed at reducing losses, safety improvement, increasing motivating and involving personnel in improvement processes [16, 17]. The first step of the 5C "Sort" method. This step allows to manage the number of items in the workplace, which leads to a reduction in unnecessary stocks and a decrease in injuries by freeing up production spaces. This step is based on the classification of items depending on belonging to a given workplace and frequency of their use in the workflow: necessary, unnecessary urgently and unnecessary with further removal. Based on the classification, a decision is made on the location of items in a particular workplace. The second step is to keep order. This step allows to place items in the workspace in such a way as to minimize losses during their use and search by the personnel of a medical organization. Item placement involves determining a location for each item and displaying the item using visualization tools. All measures for the rational arrangement of workplace/space items contribute to reducing losses both from medical care in the process of performing work, and from patients in the process of receiving medical services in a medical organization. The third step "Keep clean" reflects the sanitary and epidemiological requirements for medical organizations and includes keeping workplaces/spaces clean and constant readiness for use. The fourth step "Standardization" allows to work out a workplace standard that regulates the location of items, the number of items and control, as well as instructions

First visit

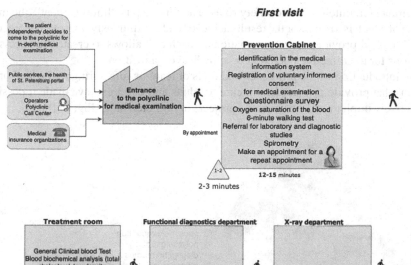

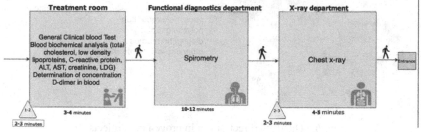

Second visit

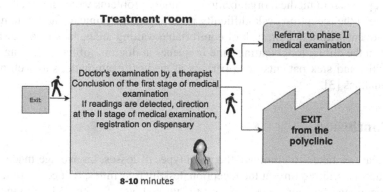

Process time = 55 minutes
Efficiency coefficient = 78%

Fig. 5. An example of a target state map for one of the implemented improvement projects

for equipment maintenance and safety rules. The fifth step is "Improvement", the main purpose of which is to monitor the results achieved and continuously improve the process. The 5C method provides for a systematic approach and allows to create the necessary conditions for the effective operation of a medical organization.

The introduction of the principles and tools of lean manufacturing in medical organizations that provide primary health care to adults and children have made it possible to effectively implement improvement projects in St. Petersburg (Fig. 6) [8, 10].

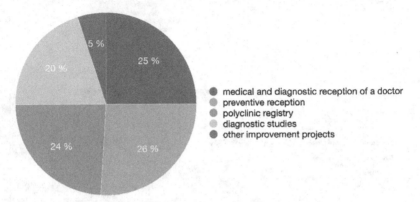

Fig. 6. The main directions of improvement projects

At the stage of implementation of improvement projects, while introducing an innovative approach in medical organizations, primary problems were identified: long waiting time at the reception desk, difficulty in calling in the clinic, difficulty in making an appointment with a doctor, lack of comfortable waiting areas, lack of accessible navigation in the clinic, long waiting time in queues at doctors' offices, crossing the flows of healthy and sick patients, long periods of medical examinations as well preventive examinations [3].

4 Conclusion

The measures taken to eliminate the main types of losses, on average made it possible to reduce the waiting time at the reception desk by four times, reduce the time to call in the receptionist by four times, increase the throughput of the blood sampling room by 2 times, reduce the patient's waiting time for a specialist's examination at the doctor's office by eight times, to reduce the time of making an appointment for a second visit to the doctor by five times, to increase the time the doctor works directly with patients by half, to reduce the number of medical examinations and preventive examinations to three visits. The application of the principles and tools of lean manufacturing made it possible to ensure the efficient and rational use of the resources of a medical organization, achieve high labor productivity, increase patient satisfaction with the quality and availability of medical care.

Thus, the introduction of an innovative approach based on the principles of lean manufacturing in medical organizations providing primary health care to adults and children allowed minimizing risks, eliminating losses and creating conditions that add value in the process of interaction of a patient and a medical organization.

References

1. Bogomolov, A.: Information technologies of digital adaptive medicine. Inf. Autom. **20**, 1154–1182 (2021)
2. Burgess, N., Radnor, Z.: Evaluation of lean manufacturing in healthcare. Int. J. Assess. Qual. Med. care. **26**, 220–235 (2013)
3. Chentsov, D., Smirnova, V., Orel, O.: The experience of implementing lean manufacturing in St. Petersburg children's polyclinics. Russ. Pediatr. J. **23**(1), 231 (2020)
4. International Standard ISO 9001:2015 Quality management system
5. Karakulina, E., Vergazova, E., Khodyreva, et al.: A new model of a medical organization providing primary health care. In: Methodological recommendations, Moscow (2019)
6. Lytaev, S.: Modern neurophysiological research of the human brain in clinic and psychophysiology. Lect. Notes Comput. Sci. **12940**, 231–241 (2021). https://doi.org/10.1007/978-3-030-88163-4_21
7. Lytaev, S.: Modeling and estimation of physiological, psychological and sensory indicators for working capacity. Adv. Intell. Syst. Comput. **1201**, 207–213 (2021). https://doi.org/10.1007/978-3-030-51041-1_28
8. Orel, V., Guryeva, N., Smirnova, V., et al.: Implementation of the pilot project lean polyclinic: first results and challenges. Med. Theor. Pract. **4**, 402–403 (2019)
9. Orel, V., Guryeva, N., Smirnova, V., et al.: Principles of lean production in a medical organization providing primary health care. Eurasian Bull. Pediatr. **1**(1), 2–7 (2019)
10. Orel, V., Guryeva, N., Smirnova, V., Sharafutdinova, L., et al.: Lean production tools in the management of the infrastructure of a medical organization providing primary health care. Med. Healthc. Organ. **5**(2), 4–10 (2020)
11. Orel, V., Nosyreva, O., Smirnova, V., et al.: Multiproject management of a primary health care medical organization Materials of the IV National Congress with international participation "Healthy children - the future of countries." Child. Med. North-West **8**(1), 257–258 (2020)
12. Orel, V., Smirnova, V., Gurieva, N., et al.: Experience in the formation of a system of knowledge of lean production tools and methods used in the implementation of improvement projects in medical organizations. Med. Healthc. Organ. **6**(3), 20–28 (2021)
13. Scott, D., Huntington, D.: A Lean tool supporting continuous improvement in Intermountain. Q. Healthc. Manag. **26**, 173–174 (2017)
14. Taiichi, O.: Toyota's Production System: Moving Away from Mass Production. Institute of Integrated Strategic Studies, Moscow (2013)
15. The national standard of the Russian Federation GOST R 56020–2020 lean manufacturing. Basic provisions and dictionary. Standartinform, Moscow (2020)
16. The national standard of the Russian Federation GOST R 56407–2015 lean manufacturing. Basic methods and tools. Standartinform, Moscow (2015)
17. The national standard of the Russian Federation GOST R 56906–2016 lean manufacturing. Organization of the workspace (5S). Standartinform, Moscow (2016)
18. The national standard of the Russian Federation GOST R 56907–2016 Lean manufacturing. Visualization. Standartinform, Moscow (2016)
19. The national standard of the Russian Federation GOST R 56908–2016 Lean manufacturing. Standardization of work. Standartinform, Moscow (2016)

20. Vumek, D., Jones, D.: Lean manufacturing: How to Get Rid of Losses and Achieve Prosperity of your Company, 7th edn. Alpina Publisher, Moscow (2013)
21. Vader, M.: Lean production tools. Alpina Publisher, Moscow (2016)
22. Yakovleva, T., Kamkin, E.G., Karakulina, E., Vergazova, E., et al.: Implementation of improvement projects using lean manufacturing methods in a medical rganization providing primary health care. Methodological Recommendations, Moscow (2019)

Workplace Health Promotion: mHealth as a Preventive Mediator Between Psychosocial Workplace Characteristics and Well-Being at Work

Vera Barbara Rick[1]([✉]), Peter Rasche[2], Alexander Mertens[1], and Verena Nitsch[1,3]

[1] Institute of Industrial Engineering and Ergonomics, RWTH Aachen University, Eilfschornsteinstraße 18, 52062 Aachen, Germany
{v.rick,a.mertens,v.nitsch}@iaw.rwth-aachen.de
[2] Institute of General Practice and Family Medicine, Ruhr-University Bochum, Universitätsstraße 150, 44801 Bochum, Germany
peter.rasche@ruhr-uni-bochum.de
[3] Product and Process Ergonomics, Fraunhofer Institute for Communication, Information Processing and Ergonomics FKIE, Campus-Boulevard 55-57, 52074 Aachen, Germany

Abstract. High levels of mental work stress have significant implications for employees and employers. Epidemiological studies consistently show links between high levels of work stress and self-reported mental and physical health problems, including depression, anxiety, cardiovascular disease, and type 2 diabetes. Therefore, helping employees to cope with mental stress is becoming more and more important. The present study examines the mediating influence of mobile health (mHealth) technology use on the relationship between psychosocial workplace characteristics and employee well-being. The investigated sample consisted of 2946 employed working adults from four different countries (United Kingdom, United States, Canada and Australia) who used a mHealth application between 2019 and 2021. The results indicate a positive indirect relationship between psychosocial workplace characteristics, mHealth use, and employee well-being, suggesting that mHealth use can have a positive impact on employee well-being and help them cope with psychosocial demands at work. The results further suggest an influence of gender and age. In the long term, mHealth technologies may provide support in everyday work to help manage psychosocial demands.

Keywords: Mental stress · Psychosocial demands · Employee well-being · mHealth

1 Introduction

Increasing digitization and the emergence of new forms of work organization has led to profound changes in our working world. Looking at the effects of these changes on our work and in particular on our work tasks, it is noticeable that mental stress is gaining in importance. The reason for this is, on the one hand, that the mental demands at work are increasing, e.g., due to work intensification, accelerated communication, dissolution of boundaries and constant reachability. On the other hand, there is a change in the actual work tasks, from formerly rather physical activities to increasingly cognitive and informational work demands [1–3].

One effect is increasing absences from work due to illness. In recent years, absenteeism, which refers to "the failure to report to work as scheduled" [4], especially due to mental illness, has increased rapidly. Mental health problems have become one of the leading causes for absenteeism from work and early retirement all over the European Region [5]. In the United Kingdom, the overall annual cost of work-related mental stress to employers is estimated to be over £26 billion, driven by increased staff turnover, performance degradation, and absenteeism [6]. In Germany, sick leave due to mental illness has more than doubled in the last 14 years. Whereas in 2006 every employed person was on sick leave for an average of 1.4 days due to a mental illness, by 2020 this number had risen to 2.99 days per employed person per year [7]. Absenteeism contributes significantly to lower productivity in the workplace and incurs substantial financial costs through health insurance claims, overtime pay, and legal claims [8]. Even though it is not only the changed working conditions and work demands that have an influence on these increased numbers of mental illnesses, there is strong evidence to believe that high mental stress in the workplace has a significant impact on the health of employees.

1.1 Psychosocial Workplace Conditions

Epidemiological studies consistently show links between high mental work demands and self-reported mental and physical health problems, including depression, anxiety, cardiovascular disease, and type 2 diabetes [9]. A poor psychosocial work environment has been found to increase the risk of sick leave and disability pensions not only due to mental disorders [10, 11] but also physical health issues [12]. Work and health are closely related, so that health and the ability to work have a bidirectional interaction and can influence each other. In addition to monetary livelihood, the positive effects of work include, for example, daily structuring, social relationships, appreciation and self-fulfilment. However, possible negative or unhealthy effects of work may result from excessive physical and psychological stress at work [13].

A number of models have been established that are suitable for describing mental stress and strain at the workplace. The basis of the ISO standard 10075, which describes work design guidelines regarding mental workload. is the stress-strain model [14]. Here, mental stress is understood as the "totality of all assessable influences that act on a person from the outside and affect him psychologically", while mental strain is understood as the "direct effect of mental stress within the individual depending on his or her current condition". Whereas physical strain describes the effects of stress on the muscular and cardiovascular systems, mental strain is the totality of all detectable influences that have a mental, e.g. cognitive and emotional effect on the working person. The terms are value-neutral, i.e. positive and/or negative effects are possible, depending on the individual reaction of the working person to the stress.

Another highly influential model in research on the relationship between work and health is the Job-Demand-Control (JDC) model, also known as job strain model. The JDC model identifies two critical aspects of the work situation: job demands and job control

[15]. In the 1980s, a social dimension was added to the model [16, 17] resulting in the Job-Demand-Control-Support (JDCS) model. Job demands refer to workload and have been operationalized mainly in terms of time pressure and role conflict, whereas job control refers to the person's ability to control his or her work activities. The model states that the most negative reactions in the form of psychological strain and illness are produced in a work environment with high demands and low control. On the other hand, high demands combined with high control lead to more learning, motivation, and skill development. Therefore, control over one's own work can mitigate the consequences of high demands. In addition, the extended model includes social integration as a crucial aspect in the development of workers' health. The JDCS model characterizes the most harmful work situation as having high demands, low control, and low support (or isolation).

One step further goes the Job Demands-Resources (JD-R) model [18, 19]. The JD-R model assumes that employee well-being is explained by work demands and work resources. High work demands deplete workers' mental and physical resources and therefore lead to energy depletion and health problems. In contrast, work resources promote engagement and off-the-job performance. Several studies have shown that work resources can buffer the effects of work demands on stress responses [19, 20]. Moreover, research has confirmed that work resources have a motivational potential especially when work demands are high [21]. Workplace resources are defined as "anything perceived by the individual to help attain his or her goals" [22] and enable employees to successfully accomplish their tasks and goals while enhancing their well-being and performance [19]. According to the JD-R model, resources at the workplace have the potential to increase well-being and to mitigate or even change the negative effects of work demands [18]. While psychological factors such as supportive managers and colleagues or role clarity are generally understood as such resources, the question arises as to what extent technologies exert an influence on the relationship of job demands and the employee health outcomes. This paper aims to provide a first approach to consider the use of mHealth technology in the context of psychosocial workplace characteristics and health outcomes.

1.2 Mobile Health Technology at Work

Mobile health (mHealth) technologies have rapidly gained popularity among the general population. MHealth technologies include wearable monitoring devices or trackers and smartphone applications (apps) designed to help people manage their own health and well-being. The potential value of mHealth in health promotion lies in its widespread appeal, accessibility and ability to reach large populations at a low cost. Not surprisingly, current research has focused on the potential benefits of mobile health apps for health prevention and care [23–25]. Mobile health has also become relevant from a legal and policy perspective, for example, the European Commission's e-health strategy identifies mobile health applications as playing a central role in the e-health action plan 2012–2020 [26]. Although mHealth apps have been a great success in both the private sector and professional healthcare [27], their use in professional settings presents difficulties. However, work is an important factor for health. Individual health behaviours are shaped by workplace culture and values, there is no clear dividing line between "work-related" and "non-work-related" illnesses, as our health behaviours span these environments and cannot be artificially separated [28]. More and more employers establish workplace health promotion programs responding to the (mental) health needs of their employees by developing and implementing workplace (mental) health programs that focus on providing health promotion services to improve employee productivity by optimizing employee health [29]. The most common outcomes related to mHealth technology at work are less absenteeism, higher psychological well-being and engagement as well as higher productivity. For example, research has shown that digital interventions can reduce depression, anxiety, and stress in the workplace [30]. Furthermore, there is evidence of a positive effect of mHealth use and psychological well-being at work [31], as well as a positive impact of mHealth interventions on employee productivity and engagement immediately and in the medium term after use [32]. While prior research has analysed direct effects of mHealth usage and health outcome, this paper now seeks to address the mediating influence of mHealth technologies in the context of psychosocial workplace characteristics and health outcomes.

1.3 Research Objective

Research has demonstrated the effectiveness of mHealth technology on the consequences of psychological stress in the workplace - direct relationships to absenteeism, well-being, and productivity have been observed. However, previous research has focused on the direct relationship to health outcomes. This paper focuses on the use of mHealth technologies in relation to psychosocial workplace characteristics and health outcomes, and seeks to examine the mediating influence of mHealth technologies on the relationship of psychosocial workplace characteristics and health outcomes. This is a step toward understanding the benefits of mobile health technologies in the work context and how they can mitigate or even change the negative effects of psychosocial work demands. Therefore, the direct relationship between psychosocial workplace characteristics and employee well-being, including the mediating influence of usage behaviour of a mHealth app, is analysed. Thus, the research question that was investigated was:

RQ1: Does the use of a mHealth app mediate the relationship between psychosocial workplace characteristics and employee well-being?

2 Method

2.1 Procedure of Data Collection

The evaluated database consists of persons who used the "HeadUp" health app between 2019 and 2021 [33]. The app is used to track the user's health data to generate customized interventions and tips based on the results and is used in terms of company's health intervention program. To do this, the app initially asks users a short questionnaire to get to know health relevant parameters covering topics like workplace and work environment, family and friends, physical and mental illnesses as well as previous illnesses in the family, nutrition habits, hobbies and leisure activities as well as demographic data such as gender and age. These questions are asked to understand and take then into account in terms of the intervention advice. The app also offers the ability to set individual goals so that the app can assist in achieving them, such as increasing activity, learning better sleep habits, or focusing on one's mental health. Furthermore, if the user agrees, it can record daily data on e.g. exercise and sleep habits and generate suitable interventions and tips, motivating and supporting the user in living a healthy life.

The app was available via App- and Google-Play Store in English. At the moment the app is still available as a white label solution companies could integrate into their health programs.

Data was retrieved from the app provider in an anonymous form as secondary data. The subjects consented to the anonymized analysis of the data. As described, the app was publicly available, which is why participants from all over the world were recorded. For the present analysis, to ensure sufficient data quality, only English-speaking countries with a sufficient sample size and western cultural background were included in the analysis in order to rule out linguistic misunderstandings and to maintain comparability of data. The procedure of data processing is explained in the following section.

2.2 Pre-processing of Data Set Used

To ensure sufficient data quality investigated data was filtered for English-speaking countries with a sufficient sample size (>100) and western cultural background were included in the analysis in order to rule out linguistic misunderstandings and to maintain comparability of data. Person living in an English-speaking country using the app in English language were expected to have sufficient command of the language to adequately use and understand the app. However, it needs to be mentioned that therefore not necessarily only native speakers were included in this analysis.

The app's measured data cover 110 different countries; after excluding all countries that did not recognize English as a national language, 17 countries remained for further analysis. Since this publication is particularly focused on working conditions and worker health, which vary greatly depending on the country's level of development, only developed countries were included in the analysis. The selection of developed countries was based on the Human Development Report 2020 [34]. After this step, eight countries remained in the analysis. The next step involves the analysis of the sample size per country. A threshold of at least 100 subjects per country was used to obtain an appropriate sample size for the following structural equation model [35]. In addition, at the individual level, only individuals who were employed at the time of app use were selected, as the analysis focuses on workplace characteristics. Four countries remained in the analysis: N = 1527 respondents from the United Kingdom, N = 713 from Canada, N = 550 from the United States, and N = 469 from Australia (in total: N = 3259 individuals). The final step involves the identification of outliers, using the one-dimensional box-plot method [36]. Outliers are defined as such if they lie outside the whiskers of the box plot diagram, i.e. are larger than 1.5 times the quartile distance in both directions. The present data set contains only outliers above the upper whisker. For the analysis of the outliers, the variable of usage frequency was used, which means that users who opened the app excessively more often in a short period of time than most of the users were excluded from the analysis. The sample used breaks down into N = 431 users living in Australia, further N = 482 are residents of the United States, N = 635 are living in

Canada and N = 1398 of the users are residents of the United Kingdom (in total: N = 2946 individuals).

2.3 Measures

The app contains two scales that are relevant for the following analysis.

The two scales used are composed of a scale for recording psychosocial workplace characteristics with five items and the general employee well-being using the WHO-5 questionnaire with five items too. In addition, log files of the app were used to analyse usage behaviour. A detailed description follows below.

Psychosocial Workplace Characteristics. The initial questionnaire of the app included five items to assess aspects of the psychosocial work characteristics are used, namely work demands ("My job is more stressful than I ever imagined"), control over one's own work ("Have freedom to decide how I do my work"), work satisfaction ("I'm satisfied with my job"), support of colleagues ("I feel comfortable asking for support") and support of the supervisor ("My boss tries to understand me"). The dimensions were selected based on the Job Demand-Control-(Support) model [16]. Each dimension is asked with a single item, which was to be answered on a 5-point Likert scale, subjects could indicate whether they *strongly agree* (5), *agree* (4), were *neutral* (3), *disagreed* (2) or *strongly disagreed* (1) with the statement.

Well-Being. The 5-item World Health Organization Well-Being Index (WHO-5) is a short and generic global rating scale measuring subjective well-being. The WHO-5 was derived from the WHO-10 [37], which in turn was derived from a 28-item rating scale [38] used in a WHO multicentre study in 8 different European countries [39]. The WHO-5 items are: "I have felt cheerful and in good spirits", "I have felt calm and relaxed", "I have felt active and vigorous", "I woke up feeling fresh and rested" and "My daily life has been filled with things that interest me". The respondent is asked to rate how well each of the five statements applies to him or her when considering the last 14 days. Each of the five items is scored from 5 (all of the time) to 0 (none of the time). From the items a raw score can be calculated (addition of the item values), which ranges from 0 (absence of well-being) to 25 (maximal well-being).

App Usage. Users' log files were analysed to determine how often the app was used. The actual opening of the app was calculated in relation to the months of use in order to be able to map both the time of use and the actual active use.

2.4 Participants

The analysed sample consisted of 2946 employed working adults. On average, the subjects were 39.69 years old (SD = 11.393 years). The sample represents an over-representation of female participants (64.8%) and breaks down into 14.6% participants living in Australia (N = 431), further 16.4% are residents of the United States (N = 482), 21.6% are living in Canada (N = 635) and finally 47.5% of the participants are residents of the United Kingdom (N = 1398). The following Table 1 gives an overview of the sample demographics.

Table 1. Descriptive statistics for the sample demographics.

Female (n, %)	1910 (64.8)
Male (n, %)	1036 (35.2)
Age in years (*M, SD*)	39.69 (11.393)
Education level	
School graduation (n, %)	896 (30.4)
Training Courses/Diploma (n, %)	1009 (34.2)
University degree (n, %)	971 (33.0)
PhD (n, %)	29 (1.0)
Country	
Australia (n, %)	431 (14.6)
Canada (n, %)	635 (21.6)
United Kingdom (n, %)	1398 (47.5)
United States (n, %)	482(16.4)

2.5 Procedure of Calculation and Evaluation of Results

To answer hypotheses and research questions different methods were used. Exploratory factor analyses (principal component analyses) and reliability analyses were calculated to verify the structure and internal consistency of the scales, using IBM SPSS Statistics version 25 was used. The research question was addressed by calculating a simple mediation model using R version 4.0.5 and package lavaan, version 0.6–9. In case of non-normally distributed data, the Satorra-Bentler scaled chi-squared test was calculated as it is robust to the violation. To make the model more robust bootstrapping with 5000 samples was used. To analyse indirect effects, the product terms of latent variables are calculated [40]. The fit of the model was evaluated using $\chi2$, Comparative Fit Index (CFI), Root Mean Square Error of Approximation (RMSEA) and Standardized Root Mean Square Residual (SRMR) [40]. CFI≈0.95 describes a good model fit, a perfect fit would correspond to a value of one, RMSEA-values ≥ 0.10 are described as unacceptable for samples >250 data points [41]. In order to quantify the correlation of the latent variables without the influence of the mediator, Pearson correlation coefficients were calculated. The effect size of the correlation is based on the following classification: $r = .10$ describes a small effect, $r = .30$ a medium effect and $r = .50$ a large effect [42]. In order to take into account any influences of demographic data, these were examined beforehand by means of correlation analyses, t-tests and ANOVAs. It was examined, on the one hand, whether age has an influence (correlation analysis), or if gender (t-test), or the country significantly affects the variables psychosocial workplace characteristics, mHealth usage and well-being.

3 Results

3.1 Scale Verification and Descriptive Statistics

Principal Component Analysis. As described, psychosocial workplace characteristics were measured using five items. To verify the structure and internal consistency a Principal Component Analysis (PCA) was calculated to extract the most important independent factors. The Kaiser–Meyer–Olkin measure of sampling adequacy is .764, representing a relatively good factor analysis, and Bartlett's test of Sphericity is significant (p < .001), indicating that correlations between items were sufficiently large for performing a PCA. Only factors with eigenvalues ≥1 were considered following the Kaiser-Guttman criterion [43, 44]. Examination of Kaiser's criteria and the scree-plot yielded empirical justification for retaining one factor with eigenvalues exceeding one, which accounts for 48.396 of the total variance.

Reliability Analysis. For reliability analysis, Cronbach's alpha was calculated to assess the internal consistency of the psychosocial workplace characteristics. The internal consistency of the scale is satisfying, with Cronbach's $\alpha = .721$, and above the threshold following Schmitt (1996). The scale used to assess well-being was the WHO-5 questionnaire, which has already been scientifically studied in numerous cases. A factor analysis was therefore not calculated, but a reliability analysis was performed. The internal consistency of the scale is satisfactory with Cronbach's $\alpha = .881$ [45]. Both scales are not normally distributed according to Kolmogorov-Smirnov test (p < .05). Therefore, in the following analysis correction procedures such as Satorra-Bentler's scaled chi-squared test are used, as it is robust to non-normally distributed data [46].

Descriptive Statistics. The descriptive statistics show that general well-being is evaluated rather positively (M = 14.23, SD = 5.00); the same applies to the psychosocial workplace characteristics (M = 3.574, SD = 0.691). Users have used the app for 390 days on average (SD = 219.207 days) and opened the app on average every two days. A more detailed overview of the descriptive statistics can be found in the following Table 2. The number of responses per item/scale varies because the subjects were not forced to answer all items.

3.2 Pre-analysis for Model Development

Correlation Analyses. In a first step, in order to quantify the correlation of the latent variables without the influence of the mediators, Pearson correlation coefficients were calculated. Employee well-being and usage behaviour are significantly positively correlated (r = .158, p < .001, n = 2941), as well as well-being is also significantly positively correlated with psychosocial workplace characteristics (r = .296, p < .001, n = 2915). Both correlations show small effects [47].

To determine whether age needs to be included in the model as a control variable, a correlation analysis was used to examine the extent to which correlations exist between age and the factors under study. Age correlates significantly with all variables studied ($p < .05$). While the effects are small in all cases, well-being is most strongly affected

Table 2. Scale verification and descriptive statistics.

	α	M	SD	Min.	Max.
Well-being	.881	14.23	5.000	0	25
Psychosocial workplace characteristics	.721	3.574	0.691	1	5
App - Days of usage [days]	–	390.080	219.207	1.000	787.000
App – Foregrounded [number of times]	–	109.970	182.095	0	2500.000
App - Usage per day [number of times/days]	–	0.40	0.39	0.00	1.71

Note. α = Cronbach's Alpha, M = Mean value; SD = Standard Deviation, "Days of Usage" represents the number of days the app was installed on the smartphone, "Foregrounded" represents the number of times the app was opened by the user, "Usage per Days" represents Foregrounded/Days of Usage

Table 3. Pearson's correlations coefficients.

	Age	Well-being	Usage behaviour	Work characteristics
Age	1			
Well-being	.189**	1		
Usage behaviour	.093**	.158**	1	
Psychosocial workplace characteristics	.088**	.296**	0.036	1

Note. **. Correlation is significant at the 0.01 level (2-tailed)

by age, with the other two variables only slightly affected. A more detailed overview of the correlation analyses can be found in the Table 3.

Country-Specific Differences. In the following, differences with regard to countries have been examined in order to be able to include corresponding influences in the mediation analysis. A single factor analysis of variance was calculated, which is robust against the already described violation of the normal distribution [48, 49]. Homogeneity of variances was asserted using Levene's Test, which showed that equal variances could be assumed in all cases (p > .05). For both general well-being and app usage behaviour, no significant differences can be identified in relation to the different countries. In contrast, however, significant differences emerge with respect to psychosocial workplace characteristics: $F(3, 2913) = 2.654$; $p = .047$; $\eta^2 = .003$. Bonferroni post-hoc analysis revealed a significant difference (p < .001) only between psychosocial workplace characteristics of the United States and United Kingdom. Employees from the United States evaluated their psychosocial workplace characteristics significantly worse than users from the United Kingdom (p = .034). However, the effect size is very low ($\eta^2 = .003$), which is why country-specific differences are not further considered in the mediation model.

Gender Specific Differences. Finally, gender specific differences are examined using an unpaired t-test. The t-test is robust to violation of the normal distribution [50, 51]. Homogeneity of variances was asserted using Levene's Test, which shows that variances are equal (p > .05). Significant differences are found for all variables studied. Male employees' rate their psychosocial working conditions significantly worse than female employees' rate, but rate their general well-being significantly better. Male users used the app significantly less often than female user. The effect sizes are associated with moderate to high effects, which is why gender differences are further analysed in the mediation model. A more detailed overview of the unpaired t-Test is given in the following Table 4.

Table 4. Unpaired t-Test

	M (SD)	Statistics	p-value	Cohen's d
Well-being	Female: 13.76 (4.998) Male: 15.10 (4.890)	t(2912) = −3.247	<.001	0.690
Usage behaviour [times/days]	Female: 0.378 (0.378) Male: 0.451 (0.416)	t(2938) = −4.827	<.001	0.392
Psychosocial workplace characteristics	Female: 3.544 (0.692) Male: 3.682 (0.416)	t(2943) = −7.007	<.001	4.960

Note. M = Mean value; SD = Standard deviation

3.3 Mediation Model

Finally, the mediating influence of mHealth use on the relationship between psychosocial workplace characteristics and well-being was examined. Responses from 2910 subjects were included in the analysis. Following the findings on differences between female and male employees, group differences were included in the analysis. Furthermore, employee age was included as a control variable. First, the entire simple mediation model shows with CFI(r) = .937, RMSEA(r) = .075 and SRMR = .034 a reasonable fit to the data, even if the CFI is somewhat low. The Chi^2 Test, on the other hand, showed a significant result, $\chi 2(13) = 200.267$, p < .001, indicating, that the predicted model and observed data differ significantly. However, since this may be attributable to the large sample size and by the size of the correlations in the model [52]. It was decided to proceed with the mediation analysis based on the other indicators pointing to a good fit.

In the following, the standardized coefficients (β) are reported to be able to ensure comparability of the groups. For both groups, female (f) and male (m) employees, an effect of psychosocial workplace characteristics on employee well-being was observed, with the effect being stronger for male employees ($\beta_m = .402$, $\beta_f = .306$; p < .001). In contrast, psychosocial workplace characteristics do not significantly predict the mediator (β_m = .027 β_f = .022; p > .05). Nonetheless, in both groups, mHealth app usage behaviour is in turn significantly related to subjective well-being, whereby differences between male and female employees are observed. While the effect size is negligible for male employees, a clear relationship is evident for female employees (β_m = .097, β_f = .306; p < .001). As described, age was used as a control variable. There are significant relationships for both groups with regard to psychological workplace characteristics and well-being, as well as a significant relationship of usage behaviour of the mHealth app and age for female employees. However, age leads to meaningful effect sizes, especially for female employees. The older the female employees are, the more frequently they use the mHealth app (β_f = .101; p < .001), furthermore the older the employees are, the better they rate their well-being (β_m = .087, p < .005, β_f = .148; p < .001) (Fig. 1).

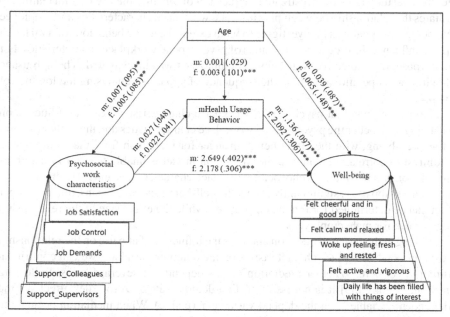

Fig. 1. Tested mediation model; unstandardized coefficients (B) and standardized coefficients in parenthesis (β) for male (m) and female (f) employees; ***: $p < .001$, **: $p < .01$, *: $p < .05$.

In a next step, for the whole sample the indirect effect was calculated. The indirect effect was calculated using the product of $a*b$. For the total effect, the indirect and the direct effect were added: $c + (a*b)$. Both the indirect effect and the total effect show a significant result for the whole sample (Table 5).

Table 5. Simple mediation analysis

	b	β	p	c′
*a*b*	0.048	.007	*	.296**
c	2.380	.343	***	
*c + (a*b)*	2.428	.350	***	

Note. Indirect effect: a* b, direct effect: c, total effect: c + (a* b), correlation coefficient: c′, b: estimate, β: standardized estimate, ***: $p < .001$, **: $p < .01$, *: $p < .05$

4 Discussion

The present study aims to investigate the question of whether the use of a mHealth app mediates the relationship between psychosocial workplace characteristics and employee well-being. The goal was to investigate to what extent the usage behaviour of a mHealth app can influence the (negative) outcomes of psychosocial workplace characteristics. For this purpose, the subjective well-being of employees was investigated. The app usage behaviour was operationalized via the frequency of app usage analysing the log files of the app.

The results show that psychosocial workplace characteristics have an influence on well-being. The better the psychosocial workplace characteristics are, the higher the subjective well-being, with the effect being stronger for male than for female employees. In contrast to correlation analysis, the mediation model is unable to identify a significant relationship between psychosocial workplace characteristics and mHealth app use. Nonetheless, app use is significantly related to well-being and here again a much stronger effect can be determined for female employees, while the effect size of the relationship is very weak for male employees.

Looking at the research question and thus the influence of app use on the relationship of psychosocial workplace characteristics on the outcome variables, we can confirm an indirect effect here. Whether mediation occurs depends on several factors. Following Baron and Kenny [53] it is necessary to first demonstrate a "zero-order effect" of the independent variable X on the depend variable Y (path c). When mediation occurs, the c′ path is smaller than the c path. This requirement is not met in the conducted mediation analysis. If we follow the requirements of Zhao et al. [54], there is only one requirement to establish mediation, that the indirect effect *a*b* is significant. This requirement is met in the conducted mediation analysis. However, the authors go on to describe the strength of mediation in terms of the measured effect size, which is very low in the model studied. In summary, it is possible to speak of mediation, but only with a very low effect size. Accordingly, there is a mediating influence of mHealth app use on the relationship between psychosocial workplace characteristics and well-being. However, further research is needed to determine whether the effectiveness is sufficient to classify mHealth technologies as a useful resource in the work context.

The studied model, however, gives some other interesting results apart from the mediation analysis. In particular, the influence of age and gender on the variables analysed should be mentioned here. The older the employees are, the more frequently they use the mHealth app. This effect, however, is only seen for female employees. Currently, there are only a few studies that focus specifically on the characteristics of users of mHealth apps, but existing literature analysed especially younger individuals as user of mHealth apps [55]. The present study would contradict this, at least to some extent, as the analysis demonstrates that older users are more frequently using the app at least in the female population. One explanation could lie in gender differences, because it is already known that usage behaviour is gender-specific, at least for mobile fitness apps. Female users are more motivated than male users to use apps where they can set individual goals and receive support in achieving them. Male users, on the other hand, tend to prefer apps that allow live tracking and sharing of these results [56]. The mHealth app studied focuses on individual support for health related goals and motivation. Based on the results for fitness apps, this concept might appeal to female users' more than male users. Another explanation could be that mHealth apps are generally more likely to be used by younger individuals, while older individuals use them more frequently when they have decided to use them. As no analyses were performed in this regard in the present study, it is not possible to answer this question conclusively. Another interesting result is the relationship between app usage and well-being. A significant correlation with moderate effect size is observed in the female sample. This means that users who use the app more frequently also have a higher subjective well-being. The results correspond to previous research [31].

Conclusively, the present study suggests that mHealth applications can provide useful support in increasing well-being, especially for older employees. This is particularly relevant in the sense that the number of older people and thus older employees is rapidly increasing worldwide [57]. The present study confirms that mHealth applications can make a meaningful contribution to the maintenance of well-being and therefore of the health of employee, thus offering a simple way to continuously support active and healthy aging at work, since access is possible anytime and anywhere and employees can be individually supported according to their individual abilities and skills. Therefore, it is of particular importance to find out which factors have an effect and what this effect looks like in order to offer the best possible support and give the opportunity to be able to work and live healthily in the long term. The present study is able to contribute to this, but more in-depth research is necessary to identify and explain the relationships.

4.1 Limitations

The findings of this study should be interpreted in light of certain limitations. Although the large data set and multi-national recruiting by the investigated app it needs to be mentioned that a proper control setting was not implemented as real world data was used for this analysis. Thus, the data set might have influences and dependencies, which were not identified due to a limited number of control variables. These include, for example, individual factors that have already been studied in connection with app usage behaviour (e.g. technical affinity) but also, for example, country-specific differences (e.g. cultural background). Participants of four different countries were involved and the sample was compiled to be as comparable as possible. However, this also means that the results are not globally valid, as they are restricted to the analysed culture. Nevertheless just industrialized western countries were investigated which might be representative in terms of their work ethos and work concepts, but further research with regard to work culture is necessary.

A further limitation is that the sample was collected with one mHealth app, limiting the generalizability of the results in terms of other mHealth apps addressing for example resilience. Furthermore, the sampling procedure was nonprobabilistic, and respondents were self-selected based on their voluntary willingness to install the app. No specific advertisement was performed. Thus, persons with the interest in their health and aim to manage their work related stress might be overrepresented within this sample. Limitation to technical requirements might also be mentioned as a limitation although the app published was within the both most frequently used operating systems. Finally, the sample is composed of employees who have used a mHealth app at least to a small extent. No control group is included, with employees who do not use an app at all.

Despite these limitations, the results presented in this article may contribute towards a better understanding of the potential of modern technologies in supporting everyday work to help manage psychosocial demands and improve mental and physical health of workers around the globe.

Acknowledgements. We would like to thank David Parfitt and HeadUp Labs Pty Ltd providing the data and the support in data preparation. The data provider had no role in the design of this study and had no role during its execution, analyses, interpretation of the data, or decision to submit results.

Funding. The analysis has been conducted within the project WorkingAge, funded by the European Union's Horizon 2020 Research and Innovation Program under Grant Agreement N. 826232.

References

1. Junghanns, G., Morschhäuser, M.: Psychische Belastung bei Wissens- und Dienstleistungsarbeit – eine Einführung. In: für Arbeitsschutz und Arbeitsmedizin, B., Junghanns, G., Morschhäuser, M. (eds.) Immer schneller, immer mehr. psychische Belastung bei Wissens- und Dienstleistungsarbeit (2013). Springer, Wiesbaden. https://doi.org/10.1007/978-3-658-01445-2_1
2. Müller-Thur, K., Angerer, P., Körner, U., Dragano, N.: Arbeit mit digitalen technologien, psychosoziale belastungen und potenzielle gesundheitliche konsequenzen. Zeitschrift für medizinische Prävention **53**, 388–391 (2018)
3. Treier, M.: Gefährdungsbeurteilung psychischer Belastungen: Begründung, Instrumente, Umsetzung. Springer Fachmedien Wiesbaden, Wiesbaden (2019). https://doi.org/10.1007/978-3-658-23293-1
4. Johns, G.: Absenteeism and presenteeism: not at work or not working well. In: The SAGE Handbook of Organizational, vol. 1, pp. 160–177 (2008)
5. Mental health Europe: mental health & work (2018). https://www.mhe-sme.org/what-we-do/mental-health-work/. Accessed 25 Jan 2022
6. Personage, M., Saini, G.: Mental Health at Work. The business costs ten years on, London (2007)
7. Gesundheitsreport. Arbeitsunfähigkeit 2021. https://www.tk.de/resource/blob/2103660/ffbe9e82aa11e0d79d9d6d6d88f71934/gesundheitsreport-au-2021-data.pdf

8. Darr, W., Johns, G.: Work strain, health, and absenteeism: a meta-analysis. J. Occup. Health Psychol. **13**(4), 293 (2008). https://doi.org/10.1037/a0012639
9. Ganster, D.C., Rosen, C.C.: Work stress and employee health: a multidisciplinary review. J. Manag. **39**(5), 1085–1122 (2013). https://doi.org/10.1177/0149206313475815
10. Kivimäki, M., et al.: Psychosocial work environment as a risk factor for absence with a psychiatric diagnosis: an instrumental-variables analysis. Am. J. Epidemiol. **172**(2), 167–172 (2010). https://doi.org/10.1093/aje/kwq094
11. Samuelsson, Å., Ropponen, A., Alexanderson, K., Svedberg, P.: Psychosocial working conditions, occupational groups, and risk of disability pension due to mental diagnoses: a cohort study of 43,000 Swedish twins. Scand. J. Work Environ. Health, 351-360 (2013). https://doi.org/10.5271/sjweh.3338
12. Virtanen, M., Vahtera, J., Pentti, J., Honkonen, T., Elovainio, M., Kivimäki, M.: Job strain and psychologic distress influence on sickness absence among Finnish employees. Am. J. Prev. Med. **33**(3), 182–187 (2007). https://doi.org/10.1016/j.amepre.2007.05.003
13. Müller-Bagehl, S., Nordbrock, C., Schütte, M.: Arbeitsprogramm psyche: stress reduzieren - potenziale entwickeln. https://www.gda-psyche.de/DE/Service/English/english_node.html. Accessed 14 Jan 2022
14. Rohmert, W., Rutenfranz, J.: Arbeitswissenschaftliche beurteilung der belastung und beanspruchung an unterschiedlichen industriellen arbeitsplätzen. Der Bundesminister für Arbeit und Sozialordnung (1975)
15. Karasek, R.A.: Job demands, job decision latitude, and mental strain: implications for job redesign. Adm. Sci. Q. 285-308 (1979). https://doi.org/10.2307/2392498
16. Johnson, J.V., Hall, E.M.: Job strain, work place social support, and cardiovascular disease: a cross-sectional study of a random sample of the Swedish working population. Am. J. Public Health **78**, 1336–1342 (1988)
17. Johnson, J.V., Hall, E.M., Theorell, T.: Combined effects of job strain and social isolation on cardiovascular disease morbidity and mortality in a random sample of the Swedish male working population. Scand J Work Environ Health, 271-279 (1989). https://doi.org/10.5271/sjweh.1852
18. Demerouti, E., Bakker, A.B., Nachreiner, F., Schaufeli, W.B.: The job demands-resources model of burnout. J. Appl. Psychol. **86**(3), 499 (2001). https://doi.org/10.1037/0021-9010.86.3.499
19. Bakker, A.B., Demerouti, E.: The job demands-resources model: state of the art. J. Manag. Psych. (2007). https://doi.org/10.1108/02683940710733115
20. Bakker, A.B., Demerouti, E., Euwema, M.C.: Job resources buffer the impact of job demands on burnout. J. Occup. Health Psychol. **10**(2), 170 (2005)
21. Bakker, A.B., Hakanen, J.J., Demerouti, E., Xanthopoulou, D.: Job resources boost work engagement, particularly when job demands are high. J. Educ. Psychol. **99**, 274 (2007)
22. Halbesleben, J.R.B., Neveu, J.-P., Paustian-Underdahl, S.C., Westman, M.: Getting to the "COR" understanding the role of resources in conservation of resources theory. J. Manag. **40**, 1334–1364 (2014)
23. Han, M., Lee, E.: Effectiveness of mobile health application use to improve health behavior changes: a systematic review of randomized controlled trials. Healthc. Inf. Res. **24**, 207–226 (2018)
24. Rasche, P., et al.: others: The aachen falls prevention scale: multi-study evaluation and comparison. JMIR Aging **2**, e12114 (2019)
25. DiFilippo, K.N., Huang, W.-H., Andrade, J.E., Chapman-Novakofski, K.M.: The use of mobile apps to improve nutrition outcomes: a systematic literature review. J. Telemed. Telecare **21**(5), 243–253 (2015). https://doi.org/10.1177/1357633X15572203

26. European commission: communication from the commission to the parliament, the council, the European economic and social committee and the committee of the regions, health action plan 2012–2020 – innovative healthcare for the 21st century. European Union, Brussels (2012). https://www.tandfonline.com/doi/pdf/10.1080/01972243.2018.1438550. Accessed 16 Nov 2021

27. Krishna, S., Boren, S.A., Balas, E.A.: Healthcare via cell phones: a systematic review. Telemedicine e-Health **15**, 231–240 (2009)

28. Punnett, L., Cherniack, M., Henning, R., Morse, T., Faghri, P.: CPH-new research team: a conceptual framework for integrating workplace health promotion and occupational ergonomics programs. Public Health Rep. **124**, 16–25 (2009)

29. Goetzel, R.Z., Shechter, D., Ozminkowski, R.J., Marmet, P.F., Tabrizi, M.J., Roemer, E.C.: Promising practices in employer health and productivity management efforts: findings from a benchmarking study. J. Occup. Environ. Med. **49**, 111–130 (2007)

30. Stratton, E., Lampit, A., Choi, I., Calvo, R.A., Harvey, S.B., Glozier, N.: Effectiveness of eHealth interventions for reducing mental health conditions in employees: a systematic review and meta-analysis. PLoS One **12**, e0189904 (2017)

31. Carolan, S., Harris, P.R., Cavanagh, K.: Improving employee well-being and effectiveness: systematic review and meta-analysis of web-based psychological interventions delivered in the workplace. J. Med. Internet Res. **19**, e271 (2017)

32. Stratton, E., Jones, N., Peters, S.E., Torous, J., Glozier, N.: Digital mHealth interventions for employees: systematic review and meta-analysis of their effects on workplace outcomes. J. Occup. Environ. Med. **63**, e512–e525 (2021)

33. HeadUp labs pty ltd: HeadUp labs (2020). https://headupsystems.com/. Accessed 4 Nov 2021

34. Conceição, P.: Human Development Report 2020. The next frontier. Human Development and the Anthropocene (2020). http://hdr.undp.org/sites/default/files/hdr2020.pdf

35. Backhaus, K., Erichson, B., Gensler, S., Weiber, R., Weiber, T.: Multivariate Analysemethoden: Eine anwendungsorientierte Einführung. Springer Fachmedien Wiesbaden, Wiesbaden (2021). https://doi.org/10.1007/978-3-658-32425-4

36. Bortz, J., Schuster, C.: Statistik für Human- und Sozialwissenschaftler. Springer Berlin Heidelberg, Berlin, Heidelberg (2010)

37. Bech, P., Gudex, C., Johansen, K.S.: The WHO (Ten) well-being index: validation in diabetes. PPS **65**(4), 183–190 (1996). https://doi.org/10.1159/000289073

38. Warr, P., Banks, M., Ullah, P.: The experience of unemployment among black and white urban teenagers. Br. J. Psychol. **76**(1), 75–87 (1985). https://doi.org/10.1111/j.2044-8295.1985.tb01932.x

39. Staehr, J.K.: Multicentre Continuous Subcutaneous Infusion Pump Feasibility and Acceptability Study Experience. WHO Regional Office for Europe, Copenhagen, Copenhagen (1989)

40. Kline, R.B.: Principles and Practice of Structural Equation Modeling. Methodology in the Social Sciences. Guilford Press, New York (2016)

41. Bühner, M.: Einführung in die Test - und Fragebogenkonstruktion, 2nd edn. Pearson Deutschland GmbH. (2011)

42. Cohen, J.: Statistical Power Analysis for the Behavioral Sciences. Academic press, Cambridge (1988)

43. Guttman, L.: Some necessary conditions for common-factor analysis. Psychometrika **19**, 149–161 (1954). https://doi.org/10.1007/BF02289162

44. Kaiser, H.F.: The application of electronic computers to factor analysis. Educ. Psychol. Measur. **20**, 141–151 (1960)

45. Schmitt, N.: Uses and abuses of coefficient alpha. Psychol. Assess. **8**(4), 350 (1996). https://doi.org/10.1037/1040-3590.8.4.350

46. Satorra, A., Bentler, P.M.: Corrections to Test Statistics and Standard Errors in Covariance Structure Analysis. Sage Publications, California (1994)
47. Cohen, J.: A power primer. Psychol. Bull. **112**(1), 155 (1992). https://doi.org/10.1037/0033-2909.112.1.155
48. Blanca Mena, M.J., Alarcón Postigo, R., Arnau Gras, J., Bono Cabré, R., Bendayan, R.: Non-normal data: Is ANOVA still a valid option? Psicothema **29**(4), 552–557 (2017)
49. Glass, G.V., Peckham, P.D., Sanders, J.R.: Consequences of failure to meet assumptions underlying the fixed effects analyses of variance and covariance. Rev. Educ. Res. **42**, 237–288 (1972)
50. Wilcox, R.R.: Introduction to Robust Estimation and Hypothesis Testing. Academic press, Cambridge (2011)
51. Rasch, D., Guiard, V.: The robustness of parametric statistical methods. Psychol. Sci. **46**, 175–208 (2004)
52. Kenny, D.A.: Mediation. (2021). http://davidakenny.net/cm/mediate.htm. Accessed 14 Jan 2021
53. Baron, R.M., Kenny, D.A.: The moderator-mediator variable distinction in social psychological research: Conceptual, strategic, and statistical considerations. J. Pers. Soc. Psychol. **51**, 1173 (1986)
54. Zhao, X., Lynch, J., Chen, Q.: Reconsidering baron and kenny: myths and truths about mediation analysis. J. Consum. Res. **37**(2), 197–206 (2010)
55. Mosa, A.S.M., Yoo, I., Sheets, L.: A systematic review of healthcare applications for smartphones. BMC Med. Inform. Decis. Mak. **12**, 1–31 (2012)
56. Klenk, S., Reifegerste, D., Renatus, R.: Gender differences in gratifications from fitness app use and implications for health interventions. Mobile Media Commun. **5**, 178–193 (2017)
57. Mamolo, M., Scherbov, S.: Population Projections for Forty-Four European Countries: The Ongoing Population Ageing. Princeton, Citeseer (2009)

Designing an Engagement's Technological Tool: User Needs and Motivations in a Humanized Way

Juliana Salvadorinho[1,2] , Andreia Vitória[1] , Carlos Ferreira[1,2] ,
and Leonor Teixeira[1,2(✉)]

[1] Department of Economics, Management, Industrial Engineering and Tourism, University of
Aveiro, 3010-193 Aveiro, Portugal
{juliana.salvadorinho,atvitoria,carlosf,lteixeira}@ua.pt
[2] Institute of Electronics and Informatics Engineering of Aveiro, University of Aveiro, 3010-193
Aveiro, Portugal

Abstract. The digital revolution is leading to the overwhelming consumption of
technology by companies, without the people who constitute them being considered the key factor to consider within this innovation. Even with more technological resources, companies must continue to readapt the context so that their
human resources can relate in an environment that aspires to be so autonomous.
For there to be greater adaptation and motivation on the part of company employees to what this digital transformation brings, it is essential to promote solutions
that at the same time determine an adequate engagement factor. Therefore, this
paper refers to the conceptualization of a technological tool that supports and
promotes the concept of engagement throughout the organization. For that purpose, a set of requirements taken from the literature were confronted with outputs
from structured interviews of people belonging to a Portuguese organization. The
results obtained made it possible to adjust the requirements, contributing to the
creation of 3 modules, which are social collaboration, supervision support and
questionnaires.

Keywords: Industry 4.0 · Human resource 4.0 · Requirements · Engagement

1 Introduction

The Fourth Industrial Revolution (4thIR) moves organizations to new challenges due
to the power of technologies that can change the organizational value [1, 2] and have
influence on physical processes, information flows and on the way people work (human
capital) [1, 3–5].

It is known that an organization's performance and competitiveness mainly depends
on how its employees are handled and engaged in daily activities [6] and, nowadays,
several managers are including Industry 4.0 implementation in their strategy to boost
productivity [7]. However buying technology is possible, the same cannot be said about
engagement regarding people [8].

V. G. Duffy (Ed.): HCII 2022, LNCS 13320, pp. 266–279, 2022.
https://doi.org/10.1007/978-3-031-06018-2_19

The work engagement definition is settled in what we consider to be a rewarding work-related state of mind, represented by an affective-motivational tool, guiding to encouraging job posture in employees [9, 10]. Four courses of action have emerged as being the determinants to increase engagement [10–15], they are: (i) knowledge sharing (using collaborative platforms); (ii) information visualization; (iii) participatory design (where collaborators can contribute with ideas to design their workstation); and, finally, (iv) training and learning.

There are already some application prototypes mentioned in the literature that promote this concept, such as knowledge sharing platforms [16] and even picking processes in intralogistics that support visualization by employees [17]. Both solutions are based on a gamification structure that aims to award points when the employee interacts with the technological system. Literature already accepts the gamification process as being able to increase motivation, engagement and, in turn, the worker's performance [18–21]. This process falls in the redesign of user interfaces and operational processes, designing motivational and enjoyable elements for monotonous flows [17, 22].

Currently, the only way to assess workforce engagement is by using traditional survey techniques [23] (such as, Utrecht Work Engagement Scale [24] and Gallup consultant surveys). In this way, there are no mechanisms in the industrial environment capable of collecting data, which, properly treated, can predict employee engagement and help organisations (i.e. human resources department) to recognise when the employee is about to leave the company.

Given the complex nature of this type of solutions (technologies that promote and allow the assessment of engagement), the development of this type of tools is also quite complex. As such, the methodological approach to understand the requirements and develop the solutions implies a strong cooperation of the workers in a logic of co-creation and co-design. Additionally, to create technological tools capable of position the human at the centre of the development and, at the same time, capable of fostering the work engagement, humanization techniques should be aggregated to the development phase. The humanization of digital technology is a process of developing a product or service based on technology for people, where qualities or values of the human aspect are contemplated. The human-centered design (HCD) and the participatory design (PD) already focuses on these characteristics, considering for that the usability, functionality, reliability, and emotional aspects of design [25].

Thus, this paper intends to collect user needs and motivations by checking a set of requirements (capable of integrating a technological platform) from the literature and, considered as good practices in terms of increasing work engagement, with outputs from structured interviews carried out in a Portuguese organization belonging to the chemical industry.

The remainder of this work is structured in the following way. Section 2 presents a theoretical background for the concepts related to industry 4.0, human resource 4.0, and workforce engagement, in order to get a perspective of what is being done related to the operator 4.0 engagement. In Sect. 3, the discussion about the user needs for the technological tool is exposed and the last section summarizes the main conclusions and some future work.

2 Theoretical Background

2.1 HR4.0: The Human Factor in the Digital Paradigm

Industry 4.0 is a concept that is very much correlated with interconnectivity among departments in an organization. This digital revolution considers intelligent production systems as self-adaptive processes and real-time communication, managing the value chain throughout the product life cycle [26]. It aims to rebuild the industrial value chain through the decentralization of production, using shared facilities in the integrated global industrial system [27].

The new value chains are equipped with complex cyber-physical networks where information flows continuously, offering almost instantaneous feedback to employees [28, 29]. New interactions between operators and machines have been created, which have strongly contributed to relevant changes in the management of human resources, in a new digital paradigm [30, 31]. To provide an intelligent workforce in these emergent environments, workers must be integrated with I4.0 technologies [26], making it necessary to identify new skills for employees, phenomenon known as Operator 4.0 [30, 31].

The operator has influence on the processes, as such it must be an aspect to be considered in the scope of Industry 4.0. The information collected by the internet of things (based on a network of physical objects that are implanted with sensors, software, and other technologies, capable of connecting and exchanging data with other devices and systems over the internet) devices does not capture the sources of variation in the processes and, in this way, human being disposes cognitive flexibility which the machine lacks [28].

The emergence of digital paradigm, the globalization of workforce which causes the increase in the turnover, have also been emerging. This phenomenon has a direct consequence in the loss of skills by the company, with impact in the organizational knowledge. Since the creation of value in industry 4.0 can be profitably achieved through the adoption of technologies that end up placing human beings at the centre of the innovation process, these losses must be prevented [32]. To retain key knowledge in organisations, it is important to start by preserving the individual knowledge holders. Thus, people must be retained, and organizations must focus on fostering work engagement. In fact, some studies in this area indicate that employee engagement has a constructive correlation with productivity, profitability, employee retention, safety, and customer satisfaction, and additionally, is linked with the individual's involvement and enthusiasm for work [23, 33].

2.2 Workforce Engagement: Concept and Applications

The level of participation in the organization activity and value creation will determine the engagement amount, through which the employee expresses him/herself [34]. In Saputra et al. [35] the authors attest that work engagement, in its holistic form, can be classified in physical terms (where there is a willingness to use health, fitness and physical resistance to do the job), emotional (where the individual shows willingness to use feelings of pride, joy and dedication to perform the work), intellectual (individual is willing to use thought, creativity, concentration and focus to do work) and spiritual (individual's willingness to give of his devotion, help to others and life purpose to perform the work).

It should be noted that there are differences between the concepts of engagement and organizational commitment, both of which collide in practice, since without engagement there is no organizational commitment, and the opposite can also be observed. Commitment differs in that it is based on the intensity of an individual's identification and involvement with a particular organization, denoting a strong belief in the acceptance of an organization's goals and values, a willingness to exert considerable effort on behalf of the organization, and a desire definitive decision to maintain organizational affiliation [36].

When it comes to measuring and tracking employee engagement, most companies still measure engagement annually, applying traditional survey techniques. While these practices provide a wide range of insights into the dimensions and impact of engagement, taking advantage of technologies can bring benefits [23]. To determine fluctuations or perhaps factors that may influence engagement in more real time, pulse surveys can also be used to track the same dimensions as the annual survey [23].

Gamification is currently the most emerging approach in the literature to enhance human motivation and, therefore, employee engagement, using game design elements in non-game contexts [37]. This concept is based on the Self Determination Theory (SDT) which states that every human being needs to feel autonomy, competence, and relatedness achieve self-determined motivation, well-being and growth. In this way, elements and actions that provide these characteristics must be incorporated to construct a human-centered work and learning environment [20].

Four dimensions were established to increase engagement and some of them include the gamification concept [10, 11, 13, 15]: i) **knowledge sharing and communication** that can be fostered through collaborative social platforms, expanding knowledge sharing among workers and support them in problem solving situations; ii) **visualization of information** through augmented reality (AR) and even virtual reality (VR) glasses, providing context-related information in the workplace; iii) **participatory design** (involving operators) using 3D simulation software to simulate work and tasks (later 3D-PD), providing collaborators the possibility to co-design the workplace and planning work practices with other stakeholders; and iv) **employee training** closely related to Learning Factories, where the participants gain skills through self-learning processes organized in a technological learning environment, using a training platform.

Specifically, social collaboration combined with gamification strategy is already realized by the literature as a potential solution for increasing employee engagement, since the combination creates an attractive package for participation and interaction with technology. The idea of creating a friendly and pleasant environment between colleagues, motivating them to interact with each other makes it possible to: enhance crowd sourcing, drive innovation, and improve employee performance [16].

Within the scope of training, the combination of gamification and augmented reality through the training platform promotes incentives for a more effective and enjoyable teaching. Each trainee has performance evaluation methods, as well as cumulative perceptions about the effectiveness of the training, where in each game (using AR) there are achievements and the points earned by the employees are synonymous with the increase in their performance and participation in the sessions [38].

3 Practical Case

3.1 Context Goals and Methods

The main objective of this paper is to carry out a needs appraisal for the modelling of a technological tool capable of assessing and promoting human resources' work engagement. To this end, the methods followed included a review of what is being researched in the academic world about this topic and interviews conducted within a Portuguese organization belonging to the chemical industry, whose production focus is flush toilets, in order to validate a previous tool concept constructed based on literature review.

The literature review enabled the contextualization of the engagement phenomenon associated with industrial digitalization, with the identification of potential predictors, as well as techniques to support the promotion of this emotional state.

The interviews were conducted after this primary awareness and a set of requirements that came from the literature (regarding potential modules integrating the technological tool) were taken to these interviews, to understand the receptiveness of employees to these features. With the feedbacks obtained the requirements were adjusted, thus following a user-centered design methodology.

The Data Collection Instrument (Semi-structured Interview). Given the disruptive nature of engagement-related applications, a set of semi-structured interviews were conducted with a view to a qualitative analysis of a concept already grounded on the exploratory literature review. a script was used to conduct the interview with the following specific five objectives: (I) to characterize the respondents taking into account their profiles in the company and familiarity with the technology; (Ii) to discuss the concept of engagement and the organization's practices to increase this factor in face of the respondents' perception; (Iii) to understand the receptiveness of a module to launch questions from questionnaires (of engagement and predictors of it) based on the gamification process; (Iv) to envision the respondents' opinion towards the construction of a social collaboration module for knowledge sharing and submission of improvement suggestions; and, (V) to verify the receptivity of a supervisory support module (focusing on competency maps and individual development plans and tasks to be performed). It should be noted that all interviews were conducted by the researcher and recorded with the Consent of the Interviewees. Due to individual availability conditions, two interviews were conducted through the TEAMS communication software and other interviews were carried out at the interviewees' premises.

The Sample. The interviews encompassed the participation of 9 people (see Table 1) most related to management positions, being human resources, finance, product development, engineering, industrial planning, quality, continuous improvement, commercial departments and, administration. Management positions were selected, as they are more related to leadership and team management statutes.

Table 1. Characterization of the respondents

Cod	Interviewed Profile	Age	Familiarity with technology[a]	Interview duration (min.)
O1	Managing complaints in the quality department	30–40	4	30
O2	Administrator (follows sales, marketing, design and development and purchasing departments)	30–40	4	45
O3	Design engineer in the commercial department	20–30	5	25
O4	Cash-flow officer and credit control of foreign market customers	40–50	4	30
O5	Mechanical engineer in the product development department	30–40	4	31
O6	Planning orders coming from the commercial side in the industrial planning department	30–40	5	32
O7	Training, reception and performance evaluation in the human resources department	20–30	5	32
O8	Mold analysis with product development in the engineering department	30–40	5	36
O9	Continuous Improvement Engineer	20–30	5	33

[a]Rate on a scale of 1 to 5, where: 1 - I have never contacted with technology; 2 - I have contacted with technologies, but I don't use them; 3 - I contact with technologies, but with difficulties; 4 - I contact with technologies with some ease; 5 - For me it is very easy to contact with technologies.

3.2 Results and Discussion

This chapter will present the main results and discussion around the specific objectives identified above.

Concept of Engagement and Organizational Practices. Most of those interviewed associated engagement with high involvement in doing the job well and even exceeding expectations. In addition, the idea that someone with a high level of engagement is someone who wears the shirt of the company was often mentioned.

(…) it is a person with a high level of commitment to the company (…) completely involved in what are the objectives and purpose of the company itself. (O1).

(…) the word brings me the dedication and commitment that the person has. It is a very motivated person and wants to give a lot of himself/herself in the company where he/she works. (O6)

It should be noted that there is an overlap in the understanding of what engagement is and what organizational commitment is. Therefore, an explanation and clarification of these two concepts was needed after this question.

As previously referred, engagement can be fostered along four dimensions, these being communication and knowledge sharing, information visualization, participative design (where employees are involved in the construction of their workstation) and training [10–14]. In addition, the concept of gamification is closely associated with engagement practices in digital transformation. From the interviewees' perspective, engagement is fostered in various ways, such as: using Lean tools that are present on the shop floor, aimed at visualizing information; sharing the organization's objectives with all its layers; fostering dialogue and proximity between people throughout the company; evaluating employees in an appropriate way, as well as giving follow-up to the job and its worker; and, finally, recognizing collaborators aligned with the company's reward system.

(…) welcoming employees is essential, as is monitoring and performance evaluation (…) (O7)

(…) we already have very interesting things, namely the daily kaizens so that people can talk about their difficulties, do brainstorms. These are meetings that happen daily on the factory floor. (O9)

Based on these two inputs, literature review and interviews, three major areas were denoted as enhancing engagement (see Fig. 1), these being social collaboration, skills management and individual development plans, as well as support from on-the-job supervision.

Therefore, based on these three areas, requirements for a technological tool were considered, to foster work engagement.

Survey module. Considering that the only valid way to assess engagement is through questionnaires, one of the system requirements is based on the launch of a question daily (the Gallup 12-question questionnaire will be used and others that intend to evaluate

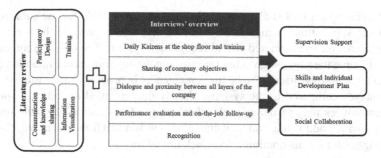

Fig. 1. Mechanisms to increase engagement

predictors of engagement). This requirement is supported in a virtual recognition system, in which, after answering the question, the person earns points. Overall, the receptivity was positive and the concept of gamification (virtual recognition system) was held in high regard.

> It was funny, but it all depends on how long it takes, but if it didn't take too long, yes, I would be open to it. (O4)

Social Collaboration Module. For the social collaboration module several requirements were defined during the literature review and then checked against the interviews carried out (see Table 2). The aim is that employees ask questions in a platform and direct them to the experts, enabling them to answer. Furthermore, these questions will be available to all employees from other areas, so that they may also comment. Employees can also attach demonstration videos to facilitate interpretation. It should be noted that all of these procedures are associated with the virtual recognition system, closely related to gamification, which distributes points to people who actively interact with the platform. People's feedback was positive, but there was the suggestion that there should be a limit to the number of questions to be asked and answered per person and, to avoid fruitless discussions, comments and interactions should be filtered.

> I think it's a good idea (…) I think it should be guided in terms of the number of questions people can ask, or even the amount of time the person responding can answer (…) tendentially, those who participate in the tools are always the same people and participate a lot, so it has to be something marked. (O2)
>
> (…) it is also necessary to verify the answers, so that there are no answers without content. (O2)

Thus, the readjustment was made so that each person would have a limit to the number of questions they could ask and answer, and that they would have to use their recognition system (buying questions with points, for example) if they wanted to exceed these limits. In addition to this, it was decided to create a filtering process on the platform with warnings for the areas of expertise, so that the comments/questions could be validated and only after this step are points awarded.

The technological tool is also intended to integrate a module for the submission of improvement suggestions, which will work in a very similar way to the previous one described, also with an associated virtual recognition system. The only difference is that here we will have the suggestion submitted passing through different evaluation phases, being them: "new suggestion", "to be implemented", "in progress" and "implemented". The advantages compared to the systems already implemented in some companies is that the employees may visualize each other's suggestions and at the same time give suggestions which add value, and they may also envision in a transparent way the status of these suggestions, thus obtaining feedback in real time.

Table 2. Social collaboration module requirements

Requirements	Interviews' overview	Revised requirement
- Consult "experts" in specific tasks and directly question these people	People agreed on the existence of a knowledge sharing platform, where help could be requested	–
- Ask questions selecting the area of expertise		
- Comment on questions from other colleagues	It is necessary to limit the number of questions that people can ask, as well as the time for answering	Limit the number of questions each person can ask and answer (inform about the number of questions and answers still available)
- A notice is sent to employees belonging to the area of the question and they have a certain time to respond		
- Any employee will be able to upload task demo videos to the platform	People agreed that videos to replace working instructions are very useful and easier to understand	–
- Monitor the group/departmental progress regarding collaboration within the digital platform	The answers need to be verified so that fruitless discussions are not created	The platform must present a filter process in which questions and answers must be evaluated and validated
Update the recognition system each time a question is answered or commented		

Supervision support module. Part 1 of supervision support module (see Table 3) was also on the agenda and the idea is that it should be associated with a method of establishing objectives by the supervisor, with a start date and end date, and in which employees could change the status of the objective.

Having goals and performance evaluations and open discussions about goals are engagement solutions (…) in my workstation it would make sense, to have records where this check-in could be carried out. (O3)

"We already had several physical boards, but then there is no feedback or there is no follow-up, so it ends. In this way, that part would have to be ensured" (O5)

According to the interviews and feedbacks obtained, the requirements were revisited and changed, so that the objectives have several phases, these being "in acceptance", "to be executed" (they have been accepted for follow-up), "in progress" and "executed". It was emphasized that this method is interesting for review tasks and that these objectives should also be able to be directed to the supervisor by the employees.

(...) from my perspective it is an effective way of reviewing some tasks (...) (O2)

To facilitate the visualization of the time to accomplish the objectives/tasks a color system will be added, in which green is within the time limit, yellow is close to the limit and red is the deadline has passed. When it is a task carried out by the employee, the supervisor will also receive a notification at the end of the task to evaluate and give feedback on the employee's performance.

Table 3. Supervision support module (tasks)

Requirement	Interviews' overview	Revised requirement
-The supervisor must be able to establish performance targets (OKRs) for the employee	Employees agreed that it would be interesting to have a task tracking system, in the sense of having reminders. They also thought it would be very useful for reviewing tasks by the line manager	The tasks will follow several states, being "in acceptance", "to be executed" (they have been accepted for follow-up), "in progress" and "executed". A start date and an end date will also be stipulated from the beginning and as time passes tasks will change color (considering the end date)
-The employee must be able to update the status of the objective applied by the supervisor		
-Upon the employee's change of status, the supervisor must receive a notice and then the objective assessment functionality be made available		

Part 2 of the supervision support module (see Table 4) aims to allow employees to access their digital skills map, as well as their individual development plan which, currently in most companies, is prepared once a year, without any follow-up of its progress. Thus, the initial idea consisted of submitting a passport to the system of skills and objectives to be developed throughout the year and that these would be monitored through a progress bar, with inputs from the supervisor and from the employee. Receiving the inputs from the interviews, a new tool was presented, which consists of a moment per month of evaluation of the employees' failures, successes, goals and action plans (for these goals and also for aspects of the personality that they want to improve). In addition, the bidirectional assessment is carried out at this point, receiving feedback from the employee as well as the supervisor.

> We already have the jour fix and the feedback is fantastic, I'm really enjoying it (…) we talk about our successes, our failures and then we can take actions to combat that. Then we have the opportunities, opportunities for improvement for the department and the organization itself. We also talk about aspects of the personality that we want to improve. Imagine that I am super shy and afraid of speaking in public, in this tool we elaborate actions to get around this and overcome my fear. We also have employee-supervisor and supervisor-employee evaluation (…) once a month is ideal. (O6)

The idea now is to include the progress bar in this method, thus leaving the system with a proper monitoring process and leaving it up to the user to determine the frequency.

Table 4. Supervision support module (skills map and individual personal development plan)

Requirement	Interviews' overview	Revised requirement
- Every month the employee must assess the supervisor performance, as well as from the supervisor to the employee (a notification must be sent)	A tool was presented called jour fix where employees have an excel file that they fill in every month, once, where they establish successes, failures and then take actions to combat them. In this tool they also talk about aspects of their personality that they want to improve and elaborate actions to get around this. The employee-supervisor and supervisor-employee evaluation is also carried out here	The platform will integrate a process (each team choose the frequency) of filling in the fields investigated in the jour fix (failures, successes, personality aspects and actions that will follow a PDCA- Plan, Do, Check and Act strategy) and will issue a warning to the actors involved in the process. In addition, a monthly two-way evaluation will also be adopted

4   Final Remarks and Future Work

As for the output generated by the applied methodology, it was generally agreed that the gamification strategy benefits engagement promotion tools. Furthermore, it was noted that the areas of greatest focus for this concept were social collaboration, supervisory support and skills, and individual development plans, the latter of which was integrated into supervisory support, which led to the creation of 3 modules: questionnaire launching (in a gamified way), social collaboration based on a knowledge sharing platform, and support from supervision focused on task tracking, and in skills visualization and individual development plans.

Thus, we intend to create a technological tool that: i) enables the daily launch of questions that are part of engagement evaluation questionnaires and predictors; ii) enables the sharing of information between employees, through questions and answers, prioritization of questions and a filtering process of what adds value to the organization; iii) allows employees to submit suggestions for improvement to their organization, where they can view those of their colleagues and comment on them, all of this being subject, later, to a filter by management; iv) has a follow-up of tasks and objectives set by the supervisor to the employee and vice-versa, while feedback is presented at the end of the task/objective; and, finally iv) offers the employee the possibility to access his/her skills and to follow (in a frequency desired by her/him and the supervisor) the progress regarding his/her individual development plan. This type of tool can support organizations in monitoring the engagement of their employees, in promoting it, and based on the outputs of the tool, in determining strategic measures to preserve their human capital.

In the very volatile digital transformation we live in it, becomes imperative to pay attention to the workforce and, above all, to preserve which is the knowledge of the organization. Therefore, it is necessary to expand tools that promote engagement and evaluate it in order to prepare management for potential exits, but also to retain the tacit knowledge that is in people's heads and that can sometimes threaten survival, when it is not properly transposed to explicit and, therefore, integrated into the company's knowledge repository.

As future work, it is intended to extend the study to other organizations with different contexts in order to validate the previously identified requirements and create personas that may highlight different needs and motivations and, consequently, to design and implement a tool that truly serves the largest organizational fabric to support the adequacy of human resources to the new digital reality.

Acknowledgements. The present study was developed in the scope of the Project Augmented Humanity [POCI-01–0247-FEDER-046103 e LISBOA-01–0247-FEDER-046103], financed by Portugal 2020, under the Competitiveness and Internationalization Operational Program, the Lisbon Regional Operational Program, and by the European Regional Development Fund.

References

1. Flores, E., Xu, X., Lu, Y.: Human capital 4.0: a workforce competence typology for Industry 4.0. J. Manuf. Technol. Manag. **31**(4), 687–703 (2020). https://doi.org/10.1108/JMTM-08-2019-0309
2. Cimini, C., Boffelli, A., Lagorio, A., Kalchschmidt, M., Pinto, R.: How do industry 4.0 technologies influence organisational change? an empirical analysis of Italian SMEs. J. Manuf. Technol. Manag. (2020). https://doi.org/10.1108/JMTM-04-2019-0135
3. Liboni, L.B., Cezarino, L.O., Jabbour, C.J.C., Oliveira, B.G., Stefanelli, N.O.: Smart industry and the pathways to HRM 4.0: implications for SCM. Supply Chain Manag. **24**(1), 124–146 (2019). https://doi.org/10.1108/SCM-03-2018-0150
4. Neumann, W.P., Winkelhaus, S., Grosse, E.H., Glock, C.H.: Industry 4.0 and the human factor – a systems framework and analysis methodology for successful development. Int. J. Prod. Econ. **233**, 107992. (2021). https://doi.org/10.1016/j.ijpe.2020.107992

5. Li, D., Landström, A., Fast-Berglund, Å., Almström, P.: Human-centred dissemination of data, information and knowledge in industry 4.0. Procedia CIRP **84**, 380–386 (2019). https://doi.org/10.1016/j.procir.2019.04.261

6. Tortorella, G., Miorando, R., Caiado, R., Nascimento, D., Portioli Staudacher, A.: The mediating effect of employees' involvement on the relationship between Industry 4.0 and operational performance improvement. Total Qual. Manag. Bus Excell. **32**(1–2), 119-133. (2021). https://doi.org/10.1080/14783363.2018.1532789

7. Erro-Garcés, A.: Industry 4.0: defining the research agenda, Benchmarking (2019). https://doi.org/10.1108/BIJ-12-2018-0444

8. Gates, D.: Industry 4.0: it's all about the people, industry 4.0: it's all about the people, no. May. KPMG, pp. 1–2, (2017)

9. Gaur, B.: HR4.0: an analytics framework to redefine employee engagement in the fourth industrial revolution, In: 2020 11th International Conference on Computing, Communication and Networking Technologies, ICCCNT 2020 (2020). https://doi.org/10.1109/ICCCNT 49239.2020.9225456

10. Kaasinen, E., et al.: Empowering and engaging industrial workers with operator 4.0 solutions. Comput. Ind. Eng. **139**, 105678. (2020). https://doi.org/10.1016/j.cie.2019.01.052

11. Ahram, T., Karwowski, W., Taiar, R. (eds.): IHSED 2018. AISC, vol. 876. Springer, Cham (2019). https://doi.org/10.1007/978-3-030-02053-8

12. Suh, A., Wagner, C.: How gamification of an enterprise collaboration system increases knowledge contribution: an affordance approach. J. Knowl. Manag. **21**(2), 416–431 (2017). https://doi.org/10.1108/JKM-10-2016-0429

13. Armstrong, M.B., Landers, R.N.: Gamification of employee training and development. Int. J. Train. Dev. **22**, 162-169. (2018). https://doi.org/10.1111/ijtd.12124

14. Pereira, M., Oliveira, M., Vieira, A., Lima, R.M., Paes, L.: The gamification increase employee skills through interactives work instructions training. Procedia Comput. Sci. **138**, 630–637 (2018). https://doi.org/10.1016/j.procs.2018.10.084

15. Salvadorinho, J., Vitória, A., Marques, J., Varum, C., Ferreira, C., Teixeira, L.: Human resource 4.0: a vision of a technological tool to assess and foster employee engagement. In: Proceedings of the International Conference on Industrial Engineering and Operations Management, Monterrey, Mexico, November 3–5, 2021 (2021)

16. Lithoxoidou, E., et al.: A novel social gamified collaboration platform enriched with shop-floor data and feedback for the improvement of the productivity, safety and engagement in factories. Comput. Ind. Eng. **139**, 11 (2020). https://doi.org/10.1016/j.cie.2019.02.005

17. Schuldt, J., Friedemann, S.: The challenges of gamification in the age of Industry 4.0: focusing on man in future machine-driven working environments, In: IEEE Global Engineering Education Conference EDUCON, no. April, pp. 1622–1630 (2017). https://doi.org/10.1109/EDUCON.2017.7943066

18. Obaid, I., Farooq, M.S.: Gamification for recruitment and job training: model, taxonomy, and challenges. IEEE Access **8**, 65164–65178 (2020). https://doi.org/10.1109/ACCESS.2020.298 4178

19. Hammedi, W., Leclercq, T., Poncin, I., Alkire, L., Nasr, N.: Uncovering the dark side of gamification at work: Impacts on engagement. J. Bus. Res. **122**, 256-269. (2021). https://doi.org/10.1016/j.jbusres.2020.08.032

20. Ulmer, J., Braun, S., Cheng, C.T., Dowey, S., Wollert, J.: Human-centered gamification framework for manufacturing systems. Procedia CIRP **93**, 670–675 (2020). https://doi.org/10.1016/j.procir.2020.04.076

21. Passalacqua, M., et al.: Playing in the backstore: interface gamification increases warehousing workforce engagement. Ind. Manag. Data Syst. **120**(7), 1309–1330 (2020). https://doi.org/10.1108/IMDS-08-2019-0458

22. Kumar, H., Raghavendran, S.: Gamification, the finer art: fostering creativity and employee engagement. J. Bus. Strategy **36**(6), 3–12 (2015). https://doi.org/10.1108/JBS-10-2014-0119

23. Burnett, J.R., Lisk, T.C.: The future of employee engagement: real-time monitoring and digital tools for engaging a workforce. Int. Stud. Manag. Organ. **49**(1), 108–119 (2019). https://doi.org/10.1080/00208825.2019.1565097

24. Schaufeli, W.B., Bakker, A.B., Salanova, M.: The measurement of work engagement with a short questionnaire: a cross-national study. Educ. Psychol. Meas. **66**(4), 701–716 (2006). https://doi.org/10.1177/0013164405282471

25. Nurhas, I., Pawlowski, J.M., Geisler, S.: Towards humane digitization: a wellbeing-driven process of personas creation, In: ACM International Conference Proceeding Series, pp. 24–31 (2019). https://doi.org/10.1145/3328243.3328247

26. Çınar, Z.M., Zeeshan, Q., Korhan, O.: A framework for industry 4.0 readiness and maturity of smart manufacturing enterprises: a case study. Sustainability **13**(12), 6659. (2021). https://doi.org/10.3390/su13126659

27. Zhang, C., Chen, Y., Chen, H., Chong, D.: Industry 4.0 and its implementation: a review. Inf. Syst. Front. (2021). https://doi.org/10.1007/s10796-021-10153-5.

28. Villalba-Diez, J., Ordieres-Meré, J.: Human–machine integration in processes within industry 4.0 management. Sensors **21**(17), 1–17 (2021). https://doi.org/10.3390/s21175928

29. Kadir, B.A., Broberg, O.: Human-centered design of work systems in the transition to industry 4.0. Appl. Ergon. **92**, 103334 (2021). https://doi.org/10.1016/j.apergo.2020.103334

30. Gallo, T., Santolamazza, A.: Industry 4.0 and human factor: how is technology changing the role of the maintenance operator? Procedia Comput. Sci. **180**(2019), 388–393 (2021). https://doi.org/10.1016/j.procs.2021.01.364

31. Valentina, D.P., Valentina, D.S., Salvatore, M., Stefano, R.: Smart operators: how Industry 4.0 is affecting the worker's performance in manufacturing contexts. Procedia Comput. Sci. **180**(2019), 958–967 (2021). https://doi.org/10.1016/j.procs.2021.01.347

32. Salvadorinho, J., Teixeira, L.: Organizational knowledge in the I4.0 using BPMN: a case study. Procedia Comput. Sci. **181**, 981–988 (2021). https://doi.org/10.1016/j.procs.2021.01.266

33. Whittington, J.L., Galpin, T.J.: The engagement factor: building a high-commitment organization in a low-commitment world. J. Bus. Strategy **31**(5), 14–24 (2010). https://doi.org/10.1108/02756661011076282

34. Alshammari, H.: Workplace productivity through employee workforce engagement: a review study. Int. J. Bus. Soc. Sci. **6**(12), 156–162 (2015)

35. Saputra, N., Sasmoko, S.B.A.: The holistic work engagement: a study in indonesia oil palm industry. Int. J. Eng. Technol. **7**(4), 1–7. (2018). https://doi.org/10.14419/ijet.v7i4.9.20607

36. Caught, K., Shadur, M.A., Rodwell, J.J.: The measurement artifact in the organizational commitment questionnaire. Psychol. Rep. **87**, 777–788 (2000)

37. Alla, A., Nafil, K.: Gamification in IoT application: a systematic mapping study. Procedia Comput. Sci. **151**, 455–462 (2019). https://doi.org/10.1016/j.procs.2019.04.062

38. Lithoxoidou, E.E., et al.: Improvement of the workers' satisfaction and collaborative spirit through gamification. In: Kompatsiaris, I., et al. (eds.) INSCI 2017. LNCS, vol. 10673, pp. 184–191. Springer, Cham (2017). https://doi.org/10.1007/978-3-319-70284-1_15

Digital Human Modeling in Interactive Product and Service Design

Auditing and Testing AI – A Holistic Framework

Nikolas Becker[✉] and Bernhard Waltl

Gesellschaft für Informatik e.V. (GI), Bonn, Germany
nikolas.becker@gi.de

Abstract. This paper describes a framework that can be used to assess and analyze AI systems in terms of risk. The framework addresses the structure and components of AI systems at five layers and allows taking a holistic view of AI systems while focusing on specific aspects, such as discrimination or data.

Keywords: AI · Testing · Auditing · Safety · Fairness · Lifecycle · Framework

1 Introduction

Artificial intelligence (AI) is present all areas of digital societies. This applies to the work and occupational context, but also to the private sphere. It is becoming increasingly apparent that the use of AI or AI-based systems leads to a tension. This tension has many facets and levels. It ranges from inadmissible discrimination, data protection violations and insufficient labeling of an AI system to a lack of information for data subjects and a lack of alternatives that make an "opt-out" practically impossible. For consumers and data subjects, this often results in risks that cannot be controlled.

From a business perspective, on the other hand, the use of AI systems is attractive for several reasons. In most cases, the focus is on application scenarios involving algorithmic decision-making. Data is used here to optimize or automate decisions. However, it is not always true that larger amounts of data necessarily lead to better decisions by AI systems. However, the amount of data available makes it possible to use new technologies that are very powerful in specific application areas and redefine the state of the art. Especially in complex use cases, where the use of AI systems has not or hardly been done so far, new and exciting possibilities arise. One area here is personnel and talent management with use cases such as automated personality assessment based on the CV or AI-based background checks.

Analysis of the opportunities and risks arising from the use of AI systems shows [1] that strategies and methods for minimizing the risks posed by AI systems are not currently being developed at the same rate as AI systems have evolved. This makes it all the more important for research in the field to catch up. It is at this interface that this work aims to contribute.

This paper describes a framework that can be used to assess and analyze AI systems in terms of risk. The framework addresses the structure and components of AI systems at five layers and allows taking a holistic view of AI systems while focusing on specific aspects, such as discrimination or data. Starting from the framework, the importance of

© The Author(s), under exclusive license to Springer Nature Switzerland AG 2022
V. G. Duffy (Ed.): HCII 2022, LNCS 13320, pp. 283–292, 2022.
https://doi.org/10.1007/978-3-031-06018-2_20

auditing and testing is underlined and the notion of AI audit is introduced. The AI audit is based on a software audit. However, it addresses the characteristics of an AI system in particular. It is particularly important to note that an AI system is a software-intensive and socio-technical system. Looking at many a discussion in recent years, one might get the impression that AI is something opaque and "magical." This is not the case. With the same methods that researchers and developers use to research and develop AI systems, progress can also be made in the area of explainability and transparency. Interdisciplinary collaboration and exchange across disciplines is critical. Explainability and transparency of AI systems are research areas with complex questions that cannot be answered by computer scientists and engineers alone.

2   Structure and Components of AI Systems

In order to fully grasp and understand the functioning of AI systems, a holistic approach is required. Holistic means, in this context, that all technical components, but also the socio-technical components of the development process of the AI system must be considered [2]. Since an AI system is a software-intensive system, it is subject to similar laws as other software systems, which have been analyzed and developed in computer science for decades [3]. This regularity also includes in particular:

- Analysis of the use scenario and description of the use case
- Life cycle of software intensive systems
- Design and structure of the ADM system,
- Emerging decision structures
- Decisions made

These different areas of an AI system must be made transparent in order to understand, comprehend and evaluate the behavior of the AI system. The framework developed in the context of this work maps these five layers of AI systems. Consequently, these layers can also be used to derive indications and criteria for recognizing potential misbehavior, i.e., a deviation from the expected behavior.

A closer look reveals that the different areas are interdependent or intertwined. This can be illustrated, for example, by the decision made by an AI system: the decision is usually dependent on the data provided (input) and the underlying decision structure (e.g., the trained ML model). The data is pre-processed and converted into a form so that it can be processed by the decision structure. The output of the decision structure is therefore based on the input data and the decision structure. This, along with other factors (see below), must be taken into account. These dependencies are shown as in Fig. 1.

Figure 1 depicts the five layers, each with three subsystems or subareas that are significant for AI systems. In the following sections, the respective layers and their subsystems are presented and discussed in detail. The figure also shows the role of the typical users or interacting and affected persons. These interact in fact only with selected sub-areas of the AI system, namely with layer 3 "ADM systems" and layer 5 "decision". The directions of the arrows also indicate the primary flow of information. While users

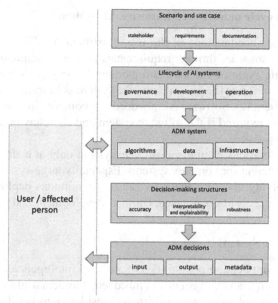

Fig. 1. Holistic overview of the creation process, components and sub-components, of an AI system.

communicate bilaterally with the ADM system, the information flow at the decision layer is generally one-way. The user has already provided his data and receives the resulting decision after appropriate preprocessing and processing by the decision structure.

2.1 Layer 1: Scenario and Use Case

The use of any AI system is based on fundamental decisions and analyses with regard to the scenario and the use case. The scenario is described and important decisions as well as motivations and motives for the deployment of AI are identified, which can be of economic or technical nature [4, 5]. In general, data intensive decisions, consistent decisions, and cost-favorable decisions are attractive for the use of AI, not only but also in HR [6].

The use case represents the description of a system from the point of view of the actors. The group of actors includes not only the affected persons, but also employees who work with the system, administrators who monitor and configure the system, and other users of the AI system. Use cases can also be described graphically in diagrams. The standard in the Modeling (UML) area provides for the diagram type "Use Case Diagram" for this purpose. The use case is crucial and can be the main entry point for analyzing the overall system. In the analysis, the descriptions of the stakeholders, the requirements and the documentation are of central importance.

2.2   Layer 2: Lifecycle of Software-Intensive AI Systems

In addition to basic specifications of the use of artificial intelligence as well as the specification of the software through requirements and documentation, an exact consideration of the life cycle of software is important. In previous considerations, often only the present software or the present software system is examined. In practice, however, this is insufficient [7]. Software is embedded in a complex life cycle. Transparency over the life cycle is required if the software system and its behavior are to be made as comprehensible as possible.

Previous considerations examine a software system only at a single point in time, which can be insufficient for complex systems. Especially large systems and platforms are constantly evolving, they are characterized by "continuous deployment". The life cycle includes the aspects of governance, (further) development and operation.

2.3   Layer 3: ADM System

Based on the basic application possibilities of artificial intelligence for a use case and the life cycle in which an AI system is embedded, the actual algorithmic decision-making (ADM) system plays a central role in the considerations [8]. This is the software system around which the life cycle from layer 2 revolves. It is the result of a complex development process. With modern software-intensive systems, the development process is never complete, but is continuously developed. In order to make the behavior of such a system transparent and to be able to evaluate it accordingly, it is necessary to recognize and take this dynamic into account. However, one can limit the considerations of the life cycle and focus on the three crucial components algorithms, data and infrastructure when it comes to analyzing the behavior of an ADM system.

2.4   Layer 4: Decision-Making Structures

Embedded in the ADM systems of layer 3 are the so-called decision-making structures. These are areas that enable concrete decisions (c.f. layer 5). The decision-making structures are often related to the algorithms used for decision-making (c.f. layer 4) [9]. They represent the results of the implementation or the implementation of the algorithms and thus concrete characteristics of the algorithms.

The decision-making structures thus result from the algorithms used and the available data. They represent the "trained models" in the field of machine learning. As briefly described in Sect. 3.4, there are different classes of algorithms. A trained model can take different forms depending on the algorithm used: rule-based, decision trees, ensemble of decision trees, statistical methods and probability distributions, neural networks, etc. Within the rule-based procedures, the use and use of decision trees is very well established. Decision trees do not necessarily have to be created by humans, but can also be created automatically by algorithms. The results of more complex algorithms, such as the result of training neural networks, can no longer be carried out by humans. Their creation is left exclusively to software systems. The result of the creation process, the decision tree, is an essential area of an AI system and is studied by the research area Explainable AI (XAI).0 [10] A key finding is that not all decision-making structures are equally suitable for interpretation by humans. However, there are additional methods and procedures to make underlying decision-making structures explainable, testable and auditable [11].

Three areas play a central role in decision-making structures, which are focused on in the context of auditing and testing, which are proposed in the Assessment List for Trustworthy AI by the HLEG AI of the European Commission: accuracy, interpretability and explainability, as well as robustness [12].

2.5 Layer 5: ADM Decisions

The decisions of an AI system derive from decision-making structures. They are the outputs of an AI system, which are reported back to the user. The processes on layers 1–4 are usually not accessible to the user. Those are important and necessary during the creation process and during further development. The decision, on the other hand, is prompted to the end user. It does not necessarily have to be communicated directly by algorithms and the developed decision-making structures. Decisions may also be communicated indirectly, e.g. by a third person. A significant advantage of the dedicated separation of the decision structure from the decision in the context of auditing and testing lies in the improved and more appropriate analysis of the underlying processes. This is particularly evident in the fact that there are numerous methods to analyze the decision-making structures independently of a specific decision or to make them transparent.

A decision is the process in which a decision tree produces an output based on input data. Various metadata can also be taken into account or generated. These are relevant from two points of view: on the one hand, metadata can be taken into account on the input side and thus included in the decision-making process. On the other hand, metadata can be created in addition to the output of a decision. This is the case, for example, if, in addition to a decision, the confidence with which a decision was made is also calculated. In the context of the decisions, the three areas of input, output and metadata play a central role, which are focused on in the context of auditing and testing [13].

3 Auditing and Self-assessments of AI Systems

To ensure quality and to prove the presence or absence of certain properties, there are already established methods that complement each other with their properties and in combination become a suitable means of quality management. In other areas and countries, such as the financial sector, the areas of auditing, testing and certification are established and anchored in the laws accordingly [14].

Auditing can be distinguished into external audits on the one hand and the internal audits on the other. A special form of the internal audit is the self-assessment. Testing is a common method for ensuring defined requirements and measuring quality, especially for software systems or software-intensive systems. This can also be applied to software and algorithms in the field of AI [15].

The superordinate area of proof and certification is the component of quality management that provides information about a successful or unsuccessful performance of an audit or a test procedure. Under certain circumstances, certificates can be issued that represent a kind of test seal confirming that certain standards (consensus) were met during the audit. In many cases, this also includes that the verifying organizational unit is accredited. This means that it has the technical, organizational and procedural capabilities to meet the standard during the verification. This accreditation is issued or certified by accreditation bodies. In the area of AI in the world of work, there are already some standards from national and international companies and authorities [16].

3.1 Audit and Audit Program

According to IEEE Standard 1028–2008 (software) audits are "an independent evaluation of conformance of software products and processes to applicable regulations, standards, guidelines, plans, specifications, and procedures [17]." If audits are carried out in a larger and strategic context, it is necessary to align the audits with their different objectives to a common and overarching goal. Audit programs exist for this purpose. The audit program must be distinguished from the audit plan. While the audit plan is a description of the activities and processes to be carried out within an audit, the audit program is the overarching classification, coordination and planning of a set or series of audits. The audit program is characterized by three core aspects:

1. Strategic classification and alignment: This includes the consideration of corporate goals and requirements that go beyond the AI system to be audited. Among the influencing factors that can be taken into account here are, for example, a company's digitization and data strategy, IT infrastructure goals (cloud and on-prem) and higher-level IT projects (cloud data hubs, lakes and warehouses).
2. Alignment and coordination: This includes the consideration of all planned audits and, in particular, the alignment of the objectives pursued in each case and the core areas of the respective audits. Here, focal points, e.g., data and data stocks, interpretability of ML models, etc., can be set and taken into account.
3. Planning and preparation: This includes consideration of the specific aspects relevant to the execution, such as trigger events for audits and the resources required for execution and preparation. Whether the audits are carried out at regular intervals or on demand and which resources, in particular personnel and infrastructure, are required and at what point in time they are made available.

3.2 AI Audit

The AI audit represents the application of auditing with the proven, tested and accepted procedures and approach to AI systems. The characteristics of AI systems are taken into account. In particular, this concerns the structure of AI systems as well as the complex interaction of different components and subsystems, which in combination yield more than is revealed by the analysis of the subsystems. The most prominent example is the interaction of data and algorithms: neither by the isolated consideration and analysis of the data set nor by the fully described algorithm is the behavior of a decision structure or a trained ML model predictable. Only the combination of algorithm and data determines the degrees of freedom (variables) created in the algorithm. The behavior of the decision structure is the emergence that results from the interaction of subsystems.

Subject of an AI audit is therefore necessarily the AI system in its entirety. The characteristics of the AI audit furthermore concern the design and implementation of the audit involving the five layers. The individual layers and the components within them can be considered to varying degrees, depending on the objective. However, neglecting them will result in an incomplete analysis.

An AI audit requires the appropriate resources and methodological competencies. As an additional challenge to auditing a conventional software system, it is above all the data centricity of AI systems that makes the AI audit particularly complex. The analysis of large data sets must be possible and therefore requires appropriate tools (big data) and expertise (data literacy, statistics, data analytics, data science, etc.). The AI audit can be further subdivided into an external and internal AI audit and a self-assessment.

3.3 External AI Audit

The external AI audit is characterized by the fact that the auditing organizational unit is located outside, i.e., organizationally separate and without influence from the audited organization. This must be taken into account when drawing up the audit plan, as it has an impact on the provision of information, including data.

3.4 Internal AI Audit

The internal KI audit is characterized by the fact that the auditing organizational unit is not located outside the audited organization. The internal KI audit can therefore also be carried out by the internal audit department or another accredited organizational unit.

3.5 AI Self-assessment

The AI self-assessment is a special form of the internal AI audit. The self-assessment also runs according to a system defined ex ante and the test criteria must still be measurable and ascertainable. The audit criteria must again be designed in such a way that the AI system is evaluated holistically and completely. This also includes subsystems (including data sets). The test criteria must be selected in a way that also allows conclusions to be drawn about the emergent properties.

In contrast to the external or conventional internal audit, the responsibility for carrying out the assessment lies with the organizational unit that is also responsible for developing the AI system. This has the disadvantage that a conflict of interest of the acting persons cannot be excluded. Therefore, the AI self-assessment does not necessarily enjoy the same credibility as an external AI audit or the traditional internal audit. The organizational unit responsible for the conception and (further) development can also delegate the AI self-assessment (or parts of it) and hand it over to a central department, for example. Depending on the design of the handover, however, it remains a self-assessment, even if the assessment of the test criteria has been delegated. The decisive factor is the planning and preparation as well as the ultimate responsibility, which cannot be delegated or divided within the framework of the self-assessment. The core characteristic of self-assessment is that responsibility lies with the organizational unit that is also responsible for the design and (further) development of the AI system.

However, a significant advantage is the relatively low organizational effort (overhead) with which an AI self-assessment can be carried out. Another advantage is that the test criteria are known to the project team members and they are thus sensitized to such issues as part of the project work. In addition, the test criteria can be adapted and updated by the project team if it becomes apparent during the assessment that the criteria are not adequate. The criteria catalog, e.g., checklist, thus becomes an implicit part of the development of the AI system. Sprawling and cumbersome self-assessment procedures, on the other hand, can quickly be perceived as additional overhead. Attention must be paid to appropriateness, i.e., the right ratio between benefit and effort.

4   Layers of AI Audits

The holistic model of an AI system provides a basis for the application of auditing and testing procedures. As explained above, an AI system is a complex and software-intensive system. Among other things, this means that the effects of decisions and changes at one point in the overall system become noticeable at another point. For example, the choice of algorithm in layer 3 has an impact on the metadata available in layer 5. If the algorithm is changed during further development because it is replaced by a new type of algorithm, this may mean that required metadata can no longer be provided in the future. This is due to the fact that some of the algorithms are based on completely different principles. For example, decision trees, Bayesian networks and neural networks implement different mathematical rules, which means that the output of the algorithms must be interpreted and processed differently. This example is intended to show that a holistic approach that can address the peculiarities of the subsystems is essential when it comes to understanding an AI system.

Figure 2 shows the resulting overall system again, including the expansion of auditing and testing procedures. It is undisputed that both auditing procedures and testing procedures will continue to evolve as research in the field continues. The four test procedures in Fig. 2 are by no means a complete overview of the test procedures available for software-intensive systems. In addition, it is to be expected that the trend of the last years continues and there will be beside the past methods for the test of software-intensive systems still further and presumably on the test of algorithms highly-specialized test procedures. Especially if these test procedures are helpful to implement legal requirements or to develop systems more efficient and robust.

Figure 2 also shows that neither auditing nor testing procedures are always limited to the application and analysis of one component or one layer. It is possible for the procedures to analyze multiple components simultaneously and across multiple layers. Thus, test procedures can not only provide information about the functioning of the algorithm (layer 3), but also provide insight into the functioning of the decision structure (layer 4) and enable an analysis of the output as well as metadata (layer 5). Analogously, this also applies to auditing procedures. As shown, the procedures of testing and auditing are not mutually exclusive, but complement each other. It can make sense to use selected test procedures as part of an audit in order to obtain objective evidence that could not be generated using only classic audit methods (e.g., software code review).

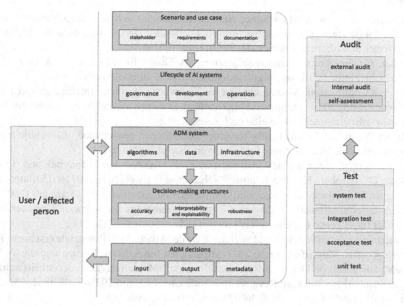

Fig. 2. Holistic overview of an AI system as a basis for locating auditing and testing procedures.

References

1. Zweig, K., Hauer, M., Raudonat, F.: Anwendungsszenarien: KI-Systeme im Personal- und Talentmanagement, ExamAI – KI Testing & Auditing. Gesellschaft für Informatik, Berlin (2020)
2. Waltl, B., Vogl, R.: Explainable artificial intelligence – the new frontier in legal informatics. Jusletter IT **4**, 1–10 (2018)
3. Broy, M., Kuhrmann, M.: Einführung in die Softwaretechnik, Springer, Heidelberg https:// doi.org/10.1007/978-3-662-50263 (2021)
4. Why AI is the future of growth, Accenture, 2016. The economic impact of the automation of knowledge work, robots and self-driving vehicles could reach between EUR 6.5 and EUR 12 trillion annually by 2025 (including improved productivity and higher quality of life in ageing populations). Source: Disruptive technologies: Advances that will transform life, business, and the global economy, McKinsey Global Institute (2013)
5. AI is part of the Commission's strategy to digitise industry (COM(2016) 180 final) and a renewed EU Industrial Policy Strategy (COM(2017) 479 final)
6. Russel, S., Norvig, P.: Artificial intelligence: a modern approach (2002)
7. Handelsblatt. Kartellamt rügt Lufthansa: Solche Algorithmen werden ja nicht vom lieben Gott geschrieben. https://www.handelsblatt.com/unternehmen/handel-konsumgueter/kartel lamt-ruegt-lufthansa-solche-algorithmen-werden-ja-nicht-vom-lieben-gott-geschrieben/207 95072.html. Accessed 28 Dec 2017
8. Waltl, B., Vogl, R.: Increasing transparency in algorithmic- decision-making with explainable AI. Datenschutz und Datensicherheit - DuD **42**(10), 613–617 (2018). https://doi.org/10.1007/ s11623-018-1011-4
9. Nguyen, G., et al.: Machine learning and deep learning frameworks and libraries for large-scale data mining: a survey. Artifi. Intell. Rev. **52**(1), 77–124 (2019)

10. Došilović, F.K., Brčić, M., Hlupić, Nikica.: Explainable artificial intelligence: a survey. In: 2018 41st International Convention on Information and Communication Technology, Electronics and Microelectronics (MIPRO). IEEE (2018)
11. Molnar, C.: Interpretable machine learning. A Guide for Making Black Box Models Explainable. https://christophm.github.io/interpretable-ml-book/ (2019)
12. European Commission, Assessment List for Trustworthy Artificial Intelligence (ALTAI) for self-assessment, 2021, c.f. https://digital-strategy.ec.europa.eu/en/library/assessment-list-tru stworthy-artificial-intelligence-altai-self-assessment
13. Schelter, S., et al.: Automatically tracking metadata and provenance of machine learning experiments. Machine Learning Systems Workshop at NIPS (2017)
14. Comptroller of the Currency Administrator of National Bank Internal and External Audits: Comptrollers Handbook. https://web.archive.org/web/20101107160153/http://www.ffiec.gov/ffiecinfobase/resources/audit/occ-hb-internal_external_audits-intro.pdf (2003)
15. Jöckel, L., et al.: Towards a Common Testing Terminology for Software Engineering and Artificial Intelligence Experts. arXiv preprint arXiv:2108.13837 (2021)
16. Bundesministerium für Arbeit und Soziales KI in der Arbeitswelt: Potenziale erkennen, Transparenz schaffen, Zugriff am 13.10.2021. https://www.bmas.de/DE/Europa-und-die-Welt/Europa/MySocialEurope-Deutsche-Ratspraesidentschaft/Meldungen/ki-in-der-arbeitswelt.html
17. IEEE Standard for Software Reviews and Audits, in IEEE Std 1028–2008, pp.1–53. https://doi.org/10.1109/IEEESTD.2008.4601584. Accessed 15 Aug 2008

Towards Situated AMR: Creating a Corpus of Gesture AMR

Lucia Donatelli[1]([✉]) [iD], Kenneth Lai[2] [iD], Richard Brutti[2] [iD],
and James Pustejovsky[2] [iD]

[1] Saarland Informatics Campus, Saarland University, Saarbrücken, Germany
donatelli@coli.uni-saarland.de
[2] Brandeis University, Waltham, MA, USA
{klai12,brutti,jamesp}@brandeis.edu

Abstract. In this paper, we extend Abstract Meaning Representation (AMR) in order to represent situated multimodal dialogue, with a focus on the modality of gesture. AMR is a general-purpose meaning representation that has become popular for its transparent structure, its ease of annotation and available corpora, and its overall expressiveness. While AMR was designed to represent meaning in language as text or speech, gesture accompanying speech conveys a number of novel communicative dimensions, including situational reference, spatial locations, manner, attitude, orientation, backchanneling, and others. In this paper, we explore how to combine multimodal elements into a single representation for alignment and grounded meaning, using gesture as a case study. As a platform for multimodal situated dialogue annotation, we believe that Gesture AMR has several attractive properties. It is adequately expressive at both utterance and dialogue levels, while easily accommodating the structures inherent in gestural expressions. Further, the native reentrancy facilitates both the linking between modalities and the eventual situational grounding to contextual bindings.

Keywords: AMR · Gesture annotation · Multimodal dialogue · Meaning representation

1 Introduction

As multimodal interactive systems become both more common and more sophisticated, people come to use them with increasing expectations that their interactions will approximate aspects of typical interactions with another human.

This work was supported in part by NSF grant DRL 2019805, to Dr. Pustejovsky at Brandeis University, and an NSF Student Grant to Kenneth Lai, Richard Brutti, and Lucia Donatelli, also funded by NSF grant DRL 2019805. We would like to express our thanks to Nikhil Krishnaswamy for his comments on the multimodal framework motivating the development of Gesture AMR. The views expressed herein are ours alone.

V. G. Duffy (Ed.): HCII 2022, LNCS 13320, pp. 293–312, 2022.
https://doi.org/10.1007/978-3-031-06018-2_21

Human-computer interaction (HCI) and human-robot interaction (HRI) involve communicating intentions, goals, and attitudes through multiple modalities beyond language, including gesture, gaze, facial expressions, and situational awareness. With this increased interest in multimodal interaction comes a need for capturing, representing, and annotating the data that encodes these different modalities during such interactions.

A representation language suitable to this task should, at a minimum, both accommodate the structure and content of the different modalities, as well as facilitate alignment and binding across the modalities. However, it is also important to make a distinction between the alignment of information from multiple channels in a multimodal dialogue (language, gesture, gaze), and the actual situated grounding of an expression to the local environment, be it a situated context, an image, or a formal registration in a database. Therefore, such a meaning representation should also have the basic facility for situated grounding in the context; e.g., explicit mention of object and situational state in context.

In this paper, we explore extending Abstract Meaning Representation (AMR) [4] to situated interaction with a focus on the gesture modality. AMR is a graph-based meaning representation that expresses the meaning of a sentence in terms of its predicate-argument structure. AMRs were designed to be easy for humans to annotate (supporting the creation of corpora), and easy for computers to parse. An example AMR for the English language sentence "Put that block there" is shown in PENMAN [55] notation in example (1) below.[1]

(1) a. Put that block there.

    b. ```
    (p / put-01
        :mode imperative
        :ARG0 (y / you)
        :ARG1 (b / block
            :mod (t / that))
        :ARG2 (t2 / there))
```

    c.

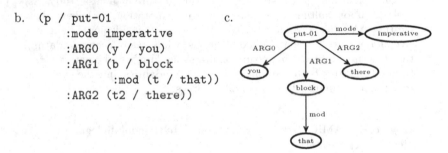

    d.  instance($p$, put-01)∧instance($y$, you)∧instance($b$, block)∧instance($t$, that)∧
instance($t2$, there) ∧ ARG0($p, y$) ∧ ARG1($p, b$) ∧ mod($b, t$) ∧ ARG2($p, t2$) ∧
mode($p$, imperative)

AMR was designed to represent meaning in language as text. As such, the AMR in example (1) does not represent the gesture that may accompany the speech, such as that shown in Fig. 1. While the AMR for the spoken sentence

---

[1] We gloss over the formal interpretation of the imperative mode in such contexts. However, two avenues are particularly aligned to our approach here: the use of SDRT relations for how the speech act relates to the mentioned action as developed in [43]; and the theory developed in [5], where imperatives are direct actions in the world.
```

Fig. 1. Person instructing an avatar through camera in a shared task of block assembly.

above conveys basic information about the desired action and the object upon which that action operates, the gesture specifies a precise block and spatial location where that block should be located. Additional gestural representations can specify the manner of motion, such as whether the "put" action is slow or fast, and clarify whether the addressee has understood the instructions correctly with gestural backchanneling. It has yet to be explored how AMR could be extended to represent meaning conveyed by additional communication modalities such as gesture, gaze, or facial expression.

In this paper, we explore how to combine multimodal elements in single representation for alignment and grounded meaning using gesture as a case study. We discuss AMR and several proposed extensions to the formalism to accommodate domains beyond textual language in Sect. 2; these extensions serve as inspiration for the development of Gesture AMR. We review existing approaches to gesture meaning and annotation in Sect. 3 before outlining the specifications of Gesture AMR in Sect. 4. We then discuss the challenges of situational grounding and dynamic updating present in multi-agent interaction and how Gesture AMR can accommodate these in Sect. 5. We conclude and discuss remaining challenges for future work in Sect. 6.

2   Situating Abstract Meaning Representation

Abstract Meaning Representation (AMR) is a general-purpose meaning representation that has become popular for its simple structure, ease of annotation and available corpora, and overall expressiveness [4,38]. Specifically, AMR focuses on representing the predicative core of a sentence as an intuitive representation of the semantics of a sentence, advantageous for parsing and matching algorithms. For the sentence in (1a), the predicate and its arguments are represented as nodes in the AMR graph in (1c), while the edges represent the relations between the predicate and each of its arguments. PENMAN notation in (1b) provides a more readable version of the AMR [55]. The AMR captures verb senses, coreference, and several aspects of argument and modifier structure. Here we review several previous and ongoing extensions to AMR that seek to enhance the formalism's expressive capacity. These extensions provide an outline for how to extend AMR to gesture and other non-verbal modalities. We then discuss the challenges in extending AMR to gesture before turning to the meaning of gesture in Sect. 3.

2.1   Extensions to AMR

Making AMR More Logically Meaningful. By design, AMR emphasizes argument structure over logical structure, distinguishing it from several other meaning representations based on formal semantic frameworks [23, 32]. Although AMRs can be represented as conjunctions of logical triples, as seen in (1d), such representations cannot always be used directly for drawing valid inferences such as textual entailment or contradiction. Quantifiers, for example, are not given any special semantics, being represented as simple modifiers. Several proposals have been put forth to provide AMRs with more meaningful logical forms, driven both by parsing and theoretical concerns [2, 11, 12, 42, 65, 73, 75]. In contrast, [24] argue that any purely graphical representation of meaning is unable to capture basic natural language semantics such as Boolean operators. Instead, the authors propose layering graphs based on the Resource Description Framework (RDF) [69] and named graphs [17] such that the interaction between different layers can capture Booleans (such as negation and disjunction), modals and irrealis contexts, distributivity and quantifier scope, co-reference, and sense selection [31]. For this paper, it is important to note that AMR in its standard form does not represent quantifier scope in any way. This is important when looking at the interaction between modalities such as gesture and language and potential scopal relations between the two [44] (see Sect. 3). Additionally, as AMR was designed for text alone, it is an open question whether its structure can adequately represent the interaction between distinct modalities and the meaning that emerges as a result of such interaction.

Dialogue-AMR. Dialogue-AMR [9] introduces a detailed schema for representing illocutionary force in AMR; it is the most extensive of the few annotation schemes that exist for AMR for spoken interaction [6, 72]. The Dial-AMR schema is specifically designed for human-robot dialogue and inferences that a robot needs to make when engaged in a collaborative navigation task. It is nevertheless flexible in its design and can be extended to other settings where understanding content and speaker intent is necessary. Dial-AMR updates standard AMR with three extensions: (i) a taxonomy of speech acts that provide coverage of the natural language found in the domain [14, 70]; (ii) annotations for tense and aspect to track task status and completion [26]; and (iii) normalizing of propositional content to standard robot concepts for downstream operationalization. The Dial-AMR corpus consists of 1122 utterance annotations on top of the Situated Corpus of Understanding Transactions (SCOUT) [51, 52], a collection of dialogues that illustrates the diversity of communication strategies in the human-robot collaboration domain. Additional work with Dial-AMR has established its suitability in a larger pipeline from spoken language input to robot control though notes that there is a need for more, varied dialogue data for the scheme to provide coverage in different domains [8]. We adapt general principles of the Dial-AMR annotation scheme, specifically the representation of speech acts (here, gesture acts), for Gesture AMR (Sect. 4).

Spatial-AMR. Spatial AMR [10] was developed for a multimodal corpus of 185 dialogues for building 3D structures in Minecraft. The schema captures fine-grained spatial semantics and object grounding strategies of previous schemata [30,64,78] with (i) spatial conceptualization relating to how eventualities and states are construed (e.g. location, orientation, configuration, extent), and (ii) 170 new or expanded spatial rolesets for PropBank. Individual utterances are grounded in space with Cartesian coordinate values that map to the Minecraft landscape; across sentences, spatial coordinates are tracked for coreference to create and ground identity chains following conventions of multi-sentence AMR (MS-AMR) [59]. Similar to Dial-AMR, though designed for Minecraft, the annotation scheme is flexible and extendable to other domains. The authors annotate a corpus of roughly 9750 sentences with Spatial AMR specifications for model training and parsing purposes. This work serves as inspiration for how to ground deictic gestures in Gesture AMR.

Multi-sentence AMR. The Multi-Sentence Abstract Meaning Representation (MS-AMR) corpus [59] is a corpus annotated on top of existing gold AMRs with extended information about coreference, implicit role reference, and bridging relationships [61]. The annotation scheme links individual AMRs together using these relationships, presenting an integrated representation of the meaning of an entire document or discourse to represent the entire propositional content of a document. Annotators are tasked with labeling clusters of variables that refer to the same entity or event over the AMRs constituting a document; this can be done by simply making explicit all numbered arguments for a given predicate as outlined in the PropBank lexicon. The corpus is composed of 293 annotated documents in total, with an average of 27.4 AMRs (429 words) per document, covering roughly 10% of the total AMR 3.0 corpus. Ongoing development of Gesture AMR will incorporate MS-AMR's representation of semantic coreference and implicit arguments across modalities.

Uniform Meaning Representation. Uniform Meaning Representation (UMR) [80] is a practical and cross-linguistically valid meaning representation designed to meet the needs of a wide range of NLP applications. UMR extends AMR with a companion document-level representation that captures linguistic phenomena such as coreference and temporal and modal dependencies that support lexical and logical inference and that often cross sentence boundaries. UMR has as a goal the extension to other languages, particularly morphologically complex, low-resource languages. Annotation experiments aimed specifically at testing the robustness of the proposed UMR annotation schemes for newly added semantic domains (temporality, modality, and aspect) and the efficiency of the annotation scheme for cross-linguistic comparability are ongoing; such experiments have been conducted in English, Arapaho, Kukama, Navajo, and Sanapaná. For English, six English texts were annotated by two independent expert annotators, amounting to 377 events expressed in 108 sentences; inter-annotator agreement for all annotation categories and language pairs was well above chance, between .64 and .94 for Cohen's kappa. These results demonstrate the effectiveness of standard AMR's design in capturing additional semantic concepts that are both cross-linguistically valid and scalable for annotation, and set an optimistic precedent for extending AMR to additional modalities.

2.2 AMR for Situated Interaction

The information typically conveyed by AMR expressions is a semantic interpretation of linguistic utterances, either spoken or written. As noted above, Spatial-AMR extends this convention somewhat and encodes the spatial relations that are present between objects in a particular situation at a given time. Situated language generally, however, introduces a number of extra-linguistic parameters that cannot easily be encoded within the basic AMR formalism. That being said, there are certain pragmatic factors and situational anchors in restricted domains, that are referenced through language or gesture, as in task-oriented dialogues, which can be usefully represented with an AMR-style representation. These include the major elements of the communicative common ground, a topic which we return to in Sect. 5.

Extending AMR to gesture specifically faces several challenges. While AMR aims to represent the semantic content of an utterance in context, gesture is a mode of expression analogous to spoken or written language. A question that arises from this analogy is whether a meaning representation should represent content independently of the mode of expression. Recent studies have cast doubt on whether different modes of expression convey the same kinds of semantic content [67]; as well as whether a coarse-grained, lexically-oriented meaning representation such as AMR can adequately capture a more underspecified morphology that gesture appears to have [19]. We discuss additional challenges posed by the semantics of gesture in the next section.

3 Representing the Meaning of Gesture

Gesture refers to the way speakers move their hands and arms when they speak and communicate information. Gesture and speech relate to each other in regular, patterned ways that can be analyzed by the relative timing of one to another, as well as how gesture enhances or complements the linguistic form of the speech content. Determining such relationships requires looking at syntactic constituency, headedness, and information structure in the linguistic signal to better understand the meaning contributed by the gesture modality [47]. Here we review previous and current semantic approaches to gesture (Sect. 3.1) before looking briefly at existing gesture annotation schemes that motivate our own (Sect. 3.2).

As an important aside, in this paper we do not consider other non-verbal components of communication such as body posture, facial expression, or gaze. Though essential to understanding global meaning and intention in communication, considering multiple non-verbal modalities together is beyond the scope of our work. By focusing on the interaction between gesture and speech, we hope to provide a case study for how to integrate other modalities into a global representation of meaning in interaction. It remains an open question whether these modalities can be isolated for their individual contributions to meaning or must be analyzed collectively to grasp the subtle interactions between their timing, scope, and ability to convey propositional and other semantic content [48].

3.1 Previous Semantic Approaches

It is important to specify the typology of gestures when defining their semantics. *Co-speech* or *co-verbal* gestures, which co-occur with spoken words, are thought to contribute to meaning and discourse in the same way as lexical items [34,56]. In this sense, co-speech gestures can themselves project illocutionary propositions distinct from speech [48]. Co-speech gestures tend to be most common in labeling gesture types (see Sect. 3.2 and Sect. 4): roughly speaking, referential gestures (iconic, metaphoric, deictic) visually illustrate some aspect of the spoken utterance, and non-referential gestures (beats) align with important words and help structure the utterance and discourse. Gestures for demonstratives in particular help clarify speech and ground language [50].

Foundational, formal work on the integration of gestural semantics in discourse and on co-verbal gesture in particular argues for gesture interpretation as dependent on its form and coherent links to accompanying linguistic context. Such interpretation assumes that gesture and speech provide complementary, inferentially related information and together compose an integrated, overarching speech act with a uniform force and consistent assignments of scope relationships [45]. For example, *depiction* can be understood as a gesture that visualizes exactly the content conveyed in speech; *overlay* relates one gesture to another when the latter continues to develop the same virtual space; and *replication* relates successive gestures that use the body in the same way to depict the same entities. Such gestural 'logical forms' allow for interpretive links in reference, content and scope to be precisely mapped and form part of a larger representation of multimodal discourse. In such accounts, gesture is often thought to be underspecified or capable of porting partial meaning in a way language cannot [20]. Language can thus serve as a disambiguating force for gesture, especially for iconic gestures [46]; this mirrors gestures disambiguating abilities with deictic expressions in language.

Additional categorical and semantic distinctions are made for *pro-speech* gestures, which fully replace spoken words and have been argued to trigger entailments, presuppositions, anti-presuppositions, scalar implicatures, and various other inferences; and *post-speech* gestures, which follow expressions they modify and can trigger inferences similar to those triggered by appositive relative clauses [67]. Such distinctions also point to gesture as *cosuppositional* in nature: in such contexts, gesture itself does not contribute at-issue semantic content but is dependent on any assertion made in the speech to be presuppositional. Finally, gesture can be analyzed for its contribution to dialogue structure: *interactive* gestures help manage turn-taking, indicate the next speaker, repair utterances, backchannel, and provide alignment between speakers [7,48,49].

Given gestures flexible and expressive nature, several researchers have argued that gesture is dimensional rather than categorical [18,57]: iconic, deictic, and other features often mix in the same gesture and assume semantic, pragmatic, and pragmatic functions simultaneously. Similarly, some approaches argue for utterance production as a multimodal process, in which gesture complements speech in communicating linguistic and symbolic representations, retrieving words, and vying for optimal expressivity [25,37,41,58,63]. Gesture may not even be communicative and used solely for speaker-internal purposes, as gesturing while on a telephone can demonstrate [7]. Treating gesture as dimensional and integrated with language for both production and comprehension reasons, such researchers argue, may allow for a more accurate assessment of how gestural movements integrate with spoken prosodic structure and discourse structure in patterned ways. Nevertheless, annotation schemes have tended for a categorical approach; a more dimensional approach to gesture in annotation is a complex and ongoing task [71].

3.2 Related Annotation Schemes

In developing an annotation scheme for gesture, we follow previous schemes that look at three main questions [47]: (i) What is the meaning of gesture? How should we assign semantic content to individual movements? (ii) How does gesture align to the linguistic signal, both semantically and temporally? (iii) How do language and gesture compose together to create meaning?

For Gesture AMR, we are influenced by annotation schemes that differentiate the following four referential forms of gestures: iconic, deictic, metaphoric, and emblematic [27,54,57]. Gesture AMR does not currently consider non-content-bearing/non-referential gestures such as 'beat' or 'rhythmic' gesture (Sect. 3.1), which may control the flow of speech or emphasize certain spoken words or phrases. We plan to investigate these types in our future work. We also draw inspiration from annotation schemes that focus specifically on the alignment and interaction of gesture and speech [1,35,39]. Importantly, such schema primarily describe the physical properties of the gestures without encoding their meaning [36,40]; we look to semantic work as described above to complement such annotations.

4 Gesture AMR

Our approach to Gesture AMR is centered around its role within the larger project of representing multimodal communication not only through language, but also through gesture, gaze, facial expressions, and situational awareness [20,28,40,53,66,81]. In order to model this communication, we must be able to situate it within a *common ground* [21,74,77,79], which includes the agents, their shared beliefs, what they jointly perceive, and their environment [63]. For this reason, Gesture AMR expressly marks the agents involved and the mode of communication, along with the content being communicated.

Unlike previous work that focuses on the physical description of gesture, we focus on the intent behind each gesture. However, our goal is to make Gesture AMR flexible enough that alignment with other, more physical, descriptions of gesture is possible in the future.

4.1 Corpus

As noted, the initial Gesture AMR specification is based on the EGGNOG corpus [82]. EGGNOG is comprised of 8 h of video across 40 participants, working in pairs on a shared task. The participants are located in different rooms connected by video and/or audio. One person *(actor)* has a set of wooden blocks, and the other *(signaler)* has a picture of a specific block arrangement. The signaler must get the actor to arrange the blocks as in the specific arrangement. EGGNOG videos are typically around 1 min long, and feature natural continuous communication. We acknowledge that gesture can be culture-and individual-specific. While there is some variation in age (from 19 to 64 years), EGGNOG participants were largely recruited from a university setting, and are all English speakers. The somewhat homogeneous group of gesturers, in combination with the task-based premise, likely limits the range of gestures exhibited in the corpus. However, the task-based premise also makes developing our Gesture AMR schema more tractable. EGGNOG has gestures annotated with multiple labels: physical descriptions of gesturing body parts and their movements, and high-level descriptions of the signaler's intent.

Given a set of EGGNOG videos, specifically those in which the participants communicate through both language and gesture, we create Gesture AMR annotations in a layer on top of the existing EGGNOG annotations. Annotators are given video and audio files of the signaler and actor, the existing annotations of the gesturer's physical movement and inferred intent, and a speech transcript. For each video, at least two annotators are instructed to create AMRs first for each spoken sentence, then for each content-bearing gesture, considering each sentence or gesture in isolation.

Annotations are done in ELAN [13], which allows for viewing the videos and existing annotation "tracks", and creating new annotations, in a unified environment. After annotating a video individually, annotators meet to discuss and compare their annotations. We then perform adjudication to create a gold standard. To measure inter-annotator agreement, we use SMATCH [15], which measures the degree of overlap between two semantic feature structures. In addition, we use the issues raised by the annotators to refine our annotation guidelines.

4.2 Annotation Guidelines

As previously mentioned, we consider the following four general types of referential gestures: iconic, deictic, metaphoric, and emblematic [27,39,54,57]. While some gestures may have aspects of multiple (or none) of these types [34], we believe that the above classification serves as a good starting point for describing the different kinds of semantic content a gesture can convey.

Fig. 2. Deictic gesture, denoting a location.

Of the above four gesture types, we did not instruct our annotators to anno-tate metaphoric gestures, which describe concepts or ideas by depicting abstract properties thereof. Because we are focusing on gestures in a task-based setting, we anticipate that depictions of entities and events will reflect their concrete properties, such as the shape of an object or the manner of an action. Thus far, we have not yet observed any gestures in the EGGNOG corpus that would best be annotated as a metaphoric gesture.

Annotations of each of the remaining three gesture types follow a canonical template:

```
(g / [gesture]-GA
  :ARG0 (s / signaler)
  :ARG1 [content]
  :ARG2 (a / actor))
```

A Gesture AMR is anchored by a gesture act (GA), where in this project, [gesture] can be deixis, icon, or emblem. This is similar to how the top node in a Dialogue-AMR represents a speech act [9]. The ARG0 represents the gesturer, ARG1 represents the semantic content of the gesture, and ARG2 corresponds to the addressee. In our task-based setting, gestures will generally serve as instructions or other communication on the part of the signaler directed towards the actor; we can thus fill in ARG0 and ARG2 with (s/signaler) and (a/actor), respectively. Each gesture form is associated with a corresponding kind of semantic content, as described below.

Deictic Gesture. Deictic gestures denote objects or locations in space through pointing. We represent the object or location as the ARG1 in the same manner as in a language AMR. For example, Fig. 2 shows a signaler pointing to a location on the table. The corresponding Gesture AMR is as follows:

```
(d / deixis-GA
  :ARG0 (s / signaler)
  :ARG1 (l / location)
  :ARG2 (a / actor))
```

Fig. 3. Iconic gesture, denoting a "slide forward" action.

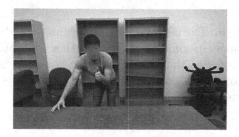

Fig. 4. Emblematic gesture, denoting positive acknowledgment.

Currently, for ease of annotation, we do not require the annotators to include any additional detail regarding the location (e.g., Cartesian coordinates), or if the gesture is aimed at an object, any specific information about the object beyond that it is, for example, a block.

Iconic Gesture. Iconic gestures depict concrete properties of the objects or actions to which they refer. Figure 3 shows a signaler making a forward pushing motion with her hands, indicating that she wants the actor to slide a block forward. This can be represented in Gesture AMR as follows:

```
(i / icon-GA
   :ARG0 (s / signaler)
   :ARG1 (s2 / slide-01
           :direction (f / forward))
   :ARG2 (a / actor))
```

In this example, the content of the gesture consists of an action, "slide", derived from the manner of the signaler's hand motions, and a direction, "forward", which comes from the forward direction of the motion. Action predicates are currently drawn from PropBank [60]; future applications of Gesture AMR may instead define their own lexicons of standardized concepts. Although it is clear in context that the object the signaler wants the actor to slide forward is a block, the gesture itself does not indicate what the object is, so it does not appear in the Gesture AMR.

Fig. 5. Gesture with both iconic ("block") and deictic (location) elements.

Emblematic Gesture. The meaning of an emblematic gesture is conventional, agreed upon by members of some community, rather than being directly related to its form. For example, a "thumbs up" gesture is commonly used in English-speaking countries to express positive acknowledgment; this is shown in Fig. 4. In Gesture AMR, this is represented as:

```
(e / emblem-GA
  :ARG0 (s / signaler)
  :ARG1 (y / yes)
  :ARG2 (a / actor))
```

Gesture with Multiple Meaning Components. Some gestures may contain aspects of more than one of the above gesture types. Figure 5 shows a signaler simultaneously outlining a square with his hands, and moving them towards a specific location on the table. The orientation of the hands is interpreted as an icon of a block, while the locational component is an example of deixis. We annotate both components of the meaning, and incorporate them into a (g / gesture-unit) as follows:

```
(g / gesture-unit
  :op1 (i / icon-GA
          :ARG0 (s / signaler)
          :ARG1 (b / block)
          :ARG2 (a / actor))
  :op2 (d / deixis-GA
          :ARG0 s
          :ARG1 (l / location)
          :ARG2 a))
```

4.3   Initial Annotation Evaluation

As mentioned previously, adjudication between annotations to create a gold standard is ongoing as we develop a corpus of Gesture AMR on top of the

EGGNOG corpus. SMATCH is used to measure inter-annotator agreement [15]. We additionally perform manual agreement analysis for subgraphs of individual Gesture AMRs to highlight particular areas of agreement and disagreement. We also record the average time spent for annotating single Gesture AMRs and entire EGGNOG video sequences. Initial results show that individual Gesture AMRs can range between 2 min (e.g., a simple deictic gesture act) to 10 min (e.g., complex gesture units) for annotation. A one-minute EGGNOG video clip with roughly 14 gesture units can take an expert annotator 20 min to annotate, while for a novice annotator can take up to one hour. We expect the average time of annotation to decrease as annotation guidelines are clarifies and annotators have more practice.

After the gold standard speech and Gesture AMRs are created, annotators are asked to mark coreferent actions and objects across the AMRs using MS-AMR [59]. As in the previous step, at least two annotators are assigned to each video, and we periodically refine our guidelines based on annotator feedback. We again perform adjudication, evaluating the inter-annotator coreference agreement using the CoNLL-2012 F1 score [62], to create a gold standard for the MS-AMRs. Further work will evaluate implicit role agreement across speech and gesture modalities with Cohen's kappa [22].

5   Situating Gesture AMR

As mentioned in Sect. 2, AMR does not support the representation of situational knowledge in a dialogue. The extension proposed here for encoding co-speech gesture is an important step forward towards including non-linguistic communicative content, but it does not address the problems associated with situational grounding and dynamic epistemic updating that accompanies any multi-agent dialogue.

For example, in multimodal dialogue, both speech and gesture can be used in a communicative act, C, alone or in combination to reference an object, person, location, orientation, or time. When that occurs, we must have some way to mark coreference or partial coreference across the different modalities. As presented above, Gesture AMR represents the semantic content of the gesture and not its temporal sequencing. As a result, temporal alignment between gesture, language, and other modalities requires the introduction of constraints on the temporal anchoring associated with the content-based AMR expressions.

A multimodal communicative act, C, as in example 2, consists of a sequence of gesture-language ensembles, (g_i, s_i), where an ensemble is temporally aligned in the common ground [63]. Let us assume that a linguistic subexpression, s, is either a word or full phrase in the utterance, while a gesture, g, comports with Gesture AMR specifications.

(2) **Co-gestural Speech Ensemble**

$$\begin{bmatrix} \mathcal{G} & g_1 \cdots g_i \cdots g_n \\ \mathcal{S} & s_1 \cdots s_i \cdots s_n \end{bmatrix}$$

```
        CO-GESTURAL SPEECH

    HUMAN:  s₁ = Put
            g₁ = ∅
    HUMAN:  s₂ = [that block]
            g₂ = [points to the blue block]
    HUMAN:  s₃ = there.
            g₃ = [points to the purple block]
```

Fig. 6. Communicative act with speech and gesture.

```
(a) (s1c / command-00                      (b) (s1 / sentence
    :ARG0 (g / gesturer)                       :coref ((b :same-entity b4)
    :ARG1 (c2 / communicative-act                      (a :same-entity y))
      :gesture (d / deixis-GA                  :alignment ((d :overlap t)
        :ARG0 g                                           (d2 :overlap t2)
        :ARG1 (b / block                                  (d :before d2)))
          :ARG1-of (b2 / blue-01))
        :ARG2 (a / addressee))
      :gesture (d2 / deixis-GA
        :ARG0 g
        :ARG1 (b3 / block
          :ARG1-of (p / purple-02))
        :ARG2 a)
      :speech (p2 / put-01
        :mode imperative
        :ARG0 (y / you)
        :ARG1 (b4 / block
          :mod (t / that))
        :ARG2 (t2 / there))
    :ARG2 a)
```

Fig. 7. Meaning representation corresponding to the communicative act in Fig. 6.

The example in Fig. 6 combines the spoken command "Put that block there" as in example (1) with the deictic gesture shown in Fig. 1. In Fig. 7(a), we represent the communicative act, with two gesture AMRs as arguments of :gesture and a speech AMR as the argument of :speech. We additionally enclose the communicative act within a Dialogue-AMR [9] "speech act" (that, in this example, is not limited to the speech modality) that marks its illocutionary force, namely, as a command.

Then, in Fig. 7(b), we present the semantic and temporal alignments between the two modalities. Our formalism is based on that of UMR [80], which in turn bases its approaches to inter-sentential coreference and temporal markup on Multi-sentence AMR [59] and temporal dependency structures [83], respectively. Following the basic strategy employed in MultiML [29] for aligning multiple modalities, we use an AMR-native device to capture the hybrid logic reentrancy binding from [3]. We mark that the blue block being pointed to and "that block" mentioned in the speech are the same entity, as are the addressee of the gesture and "you", an implicit argument of the speech. We also mark that the first deictic gesture d temporally overlaps with the word "that", the second gesture d2 overlaps with "there", and that d occurs before d2.

5.1 Additional Considerations

Gesture provides additional meaning in the form of spatial information in ways more concisely than language. For example, in Fig. 1, a linguistic description of exactly where the speaker is pointing would need to be quite long to capture the specific location indicated with a simple pointing gesture. The spatial coordinates of such a location should be documented for a complete grounding of the Gesture AMR to the environment. In addition to more precisely specifying locations, gesture also specifies spatial elements such as start point, end point, manner, and duration of motion; size of objects; and relative position of events and objects to a speaker and to each other. Such depiction is important for conveying and interpreting meaning and grounding language to environment [16].

After our initial annotation on the EGGNOG dataset focusing on content-bearing gestures, we plan to augment our annotations with spatial information and Spatial AMR [10]. Spatial AMR adds spatial rolesets to the PropBank lexicon and is conceptualized around events and relations as construed in language; this includes whether events are static or dynamic, and it describes characteristics of relations related to location, orientation, configuration, and extent. Spatial AMR also incorporates Cartesian coordinates for mapping to physical space. This forms part of a larger question when developing Gesture AMR: are there additional "lexical" items or relations unique to meaning conveyed in gesture that are absent in language and English AMR? Future work will extend Gesture AMR to more expressive meaning categories such as beat and rhythmic gestures (Sect. 3). Additionally, annotation of Gesture AMR beyond our current task-based setting will ask whether English AMR contains meaningful linguistic concepts that cannot be expressed with gesture, such as certain modals.

6 Conclusion

This paper extends the design principles of AMR and presents a specification for Gesture AMR intended to capture the semantics of gesture. In so doing, we have reviewed previous extensions to AMR that seek to enhance the formalism's expressive capacity and suitability to domains beyond written text. We have also reviewed existing semantic and annotation approaches to gesture that motivate our own representational choices, as well as challenges faced when trying to ground a representation such as Gesture AMR in situated interaction.

As presented here, Gesture AMR and its companion corpus focus on content-bearing gesture, typically independent from the meanings represented in speech. Gesture AMR is annotated on top of the task-based EGGNOG corpus and thus covers a specific set of communicative gestures. Each Gesture AMR is based on one of four gesture act relations and contains reference to the gesturer, addressee, and the semantic content of the gesture. We introduce an additional layer of representation to capture the semantic and temporal alignment between the multiple modalities of speech and gesture (as well as to-be-described modalities). Similar to previous AMR extensions that allow for use outside of a specific domain, Gesture AMR is designed to be extensible to other types of gesture. We look forward to completing our EGGNOG annotation, and further developing Gesture AMR using a wider range of corpora that include non-task-based contexts. As natural interactions with computers and robots have to account for interpreting and generating language and gesture, evaluation of Gesture AMR will need to occur on both the interpretation and generation sides.

Extending AMR to gesture is a welcome contribution to research in situated meaning, embodied interaction, and multimodal interaction for several reasons. Gesture can play a part of either the direct content of the utterance [76] or the cosuppositional content [33,68]; representing gestural semantics in AMR thus enhances AMR's traditional use of representing propositional, sentence-level content. Continued work on Gesture AMR will additionally allow us to better evaluate how the AMR formalism can capture gesture in a dimensional manner as opposed to simply categorical; such insight can be extended to additional modalities for a robust, multimodal situated AMR, as well as contribute to larger discussion about the necessary components of any situated, multimodal meaning representation.

References

1. Allwood, J., Cerrato, L., Dybkjaer, L., Jokinen, K., Navarretta, C., Paggio, P.: The MUMIN multimodal coding scheme. In: NorFA Yearbook, pp. 129–157 (2005)
2. Artzi, Y., Lee, K., Zettlemoyer, L.: Broad-coverage CCG semantic parsing with AMR. In: Proceedings of the 2015 Conference on Empirical Methods in Natural Language Processing. Association for Computational Linguistics, Lisbon, Portugal, September 2015
3. Baldridge, J., Kruijff, G.J.M.: Coupling CCG and hybrid logic dependency semantics. In: Proceedings of the 40th Annual Meeting of the Association for Computational Linguistics, pp. 319–326 (2002)
4. Banarescu, L., et al.: Abstract meaning representation for sembanking. In: Proceedings of the 7th Linguistic Annotation Workshop and Interoperability with Discourse, pp. 178–186 (2013)
5. Barker, C.: Imperatives denote actions. In: Proceedings of Sinn und Bedeutung, vol. 16, pp. 57–70 (2012)
6. Bastianelli, E., Castellucci, G., Croce, D., Iocchi, L., Basili, R., Nardi, D.: HuRIC: a human robot interaction corpus. In: LREC, pp. 4519–4526 (2014)
7. Bavelas, J., Gerwing, J., Sutton, C., Prevost, D.: Gesturing on the telephone: independent effects of dialogue and visibility. J. Mem. Lang. **58**(2), 495–520 (2008)
8. Bonial, C., Abrams, M., Traum, D., Voss, C.: Builder, we have done it: evaluating & extending dialogue-AMR NLU pipeline for two collaborative domains. In: Proceedings of the 14th International Conference on Computational Semantics (IWCS), pp. 173–183 (2021)
9. Bonial, C., et al.: Dialogue-AMR: abstract meaning representation for dialogue. In: Proceedings of The 12th Language Resources and Evaluation Conference, pp. 684–695 (2020)

10. Bonn, J., Palmer, M., Cai, J., Wright-Bettner, K.: Spatial AMR: expanded spatial annotation in the context of a grounded minecraft corpus. In: Proceedings of the 12th Conference on Language Resources and Evaluation (LREC 2020) (2020)

11. Bos, J.: Expressive power of abstract meaning representations. Comput. Linguist. **42**(3), 527–535 (2016)

12. Bos, J.: Separating argument structure from logical structure in AMR. arXiv preprint arXiv:1908.01355 (2019)

13. Brugman, H., Russel, A.: Annotating multi-media/multi-modal resources with ELAN. In: Proceedings of the Fourth International Conference on Language Resources and Evaluation (LREC 2004). European Language Resources Association (ELRA), Lisbon, Portugal, May 2004. http://www.lrec-conf.org/proceedings/lrec2004/pdf/480.pdf

14. Bunt, H., et al.: ISO 24617-2: a semantically-based standard for dialogue annotation. In: Proceedings of the Eighth International Conference on Language Resources and Evaluation (LREC 2012), pp. 430–437 (2012). http://www.lrec-conf.org/proceedings/lrec2012/summaries/530.html

15. Cai, S., Knight, K.: Smatch: an evaluation metric for semantic feature structures. In: Proceedings of the 51st Annual Meeting of the Association for Computational Linguistics (Volume 2: Short Papers), pp. 748–752 (2013)

16. Capirci, O., Caselli, M.C., Volterra, V.: Interaction among modalities and within development (2022)

17. Carroll, J.J., Bizer, C., Hayes, P., Stickler, P.: Named graphs. J. Web Semant. **3**(4), 247–267 (2005)

18. Cartmill, E.A., Demir, Ö.E., Goldin-Meadow, S.: Studying gesture. In: Research Methods in Child Language: A Practical Guide, pp. 208–225. Wiley Blackwell Ltd., Oxford (2012)

19. Cassell, J., Kopp, S., Tepper, P., Ferriman, K., Striegnitz, K.: Trading spaces: how humans and humanoids use speech and gesture to give directions (2007)

20. Cassell, J., Sullivan, J., Churchill, E., Prevost, S.: Embodied Conversational Agents. MIT Press, Cambridge (2000)

21. Clark, H.H., Brennan, S.E.: Grounding in communication. Perspect. Soc. Shared Cogn. **13**(1991), 127–149 (1991)

22. Cohen, J.: A coefficient of agreement for nominal scales. Educ. Psychol. Measur. **20**(1), 37–46 (1960)

23. Copestake, A., Flickinger, D., Pollard, C., Sag, I.A.: Minimal recursion semantics: an introduction. Res. Lang. Comput. **3**(2–3), 281–332 (2005)

24. Crouch, R., Kalouli, A.L.: Named graphs for semantic representation. In: Proceedings of the Seventh Joint Conference on Lexical and Computational Semantics, pp. 113–118 (2018)

25. De Ruiter, J.P.: On the primacy of language in multimodal communication. In: LREC 2004 Workshop on Multimodal Corpora, pp. 38–41. ELRA-European Language Resources Association (CD-ROM) (2004)

26. Donatelli, L., Regan, M., Croft, W., Schneider, N.: Annotation of tense and aspect semantics for sentential AMR. In: Proceedings of the Joint Workshop on Linguistic Annotation, Multiword Expressions and Constructions (LAW-MWE-CxG-2018), pp. 96–108 (2018). https://doi.org/10.1207/s15516709cog0303_1

27. Ekman, P., Friesen, W.V.: The repertoire of non verbal behaviour-categories, origins usage and coding (1969)

28. Foster, M.E.: Enhancing human-computer interaction with embodied conversational agents. In: Stephanidis, C. (ed.) UAHCI 2007. LNCS, vol. 4555, pp. 828–837. Springer, Heidelberg (2007). https://doi.org/10.1007/978-3-540-73281-5_91

29. Giuliani, M., Knoll, A.: MultiML: a general purpose representation language for multimodal human utterances. In: Proceedings of the 10th International Conference on Multimodal Interfaces, pp. 165–172 (2008)

30. Gotou, D., Nishikawa, H., Tokunaga, T.: An extension of ISO-space for annotating object direction. In: Proceedings of the 12th Workshop on Asian Language Resources (ALR12), pp. 1–9 (2016)

31. Kalouli, A.L., Crouch, R.: GKR: the graphical knowledge representation for semantic parsing. In: Workshop on Computational Semantics beyond Events and Roles (SemBEaR 2018), pp. 27–37 (2018)

32. Kamp, H., Reyle, U.: From Discourse to Logic: Introduction to Model Theoretic Semantics of Natural Language, Formal Logic and Discourse Representation Theory, vol. 42. Springer, Heidelberg (2013)

33. Kendon, A.: Conducting Interaction: Patterns of Behavior in Focused Encounters. Cambridge University Press, Cambridge (1990)

34. Kendon, A.: Gesture: Visible Action as Utterance. Cambridge University Press, Cambridge (2004)

35. Kipp, M.: Anvil-a generic annotation tool for multimodal dialogue. In: Seventh European Conference on Speech Communication and Technology. Citeseer (2001)

36. Kipp, M., Neff, M., Albrecht, I.: An annotation scheme for conversational gestures: how to economically capture timing and form. Lang. Resour. Eval. **41**(3), 325–339 (2007)

37. Kita, S., Özyürek, A.: What does cross-linguistic variation in semantic coordination of speech and gesture reveal?: evidence for an interface representation of spatial thinking and speaking. J. Mem. Lang. **48**(1), 16–32 (2003)

38. Knight, K., et al.: Abstract meaning representation (AMR) annotation release 1.2.6. Web download (2019)

39. Kong, A.P.H., Law, S.P., Kwan, C.C.Y., Lai, C., Lam, V.: A coding system with independent annotations of gesture forms and functions during verbal communication: development of a database of speech and gesture (dosage). J. Nonverbal Behav. **39**(1), 93–111 (2015)

40. Kopp, S., Wachsmuth, I.: GW 2009. LNCS (LNAI), vol. 5934. Springer, Heidelberg (2010). https://doi.org/10.1007/978-3-642-12553-9

41. Krauss, R.M., Chen, Y., Gottesman, R.F.: Lexical gestures and lexical access: a process. Lang. Gesture **2**(261), 261–283 (2000)

42. Lai, K., Donatelli, L., Pustejovsky, J.: A continuation semantics for abstract meaning representation. In: Proceedings of the Second International Workshop on Designing Meaning Representations, pp. 1–12 (2020)

43. Lascarides, A., Asher, N.: Imperatives in dialogue. In: Pragmatics and Beyond New Series, pp. 1–24 (2003)

44. Lascarides, A., Stone, M.: Formal semantics for iconic gesture. In: Proceedings of the 10th Workshop on the Semantics and Pragmatics of Dialogue (BRANDIAL), pp. 64–71 (2006)

45. Lascarides, A., Stone, M.: A formal semantic analysis of gesture. J. Semant. **26**(4), 393–449 (2009)

46. Lawler, I., Hahn, F., Rieser, H.: Gesture meaning needs speech meaning to denote-a case of speech-gesture meaning interaction. In: FADLI 2017, p. 42 (2017)

47. Lücking, A.: Gesture. In: Müller, S., Abeillé, A., Borsley, R.D., Koenig, J.P. (eds.) Head-Driven Phrase Structure Grammar: The Handbook, 1201–1250 27. Language Science Press, Berlin (2021)

48. Lücking, A., Ginzburg, J.: Towards the score of communication. In: Proceedings of the 24th Workshop on the Semantics and Pragmatics of Dialogue - Full Papers. SEMDIAL, Virtually at Brandeis, Waltham, New Jersey, July 2020
49. Lücking, A., Ginzburg, J., Cooper, R.: Grammar in dialogue. In: Müller, S., Abeillé, A., Borsley, R.D., Koenig, J.P. (eds.) Head-Driven Phrase Structure Grammar: The Handbook, 1201–1250 26. Language Science Press, Berlin (2021)
50. Lücking, A., Rieser, H., Staudacher, M.: Multi-modal integration for gesture and speech. In: Brandial 2006: Proceedings of the 10th Workshop on the Semantics and Pragmatics of Dialogue (SemDial-10), Potsdam, Germany, 11–13 September 2006, p. 106. Universitätsverlag Potsdam (2006)
51. Marge, M., et al.: Applying the wizard-of-OZ technique to multimodal human-robot dialogue. In: Proceedings of RO-MAN (2016)
52. Marge, M., et al.: Exploring variation of natural human commands to a robot in a collaborative navigation task. In: Proceedings of the First Workshop on Language Grounding for Robotics, pp. 58–66 (2017)
53. Marshall, P., Hornecker, E.: Theories of embodiment in HCI. SAGE Handb. Digit. Technol. Res. 1, 144–158 (2013)
54. Mather, S.M.: Ethnographic research on the use of visually based regulators for teachers and interpreters. In: Attitudes, Innuendo, and Regulators, pp. 136–161 (2005)
55. Matthiessen, C., Bateman, J.A.: Text Generation and Systemic-Functional Linguistics: Experiences from English and Japanese. Burns & Oates (1991)
56. McNeill, D.: Gesture and Thought. University of Chicago Press (2008)
57. McNeill, D.: Hand and Mind. De Gruyter Mouton (2011)
58. McNeill, D., Duncan, S.D.: Growth points in thinking-for-speaking. Lang. Gesture (1987), 141–161 (2000)
59. O'Gorman, T., Regan, M., Griffitt, K., Hermjakob, U., Knight, K., Palmer, M.: AMR beyond the sentence: the multi-sentence AMR corpus. In: Proceedings of the 27th International Conference on Computational Linguistics, Santa Fe, New Mexico, USA. Association for Computational Linguistics, August 2018
60. Palmer, M., Gildea, D., Kingsbury, P.: The proposition bank: an annotated corpus of semantic roles. Comput. Linguist. 31(1), 71–106 (2005)
61. Poesio, M., Vieira, R., Teufel, S.: Resolving bridging references in unrestricted text. In: Operational Factors in Practical, Robust Anaphora Resolution for Unrestricted Texts (1997)
62. Pradhan, S., Luo, X., Recasens, M., Hovy, E., Ng, V., Strube, M.: Scoring coreference partitions of predicted mentions: a reference implementation. In: Proceedings of the Conference. Association for Computational Linguistics. Meeting, vol. 2014, p. 30. NIH Public Access (2014)
63. Pustejovsky, J., Krishnaswamy, N.: Embodied human computer interaction. Künstliche Intelligenz (2021)
64. Pustejovsky, J., Krishnaswamy, N., Do, T.: Object embodiment in a multimodal simulation. In: AAAI Spring Symposium: Interactive Multisensory Object Perception for Embodied Agents (2017)
65. Pustejovsky, J., Lai, K., Xue, N.: Modeling quantification and scope in abstract meaning representations. In: Proceedings of the First International Workshop on Designing Meaning Representations, pp. 28–33 (2019)
66. Schaffer, S., Reithinger, N.: Conversation is multimodal: thus conversational user interfaces should be as well. In: Proceedings of the 1st International Conference on Conversational User Interfaces, pp. 1–3 (2019)

67. Schlenker, P.: Gesture projection and cosuppositions. Linguist. Philos. **41**(3), 295–365 (2018). https://doi.org/10.1007/s10988-017-9225-8
68. Schlenker, P.: Gestural grammar. Nat. Lang. Linguist. Theory 1–50 (2020)
69. Schreiber, G., Raimond, Y.: RDF 1.1 primer (2014)
70. Searle, J.R.: Speech Acts: An Essay in the Philosophy of Language. Cambridge University Press, Cambridge (1969)
71. Shattuck-Hufnagel, S., Prieto, P.: Dimensionalizing co-speech gestures. In: Proceedings of the International Congress of Phonetic Sciences, vol. 5 (2019)
72. Shen, H.: Semantic parsing in spoken language understanding using abstract meaning representation. Ph.D. thesis, Brandeis University (2018)
73. Stabler, E.: Reforming AMR. In: Foret, A., Muskens, R., Pogodalla, S. (eds.) FG 2017. LNCS, vol. 10686, pp. 72–87. Springer, Heidelberg (2018). https://doi.org/10.1007/978-3-662-56343-4_5
74. Stalnaker, R.: Common ground. Linguist. Philos. **25**(5–6), 701–721 (2002)
75. Stein, K., Donatelli, L.: Representing implicit positive meaning of negated statements in AMR. In: Proceedings of The Joint 15th Linguistic Annotation Workshop (LAW) and 3rd Designing Meaning Representations (DMR) Workshop, pp. 23–35 (2021)
76. Stojnić, U., Stone, M., Lepore, E.: Pointing things out: in defense of attention and coherence. Linguist. Philos. **43**(2), 139–148 (2019). https://doi.org/10.1007/s10988-019-09271-w
77. Tellex, S., Gopalan, N., Kress-Gazit, H., Matuszek, C.: Robots that use language. Ann. Rev. Control Robot. Auton. Syst. **3**, 25–55 (2020)
78. Tellex, S., et al.: Understanding natural language commands for robotic navigation and mobile manipulation. In: Proceedings of the AAAI Conference on Artificial Intelligence, vol. 25 (2011)
79. Tomasello, M., Carpenter, M.: Shared intentionality. Dev. Sci. **10**(1), 121–125 (2007)
80. Van Gysel, J.E., et al.: Designing a uniform meaning representation for natural language processing. KI-Künstliche Intelligenz, pp. 1–18 (2021)
81. Wahlster, W.: Dialogue systems go multimodal: the smartkom experience. In: Wahlster, W. (ed.) SmartKom: Foundations of Multimodal Dialogue Systems, pp. 3–27. Springer, Heidelberg (2006). https://doi.org/10.1007/3-540-36678-4_1
82. Wang, I., et al.: EGGNOG: a continuous, multi-modal data set of naturally occurring gestures with ground truth labels. In: Proceedings of the 12th IEEE International Conference on Automatic Face & Gesture Recognition (2017, to appear)
83. Zhang, Y., Xue, N.: Structured interpretation of temporal relations. In: Proceedings of the Eleventh International Conference on Language Resources and Evaluation (LREC 2018). European Language Resources Association (ELRA), Miyazaki, Japan, May 2018

Trajectory Planning in Dynamics Environment: Application for Haptic Perception in Safe Human-Robot Interaction

Andres Gutierrez, Vamsi Krishna Guda, Stanley Mugisha,
Christine Chevallereau, and Damien Chablat$^{(\boxtimes)}$

Laboratoire des Sciences du Numérique de Nantes, UMR CNRS 6004,
44300 Nantes, France
damien.chablat@cnrs.fr

Abstract. In a human-robot interaction system, the most important thing to consider is the safety of the user. This must be guaranteed in order to implement a reliable system. The main objective of this paper is to generate a safe motion scheme that takes into account the obstacles present in a virtual reality (VR) environment. The work is developed using the MoveIt software in ROS to control an industrial robot UR5. Thanks to this, we will be able to set up the planning group, which is realised by the UR5 robot with a 6-sided prop and the base of the manipulator, in order to plan feasible trajectories that it will be able to execute in the environment. The latter is based on the interior of a vehicle, containing a user (which would be the user in this case) for which the configuration will also be made to be taken into account in the system. To do this, we first investigated the software's capabilities and options for path planning, as well as the different ways to execute the movements. We also compared the different trajectory planning algorithms that the software is capable of using in order to determine which one is best suited for the task. Finally, we proposed different mobility schemes to be executed by the robot depending on the situation it is facing. The first one is used when the robot has to plan trajectories in a safe space, where the only obstacle to avoid is the user's workspace. The second one is used when the robot has to interact with the user, where a mannequin model represents the user's position as a function of time, which is the one to be avoided.

Keywords: Trajectory planning · Human safety · Haptic interface · Intermittent contact interface

1 Introduction

In human-robot interaction systems, knowing how to compute a path for the robot to follow, while taking into account the human position, is a crucial task to ensure the safety of the individuals around the robot. This is where path and trajectory planning plays its role in the field of robotics, where achieving real-time behaviour is one of the most challenging problems to solve. The result is a constant demand for research into more complex and efficient algorithms that allow robots to perform tasks at higher speeds, reducing the time they need to complete them, resulting in increased efficiency. But this also comes at a cost: to achieve higher speeds and shorter times, robot actuators must work under more demanding conditions that can shorten their overall life or even damage their structure. High operating speeds can also affect the accuracy and repeatability of manipulators. Therefore, it is important to generate well-defined trajectories that can be executed at high speeds without generating high accelerations (to avoid robot wear or end effector vibrations during stopping). Path planning is the generation of a geometrical path from an initial point to an end point and the calculation of the crossing points between them. Each point of the generated trajectory is supposed to be reached by the robot end effector through a specific movement. When the robot is supposed to interact with a human, its velocity and acceleration must be zero at the end of the trajectory. Another important element to take into account is the environment in which the task or the movement is going to be performed. This is what allows the system to identify the robot's environment and the colliding objects that might be present, thus determining the areas in which the robot must be constrained or limited to ensure the safety of the user.

The Lobbybot project is a project that allows interaction between a user and a cobot. These interactions allow for the creation of a touch-sensitive interface or intermitant contact interface (ICI). The scenario used allows the user to be inside a car with the possibility to interact with its environment by getting a sensory feedback of the different surfaces thanks to a 6 faces prop providing the different textures. Due to the immersion of the user via a VR headset, the system must ensure the safety of the user, as he cannot see the location of the robot. Therefore, it is necessary to implement trajectory planning techniques to be able to avoid unwanted interactions between the robot and the user. To do this, the system must take into account the obstacles present (environment or user). A virtual mannequin is modelled using data from the HTC Vive trackers which provide an estimate of the user's position, and will give the system a model to plan the movements. Thus, the goal of the LobbyBot project is to provide an immersive VR system that is safe for the user and gives them the ability to interact with the environment at different locations, providing a new level of interaction between VR environments and the real world.

2   State of the Art

2.1   Intermittent Contact Interface

In the area of human-robot interaction and haptic perception, the ability to reproduce the sense of touch to appreciate different textures and motion sensations through the use of cobots has been addressed in [1], where a rotatable metaphorical accessory approach (ENTROPiA) has been proposed to provide an infinite surface haptic display, capable of providing different textures to render multiple infinite surfaces in VR (virtual reality). Studies in [2,3] have focused on the perception of stiffness, friction, and shape of tangible objects in VR using a wearable 2-DoF (degrees of freedom) tactical device on a finger to alter the user's sense of touch. In [4,5], a 6-DoF cobot is used in a VR environment to simulate the interior of a car, where interaction between the robot and the user is expected just at specific, instantaneous points. This proposal is to use ICIs (Intermittent Contact Interfaces) [6] to minimise the amount of human-robot interactions to increase safety. In order to use the proposed implementations in this study in a real-time environment that involves human movement, it is important to ensure the safety of both the user and the robot to avoid potential collisions or accidents. This is where it is necessary to implement proper path and trajectory planning, in order to determine a feasible path to the desired goal, while avoiding interaction with the human until said goal is reached, generating a human-robot interaction just at the desired time.

2.2   Path Planning

Path planning refers to the calculation or generation of a geometric path, which connects an initial point to an end point, passing through intermediate via-points. These trajectories are intended to be followed by the end effector of a robot in order to execute a desired task or motion. This geometric calculation is based on the kinematic properties of the robot as well as its geometry (included in its workspace). In the simplest case, path planning is performed within static and known environments. However, this problem can also be generated for robotic systems subjected to kinematic constraints in a dynamic and unknown environment.

Path planning can be done using a previously known map. This is called global planning. This method is commonly used to determine the possible paths to follow to reach the final position. It is used in the case of a known and static environment, where the position of the obstacles does not change. This operation can be performed offline, as it is based on previously known information. In the case of dynamic environments, it is necessary to perform local path planning, which relies on sensors or any other type of interface providing data to obtain updated information about the robot's environment. This planning can only be done in real time, as it depends on the dynamic evolution of the environment. Figure 1 presents the main differences between local and global path planning [7,8].

There have been multiple proposals on path planning algorithms over the years. In [9], one can find a review of the basics and workings of the most common algorithms most commonly found in the robotics literature. The main methods are the following:

- The Artificial Potential Fields (APF) approach [8] introduced by O. Khatib in 1985 and further developed by [10,11].
- The Probabilistic Road-maps approach [7] consists in generating random nodes in the configuration space (C_{space}) in order to generate a grid (so called, the road-map).

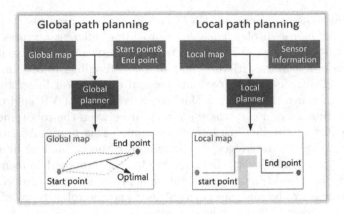

Fig. 1. Global [7] and local [8] path planning.

- The Cell Decomposition algorithms [12].
- The Rapidly Exploring Random Trees (*RRTs*) [13], introduced by S. LaValle in 2001 as an optimisation from the classical Random Trees algorithm.

2.3 Algorithm Comparison

In robotics, path planning is one of the most difficult tasks in real-time dynamic environments. Among the presented algorithms, APF and its variations offer a good adaptation to path planning in dynamically changing environments, where any obstacle entering the C_{space} generates a new repulsive field that can be taken into account to generate a new path. But the local minima problem requires the use of alternative algorithms to overcome it.

The case of PRM, it is well known for its ability to find a path without needing to explore the whole C_{space}, but it is also a graph based algorithm, which requires the use of shortest path method like A^*. It works well in static environments and can handle initial and final configuration changes, but if the objects in C_{space} change position, the connections between the nodes must be redone. Some alternatives propose to keep the previously generated nodes and recheck whether they belong to C_{free} or C_{obs}, then rebuild the graph based on this information and find a new path. This is also the case for cell decomposition methods, where the graph search has to be reconstructed again. Nevertheless, these methods have proven to be viable options in real time, capable of adapting to a dynamic environment.

Finally, regarding the RRT and RRT* methods and their alternatives, they are known to be good path planning methods, with the limitations that the generated trees are related to the initial configuration and have high computational demands. The proposal of the different alternatives allows to obtain very optimal real-time path planners. The limitations of this type of algorithms are that they require a large memory capacity, as the entire tree must be stored at all times, and that they only work in bounded environments, with unbounded and long distance environments remaining a challenge.

2.4 Setup of the Experimentation

In this section, we will present the tools used in the development of the project, such as the laboratory system, the software used, a description of the system environment as well as the laboratory setup.

System Architecture. The architecture of MoveIt is based on two main nodes, the node *move_group* and the node *planning_scene*, which is part of the first one. The *move_group* node is responsible for obtaining the parameters, configuration and individual components of the robot model being used, in order to provide the user with services and actions to use on the robot.

Within the planners available in the *OMPL* library there are:

- PRM methods (PRM [7], PRM* [14], LazyPRM [15], LazyPRM* [14,15]),
- RRT methods (RRT [13], RRT* [16], TRRT [17]), BiTRRT [18], LBTRRT [19], RRTConnect [20],
- Expansive Spacial Trees (EST) methods (EST [21], BiEST [21]).

Collision Detection. Collision checking in MoveIt is configured within a planning scene using the CollisionWorld object. Collision checking in MoveIt is performed using the Flexible Collision Library (FCL) package - MoveIt's main collision checking library.

Kinematics. MoveIt uses a plugin infrastructure, specifically designed to allow users to write their own inverse kinematics algorithms. Direct kinematics and Jacobian search are built into the RobotState class itself. The default inverse kinematics plugin for MoveIt is configured using the KDL numerical solver [22] based on Jacobians. This plugin is automatically configured by the MoveIt configuration wizard.

ROS-Industrial. ROS-Industrial is an open-source project that extends the advanced capabilities of ROS software to industrial hardware and applications. For this project, we used the ROS-Industrial-Universal-Robots metapackage [23], which provides and facilitates the main configuration files for the use of Universal Robots cobots in the ROS environment, providing the different descriptions of the robot, configuration files such as joint boundaries, UR kinematics, etc. This package also facilitates the use of the robot in MoveIt, providing the setup for its use in simulation or in real implementations.

HTC Vive. The HTC Vive is a motion tracking system that allows users to be immersed in a VR system [24]. It consists of trackers, which can attach to any rigid object, and work with the VR headset. The tracker creates a wireless connection between the object and the headset and then allows the user to represent the objects movements in a virtual world.

Laboratory Setup. The laboratory setup consists of a UR5 robotic system and a car chair in a face-to-face configuration (Fig. 2). The location and height of the robot was determined by [4] to be 75 cm above the floor. This position is optimal enough for the robot to reach all the interaction points that the system is interested in reaching. For the user, the VR headset and trackers are attached to the body (the humerus and palms), in order to obtain data and locate the user's location in the VR environment (Fig. 3).

Fig. 2. Laboratory setup

Fig. 3. Conceptual scheme of the experimental platform

3   Selection of the Optimal Trajectory Planning and Its Application

We present the setup associated with the choice of the optimal trajectory generator available within the MoveIt software and its application for the LobbyBot project.

3.1   MoveIt Setup

The installation of MoveIt consisted of configuring and defining the planning group, as well as making it compatible to work in Gazebo. The start-up phase was very important to analyse the behaviour of the different movement alternatives found in the MoveIt API. For this, it was important to configure the simulation environment in Gazebo so that we could test without compromising the real robot.

3.2   Planning Group

The planning-group is defined as the group of elements that make up the entire robotic system. These are the UR5 robot, the 6-faced prop and the robot support. These three elements are the ones that the trajectory planning algorithms must consider in order for them to avoid any collision state existing with one of these elements. The robot support was modelled to match the size of the real system that was optimally defined [4]. For the configuration of the planning-group, MoveIt has an integrated graphical interface to create all the configuration files related to the kinematics, controllers, Semantic Robot Description Format (SRDF) and other files for the usage of the robot in ROS. This interface is called *MoveIt Setup Assistant*. The MoveIt Setup Assistant creates all the mentioned files based on the robot description given to it, in this case the UR5 robot description files provided by [23] where taken and modified to include the robot support (included in the URDF definition of the robot) and also the mesh file for the prop.

3.3   User's Model

To model the user, a mannequin was defined in a URDF robot model. The main torso of the model is fixed, while the arms are structured as a serial robot with seven revolute joints, where the first three constitute the shoulder, the fourth joint represents the elbow, and the last three revolute joints represent the wrist of the arm. In the model, two small dots have been created in the humerus and palm links, which represent the location of the sensors in the user, as shown in Fig. 4. Regarding the movement of the mannequin model, a kinematic model has been developed in parallel to this project in [25], where the connection between the sensor data and the model is defined. This will allow the system to recognise the user's movements and represent it in the simulation Fig. 4.

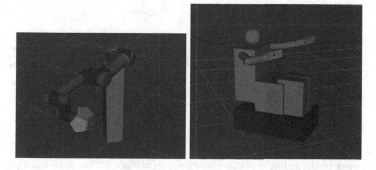

Fig. 4. Planning group and mannequin model of the user

3.4   Motions

To generate collision-free trajectories, the different algorithms implemented in the MoveIt API have been analysed. All the tasks related to planning group movement are handled by the move_group class. By specifying the planning group we want to consider, we are able to use all the different functions that the class offers for it, such as getting information about the current values of the joints, the target, configuring the planning algorithm we intend to use, and performing the planning and execution of the movements in the environment.

Types of Movement. The move_group class has the ability to perform path planning through different types of movements. These options can be chosen according to the nature of the task. For example, we can define a given pose in workspace or a desired joint value as the goal. Given the nature of the system, we will work with joint value goals, as we hope to achieve the different points in a specific configuration that provides a higher level of safety to the user (elbow up configuration for the UR5).

Another important feature is the ability to specify whether one wants to achieve each of the requested objectives or not. As the implementation will receive constantly changing goals, the best implementation is to plan and move towards said goal by allowing the system to replan if the goal changes, meaning that we do not need to reach the initial goal. To do this, the move_group class relies on the *move_group.execute(my_plan)* function to strictly reach the goal and on the *move_group.asyncExecute(my_plan)* function to execute the planned path with the possibility of re-planning during this execution.

In Fig. 5, two trajectories are calculated from an initial configuration, to an intermediate goal, and then to a final goal. In this case, by using the function *move_group.execute(my_plan)*, we ensure that the robot will completely execute each of the trajectories and achieve both goals. This is illustrated in Fig. 5, where the speeds drop to zero as the robot comes to a stop.

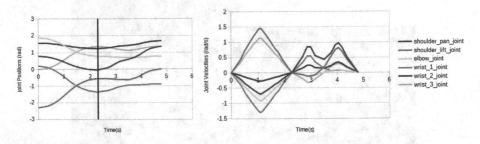

Fig. 5. Planned paths using *move_group.execute(my_plan)*: Back-to-back plans (left) and Velocities for both plans (right).

In the case of Fig. 6, we have calculated the same two trajectories as before, but using the function *move_group.asyncExecute(my_plane)*, which allows replanning during the execution of the first plane. In this case, in Fig. 6(a), we can see the two plans one after the other, while in Fig. 6(b), we show the representation of the segment that was not executed from the first plan, because a replanning scenario was set up. In this case, the current positions of the first plan were taken as the initial positions for the second plan, resulting in Fig. 6(c), showing the two plans that were executed.

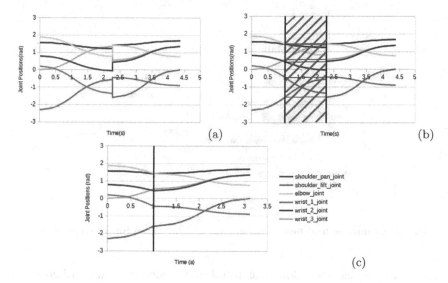

Fig. 6. Re-planned paths using *move_group.asyncExecute(my_plan)* (a) Back-to-back plans. (b) Segment not executed due to re-planning. (c) Final executed plan.

Algorithm Selection. Another parameter to select was the planning algorithm that best suited the task. As mentioned earlier, MoveIt has several built-in path planning algorithms that can be used. In order to determine the best option, we went through all the available options and performed a planning task to a desired target configuration, measuring the time required for each algorithm and recording the data. We ran each of the 12 available planning algorithms five times through nine different paths. We then took the average time it took them to find a solution, to simplify the trajectory (only for the algorithms that had this feature) and calculated the total average time. Using this data, we were able to select the algorithms that performed best with the shortest planning times (Fig. 7).

After performing these calculations, given the large difference in planning times for some of the algorithms, we select the six best algorithms to compare them on 12 trajectories (Fig. 8).

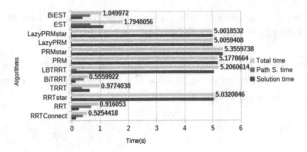

Fig. 7. Comparison of all planning algorithm's times for nine trajectories

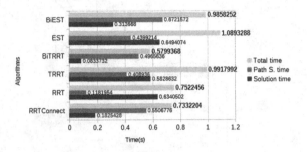

Fig. 8. Comparison of best planning algorithm's times for 12 trajectories

Another analysis that allowed us to select the algorithm which behaved the best for the implementation, was to perform an analysis on the generated trajectories with each one of the algorithms for a fixed task. Based on the six best algorithms from the previous analysis as a starting constraint, we computed the average execution time and via-points number for a set of trajectories. The BiTRRT algorithm wins for both comparisons.

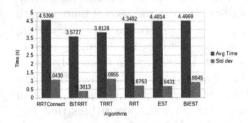

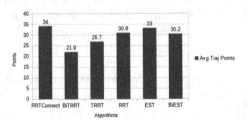

Fig. 9. Comparison of average execution times of the algorithms.

Fig. 10. Comparison of average amount of generated via-points.

This analysis was performed for the same trajectories as in the previous graphs for a total of ten iterations for each algorithm, but instead of considering only the computation time (Fig. 9), we also took into account the amount of via-points generated (Fig. 10). Between each via-point, a linear interpolation is performed in the joint space. For theses trajectories, the mannequin was placed in its seat so that it was avoided in the calculation, in order to test each algorithm's ability to plan around it. This also allowed us to see how consistent the behaviour of each algorithm was.

Unity's Virtual Environment. In parallel to the development of the project, and to better explain the developed implementation, it is important to specify how it will fit into the project. The system will receive a desired goal configuration which will be the q_{goal} for the planning algorithm, from the current q_{init} configuration. This goal selection is done in Unity by a *Point selection algorithm* which determines the interaction point the user intends to reach [26] (Fig. 11).

3.5 Planning Scene

For the definition of the planning environment and scene, MoveIt has instances that allow the manipulation and monitoring of the scene to keep it up to date. These instances are:

- PlanningSceneInterface: Is responsible for adding and removing objects in the scene.
- PlanningSceneMonitor: Takes care of keeping track of the planning_scene in order to keep it updated.

The last of these instances is absolutely necessary to perform the collision check, as we need to ensure that the scene being processed is the last one available.

3.6 Mobility Schemes

Based on the Unity information, two different motion or mobility schemes and scenarios has been proposed depending on the nature of the task we want to achieve at the moment. One for which no interaction with the user is required, and another one for when it is. These two scenarios have their own environment to consider, presenting in general two different behaviours.

Movement Outside User's Workspace. The first scenario is based on [26] where a distinction for velocity zones is made and where a plane divides the environment (space with the user and space where the user cannot go). Based on the same idea, we represented the effective working space of the mannequin as a sphere surrounding the model (Fig. 12).

The mobility scheme consists of alternating between different *"Safe positions"*. These positions are so called because they are points out of reach of the user, which means that there is no need to constrain the robot's speeds. Therefore, the movement from one point to another just has to take into account the defined sphere, as we do not want to "collide" with it. Following this idea, we

Fig. 11. Unity VR system and representation of interaction points

Fig. 12. Representation of the user's effective workspace as a sphere

have performed a calculation of all existing trajectories between the different *"Safe positions"* and stored them in a data file. This allows us to perform offline path planning, and then at runtime, depending on the initial and desired goal, we can access the pre-calculated paths to execute them directly, eliminating the computational time that would otherwise be required by performing online planning. The Algorithm 1 allows the storage of the trajectory.

Then, the second part of the device consists of loading the pre-registered data and being able to use them on demand (Algorithm 2). We wait until we know the position we want to reach. Unlike [26], we have used a spherical surface here to divide the two areas of the space instead of a plane, as this allows greater flexibility for the planning group to consider more configurations when calculating the path between points. It also allows for more feasible trajectories for the robot.

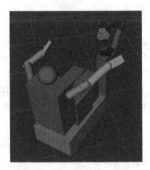

Fig. 13. Moving obstacles

Movement Inside User's Workspace. The second mobility scheme has been proposed for the scenario where the robot end effector has to go inside the user's

---

Algorithm 1. Trajectory computation and storage

Require: Number of points no_p. A counter for start point i. A counter for final point j

1: $start\_name[no_p] \leftarrow$ {Store id of the points}
2: $final\_name[no_p] \leftarrow init\_names[no_p]$ {Same id's as we are iterating through all points}
3: **for** $i < 0 \, ; \, i < no_p \, ; \, i++$ **do**
4:     **for** $j < 0 \, ; \, j < no_p \, ; \, j++$ **do**
5:         **if** $i \neq j$ **then**
6:             $\emptyset \leftarrow$ Plan_and_Exec_to($points[i]$) {Move to initial point of the plan}
7:             $plan\_array[i][j] \leftarrow$ Plan_and_Exec_to($points[j]$) {Move to desired point and keep the planned trajectory}
8:         **end if**
9:     **end for**
10: **end for**
11: {Store all as a structured message}
12: **for** $i < 0 \, ; \, i < no_p \, ; \, i++$ **do**
13:     **for** $j < 0 \, ; \, j < no_p \, ; \, j++$ **do**
14:         **if** $i \neq j$ **then**
15:             $init\_pos\_id \leftarrow start\_name[i]$
16:             $goal\_pos\_id \leftarrow final\_name[j]$
17:             $plan \leftarrow plan\_array[i][j]$
18:         **end if**
19:     **end for**
20: **end for**

---

workspace, which means that the movements have to take into account the user's model in order to avoid any collision with him. We also have to take into account that the speed of these movements must be limited, in order to ensure safety.

Unlike the first scheme, in this case the environment consists of moving obstacles, which requires constant updating of the scene and constant tracking of the objects in it (Fig. 13). For this reason, we used the images of the mannequin model to obtain its current positions and orientations in order to track their movement and link it to the objects created in the scene.

We also need to be able to determine whether a computed plan will collide or not, which requires taking several aspects into account. First, based on the calculated path to the desired goal, we check whether the path remains valid during the execution of the plan. To do so, we check for all calculated via-points of the path, whether the respective configurations are currently colliding with any other object present in the scene. If there are no collisions, we continue the execution. In the case of a collision present in any of the remaining states of the path, we instruct the robot to stop the execution of the computed path and replan it based on the updated scene information.

To test our framework, we performed an initial trajectory planning. Then, during the execution, we created an obstacle. Then, by checking the validity

Algorithm 2. Trajectory upload and execution

Require: A desired frame to go to *des_frame*. A home pose *home*. Number of elements no_e. Initial positions *init_pos_id*. Goal positions *goal_pos_id*. Planned trajectories *plan*. A counter i.

1: **for** $i < 0$; $i < no_e$; $i++$ **do**
2:    {Extract the data from the file}
3:    $start\_name[i] \leftarrow init\_pos\_id[i]$
4:    $final\_name[i] \leftarrow init\_names[i]$ {Same id's as we are iterating through all points}
5:    $plan\_array[i] \leftarrow plan[i]$
6: **end for**
7: $\emptyset \leftarrow$ Plan_and_Exec_to(*home*) {Move to home pose}
8: {Reference to home position as current}
9: $init\_frame \leftarrow$ "*home*"
10: $aux\_des\_frame \leftarrow$ "*home*"
11: **while** running **do**
12:    **if** $des\_frame == init\_frame$ **then**
13:      {The robot is in position.}
14:    **else**
15:      $aux\_des\_frame = des\_frame$ {Update the desired position}
16:      **for** $i < 0$; $i < no_e$; $i++$ **do**
17:        {Search in the list of plans the one that matches the init and final frames}
18:        **if** $(start\_name[i] == init\_frame)$ **and** $(final\_name[i] == aux\_des\_frame)$ **then**
19:          $execute(plan\_array[i])$
20:          $init\_frame \leftarrow aux\_des\_frame$
21:        **end if**
22:      **end for**
23:    **end if**
24: **end while**

---

of the trajectory, we are able to detect that an object is in collision with the planned trajectory. We then instruct the robot to stop the current execution and replan towards the same goal, taking into account the updated planning scene. This work is intended to be extrapolated to work according to the size of the

Fig. 14. Original planned path (left) and Re-planned path from detected collision (middle and right)

mannequin. Thus, we can take into account the user moving in the environment as an obstacle to be avoided (Fig. 14).

4 Conclusions

In this paper, we have presented motion generation algorithms that can be used by a cobot to create an intermittent contacts interface. A framework was presented including a UR5 cobot, ROS nodes, HTC Vive sensors and a car chair. Taking into account the objects present in the environment, a comparison of trajectory planning algorithms is presented. The selected algorithm is then used in two examples. An experimental validation is in progress and will be presented in the final version of the paper.

Acknowledgements. This research is part of LobbyBot: Novel encountered type haptic devices, a French research project funded by ANR.

References

1. Mercado, V., Marchal, M., Lécuyer, A.: ENTROPiA: towards infinite surface haptic displays in virtual reality using encountered-type rotating props. IEEE Trans. Vis. Comput. Graph. (TVCG) **27**, 2237–2243 (2019)
2. Salazar, S., Pacchierotti, C., de Tinguy, X., Macie, A., Marchal, M.: Altering the stiffness, friction, and shape perception of tangible objects in virtual reality using wearable haptics. IEEE Trans. Haptics **13**, 167–174 (2020)
3. de Tinguy, X., Pacchierotti, C., Marchal, M., Lécuyer, A.: Enhancing the stiffness perception of tangible objects in mixed reality using wearable haptics. In: IEEE Conference on Virtual Reality and 3D User Interfaces (2018)
4. Guda, V.K., Chablat, D., Chevallereau, C.: Safety in a human robot interactive: application to haptic perception. In: Chen, J.Y.C., Fragomeni, G. (eds.) HCII 2020. LNCS, vol. 12190, pp. 562–574. Springer, Cham (2020). https://doi.org/10.1007/978-3-030-49695-1_38
5. CLARTE, CNRS/LS2N, INRIA/Hybrid, and Renault, "Lobbybot project" (2020). https://www.lobbybot.fr/
6. De la Cruz, O., Gosselin, F., Bachta, W., Morel, G.: Contribution to the design of a 6 DoF contactless sensor intended for intermittent contact haptic interfaces. In: 2018 3rd International Conference on Advanced Robotics and Mechatronics (ICARM), pp. 130–135 (2018)
7. Kavraki, L., Svetska, P., Latombe, J., Overmars, M.: Probabilistic roadmaps for path planning in high-dimensional configuration spaces. IEEE Trans. Robot. Autom. **12**(4), 566–580 (1996)
8. Khatib, O.: Real-time obstacle avoidance for manipulators and mobile robots. In: IEEE International Conference on Robotics and Automation (1985)
9. Gasparetto, A., Boscariol, P., Lanzutti, A., Vidoni, R.: Path planning and trajectory planning algorithms: a general overview. In: Carbone, G., Gomez-Bravo, F. (eds.) Motion and Operation Planning of Robotic Systems. MMS, vol. 29, pp. 3–27. Springer, Cham (2015). https://doi.org/10.1007/978-3-319-14705-5_1

10. Volpe, R.: Real-time obstacle avoidance for manipulators and mobile robots. Ph.D. dissertation, The Robotics Institute, Carnegie Mellon University, Pittsburgh, USA (1990)
11. Volpe, R., Khosla, P.: Manipulator control with superquadric artificial potential functions: theory and experiments. IEEE Trans. Syst. Man Cybern. **20**(6), 1423–1436 (1990)
12. Sleumer, N., Tschichold-Gurman, N.: Exact cell decomposition of arrangements used for path planning in robotics. Technical report (2000)
13. LaValle, S., Kuffner, J.: Randomized kinodynamic planning. Int. J. Robot. Res. **20**, 378–400 (2001)
14. Karaman, S., Frazzoli, E.: Sampling-based algorithms for optimal motion planning. Int. J. Robot. Res. **30**(7), 846–894 (2011)
15. Bohlin, R., Kavraki, L.: Path planning using lazy PRM. In: IEEE International Conference on Robotics and Automation, pp. 521–528 (2000)
16. Karaman, S., Frazzoli, E.: Sampling-based algorithms for optimal motion planning. Int. J. Robot. Res. **30**, 846–894 (2011)
17. Jaillet, L., Cortés, J., Siméon, T.: Sampling-based path planning on configuration-space costmaps. IEEE Trans. Robot. **26**(4), 635–646 (2010)
18. Devaurs, D., Siméon, T., Cortés, J.: Enhancing the transition-based RRT to deal with complex cost spaces. In: Proceedings - IEEE International Conference on Robotics and Automation (ICRA), pp. 4120–4125 (2013)
19. Salzman, O., Halperin, D.: Asymptotically near-optimal RRT for fast, high-quality motion planning. IEEE Trans. Rob. **32**(3), 473–483 (2016)
20. Kuffner, J., Lavalle, S.: RRT-connect: an efficient approach to single-query path planning. In: Proceedings of the 2000 IEEE International Conference on Robotics & Automation, pp. 995–1001, April 2000
21. Hsu, D., Latombe, J.-C., Motwani, R.: Path planning in expansive configuration spaces. Int. J. Comput. Geom. Appl. **9**(4–5), 495–512 (1999)
22. Kinematics and dynamics library. http://wiki.ros.org/kdl
23. Messmer, F., Hawkins, K., Edwards, S., Glaser, S., Meeussen, W.: ROS-industrial-universal-robots. https://github.com/ros-industrial/universal_robot
24. HTC and Valve, "HTC Vive". https://www.vive.com/fr/
25. Guda, V., Chablat, D., Chevallereau, C.: Lobbybot Deliverable Report on Methogology for Motion Capture. Technical report, Ecole Centrale de Nantes, Laboratoire des Sciences de Numérique de Nantes (2021)
26. Mugisha, S., Zoppi, M., Molfino, R., Guda, V., Chevallereau, C., Chablat, D.: Safe collaboration between human and robot in a context of intermittent haptique interface. In: Proceedings of the ASME 2021 International Design Engineering Technical Conferences & Computers and Information in Engineering Conference (2021)

Improving AI Systems Through Trade-Offs Between Values

Jaana Hallamaa[✉] [iD]

University of Helsinki, Box 3, 00014 Helsinki, Finland
jaana.hallamaa@helsinki.fi

Abstract. EU regulation mechanisms are typically designed to reinforce European values of human dignity, freedom, equality, democracy, human rights, and rule of law while establishing mechanisms that mobilize products and services and supporting economic and technological development. The EU Machinery Directive 2006 has had a pivotal role in securing the quality and safety of machines and devices on the European common market. This article discusses the points of convergence and divergence of values in light of various EU regulations, particularly in relation to digital products and AI applications. To distinguish the types of value conflicts, the article refers to Erik Hollnagel's Efficiency-Thoroughness-Trade-Off (ETTO) principle and discusses how a reasonable balance between diverse values could be negotiated in designing AI-integrated devices and services.

Keywords: Usability · Safety · EU machinery directive · Efficiency-thoroughness trade-off

1 Introduction

Digitalization has become a global trend to the point that not being part of the process increases one's risk of social exclusion and economic marginalization. The developers of devices and designers of services outsource technical vocabulary as they eulogize the features of their digitalized solutions. Despite the marketing language, benefits seldom come without costs. While accessibility and ease of use help consumers make the most of their devices and applications, they also increase the possibility of misuse. A focus on easy-to-use features may also increase the number of errors caused by carelessness or inattentiveness in users.

A central reason for developing and using technology is to make everyday human activities more efficient. Because mechanized systems speed up material production, digitalizing the services offered by these systems can further accelerate the manufacture and service processes. Tasks can be performed on a larger scale and often at smaller costs than ever before.

Although this increase in efficiency has strengthened the human ability to change reality in accordance with our goals, it has also increased the negative consequences of human actions. The improved efficiency of technology-mediated tasks has undesired side effects, as accidents and disasters caused and induced by human beings now have wide-ranging, even global consequences. The double-edged nature of technology has given rise to a diverse range of safety measures aiming to mitigate risks.

The European Union (EU) is one of the most influential international institutions that play a role in developing safeguards for protecting citizens and the environment from the detrimental effects of technology-induced accidents and disasters. The EU Machinery Directive 2006 has become a central means for securing the safety of products and services. Though evaluations have shown that the Directive serves its purpose, the rapid development of digital products and AI applications has created a need to complement it with additional measures (Directive 2006/42/EC, Machinery Directive 2021).

We often make trivial mistakes and err because we can be careless, do things in a hurry, or not care to consider what a task requires (Reason 2008, 29–48). Many mishaps can be prevented with foresight, attention, steadiness, and concentration. These factors also often play a role in large-scale accidents exacerbated by technology-induced consequences. Therefore, to mitigate these risks, resources must be directed toward user safety (Reason 2008, 239–249).

The investment of resources in safety restricts their use to further the original goal, potentially making it more difficult or time-consuming to perform a task or use a device. Features essential for ideal human actions—efficiency, safety, and usability of tools and services—may conflict with each other. These conflicts become even more complex from a wider perspective as we acknowledge that individual action is a conceptual construct and presently, human actions take place within a web of codependent tasks that are interlinked to various technological systems. Human actions affect all aspects of life and well-being. In any scenario, the chosen course of action implicitly exhibits a prioritization between values.

In the following, I introduce the mechanisms instituted by the EU to safeguard public interest in the safety of products and services. I also discuss the need to update these directives to meet the requirements posed by AI-integrated devices and services. Then, I concisely discuss usability as a value, and the ways in which it may conflict with safety. Finally, I suggest that the efficiency-thoroughness trade-off (ETTO) principle introduced by Erik Hollnagel can help understand the stakes involved in conflicts between values in technology-induced human action (Hollnagel/A and Hollnagel/B).

2 EU Directives – Safeguarding Public Interest

The European Union was originally established as an economic organization after World War II. Over the past several decades, however, it has become a political community of member states based on the shared values of human dignity, freedom, equality, democracy, human rights, and rule of law [Aims and Values]. Since its inception, the EU has committed itself to protecting safety as a central public interest.[1]

The diverse interests that function as directives for the EU member states become apparent in attempts to not only further economic and political goals but also secure social values. A central way of realizing the multiple goals is to formulate directives that establish structures and mechanisms to regulate economic activities in the common

---

[1] See, for example, Bolt (2008) for the development.

market. The aim to further the various interests is expressed in the repeated intention to facilitate economic activity for the benefit of the common market, and to protect and secure the fundamental rights of EU citizens. The varying types of goals can also be expressed as a means to improve the citizens' wellbeing and facilitate technological innovation and uptake (COM/2020/64, 1).

The potential conflicts between commercial, political, and social values are mitigated by the claim that the protection of citizen rights will serve as a competitive asset in the global market. The EU Machinery Directive and the Ethical AI guidelines are both designed according to these central principles (Directive 2006/42/EC; Ethical AI).

The EU has employed regulation and standardization as central mechanisms to ensure both economic and social welfare goals are considered. One of the most important tools that affect manufacturers and citizens is the EU Machinery Directive (Directive 2006/42/EC). The speed of technological development, especially in digital solutions and technology based on artificial intelligence (AI), has created a need to review this directive, and the EU has published guidelines for doing so (COM2021/202). A separate proposal suggests harmonized rules for the development, market placement, and use of AI systems (COM/2021/206).

EU regulation and standardization mechanisms have been successful in the sense that only products that fulfil the criteria set by the directives may be sold in the common market. The CE marking is a guarantee of regulated quality and safety features. Customers can rely on products to perform their intended functions without harming or endangering their users. Supervision, spot checks by authorities, and self-regulation along with consumer awareness hold a check on the number of products and services that do not meet the standards (Directive 2006/42/EC).

The Machinery Directive is not a common topic among the public, and many EU citizens may not even be aware of its existence. Paradoxically, the efficiency of the Machinery Directive may be the very reason so few people are aware of it, as it saves them the need to worry about safety and quality standards.

2.1 EU Machinery Directive and Its Revisions

The first formulation of the Machinery Directive dates to 1989 (Directive 89/392/EEC/89).[2] The directive was amended several times (Directive 91/368/EEC, Directive 93/44/EEC, and Directive 93/68/EEC) before its second publication in 1998 (Directive 98/37/EC). Its aim was to harmonize the laws of EU member states relating to machinery. This version of the directive remained in effect until the end of 2009 (Directive 2006/42/EC).

A major revision of the document took place with the third publication of the Machinery Directive in 2006. To mark the change, the document was called the New Directive 2006/42/EC. Despite the name change, the content of the directive was derived from its previous versions. Within three years, the requirements of the New Machinery Directive were transcribed into the national legislation of each EU member state. The New

---

[2] The date of entry of the directive was 1 January, 1993, with a mandatory effective date of 1 January, 1995.

Directive 2006/42/EC establishes the regulatory basis and foundation for the harmoniza-tion of essential health and safety requirements regarding machinery within the EU. Its regulations concern not only manufacturers but also machinery distributors and users (Directive 2006/42/EC).

Annex 1 of the Machine Directive describes the basic features of safety and the mechanisms for ensuring it. For the present purpose, I will summarize the main com-ponents of the concept of safety in this directive. The starting point of the directive is the integration of safety into every product throughout its entire lifespan. Thus, safety is not a separate product quality but a principle that should direct everything from its design, construction, storage, transport, and assembly to its use, handling, and mainte-nance, and finally, to its dismantling, disabling, and scrapping (Directive 2006/42/EC). This integrated view of safety means a manufacturer must also consider any foreseeable misuse of the product. This can be done by designing and constructing the product in a way that prevents any abnormal risk-inducing use (Annex 1, Directive 2006/42/EC).

To make safety a real-life quality, the safety regulations must be translated into each product's properties following the principles listed in Annex 1. These principles do not give detailed instructions but consist of general guidelines. According to them, manufacturers are duty-bound to eliminate or reduce risks involved in the handling or use of a product. When this is not possible, they must take necessary protective measures to mitigate the residual risks and inform users about them (Annex 1, Directive 2006/42/EC).

Two principles concern the appropriate use of a product. A manufacturer must specify the type of training—if any—the safe use of the product presupposes and define the need to provide personal protective equipment for the users. These principles apply to the product, its handling, and its use until it is dismantled (Annex 1, Directive 2006/42/EC).

Another characteristic feature of the Machine Directive is its accordance with what has been dubbed the "New Approach". The New Approach document outlines the prin-ciples that manufacturers must follow if they wish to sell their products within the EU, and the mechanisms that ensure the products' compliance with these requirements (The "New Approach" 2019).

The New Approach limits the role of the EU in legislative harmonization; instead, its role is to set out the essential safety requirements through various directives and regula-tions, thereby defining the conditions for manufacturers to sell their products within the common market. It delegates the task of defining the technical specifications that cor-respond to the requirements established by the directives to trustworthy standardization organizations, such as the European Committee for Standardization (Comité Européen de Normalisation, CEN). This ensures the technical specifications are not mandatory but voluntary standards to help manufacturers fulfill the requirements. To ignore the norms is, however, not an option for the manufacturer, as the national authorities of each member state have a duty to ensure the manufactured products conform to the essential safety requirements established by the Machinery Directive (The New Approach 2019).

In 2008, the EU adopted yet another set of tools known as the New Legislative Framework to improve product safety in the common market. The aim of this legislative package is to reinforce the application and enforcement of internal market legislation (New Legislative Framework 2008).

2.2   New Challenges to Safety Regulations: AI-Equipped Products

The approach adopted in the 2006 EU Machinery Directive eliminates the need for constant updates. The general principles of the directive harmonize the essential health and safety requirements, thereby serving the two main goals: to ensure the free movement of machinery products within the internal market, and to protect those who use them. However, the rapid development of AI over the past decade has necessitated a further review of the directive. The European Commission delegated this task to the Regulatory Fitness and Performance Programme (REFIT), which published its evaluation in 2018 (Machinery Directive 2021).

In its report, the REFIT stated that there is no acute need to revise the directive, as its general principles are technology-neutral and its regulations and approaches still appear to be both relevant and effective. However, the directive may not cover risks stemming from emerging technologies, such as AI-enabled robots (Machinery Directive 2021).

The REFIT report initiated the European Commission to issue a new proposal for the regulation of machinery products (COM/2021/202) as a part of its AI package. The proposal's acceptance involves a change of instrument: defining EU regulations, the aim of which is to avoid the risk of the so-called gold plating, or incorrect transposition, of an EU directive (Gold-plating), and to ensure the member states act uniformly as they implement the norms (Machinery Directive 2021).

There is a widespread interest in emerging technologies as they are likely to affect the society at all levels. The EU digital agenda was drafted in 2010, and in 2021, the European Commission published a proposal called the Artificial Intelligence Act for harmonizing rules regarding AI applications (COM/2021/206). The same principles that have guided the formulation of the Machinery Directive have been applied in the proposal concerning harmonization of AI rules. The documents reinforce the EU's basic values, and employ a risk-based approach to ensure both safety and fundamental rights protection of its citizens (Digital Agenda; COM/2021/206).

In the following, I will summarize the problems that have been identified concerning AI-embedded systems and serve as a basis to formulate the EU regulations. I mainly refer to the European Commission's Report on the safety and liability implications of Artificial Intelligence, the Internet of Things, and robotics (COM/2020/64), though I also comment on the conceptualization of AI-related risks in the AI Act (COM/2021/206). My focus is not to present a full-scale analysis of the risks, but to identify the values that risk management aims to protect.

The Report on the safety and liability implications of Artificial Intelligence, the Internet of Things, and robotics follows the principles of the New Approach, adopts a risk-based scheme, and exemplifies an extended concept of safety, thus confirming the producers' obligation to assess and manage the risks of their products throughout their time of use (COM/2020/64, 1, 6).

The report characterizes AI, IoT, and robotics as products that can implement connectivity, autonomy, and data dependency to perform tasks without human control or supervision (COM/2020/64, 2). These autonomous features also make it possible for AI-equipped systems to improve their performance using the data they have collected during their functioning. In this sense, such systems can learn from their experience. Furthermore, products based on AI, IoT, and robotics are complex not only in terms of their composition but also in the number of economic operators involved in their supply, service, and maintenance. The unique features of AI-equipped machines justify the claim that they form new types of technological ecosystems (COM/2020/64, 2).

In relation to safety, the nature of AI-equipped systems is twofold as the adoption of AI as a part of a product may both improve safety and create new types of vulnerabilities. The use of AI often makes processes more exact, uniform, and therefore, more reliable. The movements of robots remain precise throughout their performance, and AI-equipped systems can carry out tasks without any fatigue, unlike humans. Thus, AI presents an opportunity to improve the safe execution of tasks, such as the use of robots in surgery and automated vehicles in road and sea traffic (COM/2020/64, 2). With embedded AI, products become more easily traceable, which enables surveillance authorities to locate dangerous products and identify risks across supply chains. The interactive features of AI-equipped products can also be utilized to effectively warn users of potential risks (COM/2020/64, 2–3, 5–6).

Aside from the several promising prospects, the report describes several complications stemming from specific features of AI. For an AI-equipped product, it is difficult to say which features will remain the same during its lifetime, and how adaptable they will remain within the ecosystem of other AI-enhanced products. Unlike traditional machines, AI, IoT, and robots usually change in form and function during their use. Typically, the manufacturers of such products publish updates to improve features or fix detected problems, thereby making them more effective and safer to use. However, changing some characteristics of a product may also alter the features essential to safety, necessitating its re-inspection (COM/2020/64, 7, 9). Here, the manufacturer's interest in saving costs may conflict with the public interest in ensuring safety. The novel features pose a requirement for users to regularly update the software that directs the functions of their devices and acquaint themselves with the new features (COM/2020/64, 14).

The highly specific nature of AI-equipped products makes it harder to detect the causes of potential faults, which can often only be resolved by professional experts with exclusive knowledge. The functioning of AI-integrated systems may remain opaque or unexplainable even for professionals because of the vastness of data, interplay between algorithms upon which their processes are based, and number of divergent phases of decision-making processes that they go through during their use cycles (COM/2020/64, 9).

AI applications with a built-in learning capacity can develop and improve their functions based on the data collected and processed by them. These features enable them to act autonomously and perform their functions in unprecedented ways with little human control. In the near future, more AI applications will exhibit a capacity to work without human supervision. The more autonomous the machine-learning features make the applications, the more difficult it will be to understand the underlying algorithmic processes. The inscrutability of AI-based decision making is known as the black-box effect. Features that enable autonomous decision-making processes introduce the question of human surveillance as a safety factor. As processes become intractable, it will be more difficult to identify who is responsible for what within the product chain (COM/2020/64, 14–15).

New types of risks may emerge as AI-equipped products exhibit agency (COM/2020/64, 15). Interacting with human-like machines may cause mental stress, and the selection and use of data based on visual recognition may cause the system to make faulty decisions. Traditionally, the EU safety regulations do not cover safety measures against such errors (COM/2020/64, 2, 7–8).

Connectivity can both improve safety and multiply safety risks. Although the integration of parts with distinct functions into a single system enables the monitoring of large and complex wholes, such as fire and smoke detectors, the interconnected nature of the system also makes it vulnerable to hacking, third-party control, and cyberattacks (COM/2020/64, 5–6). Although these risks are already present, they are not covered by the current EU regulations. This challenge is more complicated than coping with traditional safety concerns because all risks do not exist when a product enters the market; they may appear later (COM/2020/64, 14).

An additional factor that increases the complexity of AI-embedded products is the increasingly blurred line between products and services. The fact that products do not function without software creates new types of risks and challenges for determining liability. In settings where AI applications are integrated into large ecosystems of interacting devices and services, safety concerns arising from the system complexity reach a new level. (COM/2020/64, 13).

Traditionally, the EU product safety legislation considers the complexity of value chains along with the principle of shared responsibility, thereby imposing obligations to several economic operators. The producer bears responsibility for the safety of the final product, but the principle of shared responsibility requires cooperation between the economic operators involved in the supply chain. The challenge posed by AI-equipped products stems from the increasing complexity of supply chains. From the EU's perspective, this should not weaken user safety or the principles of liability for damage compensation resulting from defective goods. In doing so, the regulations must be designed in a way that does not inhibit innovation or discourage investors (COM/2020/64, 11–12).

The report stresses the need to complement the present EU directives to ensure the same level of protection to users and customers compared to those using traditional technologies. However, the mechanisms for such an effect should not impede continuous technological innovation but strengthen trust in emerging digital technologies and establish stable conditions to encourage investments (COM/2020/64, 16–17).

The AI Act identifies similar types of risks as the Report but lists them in passim (COM/2021/206, 11). Its focus lies in identifying second-order risks, namely those threatening systems that maintain, monitor and secure safety, and those threatening the basic values of the EU (COM/2021/206, 11, 21). The categorization of AI practices into two main categories—prohibited practices and high-risk AI systems—illustrates how the values are prioritized (COM/2021/206, 44–46).

3 Usability

Usability has become one of the core values that guides technology development. As an evaluative quality, usability applies to all types of devices, from cutlery forks to skateboards; however, the recent attention to the concept relates it specifically to software engineering (see, e.g., Nielsen & Budiu 2012). While the concept of usability is easily accessible to ordinary people in user-friendly designs and products, experts use the term to describe a set of requirements a product or system must fulfill to serve its designed purpose without harming its users or risking the safety of others. In this wider perspective, usability is tightly connected to questions on ergonomics and safety (Ahram and Karwowski 2013).

3.1 Usability as a User Value and a Design Value

The concept of usability brings together four factors: design, product, user, and product use. An analysis of the relationship between the four factors will make the possible discrepancies between the values embedded in them apparent. To do so, I will express usability with a user value and design value. Then, I will introduce some discrepancies between different values as paradoxes of usability. This will clarify some of the difficulties the revised EU Machine Directive is supposed to tackle.

In the early days of digitalization, many of my colleagues did not bother to reclaim their domestic travel expenses, as they could not do so without using a computerized refund program. They valued the time saved by refusing to use the application over the missed compensations. However, ignoring a digital application is no longer an option; it has become impossible for anyone working as a part of any company or institution to carry out everyday tasks and duties without relying on various digital applications.

A plethora of reasons make digital applications and AI systems hard to use; the irritation caused by poor design dates back to the beginning of the history of using tools. Some aspects of poor design, however, are traceable to specific features of digitalization and AI. These products and services stem from different designers and manufacturers, and each follows their own logic. Knowing how to use one such system seldom translates to an ability to use all of them. Even simple computerized chores that are not a part of one's routine duties become time-consuming obstacles for completing tasks. The specific features of recent technology create a reason for designers to rethink the standards of usability.

Not all obstacles to good usability arise from bad design. A considerable number of difficulties stem from the compromises or trade-offs between the desired and necessary features of an application or product. Under the auspices of protecting consumer rights, the users of any digital application must comply with conditions few people have the motive to read, and even fewer have the background knowledge to understand. Refusing to comply often excludes one from the service. To protect the privacy of its citizens, the EU has developed an extensive directive for data protection, known as the General Data protection Regulation (GDPR). The most concrete sign of the new protective regulation for an ordinary web user is that it has become more cumbersome to use search engines and visit different sites.

The core of digitalization is the collection, management, and processing of data. Although applications are utilized for numerous useful and constructive purposes, they can also be used for harmful and criminal activities. This has created an increasing need to protect the security of both the users of digital services and their data. The mechanisms designed to inhibit an illicit use of these systems make their proper use more difficult. Thus, ensuring safety and security worsens usability (Bradbury 2018).

Ideally, usability is a point where four factors converge: the tool, device, or system; its designed purpose; the users; and a goal they strive to achieve by using them. The importance given to each of these factors is highlighted in the different approaches used to improve usability (Groen and Noyes 2011). Usability is a quality that expresses how well a tool serves an agent and its purpose in terms of providing utility, which makes it a normative concept. A product's usability can be assessed by evaluating, for example, how easy, efficient, and accurate it is for different people to use, and how well it performs its intended function. To produce efficient tools, devices, and systems, designers should adopt usability as a central value to guide their work.

There is a tradition of extensive study on factors that play a role in usability (Ernst 2002). Psychological research has contributed to facts concerning, among others, human observation, memory, epistemology, and the ideal span of concentration, that determine several criteria of usability. Similarly, human physiology sets limits to what people experience as usable in a designed tool, device, or system (see, e.g., Acosta et al. 2011). Recently, researchers have also focused on the importance of cultural factors affecting how well the designed products serve the needs of their users (Smith-Jackson et al. 2011). As usability is not the only quality valued by manufacturers and users, the design process often employs diverse types of trade-offs between the desired objectives (Mauer and Proctor 2011).

The designers' task is complicated by the fact that different user groups may utilize the product. The groups of people who use large service systems designed for taxation, managing patient data, or recording payments have different roles and purposes for using these systems. Who are the most important users, and whose needs should be prioritized in terms of the system's usability?

3.2 The Paradox of Usability

The size of the packaging does not always match the measures of the product inside: the smaller the product, the greater the relative space reserved for instructions and user manuals. The instructions that are a central requirement of the CE standard serve the interests of several parties. They can be taken as a proof that the manufacturer has followed the common market regulations and standards, and that they make it possible for consumers to use the product adequately and safely in terms of its intended function. The user manuals also serve as criteria for proper and improper use: producer liability only covers harm connected to the proper use of their product (Directive 2006/42/EC).

The evident purpose of safety regulations and user manuals is to secure vital customer interests. Still, it is an established fact that people tend not to read user manuals (Anglim 2013; Haider and Frensch 1996; Stum 2017). There are different reasons behind this phenomenon, but the central one stems from learning psychology. A subtask—such as reading a manual—that does not seem to immediately contribute to the actions that an agent thinks will lead to the desired goal will appear as futile and a waste of time. People are motivated to engage themselves in straightforward actions instead of first concentrating on something that may not be necessary or even useful, or whose purpose is unclear. As people often have some prior experience of the activity they are aiming to perform, postponing it to read instructions may seem futile. Instead of going through the manual, they start using the new machine, device, or program (Anglim 2013; Marrazzo 2018).

Ideally, product design makes the correct use of each product self-evident, but as the design of modern products is often complex because of their multiple embedded features, a self-evident simplicity of design is seldom possible. The reluctance of people to delve into instructions before starting to use a product is the paradox of usability. The need to invest time in learning how to use a product weakens its immediate usability, although concentrating on the instructions would be most advisable to improve its long-term usability. By not reading instructions, people often act against their best interests.

The phenomenon that people tend to ignore manuals is trivial, but it brings forth a more general problem concerning usability and user interests. The Machine Directive and other EU regulations aim to improve and guarantee the safety of products, their use, and users. Manufacturers favor self-regulation, as it makes it easier and cheaper for them to distribute their products, and customers often consider regulations as unnecessary complications and signs of useless bureaucracy that hinder the smooth utilization of products.

Customers and producers typically become aware of safety issues *ex post facto*, when something bad has occurred and its cause is identified with a fault in some product, device, or practice. By defining safety as an issue of public interest, the EU has committed its different bodies to regard what securing product safety implies not only in relation to existing products, but also those that do not yet exist or have not been invented.

4   Trade-Offs Between Values

Directives and regulations are just one part of the arsenal that has been developed after WWII to mitigate risks and ensure the safety of human-machine cooperation. Safety studies is a practice-oriented field of academic study that aims to understand the underlying factors that contribute to human errors and increase the probability of risks.[3] Therefore, I introduce a practical tool developed by prominent safety scientist Erik Hollnagel. Known as the ETTO principle, this tool makes the efficiency-thoroughness trade-offs people constantly face apparent. The ETTO principle is useful in the present context as it elucidates how values central to design, production, and use of devices and services may conflict with each other, how to conceptualize the components of a conflict, and how to find ways to negotiate between them.

4.1   The ETTO Principle

The ETTO principle is derived from the fact that all human performance, both individual and collective, is curtailed by scarcity, or limited resources. Everyone has experienced how a lack of time affects the actions and performance of most tasks. Other resources that typically fall short of ideal supply include information, materials, tools, energy, and workforce. Less than perfect conditions may cause frustration. However, as it is a common condition, people usually manage to complete their tasks satisfactorily by adjusting what they do to meet their prevailing conditions. In other words, they balance the demands of a task with the available resources. Hollnagel calls the human ability to adjust performance to match the conditions as a trade-off between efficiency and thoroughness (Hollnagel/A).

---

[3] See, for example, the Journal of Safety Studies published by the Macrothink Institute, https://www.macrothink.org/journal/index.php/jss.

Such trade-offs are commonplace and characterize the execution of any type of task. Thus, the ETTO principle captures something people are intuitively familiar with. The core of the principle is the balance between efficiency and thoroughness, and Hollnagel sums it up in a simple definition: "In their daily activities, at work or at leisure, people (and organizations) routinely make a choice between being effective and being thorough, since it rarely is possible to be both at the same time. If demands for productivity or performance are high, thoroughness is reduced until the productivity goals are met. If demands to safety are high, efficiency is reduced until the safety goals are met" (Hollnagel/A).

Hollnagel defines thoroughness as a justified assumption of the necessary and sufficient conditions for performing the intended activity for a secured achievement of its objective without creating any unwanted side effects. These conditions include time, information, materials, energy, competence, tools, and so on. To achieve the requirements of thoroughness, everything needed to successfully perform a task must be available, the conditions needed for executing it must be in place, and the outcome of the action must correspond with the intended goal (Hollnagel/A).

Thoroughness often requires planning and preparation before carrying out a task, which necessarily postpones its starting point. A multitude of causes set limits to the time and resources that can be allocated to different commissions, which means the time spent in preparation restricts the time allocated for performing the actual task (Hollnagel/A).

Realizing efficiency as a value implies minimizing the resources—time, materials, money, psychological effort, physical effort, workforce, and others—to achieve an intended objective. There must be sufficient resources to achieve the goal, as allocating them scantily will lead to failure and subsequent waste of resources. Individuals typically accustom themselves to sufficient resource allocation as they adopt their routines. For organizations, functioning efficiently often requires at least some systematic planning; how much is enough is a subject that must be considered in accordance with the ETTO principle (Hollnagel/A).

The attention given to thoroughness and efficiency in any activity is a trade-off, which means it is possible to maximize only one of them at a time. Investing in thoroughness will reduce efficiency, and vice versa. To give up any of the two values is not an option either, as it is not possible to complete any activity without both. Thoroughness is always necessary to perform any action, and without efficiency, no task can be completed (Hollnagel/A).

Because thoroughness and efficiency are both crucial values in the successful completion of tasks, there is a tendency to push people to be both thorough and efficient at the same time. Hollnagel calls this demand the ETTO fallacy: while it is possible to express the requirement to maximize thoroughness and efficiency, it is impossible to fulfill it (Hollnagel/A).

The rational outcome of the trade-off depends on the priority order of the values connected to the task's performance and outcome. If safety and quality are vital for a successful performance, thoroughness must precede efficiency; conversely, in tasks where the speedy flow of production and number of completed sequences of action are the dominant concerns, efficiency prevails over thoroughness (Hollnagel/A).

Although efficiency and thoroughness are exclusive values in terms of maximization, each can be used to boost the other. Finding the most efficient way to perform a sequence of tasks is not possible without a careful analysis of the entire process and the refinement of each of its parts. One cannot be efficient now without having been thorough in the past. Likewise, being thorough currently makes it possible to act efficiently in the future. Routinizing subtasks makes any process more efficient and saves resources that can be allocated to tasks that require thoroughness to reach the best outcome. Such considerations show the ETTO principle must be complemented with the TETO principle, necessitating trade-offs in which efficiency must give way to thoroughness (Hollnagel/B, 6).

There is no standard way of determining the ideal allocation of resources between efficiency and thoroughness, as it depends on several factors, such as observed time span, currently relevant parties, goal of the activity, and so on. Typically, analyzing the causes of a major accident or catastrophe will reveal factors that were disregarded by the responsible parties, often against expert warnings. The miscalculations resulting from an improper application of the ETTO principle may result in a long-term loss of efficiency, as a major portion of the resources have to be invested in legal procedures and reparations.

4.2   Trade-Offs Between Values in AI Design

The paradox of usability discussed in Sect. 3.2 resembles the ETTO fallacy introduced by Hollnagel. Both exemplify the fact that important values connected to human action conflict with each other. Hollnagel stresses that there is an inherent conflict between thoroughness and efficiency as they require distinct types of resource allocation. Thoroughness is a value that prioritizes careful planning and precise execution, whereas efficiency stresses on performance speed and the number of completed sequences of the desired tasks.

There is a similar discrepancy between usability and safety. Even though usability and safety are both essential design values, it does not seem possible to maximize both simultaneously. The discrepancy between the two values resembles the conflict between thoroughness and efficiency: ensuring safety often means the product becomes more difficult to use.

The resemblance between the two sets of values is easy to understand, as the safe execution of a process often depends on how thoroughly it is performed. Likewise, increasing efficiency involves finding the easiest, fastest, and most effortless way to carry out the necessary actions or manufacture a product.

Negotiating between thoroughness and efficiency, and between safety and usability, must be carried out against the background of an acceptable risk and a period the agent can afford to maintain their activity. The greater the risks connected to failure and mismanagement are, the more important thoroughness and safety become. If precision is less important than completed sequences and quality plays a smaller role than the number of products, efficiency rules over thoroughness.

In Sect. 2.2, I have summarized the risks related to AI-enhanced products identified in EU documents. I will end this article with remarks concerning the conflicts of values that underlie the explicated risks, and whether tools such as the ETTO principle could help understand and mitigate them.

The EU Machinery Directive has been linked to standardization requirements and practices. It has enabled manufacturers to develop ways to design and create products that meet established safety and quality standards. When products are equipped with features based on AI, meeting the aims of the directive becomes more difficult. The contours between products and services has become opaquer and the characteristics of a product often change during its lifespan as a result of recurring updates and connectivity to other devices and systems. These features are strengths, as they help make many types of actions more efficient and precise, and services more easily available. However, the potential of misuse turns the same characteristics into weaknesses and liabilities. Thoroughness in the form of careful planning will not solve the problem.

The detection of all relevant risks is not possible, as mutability is a key feature of AI-embedded products. There may be hazards that only appear in specific contexts, or in relation to other (AI) products, services, or devices. A similar duality applies to connectivity and autonomy based on AI. These characteristics are assets that help further several goals; however, they also expose users to a wide variety of risks that may be difficult to detect before the systems are widely used.

The values the AI Act purport to protect make the application of the ETTO principle even more difficult because of their abstract nature. The Act prohibits, among other things, solutions that manipulate its users or cause them physical or psychological harm (COM/2021/206, 44). We do not yet know enough about, say, techniques based on learning algorithms that determine what we see on our screens as we connect to the Internet. The greatest harm may not be physical or psychological but social and political. The AI Act does not explicitly define measures to keep us safe from these risks.

People are reluctant to read user manuals and they may also regard protective safety measures as impediments, especially if these regulations make it more difficult for them to use a service or device. The development of AI technology has been so rapid that people now adapt to new tools long before the decision makers can identify vulnerabilities requiring protection. Thoroughness does not appear as a virtue when people rush to make use of new opportunities.

The ETTO principle does not offer a tool that would help us find an easy solutions to the trade-offs we have to make between various design values and fundamental European values. Its usefulness lies in the internal paradox it makes apparent. Our desire to have the best quality at the lowest cost is a conceptual impossibility and must therefore be refuted. The features and characteristics of AI systems are great assets and deep vulnerabilities at the same time. Because we cannot attain one without the other, we must make choices, and acknowledge that pursuing some values often involves jeopardizing others.

References

Acosta, G.G., Lange, K.M., Lagos, D.E.P., Ortez, M.R.R.: Addressing human factors and ergonomics in design process, product life cycle, and innovation: Trends in consumer product design. In: Karwowski, W., Soares, M.M., Stanton, N.A. (eds.) Human Factors and Ergonomics in Consumer Product Design: Methods and Techniques, pp. 133–154. CRC Press, Boca Raton, London, New York (2011)

Ahram, T.Z., Karwowski, W. (eds.): Advances in Physical Ergonomics and Safety. CRC Press, Boca Raton, London, New York (2013)

Aims and Values. Principles, countries, history. Principles and values. The European Union. https://european-union.europa.eu/principles-countries-history/principles-and-values/aims-and-values_en. Accessed 31 Dec 2021

Anglim, J.: Why people don't read instructions? Psychology and Neuroscience, 4 December 2013. https://psychology.stackexchange.com/questions/4831/why-dont-people-readinstructions. Accessed 30 Dec 2021

Bolt, H.M.: Europäische Chemikaliengesetzgebung. Historische Entwicklung. In: Bundesgedusundheitsblatt – Gesundheitsforschung – Gesundheitsschutz 51:12, pp. 1381–1386. (2008). https://doi.org/10.1007/s00103-008-0711-6. Accessed 18 Jan 2021

Bradbury, D.: Usability v safety: how to design our way to better security. The Guardian, 26 November 2015. file:///C:/Users/jhallama/AppData/Local/Temp/SWD(2018)160_0.pdf. Accessed 15 Dec 2021

COM/2020/64. Report on the safety and liability implications of Artificial Intelligence, the Internet of Things and robotics. COM/2020/64. https://www.europarl.europa.eu/ReData/etudes/BRIE/2021/694206/EPRS_BRI(2021)694206_EN.pdf. Accessed 05 Jan 2022

COM/2021/202. Proposal for a regulation of the European parliament and of the council on machinery products. COM/2021/202 final. https://eur-lex.europa.eu/legal-content/EN/TXT/?uri=CELEX%3A52021PC0202. Accessed 25 jan 2022

COM/2021/206. Proposal for a regulation of the European parliament and of the council laying down harmonised rules on artificial intelligence (artificial intelligence act) and amending certain union legislative acts. COM/2021/206 final. https://eur-lex.europa.eu/legal-content/EN/TXT/?uri=CELEX%3A52021PC0206. Accessed 25 Jan 2022

Digital Agenda for Europe. Fact sheets for the European Union. European Parliament. https://www.europarl.europa.eu/factsheets/en/sheet/64/digital-agenda-for-europe

Directive 89/392/EEC of 14/06/89. https://op.europa.cu/cn/publication-detail/-/publication/1732310d-dac3-4a59-924c-aee07829f1f9/language-en. Accessed 03 Feb 2022

Directive 91/368/EEC. https://eur-lex.europa.eu/legal-content/en/ALL/?uri=CELEX%3A31991L0368. Accessed 03 Feb 2022

Directive 93/44/EEC. https://op.europa.eu/fi/publication-detail/-/publication/de316709-cdbb-48b2-93e5-2b5c7f60d5d8/language-en/format-PDFA1B. Accessed 03 Feb 2022

Directive 93/68/EEC. https://eur-lex.europa.eu/legal-content/EN/ALL/?uri=celex%3A31993L0068. Accessed 03 Feb 2022

Directive 95/16/EC. https://eur-lex.europa.eu/legal-content/EN/ALL/?uri=celex%3A31995L0016. Accessed 03 Feb 2022

Directive 2006/42/EC of the European parliament and of the council of 17 May 2006 on machinery, and amending Directive 95/16/EC. https://eur-lex.europa.eu/legal-content/EN/TXT/PDF/?uri=CELEX:32006L0042&from=EN. Accessed 31 Dec 2021

Directive 98/37/EC. https://eur-lex.europa.eu/legal-content/EN/ALL/?uri=celex:31998L0037. Accessed 03 Feb 2022

Ernst, H.: Success factors of new product development: a review of the empirical literature. Int. J. Manag. Rev. **4**(1), 1–40 (2002)

Europe fit for the Digital Age: Commission proposes new rules and actions for excellence and trust in Artificial Intelligence. European Commission (2021). https://ec.europa.eu/commission/presscorner/detail/en/ip_21_1682. Accessed 26 Jan 2022

GDPR General Data Protection Regulation. GDPR.EU. https://gdpr.eu/what-is-gdpr/. Accessed 24 Jan 2022

Gold-plating. Definitions. https://www.definitions.net/definition/gold-plating. Accessed 05 Jan 2022

Groen, M., Noyes, J.: Product design: user-centered versus a task-based approach. In: Karwowski, W., Soares, M.M., Stanton, N.A. (eds.) Human Factors and Ergonomics in Consumer Product Design: Methods and Techniques, pp. 405–414. CRC Press, Boca Raton, London, New York (2011)

Haider, H., Frensch, P.A.: The role of information reduction in skill acquisition. Cogn. Psychol. **30**(3), 304–337 (1996). https://doi.org/10.1006/cogp.1996.0009

Hollnagel/A: Hollnagel, E.: The ETTO Principle. https://erikhollnagel.com/ideas/etto-principle/. Accessed 14 Jan 2022

Hollnagel/B: Hollnagel, E.: The ETTO Principle. Efficiency-Thoroughness Trade-Off. One Web Media. https://erikhollnagel.com/onewebmedia/ETTO.pdf. Accessed 25 Jan 2022

Machinery Directive: Revision of Directive 2006/42/EC. Briefing 17-09-2021. (2021). https://www.europarl.europa.eu/thinktank/en/document/EPRS_BRI(2021)694206. Accessed 07 Jan 2022

Mauer, E., Proctor, C.: Techniques to translate design research into useful, usable, and desirable products. In: Karwowski, W., Soares, M.M., Stanton, N.A. (eds.) Human Factors and Ergonomics in Consumer Product Design: Methods and Techniques, pp. 3–19. CRC Press, Boca Raton, London, New York (2011)

Marrazzo, M.: People don't read manuals (2018). https://www.researchgate.net/publication/324106690_People_don%27t_read_manuals. Accessed 30 Dec 2021

New Legislative Framework. Internal Market, Industry, Entrepreneurship and SMEs. Single Market and Standards. European Commission. https://ec.europa.eu/growth/single-market/goods/new-legislative-framework_en. Accessed 25 Jan 2022

Nielsen, J.: Usability 101: Introduction to Usability. Nielsen Norman Group, 3 January 2021. https://www.nngroup.com/articles/usability-101-introduction-to-usability/. Accessed 28 Oct 2021

Nielsen, J., Budiu, R.: Mobile Usability. New Riders Press, Indianapolis (2012)

Reason, J.: The Human Contribution: Unsafe Acts, Accidents and Heroic Recoveries. Routledge, London, New York (2008)

Smith-Jackson, T.L., Hardianto, I., Chang, G.O.: Cultural ergonomics issues in consumer product design. In: Karwowski, W., Soares, M.M., Stanton, N.A. (eds.) Human Factors and Ergonomics in Consumer Product Design: Methods and Techniques, pp. 211–222. CRC Press, Boca Raton, London, New York (2011)

Stum, L.: Seven reasons people don't read instructions. Learning Stream. Lumaverse Technologies, 11 January 2017 (2017). https://www.learningstream.com/2017/11/01/people-dont-read-instructions/. Accessed 05 Jan 2022

The 'New Approach' Reference Material. European Committee for Standardization. 2019/6/4 (2019). https://boss.cen.eu/reference-material/guidancedoc/pages/newapproach/. Accessed on 04 Jan 2022

Incremental Unit Networks for Distributed, Symbolic Multimodal Processing and Representation

Mir Tahsin Imtiaz and Casey Kennington[✉]

Department of Computer Science, Boise State University,
1910 W University Dr., Boise, ID 83725, USA
tahsinimtiaz@u.boisestate.edu, caseykennington@boisestate.edu

Abstract. Incremental dialogue processing has been an important topic in spoken dialogue systems research, but the broader research community that makes use of language interaction (e.g., chatbots, conversational AI, spoken interaction with robots) have not adopted incremental processing despite research showing that humans perceive incremental dialogue as more natural. In this paper, we extend prior work that identifies the requirements for making spoken interaction with a system natural with the goal that our framework will be generalizable to many domains where speech is the primary method of communication. The Incremental Unit framework offers a model of incremental processing that has been extended to be multimodal, temporally aligned, enables real-time information updates, and creates complex network of information as a fine-grained information state. One challenge is that multimodal dialogue systems often have computationally expensive modules, requiring computation to be distributive. Most importantly, when speech is the means of communication, it brings the added expectation that systems understand what they (humans) say, but also that systems understand and respond without delay. In this paper, we build on top of the Incremental Unit framework and make it amenable to a distributive architecture made up of a robot and spoken dialogue system modules. To enable fast communication between the modules and to maintain module state histories, we compared two different implementations of a distributed Incremental Unit architecture. We compare both implementations systematically then with real human users and show that the implementation that uses an external attribute-value database is preferred, but there is some flexibility in which variant to use depending on the circumstances. This work offers the Incremental Unit framework as an architecture for building powerful, complete, and natural dialogue systems, specifically applicable to robots and multimodal systems researchers.

Keywords: Incremental · Multimodal · Dialogue · HRI · Distributed systems

1 Introduction

The most basic and fundamental way that people communicate with each other is spoken language, specifically speech in co-located settings [10], and it follows that co-located spoken interaction will become a common setting and communication medium

V. G. Duffy (Ed.): HCII 2022, LNCS 13320, pp. 344–363, 2022.
https://doi.org/10.1007/978-3-031-06018-2_24

that people expect to use when interacting with automated systems. However, being co-located introduces important challenges: not only do people expect a system to understand speech, but also multimodal cues such as gestures, pointing, and eye gaze. Multimodal systems that incorporate such streaming information from various information sources must make sense of that information to learn from its environment and interlocutor, and make decisions about what actions to take.

In this paper, we present our recent work towards building and evaluating a multimodal system that maintains a dynamic information state and a global record of the interaction history, ensuring fast and accurate communication mechanisms between modules in the system in a distributed environment. Our work builds on the recent work of [15] that identifies five requirements for "robot-ready" spoken dialogue systems (SDS), which we generalize here to all co-located multimodal spoken dialogue interaction. A dialogue system that works on a multi-modal agent must fulfill the following requirements:

1. **modular:** the system is composed of multiple modules, and robot modules can be integrated with the SDS
2. **multimodal:** the system can take in and integrate inputs from multiple sensors and produce actions with different affordances (e.g., produce an utterance or move a drive wheel)
3. **distributive:** modules are able to reliably and quickly communicate in distributed environments
4. **incremental:** modules in the system process received inputs as much as possible, as early as possible
5. **temporally aligned:** multiple sensor inputs must be aligned temporally with each other (i.e., aligned with respect to time).

We specifically focus on the *incremental* requirement which is a way of improving speed and responsiveness of systems. Incremental processing has been recently called for as a major requirement for coupling spoken dialogue systems (SDSs) with multimodal systems (i.e., robots) to make the interactions more natural [21]. For example, SDSs often make use of automatic speech recognizers (ASRs) that transcribe a continuous audio stream from a microphone into utterance strings. Many ASR engines perform *end-pointing* in that they begin recognition when voice activity is detected then continue recognizing until a minimal amount of silence is detected; only then do they process the recorded audio stream and produce the transcribed utterance. This poses a problem when used on co-located multimodal systems such as robots because people who interact with them using speech expect them to act without delay. In this paper, we address this issue by building on the **Incremental Unit (IU)** framework to make it more amenable to multimodal, robotic systems, explained in Sect. 3.1. Since its introduction [28], the IU conceptual framework for real-time processing on spoken dialogue systems (SDS) has been taken up by the SDS research community as a viable approach to natural interactive spoken dialogue between humans and machines, resulting in multiple systems and practical toolkits [4, 23]. The IU framework is suitable for creating dialogue systems that are multimodal, can be extended to temporally align information from different channels, and keeps track of ongoing dialogue to make the most natural decision. Moreover, due to the nature of the IU framework, information passed between modules is represented symbolically, making for a potentially useful representation of the state and understanding of the unfolding interaction.

However, the primary challenge with this incremental SDS framework is that it expects all modules to exist in the same process on a single machine—a requirement that is often not feasible on multimodal platforms because they often have multiple processors distributed across a physical network to handle the processing loads. Overcoming this challenge is the main goal of this paper.

We address this shortcoming by defining and implementing an architecture for incremental processing that allows distributed modules to access incremental information from the various modules of two disparate sets of SDS modules instantiated in *ReTiCo*, an incremental SDS framework written in Python, and the *platform for situated intelligence* (PSI), written in $C\#$. When combined within the architecture we explain below, these two systems together fulfill all five multimodal SDS requirements listed above and highlight the importance of the incremental and distributed requirements. In our experiments, we built a distributed SDS using the IU framework, performed an offline, performance evaluation (Experiment 1), and evaluated our SDS using the Anki Cozmo robot platform in a navigation and visual reference Human-Robot Interaction (HRI) task with human participants (Experiment 2). Importantly, the system resulted in positive impressions from the participants. Our results show that our architecture works well despite delays in a cloud-based ASR output pointing to the possibility that even delayed modules, when incremental, are better than end-pointing. The work presented in this paper is an important step towards broader dialogue capabilities between multimodal systems, including robots, and people.

In the following section, we explain work related to ours, then we explain the incremental SDS framework that we are using. We then describe our architecture (including explanations of ReTiCo and PSI), then we explain our experiments.

2   Related Work

Several SDS frameworks exist, each of which fulfill to some degree the above five requirements, and which have been tested on multimodal or robotic platforms. InproTK [4] is the closest to handle all of the requirements. InproTK is an implementation of the IU framework implementation (Java), which was extended to include distributive and multimodal processing [14] (though this caused issues with the connectedness with the IU framework as we explain below) and was further extended to include a form of temporal alignment [13], but it is dependent on a specific implementation of the IU framework. Moreover, InproTK has only been used in one simple robotic framework [11].

ReTiCo is another modular implementation of the IU framework (Python), recently extended to work distributively, works with multimodal sensors, and has been evaluated on multiple robot platforms [15]. However, ReTiCo does not have native support for temporal alignment. In contrast, the PSI framework is inherently modular, multimodal, temporally aligned at the level of the sensor-originating time, has been evaluated on robot platforms, and has several options for distributing computation [6]. However, the PSI framework does not yet build on any incremental framework–something we address here. We also point out [25] that focused on capturing interaction patterns in their system, including dialogue, but their model was not incremental.

Also similar to our work is the platform MultiBot presented in [22], but that model does not work incrementally nor does it consider temporal alignment. The OpenDial toolkit gives researchers the ability to model dialogue states and has been evaluated on robotic platforms [19], but its incrementality has not been systematically evaluated. PaMini [26] is a framework for mixed-initiative dialogue for robot platforms, but it is not incremental.

In no case does a single platform or framework address all five requirements (including ROS, an open source collection of software frameworks for robot software development). In this paper, we propose combining two of the platforms, PSI and ReTiCo, and address the issue of global sharing of incremental information.

3   Architecture: Distributed Incremental Unit Framework

In this section, we describe our architecture. We first explain the Incremental Unit framework, then the two platforms–ReTiCo and PSI–that we use. Following that, we describe how our architecture overcomes the shortcomings of the two platforms used in isolation and how it fulfills the five requirements of multimodal SDS.

3.1   The Incremental Unit Framework

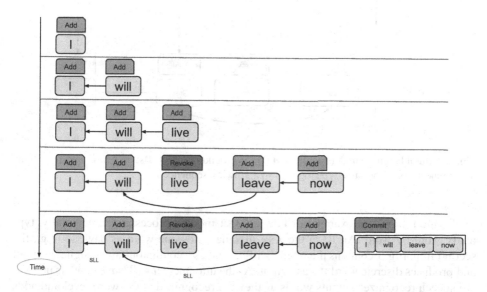

Fig. 1. Example of SLLs, and Add, Revoke and Commit operations for an incremental speech recognizer.

Following [14], the *Incremental Unit* (IU) framework [28] is a conceptual approach for incremental processing on SDSs. At its basis, the IU framework consists of a network of processing *modules*. Modules take in input data on their *left buffers*, process the input, then produce output on their *right buffers*. A critical part of the IU framework is how the data are packaged and processed. The data are packaged as the payload of *incremental units* (IUs) which are passed between modules—each IU holds a discrete amount of information. Another critical part of the framework is that the IUs themselves are interconnected via *same-level links* (SLL)—allowing the linking of IUs as a growing sequence, and *grounded-in links* (GRIN)—which allow that sequence to convey what IUs directly affect it. Ideally, IUs (e.g., produced from a sensor or processing module) can be guaranteed to be correct, but it is often the case that an IU that has been outputted to the next module needs to be updated in light of new information. To make this possible, the framework makes use of three operations: IUs can be *added* to the IU network, but can be later *revoked*, and also *committed* when a module can guarantee that an added IU will not be revoked.

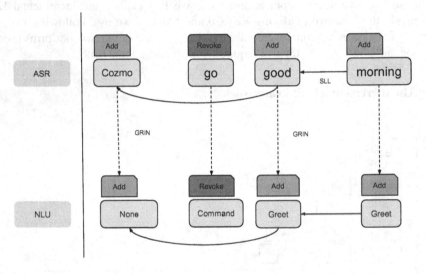

Fig. 2. Natural language understanding (NLU) IUs ground into ASR IUs; each has same-level links that connect IUs of the same type together in a growing sequence.

Figure 1 shows an example of how an ASR module processes incrementally, typically word-by-word. An IU in the ASR module holds one word as payload (e.g., the second IU in Fig. 1 contains the word "will"). It takes a continuous audio signal as input and produces discrete word IUs as output. As the utterance *"I will leave now"* is uttered, the speech recognizer outputs words as they are recognized at the word level and adds them to the IU network. The recognizer misrecognizes the word *live*, but in light of new information from the unfolding utterance, revokes *live* and replaces it with *leave*. Horizontal arrows show SLLs; i.e., how the IUs are related to each other temporally, and at the end of the utterance, when the recognizer knows it will no longer revoke, it marks all of the IUs (the uttered sentence) as committed.

Figure 2 showcases the GRIN links between the ASR and a natural language under-standing (NLU) module: the ASR module outputs word IUs to the natural language understanding module which, in lock-step with the ASR module, outputs a semantic abstraction over the utterance that is useful to downstream decision-making modules; the language understanding IUs *ground into* (GRIN) the ASR IUs as their existence gives rise to the corresponding language understanding IUs—all of which are added to an ever-growing network of IUs linked through SLLs and GRINs.

The IU framework can take advantage of up-to-date information, yet have the poten-tial to function in such a way that users perceive it as more natural. This manner of pro-cessing should not be surprising as psycholinguistic research has shown that humans comprehend utterances as they unfold and do not wait until the end of an utterance to begin the comprehension process, particularly in multimodal, co-located settings, like those between people and robots [31]. Moreover, it has been shown that people per-ceive incremental SDSs being more natural than non-incremental systems [1,2,17,29] and offer a more human-like experience [9], thus motivating the adoption of incremen-tal SDS for human-robot interaction settings. All of the modules that we use in this research are realized as modules in an incremental SDS.

3.2   The IU Network as Dynamic Information State

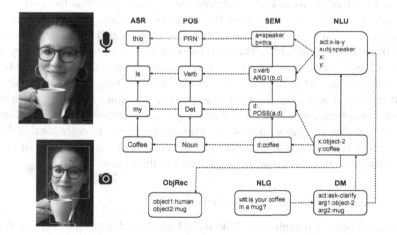

Fig. 3. Example of multimodal information state representation represented as a network of IUs. Each node is an IU; nodes can either be connected via same-level links (solid lines) or grounded-in links (dashed lines).

An incremental SDS creates a complex network of information, adding, relating, and updating micro-information with each other, generating a holistic representation of an entire interaction. Each IU created by any given module can use all information accessible to it through the IU network. For example, Fig. 2 shows how a *"Greet"* language understanding dialogue act is found not only by traversing the SLL, but also by following GRINs and traversing the SLL from a different IU type. This traversal option may or may not be used depending on how each module is designed. The entire IU network can be seen as a traversable growing representation of the unfolding interaction between a system and a human and can be interpreted as a representation of a fine-grained information state [18].

To further illustrate, Fig. 3 shows an example of a multimodal system that has an ASR, an object recognizer (ObjRec), a part-of-speech tagger (POS), a semantic parser (SEM), a natural language understanding (NLU) module, a dialogue manager (DM) that makes decisions about which action the system should take next, and a natural language generation (NLG) module that produces system utterances. The same-level links (solid lines) show how IUs in a single module connect to each other over time, and the grounded-in links (dashed lines) show how information from a module effects the processing of another module. For example, by the time the user said *"this is"*, the POS, SEM, and NLU processed in lock-step with the incremental ASR, resulting in the NLU predicting the dialogue act and what is expected next—information which is then filled once the user finishes the noun phrase *"my coffee"*. Based on the NLU IUs, the DM makes a decision to ask a clarification about the object as it heard the word *"coffee"*, but ObjRec observed a "mug".

The dynamic updates happen as the utterance unfolds. This, we conjecture, can represent a kind of *gestalt* that changes dynamically; i.e., taken together, the entire network of IUs and their relations to each other are more informative than the individual IUs or individual communication between the modules, and these representations change dynamically (i.e., more information and relationship between them are revealed in real-time as the interaction unfolds). The usefulness of this representation goes beyond the content of the IU network itself; prior work has shown that the *add* and *revoke* operations that alter the network are also informative to the system. For example, when an ASR revokes a word but the system has already formulated and begun a spoken response, the system can produce a disfluency (e.g., *uh*), followed by a correction [7].

This highlights the importance of our work in this paper: in order for this dynamic information state to be available, the IU network must maintain the history of the interaction even when modules are distributed across multiple processes.

3.3   Platform for Situated Intelligence (PSI)

PSI [6] is a framework (developed at Microsoft Research) that affords easy development and study of multimodal and integrative AI systems. PSI works by providing a parallel programming model centered around data streams, enables easy development and connection of modules while keeping the performance properties of a natively written system, and encapsulates various AI technologies allowing quick composition of complex AI applications. One of the main reasons to bring PSI into our research is because it addresses the temporal alignment requirement for a multimodal SDS and adds to that the capability of meaningful early stream fusion. Temporal alignment is important for multimodal interaction to realize correlation between different sources of data (e.g., to understand the question *"What color is the object in front of you?"* a system needs visual and auditory inputs to be aligned together to understand the context of the inter-action). This feature has not been introduced before in any other frameworks as effi-ciently as PSI (including ROS). In addition to this, PSI offers tools and APIs enabling multimodal data visualization and analysis in real-time.

Although PSI is designed to handle continuous sensor inputs natively, it does not adhere to the IU framework. We extended PSI to be amenable to the IU framework by adding a requirement that all output from all modules must be packaged as IUs, and that each unit must maintain SLLs and GRINs. Each IU also has an IU-creation timestamp and whether or not they are *add, revoke,* or *commit* edits to the IU network. With these additions, PSI can function as an IU framework directly. However, this alone does not address the problem that a network of IUs generated by PSI will be accessible across distributed modules. To address this, we turn to ReTiCo.

3.4 ReTiCo

ReTiCo [23] is a SDS platform based on the IU framework. ReTiCo enables the con-struction of incremental SDSs providing a wide range of incremental modules. ReTiCo is user-friendly and allows construction of a SDS with a few lines of code initializing modules and connecting them according to their left and right buffers. While ReTiCo is an implementation of an easy-to-use standard IU framework, it is missing some of the key features required for research for multimodal SDS; namely, it is missing the appro-priate mechanisms that can work with concurrent data streams coming from different modules and standard data storage facilities for data analysis.

The motivations for using both PSI and ReTiCo are to fulfill all five multimodal SDS requirements with the added benefit of affording researchers the ability to use mod-ules written in $C\#$ as well as Python. However, as noted above, the requirement of incrementality using the IU framework and the requirement of distributive modules are at odds with each other because the IU network needs to be maintained and remain accessible to all distributed modules. Addressing this problem is one of the primary contributions of this paper.

3.5 Maintaining the IU Network Across Distributed Modules

As the two platforms are written in different programming languages and various mod-ules distributed across potentially multiple instances of each platform, communica-tion between the modules needs to be fast and reliable. Both platforms have bindings for ROS which HRI researchers are familiar with, but we opted to use ZeroMQ as a message-passing bus because of its speed and because it is easy to integrate in many programming languages.

Both PSI and ReTiCo have multiple modules that create IUs then add or revoke them. Modules are responsible for connecting the IUs together as a sequence using SLLs and, more importantly, maintaining which input IUs that current IUs ground into (i.e., GRINs). This is impossible if a distributed module created the originating IU that must now be grounded into, though the module itself is a remote process. Addressing this is important as modules often need to traverse the IU network to make decisions about processing. We maintain the IU network across distributed modules by creating a query language that acts as a mediator between modules and compare two different storage mechanisms accessible to all modules—a fast database *Redis* and a data structure native to PSI. We first explain the query language, then explain the two storage variants.

3.6   IU Network Query Language

The query language is simple: storage mechanisms simply store IUs, their edit types (i.e., add, revoke, or commit), SLLs and GRIN information, and the timestamp. Each IU has a globally unique ID that identifies it, making storage access faster and more direct. IUs are transported across ZeroMQ as serialized objects (i.e., JSON) with unique identifiers for SLL and GRIN references. This can be achieved using four functions that are accessible from any module:

– **InsertIU:** Insert an IU to the IU network (i.e., the storage)
– **RetrieveIU:** Given the ID or key of the IU[, return that particular IU
– **GetPreviousIU:** Given the ID or key of an IU, return the previous IU of that partic-
  ular IU
– **GetGroundedInIU:** Given the ID of a particular IU, return the grounded IU of a
  particular IU

3.7   Shared Redis Storage

In this storage variant, we attempted a shared, third-party data storage for fast access. One of the fundamental issues in any distributed system is achieving sequential consistency with concurrent operations. In any given IU network, no IU is generated before the IU it links to (either via SLL or GRIN), and modules have obvious latency between them. Therefore, an implementation of a shared data storage for a distributed IU network will likely achieve sequential consistency since we are only dealing with one logical data server. For this approach, we used the popular data-structure-project Redis [8], a key-value database implementation known to be relatively fast, efficient, and supports shared memory [30].

3.8   Native PSI Storage

We also implemented a construction of the entire IU network in a single data structure directly accessible to one of the platforms, though indirectly accessible via the query language to the other platform. We opted to use PSI to maintain the IU network because of fast data storage capabilities native to C#. In this way, PSI holds and views the entire IU network directly, whereas ReTiCo queries PSI to retrieve certain information from the network when needed.

4   Experiment 1: Systematic Evaluation of Architecture

The first experiment focuses on the two IU network storage approaches. We systematically construct a distributed multimodal SDS and evaluate it for consistency and efficiency given each network storage approach.

4.1 PSI **Modules**

As shown in Fig. 4, the total network has been split between the two frameworks, each doing a share of the processing. In the network, PSI is responsible for voice activity detection, meaningful stream fusion of incoming foreign and native data, object detection from image data, and speech recognition from audio data. Furthermore, as PSI can perform temporal alignment of sensor streams, we used PSI to fuse incoming microphone stream received from ReTiCo with voice activity detection stream generated in PSI. This demonstrates that meaningful stream fusion can be done in the distributed environment. We used Azure Cognitive Speech services to implement a speech recognition module that produces word-level IUs. The object detection module uses the Google MaskRCNN for proper object detection on camera streams.

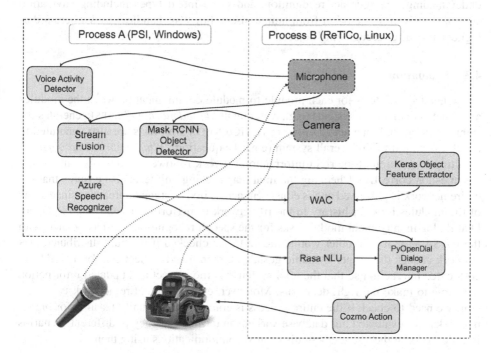

Fig. 4. Overview of the multi-framework, multimodal, incremental, distributed network; the two processes communicate with each other using ZeroMQ. All modules pass IUs to connected modules, and all IUs are stored in either Redis or native PSI storage mechanisms.

4.2 ReTiCo **Modules**

ReTiCo has existing implementations of several common SDS modules; we use ReTiCo in the network to support those modules. Specifically, ReTiCo is responsible for reading sensor inputs (microphone and camera), natural language understanding, dialog management, and sending the final signal to the robot to produce an action. The RASA NLU module [5] in ReTiCo receives ASR IUs from PSI and generates IUs with a computable, semantic abstraction over the unfolding utterance (i.e., a key-value semantic frame). The output from RASA is sent to PyOpenDial [12,20] module for dialogue management; i.e., decisions as to what actions–including robot and dialogue actions–to take next.

The Keras Object Feature Extraction module takes in IUs from Google MaskR-CNN in PSI to produce a vector that acts as object representations into the words-as-classifiers (WAC) [16]. In addition to the IUs from Keras Feature Extractor, WAC also receives ASR results from PSI. WAC is a grounded model of lexical semantics that can link uttered words to the physical world (e.g., *"pick up the red box"* would use WAC to resolve which object is the red box in a scene). The output from WAC is also sent to the PyOpenDial module for dialog management. Taken together, RASA handles language understanding, dialogue act recognition, and some intent types including navigation commands given to the robot from human users, but WAC handles cases where a dialogue act requires recognizing objects.

4.3 Evaluation

We generated unit tests for each module-to-module communication when the modules are situated in different systems (e.g., ASR output *"Good morning"* in PSI generates the right and final dialogue act *"Greet"* in ReTiCo NLU). Unit tests are also generated to check the output of the overall system (e.g., the question *"What color is that object?"* resulting in creation of the right information network followed by the robot answering the question correctly). Checking the final output using unit tests also ensures that the entire network is preserved and is consistent across both storage approaches since some of the modules look for history in the IU network to perform correctly (e.g., PyOpen-Dial dialog management module asks for the speech recognition word associated with the RASA NLU IU). In other words, the unit tests checked if the built distributed SDS network creates the proper dynamic gestalt we mentioned in Sect. 3.2 for a simulated co-located interaction so that the total system has the correct and updated information real-time to make the right decisions. Moreover, even if the entire network is consistent, we need to check if the entire process is efficient and actually feasible for bigger networks. We evaluated our database variants in terms of latency in different scenarios in order to learn the efficiency of distributed communications using them.

4.4 Results

Table 1 shows the latency of all the functions available for the IU network query language. We can see that either of the storage types is preferable to the native process (the native type storage was implemented in PSI while the shared storage was hosted in the same machine as ReTiCo). However, both types mentioned have very low communication latency for retrieval of data overall from the IU network. This demonstrates that we can achieve an efficient distributed IU network. In other words, we can establish a full incremental and distributed SDS using this framework.

Experiment 1 establishes that our implementations work in a stand-alone SDS. In Experiment 2, we extend the SDS to work with robot modules.

Table 1. Latency of different IU store functions for PSI (top) and ReTiCo (bottom)

Function	Store type	Latency
RetrieveIU	Native (C#)	0.003 ms
PSI	Shared (Redis)	6.249ms
GetPreviousIU	Native (C#)	0.007 ms
PSI	Shared (Redis)	12.513ms
GetGroundedInIU	Native (C#)	0.005 ms
PSI	Shared (Redis)	10.498 ms
RetrieveIU	Native (C#)	15.661 ms
ReTiCo	Shared (Redis)	0.098 ms
GetPreviousIU	Native (C#)	16.659 ms
ReTiCo	Shared (Redis)	0.331 ms
GetGroundedInIU	Native (C#)	16.570 ms
ReTiCo	Shared (Redis)	0.163 ms

5 Experiment 2: Live, Interactive Study with Human Participants

This second experiment moves to actual human-robot interaction in order to evaluate the system made up of SDS and robot modules that operate on the distributed IU network in order to evaluate the system in a practical setting. Although the different storage variants explained above work effectively with offline load tests, it is important to evaluate how all the different complexities of the modules affect interaction with humans when we deploy the distributed system on a real robot. The goal of this experiment is to verify that our system works in an interactive, incremental dialogue task by evaluating how well a robot performs a task from human instructions as well as the human perceptions of the robot. This experiment confirms the potentiality of the IU framework for generating a dynamic information state efficiently and consistently because only then an actual interaction between a robot and human in a co-located task setting will receive positive feedback, Moreover, since the effectiveness of incremental systems over non-incremental systems is already proven, we focused on observing the optimal way of distributed incremental unit network implementation instead of comparing with a non-incremental system.

5.1 Task, Setting, and System

We opted to use the Anki Cozmo (now owned by Digital Dream labs) robot. Cozmo has track wheels for locomotion, a simple lift, a moveable head with a camera and OLED animated eyes, and a simple speech synthesizer with a young-sounding voice. Moreover, Cozmo already has bindings for ReTiCo and has a Python SDK. These attributes make the robot suitable for capturing human perception of the robot's anthropomorphic characteristics. Figure 5 shows the task setting of the Cozmo robot for our experiment design. Cozmo is placed by the experimenter in the middle of a table with several

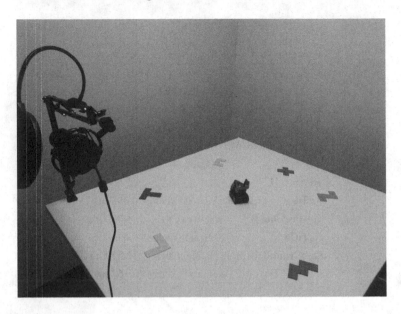

Fig. 5. Cozmo robot in its task setting. Participants were seated near the microphone (left) where they greeted Cozmo, then gave it instructions to navigate to objects and ask about their colors. Participants tracked how many times Cozmo successfully "understood" their requests.

objects of various shapes and colors randomly placed around it on the table. The goal is for Cozmo to navigate to as many objects as possible and identify their color. Participants were tasked with greeting Cozmo (e.g., *hello*), helping Cozmo navigate (e.g., *turn left, drive straight, look up*), and ask about colors (e.g., *what color is that?* or *is that red?*).

There are two input modalities: speech via microphone and images via Cozmo's camera (we can also track the internal states of Cozmo like wheel speed, lift height, head rotation, but it wasn't necessary for this task setup). We use the Azure Cognitive Speech Services API on PSI for incremental ASR, MaskRCNN for object detection (also in PSI), VGG19 to represent the objects, WAC for grounded color recognition, RASA for mapping from utterances to dialogue acts (including navigation), PyOpenDial for making decisions, and an action module that controls Cozmo's actions including driving, lift, head, and synthesized speech controlled by PyOpenDial.

For this second experiment, we then performed an A/B test using the same system as mentioned in Sect. 4, but compared our two different implementations of our IU shared storage—Redis and the native PSI implementation.

5.2 Participant Recruitment

We recruited fourteen study participants (following COVID restrictions) to interact with the Cozmo robot two times, once for each setting. After the participant signed an informed consent, the experimenter explained that the task was to help Cozmo navigate close to and identify objects' colors. The participant was then given ten minutes to interact with Cozmo and keep track of the number of times Cozmo correctly moved to and identified objects. Following each ten-minute interaction, the participants were asked to fill out a questionnaire that contained all the questions from the Godspeed Questionnaire [3] (a likert-scaled questionnaire with 24 questions ranging from negative to positive ratings of a robot's anthropomorphism, animacy, likeability, perceived intelligence, and perceived safety) along with additional questions related to our particular format of task setting. The additional questions are as follows:

- How many times did the robot respond (and correctly) to your request/command?
- How many times did the robot correctly identify an object's color?
- How many times were you able to help the robot make it to the desired object?
- Do you think the robot responded to you within reasonable amount of time?

Participants were randomly assigned the Redis or PSI (native) implementation first. The experimenter remained present near the task setting to monitor the state of the robot, troubleshoot any problems that might arise, and answer any questions or queries the participants might have over the course of the interaction with the robot. The experimenter was permitted to offer a constrained set of coaching tips to the participant during the interaction. Following each interaction, the user moved to the experimenter's seat to complete the related questionnaire on the experimenter's laptop. Following the completion of both interactions and subsequent questionnaires, the participant was paid a nominal compensation.

The study participants were mostly university students recruited from the department of Computer Science at Boise State University, although nearly one third of the participants were from different disciplines. Five of the participants were female, nine were male; 57% of the participants were native speakers, and the remaining participants were near-native.

5.3   Results

Table 2. Mean of participant responses for task-specific questions.

Question	Redis	Native
How many times did the robot respond to your request/command?	4.36	4.21
How many times did the robot respond correctly to your request/command?	4.43	4.36
How many times did the robot correctly identify an object color?	4.43	4.21
How many times were you able to help the robot find the desired object?	4.79	4.43
Do you think the robot responded to you within reasonable amount of time?	3.98	3.79

Table 2 and 3 show responses for the questions in the overall questionnaire where the values range from one to five (one being the most negative and five being the most positive). Table 2 specifically shows the responses for the "task-setting" specific questions; i.e., measures for how well the robot performed its tasks objectively. There are not big discrepancies here, though the responses favor the Redis implementation. The participant responses to the subjective Godspeed questionnaire in Table 3, however, tell a more mixed story. The responses are sorted into two bins—preference for Redis (top) and Native (bottom). Though there are some cases where either implementation is preferred, the results are not significant enough to conclude that the participants perceived any real difference between the two implementations. This is a positive result as it could mean (as a negative cannot be proven) that developers could use either implementation depending on their needs, and it will not affect the outcome of the task. This forms a basis that our two implementations worked well generally, and the overall SDS still receives positive reaction from the users despite choosing a cloud-based ASR—as long as it is incremental—which in addition adds to the importance and efficiency of the IU framework.

Table 3. Mean of participant responses for Godspeed questions; top section shows responses preferring Redis, bottom section shows responses preferring the Native variant.

Question	Redis	Native
Fake/Normal	3.79	3.50
Stagnant/Lively	3.57	3.36
Mechanical/Organic	2.08	2.07
Inert/Interactive	3.93	3.86
Apathetic/Responsive	3.86	3.57
Unpleasant/Pleasant	4.50	4.43
Incompetent/Competent	3.79	3.64
Ignorant/Knowledgeable	3.79	3.57
Foolish/Sensible	3.57	3.43
Dislike/Like	4.36	4.50
Unfriendly/Friendly	4.21	4.29
Unkind/Kind	3.86	3.93
Awful/Nice	4.43	4.50
Unintelligent/Intelligent	3.50	3.64

Table 4 shows how objective task measures correlate with participants' subjective impressions of the robots from the Godspeed questionnaires. The correlation is calculated using Pearson correlation coefficient. This table shows a more nuanced result as it shows how task success affects important perceptions of robots, and here we see which implementation is favored (even though, of course, participants did not know anything about the differences in the underlying implementations). The Redis implementation has a high positive correlation with the number of times an object's color was correctly identified and how *responsible* the participants perceived the robot. Also high for

Redis was the time response with *naturalness, elegance, friendliness*, and whether or not they liked the robot or thought the robot was nice. Taken together, timely incremental responses give participants a positive impression of the robot, even to the degree that it makes them assign *responsibility* (a slow-to-respond robot is seen as irresponsible) and if the robot is *nice* and *likable*.

Table 4. Correlations between task measures (number of correctly identified colors–color; number of correctly executed navigations–nav; general responsiveness–response; timely execution–time) and subjective scores from the questionnaire for correlations above 0.5 for at least one of the implementations (Native and Redis).

Task measure	Question	Redis	Native
Color	Responsible/irresponsible	0.56	0.27
Color	Friendly/unfriendly	0.34	0.55
Color	Begin calm/agitated	0.23	0.78
Nav	Natural/fake	−0.17	0.63
Nav	Conscious/unconscious	−0.34	0.6
Nav	Nice/awful	0.06	0.55
Nav	Responsible/irresponsible	0.04	0.82
Nav	Sensible/foolish	−0.27	0.59
Response	Competent/incompetent	0.4	0.52
Response	Lively/stagnant	0.28	0.52
Response	Interactive/inert	0.2	0.47
Response	Friendly/unfriendly	0.22	0.7
Response	Competent/incompetent	0.05	0.65
Response	Knowledgeable/ignorant	0.05	0.5
Response	Responsible/irresponsible	0.353	0.76
Response	Sensible/foolish	0.28	0.46
Response	Begin calm/agitated	−0.17	0.52
Response	End calm/agitated	0.00	0.66
Time	Attracted	0.3	0.59
Time	End calm/agitated	0.21	0.65
Time	Natural/fake	0.57	0.35
Time	Elegant/rigid (movement)	0.56	0.19
Time	Like/dislike	0.61	0.56
Time	Friendly/unfriendly	0.55	0.7
Time	Nice/awful	0.67	0.28

All other correlations were higher for the Native implementation, showing that it was not simply the case that some participants who happened to interact with the robot for one setting were judging more harshly than for the other implementation. Table 4 shows that there are some correlations that are not only high (positive values denote the positive attributes), they are significantly higher than the Redis correlation for numbers of correctly identified objects by color with the participant beginning the interaction feeling calm; similarly for numbers of correct navigation with *natural, conscious, sensible*; responsiveness with *friendly, responsible*, beginning and ending calm; and timeliness of executions with ending calm. Taken together, the participants seem to be more forgiving of Redis as their responses only correlate with some of the task measures, and the Redis implementation yielded similar objective results in terms of task success, but the Native PSI implementation is highly correlated with several of the task measures. We take this to mean that the slightly slower responses of the Native implementation were noticeable to task fluidity, and that affected how the participants perceived the robot as *natural, sensible, friendly*, and how calm it made them feel. Even the small differences in latency caused the participants to be more critical of the Native implementation. In other words, better performance is desirable although performance difference with another approach is minor. These results verify to some extent the results in [24] and [27] that showed how robot movements affect human perceptions of those robots–in this case, any processing delay in understanding and responding to spoken utterances was perceived negatively.

These results highlight the importance of incremental processing in robot-ready SDS. That is, when humans interact with systems that wait as input is received, their expectations of those systems diminish, resulting in the potential for interactions that are not natural. We interpret these results to mean that incremental processing can help improve natural dialogue with robots.

6   Conclusion

In this paper, we demonstrated the utility of the IU framework for building a multimodal SDS. We addressed and fulfilled all requirements of multimodal dialogue by solving the issue of maintaining a distributed IU network across the ReTiCo and PSI frameworks for SDS. We emphasized the importance of the capability of the IU framework of creating a holistic representation of an interaction in a multimodal setting despite being distributed. We showed that an implementation based on the Redis attribute-value database can be used to solve the problem of distributive IUs, but we also observe that the Native C# storage implementation in the PSI was less preferred or viewed less positively in Experiment 2 from the human participants, given the setting and task of interacting with an Anki Cozmo robot. As an increasing amount of research and development of multimodal, spoken dialogue systems, and more general models for machine learning and deep learning are written and maintained in Python, our work makes it easier for researchers and developers to use ReTiCo in conjunction with PSI for adding SDS capabilities to their multimodal systems. These two frameworks connected together with the extended IU framework is now a useful tool to the multimodal SDS community to build appropriate and efficient SDSs that are incremental, distributed, and multimodal, and can be used to carry out important and significant research.

For future work, we will evaluate our system on more robotic platforms under more varied tasks that require more dialogue between the robot and humans. Our framework also does not include a systematic way of generating natural language utterances; for now, verbal responses must be template-based.

References

1. Aist, G., et al.: Software architectures for incremental understanding of human speech. In: Proceedings of CSLP, pp. 1922–1925 (2006)
2. Asri, L.E., Laroche, R., Pietquin, O., Khouzaimi, H.: NASTIA: negotiating appointment setting interface. In: Proceedings of LREC, pp. 266–271 (2014)
3. Bartneck, C., Kulić, D., Croft, E., Zoghbi, S.: Measurement instruments for the anthropomorphism, animacy, likeability, perceived intelligence, and perceived safety of robots. Int. J. Soc. Robot. 1(1), 71–81 (2009)
4. Baumann, T., Schlangen, D.: The InproTK 2012 release. In: NAACL-HLT Workshop on Future Directions and Needs in the Spoken Dialog Community: Tools and Data (SDCTD 2012), pp. 29–32 (2012)
5. Bocklisch, T., Faulkner, J., Pawlowski, N., Nichol, A.: Rasa: open source language understanding and dialogue management. In: Proceedings of the 31st Conference on Neural Information Processing Systems (2017). http://alborz-geramifard.com/workshops/nips17-Conversational-AI/Papers/17nipsw-cai-rasa.pdf, http://arxiv.org/abs/1712.05181
6. Bohus, D., Andrist, S., Jalobeanu, M.: Rapid development of multimodal interactive systems: a demonstration of platform for situated intelligence. In: Proceedings of the 19th ACM International Conference on Multimodal Interaction, pp. 493–494 (2017)
7. Buß, O., Schlangen, D.: DIUM-an incremental dialogue manager that can produce self-corrections. In: Proceedings of SemDial 2011 (Los Angelogue) (2011)
8. Carlson, J.L.: Redis in Action. Manning Publications Co. (2013)
9. Edlund, J., Gustafson, J., Heldner, M., Hjalmarsson, A.: Towards human-like spoken dialogue systems. Speech Commun. 50(8–9), 630–645 (2008). https://doi.org/10.1016/j.specom.2008.04.002
10. Fillmore, C.J.: Pragmatics and the description of discourse. Radical Pragma. 143–166 (1981)
11. Hough, J., Schlangen, D.: It's not what you do, it's how you do it: grounding uncertainty for a simple robot. In: Proceedings of the 2017 Conference on Human-Robot Interaction (HRI2017) (2017)
12. Jang, Y., Lee, J., Park, J., Lee, K.H., Lison, P., Kim, K.E.: PyOpenDial: a python-based domain-independent toolkit for developing spoken dialogue systems with probabilistic rules. In: Proceedings of the 2019 Conference on Empirical Methods in Natural Language Processing and the 9th International Joint Conference on Natural Language Processing (EMNLP-IJCNLP): System Demonstrations, pp. 187–192. Association for Computational Linguistics, Hong Kong, China, November 2019. https://doi.org/10.18653/v1/D19-3032, https://www.aclweb.org/anthology/D19-3032
13. Kennington, C., Han, T., Schlangen, D.: Temporal alignment using the incremental unit framework. In: Proceedings of the 19th ACM International Conference on Multimodal Interaction, ICMI 2017, pp. 297–301. ACM, New York (2017). https://doi.org/10.1145/3136755.3136769
14. Kennington, C., Kousidis, S., Schlangen, D.: InproTKs: a toolkit for incremental situated processing. In: Proceedings of the 15th Annual Meeting of the Special Interest Group on Discourse and Dialogue (SIGDIAL), pp. 84–88. Association for Computational Linguistics, Philadelphia (2014). http://www.aclweb.org/anthology/W14-4312
15. Kennington, C., Moro, D., Marchand, L., Carns, J., McNeill, D.: rrSDS: towards a robot-ready spoken dialogue system. In: Proceedings of the 21st Annual SIGdial Meeting on Discourse and Dialogue. Association for Computational Linguistics, Virtual (2020)

16. Kennington, C., Schlangen, D.: Simple learning and compositional application of perceptually grounded word meanings for incremental reference resolution. In: Proceedings of the 53rd Annual Meeting of the Association for Computational Linguistics and the 7th International Joint Conference on Natural Language Processing (Volume 1: Long Papers), pp. 292–301. Association for Computational Linguistics, Beijing, July 2015. https://doi.org/10.3115/v1/P15-1029, https://www.aclweb.org/anthology/P15-1029

17. Kennington, C., Schlangen, D.: Supporting spoken assistant systems with a graphical user interface that signals incremental understanding and prediction state. In: Proceedings of the 17th Annual Meeting of the Special Interest Group on Discourse and Dialogue, pp. 242–251. Association for Computational Linguistics, Los Angeles, September 2016. http://www.aclweb.org/anthology/W16-3631

18. Kennington, C., Schlangen, D.: Incremental unit networks for multimodal, fine-grained information state representation. In: Proceedings of the 1st Workshop on Multimodal Semantic Representations (MMSR), pp. 89–94. Association for Computational Linguistics, Groningen, Netherlands, June 2021. https://aclanthology.org/2021.mmsr-1.8

19. Lison, P., Kennington, C.: OpenDial: a toolkit for developing spoken dialogue systems with probabilistic rules. In: 54th Annual Meeting of the Association for Computational Linguistics, ACL 2016 - System Demonstrations (2016)

20. Lison, P., Kennington, C.: Incremental processing for a neural conversational model. In: Proceedings of SemDial (2017)

21. Marge, M., Espy-Wilson, C., Ward, N.: Spoken language interaction with robots: research issues and recommendations, report from the NSF future directions workshop. arXiv preprint arXiv:2011.05533 (2020)

22. Marge, M., et al.: A research platform for multi-robot dialogue with humans. In: Proceedings of the 2019 Conference of the North American Chapter of the Association for Computational Linguistics (Demonstrations), pp. 132–137. Association for Computational Linguistics, Minneapolis, Minnesota (2019). https://aclanthology.org/N19-4023, https://doi.org/10.18653/v1/N19-4023

23. Michael, T., Möller, S.: ReTiCo: an open-source framework for modeling real-time conversations in spoken dialogue systems. Studientexte Sprachkommun.: Elektron. Sprachsignalverarbeitung 2019, 134–140 (2019)

24. Novikova, J., Ren, G., Watts, L.: It's not the way you look, it's how you move: validating a general scheme for robot affective behaviour. In: Abascal, J., Barbosa, S., Fetter, M., Gross, T., Palanque, P., Winckler, M. (eds.) INTERACT 2015. LNCS, vol. 9298, pp. 239–258. Springer, Cham (2015). https://doi.org/10.1007/978-3-319-22698-9_16

25. Peltason, J., Riether, N., Wrede, B., Lütkebohle, I.: Talking with robots about objects. In: Proceedings of the Seventh Annual ACM/IEEE International Conference on Human-Robot Interaction - HRI 2012, p. 479. 7th ACM/IEEE Conference on Human-Robot-Interaction (2012)

26. Peltason, J., Wrede, B.: Pamini: a framework for assembling mixed-initiative human-robot interaction from generic interaction patterns. In: Proceedings of the SIGDIAL 2010 Conference, pp. 229–232. Association for Computational Linguistics, Tokyo, September 2010. https://www.aclweb.org/anthology/W10-4341

27. Plane, S., Marvasti, A., Egan, T., Kennington, C.: Predicting perceived age: both language ability and appearance are important. In: Proceedings of SigDial (2018)

28. Schlangen, D., Skantze, G.: A general, abstract model of incremental dialogue processing. Dialogue Discour. 2, 83–111 (2011). https://pub.uni-bielefeld.de/record/2095091

29. Skantze, G., Schlangen, D.: Incremental dialogue processing in a micro-domain. In: Proceedings of the 12th Conference of the European Chapter of the Association for Computational Linguistics on EACL 2009 (April), pp. 745–753 (2009). https://doi.org/10.3115/1609067.1609150, http://portal.acm.org/citation.cfm?doid=1609067.1609150

30. Sun, S., Gong, J., Zomaya, A.Y., Wu, A.: A distributed incremental information acquisition model for large-scale text data. Clust. Comput. **22**(1), 2383–2394 (2017). https://doi.org/10.1007/s10586-017-1498-8

31. Tanenhaus, M.K., Spivey-Knowlton, M.J.: Integration of visual and linguistic information in spoken language comprehension. Science **268**(5217), 1632 (1995). https://doi.org/10.1126/science.7777863

Use of Virtual Reality for Safety Training: A Systematic Review

Sameeran G. Kanade$^{(\boxtimes)}$ and Vincent G. Duffy

Purdue University, West Lafayette, IN 47906, USA
{kanade,duffy}@purdue.edu

Abstract. The purpose of this study was to explore the use of virtual reality in safety training. This study used various data analysis tools to perform a systematic literature review to explore the use of virtual reality for safety training. Metadata was extracted from various databases like Scopus, google scholar through Harzings' Publish or Perish, and web of science. This data was then analyzed using VOSviewer, MAXQDA, BibExcel and Citespace. Mendeley was used to generate a bibliography. The review showed that virtual reality can be used effectively for safety training. Various studies prove that virtual reality training is superior to traditional training techniques and can actively engage learners leading to better learning outcomes. Some of the limitations of this technology like access to head-mounted displays (HMDs), language barriers and evaluation techniques have also been reviewed. Ideas for future work in this topic area have been proposed. This article demonstrates the use of various bibliometric analysis tools for a systematic literature review and discusses the potential of VR for safety training in the near future.

Keywords: Virtual reality · Safety training · VOSviewer · MAXQDA · Citespace · BibExcel · Mendeley

1 Introduction

The ability to identify risks and gauge the magnitude of risks depends on the effectiveness of the safety training that an employee receives. Training with low engagement has a negative impact on worker safety. Researchers have started exploring the use of AR/VR technologies to make the content of safety training programs more engaging (Sacks et al. 2013). The focus of using these technologies is to enhance ergonomics, risk identification, skill transfer, and workforce training (Li et al. 2018). One of the major advantages of using VR for training is the ability to provide a realistic work environment to the trainees when they experience the virtual environment (Stanney 2012). Recently, there have been studies that demonstrate the benefits of using VR applications in education and training. The increasingly easy availability of HMDs (head-mounted displays) is another reason the interest in using VR for safety training has gone up (Buttussi and Chittaro 2018).

Figure 1 shows the country-wise analysis of publications that was carried out using tools provided by the Scopus database. It can be seen that the top five countries which

V. G. Duffy (Ed.): HCII 2022, LNCS 13320, pp. 364–375, 2022.
https://doi.org/10.1007/978-3-031-06018-2_25

publish research articles in this field are the USA, China, UK, Australia, and Finland. One of the reasons for this could be the ease and availability of HMDs and VR content in these countries.

Documents by country or territory

Compare the document counts for up to 15 countries/territories.

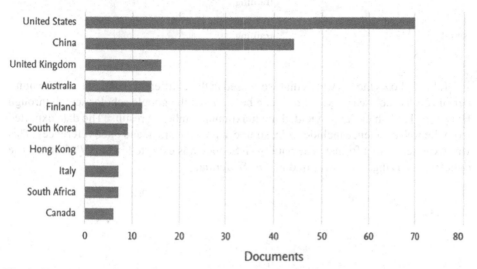

Fig. 1. Number of publications in the topic area based on the location of research ("Scopus," n.d.)

2   Purpose of Study

This study aims to conduct a systematic literature review of articles that explore the feasibility of using virtual reality systems for safety training. Information visualization techniques like Building Information Modeling (BIM), and VR/AR technologies are being implemented tentatively to enhance overall safety management in general and safety training in particular (Li et al. 2018). This study is an attempt to summarize the efforts made in this direction and to find out if these efforts have been successful. Various tools which are capable of analyzing metadata like VOSviewer, CiteSpace, BibExcel, and MAXQDA have been used.

3   Research Methodology

3.1   Data Collection

The systematic literature review was carried out by extracting metadata from various databases and then analyzing it. A similar methodology has been used to pick out articles for review by Kanade et al. and Roach et al. (Kanade and Duffy 2020; Roach and Duffy 2021).

Table 1. Keyword search in various databases and the number of results

Database	Keywords used	Number of results
Web of science	"Virtual reality" AND "safety training"	161
Scopus	"Virtual reality" AND "safety training"	254
Harzings' publish or Perish (Google scholar)	"Virtual reality" AND "safety training"	940

Table 1 shows the keywords that were used in three different databases and the number of results each search yielded. It can be seen that the google scholar search through Harzings' Publish or Perish yielded the maximum number of results. The data exported from the web of science includes title, source, author, abstract, and cited references. This was exported in text format. The data from Scopus was exported in "CSV" format. The data from Harzings' was exported in "WoS" format.

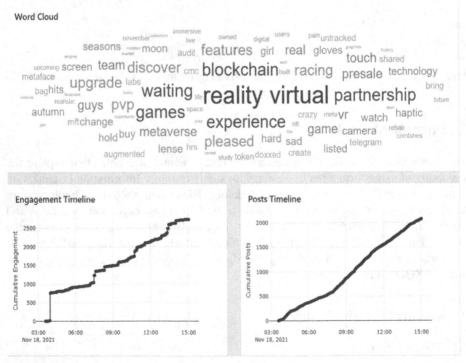

Fig. 2. Results from Vicinitas analysis based on the Twitter feed for the keyword "Virtual reality"

3.2 Engagement Measure

Vicinitas is a data mining tool that helps us measure the engagement level in a topic area based on Twitter activity. This tool was used to gauge the engagement of Twitter users in the area of virtual reality. A "hashtag/keyword tweets" search was carried out using the keyword "virtual reality". The results are shown in Fig. 2.

The engagement timeline and the timeline of the post demonstrate an increasing interest in the general topic area of virtual reality.

3.3 Trend Analysis

The metadata that was obtained from Scopus was analyzed to capture the interest of the scientific community in pursuing research related to the use of virtual reality in safety training. Trend analysis was carried out to compare the number of publications in this topic area year over year and the results can be seen in Fig. 3.

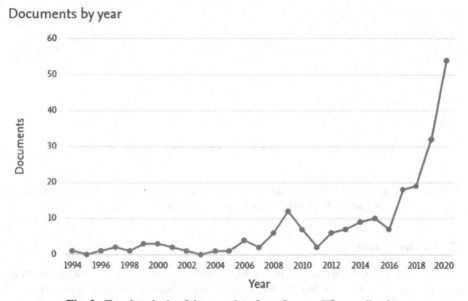

Documents by year

Fig. 3. Trend analysis of the metadata from Scopus ("Scopus," n.d.)

It can be seen from the trend analysis that the number of publications in this topic area has been increasing year over year. A substantial increase in the number of publications is seen after 2016 which suggests that the interest in the application of virtual reality for safety training has increased in the last five years.

4 Results

4.1 Co-citation Analysis

Co-citation analysis is used to find articles that have been cited together in another article. This provides information regarding the degree of connectivity between articles.

VOSviewer was used to perform co-citation analysis. Metadata was extracted from Scopus in "CSV" format. This extracted file had 254 articles. For the article to be considered in the analysis, it had to be cited at least 6 times. This criterion was satisfied by 6 articles. The resulting clusters are shown in Fig. 4.

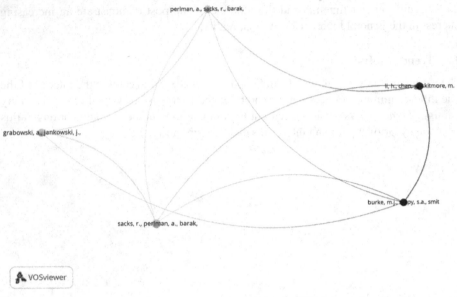

Fig. 4. Co-citation analysis using VOSviewer ("VOSviewer," n.d.)

Out of the six articles that met the criterion, only five are part of the clusters. These five articles were chosen for further review in the discussion section.

4.2 Content Analysis

Content analysis was carried out using VOSviewer to analyze the metadata extracted from Harzings' Publish or Perish. 940 results were obtained using a keyword search in Harzings'. These results were exported in WoS format ("Harzing Publish or Perish," n.d.). This file was then imported into VOSviewer and content analysis was carried out. This was done by choosing the "create map based on network data" option. The link strength was set at zero as the aim was to capture as many words as possible. A total of 88 words fulfilled the set parameter. The results are shown in Fig. 5.

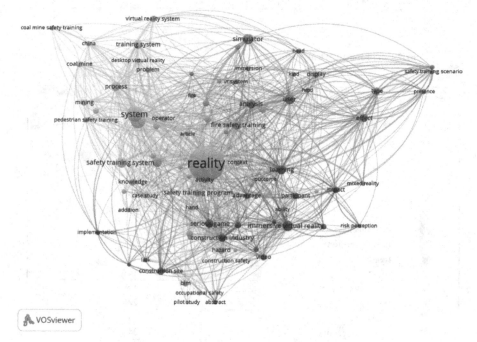

coal mine safety training virtual reality system
china training system simulator
  desktop virtual reality head
coal mine problem immersion kind display safety training scenario
process vr system presence
mining fire analysis head
  system operator use effect
pedestrian safety training fire safety training
  article
safety training system reality context learning
knowledge activity outcome mixed reality
case study safety training program advantage impact
addition hand participant ability
  serious game immersive virtual reality risk perception
implementation construction industry
  hazard
  construction safety
  construction site
  bim
  occupational safety
  pilot study abstract

VOSviewer

Fig. 5. Content analysis using metadata from Harzings' Publish or Perish ("VOSviewer," n.d.)

It can be seen from the cluster analysis that words like virtual reality display, safety training scenario, presence etc., occur prominently as nodes in the clusters. The words that occur the most can be seen in Fig. 6. The words in the clusters indicate the important words in a topic area. These words can be used as a reference point when literature related to a topic area is reviewed.

4.3 Pivot Table

The metadata extracted from Harzings' Publish or Perish was also used to generate a pivot table using BibExcel. BibExcel is a software tool that can analyze metadata to generate various forms of pivot tables. In this study, it was used to generate a "leading authors" table. This helps identify the authors who have published the most in a given topic area. The metadata from Harzings' was imported in BibExcel and analysis was carried out. The results were then exported to an excel file to generate a table. The table generated using this process is shown in Table 2.

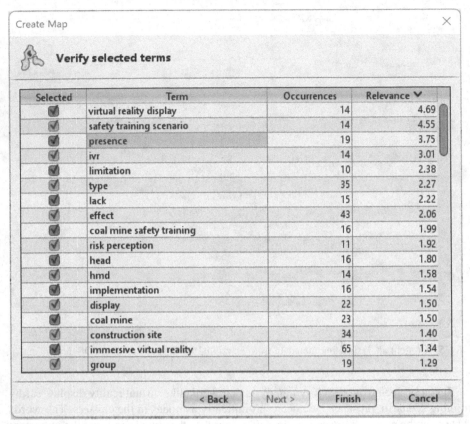

Fig. 6. Keywords from content analysis using VOSviewer ("VOSviewer," n.d.)

Table 2. Leading authors table using BibExcel ("BibExcel," n.d.)

Author name	Number of publications
Pedram S	10
Zhang H	9
Perez P	9
Gheisari M	9
Schwebel DC	8
Lucas J	8
Pedro A	7

4.4 Cluster Analysis

It can be seen in Fig. 4 that the co-citation analysis in VOSviewer has one limitation. It does not provide names for the clusters. This limitation can be overcome using CiteSpace

("CiteSpace," n.d.). CiteSpace is a software tool that can be used to perform co-citation analysis and extract labels for the clusters. It can also be used to generate a citation burst diagram that indicates the period during which a particular article was cited the most. To perform the analysis in CiteSpace, a keyword search was carried out in web of science which yielded 161 results. These results were exported along with cited references in text format. This folder was opened in CiteSpace, and co-citation analysis was carried out. Labels for the clusters were extracted using keywords. The results are shown in Fig. 7.

The names of the clusters represent the articles in a particular cluster. This helps identify various sub-topics within a topic area. It also helps identify articles within a sub-topic.

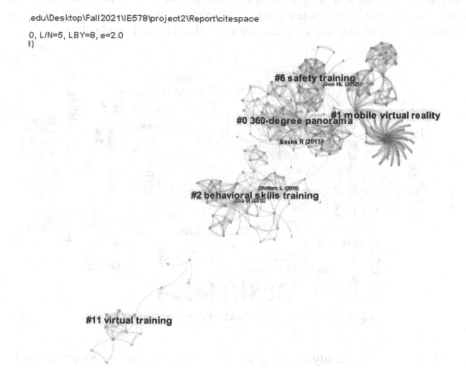

Fig. 7. Cluster analysis with labels extracted using keywords ("CiteSpace," n.d.)

Top 2 References with the Strongest Citation Bursts

References	Year	Strength	Begin	End	2000 - 2020
Guo HL, 2012, ACCIDENT ANAL PREV, V48, P204, DOI 10.1016/j.aap.2011.06.002, DOI	2012	3.94	2015	2018	
Sacks R, 2013, CONSTR MANAG ECON, V31, P1005, DOI 10.1080/01446193.2013.828844, DOI	2013	3.6	2018	2020	

Fig. 8. Citation burst diagram using CiteSpace ("CiteSpace," n.d.)

A citation burst was generated using CiteSpace. The two articles that are displayed in Fig. 8 are currently experiencing a citation burst. The fact that only two articles show up in the burst diagram demonstrates that the use of VR for safety training is a relatively new phenomenon.

At the end of this analysis, all the articles chosen for further review were saved in Mendeley to generate a reference list ("Mendeley," n.d.). The list included 5 articles from co-citation analysis which was performed using VOSviewer, 1 chapter from the handbook of human factors and ergonomics, 2 articles from citation burst, and 1 article from google scholar search.

4.5 Content Analysis Using MAXQDA

Once all the articles which were selected for the review were downloaded, content analysis based on the text of these articles was carried out. A word cloud was generated which indicates the keywords in a given set of articles. This helps decide the keywords for this literature review. The generated word cloud can be seen in Fig. 9.

Fig. 9. Word cloud using MAXQDA ("MAXQDA," n.d.)

The five most frequently occurring words from this analysis were training, safety, VR, construction, and virtual. Unlike the content analysis from VOSviewer which uses link strength as the parameter, MAXQDA provides information regarding the frequency of words which is helpful. These words were then used for lexical search that was carried out in the articles that were chosen for review in the discussion section. This helps in giving special attention to the part of the article that is related to the topic being reviewed.

5   Discussion

Human error is a major cause of accidents in the construction industry. These errors are caused due to the carelessness and lack of awareness of the workers (Perlman et al. 2014). This can be overcome to a certain extent by imparting safety training to these workers.

Historically, safety training has been imparted using chalkboards, handouts, and computer presentations. Use of these traditional techniques for safety training results in the trainees lacking comprehensive knowledge of on-site construction tasks, and a grasp of complexities involved in a construction project (Li et al. 2018). A major reason for these below-par training outcomes is the passive nature of these training programs. Research suggests that training programs should include the active participation of learners to improve learning outcomes (Burke et al. 2006). The use of virtual reality in safety training has the potential to ensure the active participation of learners and improve training outcomes.

Renganayagalu et al. have conducted a literature review that focuses on the effectiveness of virtual reality using head-mounted displays in professional training. The findings from this review suggest that the acceptance of VR as a training method is high amongst trainees. It was found that VR is useful for cognitive skill training like spatial memory, learning, and psychomotor skills. VR was also found to be a good alternative for on the job training (Renganayagalu et al. 2021). This has application in the construction industry where safety training takes place in a hands-off off-site environment (Guo et al. 2012). Grabowski et al. have conducted a pilot study that involves training coal miners using VR. In this study, head-mounted displays with differing levels of immersive experience were also compared. A highly immersive VR with a wide field of view was found to be more effective in most cases. Trainees felt the positive effects of training even three months after the training (Grabowski and Jankowski 2015). Li et al. have proposed the use of a 4D interactive safety assessment system that can help workers visualize the results of their action in a specific situation and evaluate the correctness of their action. This will contribute to the iterative learning process of the trainees (Li et al. 2012). These studies provide evidence to confirm the effectiveness of using VR in safety training. A few studies also demonstrate improved retention of the training material a few months after the training.

All these studies have focused on improving the learning outcomes of the training program by actively engaging the learner in the training process. Most of the studies prove that VR manages to actively engage trainees and improve training outcomes. Virtual reality can also be used to present hazards to the trainees without compromising their safety (Sacks et al. 2013). However, there are challenges in evaluating the effectiveness of VR/AR systems. Most of the evaluation techniques involve subjective questionnaires. This makes it difficult to generalize the results from these studies as the measures are not objective.

6 Conclusion

The review demonstrates the tremendous potential that VR has in the area of safety training. Virtual reality training can engage trainees actively thereby improving the learning outcomes and retention of the knowledge over a longer period of time. VR can also replace on the job training by creating immersive virtual environments. This is particularly helpful in training for hazardous jobs. Research indicates that virtual reality training is superior to traditional training techniques in imparting knowledge to the learner. However, several limitations hinder the universal use of VR for training. Although access to

HMDs (which are necessary to create high fidelity virtual environments) has gone up, they are still not widely available in the developing world as seen in Fig. 1 which shows the list of countries with the highest number of publications in this topic area. Most of the VR content is available in English. This might be problematic in countries where most of the workforce does not understand English. Evaluating the effectiveness of VR training is another limitation that needs to be overcome for it to become widely accepted as a better training method.

7 Future Work

The review indicates that a majority of studies involving the use of virtual reality in safety training are related to the construction industry. However, there are many other areas like warehouse safety, driver safety etc., where VR can be used as an effective training technique. These applications can be explored in future studies. One of the limitations in various studies was the evaluation technique used to gauge the efficacy of VR training as most of the studies use subjective measures for this purpose. Recently, HMDs have been integrated with eye-tracking systems which can measure the engagement patterns of the users. This opens up an interesting area of research where technologies like eye-tracker and facereader can be used to develop objective measures to gauge the efficacy of VR training.

A keyword search was carried out on the National Science Foundation's website to see if efforts are being made to develop better evaluation techniques for VR training

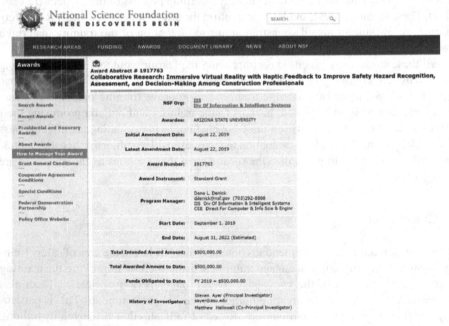

Fig. 10. A screenshot from the NSF website that shows the approval of a research project that focuses on developing objective measures for the evaluation of VR training

systems. A research proposal that is trying to evaluate if virtual reality training is resulting in better training outcomes using haptic feedback (which is an objective measure) has been approved by NSF. A screenshot has been shown in Fig. 10. This shows that research in the near future will focus on developing objective measures to evaluate the efficacy of virtual reality training.

References

BibExcel. n.d. https://homepage.univie.ac.at/juan.gorraiz/bibexcel/

Burke, M.J., Sarpy, S.A., Smith-Crowe, K., Chan-Serafin, S., Salvador, R.O., Islam, G.: Relative effectiveness of worker safety and health training methods. Am. J. Public Health **96**(2), 315–324 (2006). https://doi.org/10.2105/AJPH.2004.059840

Buttussi, F., Chittaro, L.: Effects of different types of virtual reality display on presence and learning in a safety training scenario. IEEE Trans. Vis. Comput. Graph. **24**(2), 1063–1076 (2018). https://doi.org/10.1109/TVCG.2017.2653117

CiteSpace. n.d. http://cluster.cis.drexel.edu/~cchen/citespace/

Grabowski, A., Jankowski, J.: Virtual reality-based pilot training for underground coal miners. Saf. Sci. **72**, 310–314 (2015). https://doi.org/10.1016/j.ssci.2014.09.017

Guo, H., Li, H., Chan, G., Skitmore, M.: Using game technologies to improve the safety of construction plant operations. Accid. Anal. Prev. **48**, 204–213 (2012). https://doi.org/10.1016/j.aap.2011.06.002

Harzing Publish or Perish. n.d. https://harzing.com/resources/publish-or-perish/windows

Kanade, S.G., Duffy, V.G.: A systematic literature review of game-based learning and safety management. In: Duffy, V.G. (ed.) HCII 2020. LNCS, vol. 12199, pp. 365–377. Springer, Cham (2020). https://doi.org/10.1007/978-3-030-49907-5_26

Li, H., Chan, G., Skitmore, M.: Visualizing safety assessment by integrating the use of game technology. Autom. Constr. **22**, 498–505 (2012). https://doi.org/10.1016/j.autcon.2011.11.009

Li, X., Yi, W., Chi, H.L., Wang, X., Chan, A.P.C.: A critical review of virtual and augmented reality (VR/AR) applications in construction safety. Autom. Constr. **86**, 150–62 (2018). https://doi.org/10.1016/j.autcon.2017.11.003

MAXQDA. n.d. https://www.maxqda.com/

Mendeley. n.d. https://www.mendeley.com/

Perlman, A., Sacks, R., Barak, R.: Hazard recognition and risk perception in construction. Saf. Sci. **64**, 13–21 (2014). https://doi.org/10.1016/j.ssci.2013.11.019

Renganayagalu, S.K., Mallam, S.C., Nazir, S.: Effectiveness of VR head mounted displays in professional training: a systematic review. Technol. Knowl. Learn. **26**(4), 999–1041 (2021). https://doi.org/10.1007/s10758-020-09489-9

Roach, A.L., Duffy, V.G.: Emerging applications of cognitive ergonomics: a bibliometric and content analysis. In: Stephanidis, C., et al. (eds.) HCII 2021. LNCS, vol. 13096, pp. 77–89. Springer, Cham (2021). https://doi.org/10.1007/978-3-030-90328-2_5

Sacks, R., Perlman, A., Barak, R.: Construction safety training using immersive virtual reality. Constr. Manag. Econ. **31**(9), 1005–1017 (2013). https://doi.org/10.1080/01446193.2013.828844

Scopus. n.d. https://www.scopus.com/search/form.uri?display=basic&zone=header&origin=#basic

Stanney, K.M.: Virtual environments. In: Handbook of Human Factors and Ergonomics, 4th edn (2012)

VOSviewer. n.d. https://www.vosviewer.com/

Value Creation and Value Acquisition Under Open Innovation--Theoretical Review and Future Research Directions

Guangzong Liu[✉]

Guizhou University of Commerce, Guiyang, Guizhou, China
46461905@qq.com

Abstract. Any open innovation business model must consider the relationship between value creation and value acquisition of all participants in the value network. Based on Chesbrough's point of view, this paper reviews the literature on the value creation and value acquisition mechanisms under the open innovation model, and summarizes the following five aspects: the dominant logic of corporate technological innovation; the possession system of open innovation; open innovation Innovative organizational model; value network of open innovation; relationship between open innovation and performance; creation and transfer of organizational knowledge. On this basis, the future research direction is proposed: the innovation mechanism of small and micro enterprise teams under open innovation, and the future research prospects are proposed from five aspects.

Keywords: Collective bridge · Disruptive innovation · Dynamic knowledge integrating capabilities · Democratizing innovation · Knowledge transfer performance

1 Introduction

Most people think that innovation is a gift, is that true? Clayton Christensen, a professor of innovation management at Harvard University, summed up the previous research results and conducted long-term research on these results and came to the conclusion that innovation ability is not entirely a talent, and this special skill can be completely achieved through Acquired through development, two-thirds of the innovation ability is acquired through acquired learning. Most innovative entrepreneurs use the "melting pot aggregation method" to build innovative teams: talents specializing in the industry, bring together talents with different professional backgrounds, let them motivate each other, let them think across disciplines and fields, and have advantages Complementary teams are more discoverable, foster innovation, and learn from each other's strengths. Einstein called this kind of thinking a constructive "combination game." Once unfamiliar disciplinary concepts and ideas are combined with their own specialties, they Creativity will be generated, through connection thinking, across knowledge fields, industries and regions, to carry out bold exploratory imagination, and then lead to innovative business models or ideas (Likai 2016).

V. G. Duffy (Ed.): HCII 2022, LNCS 13320, pp. 376–390, 2022.
https://doi.org/10.1007/978-3-031-06018-2_26

2 Theoretical Review About Value Creation and Value Acquisition Under Open Innovation

Any open innovation business model must consider the relationship between value creation and value acquisition by all participants in the value network (Chesbrough 2003). Regarding the mechanism of value creation and value acquisition under the open innovation model, relevant research can be summarized as follows:

2.1 Research on Dominant Logic of Company's Technological Innovation

Porter's 1991 study found that most of the resource-oriented literature is introverted: companies should be the best in their field, and incentives tend not only to high-performance spirits, but also to (potentially) invent out-of-place. While Prahalad and Hamel explicitly pointed out the effectiveness of Japanese firms' acquisition of external knowledge as an important way to build competitiveness between the 1970s and 1980s, large technology firms remained dominated by closed innovation, which is The prevailing way in which technological innovation exists (Chesbrough and Vanhaverbeke 2006). Teece (1986) distinguishes between technological innovation and complementary assets that commercialize innovation (Teece 1986), and he develops a framework of possibilities, synthetic insights from resource- and transaction-cost-based theory, to determine whether complementary assets Should it be outsourced, whether it can be through alliances or licensing agreements, or whether it can be developed independently. While Cohen and Levinthal (1990) regard open innovation as an upcoming new direction, external knowledge sources are often the key to the innovation process (Cohen and Levinthal 1990). The two scholars pointed out that internal R&D has two functions, the first is to provide improved technology and innovation of new technologies; the second is the ability to absorb relevant knowledge emerging from the external environment. Cohen and Levinthal (1990) and Rosenberg (1990) pointed out that the R&D process is inevitably related to knowledge spillovers, and that internal R&D builds absorptive capacity, which is a way to acquire spillover knowledge from external R&D. As large firms continue to invest in R&D and rapidly expand their global technology base, these firms must acknowledge that the growing sharing of relevant technical knowledge is accumulating externally (Chesbrough and Vanhaverbeke 2006). Chesbrough (2003) argues that large companies keep changing in the above-mentioned technological innovation environment, and although some reluctantly tend to the internationalization of cooperative R&D, a special feature of this transition has become a trend (Gerybadze and Reger 1999; Kuemmerle 1999; Boutellier and Gassmann 2000; Kim and Park 2003). Brusoni and Prencipe (2001) explored the development of aircraft engine control systems, showing that development requires the mobilization and maintenance of a loosely coupled network organization whose key feature is system integration (Brusoni and Prencipe 2001). Chesbrough (2003) pointed out that structural knowledge will become increasingly important when knowledge is popularized, and fundamental changes have taken place in the way companies create and acquire value. Under the open innovation model, the company uses both internal and external valuable knowledge to accelerate internal innovation, and use external innovation to expand the market, and its commercialization path can be carried out within the company or outside the company (Chesbrough

2003). Chesbrough and Heaton (2020) studied China's "One Belt, One Road" strategy and found that whether state-owned enterprises, private enterprises or foreign-funded enterprises, in the fields of high-speed railway and semiconductor industry, they all follow the national policy-oriented open from the inside to the outside. Innovation, the central government plays a leading role in open innovation activities and plays the role of capacity coordinator (Chesbrough and Heaton 2020).

2.2 Research on Possession System Under Open Innovation Model

In open innovation, as an important part of the possession system, intellectual property evolves with the change of the company's possession behavior. The era of the Internet and the information economy has had a fundamental impact on the company's business model and strategic behavior. The company's emphasis on inter-organizational relationships and the use of open innovation models have prompted it to establish and use more flexible intellectual property rights, so as to help companies transform from open innovation. Profits from innovation play an important role in guaranteeing and motivating (Wang 2010). The company's focus on the stock of knowledge should shift to how to increase the flow of knowledge (Boisot 1998). The best way to protect intellectual property is to use it and innovate further. It is not enough to just invent and patent (Sawhney and Prandelli 1998). 2000). For innovative companies, whether or not to own intellectual property is not the purpose. The real purpose is to create an incentive mechanism through intellectual property and efficiently use knowledge to create and capture value. Wang (2010) proposed the concept of relational intellectual property, emphasizing that over time, companies and their competitors are ultimately competing to establish cooperative relationships (Huston and Sakkab 2006). The use of internal and external knowledge resources is a necessary condition for the open innovation paradigm (Chesbrough 2003). Intellectual property protection provides a platform for the transfer of knowledge resources from inventive activities, and changes in intellectual property have strengthened the rights of intellectual property owners and the economic value of intellectual property (Graham and Mowery 2006). In addition to companies as a possible external source of innovation, another important source of knowledge and technological innovation is universities. Current research has demonstrated that industrial innovation relies on university research. Industrial patents heavily cite basic research produced by universities, and citation linkages between universities and industry have been increasing (Narin and Olivastro 1991; Narin and Hamilton 1997). Without the support of basic scientific achievements of universities, industrial innovation will become "cook without rice". Universities have become the most important source of external technology (Tidd and Trewhella 1997). Private scientific research in corporations differs from open scientific research in universities in that private science is characterized by obtaining appropriate rents from research while restricting external access to knowledge (Partha and David 1994; David 1998). University researchers hope that others will recognize the value of their work and build upon it. However, attention to intellectual property comes from companies to which innovations are flowing, and companies are hesitant to make these investments if they fear imitation and appropriation of innovations without intellectual property protection (Thursby and Jensen 2001). Some scholars have argued that increased protection of intellectual property rights by universities will increase the company's negotiation costs, and exclusive licensing will limit a group of subsequent innovators (Fabrizio 2006). Intellectual property concerns create insurmountable barriers for companies to join universities to form research partnerships (Hall and Ziedonis 2001). Fabrizio (2006) conducted an empirical survey of patent activity in the United States from 1975 to 1995 and found that patent grants to university researchers did not restrict companies from using public science to continue to innovate in this technology area. The increase in the grant of patents themselves did not limit the use of university research to only a few companies. However, the pace of knowledge transfer and utilization has slowed as companies become more reliant on university research results and these results are more and more associated with formal intellectual property ownership. Therefore, companies need to have the ability to understand cutting-edge science (Rosenberg 1990), that is, absorptive capacity (Cohen and Levinthal 1989). The superior innovation behavior of firms benefits from superior internal basic research, firm-university collaboration, and superior absorptive capacity (Fabrizio 2006). In conclusion, formal intellectual property protection may be beneficial in encouraging companies to invest in university technology, but there are also potential adverse effects, such as slowing technology transfer and encouraging university researchers to keep secrets. The increase of patents will not solve the problem of knowledge transfer by itself, and the research results of universities themselves cannot ensure the transfer of technology to industry. Therefore, the interaction between university researchers and company researchers and the company's continuous investment in basic science are very important to the process of knowledge and technology transfer.

2.3   Research on Organizational Model of Open Innovation

Marcel et al. (2019) divided open innovation models into four types from two dimensions: business technology development model and intellectual property strategy: open business ecosystem model, open intellectual property system model, open source model, and open through mergers and acquisitions mode of innovation (Bogers and Chesbrough 2019). Zhang Feng (2012) divided the open innovation model into inward innovation and outward innovation. Enkel (2020) divided open innovation into inward, outward and hybrid innovation. Hybrid innovation refers to the combination of a company from the inside out (bringing ideas to market) and the outside-in (gaining external knowledge) to create value with complementary collaborators through alliances, partnerships, and joint ventures. Based on specific value innovation methods, companies need to adopt various effective organizational models to support the realization of the value creation process (Wang and Zeng 2011). Many new organizational models are employed in different types of open innovation. Introverted innovation models include: innovation network (Dittrich and Duysters 2007), "Lianfa" model (Dodgson and Gann 2006; Huston and Sakkab 2006), "identification and acceleration" model (Tao and Magnotta 2006), creative competitions (Piller and Walcher 2006), community-based peer production (Reichwald and Stotko 2005), and crowdsourcing models (Howe 2008; Kohler and Chesbrough 2020). External-oriented innovation models include: spin-offs (Chesbrough 2007; Chesbrough and Garman 2009), intellectual property exchange (Chesbrough 2006; Lichtenthaler and Ernst 2007), and cross-industry innovation (Enkel and Gassmann 2010). Hybrid innovation models include: alliances and collaborations (Chiaromonte 2006), open resource development projects (Hippel and Krogh 2003), and innovation intermediaries (Lakhani 2008). Many organizational models are based on information technology and tools. These technological tools essentially improve the interface between companies and external partners (Dodgson and Gann 2006), and provide powerful support for large-scale, distributed and virtual knowledge exchange and creation (Gassmann and Zedtwitz 2006). 2003; Fetterhoff and Voelkel 2006). Rohrbeck and Hölzle (2009) examined and summarized commonly used innovation tools through case studies combined with the types of innovation processes and innovation models, such as foresight workshops, executive forums, customer integration, guild programs, corporate venture capitalists, online platforms, and test markets (Rohrbeck and Hölzle 2009). Commonly used technologies and tools include: enabling technologies or innovation technologies (Von Hippel and Katz 2002), data mining and search, user toolboxes (Dodgson and Gann 2006) or blogs, wikis and Virtual Lab. (2020) put forward the maturity model of the open innovation model in the digital age. Through the theoretical review of the past 30 years, the theoretical viewpoints have been developed from closed to open to dynamic, and the open innovation model is correspondingly divided into three stages.: Traditionalism, Modernism and Visionary (Enkel and Bogers 2020).

2.4   Research on Value Network of Open Innovation

The value in the network is generated by cooperation, and the total value created by the network directly depends on the degree to which the goals of the partners are combined and the partners' commitment to invest in complementary resources (Teece 1986). Chesbrough (2003a) defines open innovation from the perspective of large firms. Vanhaverbeke (2006) believes that analysis from different levels can broaden the scope of open innovation, and summarizes five levels of analysis. The first layer is the internal organizational network. Extensive literature describes how internal organizational networks stimulate innovation (Nonaka and Takeuchi 1995; Szulanski 1996; Tsai and Ghoshal 1998; Hansen 1999; Foss and Pedersen 2002; Lagerström and Andersson 2003). However, they did not analyze these internal organizational networks in the context of open innovation. The SECI model and "field" theory proposed by Yujiro Nonaka revealed the mechanism of knowledge creation and transformation in the company's internal organizational network, and the concept of open innovation was added to the later research, which expanded the SECI model and "field" theory. connotation. The second level is the company level. Christensen (2006) reviewed the development process of the overall technological innovation of large technology-intensive companies in the world during the 10–20 years since the end of the 1980s. The study found that the absorptive capacity of the company enables the company to obtain benefits from the external technological development of the supply chain. profit and discover new opportunities from scientific and technological breakthroughs outside the company. The core technology of large companies plays an increasingly small role in the overall technology. As large companies increasingly play the role of innovation architects and market coordinators in increasingly fragmented value chains, they have had to develop integrative capabilities for the integration of systems involving experience-based and firm-specific structural knowledge. With the increasing sharing of relevant innovation knowledge and the development of external large-scale corporate components, dynamic capabilities (Teece and Pisano 1997), that is, the ability to restructure corporate knowledge and resource bases, have become the core assets of system integration capabilities. The diverse and highly dynamic nature of integrated capabilities cannot be reflected in a central laboratory or an isolated business unit, but must be reflected in changes in organizational mandates and mobilization of external relationships (Brown and Eisenhardt 1997; Galunic and Eisenhardt 2001). West and Gallagher (2006) studied the open innovation model of open source software and pointed out that when open source software reflects the partial commoditization of the whole complex system, the value acquisition of enterprises shifts from selling software licenses to selling software support services. This model of open innovation creates a mechanism whereby a company can be rewarded for its part of the system's value creation. The third layer is open innovation at the bilateral level. Bilateral level means that two or more companies join each other through contractual or non-contractual alliances, corporate venture capital, etc. Open innovation is primarily based on non-arm-length relationships between firms (Vanhaverbeke 2006), which can leverage bilateral level perspectives, alliance management experience (Lynch 1993; Bamford and Ernst 2002) and external firm risk-benefit (Keil 2002). The fourth level is the inter-organizational network. Inter-organizational relationships and networks are a key dimension of open innovation. When a company is highly dependent on other organizations to provide new technologies or needs the help of other organizations to bring their new technologies to market, open innovation focuses on managing the company's external network (Vanhaverbeke 2006). Barney (1991) pointed out that each member of the network has a variety of complementary resources and capabilities for new products to be put on the market, and the value network can bring them together. Building value networks is related to dynamic capabilities (Teece and Pisano 1997; Eisenhardt and Martin 2000), because dynamic capabilities can coordinate and reorganize these resources in different ways and create value. The fifth layer is the national innovation system or regional innovation system. The government's system will become a help or resistance for local innovative companies. Academia debates whether innovation systems have an impact on innovation at the national, regional or supranational level. But there is no doubt that external, geographically limited innovation systems are an important factor in corporate innovation. Cooke (2005) pointed out that open innovation is a key element in explaining how regional innovation systems and clusters are organized to enhance global effectiveness. Research has shown that membership in regional economic groups can increase innovation returns (Bunker Whittington and Owen-Smith 2004). Numerous studies have shown that regional networks have an effect on both high-tech industries and industries such as clothing, shoes, knitting, and winemaking (Vanhaverbeke 2006). The elements in the regional network mainly include: universities, venture capitalists and core enterprises (Vanhaverbeke 2006). Maula and Keil (2006) expounded open innovation in the context of systematic innovation through case studies, and proposed that the systematic characteristics of innovation are an important driving force in the process of open innovation. In industries such as electronic information, the systemic nature of innovation requires companies to expand their innovative behavior, not just use internal resources. The primary shared resources required for the success of system innovation are those outside the company. The core company lacks direct control over external resources and needs an indirect management mechanism. The process of external resource allocation is completely different from the content resource allocation process (Maula and Keil 2006). Vanhaverbeke and Cloodt (2006) took the commercialization of new products in the agricultural biotechnology industry as the research content, and vividly called the inter-organizational network "value constellation" and proposed a corresponding theoretical model. The two scholars argue that core companies build value constellations through acquisitions, licensing agreements, non-equity alliances, joint ventures, contracts, and other collaborations that go beyond "arm-length relationships." Research shows that open innovation is not only applicable to the communications industry, but also to the agricultural biotechnology industry. Lundvall (1992), Nelson (1993), and Montobbio (1999) all mentioned the importance of a "national innovation system", in which the government acts as an "innovation sponsor" to provide external resources for innovation without capturing the full benefits of innovation (Chesbrough 2003), both companies and their affiliates can benefit from shifting government policies to civilian applications (Nelson 1993; Bresnahan and Malerba 1999). Aarikka-Stenroos and Ritla (2017) systematically reviewed the literature on the network management of ecosystems and proposed four ways of ecosystem development: (a) competition and evolution; (b) emergence and destruction; (c) stable business Communication; (d) value co-creation (Aarikka-Stenroos and Ritala 2017).

2.5 Research on Relationship Between Open Innovation and Performance

Hippel (1986), Urban and Hippel (1988), and Herstatt and Hippel (1992) believe that users, especially lead users, participate in innovation, which can provide manufacturers with valuable new product ideas and prototype designs. Analysis of lead user needs and solutions increases innovation efficiency. Cai Ning and Yan Chun (2013) confirmed that financial performance and strategic performance represent different types of benefits that companies obtain from open innovation. Zhang Feng (2012) considered through literature review that the relationship between external resource acquisition and performance has not reached a consistent conclusion in empirical research. For example: Yu Kaile and Wang Tiemin (2008) studied the case of Nanjing Automobile Group's acquisition of Rover, and the results show that open innovation based on mergers and acquisitions may have a positive impact on the company's independent innovation. Monteiro et al. (2011) based on the UK innovation survey data showed that both formal and informal access to external resources can help improve innovation performance. Motohashi (2005) found that, in cooperation with universities, new technology-based small companies with excellent innovation management capabilities are more efficient than large companies. (2009) used the revised knowledge production function to analyze the spillover effect of knowledge production in colleges and universities and found that the spillover effect of knowledge production in colleges and universities significantly improved the company's innovation ability. Stuart and David (2006) studied intellectual property management issues in the US software industry from 1987 to 2003. The study concluded that when software companies carry out open innovation activities, strong patent rights protection may have a negative impact on the performance of innovation activities. Johnsen and Ford (2000) pointed out that excessive use of external innovation resources may affect the strategic position of the company's internal research and development, resulting in the control of key technologies by partners. Luo Wei (2001) pointed out that once the cooperation fails, many of the company's dedicated asset investment and previous efforts for cooperation will be in vain. (1997) pointed out that the problem of information leakage is the most serious when cooperating with potential competitors, and this problem is unavoidable even when cooperating with non-competitors. Johnsen and Ford (2000) and Belderbos et al. (2004) pointed out that sensitive business information and technical knowledge may be leaked to competitors through common suppliers or users. Laursen and Salter (2006) found an inverted U-shaped relationship between external resource acquisition and innovation performance, rather than a simple linear or positive relationship, due to the limited internal absorption. (2010) based on a survey of 305 Belgian manufacturing companies and found that the diversity of technology alliances will improve product innovation performance, which in turn will have a positive impact on financial performance in the long run, but in the short term will be due to increased costs. negatively impact financial performance. Based on the inconsistency of the above research conclusions, some scholars have begun to explore the intermediate mechanism between external resource acquisition and performance. For example, Huang and Rice (2009) found that the inter-organizational network had a positive impact on performance, and technology purchases had a negative impact on performance, but the interaction between absorptive capacity and both had a positive impact on performance. Other scholars have examined the role of other variables such as relational ability, marketing ability, and production ability (Su and Tsang 2009). The other is the "invent not here" view, which holds that the stronger a company's R&D capabilities, the greater the obstacles to open innovation. R&D capability has a negative moderating effect on the relationship between external resource acquisition and performance (Laursen and Salter 2006).

Existing research mainly analyzes four of the five research levels of open innovation, namely organizational level, inter-organizational value network, industry and sector, national or regional innovation system, and for individuals and teams in an open innovation environment. Less attention has been paid to the issues of value creation and value acquisition at the level, and there has not been a lot of research on the innovation mechanism of small and micro teams under open innovation.

3 Future Research Directions

Open innovation research focuses on corporate behavior (Chesbrough and Vanhaverbeke 2006) and is about the flow of knowledge between firms (Chesbrough 2003). Tassey (1992) proposed three types of knowledge creation: basic research, applied research and experimental development. Stokes (1999) divided scientific research into four quadrants from the two dimensions of knowledge-seeking and application-oriented: pure basic research, application-oriented basic research (Pasteur quadrant), interest-oriented research and pure research. Application-oriented research. Ruttan (2001) proposed a new quartet based on Stokes research in two dimensions: knowledge production type and knowledge attributes: application-inspired basic research, the Pasteur quadrant; industry-initiated applied research and technology Development, the Edison quadrant; government-sponsored applied research and technology development, the Qian Xuesen quadrant or Rickover quadrant; and curiosity-driven basic research, the Bohr quadrant.

Martin et al. (2007) used organizational learning theory to divide knowledge creation modes into: exploring new knowledge (exploratory learning), compiling knowledge and combining old knowledge creation modes. The theory of organizational knowledge creation is not only used to explain the nature of the company's knowledge assets and the strategy of knowledge management, but can also complement the knowledge base view of the company (Grant 1996) and the dynamic capability theory (Teece and Pisano 1997) connotations (Nonaka and Toyama 2003; Nonaka and Von Krogh et al. 2006; Nonaka and Von Krogh 2009). Knowledge transfer is a dynamic interactive process between knowledge owners and knowledge receivers (Gilbert and Cordey-Hayes 1996). Scholars have mainly carried out research on the types of knowledge transfer and the mechanism of knowledge transfer. Ye Weiwei and Chen Yufen (2015) divided the types of knowledge transfer into three levels: individual and individual, individual and organization, and organization and organization. At the individual and individual level, Li Jinhua and Sun Dongchuan (2006) proposed a knowledge dissemination model different from the Cowan model to examine the speed of knowledge dissemination under different network structures. The greater the degree of localization, the faster the diffusion of knowledge in the network and the more uniform the distribution of knowledge. However, if the pressure effect of the neighboring environment is deliberately highlighted and some changes are made to the diffusion mechanism, the small-world network (Watts and Strogatz 1998) properties can be brought into play immediately. At the individual and organizational level, Hippel (2005) put forward the concept of democratizing innovation based on the analysis of open source technology. The study pointed out that creativity is mainly generated from the cognitive and emotional processes at the individual level, so dynamic individual participants are particularly interested in innovation. important. Chatterji and Fabrizio (2014) argue that user knowledge, like other external knowledge, can enhance the ability to innovate because users have specific motivations, experiences, and knowledge systems that are difficult for companies to replicate. Research shows that the type of users determines whether the result of product innovation is continuous innovation or breakthrough innovation, and at the beginning of the product life cycle, joint research and development with users will produce higher innovation performance. Joint development that incorporates the knowledge of external users can either lead to breakthrough innovations or fail. Because joint development with users is carried out under conditions different from the company's existing operating mechanism, the company also needs to face corresponding organizational change challenges (Chatterji and Fabrizio 2014). As an important form of the social network of the R&D team, network centrality plays an important role in the transfer of individual knowledge and the creation of team knowledge resources. It represents the effective transfer of individual knowledge within the R&D team and is a measure of the quality of the team's social network. Network centrality focuses on exploring the effect of knowledge transfer within a team, while collective bridges and cross-boundary structures explore how R&D team knowledge can effectively transfer across its own boundaries to other R&D teams. Zhao and Anand (2013) critiqued the utility of cross-boundary structures in dealing with systematic and complex cross-team knowledge transfer tasks, arguing that cross-boundary structures can only effectively handle simple and decentralized team knowledge transfer tasks, but when knowledge is complex When the property exceeds a certain threshold, the transboundary structure will be powerless (Zhao and Anand 2013). The two scholars reviewed and criticized the main theoretical viewpoints of knowledge transfer and constructed the collective bridge theory on this basis to deal with the problem of how to effectively transfer knowledge in complex teams and put forward corresponding propositional hypotheses. At the organizational and organizational level, Yujiro Nonaka (2003) revised the previous theory under the influence of the open innovation model and proposed that the company is a fusion of various types of A dialectical unity of contradictions, the organization is no longer composed of small tasks and a collection of tasks aimed at accomplishing specific goals, but an organic configuration of knowledge creation composed of "fields". "Fields" are not limited to a single organization, and "fields" can be created across organizational boundaries. Organization members can transcend organizational boundaries to participate in the "fields" of knowledge creation and transformation, and even when the "fields" in the network are interconnected, they can transcend the boundaries of the original "fields" (Nonaka and Toyama 2003).

The tacit knowledge exchange (TKE) within an open innovation team and among its stakeholders is a key factor in the success of the ultimate co-value creation. Tacit knowledge exchange has been recognized as a crucial prerequisite for achieving breakthrough innovations (Noble and Durmusoglu 2019). The essence of future enterprise competition is the competition of employees' entrepreneurial passion. How to stimulate employees' entrepreneurial passion and convert this passion into user value? The user experience interaction system points out a new direction for employees' entrepreneurial and innovative behaviors. As the node of user value creation and the basic unit of user value measurement, the small and micro team of an enterprise is the carrier of the user experience interaction system. In the small and micro team, the role of employees is transformed into "interface people", and they need to have interface capabilities, that is, the ability to continuously and dynamically absorb and optimize first-class resources. The new user value creation model requires a new structure and system to match it. However, traditional hierarchical management emphasizes the top-down allocation of resources around goals. In an open innovation environment, such a structure and system cannot evaluate user resources and team innovation behaviors, match user needs with breakthrough technological innovations, and create user value, leading to some entrepreneurship and innovation practices within the company. Activities and the enthusiasm of small and micro team members are suppressed, and the small and micro team loses the structure and institutional basis for survival. Therefore, it is natural for management scholars to study the innovation mechanism of enterprise small and micro teams under open innovation. The scientific research issues that still need to be further explored are:

(1) In the process of internal knowledge transfer, how to realize the dynamic integration of small and micro team knowledge?
(2) How to effectively transfer knowledge between small and micro teams?
(3) How can democratized innovation be matched with small and micro teams to achieve breakthrough innovation?

3.1 Research on Influence of Network Centrality on the Effect of Knowledge Transfer Within Small and Micro Teams

Based on the research deficiencies of Ibarra (1993) and Zhou Mi et al. (2009): 1. Participation in technological innovation is a process rather than a result, and the outcome variable of network centrality is knowledge transfer effectiveness; 2. Network trust mediates network centrality and knowledge transfer effectiveness The effect has not been proven. Therefore, it is more reasonable to use the network trust, which reflects the quality of the R&D small and micro team member relationship, as a moderator variable to examine the influence of network centrality on the knowledge transfer effectiveness of small and micro teams.

3.2 Research on Fuzzy Comprehensive Evaluation of R&D Team's Dynamic Knowledge Integration Ability

The connotation of dynamic knowledge integration ability is defined through literature review research, which mainly includes concepts and dimensions. Then, clarify the principles for establishing the evaluation index system. Select typical small and micro teams as the research object to carry out a case study of fuzzy evaluation of dynamic knowledge integration ability. Finally, the comprehensive analytic hierarchy process (AHP) and fuzzy analysis theory are used to construct the evaluation index set and evaluation level, determine the index weight, construct the judgment matrix, perform fuzzy matrix synthesis, calculate the overall score and each first-level index score, and analyze the results. The evaluation of dynamic knowledge integration ability is to use historical and current data to evaluate the current situation of knowledge integration of small and micro teams in order to find problems and put forward suggestions for improvement.

3.3 Research on Influence of Dynamic Knowledge Integration Ability on Innovation Performance of Small and Micro Teams

Taking the logical relationship between knowledge resources, dynamic knowledge integration capabilities and small and micro team innovation performance as the main line, adopting the exploratory single case study method, selecting typical small and micro teams as the research object, and discussing the process of small and micro team knowledge resource transformation And the relationship between the impact on the innovation performance of small and micro teams, build a theoretical model of the transformation process of knowledge resources under the action of dynamic knowledge integration capabilities and the impact on the innovation performance of small and micro teams. Based on the constructed theoretical model, typical small and micro teams are selected as samples, and the comparative and revised interpretation construction case analysis method is used to conduct multi-case research hypothesis testing. The purpose is to continuously revise the original research hypothesis until the case and research hypothesis are formed. matching, thereby enhancing the credibility and applicability of the theory.

3.4 Research on Effect of Collective Bridge and Cross-Border Structure on the Effect of Knowledge Transfer Between Small and Micro Teams

Referring to the theoretical framework and five research hypotheses of Zhao and Anand (2013), on the basis of mature scales related to knowledge transfer, combined with the collective bridge theory to develop the required measurement scales for research, taking typical small and micro teams as the survey objects, conduct research. Collect, organize and analyze data, verify research hypotheses, and explore the role of collective bridges and cross-border structures on the effectiveness of knowledge transfer between small and micro teams under the adjustment of knowledge complexity.

3.5 Research on Adaptation of Democratized Innovation and Breakthrough Innovation of Small and Micro Teams

A case study method is used to construct a comparative and revised interpretation to study how the collective bridge and cross-border structure and the user community can be effectively connected to make democratized innovation an important driving force for the breakthrough innovation of small and micro teams. Select a typical small and micro team as the case study object, carry out investigation and research on the cooperative innovation activities between the small and micro team and the leading users in the user community, verify the initial research hypothesis based on the results of the case analysis, and explore the organization in an open innovation environment. How to change the structure to meet the adaptability requirements of democratized innovation and breakthrough innovation of small and micro teams.

4 Conclusion

With the gradual maturity of open innovation, open innovation is no longer a simple screening of external ideas, nor is it just a study of macro issues such as models, intellectual property rights, and value networks, but should focus on micro issues: How value creation and value acquisition can be realized at the level of small and micro teams of enterprises. Future research needs to conduct in-depth discussions on the above research directions in the selection of typical enterprise cases, and enrich the theory of open innovation.

References

Aarikka-Stenroos, L., Ritala, P.: Network management in the era of ecosystems: systematic review and management framework. Ind. Mark. Manag **67**, 23–26 (2017)

Bamford, J., Ernst, D.: Managing an alliance portfolio. McKinsey Q. 3(8), 25–35 (2002)

Bogers, M., Chesbrough, H., et al.: Strategic management of open innovation: a dynamic capabilities perspective. Calif. Manag. Rev. **62**(1), 77–94 (2019)

Boisot, M.H.: Knowledge Assets: Securing Competitive Advantage in the Information Economy. OUP, Oxford (1998)

Boutellier, R., Gassmann, O., et al.: Managing global innovation: uncovering the secrets of future competitiveness (2000)

Bresnahan, T.F., Malerba, F.: Industrial dynamics and the evolution of firms' and nations' competitive capabilities in the world computer industry. Sources of industrial leadership: studies of seven industries, pp. 79–132 (1999)

Brown, S.L., Eisenhardt, K.M.: The art of continuous change: linking complexity theory and time-paced evolution in relentlessly shifting organizations. Adm. Sci. Q. **42**, 1–34 (1997)

Brusoni, S., Prencipe, A., et al.: Knowledge specialization, organizational coupling, and the boundaries of the firm: why do firms know more than they make? Adm. Sci. Q. **46**(4), 597–621 (2001)

Bunker Whittington, K., Owen-Smith, J., et al.: Spillovers versus embeddedness: the contingent effects of propinquity and social structure. Stanford University (2004)

Chesbrough, H.W., Garman, A.R.: How open innovation can help you cope in lean times. Harvard Bus. Rev. **87**(12), 68–76, 128 (2009)

Chesbrough, H.: Open business models: how to thrive in the new innovation landscape. Harvard Bus. Rev. **1** (2006)

Chesbrough, H.: The market for innovation: implications for corporate strategy. Calif. Manag. Rev. **49**(3), 45–66 (2007)

Chesbrough, H., Heaton, S., et al.: Open innovation with Chinese characteristics: a dynamic capabilities perspective. R&D Manag. **51**(3), 247–259 (2020)

Chesbrough, H., Vanhaverbeke, W., et al.: Open Innovation: Researching a New Paradigm, pp. 34–35. OUP, Oxford (2006)

Chiaromonte, F.: Open innovation through alliances and partnership: theory and practice. Int. J. Technol. Manag. **33**, 111–114 (2006)

Cohen, W.M., Levinthal, D.A.: Innovation and learning: the two faces of R & D. Econ. J. **99**(397), 569–596 (1989)

Cohen, W.M., Levinthal, D.A.: Absorptive capacity: a new perspective on learning and innovation. Adm. Sci. Q. **35**, 128–152 (1990)

David, P.A.: Common agency contracting and the emergence of "open science" institutions. Am. Econ. Rev. **88**(2), 15–21 (1998)

Dittrich, K., Duysters, G.: Networking as a means to strategy change: the case of open innovation in mobile telephony. J. Prod. Innov. Manag. **24**(6), 510–521 (2007)

Dodgson, M., Gann, D., et al.: The role of technology in the shift towards open innovation: the case of Procter & Gamble. R&D Manag. **36**(3), 333–346 (2006)

Eisenhardt, K.M., Martin, J.A.: Dynamic capabilities: what are they? Strateg. Manag. J. **21**(10–11), 1105–1121 (2000)

Enkel, E., Bogers, M., et al.: Exploring open innovation in the digital age: a maturity model and future research directions. R&D Manag. **50**(1), 161–168 (2020)

Enkel, E., Gassmann, O.: Creative imitation: exploring the case of cross-industry innovation. R&D Manag. **40**(3), 256–270 (2010)

Fabrizio, K.: The use of university research in firm innovation. In: Open innovation: Researching a New Paradigm, pp. 134–160 (2006)

Fetterhoff, T.J., Voelkel, D.: Managing open innovation in biotechnology. Res. Technol. Manag. **49**(3), 14–18 (2006)

Foss, N.J., Pedersen, T.: Transferring knowledge in MNCs: the role of sources of subsidiary knowledge and organizational context. J. Int. Manag. **8**(1), 49–67 (2002)

Galunic, D.C., Eisenhardt, K.M.: Architectural innovation and modular corporate forms. Acad. Manag. J. **44**(6), 1229–1249 (2001)

Gassmann, O., Zedtwitz, M.: Trends and determinants of managing virtual R&D teams. R&D Manag. **33**(3), 243–262 (2003)

Gerybadze, A., Reger, G.: Globalization of R&D: recent changes in the management of innovation in transnational corporations. Res. Policy **28**(2), 251–274 (1999)

Graham, S.J., Mowery, D.C.: The use of intellectual property in software: implications for open innovation. In: Open Innovation: Researching a New Paradigm, pp. 184–204 (2006)

Hall, B.H., Ziedonis, R.H.: The patent paradox revisited: an empirical study of patenting in the US semiconductor industry, 1979–1995. RAND J. Econ. **32**, 101–128 (2001)

Hansen, M.T.: The search-transfer problem: the role of weak ties in sharing knowledge across organization subunits. Adm. Sci. Q. **44**(1), 82–111 (1999)

Hippel, E.V., Krogh, G.V.: Open source software and the "private-collective" innovation model: issues for organization science. Organ. Sci. **14**(2), 209–223 (2003)

Howe, J.: Crowdsourcing: How the Power of the Crowd is Driving the Future of Business. Crown Publishing Group, New York (2008)

Huston, L., Sakkab, N.: Connect and develop. Harvard Bus. Rev. **84**(3), 58–66 (2006)

Huston, L., Sakkab, N.: Connect and develop: Inside procter & gamble's new model for innovation. Harvard Bus. Rev. **84**(3) (2006)

Keil, T.: External Corporate Venturing: Strategic Renewal in Rapidly Changing Industries. Praeger Pub Text, Westport (2002)

Kim, K., Park, J., et al.: The global integration of business functions: a study of multinational businesses in integrated global industries. J. Int. Bus. Stud. **34**(4), 327–344 (2003). https://doi.org/10.1057/palgrave.jibs.8400035

Kohler, T., Chesbrough, H.: Motivating crowds to do good: how to build crowdsourcing platingforms for social innovation. NIM Mark. Intell. Rev. **12**(1), 43–47 (2020)

Kuemmerle, W.: Foreign direct investment in industrial research in the pharmaceutical and electronics industries—results from a survey of multinational firms. Res. Policy **28**(2), 179–193 (1999)

Lagerström, K., Andersson, M.: Creating and sharing knowledge within a transnational team—the development of a global business system. J. World Bus. **38**(2), 84–95 (2003)

Lakhani, K.R.: InnoCentive. com (A). Harvard Bus. Sch. Case **608**, 170 (2008)

Laursen, K., Salter, A.: Open for innovation: the role of openness in explaining innovation performance among UK manufacturing firms. Strateg. Manag. J. **27**(2), 131–150 (2006)

Lichtenthaler, U., Ernst, H.: External technology commercialization in large firms: results of a quantitative benchmarking study. R&D Manag. **37**(5), 383–397 (2007)

Lynch, R.P.: Business Alliances Guide: The Hidden Competitive Weapon. Wiley, Hoboken (1993)

Maula, M., Keil, T., et al.: Open innovation in systemic innovation contexts. In: Open Innovation: Researching a New Paradigm, pp. 241–257 (2006)

Narin, F., Olivastro, D.: The technological utilization of European science. In: Proceedings of Joint EC-Leiden Conference on S&T Indicators (1991)

Narin, F., Hamilton, K.S., et al.: The increasing linkage between US technology and public science. Res. Policy **26**(3), 317–330 (1997)

Nelson, R.R.: National Innovation Systems: A Comparative Analysis. Oxford University Press, Oxford (1993)

Noble, C.H., Durmusoglu, S.S.等: 开放式创新: 基于PDMA的新产品开发要素分析. 北京, 化学工业出版社 (2019)

Nonaka, I., Takeuchi, H.: The Knowledge-Creating Company: How Japanese Companies Create the Dynamics of Innovation. Oxford University Press, Oxford (1995)

Partha, D., David, P.A.: Toward a new economics of science. Res. Policy **23**(5), 487–521 (1994)

Piller, F.T., Walcher, D.: Toolkits for idea competitions: a novel method to integrate users in new product development. R&D Manag. **36**(3), 307–318 (2006)

Reichwald, R., Stotko, C.M., et al.: Distributed mini-factory networks as a form of real-time enterprise: concept, flexibility potential and case studies. In: The Practical Real-Time Enterprise, pp. 403–434. Springer, Cham (2005)

Rohrbeck, R., Hölzle, K., et al.: Opening up for competitive advantage–how Deutsche Telekom creates an open innovation ecosystem. R&D Manag. **39**(4), 420–430 (2009)

Rosenberg, N.: Why do firms do basic research (with their own money)? Res. Policy 19(2), 165–174 (1990)

Sawhney, M., Prandelli, E.: Communities of creation: managing distributed innovation in turbulent markets. Calif. Manag. Rev. 42(4), 24–54 (2000)

Su, Y., Tsang, E.W., et al.: How do internal capabilities and external partnerships affect innovativeness? Asia Pac. J. Manag. 26(2), 309–331 (2009)

Szulanski, G.: Exploring internal stickiness: impediments to the transfer of best practice within the firm. Strateg. Manag. J. 17(S2), 27–43 (1996)

Tao, J., Magnotta, V.: How air products and chemicals "identifies and accelerates." Res.-Technol. Manag. 49(5), 12–18 (2006)

Teece, D.J.: Profiting from technological innovation: Implications for integration, collaboration, licensing and public policy. Res. Policy 15(6), 285–305 (1986)

Teece, D.J., Pisano, G., et al.: Dynamic capabilities and strategic management. Strateg. Manag. J. 18(7), 509–533 (1997)

Thursby, J.G., Jensen, R., et al.: Objectives, characteristics and outcomes of university licensing: a survey of major US universities. J. Technol. Transf. 26(1–2), 59–72 (2001)

Tidd, J., Trewhella, M.J.: Organizational and technological antecedents for knowledge acquisition and learning. R&D Manag. 27(4), 359–375 (1997)

Tsai, W., Ghoshal, S.: Social capital and value creation: the role of intrafirm networks. Acad. Manag. J. 41(4), 464–476 (1998)

Vanhaverbeke, W.: The interorganizational context of open innovation. In: Open Innovation: Researching a New Paradigm, pp. 205–219 (2006)

Von Hippel, E., Katz, R.: Shifting innovation to users via toolkits. Manag. Sci. 48(7), 821–833 (2002)

Likai, L.: Open Innovation: Big Collaboration Changes the World. Sanlian Publishing House, Shanghai (2016)

Wang, J.: The possession system under open innovation: a discussion based on intellectual property. Res. Manag. (1), 153–159 (2010)

Wang, J., Zeng, T.: Open innovation: a cognitive framework based on value innovation. Nankai Manag. Rev. (2), 114–125 (2011)

NetImmerse - Evaluating User Experience in Immersive Network Exploration

Kay Schröder[1,2(✉)] ⓘ, Steffi Kohl[2,3] ⓘ, and Batoul Ajdadilish[2] ⓘ

[1] Human Computer Interaction Center, RWTH Aachen, Aachen, Germany
[2] Human Data Interaction Lab, Zuyd University of Applied Sciences,
Heerlen, Netherlands
`kay.schroder@zuyd.nl`
[3] Maastricht University, Maastricht, Netherlands

Abstract. The increasing amount of interconnected data has given rise to a need among researchers and practitioners to develop new approaches to visualizing network structures. The intricacy of such structures vastly exceeds the capacity of most conventional approaches to network visualization in terms of dimensional and resolution restrictions, as they are mostly presented as two-dimensional with on a limited size screen. An additional limitation of traditional network visualization tools from a human–computer interaction standpoint is the limited interaction itself where immersion and "deep-diving" into high-dimensional data is not possible. We built NetImmerse, an application to visualize network data in a virtual environment with the ability to overview, zoom, and request details on-demand. Within the virtual space, users can either walk around the 3D data representation or rotate and move the representation using the two controllers. We tested the application with users and simulated a representative use case. NetImmerse enabled the participants to gain accurate insights based on the defined task. Participants indicated a PU of 5.25 and a PEOU of 5.46. We believe that NetImmerse is an engaging platform for multi-dimensional data exploration and may result in better insights and enhanced network data exploration.

Keywords: Immersive analytics · Network visualization · Virtual reality

1 Introduction

The increasing amount of interconnected knowledge [5,6,8,41] has given rise to a need among researchers and practitioners to develop new approaches to visualizing network structures, while the visual complexity poses a significant challenge. In the most commonly used tools [1–3], the data are presented on two-dimensional devices. The complexity of such representations vastly exceeds the capacity of most conventional approaches to network visualization in terms of dimension and resolution for two main reasons. First, the number of individual

V. G. Duffy (Ed.): HCII 2022, LNCS 13320, pp. 391–403, 2022.
https://doi.org/10.1007/978-3-031-06018-2_27

nodes, especially the edges, produces visual clutter within the given space. Second, the interaction with those complex structures poses a significant challenge from a human–computer interaction point of view. Those traditional tools do not allow users to be truly "connected" to the visualization or fluid interaction between humans and network data.

To reduce the visual complexity, different approaches like forced edge bundling [36], citerattigan2007graph, aggregation [32] or removing objects have been applied to help users to better understand connections and relationships through visual clutter mitigation or reduction. From a human–computer interaction standpoint, those tools have limitations as immersion and "deep-diving" into high-dimensional data is not possible.

To overcome these limitations with alternative strategies, researchers have begun to pursue virtual reality (VR) as a means by which to explore networks in a three-dimensional space [34,44]. Driven by the advancing technical developments, they are following the lead of researchers exploring other research applications of VR visualizations [9,10,12,18,27].

Within this project, we developed a working prototype of NetImmerse, a virtual reality exploration tool designed to make complex and large networks more accessible to researchers. We demonstrate the tool with the network data of a social media page as an illustrative use case. We used this data as a case study as many people are familiar with the workings of such platforms. Through this, we hope to make the purpose and utility of the tool accessible to a broader audience.

The rest of this paper is organized into five sections. Section 2 reviews the literature on network visualization in VR. The development of NetImmerse is described in Sect. 3, followed by the details of the user evaluation study in Sect. 4. Section 5 discusses the results before the conclusion is presented in Sect. 6.

2 Related Work

2.1 Visualizing Data in Three Dimensions

There is a long-standing debate in the research community about the added value of three-dimensional representations and visualizations of data [31,39,42]. Early [11] and later [17] studies have shown that a spatial position is the most effective way to map information within a 2D space. The extension of the two-dimensional space with a third dimension used to plot additional data attributes has proven to be problematic on two-dimensional displays, which are called "2.5D" in the literature [31,39]. The primary reason for this drawback, according to perception research, is the lack of depth cues that play a major role in interpreting three-dimensional (3D) objects and visualizations.

The presence of these cues not only provides a complete and more perceptible representation of spatial information but can also increase the performance and accuracy of 3D visualizations [28,46]. Ware did not discuss the cue–self-motion parallax as he used a static, non-head mount display in the lab setting for his stereoscopic view experiments. Instead, he described the effect of kinetic depth, which has a similar effect from a static point of view as it is a similar concept to the stereoscopic disparity. As the lack of those visual cues is limited to two-dimensional displays, the initial concerns might not be relevant. The context of use in virtual reality enables users to really perceive a visual representation three-dimensional due to the stereoscopic disparity used within head mount display. Recent technological developments have allowed the use of stereoscopic head-mounted displays in human data interaction that provide those capabilities. Recent studies have shown that 3D data representations do not perform worse than 2D representations, and both can be used to enhance decision making in specific contexts of use [20, 35, 47].

2.2 Network Data in Virtual Reality

Network research has made extensive use of visualizations with actors being represented as nodes and the relationship between them represented as ties. Visual clues for the directionality or weight of the tie are often used, ranging from arrows to color changes [19]. While the layout of early networks was determined by the artistic and analytic eye of the author, modern network representations make use of underlying algorithms for optimized layout structures [24, 30]. Using these technology advances, network researchers have long tried to go beyond simple 2D representations of networks. Some of the initial investigations on comprehension of network information in virtual reality displays were done in the early 1990s. One report of an early experiment showed that compared to a 2D view, network information was perceived more effectively in virtual reality [45]. Graph comprehension studies showed that visualizing graphs in three dimensions had great benefits, supporting human perception capabilities [16, 46]. However, the type of displays available to date has played a limiting role in visualizing big data with complex structures. With the advent of VR technologies, more researchers are now investigating the potential possibilities for data comprehension. The nature of complex networks makes them ideal for exploration via virtual reality technology [33]. As a result, *immersive analytics* has been established as a new research field and as a relatively unexplored field that would benefit from more basic research in many aspects [22].

Kraus et al. [21] provide a comprehensive comparison and categorization of published works to date in the field of immersive analytics with abstract 3D visualizations and present an overview of current trends, gaps and challenges in this research domain. They argue that because network visualizations offer much freedom in creating visual representations, findings and conclusions are domain-specific and can not be generalized. Moreover, techniques might be limited to only one device and not applicable to another device with different technical specifications. Further, the literature indicates several open research areas for immersive analytics in VR environments, such as the context of the specific data set, VR attributes, suitable visualization and interaction techniques, and evaluation of those techniques compared to the conventional desktop systems [15].

2.3 Existing Approaches

Today, some initial exploration studies aim to investigate the potential of network visualization in VR for research purposes. An example of this is $BrianX^3$, a virtual platform for discovery and analysis patterns in the brain network. In the study, participants were able to interact with whole network structures and highlight subsections of the network. The research showed that this way of interacting with the data enabled participants to discover meaningful patterns and build research hypotheses around them [4]. Other examples in the field of immersive analytics include *VRige*, a virtual reality graph visualizer that enables visualization, exploration, and tagging of social networks in the domain of law enforcement. The participants using the tool showed greater structural information retention [14]. *VRNetzer*, a VR platform that facilitates the interaction between human intuition and exploration of large networks, demonstrated that VR could help to interpret increasingly large and complex data sets [33]. *XIM* is a system for exploration and understanding of large network data sets through embodied navigation and natural gestures using the immersive mixed reality space. Studies showed that by using these natural gestures, participants could retain more information about the structure of the network data [7].

Collectively, these studies outline a critical role for VR in supporting research. Because virtual environments provide a sense of spatial immersion and awareness, the existing tools suggest that they contribute to cognitive processes during data analysis task [7,14,47]. Further, there is encouraging evidence that a 3D VR visualization of networks improves participants' confidence in observing and understanding the relationships in networks [4,43].

3 NetImmerse

3.1 Research Motivation

NetImmerse addresses various challenges with network exploration in VR, as highlighted by Ens et al. [15]. They outline research challenges that need to be addressed to be able to build productive and effective applications for immersive analytics. Our main focus in the current research is *interacting with immersive analytics systems*. Within this theme, we mainly were interested in the subchallenges of *supporting transitions around immersive environments* while *coping with immersive analytics interaction complexity*.

Specifically, we draw inspiration from Sorger et al. [40] who proposed a novel approach for the exploration of large dynamic graphs in virtual reality via overview and detail navigation. The result of their case study was encouraging, demonstrating the potential for this approach. In line with this, Kuznetsov et al. [23] conducted a study to investigate whether immersive virtual reality can serve as an effective medium to support complex analysis. They built a novel VR-based system that enables users to interact with the visualized graph layout with multi-node selection. It enables the user to convert the graph into a more manageable form by selecting nodes and highlighted edges. The usability of the system afforded greater comprehension of complex data.

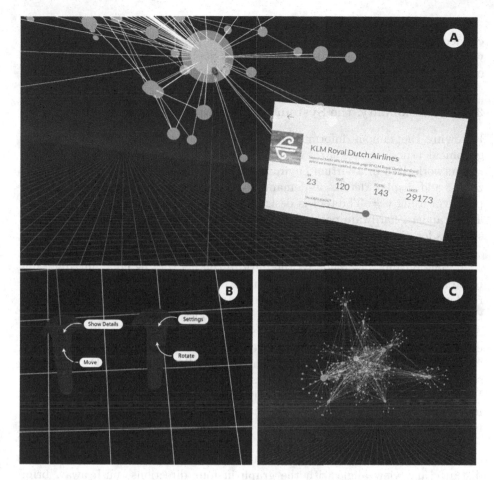

Fig. 1. Several screenshots of the application showing functionalities. A) shows the metadata display while selecting a social network data node. The info window shows additional metrics like in- and outbound traffic, likes and total traffic. B) The controller with tooltips describing the possible interactions. C) Network exploration view with disabled meta display.

3.2   Data

As an illustrative example, we present a working prototype with publicly available data collected from the Facebook page of the airline Royal Dutch KLM. Specifically, the data were collected by seeding first-degree connections of the KLM Facebook page, then all regional KLM pages within this network (e.g., KLM USA, KLM UK) were seeded for their first-degree connections. Display pictures for each page in the network were read in using the page URLs.

The resulting network is a directed, unweighted, uni-level graph with bilateral connections enabled. Edge direction represents page "likes" on Facebook (i.e., who likes whom), with bilateral connections representing pages that like each other. The network comprises 321 nodes connected by 1110 edges.

3.3   Functionality, the System and the Application

Following the famous information-seeking mantra in designing an advanced graphical user interface [37], we built NetImmerse, an application to visualize network data in a virtual environment with the ability to overview, rotate, zoom, and display details-on-demand. NetImmerse is developed on the Unity platform using C#. The tool is designed to operate with HTC Vive hardware. The standard hardware package includes a visor, two controllers and two base stations for space plotting and movement tracking.

To support quick orientation and to represent the nature of the data and their relationships, we rendered the data to the network as node-link diagrams using a force-based layout algorithm. In the first visual representation, nodes are rendered as spheres of different diameters, and edges are represented as lines. In the second representation (a directed graph), nodes are rendered as hexagons of different diameters. When a node is selected, the direction of each highlighted edge shows whether it is an inward or an outward edge.

Within the virtual space, users can either walk around the 3D data representation or rotate and move the representation using the two controllers. Prior VR studies found an advantage for coupling physical movement (such as moving around a 3D data representation) with virtual movement (such as using hand-held input devices) [13,38].

The user can navigate and interact with the visualized graph using the two controllers. On the right controller, with the touchpad, the user can adjust the distance and view angle with the graph in four directions (push away, bring forward, move to the left, and move to the right). With the menu button, the user can see detailed information of a selected node (details-on-demand). On the Left controller (with the touchpad), the user can turn the graph around in four directions (to its left, right, up, and down). The menu button is used to change the graph visualization, switching between different representations and layouts of the same data set. When the user surfs the graph with the pointer, the edges will be highlighted to show the relationship of the selected node to the whole network (Fig. 1).

4 Study - User Evaluation

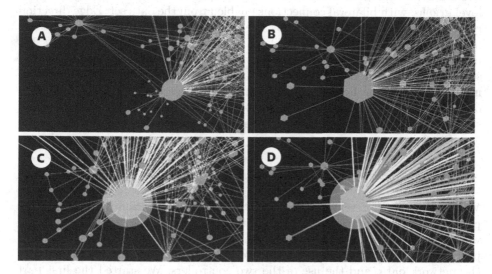

Fig. 2. Overview of the tested stimuli: A), C) Sphere nodes with regular color highlighting. B), D) Hexagon nodes with gradient highlighting.

4.1 Participants

Participants (n = 4; male = 75%) were recruited to conduct the user study. The mean age of our participants was 37.5 years (SD = 4.5). The average height was 175.25 cm (SD = 3.8). All participants were novice VR users; one participant had incidental VR experience, and three users had none. No participant had any form of color blindness (e.g., deuteranomaly), and one of the participants indicated nearsightedness as a sight impairment. Two participants indicated advanced proficiency for network analytics, and two indicated no proficiency, providing us with a heterogeneous proficiency base to draw feedback from. We believe that receiving feedback from a heterogeneous group is an advantage in this case as a tool like NetImmerse would be used by experts and less experienced researchers alike. We want to incorporate feedback from these groups as early as possible because their needs and experiences might differ significantly.

4.2 Stimuli

As an illustrative case study, we used publicly available data collected from the Facebook page of the airline Royal Dutch KLM. Specifically, the data were collected by seeding first-degree connections of the KLM Facebook page, then all regional KLM pages within this network (e.g., KLM USA, KLM UK) were seeded for their first-degree connections. Display pictures for each page in the network were read in using the page URLs. We used NetImmerse to generate two different versions of the network. Both graphs are directed, unweighted, unilevel graphs, with bilateral connections enabled from the data set. Edge direction represents page "likes" on Facebook (i.e., who likes whom), with bilateral connections representing pages that like each other. The network comprises 321 nodes connected by 1110 edges. The spatial distribution of the nodes was presented in a force-directed iterative layout. We generated a baseline graph with no visual distinction between indegree and outdegree using circular nodes, and one network with changes to the network visual representation of the same data set with a distinction between indegree and outdegree edges and hexagon nodes (see Fig. 2).

4.3 Procedure

We simulated a representative use case to test the application with the participants. For the initial training stage and the first stage of the study, participants were only exposed to the baseline graph. In the initial training stage, we allow participants to become familiar with the VR environment, the visualization of the network data, and the use of the two controllers. We started the first part of the study when each participant felt comfortable using the controllers and could interact confidently with the data visualization. Participants were provided with three analytical tasks and were given enough time to complete each task. We defined the tasks in two different levels, high-level and low-level tasks. More specifically, we asked the participants to complete two topology-based tasks (finding hubs), one attribute-based task, and one high-level task [25]. For the last stage of the study, participants interacted with the second visual representation of the same graph. Participants were once again asked to explore the data. They were given 5 min to report any new insights compared to the mental model of the previous visualization of the data set. To prevent any potential motion sickness in the participants, we made sure to define the first three tasks so that they would be completed within 20 min and limited the total time within the VR environment to 25 min.

User Evaluation. To assess NetImmerse, participants were asked to verbalize their experience during the experiment. We followed the suggestion for deploying a "think aloud" protocol and insight-based evaluations of data visualizations in VR studies [29]. Therefore, we transcribed the participants "think aloud" from audio recordings of each session to analyze the data obtained from the study. In addition, participants were asked to complete a questionnaire after the study. We assessed perceived ease of use (PEOU), perceived usefulness (PU) [26] and task self-assessment (TSA). Further, we asked participants to reflect on NetImmerse in terms of the factors: fun, enjoyable, interesting, absorbing, and boring. All measures were taken on a 7-point Likert scale.

5 Results

The results of the questionnaire are displayed in Fig. 3.

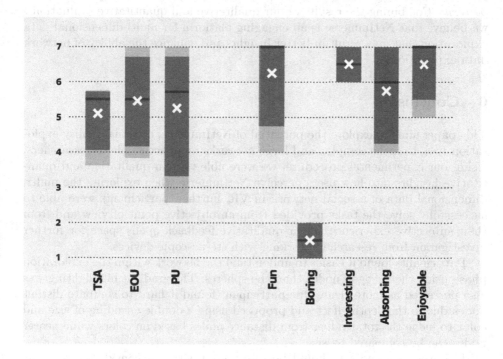

Fig. 3. Boxplots displaying the results of the user evaluation study showing task self assessment (TSA), perceived ease of use (PEOU), perceived usability (PU) and the reflection measures fun, boring, interesting, absorbing and enjoyable. The middle line of the box represents the median, the x in the box represents the mean.

Overall, NetImmerse was perceived as fun (M = 6.25, SD = 1.5), enjoyable (M = 6.5, SD = 1), absorbing (M = 5.75, SD = 1.5), interesting (M = 6.5, SD = 0.58) and not boring (M = 1.5, SD = 0.58). Users indicated a PU of 5.25 (SD = 1.89) and a PEOU of 5.46 (SD = 1.32). During the experiment, participants could gain accurate insights for the defined task based on objective performance evaluation (100% correctness of participants) and per subjective task performance, for which participants indicated a TSA of 5.09 (SD = 0.99)).

Evaluating the qualitative feedback, we conclude that participants found it easier to understand the network within the exploration phase while using the hexagon nodes instead of the spheres. One participant found it hard to compare distant nodes due to the depth effect and proposed using a double encoding of size and color to judge the total values from distance nodes based on colors while nearer nodes can be compared by size. Moreover, the gradient highlighting in the second visualization was also perceived as useful, confirmed by a participant explaining that: *When I select a node, I see incoming and outgoing lines in two different colors (...) it makes it very clearer (...) more than previous one.* Another participant highlighted the advantages of the visualization for pattern recognition, stating that: *The colors (...) make it slightly easier to find unknown patterns.* Combining the results of our qualitative and quantitative evaluations, we believe that NetImmerse is an engaging platform for multi-dimensional data exploration that may result in better insights and enhance the ability of network data exploration.

6   Conclusion

This paper aims to explore the potential of NetImmerse, a virtual reality exploration tool, to make complex and large networks more accessible to researchers. Using our experimental procedure, we were able to gain qualitative and quantitative insights into how users perceive NetImmerse when exploring the multi-dimensional data of a social network in VR. Further, participants were able to successfully solve the tasks provided from an objective point of view and from their subjective experience. Their qualitative feedback opens space for further investigation from researchers working with stereoscopic devices.

Participants found it easier to understand the network within the exploration phase using the hexagon nodes than the spheres. The gradient highlighting was also perceived as more clear. One participant found it hard to compare distant nodes due to the depth effect and proposed using a double encoding of size and color to judge the total values from distance nodes based on colors while nearer nodes can be compared by size.

However, our findings should be interpreted with the consideration of the small sample size in our initial study. More research needs to be done with increased sample size, additional tasks as well as additional visual encodings to understand better how immersive network analytics could be improved.

Future studies should also assess additional contexts of use, such as mixed reality, to evaluate if the level of immersion also influences the efficiency within related visual exploration scenarios. Also, long-term studies exposing the network to user multiple times would help to investigate the use of immersive technology in understanding abstract data structures (such as networks) under consideration of learning effects and potential additional in-depth feedback.

Acknowledgement. We would like to express our appreciation to Dr Benjamin Lucas for his valuable and constructive suggestions during the planning and development phase of this research work and providing the network data used in this study.

References

1. www.graphviz.org/
2. www.cytoscape.org/
3. www.gephi.org/

4. Arsiwalla, X.D., et al.: Network dynamics with BrainX3: a large-scale simulation of the human brain network with real-time interaction. Front. Neuroinform. **9**, 2 (2015)
5. Barabási, A.L., Gulbahce, N., Loscalzo, J.: Network medicine: a network-based approach to human disease. Nat. Rev. Genet. **12**(1), 56–68 (2011)
6. Barabási, A.L., et al.: Network Science. Cambridge University Press, Cambridge (2016)
7. Betella, A., et al.: Understanding large network datasets through embodied interaction in virtual reality. In: Proceedings of the 2014 Virtual Reality International Conference, pp. 1–7 (2014)
8. Boccaletti, S., Latora, V., Moreno, Y., Chavez, M., Hwang, D.U.: Complex networks: structure and dynamics. Phys. Rep. **424**(4–5), 175–308 (2006)
9. Bramlet, M., Wang, K., Clemons, A., Speidel, N.C., Lavalle, S.M., Kesavadas, T.: Virtual reality visualization of patient specific heart model. J. Cardiovasc. Magn. Reson. **18**(422), 1–2 (2016)
10. Calì, C., et al.: Three-dimensional immersive virtual reality for studying cellular compartments in 3D models from EM preparations of neural tissues. J. Comparat. Neurol. **524**(1), 23–38 (2016)
11. Cleveland, W.S., McGill, R.: Graphical perception: theory, experimentation, and application to the development of graphical methods. J. Am. Stat. Assoc. **79**(387), 531–554 (1984)
12. Deering, M.F.: HoloSketch: a virtual reality sketching/animation tool. ACM Trans. Comput.-Hum. Interact. (TOCHI) **2**(3), 220–238 (1995)
13. Drogemuller, A., Cunningham, A., Walsh, J., Cordeil, M., Ross, W., Thomas, B.: Evaluating navigation techniques for 3D graph visualizations in virtual reality. In: 2018 International Symposium on Big Data Visual and Immersive Analytics (BDVA), pp. 1–10. IEEE (2018)
14. Drogemuller, A., Cunningham, A., Walsh, J., Ross, W., Thomas, B.H.: VRige: exploring social network interactions in immersive virtual environments. In: Proceedings of the International Symposium on Big Data Visual Analytics (BDVA). IEEE, NJ, USA (2017)
15. Ens, B., et al.: Grand challenges in immersive analytics. In: Proceedings of the 2021 CHI Conference on Human Factors in Computing Systems, pp. 1–17 (2021)
16. Fonnet, A., Prie, Y.: Survey of immersive analytics. IEEE Trans. Vis. Comput. Graph. **27**, 2101–2122 (2019)
17. Heer, J., Bostock, M.: Crowdsourcing graphical perception: using mechanical turk to assess visualization design. In: Proceedings of the SIGCHI Conference on Human Factors in Computing Systems, pp. 203–212 (2010)
18. Kenderdine, S., Nicholson, J.K., Mason, I.: Modeling people and populations: exploring medical visualization through immersive interactive virtual environments. In: Metabolic Phenotyping in Personalized and Public Healthcare, pp. 333–367. Elsevier (2016)
19. Knoke, D., Yang, S.: Social Network Analysis. Sage Publications, Thousand Oaks (2019)
20. Kotlarek, J., et al.: A study of mental maps in immersive network visualization. In: 2020 IEEE Pacific Visualization Symposium (PacificVis), pp. 1–10. IEEE (2020)
21. Kraus, M., et al.: Immersive analytics with abstract 3D visualizations: a survey. In: Computer Graphics Forum. Wiley Online Library (2021)
22. Kraus, M., Klein, K., Fuchs, J., Keim, D.A., Schreiber, F., Sedlmair, M.: The value of immersive visualization. IEEE Comput. Graph. Appl. **41**(4), 125–132 (2021)

23. Kuznetsov, M., et al.: The immersive graph genome explorer: navigating genomics in immersive virtual reality. In: 2021 IEEE 9th International Conference on Serious Games and Applications for Health (SeGAH), pp. 1–8. IEEE (2021)

24. Kwon, O.H., Crnovrsanin, T., Ma, K.L.: What would a graph look like in this layout? A machine learning approach to large graph visualization. IEEE Trans. Vis. Comput. Graph. **24**(1), 478–488 (2017)

25. Lee, B., Plaisant, C., Parr, C.S., Fekete, J.D., Henry, N.: Task taxonomy for graph visualization. In: Proceedings of the 2006 AVI Workshop on BEyond Time and Errors: Novel Evaluation Methods for Information Visualization, pp. 1–5 (2006)

26. Marangunić, N., Granić, A.: Technology acceptance model: a literature review from 1986 to 2013. Univ. Access Inf. Soc. **14**(1), 81–95 (2014). https://doi.org/10.1007/s10209-014-0348-1

27. McGhee, J., Thompson-Butel, A.G., Faux, S., Bou-Haidar, P., Bailey, J.: The fantastic voyage: an arts-led approach to 3D virtual reality visualization of clinical stroke data. In: Proceedings of the 8th International Symposium on Visual Information Communication and Interaction, pp. 69–74 (2015)

28. McIntire, J.P., Havig, P.R., Geiselman, E.E.: Stereoscopic 3D displays and human performance: a comprehensive review. Displays **35**(1), 18–26 (2014)

29. Millais, P., Jones, S.L., Kelly, R.: Exploring data in virtual reality: comparisons with 2D data visualizations. In: Extended Abstracts of the 2018 CHI Conference on Human Factors in Computing Systems, pp. 1–6 (2018)

30. Moody, J., McFarland, D., Bender-deMoll, S.: Dynamic network visualization. Am. J. Sociol. **110**(4), 1206–1241 (2005)

31. Munzner, T.: Process and pitfalls in writing information visualization research papers. In: Kerren, A., Stasko, J.T., Fekete, J.-D., North, C. (eds.) Information Visualization. LNCS, vol. 4950, pp. 134–153. Springer, Heidelberg (2008). https://doi.org/10.1007/978-3-540-70956-5_6

32. Noel, S., Jajodia, S.: Managing attack graph complexity through visual hierarchical aggregation. In: Proceedings of the 2004 ACM Workshop on Visualization and Data Mining for Computer Security, pp. 109–118 (2004)

33. Pirch, S., et al.: The VRNetzer platform enables interactive network analysis in virtual reality. Nat. Commun. **12**(1), 1–14 (2021)

34. Royston, S., DeFanti, C., Perlin, K.: A collaborative untethered virtual reality environment for interactive social network visualization. arXiv preprint arXiv:1604.08239 (2016)

35. Schroeder, K., Ajdadilish, B., Henkel, A.P., Calero Valdez, A.: Evaluation of a financial portfolio visualization using computer displays and mixed reality devices with domain experts. In: Proceedings of the 2020 CHI Conference on Human Factors in Computing Systems, pp. 1–9 (2020)

36. Selassie, D., Heller, B., Heer, J.: Divided edge bundling for directional network data. IEEE Trans. Vis. Comput. Graph. **17**(12), 2354–2363 (2011)

37. Shneiderman, B.: The eyes have it: a task by data type taxonomy for information visualizations. In: The Craft of Information Visualization, pp. 364–371. Elsevier (2003)

38. Simpson, M., Zhao, J., Klippel, A.: Take a walk: evaluating movement types for data visualization in immersive virtual reality. In: Workshop on Immersive Analytics. IEEE, Vis (2017)

39. Smallman, H.S., John, M.S., Oonk, H.M., Cowen, M.B.: Information availability in 2D and 3D displays. IEEE Comput. Graph. Appl. **21**(5), 51–57 (2001)

40. Sorger, J., Waldner, M., Knecht, W., Arleo, A.: Immersive analytics of large dynamic networks via overview and detail navigation. In: 2019 IEEE International Conference on Artificial Intelligence and Virtual Reality (AIVR), pp. 144–1447. IEEE (2019)
41. Strogatz, S.H.: Exploring complex networks. Nature 410(6825), 268–276 (2001)
42. Van Wijk, J.J., Van Selow, E.R.: Cluster and calendar based visualization of time series data. In: Proceedings 1999 IEEE Symposium on Information Visualization (InfoVis 1999), pp. 4–9. IEEE (1999)
43. Varga, M.N., Merrison-Hort, R., Watson, P., Borisyuk, R., Livingstone, D.: Tadpole VR: virtual reality visualization of a simulated tadpole spinal cord. Virtual Reality 25(1), 1–17 (2021)
44. Villaveces, J.M., Koti, P., Habermann, B.H.: Tools for visualization and analysis of molecular networks, pathways, and-omics data. Adv. Appl. Bioinform. Chem.: AABC 8, 11 (2015)
45. Ware, C., Franck, G.: Viewing a graph in a virtual reality display is three times as good as a 2D diagram. In: Proceedings of 1994 IEEE Symposium on Visual Languages, pp. 182–183. IEEE (1994)
46. Ware, C., Mitchell, P.: Visualizing graphs in three dimensions. ACM Trans. Appl. Percept. (TAP) 5(1), 1–15 (2008)
47. Widjojo, E.A., Chinthammit, W., Engelke, U.: Virtual reality-based human-data interaction. In: 2017 International Symposium on Big Data Visual Analytics (BDVA), pp. 1–6. IEEE (2017)

The Pension Story - Data-Driven Storytelling with Pension Data

Kay Schröder[1,2](✉) [ID], Poornima Belavadi[2] [ID], Martina Ziefle[2] [ID], and André Calero Valdez[2,3] [ID]

[1] Human Data Interaction Lab, Zuyd University of Applied Sciences, Heerlen, The Netherlands
kay.schroder@zuyd.nl
[2] Human Computer Interaction Center, RWTH Aachen, Aachen, Germany
[3] Institute for Multimedia and Interactive Systems, University of Lübeck, Lübeck, Germany

Abstract. Due to global socio-economic changes, the European pension systems require several reforms that call for more active roles from the citizens. Past research has shown that traditional pension communication is often not read and understood by the majority of the population. Furthermore, the general interest of the people to learn about pension information is low. As a consequence, the accessibility of pension information poses a significant challenge. To address this challenge, we try to find out if data visualization can help in the perception of the complexity of pension data, and if a narrative can facilitate the understanding within a particular context in this research study. A data-driven storytelling application was built aiming to bridge the knowledge gap about the pension data among the citizens. In this paper, we describe the visualization and narrative structure development process with domain experts. We tested the application individually customized to ten test subjects and found out that the developed data story enhances the understanding, user satisfaction, and accessibility of this information.

Keywords: Information visualization · Storytelling · Pension data

1 Introduction

A changing labor market, increased life expectancy, and the increasingly aging population in Europe require fundamental pension reforms [14]. In the Netherlands, the government set the course for changing the Dutch pension system in 2016. The revision of the system and further development of the pension sector could significantly impact the various stakeholders over the next ten years. Therefore, it is essential to communicate about the development of the pension sector to all of the different stakeholders. However, communicating efficiently through the available communication channels is one of the biggest challenges faced by the pension sector [16].

V. G. Duffy (Ed.): HCII 2022, LNCS 13320, pp. 404–415, 2022.
https://doi.org/10.1007/978-3-031-06018-2_28

So far, the pension sector has been using the traditional communication channels, e.g., post mail, to communicate information to their clients. However, these conventional communication channels no longer suffice. Although the communication style has changed from a physical letter to a digital e-mail combined with a personalized online environment in recent years, it appears that written information (including the uniform pension overview that everyone receives annually) and annual reports are often not read or understood by people. There are two main reasons for this: first, the interest to deal with it directly is low for many people because the payout event is far in the future [22,24]. Second, understanding financial data and its context is challenging for many people [4,5,12,23]. The underlying reason for this may be that the information provided consists mainly of text and numbers [18]. With the reform of the current pension system, new ways of communication will be possible.

In this study, we focus on the second aspect: *understanding*, by the aid of visualizations we propose to improve the understanding of pension information. Visualization has been getting more attention within the pension communication sector in the last years [6,21]. As it is known that our brain can process and remember visual information much faster than text and numbers. In addition, we investigate whether adding narrative structures can enhance the visualizations to further aide the process of understanding the underlying data in context [8,9].

In this paper, we describe the process, findings, and the resulting data story of the participatory design process that we applied to develop the data story with domain experts. We conclude the finding of our qualitative evaluation study that we conducted with ten participants testing the resulting individualized pension stories. We found out that all test subjects have very little or no knowledge of their pensions and pensions in general. Moreover, questions related to interaction and behaviour indicate that their general interest in learning about pension is low. After the stimuli (a data story from approximately 1 min), nearly all subjects were able to explain how the pension system works in general and how their pension fund is generated over years. Furthermore, their follow-up questions indicate that their general interest in learning about pension increased. Additionally, we also tested visualization literacy and financial literacy. We could state that all test persons passed the visualization literacy questions successfully, from which we conclude that all of them understand the visualization method. Surprisingly, one of three test persons could not answer all financial literacy questions correctly, irrespective of the pension knowledge questions correctly reproduced in the last step, which was surprising as it was expected that the questions on pension knowledge and financial literacy questions were closely related.

2   Related Work

While there are several studies conducted to facilitate understanding of pension data for domain experts in the context of financial data visualization, the use of data visualization to reach a broader audience regarding pension information is still not well understood.

2.1 Visualizing Pension Fund Data

An overarching research question in the financial sector is how can visualizations help the experts in the field to work efficiently with complex financial information. To answer the questiong from the visualization research point of view, we first distinguish between the two objective: *Visually analyze pension data* for domain experts, e.g., for portfolio managers and *presentation of the analysed data* to the stakeholders or citizens like clients from pension funds or connected organizations. While both the contexts aim at domain experts with specific domain knowledge, they give an overview of possible design-space considerations.

Aiming at presenting annual report data, Rodriguez et al. [17] propose multiple variations of area, bar and line charts and more specific combinations like fold-over stacks, directional waterfall or position folded bar charts. Most of the examples aiming on comparison tasks or visualizing temporal changes and therefore mostly used a spatial encoding. Schroeder et al. [19] proposed a combination of bubble chart and bee-swarm plot to help asset managers identify potential financial risks in pension portfolios through regular computer displays or mixed reality devices. Lugmayr et al. [11] proposed to use virtual reality technologies to put investment data into context. However, the expected audience in this case had a high financial and domain literacy and were able to extract the right information from the proposed information systems.

2.2 Visualizing Pension Information

One of the rare examples of how financial information could be visualized to enhance understanding and decision making was given by Cox et al. [6]. The authors use infographics to visualise key mutual fund disclosures and study if the infographics effect the investment decisions of novice, intermediate and expert investors. They use infographics to highlight the risks and the rates of choosing a particular mutual fund and assist the investors in choosing and comparing them with others. They report that the infographics did help in improving the decisions made by the novice investors who represent a large population of people who find financial decision making difficult in the real world. Although not much effect was seen among the intermediate and the expert investors' decisions. Another example proposed to use metaphors in combination with pension data to facilitate understanding and engagement from citizens by Schroeder et al. [20]. Although the paper uses narrative structure to help in explaining the dutch pension systems to users, the quantitative context was primarily explained in textual form. The metaphors helped user to link the abstract context to his individual experience, however, it does not directly facilitate the understanding of the abstract concept itself.

3 Method

In this section, we describe the design process that was followed to bring forward the final visual story on pension funds. In addition we also discuss the user study design plan to investigate if the generated visual stories improved the understanding on pension funds among the users.

3.1 Domain Problem Characterization

The development of the narrative structure took place in a participatory design process. Together with domain experts from the pension sector we conducted a mixed research group workshop to explore viable design and storytelling options under consideration of prior domain knowledge. The group consists out of two academic researchers with background in information visualization & HCI and five domain experts (a market researcher, three pension communication professionals and a pension expert).

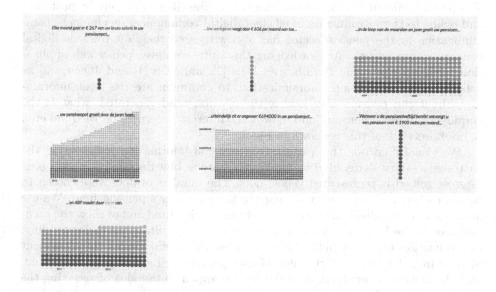

Fig. 1. The individual steps of the data story, starting with the monthly spending towards building a total pension pot and finally getting a fixed amount per month (text in figure in Dutch keeping the language of the target users in mind).

3.2 Narrative Structure

The domain experts with in-depth pension communication knowledge, work for one of the worldwide biggest pension funds which has more than 3 million members from a wide range of demographic backgrounds, provided a comprehensive perspective on the Dutch pension market. As outcome of this workshop we collected best practices from the domain experts regarding the data story structure, content and ordering. Furthermore we also discussed potential pitfalls, lessons learned, and promising future approaches in designing dynamic data visualization/storytelling based on their internal market research projects from the previous years. The findings of the practitioners were consistent with the proposed strategy that we found in the recent studies [7,14,15]. The story development followed a participatory design process with iterative validation steps, which involved domain experts as well as end users to ensure the validity of the narrative choices, the approach was similar to that followed by [25].

3.3   Visualization Design

One of the goals in the workshop was to understand the communication measures that were currently being practiced by the pension sector through which they conveyed important information about the pension funds to their clients. The pension information was communicated to the clients annually by post mail and owing to the introduction of efficient digital communication channels, communication in the pension sector has also witnessed the shift towards digital communication means. Acknowledging this shift, we developed a web application in JavaScript using the libraries D3js [2], animeJS [1] and JQuery [3] as a basic model of pension communication, to communicate the basic information about the pension like: how is the pension fund generated, what is the employer's in one's pension fund, how is the interest generated on the fund etc., A brief overview of this is shown in Fig. 1.

We visually encode the quantitative financial information representing the customer's salary share, his/her employer's share as blue dots and the additional interest gained is represented yellow dots. The number of dots were chosen to depict each party's approximate share to the customer's pension fund. We use animations to highlight the three parts of the pension fund and to show the accumulation of the fund over years until retirement. To facilitate the understanding, the animation logic was built closer to the user's mental model, the movement of dots from left mapped the idea of user giving the money to pension fund, and the movement of the dots to the right mapped to the idea of receiving the pension money. The addition of the interest amount was shown as dots stacking from the top. The animation ends with the final view of monthly annuity that the customer would get from the pension fund after his retirement.

4   User Study

We conducted a user study with 10 participants to evaluate the subjective and objective effects of the visualization. The procedure is illustrated in Fig. 2.

4.1   Participants

Participants (n = 10) were recruited from a pool of clients from one of the world's biggest pension providers. Formerly the clients had agreed to participate in market and research studies. After the experiment, each participant received

a leisure voucher from the local tourist association as compensation for participation. All the participants are currently employed and between 38 and 55 years
of age. Four of them were female and six were male. A convenient sampling approach was applied to choose the participants and they voluntarily agreed to join
the study. 9 out of 10 participants were working full-time (36 h/week), and one
participant was working part-time (28,8 h/week). One participant had dyslexia.
Three participants used mobile phones, the rest tablets or regular computers.
One participant withdrew from the experiment due to health reasons.

4.2 Procedure

Based on the personal information of the test subjects (birthday, pension start
year, salary grade and temporal extent of the employment relationship) a
custom-made data story was developed. We tried to avoid the feelings or prej-
udices provoked by apparent deviations between the presented pension scenario
and the individual scenario, which influence the results. In the first step, users
were introduced to the procedure and background of the experiment and consent
that the session can be recorded to transcribe the answers accurately. In every
interview at least 2 researchers were present, one conducting the interview with
the camera switched on and the other documenting and following all events in
writing with the camera and microphone switched off. Table 1 shows a sample
of the questions asked in the user study.

Before presenting the data story, a pre-experiment survey was conducted
where participants were informed about the conditions and background of the
experiment. We then asked the general demographic information of the participant to confirm the correctness of the background data so that the presented
individualized story matched with the participant. The experiment was divided
in 5 parts:

1) General Aspects. Participants were first asked about general conditions
that could influence the results; we noted the devices that were used to see the
story and added additional notes it necessary.(e.g. dyslexia) Following, general
knowledge about pensions and the pension provider were asked, and the related
associations and possible emotions (e.g., fear) were noted. Additionally, participants were asked to summarize previous interactions with pension information
resources (e.g., an online information system that overviews the individual pension) and the pension provider.

2) Knowledge Questions About Pensions. In the next step, we asked the
participants to describe their understanding of how the pension allowance was
made up in terms of accumulation and total savings.

3) Presenting the Pension Story. After a general introduction of the data
story, we conducted a think-aloud protocol with the participants while there
were looking at the storytelling application.

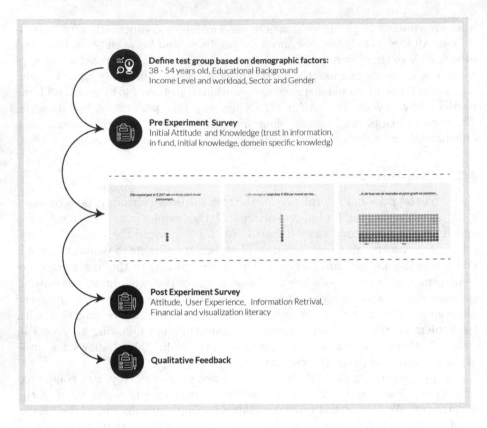

Fig. 2. Overview of the user study design conducted to study the effect of the pension fund visual story on understanding of the user.

4) Evaluating Perception, Knowledge Retrieval, and Conclusions.
After viewing the data story, we collected the initial feedback, the findings that the participants draw out of the data story, their perceived ease of use, and the level of conformity with their previous knowledge. Further, we collected subjective feedback and potentially triggered a follow-up question.

5) Measuring Financial and Visualization Literacy. To understand if the test subjects were able to understand the visualization in general, we tested the visualization literacy [10] to validate if users understand the individual elements of the visualization as their overall meaning. Finally, we measured the financial literacy according the scale from [13] and concluded the interview with an open-ended feedback question.

5   Results

In this section, we summarize the findings from the qualitative user study. A total of 6 people were involved in the qualitative data collection. Between 2 and 3 researchers were present at each interview. At the end of the experiment, all results were discussed together and summarized based on a common consensus. To sum up, most test subjects knew little to nothing about annuities. Only a few of them indicated that they had contacted their pension fund in connection with life events such as a divorce or a house purchase. About half of the total number of participants had consulted the general information websites to get an overview of pension structure and background information. Therefore, it is not surprising that the majority had no or neutral associations with annuities and the pension fund in question.

5.1   Initial Knowledge

A low level of basic interest was reflected particularly clearly in the pension-related question block: General knowledge questions about the structure could not be answered completely correctly by any test participant. Only 4 of 9 subjects knew that there was also an employer component; the rest thought that only they paid money into their pension or had no idea. Two subjects were able to indicate the amount they pay per month to pension contributions. When asked, all subjects could imagine that the money was invested, but how and in what amount was unclear to all participants.

5.2   Knowledge Retrieval After Stimuli

After the participants were shown the animation, all participants were able to reproduce the structure of the pension fund generation process correctly. The employer's share was explicitly named by 7 participants. One person had problems reading the texts, which can be explained by the fact that they had problems reading the small letters as they viewed the data story on a mobile phone. Five participants responded clearly to the net pension. All participants found the animation easy to understand and the content clear. The pictures of the animation formed the foundation of the understanding of the content, while the texts supported the contextual understanding. Only two participants stated that they did not learn anything new. However, we found that these participants had answered the content questions incorrectly before the animation and correctly afterward, which indicates a variance between their perception and our observation. The compound interest effect was clear for 7 participants; two participants gave a correct answer immediately after the animation, but could not remember it later. This could possibly be due to the fact that the new question was not understood correctly. One participant saw the interest but did not want to believe that it belonged to the pension payment amount. The same respondent was initially strongly convinced that the interest was not part of their retirement savings. What is striking here is that even though they understood the information correctly, their initial opinion hardly changed.

Table 1. Table showing the sample of questions asked in the user study (translated from Dutch)

Personal questions	
Can you introduce yourself?	
What do you know about pension?	
How do you think about retirement? What feeling does it evoke in you?	
What are your views about ABP?	
Have you contacted ABP or looked up ABP information? if yes, What for? What do you think about it?	
Do you log in to myABP? What information did you look for?	
Knowledge and questions about pension contributions	
Which parties play a role in depositing the money for your retirement fund?	
Do you pay for your retirement monthly? Do you know approximately how much you pay?	
What happens to your deposit money? What role does ABP play in handling your deposit money?	
In what ratio do each of the parties deposit money to your retirement fund (in percent)? How did you come up with the number? Where did you find the information?	
After watching the Pension story	
Can you tell what you saw here? What does it mean to you?	
Was the animation easy to understand? What were the clear and unclear aspects of the animation	
Does the information in this animation match what you already know about your retirement?	
You now saw a picture about the ratio of deposits in your pension pot. Do you know what are the three parties involved? Does your answer about the ratio change?	
If you look at the growth of your pension, when does your pension grow the most?	
Does the animation appeal to you? Why?	
Do you want to learn more about pension now?	

5.3   Subjective Feedback

8 out of 9 participants found the form clear. Two participants said it could be a little more appealing. ("I am missing a bit of 2021 vibe"). As further suggestions for improvement, one stated that the color contrast between the blue tones could be more robust. A voice-over was also recommended in combination with the existing text. One participant found the animation unappealing and difficult to follow, the test person was the only one who did not have a device with sufficient display size (cell phone) and therefore had problems reading the content. The

emotional response to the story was neutral to motivating (1), satisfied (2) and hard to believe (1). 7 out of 9 participants wanted to know more about their pension funds after viewing the pension data story, more detailed information about investments was explicitly mentioned by 6 participants, one participant wanted to know how the monthly pension is calculated, another wanted to know what his pension fund would look like if he retired earlier.

5.4   Literacy

3 out of 9 participants were not able to answer all financial literacy questions correctly. The visualization literacy questions were nevertheless answered correctly by all the participants.

6   Discussion and Conclusion

One of the challenges being faced by the pension sector is to make their clients foresee the future and prepare for the time after retirement. Although most of the working population understand finances early on, they think about retirement and take interest in understanding the pension plans only in the later stages of life or at the times of major events (marriage or divorce) in their life as suggested by one of the participants in our study. Even then, majority of them struggle to understand how the pension is calculated and don't pay attention to or find it difficult to understand the information letters sent to them via post.

New methods should be devised to increase the interest among the people and build their engagement towards understanding the pension plans and help them make better decisions. We propose using visualizations to communicate with the clients. As the phrase goes "a picture can speak a thousand words", visual cues are perceived and understood better by people from different cultural and educational backgrounds. With the communication channel shifting towards digital modes, visual cues with animations can be used to create the interest, explain a complex idea to the people. In this paper, we use a basic visualization and animation to make the users understand how pension fund is created. We conducted a user study (n = 10) to test if the visual data story increased the understanding of the people in this regard. The results showed that, majority of the users were able to understand the structure of the pension fund, which they did not know before viewing the visualization.

One interesting aspect the caught our attentions was that the initial bias of one user about interest amount not being part of the pension fund did not change despite him answering correctly in the post test that the interest was part of the pension fund, which makes us ask the question whether there is no correlation between understanding and bias. This could be further investigated with a bigger test group. In this paper, we have done a preliminary study to test if visualizations are effective in increasing user understanding. This could be elaborated in the future to have more metaphors and visual cues and test what visualizations are best suitable for this domain problem. More work has to be done to evaluate the different possible narrative structures for the pension problem. This work shall be extended to test the role of interactions along with visualizations among different target user groups.

References

1. AnimeJS - a javescript animation library. https://animejs.com/. Accessed 29 Dec 2021
2. D3js - Data Driven Documents. http://www.d3js.org. Accessed 29 Dec 2021
3. JQuery - a javascript libary. https://jquery.com/. Accessed 29 Dec 2021
4. Bernheim, D.: Do households appreciate their financial vulnerabilities? An analysis of actions, perceptions, and public policy. Tax Policy Econ. Growth **3**, 11–13 (1995)
5. Bernheim, D.: Financial illiteracy, education and retirement saving. Living with Defined Contribution Pensions, vol. 3868 (1998)
6. Cox, R., De Goeij, P.: Infographics and financial decisions. Netspar Industry Paper Series (2020)
7. Dinkova, M.: Brace yourselves, pension is coming: consumption, financial literacy and tailored pension communication. Ph.D. thesis, Utrecht University (2019)
8. Elling, S., Lentz, L.: Tien jaar upo.: een terugblik en vooruitblik op inhoud, doelen en effectiviteit. Netspar Design Paper (102), 1–42 (2018)
9. Lentz, L., Pander Maat, H.: De gebruiksvriendelijkheid van het uniform pensioenoverzicht. Netspar Occasional Papers (2013)
10. Locoro, A., Fisher, W.P., Mari, L.: Visual information literacy: definition, construct modeling and assessment. IEEE Access **9**, 71053–71071 (2021)
11. Lugmayr, A., Lim, Y.J., Hollick, J., Khuu, J., Chan, F.: Financial data visualization in 3D on immersive virtual reality displays. In: Mehandjiev, N., Saadouni, B. (eds.) FinanceCom 2018. LNBIP, vol. 345, pp. 118–130. Springer, Cham (2019). https://doi.org/10.1007/978-3-030-19037-8_8
12. Lusardi, A., Mitchelli, O.S.: Financial literacy and retirement preparedness: evidence and implications for financial education. Bus. Econ. **42**(1), 35–44 (2007)
13. Lusardi, A., Mitchell, O.S.: Financial literacy around the world: an overview. J. Pension Econ. Finance **10**(4), 497–508 (2011)
14. Merton, R.C.: The crisis in retirement planning. Harv. Bus. Rev. **92**(7/8), 43–50 (2014)
15. Myriam, L., Devolder, P.: Pension communication: digitalization and real power on people's behavior
16. Prast, H., Teppa, F., Smits, A.: Is information overrated? Evidence from the pension domain (2012)
17. Rodriguez, J., Kaczmarek, P.: Visualizing Financial Data. Wiley, Hoboken (2016)
18. Schroeder, K., Ajdadilish, B., Calero-Valdez, A.: Towards bridging the gap between privacy terms and humans through information visualization. PinG Privacy in Germany (2021). https://doi.org/10.37307/j.2196-9817.2020.01.17
19. Schroeder, K., Ajdadilish, B., Henkel, A.P., Calero Valdez, A.: Evaluation of a financial portfolio visualization using computer displays and mixed reality devices with domain experts. In: Proceedings of the 2020 CHI Conference on Human Factors in Computing Systems, pp. 1–9 (2020), https://doi.org/10.1145/3313831.3376556

20. Schroeder, K., Kohl, S., de Jongh, F., Putzu, M., Ziefle, M., Calero-Valdez, A.: Rethinking pension communication - the role of methaphors in information visualization. In: Duffy, V.G. (ed.) International Conference on Human-Computer Interaction, vol. 13320, pp. 416–429. Springer, Cham (2022)
21. Strikwerda, J., Holleman, B., Hoeken, H.: Supporting pension participants. Netspar Industry Paper Series (2021)
22. Van Els, P.J., Van den End, W., Van Rooij, M.C., et al.: Pensions and public opinion: a survey among Dutch households. De Econom. **152**(1), 101–116 (2004)
23. Van Rooij, M.C., Kool, C.J., Prast, H.M.: Risk-return preferences in the pension domain: are people able to choose? J. Public Econ. **91**(3–4), 701–722 (2007)
24. Van Rooij, M.C., Lusardi, A., Alessie, R.J.: Financial literacy, retirement planning and household wealth. Econ. J. **122**(560), 449–478 (2012)
25. Weijers, M., Bastiaenen, C., Feron, F., Schröder, K., et al.: Designing a personalized health dashboard: interdisciplinary and participatory approach. JMIR Format. Res. **5**(2), e24061 (2021). https://doi.org/10.2196/24061

Rethinking Pension Communication – The Role of Metaphors in Information Visualization

Kay Schröder[1,2]([✉])(iD), Steffi Kohl[1](iD), Frederique de Jongh[1](iD), Marco Putzu[1](iD), Martina Ziefle[2](iD), and André Calero Valdez[2,3](iD)

[1] Human Data Interaction Lab, Zuyd University of Applied Sciences, Heerlen, Netherlands
kay.schroder@zuyd.nl
[2] Human Computer Interaction Center, RWTH Aachen, Aachen, Germany
[3] Institute for Multimedia and Interactive Systems, University of Lübeck, Lübeck, Germany

Abstract. Pensions are the most important source of income for the elderly. However, old age poverty is a growing issue and conventional communication channels seem insufficient to inform people about how their current decisions will impact their future pensions. This paper provides a practical approach to addressing pension literacy through data visualization via metaphoric storytelling. Information visualizations aid in both communicating complex phenomena and serve an educational role. In particular, metaphors have been widely applied for educational purposes. We recruited participants (N = 11) for a qualitative user study. Participants' prior knowledge of pensions was assessed before presenting them with an animated information visualisation about pensions using a tree metaphor. After the stimulus presentation, a semi structured interview was conducted with the participants to assess differences in pension literacy and to gather feedback on the visualisation. These interviews indicate that the used metaphor successfully communicated information about the pension system. The results of the study indicate that metaphors enable participants to immerse themselves in the story and think of scenarios in which their pension decisions affect them, going thereby beyond simple knowledge recall. This provides evidence that this type of data visualization might be suitable to communicate and educate about abstract, long-term phenomena such as climate change and the spread of infectious diseases.

Keywords: Information visualization · Storytelling · Pension data

1 Introduction

Pensions are the key dimension against poverty and social exclusion for the elderly as they are the most important source of income for this group [23].

V. G. Duffy (Ed.): HCII 2022, LNCS 13320, pp. 416–429, 2022.
https://doi.org/10.1007/978-3-031-06018-2_29

However, the 2021 pension adequacy report of the Social Protection Committee and European Commission indicates that old age poverty is a growing issue within the EU [4]. Existing pension systems are based on the assumption that people will act rationally, following incentives and measures, such as working longer and avoiding part-time positions. However, research shows that people do not react as expected [19]. Despite the impact on their pension, individuals leave the labor market too early, even before retirement age. Surveys show that individuals do not think about their pension [16,24] and have low interest, knowledge, or awareness of pensions [23]. Conventional communication channels no longer suffice. Myriam and Devolder [19] conclude that digitization of pension communications improves the understanding and the accessibility of the information. However, the field remains mute on how this communication should be designed. It is essential to review whether traditional communication strategies transfer well into a digital context.

Collaborating with a large Dutch pension fund, we assess a common method of information communication they use in traditional media and in their digital communication: metaphors. A metaphor is an oversimplification in which one phenomenon (source) is understood by conceptualizing in terms of a different phenomenon (target) [14]. For example, water flowing from a lake through pipes can be used to explain electricity from a battery running through a circuit [10]. We are expected to have a rudimentary knowledge of both batteries and water to understand this concept.

In a participatory design approach, we develop a new animated metaphor story that satisfies the developed criteria and communicates the key messages the pension fund is trying to express to their customer base. We assess this metaphor qualitatively and conclude that a metaphor-driven data story based on pension data can enhance pension communication.

The rest of this paper is organized into five sections. Section 2 reviews the literature on visual metaphors with a special focus on pensions. The method used in this study is described in Sect. 3, followed by the details of the qualitative user study in Sect. 4. Section 5 discusses the results before the conclusion is presented in Sect. 6.

2 Related Work

2.1 Towards Understanding Pension Data

Efficient communication of pension information within the available channels poses a significant challenge [1,2,17,22,31]. Overcoming these difficulties is of vital importance for the years to come [19]. One possible cause of the underlying difficulties might be how information is presented, which is mostly in the form of text and numbers [25]. Therefore, it is not surprising that new forms of presentation with visual means are receiving more attention within the pension domain. For example, Cox et al. [5] suggest using infographics to support financial decisions. As this field of research is relatively new within financial decision making, others propose learning from disciplines with a comparable domain like health [28]. In the past, most of those approaches presented information in a static manner, which might be inefficient as the underlying process is time based and dynamic [7]. Prast [21] suggests an interactive tool on the pension system containing imagery of pension ownership, outcome estimations, an individual's payments, and how the pension changes over time. This tool might enable users to obtain a better grasp of the risks in their personal situation.

However, animated or interactive visualization of pension data is still very rare. Schroeder et al. [26] developed and evaluated interactive pension data visualization applications for domain experts in two and three-dimensional displays and found that both contexts can be beneficial. More recent work investigated the use of storytelling with pension information to facilitate understanding of individual pension data for citizens [27]. In the latter example, the information was presented solely by showing the visualized data, contextualized through text.

2.2 Contextualization Through Images

A growing body of research utilised metaphors for information visualization [15] and metaphors have been used in the past to communicate about the Dutch pension system [30]. Here, the focus lies on communicating investment uncertainty rather than explaining the financial flows. Although the authors claim the metaphor sufficiently communicates about pension risks, opponents state it might oversimplify and be too positive about the claims made [21].

As described in the introduction, water flowing through a pipe can be considered as a metaphor for understanding electricity flowing through a wire. Here, a property of model transfer takes place, moving attributes from one domain to another. The attributes in question are the finite capacity of pipes, indicating that wires also have a finite capacity and, therefore, a maximum amount of electricity can run through them. This inheritance of properties can be positive if accounted for, or can be negative ans cause misconceptions [12,15]. This can also be seen as a bias because it creates boundaries defined by the creator. Furthermore, it is a possibility that people either misunderstand or do not understand the intended metaphor at all. A model transfer will then be a misconception or non existent [20]. In one experiment on pension system communication and early retirement, manual laborers were used as a metaphor to communicate deserving tired workers. Once a different persona was used to symbolize under-served deserving elders, participants had a hard time adjusting because their understanding of the needs changed accordingly [11].

2.3 Visual Metaphors

The concept of metaphors refers to conveying a message through images. This message is not direct as it is implied through symbols and how these symbols are positioned. Implicit communication carries the risk of misinterpretation of a message [20]. Traegus [29] explores individual and holistic characteristics of an effective explanation by discussing explanatory frameworks. He states that the very basis of explaining unfamiliar concepts is to compare them to familiar

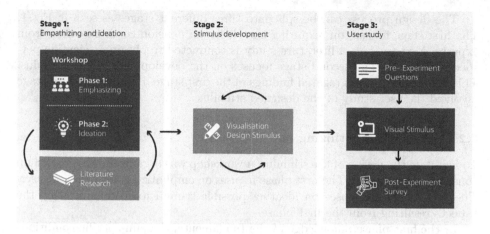

Fig. 1. The individual steps of the story generation and evaluation process as described in Sect. 2.

concepts and processes. For that reason, metaphors are important components in explanatory frameworks. Fry et al.'s [8] research has shown that by designing visualizations that are aligned to "system 1 thinking" [13], metaphors and narrative visualizations can communicate financial concepts in a way that also helps improve financial literacy. Lusardi's research [18] evaluated four educational programs about improving financial literacy. These consisted of an informational brochure, an interactive visual tool, a written narrative, and a video narrative. Outcomes of these evaluations showed how all the programs increased self-efficacy and how interactive programs can be particularly effective in improving financial literacy. Video narratives and visual tools appeared to be most beneficial in terms of financial literacy and financial self-efficacy through the vicarious and mastery experience.

3 Method

The method section presents the methodology followed to develop the visual stimuli used in this research. In Sect. 5, we overview the method used in the user study.

3.1 Participatory Design Process

We used a participatory design process to foster a holistic understanding and integrate domain knowledge from all relevant disciplines with domain experts. This methodology was also applied in other domains with similar challenges [32]. An interdisciplinary research group consisted of two industrial designers focusing on collaborative design methods, one information visualization researcher, four pension communication experts from different pension funds, and a researcher with a background in psychology.

The design process can be split into three different stages as seen in Fig. 1. The first stage focuses on acquiring knowledge on pension communication from experts. Next to that, a literature study is conducted to obtain a scientific perspective on this. The second stage focuses on the development of the stimulus. This is based on the aggregated findings of the first stage. Finally, the third stage involved the user study of the designed stimulus.

3.2   Stage 1: Empathizing and Ideation

To facilitate the design of the stimulus, a workshop was organized. This workshop consists of two phases. The first phase focuses on emphatizing with the end-user. The second phase focuses on ideating possible stimuli for communicating the aspects resulting from the first phase.

In the first phase, knowledge of the fundamental domain-specific conditions was shared. Based on the insights of the participants, lessons learned were distilled, resulting in an overview of insights and challenges covering topics such as the information visualization methodologies, levels of activation and demographics of the target group.

Synthesizing the knowledge gained from the collaboration with the domain experts and with the reviewed literature [6,9,19], three communication guidelines were established for the material, namely:

1. Simple and neutral communication
2. Specific monetary amounts
3. Personalized information

In addition to the communication guidelines, three key messages to be communicated through the visualization were generated:

1. Which money ends up in the pension fund
   This money originates both from the future retiree and the employer. The employer actually contributes a larger amount than the future retiree, which is often not known by the Dutch.
2. Growth of money over time
   Money placed in a pension fund is invested by the pension organization to create interest.This is an exponential relationship, which is hard for individuals to grasp.
3. The monthly retirement income of the individual
   It is assumed this will remain stable as the individual grows older rather than increase. Incomes generally increase as employees become more experienced, but this is not a guarantee that can be made in these visualizations.

An idea generation session was held in the second part of the workshop. The aim of the idea generation session was to generate a data story based on the generated key messages. During this part of the workshop, different kinds of data visualizations within a range of comparable contexts to pensions were shown as a source of inspiration. Next to that, design cards with triggering questions and self-formulated triggering questions about pensions were presented to the participants to stimulate idea generation. All participants were given time to generate ideas with the help of the provided material and the three earlier defined key messages from the first workshop. These ideas were presented to one another, and the group had an opportunity to build upon each others' ideas. All ideas were documented, resulting in an overview of ideas focusing on the story the visualization should tell, the interaction that the target group should have with the visualization and metaphors that are suitable for the pension context.

3.3   Stage 2: Stimulus Development

Design. The design was developed through an iterative process. The final stimulus is an animation consisting of both text and visual elements. The duration of the animation is 90 s. The text and visual elements are presented dynamically, which results in several screens with different types of information. An overview of the screens is presented in Fig. 2. No interactivity was included in the final stimulus. The story, symbolism and aesthetics of the visualization will be discussed in the next section.

Story. The storyline resulting from the key messages generated in the workshop is threefold. First, the contributions of both employer and employee are presented. Second, what happens to these contributions is detailed. Finally, a total amount of pension is presented. The way these are presented was designed to be in line with the three communication requirements: simple and neutral, actual net amounts, and personalized. Net amounts of contribution and pension and information about the contribution of all parties are retrieved from the domain experts. This eventually led to the following bilingual textual story:

> **Dutch:** *Elke maand gaat er €201 van uw bruto salaris in uw pensioenpot. Uw werkgever voegt daar €456 per maand aan toe. In de loop van de maanden en jaren groeit uw pensioen en [naam van pensioenfonds] maakt daar meer van. Uw pensioenpot groeit door de jaren heen. Uiteindelijk zit er ongeveer €522.000 in uw pensioenpot. Wanneer u de pensioenleeftijd bereikt ontvangt u een pensioen van €1400 netto per maand.*

> **English:** *Every month, €201 from your salary is saved for your pension. In addition, your employer adds €456 per month. Over the months and years, your pension grows, and [name of pension fund] generates interest. Over the years, the pension pot grows. In the end, it will be €522,000 all together. When you reach the retirement age, you get a fixed amount of €1,400 per month.*

The Dutch version of the textual story was used during data collection. The text is aligned with the Dutch B1 level, which is representative of the target group.

Symbolism and Aesthetics. The visual story is conveyed metaphorically. During the first phase of the workshop, domain experts expressed difficulties with conveying pension stories. Based on the reviewed literature, metaphors might help to increase the understanding of pension [30]. To the best of our knowledge, this has only been assessed with a single study, and no replications have been conducted. From a practitioner's point of view, the domain experts expressed that the biggest challenge arises in finding the right metaphor. During the workshop, they expressed that some metaphors, such as coins and a piggy bank, have not worked in the past. Even though a piggy bank is a well-known metaphor representing savings, it is considered insufficient in this context as the pension story is about more than savings. Concluding from the workshops, we decided to develop a new metaphor for the means of this study.

During the second phase of the workshop, participants came up with metaphors that are not directly linked to pensions but do represent a process of change and growth over time. This resulted in the ideas of using the weather or the growth of plants as metaphors. These ideas were developed further during the iterative last stage of the workshop. The final metaphor decided on was the growth of an apple tree. In this visual story, watering cans symbolize the employer and employee contributions, and the growth of apples symbolizes the result of interest that is generated. The choice of the apple tree is based on two Dutch sayings: *Een appeltje voor de dorst* (*A rainy day fund*) and *De vruchten ergens van plukken* (*Reap the fruits of your labor*).

The aesthetics of the visual story are based on the colors and style that are in line with the corporate identity and of the collaborating pension fund, signaling trust and recognition. Colors are used to represent the different parties (dark blue—employee, light blue—employer, red—pension fund) and to emphasize the contributions of these parties in the text as seen in Fig. 2.

4   Stage 3: User Study

The goal of the study was to understand preconceived notions of the pension system and how a visual stimulus conveying the pension system through a metaphor is perceived by participants grasping a greater understanding of the pension system. The designed data visualization has been evaluated qualitatively to better understand how participants perceive and experience this visual stimulus.

4.1   Participants

Eleven participants were interviewed, aged between 32 and 55 (64% men, mean age 46, SD = 6.9). All participants are members of the same pension fund. The experts involved in this research work for this fund. The presented contributions are approximated based on the publicly available wage agreement of the participants. Recruitment of these participants was based on pension fund similarity as the designed data visualization is based on the corporate identity of this pension fund, signaling trust and recognition. Finally, all participants have completed a

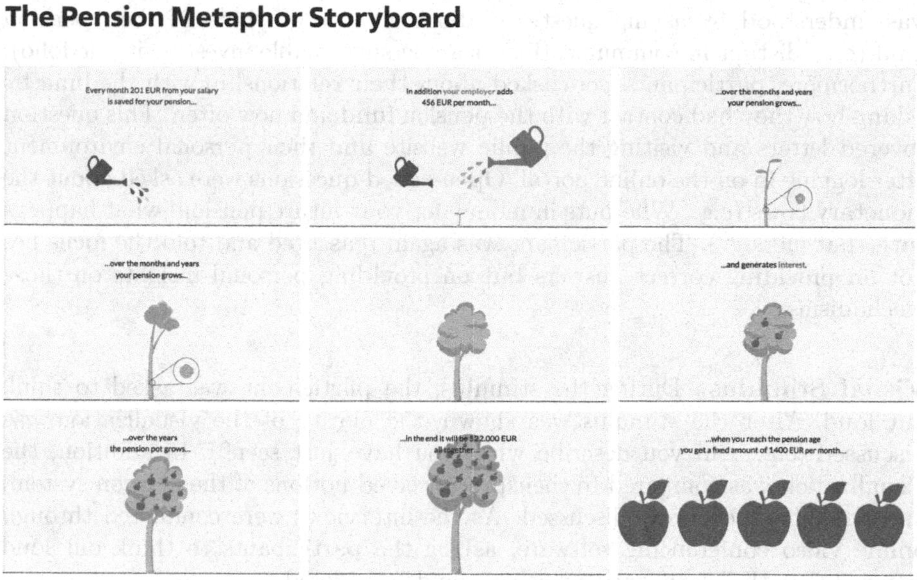

The Pension Metaphor Storyboard

Fig. 2. Storyboard (Color figure online)

Dutch bachelor degree. There appeared to be no clustering of participants based on differences in prior pension knowledge. This is based on the financial literacy questions post-experiment and on insights obtained during the interview about their preconceived notions of the pension system.

4.2 Procedure

The procedure of the user study is visually outlined in the last step of Fig. 1. Each interview lasted approximately 30 min and was conducted using online video conferencing software in which both audio and video streams were recorded. First, the participant was introduced to the study. As a second step, participants were asked to answer demographic questions and questions about their current understanding of the pension system. Then, the visual stimulus was shown. Participants were asked to think out loud while viewing the visual stimulus. A post-interview was conducted afterward.

Pre-experiment Questions. Control variables covering demographics, such as age, education level, work, and family situation, were collected first. Then the participants were asked to share their current understanding and associated feelings with regards to the pension fund and system. The interviewer stressed that these questions were focused on their perception rather than their knowledge of pensions. Questions such as "What do you think of pensions?" were asked in this step. The relationship between the participant and the pension fund was understood by asking questions about what they think of their pension fund (e.g., distant in communication or a non-sustainable investment portfolio). Furthermore, participants were asked about their relationship with the fund by asking how they had contact with the pension fund and how often. This question covered letters and visiting the public website and their personal environment after logging in on the online portal. Open-ended questions were asked about the monetary flows (e.g., Who puts in money for your future pension, what happens with that money?). The participant was again reassured and told the focus lies not on providing correct answers but on providing personal insights on those mechanisms.

Visual Stimulus. During the stimulus, the participant was asked to think out loud. After the stimulus was shown, the clarity of the visualization was discussed (e.g., can you describe what you have just seen?). In addition, the visualization was compared to their preconceived notions of the pension system, and the differences were discussed. As the interviews were conducted through online video conferencing software, asking the participants to think out loud ensured that the visualization was seen and considered.

Post-experiment Survey. After the participants had observed the stimulus, whether the visualization met their preconceived notions of the Dutch pension system was determined. In addition, participants were asked about the objects used, and more in-depth questions were asked regarding the symbolism (e.g., Can you explain what the apples/tree/watering can symbolize?) and what the colors represent. These questions were asked to learn whether participants understood the metaphor in this particular context. Participants were asked for suggestions about further improving the visualization. This was asked to empower the participant to share thoughts regarding topics that have not been covered by the asked questions. Finally, the participants were asked multiple-choice questions about financial literacy. These questions are used as control variables for financial literacy.

4.3   Analysis

The interviews were recorded and transcribed by the researchers. Considering the relatively small sample size (N = 11), the data integrity was maintained. Answers to the posed questions have been summarized as transcript summaries and placed in a spreadsheet to create a legible overview for all researchers involved. Furthermore, researchers made notes during the interview to revisit during the analysis. The research team analyzed the data together in order to minimize biases. During the analysis, the analytical focus was on the participant's perception of pensions and the Dutch pension system rather than knowledge of Dutch pensions. Considering the scarcity of research in this domain, a data-driven approach was used to derive emerging codes and themes through the data analysis. These are topics that are direct consequences of the posed question topics.

Looking at the quantitative control test on financial literacy, 10 of 11 participants answered these three questions correctly. Only one participant answered only two of three questions correctly. Based on these initial results, no outliers can be detected in terms of participant financial literacy. After conducting the interviews, it appeared that another participant had prior work knowledge in the pension field. This has been taken into account in the analysis of the findings.

5 Results

The participants' knowledge prior to the visual stimulus was assessed based on the pre-test questions. Two of three questions used as the control variable on financial literacy were answered correctly by all participants. One question was answered correctly by ten of eleven participants. Based on this, it can be stated that the financial literacy of all participants was good. All participants know their pension fund and understand its purpose.

Based on the participants' descriptions of their feelings towards their pension fund, two main characteristics can be observed: *trustworthy* and *old-fashioned*. Few participants mentioned a negative association with their pension fund in terms of its investments in particular industries. All participants indicated they had been in contact with their pension fund at some point in their lives. The majority indicated that their only point of contact was the letters they receive from their pension fund on a yearly basis. Some have reached out to the pension fund themselves to get answers to questions raised by life-changing events such as marriage or divorce. Three themes distilled from the rest of the interviews are discussed below.

5.1 Ratio of Contribution

All participants are aware that a part of their salary is set aside for their pension. Only one participant did not know that the employer also contributes to the employee's pension. However, none of the participants either knew or had a correct view of the ratio of the employee and employer contributions. All participants know that their pension fund invests the contribution.

In the visual stimulus, the contributions of the employee and the employer are described numerically. After viewing the visual stimulus, all participants knew the employee's and employer's contribution and the ratio thereof. In addition, all participants were able to recall the approximate amount of the accrued pension and the net amount of their pension. They were all able to exactly reproduce the numbers and express the ratio. Almost all participants expressed that the employer's contribution was higher than expected.

The pension fund's contribution has only been shown visually (apples that grow in the tree) and not numerically. After viewing the visual stimulus, it remained unclear to the participants what the contribution of their pension fund is exactly and this raised questions. Other questions that arose throughout the interview are related to whether the ratio would change over time, whether this information would still be relevant in 20 years, and what impact life-changing events would have on this scenario.

5.2   Metaphor

During the interview, it became clear that all participants understood the metaphor. They describe that the apple represents interest, the tree represents the contributions from themselves and their employer, and that the watering cans represent the contributing parties. When discussing the metaphor, the apple seemed to draw the most attention from the participants.

Three participants connected the metaphor of the apple to two Dutch proverbs which apples or fruits are part of: *'Een appeltje voor de dorst'* (a rainy day fund) and *'De vruchten ergens van plukken'* (reap the fruits of your labor). Four participants mentioned that the metaphor of the tree is very suitable in this context as it meets the expected and desired image of pension funds. In addition, the participants mentioned that a tree represents healthy growth and stability.

Different questions raised by more than one participant about the metaphor were: *What would happen to my tree when I die?, How do the apples grow exactly? Do they grow healthy?,* Is there something I can do to make the apples grow? and *Can I pick the apples earlier?* The participants expressed that these were not questions that they thought of before viewing the visual stimulus.

5.3   Design

Many comments were made about the colors used in the visual stimulus. The most discussed object was the yellow tree. Participants expressed that the tree should be green and brown. On the one hand, this had to do with the fact that the tree should have "regular" colors. On the other hand, participants expressed that the tree color had been used to indicate the difference in contribution from employee and employer, as discussed earlier. Furthermore, the color scheme as a whole was not appreciated. Participants described it as *boring* and *not colorful.*

Participants expressed confusion about the speed and the size of objects within the animation. The speedy growth of the apples did not represent the participants' perception of the time required to grow a pension. In addition, the total size of the tree was not considered representative of the total amount of a pension.

6   Conclusion

This paper aims to research the potential of metaphors as an alternative to quantitative data visualization approaches in pension communication. Due to regulatory changes in the Dutch pension system, employees will have more control and ownership of their pension fund. As about 79% of the Dutch working-age people have an incorrect understanding of how pension funds work, it is important to improve pension literacy. The research team created a personalized dynamic visualization of the pension fund, which is told through metaphors aligned with Dutch proverbs. A qualitative study evaluated this visualization with eleven participants. All participants understood the metaphor correctly and were able to explain what they observed.

Our research has two main findings. Primarily, we show that metaphors seem to be a fitting approach to explaining the Dutch pension system. Metaphors can help link a more abstract concept to an individual experience. Through the metaphor, the participants were inclined to think of their own situation and understand the pension system as a whole. This might indicate that participants have surpassed superficial thinking about their pension and are able to question their individual situation through wonderment [3].

Secondly, numerical values used in the data visualization, such as net monthly pension upon retirement or monthly contribution from the employer, appeared to play a stronger role in the comprehension of the pension fund than the metaphor itself. The participants were able to recall these numerical values in the discussion after viewing the visualization. The combination of a metaphor and concrete descriptions might be beneficial in understanding complex and abstract phenomena as they complement each other. Concrete descriptions aid in the general understanding, whereas the metaphor contributes to the role of an individual in this complex phenomenon.

6.1   Limitations

The designed data visualization utilized the colors present in the corporate identity of the pension fund to meet expectations of trust and recognition. However, many participants stated these colors were out of place and raised questions rather than providing recognition. The color used for the tree had a particularly negative impact on the participants' experiences. Still, this does not appear to have negatively influenced the understanding of the pension fund explanation as a whole. Properties of model transfer apply in this case of metaphors. Both predestined attributes and abundant attributes of the source are translated to the field of application. By suggesting the metaphor as a model image function, abundant attributes can be introduced to the concept. This property has both wanted and unwanted effects. On the one hand, it provides learning opportunities to transfer known properties from one domain to another. On the other hand, it also holds true for unwanted or unknown properties, thereby including more uncertainty in the designed data visualization. In the case of this study, the representation of apples as money in the pension fund unintentionally indicated that the pension fund could be accessed before the retirement age is reached.

6.2   Future Research

The studied metaphor caused participants to think about the pension fund in their own situation. It is unclear whether that reaction was caused by this specific metaphor or by the dialogue about pensions in general. Possible explanations are that the animation itself caused the participants to consider their own situation, or that such consideration was an effect caused by the metaphors. Future studies should attempt to isolate this effect by comparing metaphors to non-metaphorical data visualizations in this domain.

Pension research is extensively covered in the scientific literature. Upon transferring this type of study to different fields, research needs to be conducted on the variables that need to be disclosed and the metaphor itself that could complement the data story.

The results of this study show the potential for the application of metaphorical data visualization to comparable abstract processes in the public sector such as regulations and laws and for similarly complex and abstract phenomena such as climate change and the spread of infectious diseases.

References

1. Bernheim, D.: Do households appreciate their financial vulnerabilities? An analysis of actions, perceptions, and public policy. Tax Policy Econ. Growth **3**, 11–13 (1995)
2. Bernheim, D.: Financial illiteracy, education and retirement saving. In: Living with Defined Contribution Pensions, vol. 3868 (1998)
3. Chin, C.: Student-generated questions: encouraging inquisitive minds in learning science (2002)
4. Directorate-General for Employment, Social Affairs, Inclusion (European Commission): 2021 pension adequacy report: current and future income adequacy in old age in the EU, vol. 1. Publications Office (2021). https://doi.org/10.2767/013455
5. Cox, R., De Goeij, P.: Infographics and financial decisions. Netspart Industry Series, Nueva Zelanda (2020)
6. Debets, S., Prast, H., Rossi, M., van Soest, A.: Pension communication in The Netherlands and other countries (2018)
7. Fouh, E., Akbar, M., Shaffer, C.A.: The role of visualization in computer science education. Computers in the Schools 29(1–2), 95–117 (2012)
8. Fry, A., Wilson, J., Overby, C.: Teaching the design of narrative visualization: using metaphor for financial literacy and decision making. In: Conference Paper, DRS/Cumulus, 2nd International Conference for Design Education Researchers, Oslo (2013)
9. Fuentes, O., Lafortune, J., Riutort, J., Tessada, J., Villatoro, F., et al.: Personalized information as a tool to improve pension savings: results from a randomized control trial in Chile. Doc. Trabajo IE-PUC **483**, 1–50 (2017)
10. Gentner, D., Gentner, D.R.: Flowing waters or teeming crowds: mental models of electricity. In: Mental models, pp. 99–129 (1983)
11. Hagelund, A., Grødem, A.S.: When metaphors become cognitive locks: occupational pension reform in norway. Policy and Society **38**(3), 373–388 (2019)
12. Inayatullah, S., Izgarjan, A., Kuusi, O., Minkkinen, M.: Metaphors in futures research (2016)

13. Kahneman, D., Patrick, E.: Thinking, fast and slow. Penguin Books, Allen Lane (2011)
14. Lakoff, G., Johnson, M.: The metaphorical structure of the human conceptual system. Cognitive science 4(2), 195–208 (1980)
15. Li, Y.-N., Li, D.-J., Zhang, K.: The impact of metaphors on information visualization. J. Visualization **20**(3), 487–504 (2016). https://doi.org/10.1007/s12650-016-0371-9
16. Lusardi, A., Mitchell, O.S.: Financial literacy around the world: an overview. J. Pension Econ. Financ. **10**(4), 497–508 (2011)
17. Lusardi, A., Mitchelli, O.S.: Financial literacy and retirement preparedness: Evidence and implications for financial education. Bus. Econ. **42**(1), 35–44 (2007)
18. Lusardi, A., Samek, A., Kapteyn, A., Glinert, L., Hung, A., Heinberg, A.: Visual tools and narratives: New ways to improve financial literacy. J. Pension Econ. Financ. **16**(3), 297–323 (2017)
19. Myriam, L., Devolder, P.: Pension communication: digitalization and real power on people's behavior
20. Petridis, S., Chilton, L.B.: Human errors in interpreting visual metaphor. In: Proceedings of the 2019 on Creativity and Cognition, pp. 187–197 (2019)
21. Prast, H.: Pension risk communication in the Netherlands. Technical report, Discussion Paper DP 01/2020 (2020)
22. Prast, H., Teppa, F., Smits, A.: Is information overrated? Evidence from the pension domain (2012)
23. Prast, H.M., van Soest, A.: Financial literacy and preparation for retirement. Intereconomics 51(3), 113–118 (2016)
24. van der Schors, A., Crijnen, C., Schonewille, G.: Geldzaken in de Praktijk 2018–2019 (2019)
25. Schroeder, K., Ajdadilish, B., Calero Valdez, A.: Towards bridging the gap between privacy terms and humans through information visualization. PinG Privacy in Germany (2021). https://doi.org/10.37307/j.2196-9817.2020.01.17
26. Schroeder, K., Ajdadilish, B., Henkel, A.P., Calero Valdez, A.: Evaluation of a financial portfolio visualization using computer displays and mixed reality devices with domain experts. In: Proceedings of the 2020 CHI Conference on Human Factors in Computing Systems, pp. 1–9 (2020). https://doi.org/10.1145/3313831.3376556
27. Schroeder, K., Belavadi, P., Ziefle, M., Calero Valdez, A.: The pension story - Data-driven storytelling with pension data. In: Duffy, V.G. (ed.) International Conference on Human-Computer Interaction, vol. 13320, pp. 404–415. Springer, Cham (2022)
28. Strikwerda, J., Holleman, B., Hoeken, H., et al.: Supporting pension participants: three lessons learned from the medical domain for better pension decisions. Netspar Design Paper 167 (2021)
29. Treagust, D.F., Harrison, A.G.: In search of explanatory frameworks: An analysis of Richard Feynman's lecture 'Atoms in motion'. Int. J. Sci. Educ. **22**(11), 1157–1170 (2000)
30. Van Hekken, A., Das, E.: Getting the picture: A visual metaphor increases the effectiveness of retirement communication. Futures **107**, 59–73 (2019)
31. Van Rooij, M.C., Kool, C.J., Prast, H.M.: Risk-return preferences in the pension domain: are people able to choose? J. Public Econ. **91**(3–4), 701–722 (2007)
32. Weijers, M., Bastiaenen, C., Feron, F., Schröder, K., et al.: Designing a personalized health dashboard: interdisciplinary and participatory approach. JMIR Format. Res. **5**(2), e24061 (2021). https://doi.org/10.2196/24061

Knowledge and Competencies for Human-Centered and Productive AI Work Design

Sebastian Terstegen[✉], Stephan Sandrock, and Sascha Stowasser

ifaa – Institute of Applied Industrial Engineering and Ergonomics, Uerdinger Straße 56, 40474 Düsseldorf, Germany
{s.terstegen,s.sandrock,s.stowasser}@ifaa-mail.de

Abstract. Artificial intelligence (AI) is already part of many things we use every day. AI opens new opportunities and possibilities for our work and our lives. The research project en[AI]ble is currently investigating which knowledge and competencies about AI are necessary to design this technology in a human-friendly, health-promoting and productive way in a company. A training program to being developed and tailored to the needs of SMEs will specifically enable managers, employees and works councils in SMEs as well as consultants to realistically assess AI applications and enable AI use that is profitable for all sides. This qualification will add AI competencies to the existing domain knowledge, by which is described the existing competencies as well as specialized knowledge of the target groups. In this paper, the core elements of this qualification and the reference to regulatory initiatives regarding AI will be presented.

Keywords: Artificial intelligence · Qualification · Work design

1 On the Importance of Artificial Intelligence for the World of Work

During Industry 4.0 and ongoing digitization in the production industry, intelligent networking of various IT systems as part of vertical integration and the use of networked cyber-physical systems are generating extensive data streams that can be combined and used economically for a wide variety of evaluations. The resulting data volumes can be systematically analyzed with the aid of appropriate techniques for the purpose of process or product innovation and the development of new business models. The intelligent use of this data is usually associated with the terms Big Data, Digital Twin, Smart Data or Data Mining. However, the mere existence of data does not yet mean process improvement or data-driven innovation, for example, the improvement of existing business models or the generation of new ones.

Due to increased computer performance, very dynamic research and progress achieved in application in recent years, machine learning techniques based on artificial intelligence methods are nowadays mostly used for these evaluations and data analyses.

V. G. Duffy (Ed.): HCII 2022, LNCS 13320, pp. 430–442, 2022.
https://doi.org/10.1007/978-3-031-06018-2_30

Since machine, plant and process data are available as part of the digital transformation, Industry 4.0 has created a central prerequisite for artificial intelligence methods to now find their way into industrial production processes as an extension of digitization and enable additional productivity gains here [1].

1.1   Definition and Delimitation of the Definition Artificial Intelligence

However, it is difficult to define the term AI clearly and unambiguously, as there is no universally accepted definition that is consistently used by all stakeholders.

AI as a Subfield of Computer Science. First, AI is a subfield of computer science. In this scientific domain, systems, methods, and algorithms are developed that emulate cognitive abilities such as learning, planning and problem solving and realize them in a computer. AI research pursues both engineering and cognitive science goals. Depending on the application, it focuses either on computer science, data mining, mechatronics and engineering, or on cognitive science, linguistics, psychology, and neuroscience and bioscience. Knowledge from the field of mechatronics, for example, is required in the development and deployment of autonomous robotic systems. Another application area is in the direction of cognitive science: speech recognition systems based on AI require domain knowledge from linguistics, psychology, but also from neuroscience and bioscience. Functionalities of artificial intelligence and learning systems are often based on the principles of the human brain. This requires basic neuroscientific and bioscientific knowledge and domain knowledge to (further) develop such systems. In Germany AI – in German KI – is therefore also commonly used as an abbreviation for so-called "future computer science" – in German "künftige Informatik". This is understood as the realization of intelligent behavior and underlying cognitive abilities on computers.

Artificially Intelligent Computer Systems. At the same time, the term artificial intelligence is also used to describe computer systems that exhibit human-appropriate behavior or behave in such a way that human intelligence could be assumed. Basically, a distinction is made between strong and weak artificial intelligence. A "strong" AI system would have the same intellectual skills as humans or could even surpass them; "weak" AI is focused on solving concrete application problems based on methods from mathematics and computer science [2].

In contrast to strong artificial intelligence, systems that have weak artificial intelligence appear to act intelligently in a specific, narrowly defined environment. Accordingly, AI technologies are to be understood as procedures and methods that enable technical systems to acquire data and thus to perceive their environment and recognize situations, to interpret these data and draw conclusions, to process data or what is perceived, to solve problems independently, to plan and make decisions and act accordingly, and to learn from the consequences of these decisions and actions [3–5]. The capabilities of these systems may exceed human capabilities in the application domain for which they were developed. A strong artificial intelligence system does not (currently) exist and is rather hypothetical. The currently available artificial intelligence systems all represent weak artificial intelligence.

In addition to popular examples such as strategy or quiz games, medical diagnostic systems or AI in product recommendation, there are also modern systems and algorithms of weak AI that are used in machines, robots or software systems and enable them to independently process and solve abstractly described tasks and problems. The individual execution and calculation steps are not programmed by humans but are developed by the learning ability of the systems themselves. Thus, the systems can also adapt to changing environmental conditions. Examples of such AI systems can be found in image recognition, in production, in assistance systems, in assembly or in human-robot collaboration. Due to functionally integrated mechanics, electronics and control technology, today's industrial robots, for example, can already be operated easily and intuitively, and humans and machines can work together effectively. With the help of AI and the equipment with sensors, robots are to become "smarter" and enabled to see, hear and feel. The aim of the development is that industrial robots could be controlled intuitively via simple commands or gestures without any great programming effort and to learn independently from "human colleagues" by imitating complete work processes.

Machines or systems developed using the machine learning method perform calculation steps automatically and without explicit programming of a concrete solution path. Thus, the methods and algorithms can learn from sample data and develop models that can then be applied to new, previously unknown data. Machine learning is mostly done with artificial neural networks (ANN). ANNs are computational models that replicate elements and structures of the human brain, particularly neurons - layers of nodes. Individual connections between artificial neurons realized in software have a numerical weighting that is adjusted during the training process. As the number of layers grows, more abstract representations of the input emerge, so the computed results get better and better. With a very high number of layers very complex patterns can be represented, and training data can then be used to detect such patterns in the data under investigation. Such machine learning methods, based on very complex ANNs, are also referred to as deep learning methods. They are used in nearly all modern AI systems, such as data mining or smart data analysis. A platform established by the German government as part of its high-tech strategy (www.plattform-lernende-systeme.de) therefore more accurately refers to weak AI systems as learning systems. The platform defines learning systems as *"machines, robots, and software systems that perform abstractly described tasks autonomously based on data that serve as their learning basis, without each step being specifically programmed by humans."* (translated from German). Learning systems solve tasks by using models trained by learning algorithms, with which they can continue learning during operation, to improve the previously trained models and to expand their knowledge base.

1.2   Status of Implementation in Operational Practice and Requirements for Qualification and Competencies

Despite the facts that AI procedures and methods have been researched for decades, that significant progress has been made in the application of AI especially in recent years due to increased computing power and very dynamic research, and that in the context of digital transformation, machine, plant and process data are available in most companies with which machine learning procedures can function efficiently, there seems to be reluctance to use AI in (industrial) companies.

Study on the Use of AI in Companies. A study by the Fraunhofer Institute on the use of artificial intelligence in companies, for example, concludes that only a few AI applications have been used productively in industrial and service companies in Germany to date [6]. In the period from January to February 2019, 309 companies were surveyed on the impact of artificial intelligence on the work of the future.

75% of the companies surveyed are currently involved with AI, i.e. they are gathering detailed information about artificial intelligence (35%), have analyzed the potential of artificial intelligence for their company (10%) or are partially preparing (14%) to introduce artificial intelligence in the company. However, only 16% of the companies already have at least one concrete AI application in use. This result can be explained by the fact that the companies surveyed do not attach great importance to artificial intelligence for their company (average 3.2 on a scale of 1, very low, to 5, very high).

In addition, respondents expect the application of AI to change the division of labor between humans and technology; for example, most respondents believe that the use of AI will lead to automation of simple tasks and that AI will take over human tasks in data analysis (average 4.2 on a scale of 1, very low, to 5, very high).

However, the reluctance of industrial companies to use AI can also be attributed to a possible shortage of AI specialists. For example, the respondents assume that their company will have a rather large demand for specialists for the efficient use of AI systems in the next five years. The recruitment of AI specialists and the corresponding qualification of the company's own personnel thus appear to be a prerequisite for the productive use of AI applications in the company. This is also confirmed by the question about the obstacles to the introduction of artificial intelligence in the company: the lack of competence in the company is cited as an obstacle (average 3.5 on a scale of 1, does not apply, to 5, applies); in addition, the companies surveyed state that high requirements for data protection and data security make the introduction of AI applications difficult (average 3.7 on the above-mentioned scale) and that no tailored AI solutions are available (average 3.6 on the above-mentioned scale).

Study on AI in Germany. The trade association Bitkom sees the main reason for the sluggish use of artificial intelligence in industrial companies less as a lack of knowledge than as a massive implementation problem (see, among others, [7, 8]).

In a Bitkom study, 73% of the 603 companies surveyed (with a company size of 20 employees or more) consider artificial intelligence to be an important technology of the future, but only 6% of companies are already using AI, while 22% are planning to use AI applications or are looking into the technology. Reluctance to embrace AI is more pronounced among smaller companies than larger ones. Only 53% of companies with up to 99 employees see AI as an opportunity for themselves, while around 74% of medium-sized companies (100 to 1999 employees) and as many as 84% of large companies (more than 2000 employees) perceive AI as an opportunity. On the other hand, 14% of all companies assume that AI will have no impact at all on their respective business models.

The study also reveals the companies' fears: 28% see AI as a threat to their own company, 17% even see their existence threatened, and 81% fear that foreign digital companies could use their lead in AI to become a serious competitor to German core industries such as the automotive sector. This is because only around 38% of the companies surveyed rank Germany among the world leaders in AI research and consider the German government's AI initiative launched in 2018 to be sufficient to prepare the economy and society for AI.

Bitkom derives from this four demands on politics or proposes corresponding measures that focus on AI research (Bitkom et al. 2020): Fill AI professorships not only in computer science, but also in other disciplines, in order to promote the plurality of AI research and underline the role of AI as a key technology; diversity in filling AI professorships; promote existing regional strengths, i.e. strong AI locations, when filling new AI professorships; create so-called "Chairs 2.0", where AI professors can teach and research locally only part-time and at the same time manage their own start-up.

Study on AI Qualification. An international study commissioned by Microsoft, in which about half a million English-language articles were evaluated and interviews were also conducted with around 12,000 specialists and managers from 20 countries in March 2020, investigated the connection between the successful use of AI in the company and the qualification or competencies of the employees (see, among others, [9]).

The study concludes that companies were able to introduce and apply AI in the company as part of pilot projects successfully if they simultaneously qualified their own employees and established or promoted a corresponding learning culture. The study results also showed that the need for AI specialists is growing; in the next six to ten years, companies would need roughly twice as many AI specialists as are currently employed in the companies. For this reason, almost 94% of the executives surveyed who are already using the first AI applications in their companies say that they are actively training their employees and building up the relevant skills or are at least planning these training measures. According to the study, this commitment is justified by a fundamentally positive assessment of the use of AI. Around 85% of managers in these companies (80% in Germany) derive direct benefit from the use of AI. In companies with a low level of AI maturity, on the other hand, only around 59% of executives (71% in Germany) see an opportunity in AI. The survey of employees paints a different picture. In companies with a higher level of AI maturity, i.e., where AI technology is increasingly being used, only 46% (42% in Germany) of employees claim that AI complements or enriches their work in a meaningful way.

Nevertheless, a large majority of employees (92%, 76% in Germany) are highly motivated to acquire or deepen their AI qualifications. In these companies, around 65% (in Germany around 50%) of employees have already taken part in corresponding qualification programs; in contrast, only 38% (in Germany 21%) of employees in companies with a low level of AI maturity have done so.

Overall, the picture is unbalanced: On the one hand, AI technology, and here in particular machine learning methods, are well developed. A broad spectrum of AI applications also illustrates the benefits of using AI for the purpose of increasing productivity as well as cognitive relief (for example, through AI-based assistance systems) or physical relief (for example, through intelligent AI robots) for the employees who use these AI systems. On the other hand, AI is slow to be tested, applied, and deployed in industrial companies. Barriers to the effective application of AI are being removed only hesitantly.

2 AI Qualification for Productive and People-Oriented Work Design

Even though AI can be technically defined and explained, even experts disagree about where and to what extent AI will influence our work and our lives. In order to be able to answer this as an employee, entrepreneur or employee representative at least approximately for the respective area of responsibility within the company, criteria should be known in order to be able to recognize the developments related to AI, to be able to perceive its opportunities and dangers and to be able to use it humanely and productively in companies.

For small and medium-sized enterprises (SMEs) in particular, many training and consulting offers are already available to help them expertly evaluate and apply the possibilities of AI for their purposes. However, the majority of these offerings focus on technical issues related to AI. As a result, a gap remains: Companies and their employees usually find it difficult to identify meaningful AI applications for their value creation, to evaluate them strategically, and to design and use them in a productive and people-friendly manner.

The en[AI]ble project aims to close this gap by offering a supplementary qualification program. By means of an AI qualification tailored to the needs of SMEs, managers, employees and works councils in SMEs as well as consultants are to be specifically enabled to realistically assess AI applications and to enable a profitable AI use for all sides in the companies. This AI qualification will add AI competencies to the respective existing domain knowledge, which is used here to describe existing competencies as well as specialized knowledge of the target groups.

2.1 Topic Area Health

The topic of health is an important criterion of work design with AI in the context of the AI qualification to be developed. The digital transformation with AI technology is fundamentally changing the working conditions for managers and employees in companies. This not only affects work equipment and work processes, but also has an impact on all areas of the company – from strategy to work organization, leadership to health-promoting working conditions. The changes brought about by AI open opportunities for companies to make working conditions more productive and health-promoting. Those who use AI in all areas of application have a wide range of opportunities to improve the health, satisfaction and motivation of their managers and employees and thus increase productivity and competitiveness. Without an appropriate design of AI, however, additional hazards and stresses can arise.

If aspects of the health-related design of AI are taken into account from the outset, opportunities arise for the company, among other things, that e.g., managers and employees are relieved of routine tasks and can work more productively, mental and physical demands are optimized or reduced (for example, through digital AI assistance systems, intelligent robots), and that data can be used almost in real time and for needs-based measures [5].

If, on the other hand, aspects of the health-related design of AI are not being taken into account, measures of workplace health promotion cannot be sufficiently considered. As a consequence, the use of AI may not be accepted by managers and employees, health hazards due to AI are not mitigated and this may lead to illnesses, accidents and incidents. New forms of potential health hazards from AI include: Dealing with complexity and less room for maneuver due to standardized processes. In this context, there is a possibility that the potential of AI-supported assistance systems and intelligent work equipment for mental and physical relief may not be exploited.

2.2 Core Elements of the AI Qualification

On the basis of surveyed needs and requirements for AI knowledge and AI competencies as well as comprehensive research and evaluations of specialist literature and the analysis of existing qualification offers for AI support, the en[AI]ble project team is currently developing an AI qualification. Target groups are employees, managers and works councils from companies who want to expand their competencies with AI competencies, as well as consultants in intermediary organizations who advise and support small and medium-sized companies and works councils.

The AI qualification is intended to provide basic competencies for criteria for the productive and health-oriented design of AI applications. These competencies are to be integrated into the existing domain knowledge of the target groups so that they can take the topic of AI into account and incorporate it into their existing tasks. Therefore the focus lays not only on the technological potential of AI, but also on its economic, organizational and personnel policy implications in the operational landscape. Against the background of the high development dynamics in the field of AI, medium-sized companies in Germany are to receive continuous support with the following core elements of the qualification measure.

Experimental Spaces Create Competence in Companies for the Planning, Implementation and Evaluation of AI Projects. The focus of the expanded competencies is not on specialized technological knowledge, but on imparting AI knowledge in socio-technical contexts, the exchange of experience about process and work design, and project competence. This requires new formats with experimental spaces in which companies and stakeholders can directly implement their projects. Products, services and complex solutions are created in close cooperation with universities, technical colleges and vocational schools. The participants are not customers, but partners in a consortium.

Institutions, organizations, and associations will formulate offers that, in addition to the technological tasks, focus on the preventive aspects of working with new AI-based solutions. Three different application scenarios characterize what is happening with AI in companies: 1. solutions and things that are already being used in the company and contain AI; 2. solutions and things that are being purchased and for which it is necessary to check whether AI is contained; 3. AI applications that are to be implemented and used in the company.

In the three scenarios, a systemic and holistic approach involving the stakeholders is required. The guiding criteria for data handling and process design are data sovereignty, transparency and explainability. Project competencies will serve these criteria. "Data sovereignty" is understood here as that a user of AI knows what happens to his or her collected data and consents to its use. "Transparency" refers to the property that the actions and functions of the system are traceable. The requirement for maximum transparency is often not fully achievable because many models are so complex that users of AI cannot see through the processes. This is precisely where the third criterion comes in, "explainability." The company needs the competence to explain regularities, processes and their backgrounds and thus to get all stakeholders "on board". Companies and individuals form an awareness of how AI works and how data is used. This does not require in-depth IT knowledge. Mastering this ability will be an important task in the "AI learning field" [5].

The Target Group of Consulting Organizations, that is, Consultants Accompany Companies and Their Employees in a Productive and Preventive Use of AI. Dealing with AI projects and accompanying AI stakeholders has become an important part of consulting services. The domain knowledge of the consultants combines with clear criteria for AI solutions and their implementation.

Consultants see their task as integrating AI into their existing competencies. An occupational safety specialist does not become a change manager and a personnel coach does not become a technology consultant. Instead, they see themselves challenged to expand their own domain knowledge to include knowledge about the effects of AI on their core competencies.

Consultants sharpen awareness of where the use of AI makes sense. They have criteria with which they can assess what is happening in the company. And they know the relevant networks and even who can assist with expertise. What is needed are design criteria that focus both on the benefits for the company's value creation process and on good working conditions and employee motivation.

All Company Players Are Trained to Recognize the Basic Functions of AI. The way how AI is used depends to a large extent on what knowledge managers and employees have about AI and how wisely and with which foresight they use and shape the new possibilities. In doing so, it is important to maintain a balance between the requirements of technology, economic efficiency and people.

In terms of how AI is built and how it works, its operators and users should know what sensors are in the "object" they want to acquire or use, and what data is collected by those sensors, where data is stored and who has access to the data, and what rules AI uses to process its data, manage its processes, and evolve.

Here it also becomes clear how important the work design competencies of the company actors are in addition to the technological competencies of the project service providers (often external). This should be the focus of further training in companies [5].

The Topics "Leadership and Culture", "Organization", "Safety" and "Health" Form Central Elements of AI Design Concepts. They are also important elements of AI training. With the introduction of AI, new requirements arise for managers: they must both effectively integrate the strengths of technical AI systems into their processes and preserve the specific skills of the people and social relationships in the company to maintain innovation capability. The roles of facilitator, trainer, coach, organizer will become even more prominent [5].

A "preventive organization" is network- and team-oriented in its nature. This requires self-organized structures. Clear objectives and goals are combined with the greatest possible leeway for the implementation of work tasks. There is often talk of learning AI; much more important are learning organizations and self-determined learning employees [5].

Data protection is about the legal questions under which conditions personal data may be collected, processed or used. Here, the stakeholders need expertise, but also an understanding of the uncertainties and fears of those involved. Data security is about the question of what measures must be taken to ensure the external protection of company data. Data security is thus a state that is to be achieved through suitable and effective measures.

The health-promoting aspects of AI should already be considered in the planning and acquisition of AI solutions and integrated into the processes to be able to design a productive and health-friendly Work 4.0. At the same time, there is a risk of increasing efficiency and productivity at the expense of health. This field of action gives rise to tasks for further training of the players. They must learn to assess the consequences, opportunities and risks inherent in newly designed work processes and forms of work [5].

Against this background, stable and powerful consulting infrastructures are emerging in the field of AI. The organizations focus on different areas and have different expertise. There is a constant exchange about the service portfolio. In this way, consulting and qualification offers are coordinated and connected with each other. The company stakeholders can thus access a multifaceted spectrum of topics that encompasses technological, economic, ergonomic and human resources fields of action.

2.3 Relation of the AI Qualification to Regulatory Initiatives

The topics identified in the EU Commission's initiative for a European legal framework for the approval and use of AI applications are an integral part of the additional AI qualification. The qualification aims to provide participants with success factors and criteria with which they can recognize developments related to AI, perceive their opportunities and risks, and use AI in their companies in a humane and economical manner.

This includes the success factor transparency: Transparency in the procedure should be ensured in all phases of the introduction of AI. Transparency can reduce fears and reservations about AI and create trust. An open information and communication policy must be used to clearly demonstrate the benefits of the AI solutions to be introduced and that the solutions include the protection of personal data and strategies against behavioral and performance controls and evoking work stress.

Another success factor is participation: This is understood as the involvement of employees in the entire process of introducing AI, considering their rights of co-determination. The aim of participation is to actively involve employees as experts in their work processes early in the introduction process of AI and thus make them co-designers and not just let them to be affected.

Qualification and Support Are Important Prerequisites for AI from the Perspective of Works Councils. However, the interviews with the target groups conducted by the en[AI]ble project team to identify the support needs for AI qualification also revealed that the successful introduction of AI and machine learning application (ML) requires the timely and comprehensive involvement of works council representatives. Only when it is possible to take a holistic view of the multifaceted topic of AI and to take the concerns and fears of employees seriously a positive relationship to the use of data-driven processes might be achieved. The works councils surveyed see that company management and employee representatives often weight the topics differently when introducing AI and ML.

In the interviews, the use of new technologies like AI, that help to safeguard the company's long-term future, was also formulated as an interest of the works councils. However, a distinction was made between the optimization of corporate processes and the optimization of employees. Increasing control, fear of job loss, work intensification and monitoring pressure are additional burdens and are decisive for the works councils' rejection of AI. One solution was seen in binding works agreements, which can ensure that, in addition to an interest in increasing efficiency and optimizing work processes, issues of health protection and data security are being considered. Since work agreements increase legal certainty when introducing AI applications, they might be also in the interest of entrepreneurs.

In the discussion about the introduction of AI and ML, the importance of qualification and further training to secure employment is emphasized. However, the question of the acceptance of AI arises less in relation to the ability to operate the systems, but in relation to a human-oriented design of the same. There is a consensus in that learning how to program self-learning systems cannot be the issue on a grand scale. And it can be stated that the software ergonomics of these new systems is better today than ever before, and so is their operation.

In addition to issues relating to the humane design of new types of work, works councils are particularly in demand where the processing, access and storage of the required data are concerned. The role of works councils in the introduction of IT systems is largely understood, at least by the representatives surveyed. The problems arise in the concrete practice and application of data protection and the design of IT systems to guarantee the criteria of data protection and to minimize performance and behavioral control to defined purposes only. Ex officio, works councils are obliged to monitor compliance with the principle of data minimization (GDPR Art. 5/1c). However, to learn independently, an algorithm must necessarily analyze and process large amounts of data (Big Data). Moderating the clash of interests and ensuring the informational self-determination of employees is the central task of the works agreements to be concluded in this field. This applies where a data lake is used to create a collection of data that is continuously fed from different sources. Where this data is collected, how it is stored, and how it is protected from unauthorized access is often beyond the knowledge of the company, especially in the case of cloud solutions.

This is also the Context for the Act to Promote Works Council Elections and Works Council Activities in a Digital Working World - the So-Called Works Council Modernization Act, Which Was Promulgated in the Federal Law Gazette in June 2021. The primary aim of this law is to counter the declining number of employee representatives in works councils, the prevention of works council elections on the part of employers, and new challenges and requirements resulting from digitalization.

However, the law also provides for extended co-determination rights of the works council regarding regulations on AI. According to §90 Works Constitution Act, the works council must be informed by the employer in good time about the planning of work procedures and work processes, including the use of AI. §Sect. 80 Works Constitution Act regulates simplified access to special expertise if the works council has to assess the introduction or use of AI in order to carry out its tasks. Since the legislator is of the opinion that questions regarding AI are complex per se and require enormous expertise, in this case even the otherwise necessary necessity test is omitted; with regard to the costs and selection of the experts, the employer and the works council must nevertheless reach an agreement. Furthermore, in addition to the existing right of co-decision on selection guidelines for hiring, transfers, regrouping and terminations, the works council has a right of co-decision as soon as AI is used in drawing up the selection guidelines [10].

General criticism of this law relates to the lack of a definition of AI and the mere insertion of the term, which in the view of many experts does not in itself constitute modernization (see, among others, [11]). The work of the works council is only "modernized" to a small extent by this law and the topic of AI in the company is not regulated in a modern way, but only "cosmetically".

The Obstacles and Challenges that P&MS and Works Councils See in the Use of AI and the Expertise They Consider Necessary Were Investigated in the En[AI]ble Reproject Mentioned Above. The surveyed specialists and managers lack a dedicated approach to the systematic use of AI, even though the topic of AI has arrived in the companies. Although they are open to the potential for improvement offered by AI, there is uncertainty about the economic viability of investments in AI applications. The development of skills among managers and employees is seen as necessary, both in terms of mastering the new technology and dealing with data. Furthermore, the effects of the use of AI on leadership behavior and corporate culture must be considered. Companies therefore have a wide range of expectations for qualified support, ranging from basic knowledge of AI, knowledge of the economic benefits and AI-related change processes, to social skills, pedagogical skills, and the ability to address uncertainties and fears about AI.

The surveyed works councils identified the identification of AI applications and the associated need for regulation as key challenges. Works councils reported, often not being involved in AI implementations, or being involved too late, whether in terms of their right to co-determination or in communication within the divisions. Works councils fear and experience increasing fears of control, job loss, elimination of activities, work intensification and monitoring pressure when AI is used. On the other hand, works councils also see the use of AI as offering greater potential for making working conditions more humane. To be able to act in a knowledgeable and targeted manner in this complex area, the surveyed works councils see a need for being supported by AI experts. These can be recruited either externally or, with the appropriate professional qualifications, internally.

From the Perspective of Labor Research, the Question of the Division of Working Tasks Between Humans and Machines Has not yet Been Conclusively Answered. The law outlined above and the accompanying extended co-determination rights of the works council in the use of AI in companies are not helpful. Instead, the task is to find a productive collaboration between humans and machines. For example, by having company representatives agree with AI developers or providers of AI systems on what goals are to be achieved for the company using AI. A company impact assessment can refer to the future work content and the resulting changes in the requirements and stress profiles of employees, qualification needs in the workforce, and the number of jobs. At the same time, the new technology and the resulting operational possibilities must not be over-regulated. In the working world of the future, courage and freedom are needed to try things out in partnership without being able to clarify in detail what the end result will be.

The en[AI]ble project with its AI qualification is aimed precisely at this in-company technical qualification of the skilled workers and works councils.

Acknowledgment. The authors would like to thank the German Federal Ministry of Labor and Social Affairs (BMAS), which is funding the en[AI]ble project as part of the New Quality of Work Initiative (INQA), the German Federal Institute for Occupational Safety and Health (BAuA), which is providing technical support for the project, and the project sponsor Gesellschaft für soziale Unternehmensberatung mbH (gsub). The authors are responsible for the content of this publication.
This publication was translated with the help of the DeepL translator.

References

1. Wangler, L., Botthof, A.: E-governance: digitalisierung und KI in der öffentlichen verwaltung. In: Wittpahl, V. (ed.) Künstliche Intelligenz, pp. 122–141. Springer, Heidelberg (2019). https://doi.org/10.1007/978-3-662-58042-4_8
2. Bundesregierung: Strategie Künstliche Intelligenz der Bundesregierung, Berlin (2018)
3. Russell, S.J., Norvig, P.: Artificial Intelligence: A Modern Approach. Prentice Hall, Upper Saddle River (1995)
4. iit (ed.): Potenziale der künstlichen Intelligenz im produzierenden Gewerbe in Deutschland. iit-Institut für Innovation und Technik in der VDI/VDE Innovation + Technik GmbH, Berlin (2018)
5. Offensive Mittelstand (ed.): Umsetzungshilfen Arbeit 4.0. Künstliche Intelligenz für die produktive und präventive Arbeitsgestaltung nutzen: Hintergrundwissen und Gestaltungsempfehlungen zur Einführung der 4.0-Technologien. Offensive Mittelstand, Heidelberg (2019)
6. Fraunhofer-Institut für Arbeitswirtschaft und Organisation IAO: Studie zum Einsatz Künstlicher Intelligenz in Unternehmen. Präsentation der Gesamtergebnisse. Fraunhofer-IAO, Stuttgart (2019)

7. Billerbeck, J.D.: Einsatz von KI geht schleppend voran. VDI nachrichten, June 2020

8. Streim, A., Alsabah, N.: Unternehmen tun sich noch schwer mit Künstlicher Intelligenz. Bitkom, Berlin (2020)

9. Unternehmen gewichten KI und Qualifizierung gleich. IT&Production, 5 June 2020

10. Bund Verlag: Das ändert sich durch das Betriebsrätemodernisierungsgesetz. https://www.bund-verlag.de/aktuelles~Das-aendert-sich-durch-das-Betriebsraetemodernisierungsgeset z~.html. Accessed 15 Sep 2021

11. Heimann, E., Klaus, S.: Betriebsrätemodernisierungsgesetz: Scheinheilige Reform der Betriebsverfassung oder tatsächliche Veränderung? https://efarbeitsrecht.net/betriebsraetemo dernisierungsgesetz. Accessed 15 Sep 2021

A Bibliometric Analysis of Intelligent Voice Interaction Based on VOSviewer

Lei Wu[✉] and Min Chen

School of Mechanical Science and Engineering, Huazhong University of Science and Technology, Wuhan 430074, People's Republic of China
lei.wu@hust.edu.cn

Abstract. VOSviewer was used as an analysis tool to sort out and analyze intelligent voice interaction. The time span was set as five years, and 12,558 results were searched in total. The database was screened by the types of papers in WOS core journal sets, and 2687 records were refined. Word frequency statistics and keyword clustering method based on author and country relationship were used to construct the atlas, and the clustering results were displayed intuitively by VOSviewer. The results show that the current studies of voice interaction mostly take behavioral experiments. Keywords of voice interaction include voice, recognition, perception, health, knowledge education, social participation, information retrieval, human-computer interface. Based on human-computer interaction research, artificial intelligence, behavior, gender keywords becomes new research trend in recent years. In the study of author distribution, Munteanu, Cosmin Clark, Leigh, Torre and Ilaria are the authors as the core, showing scattering pattern, and the correlation among authors is not very close. From the perspective of national branches, European and American regions led by the United States are the first to initiate research. In recent years, China, Spain, Australia and other countries have also emerged in the field of research.

Keywords: Intelligent voice interaction · Bibliometric · VOSviewer

1 Introduction

In the development history of interaction design, from the stage of manual work in the early agricultural society to the stage of command language, graphical user interface and multimedia in the information age, the continuous development of society has promoted the innovation of interactive experience thinking and theory. With the development of mobile internet technology, driverless cars, display technology and various artificial intelligence technologies, design methods and forms are changing. In this context, Wahl H believes that the era of relying on traditional tools such as display and keyboard for interaction is coming to an end. In the coming era of environmental interaction, it is necessary to combine technology and users with an interaction way with low cognitive load and in line with human natural interaction rules as much as possible [1]. In the field of modern interaction design, scholars and designers are trying to explore new interaction media. Optimize the existing interactive experience mode, developing more intelligent interactive tools, developing innovative interactive experience theory and design intelligent products with better user experience.

In recent years, voice interaction has gradually entered people's daily life. Wang explored the technological progress of intelligent speech [2], while Kumah-Crystal reviewed the benefits and challenges of the implementation and use of speech technology and discussed the emerging opportunities of voice assistant technology [3]. The convenience of voice interaction has made intelligent voice interaction the main way to connect people and intelligent devices. Voice interaction has been more widely used in smart home products, educational agent applications and auxiliary design due to its fast speed, high naturalness. For example, Huang compared voice interaction and gesture interaction modes in HMI experience design and summarized the potential and feasibility of voice interaction in HMI experience design [4]. Aeschlimann explored the active participation and feedback of children in the interaction between voice assistants and children in daily social life and compared the interaction with adults [5]. Filimon introduces a universal culture game called Bob, which is a skill for Amazon's software assistant Alexa. Provide users with dialogues on general cultural issues in the geographical field to enrich the interest of human-computer interaction [6]. Yang compared the recommendations of user interaction and visual transmission with those of voice transmission and revealed the relevant habits of users in choosing voice interfaces [7]. Jones proposed that personal voice assistant (PVA) can effectively reduce loneliness of the elderly at home by providing easy-to-use voice control and friendly artificial intelligence dialogues [8]. Voice interaction as an auxiliary means, many scholars are exploring the possibility of its application in the field. To have a more comprehensive understanding of current research hotspots in the field of voice interaction, VOSviewer visual analysis software used in this paper to conduct bibliometric analysis and obtain a visual knowledge map of intelligent voice interaction. Its development principle is based on the co-citation and co-citation principles of literature, and the graphical display is rich and clear. Therefore, this paper applies and sorts out the research results, discusses the main directions and contents of future voice interaction research, and provides new ideas for the innovative development of voice interaction.

2   Definition and Research Ideas of Voice Interaction

2.1   Definition of Intelligent Voice Interaction

Intelligent voice interaction includes several technical aspects. Automatic speech recognition (ASR), which converts words in human speech into computer readable input, generally includes speech signal processing, and is feasible in shielding differences of environmental noise. The user gives instructions to the machine according to the way of system design. For example, the MI speaker uses the sentence pattern of 'Xiao Ai+ work task' to make the machine convert the received speech into words, and then the words are used as the execution instructions or search terms to drive the machine to execute. Natural language processing (NLP) technology is used to transform human's natural language into a machine that can understand it. The interactive interface involves voice output from the machine to people, which is mainly used for inquiring and verifying parts that are not understood or clear. Texts generated by the computer itself or input from outside need to be turned into understandable and fluent spoken language by people through texts to speech (TTS) technology, just as the machine speaks. The technological progress and breakthrough in these aspects make the voice interaction interface intelligent.

2.2   Research Ideas

In order to explore the development and application prospects of voice interaction, the following studies are carried out in this paper. 1) Review the existing literature related to voice interaction and summarize the development process of voice interaction. 2) Web of Science (hereinafter referred to as WOS) was used as the literature source to obtain the literature on speech interaction research, and the VOSviewer analysis system was used to analyze the overall trend of the number of documents published, keyword co-occurrence network analysis, and national and regional analysis with the help of graphical means. Research institutions analyze the trend, progress, and hot spots of voice interaction research quantitatively, and provide references for the future development of voice interaction. 3) Explore the future research direction and content of voice interaction based on big data analysis.

3   Experiment Method

Voice interaction was analyzed with VOSviewer as the analysis tool. In the Web of Science database, search with "voice interaction" as the main topic, screen the paper format, retain SCI paper core journal database, refine in the past five years (2017–2021) to obtain 2687 records, and check all fields respectively. The corresponding records are output in TXT format, and the corresponding text files are imported into VOSviewer software for analysis.

Subject analysis can better understand the research direction and topic structure of existing studies. Subject analysis is conducted on the titles and abstracts recorded in the collected 2687 articles, and word analysis with a frequency of more than 15 times is screened to obtain the topic distribution as shown in Fig. 1. As can be seen from the topics can be roughly divided into three clusters. The blue part of the first cluster includes effect, speech, measure, emotion, speaker, sound, age, adult, listener, talker, and therapy. Significant effect, control group, vocalization, score, comparison, month, treatment, etc. The vocabulary in this part is mainly related to the experimental methods and tests of speech interaction. The second type of cluster includes system, user, technology, device, robot, machine, accuracy, performance, recognition, control, dataset, gesture, efficiency, speech recognition, algorithm, voice command, architecture, vehicle, object, assistant, smartphone. This part of the vocabulary is related to the carrier of speech interaction, the technology used. The red part of the third cluster includes relationship, article, practice, interview, member, teacher, team, country, intervention, woman, care, youth, focus group, focus, politic, journalist, employee, institution, creation, reader, learner and other words are related to the application group and social relationship of phonetic interaction. The three words clusters are distinct and closely related to each other.

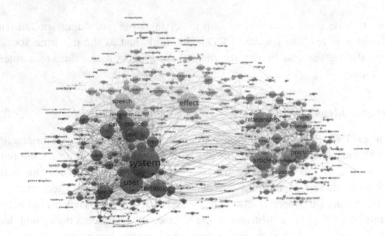

Fig. 1. Topic analysis of voice interaction

Keywords co-occurrence analysis from the literature metrology, it is the journal articles, dissertations, in the literature of two or more papers to use the same keywords phenomenon through statistical keywords co-occurrence frequency of multivariate statistical analysis, different from existing research topic, keywords co-occurrence analysis can be estimated according to the keyword's affinity-disaffinity relationship between one of the hot topics. To effectively present the results of keyword co-occurrence analysis and reflect the relationship and internal relationship between keywords, VOSviewer analysis system can be further used to construct visual network co-occurrence map for visual co-occurrence analysis. The larger the node value is, the greater the frequency of the keyword co-appearing with other keywords in the same literature, and the greater its status and role in the field of discipline research.

Table 1. High-frequency co-occurrences keywords in voice interaction

	Keyword	Occurrences		Keyword	Occurrences
1	Voice	263	11	Performance	83
2	Communication	156	12	Model	83
3	Children	143	13	Emotion	76
4	Perception	135	14	Experiences	69
5	Language	128	15	Technology	69
6	Recognition	124	16	Information	67
7	Impact	104	17	Perceptions	58
8	Gender	103	18	Health	65
9	Behavior	91	19	Participation	64
10	People	88	20	Care	62

According to the literature data acquisition method mentioned above, keywords and frequency of speech interaction research literature in 2017–2021 WOS are selected, and the results are shown in Table 1. Among them, the frequency of WOS keywords from high to low is voice, communication, children, perception, language, recognition, impact, gender, behavior, people, performance, model, emotion, experiences, technology, information, perceptions, health, participation, care. Speech interaction often involves emotion, behavior, group differences, and human-computer interaction. Voice interaction is usually associated with voice agent, voice assistant, smart phone, and vehicle-mounted system. For example, in the work of Bulthoff, the unique effect of human voice on face recognition shows that the timbre of voice will affect the memory efficiency of user's face. The recognition of strangers' faces combined with timbre can improve the familiarity of users' memory [9]. Coffey, F. et al. focused on the influence of timbre and tone use on the interaction results of healthcare professionals (HCP) with patients [10]. Huang used PAD model to study the differences between gender and seven characteristics of acoustics [11]. Different from the thematic vocabulary research, the 10 top clusters in the keyword co-occurrence analysis results are closely related to each other, presenting a cross-distribution pattern. Network visualization of co-occurrence of keywords is shown in Fig. 2.

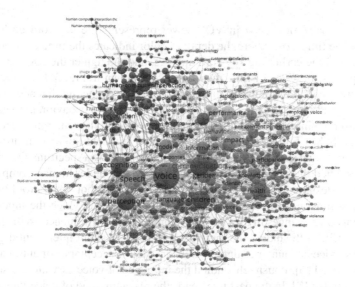

Fig. 2. Network visualization of co-occurrence of keywords.

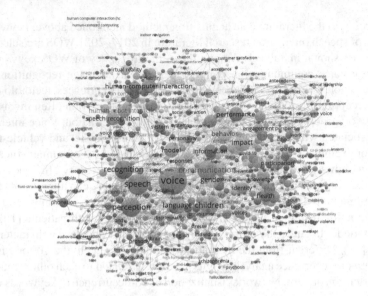

Fig. 3. Time visualization of co-occurrence of author keywords.

Density Visualization view in VOSviewer represents the keyword co-lead graph observed on the time axis, where the depth of color indicates the time distribution. The darker the color, the earlier the keyword appears, and the lighter the color, the later the keyword appears. In terms of time distribution, as shown in Fig. 3, the research focus in the past five years has gradually shifted from mobile phone intelligence, recognition technology, social interaction and other technical research to behavior, human-machine interface, machine interaction, intelligent interaction, and other emerging scientific and technological fields. For example, Schelinski (2017) studied interaction difficulties in facial recognition and speech recognition in people with autism spectrum disorder (ASD) [12]. Chen studied the emotional communication system under human-computer interaction [13]. Li designed an audio-visual integration guide robot system for blind people [14]. Hodges-Simeon studied the interpersonal attraction, in which the modulation of voice timbral color changes in the social environment and its influence on the recipient's psychology [15]. Lutfi studied the motivation of users to adopt intelligent digital voice assistant in service encounter to understand consumers' acceptance of automation technology in service [16]. Poushneh studied the influence of voice assistant personality on consumer attitude [17]. In the past five years, the research trend of voice interaction has gradually changed from the improvement of technology to the human-centered research trend such as user experience and emotional communication.

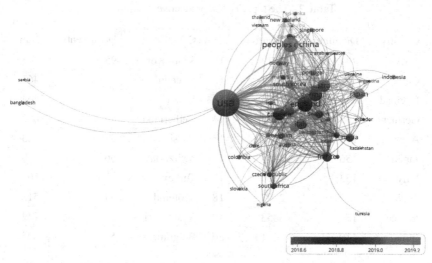

Fig. 4. Time visualization of co-authorship of countries.

In terms of the distribution of countries, the academic output of the research on speech interaction led by the United States is the largest, with 994 papers produced and 7,979 cited times, far exceeding other countries. It was followed by China (341), the UK (331), Germany (239), Australia (219) and Japan (156), as seen in Table 2. In terms of the number of citations, high-quality citations are mostly from the developed countries of the European Union, and there are also a few developing countries with high-quality censored articles, such as South Korea, Brazil and Turkey, whose article output is less than 100, and the number of citations exceeds that of China, which ranks second in article output. From the perspective of time distribution, countries that first studied voice interaction include Poland, Iran, Slovakia, etc. Recently, China, Singapore, Australia, and Japan have also gradually begun to attach importance to the study of voice interaction. Except for Serbia and Bangladesh, the research relationship between countries is relatively close, which benefits from the development of communication equipment and the trend of the internet. For example, the number one American has Google's Assistant, Amazon's Alexa and Apple's Siri. China, in second place, has Xiao du for Baidu and Xiao ai for Xiaomi. The overall research trend is from the earliest European region to the rise of Asia in recent years. Time visualization of co-authorship of countries shown in Fig. 4.

Table 2. The top 20 most productive countries.

	Country	Documents	Citations		Country	Documents	Citations
1	USA	994	7979	11	South Korea	95	2683
2	China	341	2193	12	Sweden	90	467
3	England	331	2266	13	Brazil	89	2464
4	Germany	239	3503	14	Netherlands	89	692
5	Australia	219	1226	15	Russia	88	83
6	Japan	156	2745	16	Switzerland	66	349
7	Italy	153	3160	17	Turkey	55	2509
8	Spain	143	2792	18	Scotland	54	513
9	France	131	3053	19	South Africa	53	142
10	India	119	211	20	Belgium	52	323

In the distribution study of authors, according to the distribution of authors' correlation degree, the authors munte-anu, cosmin clark, Leigh, Torre ilaria, Murad and Christine are taken as the core, showing scattering, as seen in Fig. 5. The relationships among the authors of Cosmin Clark, Leigh, Murad and Christine are relatively rich and close, while the relationships among the authors with less output are not particularly close. The output ranking of the articles is shown in Table 3, which is Munteanu, Cosmin, Clark, Leigh, Edwards, Justin, Murad, Christine, Cowan, Benjamin R. Schloegl, Stephan. As an emerging field, voice interaction has few articles produced by researchers at present, and the most scholars only produced 13 articles. Munteanu Cosmin from Univ Toronto Missis- Sauga, the author with the highest co-citation frequency, has produced 13 articles on voice interaction covering user interface [18], voice assistant, user experience design research [19], and conversation agent [20]. The most frequently cited article on voice interfaces is Porcheron wrote in 2018. This article describes how voice user interfaces (VUI) can be used as a medium to communicate between users and devices for the daily complexity of family social life. Explore how VUI can precisely order and coordinate the content of conversations [21].

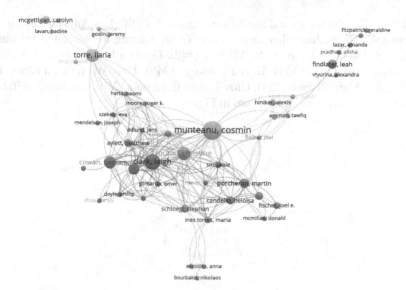

Fig. 5. Co-authorship network of productive authors.

Table 3. The top 10 most productive authors.

	Author	Country	Documents	Citations
1	Munteanu, Cosmin	Canada	13	60
2	Clark, Leigh	Wales	10	81
3	Edwards, Justin	Ireland	6	49
4	Murad, Christine	Canada	8	38
5	Cowan, Benjaminr	Ireland	7	57
6	Schloegl, Stephan	Austria	4	20
7	Aylett, Matthew	Scotland	4	23
8	Doyle, Phillp	Ireland	3	29
9	Porcheron, Martin	England	5	114
10	Juhar, Jozef	Slovakia	7	33

We also analyzed related research institutions and ranked them by the number of published articles. The top 10 institutions with the most published articles were Univ Washington (37), Univ Toronto (36), UCL (35), Univ Sydney (29), Mcgill Univ (29). Univ Melbourne (28), Univ Mich-Igan (24), Univ Calif Los Angeles (24), MIT (24), Univ Penn (22). See Table 4. There is little difference in the number of articles published in the top 10. Five of the 10 research institutions are from the United States, which is the country with the largest number of articles published by research institutions. Canada and Australia each have two institutes, with the remaining one from the UK. Among the cited articles, the most cited institution was Univ, Calif., Los Angeles (2490), with far more cited times than other institutions. The remaining top ten cited institutions from high to low were Chinese ACAD SCI (540). Georgia Inst Technol (378), Kings Coll London (361) UCL (354), Univ Edinburgh (349), Univ Washington (260), Univ Toronto (235), Univ Sydney (234), Univ British Columbia (220). As shown in Table 5. The overall distribution trend is shown in Fig. 6.

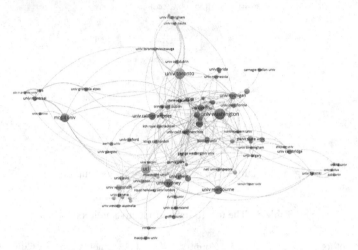

Fig. 6. Co-authorship network of productive organizations.

Table 4. The top 10 most productive organizations.

	Organization	Country	Documents	Citations
1	Univ Washington	America	37	260
2	Univ Toronto	Canada	36	235
3	UCL	England	35	354
4	Univ Sydney	Australia	29	234
5	McGill Univ	Canada	29	182
6	Univ Melbourne	Australia	28	116
7	Univ Michigan	America	24	201
8	Univ Calif Los Angeles	America	24	2490
9	MIT	America	24	99
10	Univ Penn	America	22	165

Table 5. The top 10 most-cited organizations

	Organization	Country	Citations	Documents	Total link strength
1	Univ Calif Los Angeles	America	2490	24	10
2	Chinese ACAD SCI	China	540	14	6
3	Georgia Inst Technol	America	378	11	8
4	Kings Coll London	England	361	14	6
5	UCL	England	354	35	30
6	Univ Edinburgh	England	349	12	13
7	Univ Washington	America	260	37	17
8	Univ Toronto	Canada	235	36	35
9	Univ Sydney	Australia	234	29	30
10	Univ British Columbia	England	220	14	15

4 Conclusion

This bibliometric analysis provides detailed visual bibliometric review of voice interaction by sifted through the core of SCI papers on Web of Science from 2017 to 2021. In the existing literature, the topic of voice interaction roughly covers three directions: experimental validation oriented, technical research oriented, and specific target population oriented. In keyword co-occurrence analysis, in the past five years, the research field of voice interaction has shifted from technical improvement research to human-centered research such as user experience and emotional communication. Among the countries studying voice interaction, the United States has published the most articles, and the overall research trend is developing from Europe to Asia. Among the authors studying voice interaction, most of the core authors are from European countries, so the studies are scattered and there is little correlation between the author groups. Five of the 10 institutions studying voice interaction are based in the United States.

There are also some limitations in this study. The bibliometric data is dynamic, and this study only analyzes the studies in a certain period, which can only represent the voice interaction research situation in the research period. Moreover, the selected data is only the core journal database of SCI papers in Web of Science. There are no large databases in other languages, so the conclusion of this paper only represents the objective fact of the core journal database of SCI papers, not the whole picture of voice interaction research.

Acknowledgments. The research supported by the youth foundation for humanities and social sciences of ministry of education of China, humanized design of intelligent mobile products for the elderly based on inclusive theory (20YJC760105).

References

1. Schnabel, E.-L., Wahl, H.-W., Schönstein, A., Frey, L., Draeger, L.: Nurses' emotional tone toward older inpatients: do cognitive impairment and acute hospital setting matter? Eur. J. Ageing **17**(3), 371–381 (2019). https://doi.org/10.1007/s10433-019-00531-z
2. Lu, J.X., Wang, P., Shi, H.Z., Wang, X.: Study on multichannel speech enhancement technology in voice human-computer interaction. In: Advanced Materials Research, vol. 267, pp. 762–767. Trans Tech Publications Ltd (2011)
3. Kumah Crystal Yaa, A., Pirtle Claude, J., Whyte Harrison, M., Goode Edward, S., Anders Shilo, H., Lehmann Christoph, U.: Electronic health record interactions through voice: a review. Appl. Clin. Inform. **9**(3), 541–552 (2018). https://doi.org/10.1055/s-0038-1666844
4. Huang, Z., Huang, X.: A study on the application of voice interaction in automotive human machine interface experience design. In: AIP Conference Proceedings, vol. 1955, no. 1, p. 040074. AIP Publishing LLC (2018)
5. Aeschlimann, S., Bleiker, M., Wechner, M., Gampe, A.: Communicative and social consequences of interactions with voice assistants. Comput. Hum. Behav. **112**, 106466 (2020)
6. Filimon, M., Iftene, A., Trandabăţ, D.: Bob-a general culture game with voice interaction. Procedia Comput. Sci. **159**, 323–332 (2019)
7. Yang, L., Sobolev, M., Tsangouri, C., Estrin, D.: Understanding user interactions with podcast recommendations delivered via voice. In: Proceedings of the 12th ACM Conference on Recommender Systems, pp. 190–194 (2018)
8. Jones, V.K., Hanus, M., Yan, C., Shade, M.Y., Boron, J.B., Bicudo, R.M.: Reducing loneliness among aging adults: the roles of personal voice assistants and anthropomorphic interactions. Front. Public Health **9** (2021)
9. Bülthoff, I., Newell, F.N.: Crossmodal priming of unfamiliar faces supports early interactions between voices and faces in person perception. Vis. Cogn. **25**(4–6), 611–628 (2017)
10. Coffey, F., Tsuchiya, K., Timmons, S., Baxendale, B., Adolphs, S., Atkins, S.: Analysing voice quality and pitch in interactions of emergency care simulation. BMJ Simul. Technol. Enhanced Learn. **4**(4), 196 (2018)
11. Huang, K.L., Duan, S.F., Lyu, X.: Affective voice interaction and artificial intelligence: a research study on the acoustic features of gender and the emotional states of the PAD model. Front. Psychol. **12**, 1212 (2021)
12. Schelinski, S., Roswandowitz, C., von Kriegstein, K.: Voice identity processing in autism spectrum disorder. Autism Res. **10**(1), 155–168 (2017)
13. Chen, M., Zhou, P., Fortino, G.: Emotion communication system. IEEE Access **5**, 326–337 (2016)
14. Zikang, L., Guizhi, X., Miaomiao, G.: Design and research of audio-visual fusion blind guiding robot. Laser Optoelectron. Prog. **54**(12), 121506 (2017)
15. Hodges-Simeon, C.R., Gaulin, S.J., Puts, D.A.: Different vocal parameters predict perceptions of dominance and attractiveness. Hum. Nat. **21**(4), 406–427 (2010). https://doi.org/10.1007/s12110-010-9101-5
16. Lutfi, S.L., Fernández-Martínez, F., Lucas-Cuesta, J.M., Lopez-Lebon, L., Montero, J.M.: A satisfaction-based model for affect recognition from conversational features in spoken dialog systems. Speech Commun. **55**(7–8), 825–840 (2013)
17. Poushneh, A.: Humanizing voice assistant: the impact of voice assistant personality on consumers' attitudes and behaviors. J. Retail. Consum. Serv. **58**, 102283 (2021)
18. Murad, C., Munteanu, C.: "I don't know what you're talking about, HALexa" the case for voice user interface guidelines. In: Proceedings of the 1st International Conference on Conversational User Interfaces, pp. 1–3 (2019)

19. Kaye, J.J., et al.: Panel: voice assistants, UX design and research. In: Extended Abstracts of the 2018 CHI Conference on Human Factors in Computing Systems, pp. 1–5 (2018)
20. Clark, L., et al.: What makes a good conversation? Challenges in designing truly conversational agents. In: Proceedings of the 2019 CHI Conference on Human Factors in Computing Systems, pp. 1–12 (2019)
21. Porcheron, M., Fischer, J.E., Reeves, S., Sharples, S.: Voice interfaces in everyday life. In: Proceedings of the 2018 CHI Conference on Human Factors in Computing Systems, pp. 1–12 (2018)

Author Index

Printed in the United States
by Baker & Taylor Publisher Services